Textbook on Criminal Law

Textbook on
Criminal Law

··

Twelfth Edition

Michael J. Allen

*LLB, LLM, Barrister, formerly Commissioner at the Criminal Cases
Review Commission (2002–2012) and Professor of Law,
Newcastle Law School (1996–2002)*

OXFORD
UNIVERSITY PRESS

OXFORD

UNIVERSITY PRESS

Great Clarendon Street, Oxford, OX2 6DP,
United Kingdom

Oxford University Press is a department of the University of Oxford.
It furthers the University's objective of excellence in research, scholarship,
and education by publishing worldwide. Oxford is a registered trade mark of
Oxford University Press in the UK and in certain other countries

© Michael J. Allen 2013

The moral rights of the author have been asserted

Ninth edition 2007
Tenth edition 2009
Eleventh edition 2011
Impression: 1

Public sector information reproduced under Open Government Licence v1.0
(http://www.nationalarchives.gov.uk/doc/open-government-licence/
open-government-licence.htm)

Crown Copyright material reproduced with the permission of the
Controller, HMSO (under the terms of the Click Use licence)

British Library Cataloguing in Publication Data

Data available

ISBN 978-0-19-966929-5

Printed in Great Britain by
Ashford Colour Press Ltd, Gosport, Hampshire

OUTLINE CONTENTS

DETAILED CONTENTS

NEW TO THIS EDITION

Key revisions in the twelfth edition include—

- Analysis of the latest case law developments including: *A* [2012] EWCA Crim 434, *Assange* v *Swedish Prosecution Authority* [2011] EWHC 2489 (Admin), *Ciccarelli* [2011] EWCA Crim 2665, *Clinton* [2012] EWCA Crim 2, *Dao and others* [2012] EWCA Crim 1717, *Dowds* [2012] EWCA Crim 281, *G* v *UK* [2011] ECHR 1308, *Gnango* [2011] UKSC 59, *Goddard* [2012] EWCA Crim 1756, *Inglis* [2010] EWCA Crim 2637, *JM and SM* [2012] EWCA Crim 2293, *R (Nicklinson)* v *Ministry of Justice* [2012] EWHC 2381 (Admin), *Razoq* [2012] EWCA Crim 674, *S* [2011] EWCA Crim 287, and *Seray-Wurie* v *DPP* [2012] EWCH 208 (Admin).

- Analysis of the latest statutory developments including the offence of stalking created by s. 111 of the Protection of Freedoms Act 2012 and s. 148 of the Legal Aid, Sentencing and Punishment of Offenders Act 2012 (amending s. 76 of the Criminal Justice and Immigration Act 2008).

PREFACE

Criminal law is a subject of great complexity which students find both fascinating and frustrating. The complexity is in large part caused by the uncertainty created by judges in courts at all levels, who fail to understand or adhere to fundamental principles. As a result the subject is both challenging and potentially frustrating.

Traditionally textbooks on criminal law provide much more detail than students require and may, themselves, add to the confusion. This book will seek to state clearly both the principles fundamental to criminal liability and the current state of the law in the areas covered in most criminal law courses. In addition it will highlight those areas where there are doubts, problems, or confusion. It is hoped that this book will help students both to meet the intellectual challenge which criminal law presents them and safely to negotiate those areas where frustration might creep in.

In the two years since the eleventh edition of this book was published there have been numerous developments in both statutory and case law. New cases have been incorporated into most chapters with the result that some questions posed in the eleventh edition have been answered, while new questions have arisen to which answers are now required.

Following the success of the presentational devices introduced in the ninth edition and developed in the last two editions which were designed to improve the visual impact of the text and to reinforce understanding by highlighting statutory provisions, quotations, key cases, examples, and questions, these have been retained and further developed for this edition.

Thanks are due to all the editorial staff at OUP who have assisted with the production of this edition.

The law is stated as it was on 1 December 2012.

Michael J. Allen

TABLE OF CASES

TABLE OF STATUTES

TABLE OF SECONDARY LEGISLATION

1

Introduction

1.1 Substantive criminal law

The subject matter of this book is the substantive criminal law; that is, the law which determines what is or is not a crime. This book is not concerned with the reasons why certain conduct is defined as criminal; that is a matter of moral philosophy. Neither is it concerned with the reasons why people commit crimes; that is a matter for criminologists to ponder. Likewise, the procedures by which criminals are arrested, prosecuted, convicted, and sentenced are outside the remit of this book. Similarly, the study of punishment and the efficacy of the various sentencing options available to the courts is a matter for penologists to consider.

Having excluded so much it might appear that there is little left to consider. Such a conclusion would be erroneous as the criminal law is a complex and expansive subject. Before studying it, however, it is necessary to place it in context by considering questions such as the following: What is a crime? What purpose or function does the criminal law serve? Why is particular conduct classified as criminal?

1.2 Defining a crime

A crime may be defined as an act (or omission or a state of affairs) which contravenes the law and which may be followed by prosecution in criminal proceedings with the attendant consequence, following conviction, of punishment. This definition reveals nothing of the characteristics of acts which are defined as criminal. Indeed the same act may give rise to both criminal and civil liability. For example, if D punches P he may be guilty of assault, a crime. The same act also constitutes the tort of assault which is a form of trespass to the person and D, if successfully sued by P, would be liable to pay damages. Likewise, if D sets fire to P's house he may be guilty of the crime of arson. P could also sue him for the tort of trespass to his property.

When Parliament passes legislation making a particular act criminal, the nature of that act does not change but the consequences of performing it do change. For example, until 1930 it was not an offence to take and drive away a motor vehicle without the owner's consent. Section 28 of the Road Traffic Act 1930 made this an offence and in 1968 Parliament extended this offence to cover the taking of any 'conveyance' thus including, for example, boats (see s. 12 of the Theft Act 1968). Similarly, until 1978 it was not an offence for a diner in a restaurant to make off without paying for the meal he had consumed. The mischief of customers making off without paying their bills where payment on the spot was expected was dealt with in s. 3 of the Theft Act 1978. In both these cases, the relevant act remains the same and the actor continues to be civilly liable for trespass and debt respectively. Parliament's legislative intervention, however, has meant that both these acts may also result in criminal liability.

By the same token, if Parliament enacts legislation which abolishes a particular crime, the nature of the act which previously constituted a crime remains the same; it is only the consequences of performing that act which differ. For example, s. 1 of the Sexual Offences Act 1967 provided that it would no longer be an offence for a man over the age of 21 to commit buggery or gross indecency in private with another man over that age who consented to the act. The nature of these acts did not change after 1967 but the consequence of committing them in particular circumstances changed as the criminal sanction was removed.

The definition of crime is thus of limited usefulness. It only indicates which acts are criminal by reference to consequences which may ensue from their commission; it tells us nothing about the function of the criminal law or why particular conduct is classified as criminal. The definition, therefore, is essentially concerned with the legal consequences of the act.

1.3 The function of the criminal law

The function of the criminal law is largely to set the parameters within which the criminal justice system operates. There are two aspects to this. First, the criminal justice system is a tool of social control representing the agglomeration of powers, procedures, and sanctions which surround the criminal law. The police are empowered to investigate crime, search for evidence, arrest suspected offenders, and question them. The courts are empowered to try persons charged with committing crimes and, if convicted, to sentence them. In setting the parameters within which this coercive State apparatus operates, the criminal law plays a central role; a person may only be arrested where he is suspected of committing a crime; the police may only search for evidence which points towards the commission of a crime; the courts may only try and sentence persons who are charged with, and then convicted of, committing crimes. It is crucial, therefore to define clearly what acts, omissions or states of affairs amount to crimes as all the other powers, procedures, and sanctions of the criminal justice system are dependent upon these definitions. The criminal law, accordingly, limits and controls the legitimate exercise by the State of its coercive power to investigate crime and prosecute, convict, and punish criminals. Secondly, the criminal law operates as a guide to the citizen indicating the limits of legitimate activity on his part and predicting the consequences of infraction of the criminal law.

If the power of the State is to be effectively limited and if the citizen is to be able confidently to make rational choices regarding his behaviour, the criminal law must be clear, relatively stable and accessible, that is, knowable in advance. Throughout the course of this book judicial decisions on the content and ambit of the substantive criminal law will be subjected to criticism, sometimes trenchant criticism, as there is a tendency for judges to lose sight of the wider role which the criminal law serves in their understandable desire to see persons whom they regard as 'undesirable characters' locked behind bars.

But criticism should not be confined to the judiciary; the legislature is also deserving of criticism for its hyperactivity in creating new crimes and doing so by means of ill-drafted and obscurely worded statutory provisions. The courts regularly bemoan the complexity of the legislation they are called upon to interpret and apply as well as the difficulty of tracking the state of statutory provisions which may be subject to countless amendments by various subsequent provisions with no attempt at consolidation. In *Chambers* [2008] EWCA Crim 2467 Toulson LJ launched a broadside at the legislature criticising both the volume and form of criminal statutory provisions. D had been prosecuted by Her Majesty's Revenue and Customs with an offence of fraudulent evasion of duty contrary to s. 170(1)(b) of the Customs and Excise Management Act 1979. This offence is aimed at smugglers but regulations made under the Act dealt with the circumstances in which a confiscation order could be made for evading duty. D pleaded guilty and was made subject to a confiscation order which he appealed. The prosecution relied upon the Excise Goods Regulations 1992 to contend that D's actions were caught by the legislation. At the Court of Appeal, the Court having issued a draft judgment for the parties to consider in advance of judgment being delivered, a lawyer at the Revenue and Customs Prosecution Office noticed that the 1992 Regulations had been superseded by the Tobacco Product Regulations 2001, some five years before Mr Chamber's actions which formed the subject of the prosecution. These changed the basis upon which a confiscation order would be assessed. Quashing the confiscation order the Court of Appeal complained of the problem of criminal legislation being one of 'substantial constitutional importance' stating:

64 This case also provides an example of a wider problem. It is a maxim that ignorance of the law is no excuse, but it is profoundly unsatisfactory if the law itself is not practically accessible. To a worryingly large extent, statutory law is not practically accessible today, even to the courts whose constitutional duty it is to interpret and enforce it. There are four principal reasons.

65 First, the majority of legislation is secondary legislation.

66 Secondly, the volume of legislation has increased very greatly over the last 40 years. The Law Commission's Report on Post–Legislative Scrutiny, (2006) Law Com 302, gave some figures in Appendix C. In 2005 there were 2868 pages of new Public General Acts and approximately 13,000 pages of new Statutory Instruments, making a total well in excess of 15,000 pages (which is equivalent to over 300 pages a week) excluding European Directives and European Regulations, which were responsible for over 5,000 additional pages of legislation.

67 Thirdly, on many subjects the legislation cannot be found in a single place, but in a patchwork of primary and secondary legislation.

68 Fourthly, there is no comprehensive statute law database with hyperlinks which would enable an intelligent person, by using a search engine, to find out all the legislation on a particular topic. This means that the courts are in many cases unable to discover what the law is, or was at the date with which the court is concerned, and are entirely dependent on the parties for being able to inform them what were the relevant statutory provisions which the court has to apply. This [is a] lamentable state of affairs....

While ignorance of the law may be no excuse, there is a responsibility upon the State to make the law accessible to its citizens if it wishes them to be able to order their actions in accordance with the law.

The criminal law is a series of prohibitions backed up with the threat of punishment. An understanding of the function of the criminal law requires further inquiry into the reasons why breaches of the criminal law are met with punishment and why certain behaviour is subjected to prohibition.

1.3.1 Social control and social morality

The criminal law represents the rules of social control within a society. But how are the rules determined? Is there an essential criterion which determines which behaviour merits criminal sanction? The Wolfenden Committee, *Report of the Committee on Homosexual Offences and Prostitution* (Cmnd 247, 1957) stated (at paras. 13 and 14) that the function of the criminal law is:

> to preserve public order and decency, to protect the citizen from what is offensive or injurious and to provide sufficient safeguards against exploitation or corruption of others, particularly those who are specially vulnerable because they are young, weak in body or mind or inexperienced or in a state of special physical, official or economic dependence. It is not … the function of the law to intervene in the private lives of citizens, or to seek to enforce any particular pattern of behaviour, further than is necessary to carry out the purposes we have outlined.

To this extent the criminal law is a reflection of corporate or societal morality. The wrongdoing which the criminal law seeks to punish is that which threatens the fundamental values upon which a society is founded. While it is harmful to the individual to be robbed or assaulted, it is also harmful to society as such behaviour threatens the security and well-being of that society. The criminal sanction operates then as a form of social control both punishing the offender and reasserting the mores of that society. This may be seen more clearly when the possible purposes punishment may serve are examined.

1.3.1.1 Retribution

A major purpose which punishment serves is retribution. Punishment is meted out to the offender because this is what he deserves in response to his infraction of the criminal law. This was expressed by Stephen, *A History of the Criminal Law of England* (1883) at pp. 81, 82:

> [T]he infliction of punishment by law gives definite expression and a solemn ratification and justification to the hatred which is excited by the commission of the offence, and which constitutes the moral or popular as distinguished from the conscientious sanction of that part of morality which is also sanctioned by the criminal law. The criminal law thus proceeds upon the principle that it is morally right to hate criminals, and it confirms and justifies that sentiment by inflicting upon criminals, punishments which express it.

To some extent, therefore, retribution reflects society's desire for vengeance. When people join together in a society governed by law, they relinquish their own right to retaliate to harm done to them in exchange for the protection which the law offers them. H. Gross gives expression to this view in *A Theory of Criminal Justice* (1979) (at pp. 19–20):

> But society requires that this right [to repay harm with harm] be surrendered by its members, and in exchange undertakes to protect them by laws that can be effective only if violations are punished. The bargain that is struck, then, places a moral obligation on society to punish crime as it places a moral obligation on its members to refrain from breaking the law.

Vengeance or retaliation is only one aspect of retribution. A further element is that of denunciation. The infliction of punishment signals society's disapproval of the criminal's conduct and reaffirms the values the criminal law is designed to uphold. This reflects the more modern view of the appropriate place for retribution in the criminal justice system. In *Sargeant* (1974) 60 Cr App R 74, a case concerning violent crime, Lawton LJ, after rejecting the idea of 'an eye for an eye', gave expression to this view (at p. 77):

> ...society, through the courts, must show its abhorrence of particular types of crime, and the only way in which the courts can show this is by the sentences they pass. The courts do not have to reflect public opinion. On the other hand they must not disregard it. Perhaps the main duty of the court is to lead public opinion. Anyone who surveys the criminal scene at the present time must be alive to the appalling problem of violence. Society, we are satisfied, expects the courts to deal with violence.... Those who indulge in the kind of violence with which we are concerned in this case must expect custodial sentences.

The punishment inflicted, however, must not represent a blind act of vindictive retaliation; it must be both reasoned and reasonable. The idea which has gained ascendancy in recent years is that of 'just deserts' based on the philosophical ideas of Kant. A person who commits a crime has gained an unfair advantage over the other members of society. Punishment cancels out that advantage (particularly where the court orders confiscation, restitution, or compensation) while, at the same time, it reaffirms the values of that society by visiting moral disapproval or reprobation on the offender. The punishment the criminal deserves, of course, must bear some relationship to the harm he has caused. Punishment can only be considered reasonable where the courts respect the concept of proportionality.

1.3.1.2 Deterrence

A second purpose which punishment may serve is that of deterrence, whether this be *particular* deterrence (i.e. dissuading the individual criminal from reoffending in the future) or *general* deterrence (i.e. dissuading other possible offenders from offending by the example made of each particular offender). It is difficult to assess the effectiveness of individual deterrence. Some offenders may never offend again even if they are not caught or punished; others may only be deterred where the punishment imposed is so severe that it is out of all proportion to the gravity of the wrongdoing. In relation to general deterrence, courts, in the past, sometimes imposed exemplary sentences to deter others where an offence had become prevalent or was particularly grave (see e.g. *Wilson and Tutt* (1981) 3 Cr App R (S) 102; *Poh and To* [1982] Crim LR 132). While judges may have associated severe sentences with deterrence, the connection was not necessarily valid. In *The Sentence of the Court* (5th edn, 1990) published by the Home Office, it is stated (at para. 3.3):

> The simplest way of evaluating the individual deterrent effect of sentencing is to compare the proportions of offenders undergoing different types of sentence who, when free to do so, continue to commit offences. The almost invariable conclusion of the large amount of research which has been undertaken ... is that it is hard to show any effect that one type of sentence is more likely than any other to reduce the likelihood of reoffending, which is high for all. Similarly, longer periods of custody or particular institutional regimes do not seem to have a significant effect. Studies comparing the reconviction rates of offenders given community service orders with those given custodial sentences have also shown little difference.

Different sentences therefore have little effect in deterring offenders. *The Sentence of the Court* goes on to state, however (at para. 3.4), that:

> The inference most commonly drawn from research studies is that the probability of arrest and conviction is likely to deter potential offenders whereas the perceived severity of the ensuing penalties has little effect.

Of course, detection and conviction must result in punishment if the rules are not to lose their coercive force. Whether a particular person is susceptible to coercion, however, may depend on other factors. H. Packer, *The Limits of the Criminal Sanction* (1968) observed (at p. 45):

> [T]he deterrent role of the criminal law is effective mainly with those who are subject to the dominant socializing influences of the day ... Deterrence does not threaten those whose lot in life is already miserable beyond the point of hope. It does not improve the morals of those whose value systems are closed to further modification, either psychologically ... or culturally....

Thus, the deterrent role of the criminal process is a limited one; those who are set on committing crime may not be deterred by the criminal law. For most members of society, however, the criminal law may serve to educate them on acceptable and unacceptable conduct creating thereby unconscious inhibitions against offending. Gross makes this point (at p. 401):

> The threats are not laid down to deter those tempted to break the rules, but rather to maintain the rules as a set of standards that compel allegiance in spite of violations by those who commit crimes. In short, the rules of conduct laid down in the criminal law are a powerful social force upon which society is dependent for its very existence, and there is punishment for violation of these rules in order to prevent the dissipation of their power that would result if they were violated with impunity.

1.3.1.3 Incapacitation

The third purpose which punishment may serve is that of incapacitation. If a term of imprisonment is imposed on an offender, the public are protected from further offences by him for so long as he is in prison.

1.3.1.4 Rehabilitation

The pre-1960s penal debate was premised upon the idea of rehabilitation. Probation was introduced as a disposal following conviction to give effect to this rehabilitative ideal. The idea of rehabilitation even found expression in the Prison Rules 1964 which stated that 'the purpose of the training and treatment of convicted prisoners shall be to encourage and assist them to lead a good and useful life'. So far as prison is concerned this ideal has largely been abandoned as the problems of overcrowding and underfunding have taken their toll, making the most immediate concern of prison governors that of containment. The idea of rehabilitation also underpins parole which was introduced by the Criminal Justice Act 1967.

Since the 1960s and 1970s there has been a movement away from rehabilitation as an objective of punishment. Studies on both sides of the Atlantic reveal that the recidivism rate varies little between offenders who received retributive sentences and those who received rehabilitative sentences (see e.g. Brody, *The Effectiveness of Sentencing* (Home Office Research Study No. 35, 1976)). Similarly, rehabilitation as a basis for sentencing offenders led to disparity in punishment as the sentencer was looking to the needs of the offender rather than the offence committed as the starting point in determining the appropriate sentence. This is not to say that alternatives to prison are disparaged. On the contrary, during the 1980s and early 1990s there was a growing interest on the part of the Home Office in community sentences as these may be as effective as prison, both in terms of their retributive and deterrent value, and incur a lower financial and social cost as the prisoner can serve his sentence (e.g. community service) in the community. The interest in such punishments has been revived as the current Government seeks to reduce the overall budget of the Prison Service through reducing the numbers of offenders sentenced to imprisonment.

1.3.1.5 The current approach

Until 1991 the sentencing system in England and Wales lacked a coherent rationale as retribution, deterrence, incapacitation, and rehabilitation were all advocated as the aims of sentencing, without there being any explanation of how these aims were to be reconciled or of which was to take priority if they came into conflict (see, for example *Sargeant* (1974) 60 Cr App R 74). In the late 1980s the Government began to consider the sentencing system and the relative merits of the various objectives which may be achieved through punishment. The Government's approach was set out in the White Paper, *Crime, Justice and Protecting the Public* (Cmd 965, 1990). The Government recognised that rehabilitation, while it may be sought, may not always be achieved and cannot be used as a justification for imprisonment (see paras. 2.6 and 2.7). Deterrence, while it may have immediate appeal, probably operates only with those who are law-abiding in the first place. The White Paper stated (at para. 2.8):

> But much crime is committed on impulse, given the opportunity presented by an open window or unlocked door, and it is committed by offenders who live from moment to moment; their crimes are as impulsive as the rest of their feckless, sad, or pathetic lives. It is unrealistic to construct sentencing arrangements on the assumption that most offenders will weigh up the possibilities in advance and base their conduct on rational calculation. Often they do not.

The approach the Government opted for, therefore, was one based on the idea of retribution. The White Paper stated (at para. 2.9):

> The Government's proposals therefore emphasise the objectives which sentencing is most likely to meet successfully in whole or in part. The first objective for all sentences is denunciation of and retribution for the crime. Depending on the offence and the offender, the sentence may also aim to achieve public protection, reparation and reform of the offender, preferably in the community. This approach points to sentencing policies which are more firmly based on the seriousness of the offence, and just deserts for the offender.

In 1991 the Criminal Justice Act was passed reflecting in its provisions, to a large extent, the views expressed in the White Paper. The sentencing provisions were subsequently consolidated with other sentencing legislation in the Powers of Criminal Courts (Sentencing) Act 2000. The emphasis on retribution was apparent in that the concept of proportionality was made a central principle of sentencing.

Since 2000 there have been several major pieces of legislation dealing with sentencing making for immense complexity when it comes to trying to determine whether a provision is in force, has been amended or repealed, and in trying to determine what sentence is actually available for any particular offence. (It should be borne in mind that while prosecution and conviction may occur many years after an offence was committed the court is limited to applying the law that was in force at the time of the offence.) However, the Criminal Justice Act 2003 provides a smorgasbord in s. 142 which sets out the purposes of sentencing as follows:

> (1) Any court dealing with an offender in respect of his offence must have regard to the following:
> (a) the punishment of offenders,
> (b) the reduction of crime (including its reduction by deterrence),
> (c) the reform and rehabilitation of offenders,
> (d) the protection of the public, and
> (e) the making of reparation by offenders to person affected by their offences.

The 2003 Act, by s. 167, also created the Sentencing Guidelines Council (SGC) to give guidance to the courts on sentencing. The Coroners and Justice Act 2009 replaced the SGC with the Sentencing Council (SC). The SGC and the SC have been responsible for general guidance on sentencing and guidelines for specific offences (see www.sentencingcouncil.org.uk). In its *Overarching Principles: Seriousness* Guideline, the SGC provided guidance on how a sentencer should approach an individual case when choosing from the smorgasbord of purposes:

> 1.3 The sentencer must start by considering the *seriousness* of the offence, the assessment of which will:
> • determine which of the sentencing thresholds has been crossed;
> • indicate whether a custodial, community or other sentence is most appropriate;
> • be the key factor in deciding the length of a custodial sentence, the onerousness of requirements to be incorporated in a community sentence and the amount of any fine imposed.

1.4 A court is required to pass a sentence that is commensurate with the seriousness of the offence. The *seriousness* of an offence is determined by two main parameters: the *culpability* of the offender and the *harm* caused or risked being caused by the offence.

The Guideline goes on, at 1.6 and 1.7, to set out the hierarchy of the levels of criminal culpability as intention to cause harm, recklessness as to causing harm, knowledge by a defendant of the risks his actions entail, and negligence. 'Harm' itself may be harm to individuals such as 'physical injury, sexual violation, financial loss, damage to health or psychological distress' (1.9). Where no harm has arisen from the offence, for example where the conviction is for conspiracy or attempt, the court will assess the relative dangerousness of the offender's conduct considering 'the likelihood of harm occurring and the gravity of the harm that could have resulted' (1.11). Community harm may include 'economic loss, harm to public health, or interference with the administration of justice' (1.12).

The Guideline recognises that assessing seriousness is a difficult task, particularly so where there is an imbalance between culpability and harm (1.15) as sometimes the harm that results may be greater than that intended (1.16; see, for example, constructive manslaughter **9.3.3.1** *post*) or the culpability may be higher than the harm resulting from the offence (1.16; see, for example, **Chapter 8** *post* 'Inchoate offences'). In fixing the level of culpability courts also have to factor in motive, whether the offence was planned or spontaneous or whether the offender was in a position of trust (1.17).

Particular offences have sentencing guidelines which include lists of the aggravating and mitigating factors relevant to those offences. Offence guidelines provide Sentence Ranges and Starting Points which relate to offence seriousness and which the sentencer will use as a baseline against which to factor in particular aggravating and mitigating factors. The sentencer also has to take account of the thresholds for custodial and community sentences. Section 152(2) of the Criminal Justice Act 2003 provides:

The court must not pass a custodial sentence unless it is of the opinion that the offence, or the combination of the offence and one or more offences associated with it, was so serious that neither a fine alone nor a community sentence can be justified for the offence.

Section 153(2) requires that where a fixed term custodial sentence is passed it should be for 'the shortest term that is commensurate with the seriousness of the offence'.

The threshold for community sentences is set out in s. 148(1) of the 2003 Act:

A court must not pass a community sentence on an offender unless it is of the opinion that the offence, or the combination of the offence and one or more offences associated with it, was serious enough to warrant such a sentence.

By s. 148(2) when imposing a community sentence, the court must ensure that the restriction on liberty placed on the offender is commensurate with the seriousness of the offence. Prison, accordingly, is to be reserved as a punishment for the most serious offences; but even if the custody threshold is satisfied personal mitigation factors may come into play and dictate that a fine or community penalty is more appropriate. A community sentence, however, may be passed even if the seriousness threshold is not satisfied where the offender previously has, on three or more occasions, had sentences consisting only of a fine imposed on him. In either case, however, custodial or community penalties must be tailored to offence seriousness.

Sentencing is, accordingly, an extremely complex task with courts having to evaluate and balance so many different factors when sentencing an offender for a particular offence. It is not surprising, therefore, that errors may be made and that so many appeals against sentence are pursued each year. In the year October 2010 to September 2011 the Court of Appeal received 5481 applications to appeal sentence (The Court of Appeal Criminal Division, *Review of the Legal Year 2010/2011*, para. 1.2). These complexities, however, elude politicians, commentators, and tabloid journalists when they raise a hue and cry over the latest unduly lenient sentence that provokes their ire. Inevitably, calls for further legislation and demands for greater consistency in sentencing ensue without any recognition of the fact that every offence and every offender is different and that very different sentences for two offenders convicted of the same offence may be both justifiable and consistent.

1.3.2 What conduct should be classified as criminal?

Having looked at the purposes which punishment may serve, it is necessary to consider why particular conduct is prohibited by the criminal law. What is the social morality which the criminal law reflects? Is the fact that certain conduct is regarded as immoral by the majority of citizens a sufficient justification, in itself, for making that conduct punishable by law?

To determine what is immoral is a far from straightforward task. Ideas of what is immoral vary from one society to another and from one generation to another. In any society, however, there is to be found a common core of morality which reflects standards of behaviour to which the majority of citizens in that society conform, deviations from which will provoke censure. Many of these rules of morality will be enforced by the criminal law, such as prohibitions of murder, violence to the person, sexual assaults, and theft. As Gross states (at p. 13):

> It seems obvious that those crimes of violence, theft and destruction that stand as paradigms of crime and comprise the core of any penal code are also moral wrongs. Everyone has a right to be free of such harm inflicted by others, and when murder, rape, arson, assault or [theft] is committed there is also a moral wrong since a moral duty to refrain from doing harm to others has been breached. The right to be free of such harm does not have its origin in law but in a general consensus on the rights enjoyed by any member of society, or even by any person, no matter how he lives. This consensus is a more fundamental element of society even than the law, and for that reason the violation of such a right is a moral wrong and not simply a legal wrong.

Not all rules of social morality, however, are subject to enforcement by the criminal law. Adultery may be regarded by many as immoral but it is not a crime. Lying may be immoral but it is not necessarily a crime (see **Chapter 12** *post*). Similarly, many prohibitions of the criminal law are morally neutral. There is no rule of social morality which dictates that the speed limit for vehicles in built-up areas should be 30 mph, nor does social morality dictate that seatbelts should be worn in vehicles or that persons under 18 should not be served alcohol in licensed premises. These laws may be justified on the basis that they improve safety for, or prevent harm to, citizens. They may be matters on which there is a fair degree of social consensus but this is not due to any common perception of morality.

There has long been disputation amongst legal philosophers as to what the proper sphere of the criminal law should be. The nineteenth-century philosopher J. S. Mill in his essay *On Liberty* expressed the view that the only legitimate purpose for which legal coercion could be exercised over any member of a civilised community is to prevent harm to others. The Wolfenden Committee extended this (see **1.3.1** *ante*). By contrast Lord Devlin in *The Enforcement of Morals* (1965) expressed the view that the primary function of the criminal law was to maintain public morality. In his opinion 'intolerance, indignation and disgust' were vital to a society and conduct which aroused such feelings amongst right-thinking members of society deserved suppression by means of the criminal law.

The views expressed by Lord Devlin subsequently seemed to receive approval in the House of Lords. In *Shaw v DPP* [1962] AC 220, D was convicted of conspiracy to corrupt public morals arising from his publication of the 'Ladies Directory' advertising the names and addresses of prostitutes, together with photographs and details of the 'services' they were prepared to offer. The House of Lords upheld the conviction, Viscount Simonds stating (at p. 267):

> In the sphere of the criminal law I entertain no doubt that there remains in the courts of law a residual power to enforce the supreme and fundamental purpose of the law, to conserve not only the safety and order but also the moral welfare of the State, and that it is their duty to guard against attacks which may be the more insidious because they are novel and unprepared for.

By contrast, Lord Reid, dissenting, reflected the view of Mill. He was of opinion that there was 'no such general offence known to the law as conspiracy to corrupt public morals.' Lord Reid went on to state (at p. 275):

> Even if there is still a vestigial power [in the courts to extend the law of conspiracy], it ought not, in my view, to be used unless there appears to be general agreement that the offence to which it is applied ought to be criminal if committed by an individual. Notoriously, there are wide differences of opinion today as to how far the law ought to punish immoral acts which are not done in the face of the public. Some think that the law already goes too far, some that it does not go far enough. Parliament is the proper place, and I am firmly of opinion the only proper place, to settle that. When there is sufficient support from public opinion, Parliament does not hesitate to intervene. Where Parliament fears to tread it is not for the courts to rush in.

It is rare for such a stark division to occur in the House of Lords as a result of philosophical differences of opinion regarding the function of the criminal law. While Mill's and Devlin's views are prescriptive it is clear that neither accurately describes the actual province of the criminal law. In reality the justifications for the creation of particular offences may differ. Some offences enforce morality, others are there to protect individuals from harm, and others do both. Indeed defining 'harm' is as difficult a task as defining 'morality'. Should harm be limited to physical harm to others or should the law also adopt a paternalistic approach to protect the individual from harming himself? (All these issues surfaced in the House of Lords' decision in *Brown* [1993] 2 WLR 556 concerning sado-masochism; see **10.1.1.3.1** *post*.) Attempting suicide used to be a crime, possessing prohibited drugs, riding a motor cycle without a helmet, or driving a car without wearing a seatbelt are offences. Only the perpetrator and victim will suffer from these activities. Looked at more widely, however, it may be argued that society may also suffer the cost of medical treatment and social security payments to persons maimed or debilitated by, or orphaned or widowed as a result of, these activities. The definition of 'harm' may be widened in another way to include offence to one's sensibilities and psychological harm. Offences under the Obscene Publications Acts 1959 and 1964, or offences such as indecent exposure or brothel-keeping may be regarded as causing harm in this sense apart from offending against morality.

What is clear from this brief examination is that the decision to criminalise or decriminalise particular activities, whether by judicial decision or legislation, is far from straightforward. A range of considerations may be relevant to the ultimate decision, for example, morality, economics, ethics, politics, and philosophy. Changes in morality may lead to changes in the law, for example, s. 1 of the Sexual Offences Act 1967 or the Abortion Act 1967. As views change perhaps other offences will be removed from the criminal calendar; many would argue for the legalisation of voluntary euthanasia or of the possession of cannabis.

The decision to use the criminal law to proscribe particular conduct or activities requires a balancing of moral considerations and concepts of harm as well as an assessment of the extent to which the State has a legitimate interest in controlling the acts which an individual does in private which cause harm to no one else. Even if conduct is considered immoral and harmful this will not necessarily justify criminalisation. Other considerations may be relevant such as whether the law would be enforceable and whether a criminal sanction is necessary or appropriate to achieve the end in view. For example, the connection between STDs and sexual promiscuity may be clearly established and this may lead to a change in attitudes to sexual morality. The majority of people in society may come to regard fornication, adultery, and casual sexual relationships with 'intolerance, indignation and disgust'. Greater sexual fidelity may reduce the spread of STDs and the harm to individuals and society. However, to seek to criminalise all sexual relationships outside marriage would be impossible to enforce without gross invasion of privacy; it may also be argued that the State has no legitimate interest in seeking to control private consensual sexual activity (see further *Brown* at **10.1.1.3.1** *post*). Criminalisation is also not the only possible solution to the problem; greater health education may be sufficient to reduce the spread of STDs. Moral considerations alone are not a sufficient reason for extending the reach of the criminal law. The evidence of the past 40 years also suggests that the view that it is the function of the criminal law to enforce morality is one which is in decline.

It is not possible therefore to present an equation which when applied to particular behaviour will provide the answer whether or not such behaviour should be classified as criminal. Too many factors of varying weight and relevance have to be weighed in the balance. Furthermore the answer may vary over time as public perceptions of the role of the criminal law, the role of the State, the rights of the citizen, and social morality change.

1.4 Classifying offences

There are now literally thousands of criminal offences, the vast majority being of statutory creation and of a regulatory nature. Our concern, however, is generally with the major offences (e.g. murder, manslaughter, rape, assault, theft, robbery, burglary, criminal damage, deception) and the general principles underlying criminal liability. While most offences are now of statutory creation, the criminal law originally was laid down in the decisions of the judges. Some offences, such as murder and manslaughter, are still common law offences lacking a statutory definition.

At common law, crimes were classified generally as either felonies or misdemeanours. Subsequently this classification was adopted by Parliament when it came to create offences by legislation. The principal felonies were homicide, rape, theft, burglary, robbery, and arson. A misdemeanour was any offence which was not a felony. Felonies were more serious than misdemeanours. The classification had important consequences in terms of the power of arrest and the penalties available on conviction. There was a general power of arrest without warrant in respect of felonies but not in respect of misdemeanours. On conviction of a felony the felon was liable to forfeiture of his land and goods (abolished by the Forfeiture Act 1870) and, if Parliament had declared a crime to be a 'felony without benefit of clergy', the penalty was death. Gradually the distinctions between felonies and misdemeanours were eroded by legislation. Finally, in the Criminal Justice Act 1967, all distinctions between felonies and misdemeanours were abolished.

A second mode of classification of offences relates to the mode of trial. The distinction here is between summary and indictable offences. Summary offences are less serious than indictable offences and are tried before a magistrates' court. Indictable offences are more serious and are tried in the Crown Court before a judge and jury. Many offences are triable either way (see s. 17 of and sch. 1 to the Magistrates' Courts Act 1980). The decision whether an offence should be tried summarily or on indictment where it is triable either way is made by the magistrates' court having regard to the representations made by the prosecutor and the accused and all the circumstances of the case (see s. 19 of the 1980 Act). Obvious considerations are the gravity of the offence and the sentence available to the magistrates' court as compared to that available before the Crown Court. Theft, for example, is an offence triable either way. The maximum penalty available on trial on indictment is seven years' imprisonment whereas the maximum sentence which a magistrates' court may impose is generally six months' imprisonment (see s. 31 of the 1980 Act; but should s. 154 of the Criminal Justice Act 2003 ever come into force it will be 12 months). If the court decides to proceed summarily the consent of the accused is required as he may wish to assert his right to trial by jury (see s. 20 of the 1980 Act) (note new ss. 19 and 20 have been substituted into the 1980 Act by sch. 3, para. 6 of the Criminal Justice Act 2003, not in force at the time of writing, which will alter these procedures).

1.5 Procedural issues

1.5.1 Burden and standard of proof

In criminal cases the burden of proof is on the prosecution; it is for the prosecution to prove the charge against the accused, which may also involve disproving any defence the accused may raise. The prosecution will seek to prove its case by calling evidence such as that of witnesses to the alleged offence, forensic evidence, evidence of incriminating items found in the accused's possession or in his home or car, a confession he may have made to the police, and circumstantial evidence, for example, his presence at the scene of the crime before or shortly after it was committed. If the prosecution fail to establish a prima facie case that the accused committed the alleged offence, the judge will, at the conclusion of the prosecution case, direct the jury to acquit the accused. If a prima facie case is made out, the trial will continue and the accused may call witnesses, present evidence, and testify himself if he so desires. At the conclusion of all the evidence the prosecution and defence will make their closing submissions and the judge will sum up to the jury, whose task it then is to reach a verdict. The jury are only entitled to convict the accused if the prosecution has discharged the burden of proof and satisfied them beyond reasonable doubt of the guilt of the accused. If the jury are left with a reasonable doubt as to his guilt they must acquit; they may not be satisfied that he is innocent, but if they are not sure of his guilt the case against him has not been proved.

This rule was expressed clearly in the House of Lords in *Woolmington v DPP* [1935] AC 462. D was charged with the murder of his wife who had left him. His defence was that he had gone to his wife taking the gun with him to show her and tell her that he was going to commit suicide, and in showing it to her it had gone off accidentally. The judge directed the jury that once the prosecution proved that the deceased was killed by D, it was for D to show that the killing was not murder. The House of Lords held that this was a misdirection. The accused in a criminal trial is presumed innocent until proved guilty. It was not enough to show that D had done the act, it had also to be proved that he did so with the necessary criminal intent. It was for the prosecution to prove this rather than for the defence to disprove it. Viscount Sankey LC stated (at pp. 481–482):

> Throughout the web of the English criminal law one golden thread is always to be seen, that it is the duty of the prosecution to prove the prisoner's guilt.... If, at the end of and on the whole of the case, there is a reasonable doubt, created by the evidence given by either the prosecution or the prisoner, as to whether the prisoner killed the deceased with a malicious intention, the prosecution has not made out the case and the prisoner is entitled to an acquittal. No matter what the charge or where the trial, the principle that the prosecution must prove the guilt of the prisoner is part of the common law of England and no attempt to whittle it down can be entertained.

While the overall burden of proof is upon the prosecution, the accused may have either an evidential burden or a burden of proof in respect of any defence he may seek to raise. If the accused's defence is anything more than a simple denial that he committed the alleged offence, he will bear an evidential burden to make this a live issue in the trial. The prosecution cannot be expected to anticipate all the possible defences an accused might raise. Accordingly, the burden on them to negate the accused's defence only arises when the accused has raised that defence. In *Woolmington* the accused's defence was accident; it was incumbent upon him to tender some evidence to this effect, either by testifying himself or calling other witnesses or by cross-examination of prosecution witnesses. Once he had raised this issue the prosecution was obliged to disprove it if they were to secure a conviction. Similarly, if the accused wishes to raise other defences such as self-defence, or duress, or automatism, he must discharge this evidential burden.

In some exceptional cases, however, a burden of proof is cast upon the accused in respect of certain defences he may wish to raise. The only such exception at common law is that of insanity. If D wishes to plead that he was insane at the time he committed the offence with which he is charged, he bears the burden of proving insanity. Other exceptions have been created by statute, for example, diminished responsibility (s. 2(2) of the Homicide Act 1957) or 'lawful authority or reasonable excuse' for the possession of an offensive weapon in a public place (s. 1(1) of the Prevention of Crime Act 1953). Where a burden of proof is cast upon the accused he is not required to prove his defence beyond reasonable doubt, but rather to the civil standard of proof, that is, he must prove his defence on a balance of probabilities (see *Carr-Briant* [1943] KB 607 at 610).

1.5.2 The functions of judge and jury

The judge is in overall control of the proceedings. He will decide all legal questions which may arise, for example, whether a particular piece of evidence is admissible, whether a particular witness may be compelled to testify, and whether the prosecution has raised a prima facie case against the accused. At the end of the case he will sum up to the jury. This will usually involve a summary of the evidence which each side has tendered and may involve, in addition, pointing out inconsistencies in the evidence or omissions, or points where both sides are not in dispute thereby highlighting the key issues which will have to be settled by the jury. The judge will also direct the jury on the law. He will instruct them on the necessary requirements of the offence which the prosecution must prove and the requirements of any defence the accused has raised which they must disprove or which he must prove. The jury's task then will be to determine what the facts were and apply the law to these facts to see whether all the requirements of the offence have been proved and the requirements of any defence negated by the prosecution. If the jury are satisfied beyond reasonable doubt that all these requirements have been proved or negated they will convict. If, however, the jury have a doubt as to any requirement of the offence which may not have been proved, or a requirement of the defence which may not have been negated, or, if it is a case where the defence have a burden of proof, they are satisfied that the defence have discharged that burden, they must acquit.

One problem which has arisen in recent years is the tendency of judges to avoid their responsibility to declare and explain the law to the jury. In specifying the requirements of a particular offence, it is the responsibility of the judge to explain to the jury what particular words mean. For example, the offence of burglary is committed, *inter alia*, where the accused enters a building as a trespasser, and steals therein (see s. 9(1)(b) of the Theft Act 1968). It is not sufficient for the judge blandly to state to the jury that the prosecution must prove that (i) the accused entered, (ii) that what he entered was a building, (iii) that he was a trespasser, and (iv) that he stole therein. The jury may not know what constitutes 'trespass' or what constitutes 'stealing'. Further elucidation of these concepts is therefore required on the part of the judge if the jury are to be equipped to perform their task of applying the law to the facts as they find them. In recent years, however, judges have taken a relaxed view of their own responsibilities. Where a statute uses 'an ordinary word' they have been content to leave it to juries to decide upon the meaning of that word and then apply it to the facts as they find them. Thus judges have resisted defining words like 'intention' or 'dishonesty' being content to leave it to the juries to determine what they mean. At many points in this book this judicial attitude will be subjected to criticism as it presumes a degree of linguistic ability on the part of jurors which may not actually exist. It also leaves to juries the task of determining what the law is before applying it to the case before them. This harbours the obvious danger of inconsistency between juries and, it is suggested, the even greater danger of injustice to the accused. Where the liberty of the citizen is at stake there is a great need for certainty and clarity in the law. These goals can only be attained when the judges accept their responsibility to declare and explain the law.

1.6 The European Convention on Human Rights

The Human Rights Act 1998, which came into force on 2 October 2000, gives effect in English law to the rights guaranteed in the European Convention of Human Rights and Fundamental Freedoms. Where Parliament is considering new legislation, s. 19 of the 1998 Act requires a Minister in charge of a Bill before Parliament to make a statement of compatibility or, if the Bill is not compatible with the Convention, to make a statement to this effect. As a result Parliament must now pay particular regard to the Convention to ensure that new laws do not breach the rights which it guarantees. In addition, the courts in applying all legislation must interpret it, so far as it is possible to do so, in a way which is compatible with the Convention rights (s. 3). If a compatible interpretation is not possible, the court must apply the existing law to the case before it but the High Court and appellate courts may make a declaration of incompatibility (s. 4). Where the common law conflicts with the Convention, courts are likely to override the common law because of the obligation on them, as a public authority, not to act in a way which is incompatible with a Convention right (s. 6). Accordingly, the Convention will have considerable impact on criminal courts particularly on matters relating to criminal procedure, evidence, and sentencing. It may, however, also have relevance in certain areas of the substantive criminal law. In the chapters which follow, reference to the European Convention on Human Rights and cases of the European Court of Human Rights will be made where relevant.

FURTHER READING

A. Ashworth, 'Is the Criminal Law a Lost Cause?' (2000) 116 *LQR* 223.

D. J. Galligan, 'The Return of Retribution in Penal Theory', in *Essays in Memory of Rupert Cross* (1981, ed. C. F. H. Tapper).

A. von Hirsch and J. V. Roberts, 'Legislating Sentencing Principles: the Provisions of the Criminal Justice Act 2003 Relating to Sentencing Purposes and the Role of Previous Convictions' [2004] *Crim LR* 639.

N. Lacey, 'Contingency and Criminalisation', in *Frontiers of Criminality* (1995, ed. I. Loveland).

G. Lamond, 'What is a Crime?' (2007) 27 *OJLS* 609.

D. A. Thomas, 'Form and Function in Criminal Law', in *Reshaping Criminal Law: Essays in honour of Glanville Williams* (1978, ed. P. R. Glazebrook).

D. A. Thomas, 'The Criminal Justice Act 2003: Custodial Sentences' [2004] *Crim LR* 702.

2

Actus reus

2.1 The elements of crime

2.1.1 General

The criminal law does not seek to punish people for their evil thoughts; an accused must be proved to be responsible for conduct or the existence of a state of affairs prohibited by the criminal law before liability may arise. Whether liability arises will depend further on the accused's state of mind at the time; usually intention or recklessness is required.

 Key Point

A Latin maxim encapsulates this principle—*actus non facit reum, nisi mens sit rea*—the act itself does not constitute guilt unless done with a guilty mind. The conduct or state of affairs which a particular offence prohibits is called the *actus reus* and the state of mind which the accused must be proved to have had at the time of the conduct or during the existence of the state of affairs is called the *mens rea*.

It is important to note that the terms *actus reus* and *mens rea*, are simply useful labels to be attributed to the constituent parts of any crime being analysed; they do not have any meaning in themselves. They have no greater meaning than, for example, the terms 'obverse' and 'reverse' used when describing coins. Just as the words and designs on coins will vary so too will the *actus reus* and *mens rea* of different crimes.

It is particularly important when analysing the *mens rea* of offences to realise that this term is not prescriptive. In some offences nothing short of intention to bring about the prohibited consequence will suffice (e.g. theft, **Chapter 11** *post*) whereas in others recklessness will suffice (e.g. assault, **Chapter 10** *post*). While the Latin maxim *actus non facit reum, nisi mens sit rea* is a useful tool it is not a universal truth. There are many offences, largely of a minor and regulatory nature, where *mens rea* is not required. These are called strict liability offences and are of statutory creation (see **4.2** *post*). In such cases proof by the prosecution of *mens rea* is not required in respect of at least one element of the *actus reus*.

The use of the Latin terms *actus reus* and *mens rea* has been criticised. In *Miller* [1983] 2 AC 161, 174 Lord Diplock stated that:

> it would…be conducive to clarity of analysis of the ingredients of a crime that is cre-
> ated by statute…if we were to avoid bad Latin and instead to think and speak…about
> the conduct of the accused and his state of mind at the time of that conduct, instead of
> speaking of *actus reus* and *mens rea*.

The Law Commission in its Draft Criminal Code Bill (Law Com No. 177) used the terms 'external elements' and 'fault element'. However, the terms *actus reus* and *mens rea* are so widely used that they will be retained for the purposes of exposition in this book.

While most crimes may be analysed in terms of *actus reus* and *mens rea*, a few crimes exist where these concepts merge. In some offences the *actus reus* may only be proved by proving *mens rea*. For example, s. 1(1) of the Prevention of Crime Act 1953 makes it an offence for any person, without lawful authority or reasonable excuse, to have with him in any public place any offensive weapon. Section 1(4) defines 'offensive weapon' as 'any article made or adapted for use for causing injury to the person, or intended by the person having it with him for such use'. If, for example, the accused is found carrying a pick-axe handle in a public place, the issue whether this amounts to the *actus reus* of the offence will depend on his intention at the time as this article does not fall into either of the first two categories of articles 'made or adapted for use for causing injury'. If there is no intent to use it to cause injury then there is no offensive weapon and thus no *actus reus*. In some other offences the *actus reus* implies a mental element. For example, if the accused is charged with possession of a controlled drug such as heroin or cannabis contrary to s. 5 of the Misuse of Drugs Act 1971 it is necessary to prove that he knew he possessed the thing which turns out to be the drug even though he does not know its nature (see *DPP* v *Brooks* [1974] AC 862; *Boyesen* [1982] AC 768); it is not possible to possess something if you do not know of its existence and thus in the absence of this mental element of knowledge there can be no *actus reus*.

2.1.2 Defences

So far the suggestion has been that if the prosecution prove the commission of an *actus reus* by the accused with the necessary *mens rea*, criminal liability will have been established. This ignores the fact that the accused may be able to rely upon some justification or excuse to avoid criminal liability. Do justifications or excuses, more commonly referred to as defences, form part of the definition of a crime or are they outside the definition, operating like a trump card in bridge? Glanville Williams in *Criminal Law: The General Part* (2nd edn, 1961) expresses the view that all the constituents of a crime are either *actus reus* or *mens rea* stating (at p. 20):

> *Actus reus* includes…not merely the whole objective situation that has to be proved by
> the prosecution, but also the absence of any ground of justification or excuse, whether
> such justification or excuse be stated in any statute creating the crime or implied by the
> courts in accordance with general principles.

An alternative view expressed by D. J. Lanham, *'Larsonneur* Revisited' [1976] Crim LR 276, is that a crime is 'made up of three ingredients, *actus reus*, *mens rea* and (a negative element) absence of a valid defence'. Which view is correct is not crucial; it can even be argued that both are partially correct if a distinction is drawn between justifications and excuses. A. T. H. Smith, 'On *Actus Reus* and *Mens Rea*' in *Reshaping the Criminal Law* (ed. Glazebrook, 1978), states (at p. 99):

> the distinction is that we excuse the actor because he is not sufficiently culpable or at fault, whereas we justify an act because we regard it as the most appropriate course of action in the circumstances, even though it may result in harm that would, in the absence of justification, amount to a crime.

 Example

An example of a justification is self-defence. If, for example, D is charged with unlawfully and maliciously wounding V contrary to s. 20 of the Offences Against the Person Act 1861 he may admit that he did wound V and that he intended to do so, but he would not be convicted if he did so only in response to V's murderous assault upon him. In such circumstances the wounding of V would not be unlawful as it would be justified by the defence of self-defence. As the wounding was not unlawful it can be said that there was no *actus reus*; similarly as D only intended to wound V in circumstances where this was justified, there was no intention to wound V unlawfully (see further **6.5.2.3** *post*). By contrast, if D wounded V because he was told to do so by X who was holding D's wife hostage threatening to kill her if he did not obey, D could plead the defence of duress. In this situation, D intended to wound V and did so unlawfully (as he had no justification for so doing) but the defence of duress would operate to excuse him from the consequences of conviction and punishment. There has been an *actus reus* and *mens rea* but the defence of duress is superimposed much as a trump card might be played in bridge (see further **6.2** *post*).

2.2 Defining an *actus reus*

Each crime must be looked at individually to determine what must be proved to establish its *actus reus*. In the case of a common law crime (such as murder) the definition of its *actus reus* is to be found in the decisions of the courts; in the case of a statutory crime (such as theft) the definition of the *actus reus* is to be found in the statute as interpreted judicially in decided cases. Generally, however, it is necessary to know which elements of the definition of an offence comprise the *actus reus*. **The term *actus reus* has a much wider meaning than the 'act' prohibited by the law which it implies. A useful working definition is that it comprises all the elements of the definition of the offence except those which relate to the mental element (*mens rea*) required on the part of the accused.** The definition of an offence may prohibit acts or omissions (conduct) but it may prohibit these only in particular circumstances. In some cases the definition of the offence may require particular consequences to ensue from the conduct. **A distinction which flows from this is that between 'conduct crimes' and 'result crimes'.** A 'conduct crime' prohibits conduct regardless of consequences whereas a 'result crime' prohibits particular consequences which ensue from conduct on the part of the accused. In a limited number of cases, offences prohibit particular states of affairs without reference to conduct or its consequences. The ambit of the criminal law may be illustrated by the following examples of offences.

 Example

An example of a 'conduct crime' is perjury which is committed whenever D makes a statement on oath which he does not believe to be true. The offence is committed whether or not the statement is believed. In other words, the result of D's prohibited conduct is irrelevant; it is the conduct and not the consequence which is prohibited. The relevant circumstance in the *actus reus* of this offence is that the statement is made on oath. Another conduct crime is rape, which is committed where D penetrates with his penis the vagina, anus, or mouth of another person who does not consent. The relevant circumstance in the *actus reus* of this offence is that the other person is not consenting at the time of the penetration. An example of a 'result crime' is murder where it must be proved that D's conduct caused the deceased's death. If the intended result of the death of the victim does not occur, the law of attempts, under the Criminal Attempts Act 1981, provides for a charge of attempted murder—a 'conduct crime'. An example of a 'state of affairs' offence, where the definition of the *actus reus* is concerned neither with conduct nor its consequences, is being in charge of a motor vehicle on a road or other public place while unfit to drive through drink or drugs contrary to s. 4(2) of the Road Traffic Act 1988. If D is in charge of the vehicle (a state of affairs) it matters not whether he was driving the vehicle, sitting in it, or asleep in it.

2.3 Proving an *actus reus*

It has already been stated that the criminal law does not seek to punish people for their evil thoughts or intentions. If D has the *mens rea* for a particular offence but does not bring about the *actus reus* he is not guilty of committing that offence. This is illustrated by the case of *Deller* (1952) 36 Cr App R 184.

> P was selling a car to D and accepted D's car in part exchange after D represented to him that it was 'free from all encumbrances'. D believed this representation to be false as he had previously executed a document with a finance company which purported to be a hire purchase agreement in respect of the car. If this agreement was valid the car was not free from encumbrances and D had lied to P. If, however, the agreement was in reality a loan on the security of the car it was void as it had not been registered under the Bills of Sale Act 1878 and thus D's representation would, in fact, be true. D was charged with, and convicted of, obtaining P's car by false pretences contrary to s. 32 of the Larceny Act 1916. As the jury found the agreement was a loan on the security of the car, the Court of Criminal Appeal quashed D's conviction as this agreement was void and thus the car was unencumbered. There were, accordingly, no false pretences because 'it may be quite accidentally and, strange as it may sound, dishonestly, the appellant had told the truth' (*per* Hilbery J at p. 191). D quite clearly intended to make false representations but the representations he made were true; while he had *mens rea* there was no *actus reus*. If such facts were to recur the correct charge would be *attempted* fraud by false representation.

2.4 **Conduct must be voluntary**

2.4.1 **General**

 Question

D is driving his car when suddenly, without warning, he suffers a heart attack which renders him incapable of continuing to exercise control over the vehicle. D slumps over the steering wheel and his foot pushes the accelerator pedal to the floor while the car careers through a traffic light which is showing red. The vehicle continues along the road and crashes into the rear of E's car which is stopped at a zebra crossing. E's vehicle is forced on to the crossing where it hits V breaking his leg. If D was charged with failure to stop at a red traffic light, dangerous driving, and criminal damage to E's car, and E was charged with failing to accord precedence to a pedestrian on a zebra crossing and causing V grievous bodily harm, could they be convicted, have they committed the *actus reus* of any of these offences?

Where the *actus reus* of an offence requires conduct on the part of the accused, whether an act or omission, liability will only accrue where the conduct is willed; it is not sufficient that the accused by his bodily movements performed the prohibited conduct or brought about the prohibited consequence defined by the *actus reus* of the offence. In *Bratty v A-G for Northern Ireland* [1963] AC 386 (at p. 409), Lord Denning stated that the 'requirement that it should be a voluntary act is essential, not only in a murder case, but also in every criminal case'. **In offences requiring *mens rea*, if the conduct is not willed there will also be an absence of *mens rea* on the part of the accused, but even if the offence is one of strict liability, requiring no proof of *mens rea*, it is still necessary to prove that the accused's conduct was voluntary.** To convict and impose punishment on an accused who was not responsible for his conduct would be unjust.

In the earlier example, driving through a red traffic light is a strict liability offence. There is no need to prove that D was aware that the light was red and drove through it intentionally. The only matter which the prosecution need to prove is that D was driving the vehicle when it went through the red traffic light. However, as D had been incapacitated by the heart attack, there was at the time no voluntary act of driving and thus no *actus reus*. The charge of dangerous driving would similarly fail. The charge of criminal damage would also fail as, although D's car caused damage to E's car when it crashed into it, this was not the result of a voluntary or willed act on the part of D. Had D felt warning pains before the heart attack and continued driving he might be liable, particularly if he had previously had such an attack and recognised the pains as warning symptoms.

In *Kay v Butterworth* (1945) 173 LT 191 (see also *Hill v Baxter* [1958] 1 QB 277), D was driving home after night-shift work when, overcome by sleep, he drove into a party of soldiers. He was convicted of driving without due care and attention and dangerous driving as, realising that he was becoming drowsy, he should have stopped and it was immaterial that he was not conscious of his actions when the accident happened. Humphreys J stated:

> A person, however, who through no fault of his own, becomes unconscious while driving, for example, by being struck by a stone, or by being taken ill, ought not to be liable at criminal law.

In *Bell* [1984] 3 All ER 842, further examples of involuntary conduct for which no criminal liability may arise were given by Goff LJ who stated (at p. 846):

> a motorist...[who] has been attacked while driving by, for example, a swarm of bees or a malevolent passenger, or because he has been affected by a sudden blinding pain, or because he has become suddenly unconscious by reason of a black-out, or because his vehicle has suffered some failure, for example, through a blow-out or through the brakes failing.

In this example E would be acquitted as his failure to accord precedence to a pedestrian was due to the external application of force on his vehicle which was beyond his control (see *Leicester* v *Pearson* [1952] 2 QB 668). Similarly, there was no voluntary act on E's part which caused V's injury.

In the example of D and E a distinction may be drawn between the causes of their involuntary conduct. E's conduct was caused by the external application of physical force. Another example would be where A is carving the Sunday joint when B seizes his hand holding the knife and thrusts it into C killing him. If A was charged with murder he would be acquitted as there was no voluntary act on his part. In our earlier example D's involuntary conduct was due to his loss of consciousness. Where a person does physical acts while in a state of unconsciousness this is referred to as automatism. For example, a person may perform physical acts while concussed or in a state of somnambulism or while suffering a fit or seizure. Automatism will be considered further in **Chapter 5**.

2.4.2 State of affairs offences

While most offences require voluntary conduct on the part of the accused to establish their *actus reus*, there are some offences which prohibit the existence of a state of affairs. An example given earlier is s. 4(2) of the Road Traffic Act 1988, being in charge of a motor vehicle on a road or other public place while unfit to drive through drink or drugs. For as long as the accused is in charge of the vehicle while unfit the *actus reus* is committed. This is so even though the accused may not be responsible for his unfitness, as where his soft drink has been laced with alcohol, although this may constitute a special reason for not disqualifying him from driving (see *Shippam* [1971] RTR 209; *Pugsley* v *Hunter* [1973] RTR 284).

While there may be strong public policy reasons for adopting an 'absolute liability' approach to 'situational' road traffic offences because of the obvious dangers involved to members of the public, it is questionable whether this approach should be adopted in other cases of 'state of affairs' offences. The courts, however, have not shown any reluctance to convict people of situational offences where they have not been responsible for bringing about the prohibited state of affairs.

> In *Larsonneur* (1933) 97 JP 206, L, a French citizen was required to leave the United Kingdom. She went to Eire but was deported and brought back to Holyhead by

the Irish police who handed her over to British police officers. On a charge under the Aliens Order 1920 that she 'being an alien to whom leave to land in the United Kingdom has been refused, was found in the United Kingdom' L was convicted. The Court of Criminal Appeal upheld her conviction, Hewart CJ referring to the circumstances of compulsion which brought about her return to the United Kingdom as 'perfectly immaterial'.

The Court was totally unconcerned to discover whether L had caused that state of affairs. The suspicion must be that the Court would have upheld her conviction even if a group of kidnappers had removed her from Eire and had brought her to the United Kingdom; a requirement of culpability (i.e. voluntariness) on the part of the accused leading to the creation of the state of affairs would have been desirable and could easily have been implied by the Court of Criminal Appeal in its construction of the statute.

Just when it was thought that *Larsonneur* was an aberrant decision which could be shunted into a siding and forgotten, the Divisional Court revived the controversy with its decision in *Winzar* v *Chief Constable of Kent, The Times*, 28 March 1983.

> W had been brought to hospital on a stretcher. He was diagnosed as being merely drunk and was asked to leave. When he was later found slumped on a seat in the corridor the police were summoned. They removed him to the road, concluded he was drunk and placed him in their police car. W was charged with being found drunk on the highway contrary to s. 12 of the Licensing Act 1872. The Divisional Court construed the words 'found drunk' to mean 'perceived to be drunk' and upheld his conviction on the basis that, as the purpose of the offence was to deal with the nuisance of public drunkenness, it was sufficient to establish guilt to prove that the person was drunk while in a public place; how he came to be there was considered to be irrelevant.

The report does not indicate how W came to be taken to hospital. If he had been found lying in the street originally there might be no cause for complaint. The decision, however, is expressed in broad terms and may be criticised on two bases. First, it is arguable that the officers first perceived W's condition while he was in hospital; by taking him outside to the public highway they had procured the commission of the offence. Secondly, in the absence of express words in the statute dispensing with the need to prove voluntary conduct on the part of the accused bringing into existence the prohibited state of affairs, the requirement of voluntariness should have been implied on the basis that penal statutes should be construed strictly in favour of the accused. (This is a presumption of statutory interpretation honoured more in the breach than in the observance in recent years.)

The decision in *Winzar* may be contrasted with *Martin* v *State* 31 Ala. App. 334, 17 So. 2d 427 (1944) where the Alabama Court of Appeals reversed the trial court's conviction of being drunk on a public highway on the ground that a voluntary appearance on the highway is a prerequisite of a conviction. The appellant had been in his own house drunk when police officers forcibly entered his house, carried him into the street and then arrested him. If this factual situation occurred in England the broad terms of the decisions in *Larsonneur* and *Winzar* would dictate a contrary result. It is to be hoped that courts will apply these two cases narrowly and look for culpability on the part of the accused in bringing about the prohibited state of affairs before convicting. The degree of culpability required need not be very great.

An objective requirement that the creation of the state of affairs be reasonably foreseeable at the time the accused embarked on the course of conduct which ultimately led to that state of affairs would suffice. For example, if the accused is drinking in a public house it is reasonably foreseeable that he will end up on the public highway either at closing time or if he leaves or is ejected earlier. If, however, he is drinking at home, it is not reasonably foreseeable that this will happen. Thus if Winzar had been at home unconscious from his drinking when a third party summoned the ambulance to take him to hospital, the reasonable foreseeability test would not be satisfied. If, however, he had been drinking in a public house when he collapsed the test would be satisfied, albeit the roundabout way in which he ended up on the highway could not have been foreseen at the time he commenced his drinking.

2.5 Omissions

2.5.1 General

> **Question**
>
> A, knowing that B cannot swim, pushes him into the deep end of the swimming pool intending that he should drown. C, a swimmer using the pool, ignores B's struggles and his cries for help. D, the life-guard employed by the council to rescue anyone in difficulty, ignores B's cries, believing them to be a prank of which there have been many that day. E, B's father who is swimming in the pool, also ignores B's cries, reckoning that it is time that his wimpish son either sinks to oblivion or learns to swim. B drowns. Will A, C, D, and E be liable for unlawful homicide (i.e. either murder or manslaughter depending on their *mens rea*)? A is the only one to have performed a positive act which caused B's death. C, D, and E failed to act to save B but they did not do any positive act to cause his death. If liability is to arise it would depend on there being a duty upon them to act to prevent B's death although they are not responsible for the existence of the life-threatening situation.

Generally the common law was concerned to prohibit particular results from occurring and it punished an accused for causing the prohibited result by his positive acts. Gradually the courts came to recognise limited liability for omissions where a duty to act could be implied, the accused failed to act, and the prohibited result ensued. Not all offences, however, are capable of commission by omission. It is a question for the courts whether a particular offence is capable of commission by omission (see, for example, *Firth* (1990) 91 Cr App R 217, **12.3.2.2.1** *post*). Some offences cannot be committed by omission, for example, burglary and robbery. In some offences the definition of the *actus reus* may make it clear that it may only be committed by an act. In *Ahmad* (1986) 84 Cr App R 64, A, a landlord, was charged with doing acts calculated to interfere with the peace or comfort of a residential occupier with intent to cause him to give up occupation of the premises contrary to s. 1(3) of the Protection from Eviction Act 1977. The relevant acts had been done by A without the necessary intent but he subsequently omitted to rectify the situation with the intention of causing his tenant to give up occupation of the premises. The Court strictly construed the statute holding that the requirement of doing acts could not be satisfied by an omission.

Murder or manslaughter may be committed by omission. In the earlier example D and E could be found liable for unlawful homicide provided *mens rea* could be established as the courts have recognised a duty to arise under contract (see *Pittwood* (1902) 19 TLR 37, **2.5.2.2.1** *post*) and a duty on the part of parents to care for their children and protect them from physical harm (see *Gibbins and Proctor* (1918) 13 Cr App R 134, **2.5.2.2.2** *post*). A problem in relation to D and E, however, is that they did not actually cause B's death in the sense in which causation is generally understood (see **2.6** *post*). **The courts do not appear to have grappled with the principles of causation specifically in relation to omissions**. The Law Commission in its Draft Criminal Code Bill (Law Com No. 177) specifically addresses this issue in cl. 17(1) which states: '... a person causes a result...when...(b) he omits to do an act which might prevent its occurrence and which he is under a duty to do according to the law relating to the offence'.

With regard to C, he would not be liable as there is no general duty to be a 'Good Samaritan'. The position of the common law was summarised in *Lord Macaulay's Works* (ed. Lady Trevelyan), Vol. VII, p. 497:

> In general...the penal law must content itself with keeping men from doing positive harm, and must leave to public opinion, and to the teachers of morality and religion, the offence of furnishing men with motives for doing positive good. It is evident that to attempt to punish men by law for not rendering to others all the service which it is their [moral] duty to render to others would be preposterous. We must grant impunity to the vast majority of those omissions which a benevolent morality would pronounce reprehensible, and must content ourselves with punishing such omissions only when they are distinguished from the rest by some circumstance which marks them out as peculiarly fit objects of penal legislation.

While C's disregard of B's plight and failure to render assistance may be morally reprehensible it falls outside the ambit of the criminal law.

2.5.2 Classifying omissions

 Key Point

The analysis of offences into *conduct crimes* and *result crimes* is useful when examining liability for omissions. G. P. Fletcher in *Rethinking Criminal Law* (1978) distinguishes two forms of liability for omissions. The first type he designates 'breach of duty to act', where liability may be imposed for breach of a statutory obligation to act. This relates to conduct crimes where there is no requirement for the occurrence of harm to be proved. The second type of liability which relates to result crimes he designates 'commission by omission', where liability is imposed 'for failing to intervene, when necessary, to prevent the occurrence of a serious harm such as death or the destruction of property' (at p. 421). Fletcher's classification will be used to examine the situations in which the criminal law imposes liability for omissions.

2.5.2.1 Breach of duty to act

Various statutes impose duties to act on individuals in specified circumstances. An individual finding himself in the specified circumstances who fails to perform that duty will commit an offence. For example, a motorist who, without reasonable excuse, fails to provide a police officer with a specimen of breath when required to do so under s. 6 of the Road Traffic Act 1988, or who, when at a police station, similarly fails to provide a specimen of breath, blood, or urine when required to do so under s. 7 of the 1988 Act, is guilty of an offence. The penalty for these offences of omission is the same as the offences of commission of which the motorist was suspected. Thus a motorist suspected of driving a vehicle while unfit due to drink or drugs is liable to the same penalty whether he provides the specimen which would establish his guilt or whether he refuses to provide it. Another example of an offence of omission created by statute is failure by a motorist to stop and provide his name and address to any person reasonably requiring it where his vehicle has been involved in an accident where there has been *inter alia* injury to another person or damage to another vehicle (s. 170(4) of the Road Traffic Act 1988). A more serious offence relating to non-disclosure of information is created by s. 19 of the Terrorism Act 2000. If information comes to the attention of D in the course of his trade, profession, business, or employment giving rise to a belief or suspicion that another person has committed one of a range of offences under the Act, D commits an offence if he does not disclose his belief or suspicion and the information on which it is based to the police as soon as is reasonably practicable.

The previously discussed examples are all of statutory creation where it is specifically stated that failure to perform the duty imposed by the statute is an offence. In some situations the common law has recognised an offence where a duty imposed by common law or statute has been neglected.

In *Dytham* [1979] QB 722, D, a police constable, was on duty in uniform near a club when a man was ejected from the club and kicked to death by a 'bouncer'. D took no steps to intervene and when the incident was over he drove off having told a bystander that he was going off duty. D was charged with the common law offence of misconduct whilst acting as an officer of justice, in that he had wilfully and without reasonable excuse or justification neglected to perform his duty to preserve the Queen's Peace and to protect the person of the deceased or arrest his assailants or otherwise bring them to justice. D contended that there was no such offence known to the law and that misconduct required a positive act or an element of corruption but mere non-feasance was not enough. The Court of Appeal, in upholding his conviction, placed reliance on a passage in Stephen's *Digest of Criminal Law* which stated:

> Every public officer commits a misdemeanour who wilfully neglects to perform any duty which he is bound either by common law or by statute to perform provided that the discharge of such duty is not attended with greater danger than a man of ordinary firmness and activity may be expected to encounter.

Lord Widgery stipulated the requirements of the offence as being wilful neglect not mere inadvertence, and the neglect must be culpable in the sense that it is without reasonable excuse or justification. He stated (at p. 727):

> This...element of culpability...is not restricted to corruption or dishonesty but...must be of such a degree that the misconduct impugned is calculated to injure the public interest so as to call for condemnation and punishment. Whether such a situation is revealed by the evidence is a matter that a jury has to decide.

It is interesting that Dytham was charged with a conduct crime and not the result crime of manslaughter. This is presumably because it was considered that causation could not be established as it would be impossible to prove that the victim would not have died but for Dytham's failure to perform his duty.

Misconduct in a public office would appear to be an offence applicable to all holders of public office. The nature of the offence will obviously vary depending upon the duties, statutory or common law, placed upon the office holder (see also *A-G's Ref (No. 3 of 2003)* [2004] EWCA Crim 868). Another common law offence which may be committed by omission in breach of a duty, in this case a statutory one, is cheating the revenue (see *Mavji* [1987] 1 WLR 1388).

2.5.2.2 Commission by omission

The situations examined so far have involved 'conduct crimes'. Is it possible to commit a 'result crime' by omitting to act? **Not all omissions will give rise to liability; liability will depend on there being a duty, recognised by the law, to act or intervene in the circumstances.** There are several situations in which the law has recognised the existence of such duties; these are outlined later. Most of the cases which have arisen concern murder or manslaughter. There has been some doubt whether less serious offences against the person which require the commission of an assault (i.e. in the broader sense of that term which includes a battery) may be committed by omission. There is no decision which states that an assault requires an act and J. C. Smith argues that such a requirement is unnecessary (see Smith, 'Liability for omissions in criminal law' (1984) 4 *Legal Studies* 88). The situations in which a duty may arise are not closed; new situations may give rise to the recognition of a duty.

> In *Khan and Khan* [1998] Crim LR 830 two drug dealers appealed from convictions of manslaughter arising out of their supply of heroin to the deceased and their failure to summon medical assistance when she went into a coma following her consumption of the drug. In quashing their convictions Swinton Thomas LJ stated:
>
>> To extend the duty to summon medical assistance to a drug dealer who supplies heroin to a person who subsequently dies on the facts of this case would undoubtedly enlarge the class of persons to whom, on previous authority, such a duty may be owed. It may be correct to hold that such a duty does arise....Unfortunately, the question as to the existence or otherwise of [such] a duty...was not... at any time considered by the Judge, and the jury was given no direction in relation to it.

By contrast, in *Evans (Gemma)* [2009] EWCA Crim 650 the Court of Appeal recognised the extension of the duty and upheld a conviction in similar circumstances as the trial judge had correctly identified the duty of care that could have existed, leaving it to the jury to determine whether it did exist on the facts of the case. The judge had directed the jury that if they were satisfied that D had supplied the heroin to V, she having self-injected and died from an overdose with D admitting failing to seek medical assistance when she discovered V's condition, they could convict. The Court of Appeal held that where a person creates, or contributes to the creation of, a state of affairs that he knows or ought reasonably to know has become life-threatening, a consequent duty on him to act by taking reasonable steps to save the other's life would normally arise. The supply of heroin to V represented D's contribution to the creation of the life-threatening situation. This represents an extension of the *Miller* principle as the act of supply itself did not create that situation; rather it required V to self-administer the drug in an excessive amount. The Court of Appeal affirmed that whether a situation gave rise to a duty was a question of law for the judge to determine. (See further **9.3.3.2.1** *post*).

 Question

To what extent does the decision in *Evans* conflict with the principles of causation as understood following the decision of the House of Lords in *Kennedy (No. 2)* [2007] UKHL 38, see **2.6.3.5.4** *post*).

2.5.2.2.1 *Duty arising out of contract*
Where the failure to fulfil a contractual obligation is likely to endanger lives, the criminal law will impose a duty to act. The duty will be owed not only to other parties to the contract but also to any other person whose life may be endangered. In *Pittwood* (1902) 19 TLR 37 the accused was convicted of gross negligence manslaughter following the death of a road user who was hit by a train on a level crossing. The accused was employed by the railway company to look after the crossing and ensure that the gate was shut when a train was due to pass. When the collision occurred the accused was away from his post having left the gate open. His actions were regarded as grossly negligent, and his contention that his contractual obligations gave rise to no duty to the public was dismissed as he was paid to keep the gate shut and protect the public.

2.5.2.2.2 *Duty arising out of relationship*
The existence of close relationships can give rise to a duty to act. It is generally accepted at common law (although there is little direct authority) that parents are under a duty to their children to protect them from physical harm and spouses are under a duty to aid each other (see *Smith* [1979] Crim LR 251, **2.5.2.2.3** *post*). In *Gibbins and Proctor* (1918) 13 Cr App R 134, a man and a woman, with whom he was living, were convicted of the murder of the man's child, she having starved to death because they withheld food from her. In the case of the man he had breached the duty parents owe their children. The woman, by taking money to buy food, had assumed a duty towards the child (see **2.5.2.2.3** *post*).

2.5.2.2.3 *Duty arising from the assumption of care for another*

If a person voluntarily undertakes to care for another person who is unable to care for himself, whether from infancy, mental illness or other infirmity, a duty will be owed to that person (see *Nicholls* (1874) 13 Cox CC 75). The duty may arise from an express undertaking to care for the other, as in *Nicholls* where a grandmother took into her home her grandchild after its mother died, or it may be implied as in *Instan* [1893] 1 QB 450. In the latter case D, who was without independent means, lived with her aunt who became ill and for the last 12 days of her life was unable to care for herself or summon help. D did not give her any food or seek medical assistance but she continued to live with the aunt and eat her food. D was convicted of manslaughter on the basis that by remaining with the aunt a duty was imposed on her to care for the aunt, which duty she had wilfully and deliberately left unperformed.

The principle in *Instan* has been greatly extended by *Stone and Dobinson* [1977] QB 354, so that a duty to care for another may be easily incurred although onerous or difficult to execute.

> S's sister F came to live with him and his mistress D in 1972. F was suffering from anorexia nervosa and, although initially able to look after herself, her condition deteriorated until she was confined to bed by July 1975. S was 67, partially deaf, nearly blind, and of low intelligence. D was 43 but was described as 'ineffectual and inadequate'. S and D tried to find F's doctor but failed. They took F such little food as she required. D and a neighbour once gave her a bedbath. S and D were unable to use a telephone and no one was informed of F's condition. A neighbour was unsuccessful in getting a local doctor to attend. When F died S and D were convicted of manslaughter and on appeal their convictions were upheld, the Court of Appeal being satisfied that the jury were entitled to find that S and D, by the minimal attention they had given F, had assumed a duty to care for her and had been grossly negligent in the performance of this duty as a result of which F had died.

It is unclear from the judgment whether it would have been held that S and D had incurred a duty to care for F if, when she became infirm and unable to care for herself, they had simply ignored her.

> The principle in *Stone and Dobinson* was followed in *Ruffell* [2003] EWCA Crim 122, where the Court of Appeal upheld the defendant's conviction of manslaughter. On an evening in February V was at D's house at D's invitation and both partook of a mixture of heroin and cocaine. V lapsed into unconsciousness and D engaged in some efforts to revive him—placing him by a window to get some fresh air, splashing water on his face, placing him in a bath, wrapping him in towels and placing him by a radiator. The following morning D telephoned V's mother informing her that he was sick due to drinking vodka and that he was sitting on D's doorstep. V's mother asked D to take V inside and cover him with a blanket. D agreed to do so but did not, returning to bed to sleep. Three hours later V was found on the path by workmen and neighbours. He was taken to hospital but pronounced dead three hours later. The cause of death was hypothermia and opiate intoxication. The trial judge directed the jury that they could find that D had assumed a duty of care from the fact that V was a guest in D's house and a friend of D, and that D had sought to revive him following his taking of the drugs. If they considered that D had assumed

this duty, they were entitled to consider whether putting V outside amounted to a breach of that duty. The jury convicted D and the Court of Appeal upheld the conviction endorsing the trial judge's direction to the jury.

Question

Can a person under a duty to care for another ever be released from that duty?

An issue which is left unresolved in the case law is whether a person who is under a duty to care for another, whether due to relationship or because the duty is imposed as a result of care rendered to a helpless or infirm person, may be released from that duty by the person to whom it is owed. For example, if the person wishes to die and does not want medical attention, is the 'carer' under a duty to contravene their requests and obtain medical aid? In *Smith* [1979] Crim LR 251, S was charged with manslaughter following the death of his wife. She had a marked aversion to doctors and medical treatment and would not allow her husband to seek medical attention after she had given birth to a still-born child at home. When she finally gave him permission it was too late and she died before the doctor arrived. Medical evidence was such that she could have been saved had medical aid been sought originally. In summing-up to the jury Griffiths J directed them:

> to balance the weight that it is right to give to his wife's wish to avoid calling a doctor against her capacity to make rational decisions. If she does not appear too ill it may be reasonable to abide by her wishes. On the other hand, if she appeared desperately ill then whatever she may say it may be right to override.

The suggestion seems to be that if a person is capable of making rational decisions he may release a carer from his duty of care. In this case the jury could not agree on the charge of manslaughter and were discharged from giving a verdict. This was only a first instance decision and it left unresolved the question whether a person may release another from the duty of care in anticipation of that duty arising.

Question

For example, could an ageing wife release her husband from his duty of care by telling him that if she falls ill at any time in the future she wants to be left to die at home without medical attention being called?

The answer to this question was given by the House of Lords in the course of its decision in *Airedale NHS Trust* v *Bland* [1993] 2 WLR 316. An application was made by the Trust for a declaration whether it was lawful for doctors to withdraw life-supporting medical treatment, including artificial feeding through a nasogastric tube, from a patient in one of its hospitals who was in a persistent vegetative state with no prospect of recovery or improvement, when it was known that the discontinuance of the treatment would cause his death within a matter of weeks. (Mr Bland was one of the victims of the 1986 Hillsborough Stadium disaster.) The House of Lords held that the treatment could be removed and a doctor would not be acting unlawfully in so doing (see further *R (Burke)* v *GMC* [2004] EWHC 1879 (Admin)).

Lord Goff of Chieveley, giving the leading judgment, stated several principles which apply in the treatment of patients. First, there was **no absolute rule that a patient's life had to be prolonged regardless of the circumstances.** While the fundamental principle was the sanctity of human life, this principle was not absolute. His Lordship was recognising that respect for human dignity demands that the quality of the life in question must be considered. Secondly, **the principle of self-determination required that respect be given to the expressed wishes of the patient.** Thus, if an adult of sound mind refused treatment the doctors responsible for his care had to give effect to his wishes. If the patient was incapable of communicating, an earlier expression of refusal of consent to treatment in certain circumstances would be effective. **Where, however, the patient was both incapable of communicating and had given no earlier indication of his wishes there was no absolute obligation upon the doctor to prolong his life regardless of the circumstances. The question was what was in the best interests of the patient.** Where a patient is incapable of giving consent, treatment may be provided if it is in his best interests (see *In re F (Mental Patient: Sterilisation)* [1990] 2 AC 1, **10.1.1.3.2** *post*). Likewise it may be discontinued if this is in his best interests. His Lordship considered that the question should be carefully formulated as it was not whether it was in the patient's best interests that treatment should be ended but rather whether it was in his best interests that treatment which had the effect of artificially prolonging his life should be continued. Such treatment would not be appropriate where it had no therapeutic purpose, which would be the case where it was futile because the patient was unconscious and had no prospect of any improvement in his condition.

Thirdly, **where such conditions pertained, the treatment being futile, there was no duty on a doctor to continue life-supporting treatment as it was not in the best interests of his patient.** Accordingly, although the discontinuance of treatment would amount to an omission, it would not be unlawful as it would not be in breach of duty to the patient. Similar principles applied with regard to the decision whether to put a patient on life-supporting treatment in the first place. Finally, Lord Goff emphasised that doctors in deciding whether to initiate or discontinue life-support treatment for a patient had to act in accordance with a responsible and competent body of relevant professional opinion on the principles set down in *Bolam* v *Friern Hospital Management Committee* [1957] 1 WLR 582. In *Airedale NHS Trust* v *Bland* guidance was to be found in a 'Discussion Paper on Treatment of Patients in Persistent Vegetative State' issued in September 1992 by the Medical Ethics Committee of the British Medical Association which provided four safeguards which should be observed before discontinuing life-support for such patients:

(1) Every effort should be made at rehabilitation for at least six months after injury.

(2) The diagnosis of irreversible PVS should not be considered confirmed until at least 12 months after the injury.

(3) The diagnosis should be agreed by at least two other independent doctors.

(4) Generally, the wishes of the patient's immediate family would be given great weight.

In all cases where it is decided to end life-support treatment the opinion of the Family Division of the High Court should be sought. This latter requirement might subsequently be relaxed by the President of the Family Division in light of experience.

2.5.2.2.4 *Duty arising from creation of a dangerous situation*

Where a person inadvertently and without the appropriate *mens rea* does an act which starts a chain of events which, if uninterrupted, will result in harm to another or his property (or any other interest protected by the criminal law), that person, on becoming aware that he was the cause, is under a duty to take such steps as lie within his power to prevent or minimise the risk of harm. If, before the harm occurs, he realises what he has done and with appropriate *mens rea* he fails to take such steps, he will be criminally liable. The authority for this principle is *Miller* [1983] 2 AC 161.

> D, a vagrant who was squatting in a house, awoke to find that a cigarette he had been smoking had set fire to the mattress on which he was lying. He did not attempt to extinguish the fire but moved to another room. The house caught fire. D was convicted of arson contrary to s. 1(1) and (3) of the Criminal Damage Act 1971. The House of Lords dismissed his appeal against conviction holding that when D became aware of what he had done in setting the mattress on fire he was under a duty to take such steps as were within his power to prevent or minimise the damage to the property at risk. Lord Diplock stated (at p. 181):

> > I see no rational ground for excluding from conduct capable of giving rise to criminal liability, conduct which consists of failing to take measures that lie within one's power to counteract a danger that one has oneself created, if at the time of such conduct one's state of mind is such as constitutes a necessary ingredient of the offence.

The steps which an accused is required to take to counteract the danger he has caused are such as are reasonable in the circumstances. Clearly he would not be expected to attempt to put out a raging inferno; all that might be required is a telephone call summoning the fire brigade. In the case of a minor fire he might reasonably be required to extinguish it himself if all that would be required was a bucket of water or that he stamp on it with his shoe.

In *DPP v Santana-Bermudez* [2003] EWHC Admin 2908, the Administrative Court applied the *Miller* principle in unusual circumstances. V, a police officer, sought to carry out a lawful search of D and asked him to turn out his pockets, the contents of which included some syringes. She then asked him if he was sure that he had no more needles. He lied to her and her finger was pierced by a hypodermic needle when she commenced a search of his pockets. The Administrative Court held that where someone by act or word or a combination thereof created a danger and thereby exposed another to a reasonably foreseeable risk of injury which materialised, this could amount to the *actus reus* of assault occasioning actual bodily harm. In this situation it was clearly D's duty to tell the truth. Whether a conviction would ensue would depend upon proof of intention or recklessness. This decision may appear to conflict with the Divisional Court's decision in *Fagan* v *Metropolitan Police Commissioner* [1969] 1 QB 439 (see **2.7** *post*; **10.1.1.2** *post*) where it was stated that an omission could not constitute an assault. However, the *Miller* principle is founded upon there being an initial act which creates the danger and the Court in *Fagan*, necessarily, did not address the principle as stated in *Miller*. In the instant case it would have been possible for the Administrative Court to have arrived at the same conclusion by means of the 'continuing act' analysis (see Professor Ashworth's commentary to *Santana-Bermudez* [2004] Crim LR 471).

The incidence of this duty to act arises from the creation by the accused of the dangerous situation. The House of Lords spoke in terms of a physical act on the part of the accused setting the train of events in motion. They did not address the question whether an initial omission which set in motion a train of events which placed a person or property in peril might found liability.

> **Question**
>
> D parks his car on a hill and omits to apply the handbrake. He is walking up the path to his house when he remembers this and turns to see his car start to roll down the hill towards children playing in the street. D realises the danger they are in but he hates children and decides to do nothing either to try to stop his car or warn the children of the danger. V, one of the children, is hit by his car sustaining a broken leg. If D is charged with causing grievous bodily harm with intent contrary to s. 18 of the Offences Against the Person Act 1861 would he be liable? There was no physical act on the part of D which caused the injury but rather an omission, i.e. his failure to apply the handbrake. Should the principle of *Miller* be extended?

2.6 Causation

2.6.1 General

Where an accused is charged with a result crime, it is necessary for the prosecution to prove that his acts or omissions caused the prohibited consequence. In murder or manslaughter, for example, it is necessary to prove that the accused, by his acts or omissions, caused the death of the victim. Similarly, in criminal damage, it is necessary to prove that the accused's acts or omissions caused damage to, or destruction of, property belonging to another. If the death, damage, or destruction occurred because of some other cause then the offence has not been committed even though all the other elements of the *actus reus* are present and the accused had the necessary *mens rea*. The accused, however, may be guilty of some other offence such as attempt (see *White*, **2.6.2** *post*). In the case of result crimes for which liability is strict (see **4.2.1** *post*) causation may be established even though the accused did not intend or have knowledge of the harm or was not negligent thereto (see *Southern Water Authority* v *Pegrum and Pegrum* [1989] Crim LR 442; *National Rivers Authority* v *Yorkshire Water Services* [1994] Crim LR 451; *Environment Agency* v *Empress Car Co. (Abertillery)* [1999] 2 AC 22).

The issue of causation is for the jury to decide upon. The cases which have given rise to problems have usually involved homicide. But, even in homicide cases, causation rarely becomes an issue, as how the victim came to die is usually not in dispute. Where there is a dispute it is the duty of the trial judge to direct the jury on the legal principles relating to causation, but it is for the jury, applying those principles, to decide if the causal link between the accused's conduct and the prohibited consequence has been established. Usually it will be sufficient to direct the jury 'simply that in law the accused's act need not be the sole cause, or even the main cause, of the victim's death, it being enough that his act [or omission] contributed significantly to that result' (*Pagett* (1983) 76 Cr App R 279, *per* Robert Goff LJ). Occasionally, when a particular problem relating to causation arises, such as whether the act of a third party has broken the chain of causation, it is (*per* Robert Goff LJ at p. 290):

> for the judge to direct the jury…in the most simple terms, in accordance with the legal principles which they have to apply. It would then fall to the jury to decide the relevant factual issues which, identified with reference to those legal principles, will lead to the conclusion whether or not the prosecution have established the guilt of the accused of the crime of which he is charged.

In simplifying causation for the jury, the judge may refer to the two principles of causation namely that an accused can only be convicted if they are satisfied that his conduct was both a *factual cause* and a *legal cause* of the victim's death. The discussion will centre on homicide but the principles are equally applicable to other offences where causation may be in issue.

2.6.2 Factual causation

The accused's conduct must be a *sine qua non* of the prohibited consequence. In other words it must be established that the consequence would not have occurred as and when it did *but for* the accused's conduct. This is sometimes referred to as the **'but for'** test. In *White* [1910] 2 KB 124 D put cyanide into his mother's drink with intent to kill her. Later his mother was found dead with the glass containing the poisoned drink beside her three parts full. Medical evidence established that she had died of heart failure and not from poisoning. D was acquitted of murder as he had not caused her death and thus there was no *actus reus*. He was, however, convicted of attempted murder.

The fact that factual causation is established, however, does not mean that legal causation can be established.

Example

A shows B a job advertisement. B applies for the job and C, the employer, invites her for interview. On her way to the interview B is attacked by D while walking through a park and killed. But for A showing B the advertisement she would not have applied for the job and but for C inviting her for interview she would not have been in the park and been killed as and when she was. No one would argue, however, that A's and C's acts should be regarded as legal causes of B's death. It is D's acts which are the legal cause of B's death.

2.6.3 Legal causation

Not all but-for causes are legal causes of an event. Legal causation is closely connected to ideas of responsibility and culpability. Glanville Williams in *Textbook of Criminal Law* (2nd edn, 1983) states (at p. 381):

> When one has settled the question of but-for causation, the further test to be applied to the but-for cause in order to qualify it for legal recognition is not a test of causation but a moral reaction. The question is whether the result can fairly be said to be imputable to the defendant....If the term 'cause' must be used, it can best be distinguished in this meaning as the 'imputable' or 'responsible' or 'blamable' cause, to indicate the value-judgment involved.

The discussion which follows will examine the conditions for the attribution of legal causation.

2.6.3.1 Consequence must be attributable to a culpable act

If the culpable act the accused performed did not contribute to the consequence legal causation will not be established. Thus although D may have been grossly negligent in performing an act he will not be held responsible for a prohibited consequence which would have occurred whether or not he was negligent. This is illustrated by the case of *Dalloway* (1847) 2 Cox 273.

> D was driving a horse and cart without holding the reins which were lying loose on the horse's back. A child ran in front of the cart and was killed. Erle J directed the jury that if the driver could have saved the child by using the reins they should convict him of manslaughter, but if they thought he could not have saved the child by pulling the reins they must acquit him. The jury acquitted him presumably satisfied that the child's death could not have been avoided and thus the child's death was not attributable to the accused's negligence. But for the cart being on the road the child would not have died, but driving a cart on the road is not itself a culpable act.

The principle in *Dalloway* would similarly apply on a charge of causing death by dangerous driving if the death would have occurred regardless of the manner of the accused's driving.

2.6.3.2 The culpable act must be a more than minimal cause of the consequence

In homicide the accused's act may be considered a cause of death if it has accelerated the victim's death. It is no answer to a charge of murder or manslaughter to say that the victim was dying from a fatal disease or injury and would have died within a short time had the accused not hastened his death (see *Dyson* [1908] 2 KB 454). If, however, the act of the accused produces only a very trivial acceleration of the death of the victim, it may be ignored under the *de minimis* principle (see *Hennigan* [1971] 3 All ER 133 and *Cato* [1976] 1 WLR 110). On occasions judges have stated that the accused's act must be a 'substantial' cause of the victim's death. This would tend to state the principle too favourably for the accused (see *Malcherek and Steel* [1981] 1 WLR 690). In *Pagett*, Robert Goff LJ stated that 'the accused's act need not be the sole cause, or even the main cause, of the victim's death, it being enough that his act contributed significantly to that result'. Whatever the terminology used the idea which is sought to be communicated to the jury is that **the accused's contribution to the death of the victim must be more than minimal**. The test is far from scientific as what is sought from the jury is not an exact measurement but, to use Williams' term, a 'moral reaction'; is the death of the victim morally attributable to the accused? This is, perhaps, what Devlin J had in mind when he directed the jury in *Adams* [1957] Crim LR 365.

> Dr Adams was charged with murder of one of his patients by means of administering pain-relieving drugs. Devlin J directed the jury that it did not matter that the patient's death was inevitable and that her days were numbered:

>> If her life were cut short by weeks or months it was just as much murder as if it was cut short by years. The law knows no special defence [by which doctors might be justified in administering drugs which would shorten life in cases of severe pain,] but that did not mean that a doctor who was aiding the sick and dying had to calculate in minutes, or even in hours, and perhaps not in days or weeks, the effect upon a patient's life of the medicines which he administers or else be in peril of a charge of murder. If the first purpose of medicine, the restoration of health, can no longer be achieved there is still much for a doctor to do, and he is entitled to do all that is proper and necessary to relieve pain and suffering, even if the measures he takes may incidentally shorten life.... The law is the same for all, and what I have said to you rests simply upon this: no act is murder which does not cause death. 'Cause' means nothing philosophical or technical or scientific. It means what you twelve men and women sitting as a jury in the jury box would regard in a common-sense way as the cause.

In such circumstances a jury would presumably not find causation, as their moral reaction would be that the doctor was seeking to relieve pain and only incidentally accelerated the patient's death. If, however, the pain-relieving drugs were administered not by a doctor but by the sole beneficiary under her will, and were administered to hasten the inheritance, one could assume that a jury would exhibit a different moral reaction and would find causation to be established.

2.6.3.3 The culpable act need not be the sole cause

The act of the accused need be neither the sole nor the main cause of the prohibited consequence. Other causes contributing to the consequence may be the acts of others or even of the deceased himself.

2.6.3.3.1 *The actions of third parties*

> In *Benge* (1865) 4 F & F 504, the actions of third parties contributed significantly to the deaths. D, the foreman of a track-laying crew, misread the railway timetable so that the track was up at a time when a train was due. D placed a signalman with a

flag 540 yards up the line although the company regulations specified 1,000 yards. The driver of the engine was not keeping a good lookout and several deaths resulted from the ensuing accident. D argued that if the signalman had gone the correct distance and the driver had kept a proper lookout there would not have been an accident. D was convicted of manslaughter after Pigott B directed the jury that if D's conduct mainly or substantially caused the accident it mattered not that it might have been avoided if the others had not been negligent.

The facts of cases need not be as unusual as *Benge*. For example, if A and B both attack C, A stabbing him in the lung and B stabbing him in the abdomen, both would be liable for homicide if he dies as a result of the combined effect of the wounds even though neither wound was, of itself, mortal. There are other circumstances, however, where a subsequent act may supersede an antecedent act which otherwise would have caused death. For example, A poisons B with a slow acting poison. Before it takes effect C decapitates B with an axe. In this situation C's act is the sole cause of B's death. A, however, could be charged with attempted murder (see e.g. *Rafferty* [2007] EWCA Crim 1846).

2.6.3.3.2 *The actions of the victim*

The deceased by his negligence may contribute to his own death. For example, if D is driving in excess of the speed limit when V, who is blind, walks across the road and is hit by D killing him, it matters not that V's negligence contributed to his death if D could have avoided hitting him had he been observing the speed limit (see *Longbottom* (1849) 3 Cox CC 439).

Where the victim brings about his own death this may be legally attributable to the accused where he has caused the victim reasonably to apprehend violence to himself and he has died in seeking to escape. In such a situation D will only be found to have caused V's injuries or death where V's response to D's violence or threat of violence was 'within the range of responses which might be expected from a victim placed in the situation which he was' (*Williams* [1992] 2 All ER 183, 191 *per* Stuart-Smith LJ). V's response must be 'proportionate to the threat, that is to say that it was within the ambit of reasonableness and not so daft as to make it his own voluntary act which amounted to a *novus actus interveniens* and consequently broke the chain of causation' (*Williams* [1992] 2 All ER 183, 191 *per* Stuart-Smith LJ; see also *Lewis* [2010] EWCA Crim 151). In deciding whether V's response was reasonably foreseeable the jury should bear in mind 'any particular characteristic of the victim and the fact that in the agony of the moment he may act without thought and deliberation' (*Williams* [1992] 2 All ER 183, 191 *per* Stuart-Smith LJ). (See also *Roberts* (1971) 56 Cr App R 95; *Mackie* (1973) 57 Cr App R 453; *DPP v Daley* [1979] 2 WLR 239; *Hayward*, **2.6.3.4** *post*.)

In *Marjoram* [2000] Crim LR 372, D argued on appeal that for, the purposes of the question whether a reasonable person could have foreseen the victim's attempt to escape as a possible consequence of D's assault, the reasonable person should be the same age and sex as the defendant. In this case D was aged 16. The Court of Appeal ruled that as the issue concerned the effect of the defendant's conduct on the victim's mind, the test had to be objective to avoid the absurdity where there were two defendants of one being held not to have caused the injury because he had not foreseen the victim's flight, and the other being held to have caused it because he had foreseen the victim's flight.

2.6.3.4 The accused must take his victim as he finds him

The accused cannot complain if his victim is particularly susceptible to physical injury as where, for example, he suffers from brittle bones or haemophilia; if death ensues from an injury which would not have been fatal in a person of sound health it will still be attributable to the accused. In *Martin* (1832) 5 C & P 128 Parke J stated (at p. 130):

> It is said that the deceased was in a bad state of health; but that is perfectly immaterial, as, if the prisoner was so unfortunate as to accelerate her death, he must answer for it.

The accused will be liable, even though he does not physically assault the victim, if he so frightens the victim that a pre-existing condition is exacerbated resulting in death.

> In *Hayward* (1908) 21 Cox CC 692, D, who was in a state of violent excitement, was heard to express his intention of 'giving his wife something' when she returned home. When she did so an argument ensued and D chased her from the house using violent threats. She collapsed in the road and died. Medical evidence was given that she was suffering from an abnormal condition such that any combination of fright or strong emotion and physical exertion might cause death. Ridley J directed the jury that no proof of actual physical violence was necessary, but that death from fright alone, caused by an illegal act, such as threats or violence, would be sufficient (cf. *Watson* [1989] 2 All ER 865).

The principle that the accused must take his victim as he finds him is not limited to consequences flowing from pre-existing medical or physiological conditions; it has been extended to cover the victim's mental condition or religious beliefs.

> In *Blaue* [1975] 1 WLR 1411, D stabbed a girl, the wound penetrating a lung. At hospital she was told that a blood transfusion and surgery were necessary to save her life. She died after refusing a blood transfusion as it was contrary to her beliefs as a Jehovah's Witness. Medical evidence indicated that she would not have died if she had accepted the transfusion. On appeal from his conviction for manslaughter, D argued that the deceased's refusal of a transfusion was unreasonable and broke the chain of causation. The Court of Appeal rejected this argument in categorical terms. Lawton LJ stated (at p. 1415):

> > It has long been the policy of the law that those who use violence on other people must take their victims as they find them. This in our judgment means the whole man, not just the physical man. It does not lie in the mouth of the assailant to say that the victim's religious beliefs which inhibited him from accepting certain kinds of treatment were unreasonable. The question for decision is what caused her death. The answer is the stab wound. The fact that the victim refused to stop this end coming about did not break the causal connection between the act and death.

It has been argued that had the Court of Appeal adopted the 'reasonable foresight' test used in the 'flight' cases discussed earlier there would have been no need for a value judgment to be made on the reasonableness of the victim's religious beliefs; the only issue would be whether such refusal of treatment was reasonably foreseeable. This is the position in the law of tort. Lawton LJ distinguished between crime and tort stating that 'the criminal law is concerned with the maintenance of law and order and the protection of the public generally'. Glanville Williams, in a casenote (1976) *Cambridge Law Journal* 15, observes that this argument ignores the fact that Blaue was in any event punishable severely for wounding with intent. The need to protect the public could be reflected in the sentence for such an offence just as much as in the sentence for manslaughter. In such a circumstance the label under which punishment is imposed would appear to be purely symbolic. Symbolism, however, may sometimes serve a purpose. Had the victim been unable to obtain medical assistance it would have been unarguable that the wound caused her death. Why should Blaue be allowed to avoid a conviction for manslaughter because of his victim's choice not to accept medical treatment? The victim's omission did nothing to interrupt the chain of causation flowing from Blaue's initiating act.

? Question

Could taking his victim as he finds him include holding D liable where V commits suicide following D's attack on him?

Where V commits suicide following D's attack on him, this will break the chain of causation if it is done for a reason other than the attack on him. In *Dear* [1996] Crim LR 595, the Court of Appeal accepted that if V had reopened wounds inflicted on him by D because of shame over an alleged sexual assault by V on D's daughter (which was the background to D's attack on him) rather than because of the fact of the attack (which was serious and had disfigured him), this would break the chain of causation. As the evidence to this effect was described as 'tenuous' and had been put before the jury with an adequate direction, the Court saw no grounds for overturning D's conviction of murder. The Court emphasised that death resulted from bleeding from an artery which D had severed and thus, whether or not V had reopened the wound, D's 'conduct made an operative and significant contribution to the death'. The Court, however, did not address the question whether, if the victim commits suicide because of an attack by D, it must be proved that such suicide was a reasonably foreseeable consequence of D's acts before causation can be established. In *R v D* [2006] EWCA 1139, [2006] Crim LR 923, the Court of Appeal, in quashing a conviction for manslaughter, *obiter* left open the possibility of such a conviction where it was triggered by a physical assault which represented the culmination of a course of abusive conduct, and the final assault played a significant part in causing the victim to commit suicide where the victim was someone with a fragile and vulnerable personality. The Court of Appeal left many questions unanswered in this case. The physical assault had not left any wound which could constitute an operating cause at the time of death. It is suggested, by analogy with the *Roberts* line of cases (**2.6.3.3.2** *ante*) that reasonable foreseeability should be a requirement if suicide is not to be regarded as breaking the chain of causation. It is also not clear what the position would be if the victim of an offence commits suicide due to the distress caused by an offence (for example a rape, indecent assault, or continuous harassment) and there is no wound caused by D operating at the time of death. Such offences might just cross the threshold of dangerousness for the purposes of constructive manslaughter but whether there is causation is another matter. In the absence of any operating and substantial physical cause of death flowing from D's acts, it would seem that death in such cases flows rather from V's acts. There is a difference between physical weaknesses which make a victim more vulnerable to, or beliefs which inhibit the victim from seeking medical treatment for, injuries inflicted by D and emotional factors which prompt V to do positive acts to himself or herself which become the operating and substantial cause of death.

2.6.3.5 Intervening events and acts

Between the initial act or omission of the accused which sets in motion the train of events which result in the prohibited consequence occurring, other events or acts may intervene. The question will arise whether such an event or act amounts to a *novus actus interveniens*, that is a new act which intervenes to break the chain of causation. **The general principle is that an intervention by a third party will constitute a *novus actus* where it is 'free, deliberate and informed'** (*Pagett* (1983) 76 Cr App R 279, 288, *per* Sir Robert Goff LJ, quoting Hart and Honore, *Causation in the Law*; see also *Latif* [1996] 1 WLR 104, 115, *per* Lord Steyn). A natural event will do so where it is not reasonably foreseeable. There are several situations in which it may be argued that the chain of causation has been broken.

2.6.3.5.1 *Medical treatment*

? Question

Where the accused inflicts an injury upon his victim which requires medical treatment, is he to be held liable if that treatment is improper or negligent? While it may be foreseeable that a person who is injured will require medical treatment, is it foreseeable that he might receive improper or negligent treatment?

In *Jordan* (1956) 40 Cr App R 152, D stabbed V who was taken to hospital and the wound was stitched. Eight days later V died. D was convicted of murder. On appeal fresh evidence was called which disclosed that at the time of death the wound was healed but D had died as a result of 1) a Terramycin injection to prevent infection, administered after V had shown intolerance to a previous injection, and 2) the intravenous introduction of large quantities of liquid which had caused V's lungs to become waterlogged. The treatment was described as 'palpably wrong' and the Court of Appeal quashed the conviction as, if the jury had heard this evidence, they 'would have felt precluded from saying that they were satisfied that death was caused by the stab wound'. The problem with the judgment is that no clear principle was stated for determining when the chain of causation might be broken by medical treatment. Hallett J stated (at p. 157):

> We are disposed to accept it as the law that death resulting from any normal treatment employed to deal with a felonious injury may be regarded as caused by the felonious

> injury but we do not think it necessary…to formulate… the correct test which ought to be laid down with regard to what is necessary to be proved in order to establish causal connection between the death and the felonious injury. It is sufficient to point out here that this was not normal treatment.

Treatment which is 'not normal', however, is not necessarily 'palpably wrong'.

> In *Smith* [1959] 2 QB 35, D, a soldier, stabbed V twice with a bayonet in a barrack room fight. Another soldier carrying V to the medical reception station dropped him twice. The medical staff were under pressure as others had been injured in the fight. They did not realise that one of V's wounds had pierced a lung and caused a haemorrhage and gave V treatment which, in light of this information, was described at D's trial as 'thoroughly bad and might well have affected his chances of recovery'. V died and D was convicted of murder. On appeal D's counsel sought to argue that the treatment he received was abnormal and that, if the treatment impeded the chance of V recovering, the death did not result from the wound. The appeal was dismissed, Lord Parker CJ stating (at pp. 42, 43):

> > if at the time of death the original wound is still an operating cause and a substantial cause, then the death can properly be said to be the result of the wound, albeit that some other cause of death is also operating. Only if it can be said that the original wounding is merely the setting in which another cause operates can it be said that the death did not result from the wound. Putting it in another way, only if the second cause is so overwhelming as to make the original wound merely part of the history can it be said that the death does not flow from the wound.

Where the medical treatment is negligent but the wound is still operating, it would seem that both the perpetrator of the wound and the doctor treating it could be said to have caused the death. In such a situation, however, there would be little likelihood of a prosecution for manslaughter being brought against the doctor. Where, however, the wound has healed and negligent treatment independently causes death a prosecution of the doctor may ensue.

It is arguable that had the jury been in full possession of the facts in *Jordan* they legitimately could have found that the wound was simply the setting in which the palpably wrong treatment operated to cause death. An analogous example might be where a doctor administers a drug to V mistaking him for another patient and V dies as a result.

In *Cheshire* [1991] 3 All ER 670, **the Court of Appeal shifted the point of focus away from the question whether the original wound was still an operating cause at the time of death to whether death was attributable to the acts of the accused.**

> D had shot V in the leg and abdomen. Respiratory problems had ensued necessitating a tracheotomy. V suffered further respiratory problems and infections culminating in his death two months after the shooting due to cardio-respiratory arrest. This occurred because V's windpipe had become obstructed due to narrowing where the tracheotomy had been performed, a rare but not unknown complication. The medical staff failed to diagnose and treat this problem. Although the gunshot wounds were healed at the time of death, the Court of Appeal upheld D's

conviction of murder on the basis that the respiratory complications were a direct consequence of D's *acts* which, despite medical negligence, remained a significant cause of V's death.

This is undoubtedly correct as the failure of diagnosis did not cause V to die but simply hindered measures being taken which might have kept him alive. There are similarities with *Smith* who also suffered the misfortune of misdiagnosis. The Court of Appeal was of opinion that only in the most extraordinary and unusual case would medical treatment break the chain of causation as 'treatment which falls short of the standard expected of the competent medical practitioner is unfortunately only too frequent in human experience for it to be considered abnormal in the sense of extraordinary' (*per* Beldam LJ, at p. 675). By 'extraordinary' it appears his Lordship meant 'unforeseeable'. His Lordship went on to suggest the terms in which a jury should be directed where they have to consider whether negligent medical treatment, rather than the injuries inflicted by D, were the cause of V's death (at p. 677):

> [I]t is sufficient for the judge to tell the jury that they must be satisfied that the Crown have proved that the acts of the accused caused the death of the deceased, adding that the accused's acts need not be the sole cause or even the main cause of death, it being sufficient that his acts contributed significantly to that result. Even though negligence in the treatment of the victim was the immediate cause of his death, the jury should not regard it as excluding the responsibility of the accused unless the negligent treatment was so independent of his acts, and in itself so potent in causing death, that they regard the contribution made by his acts as insignificant.

? Question

How likely is it that negligent medical treatment will break the chain of causation?

It is submitted that only in rare cases where positive treatment is given, either in terms of surgical operation or medicinal prescription, will medical negligence supervene to become an independent cause of death rendering the accused's acts 'insignificant'. Examples might be where poison is administered in mistake for a drug, or a drug is administered in an excessive quantity resulting in an overdose, or medical staff continue to administer a drug to which V has displayed intolerance and V dies as a result, or an unnecessary operation is performed in the course of which V dies. If, however, due to misdiagnosis treatment which would have been effectual if administered is not given and V dies, the death can still be linked directly to D's original act as in *Smith* and *Cheshire*. The situation is no different from that where D refuses medical treatment (**2.6.3.5.2** *post*) or where medical treatment is not available. If there is negligence in the treatment of V, for example, a doctor operating to save his life makes a mistake and V dies during the operation, D's acts will remain a cause of death as such an eventuality is not so extraordinary as to be unforeseeable; the operation was a direct result of D wounding V and thus was not independent of D's acts. The crucial issue is whether the accused's acts contributed significantly to the victim's death and, if they did, it matters not whether the medical treatment was incompetent or mistaken (see *Mellor* [1996] 2 Cr App R 245).

? Question

What would happen if D's acts prevented V from having medical treatment for an existing condition?

Where as a result of D's acts V is prevented from undergoing treatment for a condition from which he is suffering (in this case a duodenal ulcer) and he dies as a result of not receiving that treatment, D's acts remain the cause of V's death unless the decision not to treat the pre-existing condition was an 'extraordinary and unusual' one (see *McKechnie* (1992) 94 Cr App R 51).

? Question

What happens if D's act causes serious injuries to V such that he is only kept alive by a life-support machine and this is ultimately switched off?

A problem which has arisen in recent years due to advances in medical technology is that of a victim who has suffered serious injuries whose life is sustained by a life-support machine. If the machine is switched off by the doctors treating the victim, who is responsible for the death? This issue arose in two appeals heard together by the Court of Appeal: *Malcherek and Steel* [1981] 1 WLR 690. Both appellants had caused serious injuries to their victims whose lives were sustained by life-support machines. When the doctors treating the victims concluded, after extensive tests, that they were 'brain dead', they switched off the machines, whereupon the victims ceased breathing, their hearts ceased beating and their blood ceased circulating and 'conventional death' occurred. The Court of Appeal upheld the convictions for murder, Lord Lane CJ stating (at p. 696):

> There is no evidence in the present case here that at the time of conventional death, after the life-support machinery was disconnected, the original wound or injury was other than a continuing, operating and indeed substantial cause of the death of the victim.

While it was immaterial whether the doctors' actions were also causes of death, the Court of Appeal did state *obiter* that they regarded such a suggestion by counsel for the appellants as 'bizarre'. This is undoubtedly correct as when the doctors switched off the machines they merely ceased artificially to sustain lives which had been effectively ended by the initial injuries.

Malcherek and Steel dealt with switching off life-support machines where the victims are already 'brain dead'. It is assumed that the same principles apply where life-supporting treatment is removed from a patient in a persistent vegetative state (see *Airedale NHS Trust* v *Bland*, **2.5.2.2.3** *ante*). In deciding that case the House of Lords were not addressing the issue of causation, but in the course of his speech Lord Goff stated that **in discontinuing life-supporting treatment a doctor is 'simply allowing the patient to die in the sense that he [is] desisting from taking a step which might prevent his patient from dying as a result of his pre-existing condition'.** If the victim is in a persistent vegetative state as a result of the accused's act, his death after discontinuance of life-supporting treatment would also be caused by the accused's act.

2.6.3.5.2 *Neglect by the victim*

 Question

What happens if V mistreats or neglects to treat injuries D caused him and he dies?

If the victim mistreats or neglects to treat injuries perpetrated by the accused, this will not prevent legal attribution of responsibility to the accused where death results. In *Wall* (1802) 28 State Tr 51, the governor of a colony was convicted of the murder of a soldier whom he had sentenced to an illegal flogging of 800 lashes, although the soldier aggravated his condition by drinking spirits while in hospital.

MacDonald LCB directed the jury that:

> there is no apology for a man if he puts another in so dangerous and hazardous a situation by his treatment of him, that some degree of unskilfulness and mistaken treatment of himself may possibly accelerate the fatal catastrophe. One man is not at liberty to put another into such perilous circumstances as these, and to make it depend upon his own prudence, knowledge, skill or experience what may hurry on or complete that catastrophe, or on the other hand may render him service.

In *Holland* (1841) 2 Mood & R 351, D cut V severely on the finger. The wound became infected and V ignored medical advice that he should have the finger amputated or his life might be endangered. The wound caused lockjaw and V died. Maule J directed the jury that it made no difference whether the wound was instantly mortal, or whether it became so by reason of the deceased not having adopted the best mode of treatment as 'the real question is, whether in the end the wound inflicted by the prisoner was the cause of death'. The jury convicted D of murder. Medical science has advanced greatly and a refusal of treatment today in such a case might be regarded as unreasonable. The reasonableness of the victim's conduct, however, is not a relevant issue when considering causation (see *Blaue*, **2.6.3.4** *ante*). In *Dear* [1996] Crim LR 595 (**2.6.3.4** *ante*) Rose LJ stated:

> It would not, in our judgment, be helpful to juries if the law required them…to decide causation in a case such as the present by embarking on an analysis of whether a victim had treated himself with mere negligence or gross neglect, the latter breaking but the former not breaking the chain of causation between the defendant's wrongful act and the victim's death.

It would seem that the accused also has to accept his victim's phobias, irrationality, or stupidity. These matters, however, would be pertinent when sentencing an accused convicted of manslaughter where the death could easily have been avoided had the deceased not mistreated or neglected to treat the injury but, of course, they would not be relevant on a murder conviction where the only sentence available is life imprisonment.

2.6.3.5.3 *Naturally occurring events*

If D renders V unconscious and leaves him lying on a beach with an incoming tide, V's drowning will be attributable to D. In such a situation, while the original injury did not, of itself, cause death, this will not avail D as the event was objectively foreseeable as likely to occur in the normal course of events. By contrast, if D renders V unconscious and leaves him in a building and thereafter the building collapses in an earthquake, V's death will not be attributable to D as V was not left in a position of obvious danger and such an event would not be expected to occur in the normal course of events.

2.6.3.5.4 *Intervention by a third party*

The acts of a third party may intervene to break the chain of causation as where, for example, the injured victim dies when the ambulance in which he is being taken to hospital crashes, or, while in hospital he is attacked and killed by an insane patient who has escaped from the psychiatric ward. Where the act of the third party is a reasonable act of self-defence in response to the act of the accused, or a reasonable act done in the execution of a duty to prevent crime or arrest an offender, this will not break the chain of causation (*Pagett* (1983) 76 Cr App R 279). In *Pagett* D fired a shotgun at police officers attempting to arrest him while holding V against her will and using her body as a shield. The officers returned fire and killed V. D was convicted of manslaughter and his conviction upheld by the Court of Appeal. The same principle would apply if the police had returned fire hitting a bystander.

There used to be two problematic cases in this area of third party interventions. In *Environment Agency v Empress Car Co. (Abertillery)* [1999] 2 AC 22, D Co. had on its land a diesel tank which had an outlet pipe connected to it which led to a drum. The outlet pipe was controlled by a tap which was not locked. An unknown person opened the tap resulting in the contents of the tank draining into the drum, overflowing and polluting a river. D Co. was charged with causing polluting matter to enter controlled waters contrary to s. 85(1) of the Water Resources Act 1991. D Co. denied causing pollution but was convicted. The House of Lords dismissed D Co.'s appeal. Incredibly the leading judgment by Lord Hoffmann **drew no distinction between deliberate acts of third parties and interventions of nature stating that:**

> The true common sense distinction is, in my view, between acts and events which, although not necessarily foreseeable in the particular case, are in the generality a normal and familiar fact of life, and acts or events which are abnormal and extraordinary...There is nothing unusual about people putting unlawful substances into the sewage system and the same, regrettably, is true about ordinary vandalism. So when these things happen, one does not say: that was an extraordinary coincidence, which negatived the causal connection between the original act of accumulating the polluting substance and its escape. In the context of section 85(1), the defendant's accumulation has still caused the pollution.

There was something almost perverse about reasoning which concluded that D should be responsible for a result which he did not cause simply because the act of vandalism by which it was caused was not so extraordinary as to be unforeseeable. There is a major difference between a natural event and the action of a third party: the act of the third party is 'free, deliberate and informed'. In the instant case it was also malicious. In such a case D's liability ends up depending on the choices and actions of others rather than his own choices and actions. In *Kennedy (No. 2)* [2007] UKHL 38 the House of Lords confined the authority of *Empress* to strict liability pollution offences overruling a number of Court of Appeal decisions which purported to apply *Empress* to manslaughter (see *post* and see further *L* [2008] EWCA Crim 1970 and **Chapter 7**, *post*).

The second problem case was that of *Kennedy* [1999] Crim LR 65. D supplied a syringe filled with heroin to V who paid him and injected it and subsequently died. D was convicted of manslaughter. The Court of Appeal placed considerable emphasis on the fact that D's supply of the syringe amounted to encouragement to V to inject himself. A person who encourages another to commit an offence may be liable as an accessory to that offence because of the encouragement offered, not because the encouragement causes the relevant consequence—it is the principal who causes it. In the instant case, however, V, being the deceased, could not be the principal to manslaughter, only D could be that, but V's injection of himself with heroin was the immediate cause of his death (cf. *Dalby*, **9.3.3.1.2** *post*). As in the *Empress* case D merely produced the setting in which a third party's free, deliberate, and informed act intervened. D did not force, induce, or deceive V into injecting himself; his appeal should have been allowed.

In *Dias* [2001] EWCA Crim 2986, where the facts were similar to *Kennedy*, the Court of Appeal quashed the conviction of D for manslaughter as self-injection by the deceased was not unlawful and thus there was no offence which D could have encouraged. The Court, however, left unresolved whether a conviction of constructive manslaughter could have been upheld had the case been presented to the jury on the basis of unlawfully causing a noxious thing to be administered to the deceased. The Court expressed the view that the deceased's self-injection 'might well have been seen as an intervening act' which would probably have broken the chain of causation between the supply of the heroin to the deceased and his death. The Court, however, considered that this issue should have been left to the jury to determine. Unfortunately it did not enlarge on the circumstances in which self-injection would not have the effect of breaking the chain of causation. Most commentators believed that this should only arise where D forces V to inject himself or deceives V as to the nature of the substance in the syringe or V, by reason of his age or mental condition, is unable to understand what he is doing.

?   Question

Has the Court sorted out any confusion in subsequent cases?

Since the decision in *Dias* the Court of Appeal had several opportunities to clarify the uncertainties in this area but on each occasion it either avoided the issue or further added to the confusion. In *Richards* [2002] EWCA Crim 3175, which was referred to the Court of Appeal by the Criminal Cases Review Commission, the Court quashed D's conviction for manslaughter following his guilty plea at trial where he had supplied a heroin-filled syringe to V who had self-injected and died. The Court followed its decision in *Dias* reasoning that self-injection, being the causative act, was not an unlawful act and thus could not found a conviction for manslaughter.

In *Rogers* [2003] EWCA 945, the Court expressed its agreement with its decision in *Dias* and with Sir John Smith's criticisms of the reasoning in *Kennedy* (see [1999] Crim LR 65) concluding that 'in so far as that reasoning was based on self-injection being an unlawful act, it was wrong'. However, the Court upheld D's conviction for manslaughter as, in this case, D had not simply supplied the heroin-filled syringe but had, in addition, applied a tourniquet to V's arm to help raise a vein into which V then self-injected the heroin. The Court came up with the novel view that it was immaterial whether or not V was committing a criminal offence as D **'was playing a part in the mechanics of the injection which caused death'**. By so doing the Court was able to conclude, almost by a conjuror's sleight of hand, that D thereby committed the *actus reus* of the offence of administering a noxious thing contrary to s. 23 of the Offences Against the Person Act 1861 by participating in the 'injection process' (see further **10.1.4** *post*). If D was the principal, then the issue of an intervening act by V could be avoided as the s. 23 offence would amount to an unlawful and dangerous act. Of course, the Court chose to ignore the fact that however much D might tighten the tourniquet, there would be no administration until V injected the syringe and his act was 'free, deliberate and informed' and thus was an intervening act between the act of supply, or of raising a vein, and death resulting from the injection.

The Court of Appeal, however, remained impressed with their own magic and, indeed, sometimes appeared to believe that their tricks represented the reality. Following the decisions in *Dias* and *Richards*, the Criminal Cases Review Commission referred the case of *Kennedy* back to the Court of Appeal. It appeared that the conviction could not stand following the doubts expressed in *Dias* and the quashing of a conviction in similar circumstances in *Richards*. The sleight of hand of *Rogers* did not appear to apply as Kennedy had performed no act beyond supplying the heroin-filled syringe. The Court of Appeal, however, upheld the conviction in *Kennedy* while, at the same time, expressing no doubts about the decisions in *Dias* and *Richards*. Some higher order magic was surely involved here! Magic, of course, is a matter of faith and not something subject to rational explanation. The Court of Appeal's second decision in *Kennedy* [2005] EWCA Crim 685, all but defied rational explanation.

The Court, while declaring that Lord Hoffmann's dicta in *Empress* were very much confined to their context, conjured a new spell derived from a dictum of Lord Steyn's in *Latif* [1996] 1 WLR 104, at 115 where he stated:

> The free, deliberate and informed intervention of a second person, who intends to exploit the situation created by the first, *but is not acting in concert with him* is held to relieve the first actor of criminal responsibility.

Lord Steyn's dictum previously had been regarded as a statement of conventional doctrine: if a person is acting in concert there is a joint enterprise and those involved are either principals or accessories, and the act of the principal in bringing about the prohibited result cannot amount to an intervening act negating the liability of another party who has aided and abetted the principal in performing that act. The Court of Appeal, however, treated 'acting in concert' as some separate means of participation in an offence such that if it could be proved that D and V acted in concert, resulting in the s. 23 offence being committed, D could be guilty of this offence and of manslaughter (if death ensued) notwithstanding the fact that V did not commit any offence by self-injecting. In *Finlay* [2003] EWCA Crim 3868, the Court of Appeal took *Rogers* to have been based on the concept of **joint principalship**. Buxton LJ stated at para. 14:

> *Rogers* is thus clear authority for saying that if a 'helper' is in fact a joint principal with the deceased, then he can be guilty of an offence under section 23 even though the deceased is not guilty of an offence by self-administration. That follows from the classic understanding of what is meant by joint principalship, as set out in the 10th Edition of Smith and Hogan at page 161. That work of authority says:
>
> > 'A and B are joint principals where each does an act which is a cause of the *actus reus*, eg, each stabs P who dies from the combined effect of the wounds; or A and B together plant a bomb which goes off and kills P; but then each is liable for his own act, not because he has "participated" in the act of another, and each is liable to the extent of his own *mens rea*.'
>
> The learned authors finish the paragraph by saying: 'there are two principals and two offences'. The test therefore is whether each of the parties has done an act which is a cause of the *actus reus* and it was that test that was applied by this court in *Rogers*. In paragraph 7 the court said this:
>
> > '...by applying the tourniquet, the appellant was playing a part in the mechanics of the injection which caused the death. It is therefore, as it seems to us, immaterial whether the deceased was committing a criminal offence.'

This was powerful magic indeed—the magic of self-deception. Just a moment's analysis would have revealed several flaws in the reasoning. It was not immaterial to Smith and Hogan that one of the parties was not committing a criminal offence; joint principalship could only apply where (1) each party does an act which is a cause of the *actus reus*, (2) does so with the necessary *mens rea* for the offence, and (3) is liable (which in context means to conviction of a criminal offence) for his own act and not because he has participated in the act of another. In *Rogers* the Court created liability out of D's assistance in V's act of self-injection which looked remarkably like participation in the act of another. The act of V, of course, was one which V did without *mens rea* as the *mens rea* of the s. 23 offence is an intention to administer a noxious thing to **another** person or recklessness thereto. V, of course, was intending to administer to **himself** and was not acting unlawfully in doing so. Finally, joint principalship requires that each party's act be a cause of the *actus reus* of the offence. In the example of the stabbing A and B each stab P; each wound is a more than minimal cause of P's death. In the syringe cases, absent V's self-injection and there would be no administration and no death. None of the three criteria which Smith and Hogan specified for liability as a joint principal are met. To further emphasise this point another quotation from Smith and Hogan immediately following the passage quoted earlier would have assisted the Court of Appeal:

Suppose that in the bomb case, B intends (and believes that A intends) that ample warning will be given to allow the area to be cleared, whereas A intends that no warning shall be given. The bomb goes off prematurely and kills P. A is prima facie guilty of murder, B of manslaughter. Similarly where they jointly release a gas canister which B believes to contain tear gas and A knows to contain a deadly gas. There are two principals and two offences.

This passage, and the one preceding it, must be seen in the context of a further qualifying statement made by the learned authors at p. 161 that 'where there are several participants in a crime the principal is the one whose act is the most immediate cause of the *actus reus*.' In the syringe examples there are not two offences as V commits no offence; nor is D's act the most immediate cause of the *actus reus*. The conclusion, which eluded the Court of Appeal, is that D and V cannot be joint principals. The Court of Appeal in *Kennedy* was made aware of these difficulties with the concept of joint principalship by the Criminal Cases Review Commission in their reference. Their Lordships' faith in the power of magic, however, was not to be shaken as they stated, with sincere conviction, at para. 42:

If Kennedy either caused the deceased to administer the drug or was acting jointly with the deceased in administering the drug, Kennedy would be acting in concert with the deceased and there would be no breach in the chain of causation.

 Question

Does the concept of 'acting in concert' not provide a logical basis for the Court's decision?

The criminal law, prior to this decision, did not recognise 'acting in concert' as a separate mode of participation; it talked only of principals and accessories (or secondary parties) and joint enterprises. There is no joint enterprise where one of the two participants cannot be convicted of an offence. In such a situation D could be liable to conviction as the principal if he was acting through V who was an innocent agent. Where V, however, was of the age of criminal responsibility, was not mentally incompetent, and acted voluntarily (his act being free, deliberate, and informed), he was not an innocent agent. Their Lordships clearly believed that 'acting in concert' covered both joint principalship and the situation of principal and innocent agent. But V was not an innocent agent as his act was free, deliberate, and informed—he was not duped. Further he could not be a joint principal. Nonetheless the Court of Appeal considered that where D handed the heroin-filled syringe to V for V to self-inject, D and V were acting in concert in committing the s. 23 offence (even though V could not be convicted of this) and that that offence amounted to the unlawful and dangerous act which provided the basis for a conviction of D of manslaughter. **To talk of D and V being jointly engaged in administering the heroin where it was V who administered it, was both linguistically and legally inaccurate. To describe D's and**

V's actions as a '"combined operation" for which they are jointly responsible' was similarly so. To suggest that it was really a question of fact for juries to determine whether or not D and V were acting in concert, could neither cure nor excuse this error.

> **Question**
>
> What is it, then, that joint responsibility covers?

Joint responsibility refers to two or more actors being jointly liable to conviction in respect of the commission by them of an offence. In *Kennedy* (and all the other cases) V was not, and could not be, liable to conviction for the s. 23 offence. While Kennedy possessed a Class A drug, that possession was not causative of death. Glanville Williams, *Textbook of Criminal Law* (2nd edn, 1983), p. 392 observed:

> The *novus actus* rule is of fundamental importance at common law, because it under-lies the doctrine of accessoryship. If D2 incites D1 to kill V, and D1 complies, D2 has prompted (in ordinary speech, caused) D1 to perpetrate the crime, and is himself an accessory to the crime, but he has not in law caused V's death. Fletcher states the principle as follows:
>
> > 'Aiding the crime of a responsible, self-actuating perpetrator does not "cause", "control" or "determine" the latter's conduct. The accessory contributes to the crime, but the execution is not his doing.' [*Rethinking Criminal Law* (Boston 1978), 582]

If it were not for the *novus actus* rule the successful inciter would be liable as a perpetrator, which would require the law of complicity to be rewritten.

> **Question**
>
> It would appear that the Court of Appeal in trying to uphold one conviction have caused problems with several areas of the law. Has anyone had the sense to sort out this potential mess?

Thankfully *Kennedy* was appealed to the House of Lords when the Court of Appeal certified the following question of general public importance:

> When is it appropriate to find someone guilty of manslaughter where that person has been involved in the supply of a class A controlled drug, which is then freely and voluntarily self-administered by the person to whom it was supplied, and the administration of the drug then causes his death?

In *Kennedy* (*No. 2*) [2007] UKHL 38, their Lordships answered the question with a unanimous and resounding 'Never'. The House of Lords reasserted the principle that the criminal law assumes the existence of free will. Lord Bingham of Cornhill stated (at para. 14):

The law recognises certain exceptions, in the case of the young, those who for any reason are not fully responsible for their actions, and the vulnerable, and it acknowledges situations of duress and necessity, as also of deception and mistake. But, generally speaking, informed adults of sound mind are treated as autonomous beings able to make their own decisions how they will act, and none of the exceptions is relied on as possibly applicable in this case. Thus D is not to be treated as causing V to act in a certain way if V makes a voluntary and informed decision to act in that way rather than another. There are many classic statements to this effect. In his article *'Finis for Novus Actus?'* (1989) 48(3) CLJ 391, 392, Professor Glanville Williams wrote:

> 'I may suggest reasons to you for doing something; I may urge you to do it, tell you it will pay you to do it, tell you it is your duty to do it. My efforts may perhaps make it very much more likely that you will do it. But they do not cause you to do it, in the sense in which one causes a kettle of water to boil by putting it on the stove. Your volitional act is regarded (within the doctrine of responsibility) as setting a new "chain of causation" going, irrespective of what has happened before.'

In chapter XII of *Causation in the Law*, 2nd ed (1985), p 326, Hart and Honoré wrote:

> 'The free, deliberate, and informed intervention of a second person, who intends to exploit the situation created by the first, but is not acting in concert with him, is normally held to relieve the first actor of criminal responsibility.'

This statement was cited by the House with approval in *R v Latif* [1996] 1 WLR 104, 115. The principle is fundamental and not controversial.

The sleight of hand of the Court of Appeal did not fool the House of Lords who affirmed the doctrine of *novus actus interveniens* and its importance in maintaining the essential division between principals and accessories as identified by Glanville Williams. In arriving at this position, their Lordships declared that *Finlay* and *Rogers* were wrongly decided. They confirmed that Kennedy had not either administered the heroin or caused it to be administered and affirmed the decisions in *Dalby* and *Dias*.

The mess made by the Court of Appeal in its series of misguided decisions over a period of nine years was thus cleared up. What is disappointing is that it took so long for the fundamental errors made by the Court of Appeal to be recognised and remedied. It must be an issue of concern that the defendants in numerous cases were convicted of manslaughter, and that they were sentenced to lengthy terms of imprisonment when they were guilty of no homicide offence, all because senior appellate judges lacked even the most rudimentary understanding of the doctrine of causation. While Lord Bingham of Cornhill deserves some credit for belatedly rectifying the errors made by the Court of Appeal in this area, that credit should be strictly limited as when he was Lord Chief Justice he had an opportunity to nip these errors in the bud in 1998 when they first arose in the case of *Edwards* (unreported, 28 April 1998) and failed to do so. Mr Edwards' sentence of five years was also upheld.

 Question

But is there not a possible problem remaining with the conviction of Evans for gross negligence manslaughter?

An issue arising from the decision in *Evans (Gemma)* [2009] EWCA Crim 650 (see **2.5.2.2** *ante*) is whether the Court of Appeal adequately considered the principles of causation before affirming the conviction of gross negligence manslaughter. D's liability arose from her failure to take reasonable steps to save V's life following her overdosing on the heroin D had supplied, which supply created, or contributed to the creation of, the state of affairs which became life-threatening. It may be argued that it was not the supply which created the dangerous situation; rather it was V's voluntary act of self-injection which occurred after the act of supply and before the danger arose. The Court of Appeal briefly adverted to *Kennedy (No. 2)*, but did not examine the principles of causation in any detail concentrating rather on other gross negligence manslaughter cases. If the point at which the duty arose was only when the life-threatening situation had developed and D became aware of it, it may be that V's prior act of taking the heroin did not break the chain of causation. If, however, the focus is placed on the initiating act which contributed to the creation of the dangerous situation, namely the supply of the heroin, as being the point when the duty arose, then V's act of taking the heroin could break the chain of causation. As D's duty requires awareness of the existence of the dangerous situation, it is submitted that the chain of causation between the duty arising and the death occurring was not broken by any act of V as her self-administration preceded this point.

2.7 Coincidence of *actus reus* and *mens rea*

Question

If D commits the *actus reus* of an offence requiring proof of *mens rea*, at what point in time must he have had the requisite *mens rea*?

Where an offence requires *mens rea* the prosecution must prove that the accused had *mens rea* at the time he did the act which caused the *actus reus* (*Jakeman* (1982) 76 Cr App R 223). In this case D had booked two cases containing cannabis onto a flight from Accra to Rome and from there to London. The flight was diverted from Rome to Paris. D had repented of her intention to import the cannabis into England and did not claim her cases in Paris. Officials in Paris, however, sent the cases to London where the cannabis was discovered. D was charged with being knowingly concerned in the importation of cannabis. The Court rejected her defence that she had repented of her criminal intent at the time the cannabis entered England. They stated that what mattered was her 'state of mind at the time the relevant acts are done'. In this case the relevant act was booking her luggage to London, at which time she intended it to arrive in London, and it was immaterial that innocent agents at a Paris airport subsequently became instrumental in it being sent to London.

? Question

What happens if the *actus reus* is established by means of a continuing act?

Where an *actus reus* may be brought about by a continuing act, it is sufficient that the accused had *mens rea* during its continuance albeit that he did not have *mens rea* at its inception (*Fagan* v *Metropolitan Police Commissioner* [1969] 1 QB 439). In *Fagan* D accidentally drove his car onto a policeman's foot. The officer asked him to move but he delayed doing so. D was convicted of assaulting the constable in the execution of his duty. It was clear that at the time of driving onto the officer's foot D did not have the necessary *mens rea* for the offence. The Divisional Court, however, held that the assault involved a battery (unlawful application of force to another person) and that this battery continued after the car came to rest, and thus there was a continuing act of assault for which D had the necessary *mens rea* at some time during its continuance. The Court also stated that **if an act is complete, even though results continue to flow from it, the subsequent inception of *mens rea* cannot convert it into an offence**. For example, if D accidentally runs over V in his car and V sustains injuries from which he dies some time later, D's desire that V die, formed after the accident, will not convert V's death into murder. The act which caused death was complete prior to the formation of D's desire, even though the results of the act continued to flow up to the point of V's death.

If the facts of *Fagan* were to recur the accused could now be convicted under the 'duty' principle in *Miller* (**2.5.2.2.4** *ante*). The 'continuing act' principle remained relevant in some circumstances. In *Kaitamaki* [1985] AC 147 (see further *Cooper and Schaub* [1994] Crim LR 531), the Privy Council affirmed the decision of the New Zealand Court of Appeal that, for the purposes of rape, sexual intercourse is a continuing act. Thus, if D penetrated V with consent (or believing he had consent), and then declined to withdraw on consent being revoked (or on realising that V did not consent), he was guilty of rape as he had formed the *mens rea* for the offence during the continuance of the *actus reus*. The Sexual Offences Act 2003 has affirmed this approach providing in s. 79(2): 'Penetration is a continuing act from entry to withdrawal'.

? Question

What happens if there are several acts which combine to bring about a consequence and D had *mens rea* only part of the time during which those acts were committed?

The cases examined so far have involved one act to which *mens rea* may be linked. In several cases the problem has arisen of a consequence ensuing from a combination of several acts but *mens rea* did not exist for the commission of each act. Is it sufficient that the accused had *mens rea* at some stage during the course of events?

In *Thabo Meli* [1954] 1 WLR 228, the appellants struck V over the head with intent to kill him. V's body was rolled over a cliff to make his death appear to be an accident. In fact V died from exposure and not from the initial blow to the head. The appellants had *mens rea* when they struck V, but V died from the act of disposal when they did not have *mens rea* as they believed they were disposing of a corpse. The appellants were undoubtedly guilty of attempted murder but the Privy Council upheld the convictions for murder because, as they stated (at p. 230) it was:

> impossible to divide up what was really one series of acts in this way. There is no doubt that the accused set out to do all these acts in order to achieve their plan and as parts of their plan; and it is too refined a ground of judgment to say that, because they were under a mis-apprehension at one stage and thought that their guilty purpose had been achieved before in fact it was achieved, therefore they are to escape the penalties of the law.

In framing the decision in this way the Privy Council appear to have delivered a policy decision as there was no *mens rea* when the act immediately causing the death was performed. The fact that all the acts were performed in pursuance of an antecedent plan, and death ensued from the execution of that plan, appeared to be crucial to the decision of the Privy Council. In *Church* [1966] 1 QB 59, the Court of Appeal extended the *Thabo Meli* 'series of acts' doctrine to a case of manslaughter where there was no antecedent plan. In the course of a fight with V, D struck and attempted to strangle her. She fell unconscious and D, believing her to be dead, threw her into a river where she drowned. The Court of Criminal Appeal was of the opinion that it was sufficient for a conviction if the conduct constituted 'a series of acts which culminated in her death'. The Court stated *obiter* that the jury could have convicted of murder 'if they regarded the appellant's behaviour from the moment he first struck her to the moment when he threw her into the river as a series of acts designed to cause death or grievous bodily harm'. As the act of disposal is for the purpose of disposing of a body, it being the accused's belief that death had occurred already, it is difficult to see how the series of acts could be described as being 'designed to cause death'. The act which caused death was designed to dispose of a corpse! The principle the Court was endeavouring to state has been clarified by another case.

In *Le Brun* [1991] 4 All ER 673, there was neither an antecedent plan nor did D believe that he was dealing with a corpse as he attempted to drag the unconscious body of his wife away from the place where he had assaulted her following an argument in the course of which she had refused to go home. In moving his wife she slipped from his grasp and hit her head on the pavement causing a fractured skull from which she died. D was convicted of manslaughter following a direction to the jury by the trial judge that they could convict of murder or manslaughter, depending on the intention with which the original blow was struck, if D had 'accidentally dropped the victim causing her death whilst either: (a) attempting to move her to her home against her wishes..., and/or (b) attempting to dispose of her body or otherwise cover up the previous assault'. The Court of Appeal upheld D's conviction of manslaughter applying *Church*, Lord Lane CJ stated (at pp. 678, 679):

> It seems to us that where the unlawful application of force and the eventual act causing death are parts of the same sequence of events, the same transaction, the fact that there is an appreciable interval of time between the two does not serve to exonerate

the defendant from liability. That is certainly so where the appellant's subsequent actions which caused death, after the initial unlawful blow, are designed to conceal his commission of the original unlawful assault...In short, in circumstances such as the present,...the act which causes death and the necessary mental state to constitute manslaughter need not coincide in point of time.

Accordingly, the 'transaction' principle applies not only where D is disposing of what he believes to be a corpse but also when he is attempting to move V to a place contrary to her will or where D is attempting to cover up his original crime. The Court of Appeal did not expressly declare that the **'transaction' principle** is equally applicable to murder, but presumably it is.

An alternative approach to this problem is to express it as an issue of causation. If, for example, D by an assault (for which he has *mens rea*) renders V unconscious leaving him on a beach with an incoming tide and V drowns, D will be guilty at least of manslaughter as V's death was reasonably foreseeable. Why should it make any difference if D, believing V to be dead as a result of his assault on him, throws V into the water where he drowns? It is equally foreseeable by the reasonable person that V might not be dead and thus may die from drowning. D's second culpable act cannot be regarded as a *novus actus interveniens* as it is all part of the same transaction or series of acts (see Smith and Hogan, *Criminal Law* (9th edn) at p. 341). The Court of Appeal in *Le Brun* accepted that the problem could also be expressed as one of causation. However, the Court continued to focus on the later act which immediately caused death rather than regarding the original act, which was done with *mens rea*, as a cause of death. If the original act, performed with *mens rea*, is seen as a cause of death, with everything subsequent being regarded as an unbroken chain of causation, there is no problem of a lack of coincidence between *actus reus* and *mens rea*; there is no need to rely on a 'transaction principle'. **It is arguable that the transaction principle has arisen because the courts have failed to recognise that the *actus reus* of an offence comprises conduct, circumstances, and consequences.** They have treated the act which immediately led to death as the *actus reus* when it could equally be seen as the consequence flowing from the original conduct. In the South African case of *S v Masilela* [1968] (2) SA 558, Ogilvie Thompson JA came closest to this position when he described the accused's earlier acts of strangulation as 'a direct and contributory cause' of the victim's later death which resulted from carbon monoxide poisoning when the accused set fire to his house believing him to be dead; had the victim not been unconscious he could have escaped from the house.

 Question

What happens if it is not possible to determine which of D's acts caused the victim's death?

In *Thabo Meli*, *Church*, and *Le Brun* it was clear that death ensued from the second act. Where it is not possible to determine which of the two acts caused death, the accused may be convicted only if the prosecution prove that he acted with *mens rea* on both occasions (*A-G's Reference (No. 4 of 1980)* [1981] 1 WLR 705). The facts of *A-G's Reference* were that D had slapped V on the face causing her to fall down a flight of stairs and bang her head. D dragged her upstairs by a rope tied around her neck, placed her in the bath and drained off her blood before cutting up her body and disposing of the pieces. It was impossible to determine the cause of death. The Court of Appeal held that it is not necessary to prove which act caused death but the jury could only convict of manslaughter if they were satisfied *both* (i) that the fall downstairs was the result of an intentional act by the accused which was unlawful and dangerous (i.e. 'unlawful act' manslaughter), and (ii) that the act of cutting the victim's throat was an act of gross criminal negligence (i.e. gross negligence manslaughter). The same principle would apply on a charge of murder provided the accused had the requisite *mens rea* when he performed each act. For example, D hits V over the head intending to kill him but believing that V is not dead he slits his throat to complete the job before disposing of the body in an incinerator. In this example D has the necessary *mens rea* for murder when he hits V and when he slits his throat. The problem, however, with the principle in *A-G's Reference* is that it is too favourable to the accused as the jury must acquit if they are not satisfied that each act was performed with *mens rea*. It is submitted that if it is proved that the accused had the relevant *mens rea* when he performed the first act, he should be guilty of homicide as either this act caused death and thus there is no problem or, if the second act caused death, a conviction can be supported on the basis of the transaction principle or on the basis of causation, as the first act was a contributory cause of death.

FURTHER READING

L. Alexander, 'Criminal Liability for Omissions: an Inventory of Issues', in Shute and Simester (eds.), *Criminal Law Theory: Doctrines of the General Part* (2002).

H. Gross, 'A Note on Omissions' (1984) 4 *LS* 308.

B. Hogan, 'Omissions and the Duty Myth', in *Criminal Law: Essays in Honour of J. C. Smith* (1986, ed. P. Smith).

A. C. E. Lynch, 'The Mental Element in the *Actus Reus*' (1982) 98 *LQR* 109.

M. Nkrumah, '*R v Kennedy* Revisited' (2008) 72 *JCL* 117.

A. Norrie, 'A Critique of Criminal Causation' (1991) 54 *MLR* 685.

D. Ormerod and R. Forston, 'Drug Suppliers as Manslaughterers (Again)' [2005] *Crim LR* 819.

J. Rogers, 'Death, drugs and duties' [2009] 6 *Archbold News* 6.

J. C. Smith, 'Liability for Omissions in the Criminal Law' (1984) 4 *LS* 88.

J. E. Stannard, 'Medical Treatment and the Chain of Causation' (1993) 57 *JCL* 88.

G. Williams, 'Criminal Omissions—the Conventional View' (1991) 107 *LQR* 86.

3

Mens rea

3.1 **Introduction**

Where a person has performed acts or brought about consequences which constitute the *actus reus* of an offence he will generally be found guilty of the offence only if he had the necessary *mens rea* at the time he acted. The exceptions to this are offences of strict liability and offences which may be committed negligently, for example, careless driving. ***Mens rea* refers to the mental element necessary for a particular crime.** This may differ from one crime to another and the definition of each crime must be examined to determine what state of mind is required. Words used in offences to convey a requirement of *mens rea* are, for example, intention, recklessness, maliciousness, wilfulness, knowledge (together with their adjectival and adverbial variants).

Offences which require *mens rea* are generally regarded as being more serious than those which may be committed negligently or for which liability is strict. The term imports a notion of culpability or moral blameworthiness on the part of the offender. For most of the twentieth century scholars understood *mens rea* to require an advertent state of mind, whereas those offences which could be committed negligently, or for which liability was strict, imposed liability on the person who may have done the prohibited act or caused the prohibited consequence inadvertently. Towards the end of that century, however, the line of demarcation between *mens rea* and negligence became blurred as judges struggled to define the meaning of *mens rea* words. After two decades of struggling the outcome was uncertainty and confusion. This was particularly unsatisfactory in the light of the serious consequences for the individual which attend conviction for a criminal offence. It was also unacceptable in a country which purports to adhere to the principles deriving from the idea of the rule of law. J. Raz in 'The rule of law and its virtue' (1977) 93 LQR 195, at pp. 198, 199 states:

> The law must be open and adequately publicised. If it is to guide people they must be able to find out what it is. For the same reason its meaning must be clear. An ambiguous, vague, obscure or imprecise law is likely to mislead or confuse at least some of those who desire to be guided by it.

'Ambiguous', 'vague', 'obscure', and 'imprecise' are all words which could be used to describe judicial pronouncements on the meaning of words which import the requirement of *mens rea* into definitions of offences. The advent of the twenty-first century has witnessed a significant shift as the House of Lords has reconsidered the meaning of recklessness in *G* [2003] UKHL 50 and has confronted and dealt with most, if not all, of these criticisms. In respect of intention, however, some confusion remains.

3.2 Intention

3.2.1 What might intention mean?

In many offences the *mens rea* required is that of intention to cause the prohibited result. Intention is a word in ordinary use. Its meaning, however, is not clear. When dissenting in *Caldwell* [1982] AC 341, Lord Edmund Davies stated (at p. 357):

> The law in action compiles its own dictionary. In time, what was originally the common coinage of speech acquires a different value in the pocket of the lawyer than when in the layman's purse.

It is important, therefore, that technical words, such as 'intention', should be clearly defined. Unfortunately, however, to use Glanville Williams' words, 'judges decline to define [intention], and they appear to adjust it from one case to another' (see Williams, 'Oblique intention' [1987] CLJ 417). The *Concise Oxford Dictionary* defines 'intend' as 'have as one's purpose' and 'intention' as 'intending, one's purpose...object...ultimate aim'. As used in the criminal law, *intention* does not appear to have such a clear or restricted meaning. There are basically four possible states of mind which may be encompassed within the term 'intention'.

 Example

Let us assume that D has insured V's life. He decides to kill V in order to obtain the insurance moneys. D's *desire* is to kill V and his *motive* is to obtain the money. The following four examples of D killing V illustrate the four states of mind which may constitute intention.

   (i) D shoots at V in order to kill him. In this situation V's death is both desired and intended by D. The consequence of V's death may be said to be D's purpose, aim, or objective. This variety of intention is referred to as *direct intention*. Even though D may realise that his chances of hitting V may be slim because of the distance or his poor ability with a gun, this does not affect his intention which is to kill V.

   (ii) D sees V standing behind a window and shoots at V in order to kill him realising that to do so the bullet must first break the window. In this situation it may be said that D intends also to break the window as this is a necessary precondition to killing V. This may be described as *oblique intention*; breaking the window is D's subsidiary aim or secondary purpose which must be achieved if he is to achieve his ultimate aim or primary purpose. Glanville Williams in 'Oblique intention' *ante*, states (at p. 421):

Direct intention is where the consequence is what you are aiming at. **Oblique intention** is something you see clearly, but out of the corner of your eye. The consequence is (figuratively speaking) not in the straight line of your purpose, but a side effect that you accept as an inevitable or 'certain' accompaniment of your direct intent (desire-intent). There are twin consequences of the act, x and y; the doer wants x, and is prepared to accept its unwanted twin y. Oblique intent is, in other words, a kind of knowledge or realisation...Certainty in human affairs means certainty as a matter of common sense—certainty apart from unforeseen events or remote possibilities. Realisation of practical certainty is something higher in the scale than appreciation of high probability. (emphasis added)

→

➡

> While there may be a remote possibility that the window may blow open before the bul-
> let passes through it, it is clear at the time D squeezes the trigger that breaking the window
> is a practical or moral certainty.
>
> (iii) D places a bomb under V's seat timed to kill him in mid-flight as he co-pilots a plane
>   over the Atlantic. In this situation D does not desire to kill the crew or passengers on
>   the plane and their deaths are not a precondition to killing V. In the normal course of
>   events, however, their deaths will ensue as the inevitable *by-product* of D's achieve-
>   ment of his primary purpose; they are an inseparable consequence of that end. Again
>   it may be said that at the time of planting the bomb the deaths of the crew and pas-
>   sengers were morally certain if D achieved his primary purpose. Thus, this situation
>   may be regarded as another example of oblique intention.
> (iv) D shoots at V, while he is driving a bus, in order to kill him. D foresees that it is highly
>   probable that the passengers on the bus will also be injured or killed. In this situation D
>   does not desire to kill or injure the passengers; their injuries or deaths are not inevitable
>   although highly likely. Does foresight that a consequence is highly probable amount to
>   intention to bring that consequence about or does it only constitute recklessness?

There is much judicial and academic discussion about whether a consequence can
be intended if it is not desired. In the examples earlier at (ii) and (iii) it may be
argued that as D's desire was to kill V the consequences of breaking the window or
killing the crew and passengers were undesired. Norrie, 'Oblique intention and legal
politics' [1989] Crim LR 793, argues that secondary consequences flowing from D's
primary purpose may also be regarded as desired. As D seeks to bring about the primary purpose in a known set of circumstances, secondary consequences which D
obliquely intends may be regarded as desired in a broader sense in that they are part
and parcel of the package of circumstances within which D chooses to operate.

3.2.2 What should intention mean?

The Law Commission in its Draft Criminal Code (Law Com No. 177) gives the following definition of intention to cause results:

> ...a person acts—...
>
> (b) 'intentionally' with respect to—...
>   (ii) a result when he acts either in order to bring it about or being aware that it will
>   occur in the ordinary course of events...

In its commentary on the Code the Law Commission states (at para. 8.14):

> Acting in order to bring about a result is, as it were, the standard case of 'intending' to
> cause a result. But we are satisfied that a definition of 'intention' for criminal law pur-
> poses must refer...to 'the means as well as the end and the inseparable consequences
> of the end as well as the means'. Where a person acts in order to achieve a particular
> purpose, knowing that this cannot be done without causing another result, he must be
> held to intend to cause that other result. The other result may be a precondition...or it
> may be a necessary concomitant of the first result....The result will occur, and D knows
> that it will occur, 'in the ordinary course of events....unless something supervenes to
> prevent it'. It is, and he knows it is, 'a virtual certainty'. We have adopted the phrase, 'in

the ordinary course of events' to ensure that 'intention' covers the case of a person who knows that the achievement of his purpose will necessarily cause the result in question, in the absence of some wholly improbable supervening event.

The Law Commission, accordingly, defined *intention* to include the types of situation given in examples (i), (ii), and (iii) given earlier. They went on to reject (iv) as a situation involving intention stating (at para. 8.15):

A person's awareness of any degree of probability (short of virtual certainty) that a particular result will follow from his acts ought not, we believe, to be classed as an 'intention' to cause that result for criminal law purposes.

The Law Commission's definition of intention has been adopted in the House of Lords, *Report of the Select Committee on Murder and Life Imprisonment* (Session 1988–89, HL Paper 78). Professor J. C. Smith, however, is of opinion that the definition could be improved to avoid possible difficulties (see 'A Note on Intention' [1990] Crim LR 85). The most significant difficulty which he considers might arise relates to the type of situation given earlier in example (iii). If the bomber knows that bombs of the type he is using have, for example, a 50% failure rate, Smith states (at p. 86):

It may be argued that the defendant does not … intend the death of the crew because he is not virtually certain etc., that they will die—he is not aware that it will happen 'in the ordinary course of events', because there is a 50 per cent chance that it will not happen at all.

In *Legislating the Criminal Code: Offences Against the Person and General Principles* (Law Com No. 218) the Law Commission accepted Smith's argument (see paras. 7.6–7.14) and proposed the following definition of intention in the Criminal Law Bill appended to the Report:

1. … a person acts
(a) 'intentionally' with respect to a result when—

    (i) it is his purpose to cause it, or
    (ii) although it is not his purpose to cause it, he knows that it would occur in the ordinary course of events if he were to succeed in his purpose of causing some other result; …

The important point to note about the Law Commission's definition is that it both accepts that *intention* should have a meaning wider than in situations like example (i) earlier but that it should not be so wide as to encompass foresight of probability in situations like example (iv) as this is the domain of recklessness.

3.2.3 How have the courts defined intention?

3.2.3.1 The difficulty of formulating a definition

While it is easy to state the Law Commission's definition of intention and the states of mind which this encompasses, it is more difficult to glean from judicial statements a clear definition of intention. **Most of the judgments which refer to intention suffer from the defect that the judges have been neither clear nor precise in their use of language. Their judgments consequently contain inconsistencies, contradictions, and ambiguities.** There are several reasons for this. Some of the cases in which the meaning of intention has been considered have involved emotive factual situations which appear to have coloured judicial pronouncements (see e.g. *Steane* [1947] KB 997). The most important cases before the House of Lords have involved murder where their Lordships had to decide what the *mens rea* for murder is (see *Hyam* [1975] AC 55; *Moloney* [1985] 1 AC 905; *Hancock and Shankland* [1986] 1 AC 455). The meaning of intention was thus subsumed within the discussion of the *mens rea* for murder and coloured by considerations of the type of conduct which should be caught by the definition of murder. Their Lordships concluded in *Moloney* that the *mens rea* for murder was intention to kill or intention to cause grievous bodily harm. Having given this definition of the *mens rea* of murder their Lordships considered certain examples of egregious and reprehensible conduct resulting in death. They concluded that such conduct merited conviction for murder although, unrecognised by them, it did not fall within any of the three situations given in examples (i)–(iii) earlier which exemplify the meaning of intention. Their Lordships, in effect, confused policy with principle and as a result have left the principles of the criminal law in a less than satisfactory condition. One cannot ignore, however, the pronouncements of the House of Lords and the Court of Appeal. Accordingly, an attempt must be made to make some sense of the cases.

A **further problem in some of the cases dealing with intention is judicial confusion of substantive law with the law of evidence.** The substantive law lays down the facts which must be proved if the accused is to be convicted of a particular offence. For example, if D is charged with murder one of the facts which must be proved is that he intended to kill or to cause grievous bodily harm to the deceased. The law of evidence lays down rules relating to the evidence which may be admitted to prove the existence of this fact. The state of a person's mind, however, is not an easy fact to prove unless the accused provides an admissible confession in which he states what his intention or foresight was. In the absence of such a confession the jury (or magistrates in summary proceedings) are left to use their collective common sense to draw inferences from the circumstances and the natural and probable consequences of the accused's conduct in those circumstances. This is provided for specifically by s. 8 of the Criminal Justice Act 1967:

A court or jury in determining whether a person has committed an offence,—

(a) shall not be bound in law to infer that he intended or foresaw a result of his actions by reason only of its being a natural and probable consequence of those actions; but

(b) shall decide whether he did intend or foresee that result by reference to all the evidence, drawing such inferences from the evidence as appear proper in the circumstances.

Example

D is charged with murder having pushed V over a 50 metre high cliff on to rocks below where he died. At his trial, D claims he did not intend to kill or seriously injure V but that he only wished to frighten him to teach him a lesson. If the jury disbelieve D (which they undoubtedly would), they can convict him of murder only if they are satisfied beyond reasonable doubt that D intended to kill V or to cause him serious injury. They would be entitled to use their common sense to determine what a person of normal intellect would have foreseen as the outcome of such conduct. One would suggest that the inevitable consequence of such conduct is at least serious injury. They would then be entitled to infer that D is a person of normal intellect and, in the absence of any other credible explanation, that he had such foresight and that his purpose in pushing B over the cliff must have been seriously to injure or kill him.

Of course, there are many situations where consequences are merely probable or even possible rather than inevitable. This does not preclude the jury from inferring that D intended to bring about the probable or possible consequence.

 Example

D is 800 metres from V and fires a rifle at him which results in V being grazed by the bullet. D is charged with attempted murder for which the requisite *mens rea* is intent to kill. D pleads 'Not Guilty' and declines to give evidence having also remained silent when questioned by the police. In the circumstances described, death was not inevitable nor even probable. It was, however, possible. In the absence of any credible explanation as to why D fired at V, the jury would be entitled to draw such inferences as are appropriate. One reason for firing the rifle could have been to kill V. If the jury are satisfied by the evidence (which in this case includes testimony from witnesses who overheard an argument between D and V in which D threatened to kill V) that the only proper inference to draw is that D's purpose was to kill V, they may convict. If the chances of killing V decrease with distance there will come a point where D is too far away for death to be a realistic possibility. In the absence of any other evidence from which an inference of intention could be drawn, an inference of intention to kill would not be proper as the act of shooting in such circumstances does not point (with the degree of sureness required to satisfy the burden of proof) to the conclusion that D's aim or purpose was to kill V.

The appropriateness of drawing inferences also may vary depending on other evidence which is available, for example, evidence relating to the intelligence of D may be pertinent to the question whether D foresaw any particular risk which his actions involved. **But where inferences are drawn, what should not be variable is the meaning of 'intention' for the purpose of determining whether the conclusion to which the evidence points amounts to 'intention'. Intention must mean 'aim' or 'purpose'.** There has been some confusion in the cases regarding the conclusion at which a jury may arrive where they have drawn inferences from the evidence as to the defendant's state of mind (see *Moloney, Hancock and Shankland,* and *Woollin,* see **3.2.3.3** and **3.2.3.4** *post*). In particular where D's aim or purpose has not been to bring about the consequence which resulted from his acts, it would be inappropriate to permit a jury to conclude that he intended that consequence where the only appropriate inference from the evidence was that he foresaw it as possible or probable. Such a state of mind amounts to recklessness but not to intention. The cases which follow, however, are not always supportive of this proposition.

3.2.3.2 Approaching a clear definition

The cases are in agreement that intention covers situation (i) in **3.2.1** *ante* where D does an act with the aim or purpose of causing a particular result. The problem centres on situations (ii) and (iii) that is whether oblique intention will suffice where the definition of the *mens rea* element of an offence requires **intention to cause a particular result. In *Mohan* [1976] QB 1 intention was defined as 'a decision to bring about, in so far as it lies within the accused's power, [the prohibited consequence], no matter whether the accused desired that consequence of his act or not'.** James LJ also stated (at p. 11):

> ...evidence of knowledge of likely consequences, or from which knowledge of likely consequences can be inferred, is evidence by which intent may be established but it is not...to be equated with intent. If the jury find such knowledge established, they may, and using common sense, they probably will find intent proved, but it is not the case that they must do so.

In this case D was charged with attempting to cause grievous bodily harm with intent having driven a car at a policeman who was blocking his path as he endeavoured to escape. The definition of intention which the Court of Appeal gave clearly included the type of situation given in example (ii) earlier; D may not have desired to injure the policeman as an end in itself but he was prepared to do so as a precondition to escaping which was his ultimate aim or purpose. The court also excluded situation (iv) from the definition of intention. This followed dicta in *Hyam* [1975] AC 55. In that case Lord Hailsham stated (at p. 65):

> I do not believe that knowledge or any degree of foresight is enough. Knowledge or foresight is at best material which entitles or compels a jury to draw the necessary inference as to intention.

Lord Hailsham made it clear later in his judgment (at pp. 73, 74) that **intention was to be distinguished from desire and foresight of probable consequences.** He clearly included within his definition of intention, however, both types of situation given in examples (ii) and (iii) stating that intention includes 'the means as well as the end and the inseparable consequences of the end as well as the means'. Thus he went on to state:

> ...a man may desire to blow up an aircraft in flight in order to obtain insurance moneys. But if any passengers are killed he is guilty of murder, as their death will be a moral certainty if he carries out his intention. There is no difference between blowing up the aircraft and intending the death of some or all of the passengers.

After *Mohan* and Lord Hailsham's speech in *Hyam* one would have thought that the meaning of intention was clear. Situations of the type exemplified in (i), (ii), and (iii) in **3.2.1** *ante* constituted intention and situation; (iv) did not. Evidence that a consequence was foreseeable as highly probable was simply circumstantial evidence which might persuade the jury to draw the inference that the accused intended the consequence. But the question always is 'what was the accused's subjective state of mind?'. If the jury are not satisfied that the accused actually foresaw the consequence as a moral certainty in situations like (ii) and (iii) the inference of intention would not be appropriate. If the consequence was D's aim or purpose it does not matter that he only foresaw a possibility of achieving it. This view is confirmed by a reading of the case of *Pearman* (1984) 80 Cr App R 259. This distinction between what intention is and how it may be proved is consistent with s. 8 of the Criminal Justice Act 1967 (see **3.2.3.1** *ante*).

Mohan must be contrasted, however, with the cases of *Steane* and *Gillick*. In *Steane* the Court of Criminal Appeal, swayed by the emotive facts of the case, gave a narrow definition to intention confining it to purpose. D was convicted of doing acts likely to assist the enemy with intent to assist the enemy. D gave broadcasts from Germany during the Second World War. The Court of Criminal Appeal quashed his conviction as the jury had not been directed to acquit if he may have had 'the innocent intent of a desire to save his wife and children from a concentration camp'. While saving his family may have been his ultimate aim or purpose, assisting the enemy was a necessary precondition to achieving that aim. As Glanville Williams points out (see 'Oblique intention' **3.2.1** *ante*, at p. 428) his intent to save his family did not negative his intent to assist the enemy. Steane, however, did merit having his conviction quashed as the jury had not been directed on duress. The Court of Criminal Appeal, however, wrongly believed that duress might not have succeeded as a defence and thus restricted the meaning of intention to ensure Steane's acquittal. The approval of *Steane* by the House of Lords in *Moloney* [1985] 1 AC 905 added to the confusion as the case is not reconcilable with the speeches of their Lordships. In *Gillick* v *West Norfolk and Wisbech AHA* [1986] AC 112, the House of Lords balked from recognising a defence of necessity but tampered with the meaning of intention to ensure that a doctor who prescribes contraceptives for a girl under 16 would not be guilty of aiding, abetting, counselling, or procuring the offence of unlawful sexual intercourse committed by her with a man, stating that the doctor's 'clinical judgment' is a 'complete negation of the guilty mind which is an essential ingredient of the criminal offence'. But whatever the doctor's motives, if he knew that his act would promote, encourage, or facilitate unlawful sexual intercourse, he clearly intended to aid or abet that offence. (See now s. 73 of the Sexual Offences Act 2003 which expressly legislates that a doctor, in these circumstances, is not guilty of aiding, abetting, or counselling the commission of a sexual offence against the child.) As *Gillick* did not involve a criminal prosecution what was said was *obiter* but it continues to have an influence (see **3.2.3.5** *post*).

3.2.3.3 The restoration of confusion

In the 1980s the House of Lords had two further attempts at defining intention, both of which were in the context of appeals from convictions for murder. The problem with *Hyam* was that while Lord Hailsham was clear regarding the meaning of intention, there was uncertainty regarding the actual *mens rea* of murder. The other four Law Lords appeared to accept that foresight by the accused of a high probability of death or serious bodily harm resulting from his conduct would suffice to constitute the *mens rea* of murder. In *Moloney* the House of Lords declared that the *mens rea* for murder is intention to kill or to cause grievous bodily harm, nothing else will suffice. The issue to be clarified was the meaning of intention.

> In *Moloney* the issue was essentially a factual one; there was a dispute between the prosecution and the defence as to whether the appellant knew the gun was point-ing at the deceased when he fired it. The appellant's account of the incident was that he had been drinking with his stepfather when the stepfather challenged him to a competition to see who could load, draw, and fire a shotgun in the shortest time. In doing so the appellant shot his stepfather, killing him. He claimed that he had not aimed the gun and that he had no idea that in firing it he would injure his stepfather. The issue for the jury should have been a simple one as stated by Lord Bridge (at p. 917):

>> If they were sure that, at the moment of pulling the trigger…the appellant realised that the gun was pointing straight at his stepfather's head, they were bound to convict him of murder. If, on the other hand, they thought it might be true that, in the appellant's drunken condition and in the context of this ridiculous challenge, it never entered the appellant's head when he pulled the trigger that the gun was pointing at his father, he should have been acquitted of murder and convicted of manslaughter.

Either the appellant had the direct intent of killing or seriously injuring his step-father or he had not. Unfortunately the trial judge confused the issue by directing the jury that 'a man intends the consequence of his voluntary act (a) when he desires it to happen, whether or not he foresees that it probably will happen and (b) when he foresees that it will probably happen, whether he desires it or not'. The equation of intention with foresight of probability rendered an appeal inevi-table. Lord Bridge considered the direction on 'foresight of consequences' to be an example of an irrelevant direction which would only confuse a jury. If when the appellant fired the gun he knew that it was pointing at his stepfather's head, the inference was inescapable 'using words in their ordinary, everyday meaning, that he intended to kill his stepfather'.

Lord Bridge went on to consider the correct direction for all crimes where a spe-cific intent is required. (An offence of specific intent is one which requires inten-tion to be proved; recklessness will not suffice as an alternative state of mind.) Lord Bridge considered that **'the golden rule' is to 'avoid any elaboration or paraphrase of what is meant by intent, and leave it to the jury's good sense to decide whether the accused acted with the necessary intent'** (at p. 926), although an explanation that intention is something quite different from motive or desire is frequently necessary. Further explanation or elaboration should only be given where necessary to avoid misunderstanding in the light of the facts and the way the case has been presented to the jury in evidence and argument (see further *Fallon* [1994] Crim LR 519). While Lord Bridge did not express himself particu-larly clearly at this point, it would appear that he was referring to cases where the evidence suggests that the accused's ultimate aim or purpose was to bring about something other than the prohibited consequence which he had caused, that is cases where the accused had an oblique intent. In such cases, Lord Bridge stated, **foresight of a high degreeof probability is not equivalent to intention** but 'as an element bearing on the issue of intention…belongs, not to the substantive law, but to the law of evidence'. **When elaboration is required, two questions should be put to the jury** (at p. 929):

> First, was death or really serious injury in a murder case (or whatever relevant consequence must be proved to have been intended in any other case) a natural consequence of the defendant's voluntary act? Secondly, did the defendant foresee that consequence as being a natural consequence of his act? The jury should then be told that if they answer yes to both questions it is a proper inference for them to draw that he intended that consequence.

Question

Does 'natural' not mean something different to 'certain'?

Unfortunately this statement is not as clear as it might have been as the term 'natural consequence' is ambiguous. Something may be natural, in the sense of being causally connected to the original act, but it is not necessarily a certain consequence. The example often given is that conception may be a natural consequence of sexual intercourse but it is by no means certain. Lord Bridge appears to have meant to convey, however, the idea that the consequence must have been foreseen as morally certain. Earlier in his speech he stated (at p. 929):

> [Natural] conveys the idea that in the ordinary course of events a certain act will lead to a certain consequence unless something unexpected supervenes to prevent it.

Although Lord Bridge regarded as irrational rules of substantive law which sought to define intention in terms of degrees of probability, he did reveal some inconsistency when he stated (at p. 925) that the probability of the consequence taken to have been foreseen must be little short of overwhelming before it will suffice to establish the necessary intent. Such a probability, however, would appear to be indistinguishable from a consequence which is certain unless prevented by some unexpected supervening event. Lord Bridge then illustrated his point by the following example of a person who has an ultimate aim or purpose whose achievement will necessarily involve another consequence (at p. 926):

> A man, who, at a London airport, boards a plane which he knows to be bound for Manchester, clearly intends to travel to Manchester, even though Manchester is the last place he wants to be and his motive for boarding the plane is simply to escape pursuit. The possibility that the plane may have engine trouble and be diverted to Luton does not affect the matter. By boarding the Manchester plane, the man conclusively demonstrates his intention to go there, because it is a moral certainty that that is where he will arrive.

In this example, Lord Bridge states that boarding the plane 'demonstrates...intention'; he does not state that this is evidence from which intention is to be inferred. In other parts of his speech, and particularly when he framed his two-part test,

Lord Bridge did speak in terms of drawing inferences. It is his test which has subsequently been taken to have conveyed his intention. Inferring intention from foresight, rather than treating a particular degree of foresight as intention, can create confusion. In a case where the prohibited consequence was not the accused's aim or purpose, nor desired by him as an end in itself or means to an end, the task for the prosecution would be to prove what he foresaw. In the absence of an admission by the accused the jury would be left to infer this from the evidence. If they are satisfied that he foresaw death or serious injury as morally certain at the time he acted it would be correct to say he intended that result in the 'oblique' sense of the word—no further *inferring* should be required. Indeed, as it is not a case where bringing about the prohibited consequence is the accused's aim or purpose, and as intention is something distinct from motive or desire, there would not seem to be any ingredient left which might be inferred to convert foresight into intention. Doubtless juries would use their common sense and equate foresight of a consequence as morally certain with intention but it would have been much more helpful if Lord Bridge had said so clearly.

A further problem arising from *Moloney* is created by Lord Bridge himself when he provides the example of a terrorist bomber who plants a bomb in a building, giving a warning to enable the building to be evacuated, but realising that it is virtually certain that a bomb disposal squad will attempt to defuse it. If it explodes killing a bomb disposal expert Lord Bridge assumes the terrorist would be guilty of murder. While it may be virtually certain that an attempt will be made to defuse the bomb, it is not, however, certain that anyone will die; bomb disposal experts do not become experts by needlessly throwing their lives away. This example does not illustrate a case of intention to kill but rather recklessness. It may be that Lord Bridge felt that someone like this terrorist should be guilty of murder; that would necessitate a new definition of the *mens rea* of murder.

At the end of his speech in *Moloney* Lord Hailsham stated (at p. 913):

> I conclude with the pious hope that your Lordships will not again have to decide that foresight and foreseeability are not the same thing as intention although either may give rise to an irresistible inference of such....

Lord Hailsham's hopes proved to be in vain as a mere nine months later the House of Lords was considering the meaning of Lord Bridge's judgment in *Hancock and Shankland* [1986] 1 AC 455. The phrase 'natural consequence' had created judicial confusion. This is another example of a case where the only issue was one of fact but the matter was complicated by the trial judge's direction to the jury.

> The accused were miners on strike. They pushed a block of concrete and a concrete post from a bridge over a three-lane highway on which a miner was being taken to work by taxi. The block hit the taxi killing the driver. The accused were charged with murder the prosecution alleging that they intended to kill or cause serious injury. The accused's case was that their intention was only to block the road and frighten the miner as they believed the block was positioned over the middle lane when the taxi was in the nearside lane.

The issue for the jury should have been to determine which version of the facts was to be believed. If the accused were to be believed then a conviction of manslaughter would follow as there clearly was no intention to kill or cause serious injury. If, on the other hand, they disbelieved the accused and the prosecution satisfied them beyond reasonable doubt that the accused knew the block was positioned above the lane along which the taxi was driving, the inference that they intended to kill or cause serious injury would have been inescapable as one could imagine no other reason for dropping the block. **The only issue in fact was what was their aim or purpose?** If it was to kill or cause serious injury it would not matter whether they only foresaw a slight chance of success. **Unfortunately the judge complicated matters by giving the Bridge direction relating to foresight of consequences.** He did not explain that 'natural consequence' did not simply mean causally connected and thus the appeal was based on the ambiguity of this phrase. The Court of Appeal quashed the convictions for murder and the House of Lords affirmed this on the basis that the phrase 'natural consequence' required amplification. The amplification which Lord Scarman provided, however, bears little connection to the meaning Lord Bridge attributed to the phrase.

Lord Scarman stated (at p. 473):

> [Lord Bridge] omitted any reference in his guidelines to probability. He did so because he included probability in the meaning which he attributed to 'natural'...[T]he probability of a consequence is a factor of sufficient importance to be drawn specifically to the attention of the jury and to be explained. In a murder case where it is necessary to direct a jury on the issue of intent by reference to foresight of consequences the probability of death or serious injury resulting from the act done may be critically important. Its importance will depend on the degree of probability: if the likelihood that death or serious injury will result is high, the probability of that result may...be seen as overwhelming evidence of the existence of the intent to kill or injure....In my judgment, therefore, the *Moloney* guidelines as they stand are unsafe and misleading. They require a reference to probability. They also require an explanation that the greater the probability of a consequence the more likely it is that the consequence was foreseen and that if that consequence was foreseen the greater the probability is that that consequence was also intended.

A direction in terms of foresight of consequences should only be appropriate where the consequence which occurred was not the accused's direct aim or purpose. Lord Scarman did not state whether such a direction actually was appropriate in the case before him. His judgment serves to dilute the meaning Lord Bridge intended to convey in that a jury, directed in accordance with Lord Scarman's dicta, may infer intention from foresight of high probability whereas Lord Bridge would only permit such an inference where the consequence was foreseen as a moral certainty. **On a Scarman direction, different juries may arrive at different verdicts depending on whether they feel the accused's conduct should be condemned as murder.** But if foresight of a high probability is not intention, how can a jury infer intention from such foresight unless their decision is effectively a policy one, namely, that they feel that this accused, in these circumstances, deserves to be convicted of murder. Foresight that a consequence is certain to ensue is the other side of the coin of intention, but foresight of probability is a different entity entirely, namely recklessness.

The conflict between *Moloney* and *Hancock and Shankland* led the Court of Appeal to seek to restore some order to the confusion in *Nedrick* [1986] 1 WLR 1025. In that case, the appellant had a grudge against a woman. With the intention of frightening her, he poured paraffin through her letter box and on to the front door of her house and ignited it. A child died in the ensuing fire. The appellant was convicted of murder following a direction to the jury which equated foresight with intention. The Court of Appeal quashed the conviction, substituting a conviction of manslaughter. Lord Lane CJ stated two questions which might be helpful to a jury when determining whether the accused had the necessary intent (at p. 1028):

(1) How probable was the consequence which resulted from the defendant's voluntary act?

(2) Did he foresee that consequence?

Lord Lane CJ went on to explain that if the accused did not appreciate that death or serious harm was likely to result from his act, he did not intend to bring it about. If he did appreciate the risk but thought that it was only slight, then a jury might easily conclude that he did not intend to bring about the result. Lord Lane CJ continued (at p. 1028):

> On the other hand, if the jury are satisfied that at the material time the defendant recognised that death or serious harm would be virtually certain (barring some unforeseen intervention) to result from his voluntary act, then that is a fact from which they may find it easy to infer that he intended to kill or do serious bodily harm, even though he may not have had any desire to achieve that result....Where the charge is murder and in the rare cases where the simple direction is not enough, the jury should be directed that they are not entitled to infer the necessary intention unless they feel sure that death or serious bodily harm was a virtual certainty (barring some unforeseen intervention) as a result of the defendant's actions and that the defendant appreciated that such was the case.
>
> Where a man realises that it is for all practical purposes inevitable that his actions will result in death or serious harm, the inference may be irresistible that he intended that result, however little he may have desired or wished it to happen. The decision is one for the jury to be reached upon a consideration of all the evidence.

Lord Lane CJ appeared to endorse the view that it is only in cases where a consequence is foreseen as virtually certain that intention may be inferred. He expressly stated that on a murder charge if a simple direction would not suffice, the jury should be directed that they are not entitled to infer intention unless satisfied that death or serious bodily harm was virtually certain to result from D's acts and D foresaw this. Lord Lane CJ remained somewhat ambivalent about foresight of degrees of probability in between slight risk and virtual certainty in other offences requiring proof of intention. Lord Lane CJ also caused further confusion, however, in attempting to reconcile Lord Bridge's dicta with those of Lord Scarman when he spoke in terms of the probability of a consequence ensuing from the accused's act.

Following *Nedrick* the courts have continued to struggle with intention. In *Walker and Hayles* (1990) 90 Cr App R 226 the Court of Appeal expressed the view that the phrase 'very high degree of probability' meant the same as virtual certainty and held that a direction using the former could not be faulted. In *Scalley* [1995] Crim

LR 504, where the facts were similar to those in *Nedrick*, the trial judge directed the jury on the basis of Lord Lane CJ's questions as follows:

> Have the prosecution made you sure…[t]hat as to [murder] he intended to kill, or to do really serious harm (in the sense that he foresaw either death or such harm as virtually certain). If yes, convict him of murder.…

The defendant appealed on the basis that on a number of occasions the trial judge used words and phrases which tended to equate foresight with intent. The Court of Appeal allowed the appeal, Russell LJ stating:

> We do wish to emphasise that there is always a third question to be asked and resolved, whenever the problem encountered in the instant case is before a jury. We remind ourselves that Lord Lane CJ posed two questions: how probable was the consequence which resulted from the defendant's voluntary act; and secondly, did he foresee that consequence? The third question which, in all these cases, has to be asked and has to be answered, is whether, in the light of all the circumstances, including these questions of foresight, the intent either to kill or to cause serious bodily harm is made out…

The Court of Appeal gave no guidance as to what further state of mind a jury has to find to exist in order to conclude that D had the requisite intention. The use of the *Nedrick* direction indicates that it is not a case of 'intention' in the sense of aim, objective, or purpose. If foresight of a consequence as a virtual certainty is not equivalent to intention, by what process is the jury to convert it *into* intention?

In the Court of Appeal decision in *Woollin* [1997] 1 Cr App R 97, the Court approved a direction which left it open to the jury to infer intention where they were satisfied that D foresaw a substantial risk of serious harm to the victim, his three-month-old son, whom he threw four or five feet across a room in the direction of his pram causing him a fractured skull from which he died. At no time did the trial judge indicate that intention meant 'aim, objective or purpose'. It was therefore open to the jury to infer that D deliberately exposed the child to the risk of serious harm and that this amounted to 'intention' for the purposes of murder when, in fact, it only constitutes recklessness which does not suffice to support a conviction of murder. The Court of Appeal satisfied itself that it was all a matter of inferences for the jury to draw from the evidence. But the evidence and inferences drawn therefrom must result in conclusions of fact and such facts must be fitted to legal definitions if a conviction is to follow. It is for the courts to provide such definitions in clear terms so that a jury having drawn inferences knows how to characterise those facts in the light of the legal definitions. If the definition of intention is not clear juries may end up characterising inferences which point only to foresight of a risk (recklessness) as intention.

3.2.3.4 The problem resolved?

On appeal to the House of Lords, *Woollin* [1998] 3 WLR 382, their Lordships unanimously rejected the decision of the Court of Appeal and quashed the conviction of murder, substituting a conviction of manslaughter. At trial the prosecution had accepted that it had not been D's aim or purpose to kill or seriously injure his child. The case, accordingly, was not one where the simple direction on intention could suffice. Lord Steyn, giving the leading judgment, affirmed that the case had been one requiring the *Nedrick* direction relating to virtual certainty. He stated (at p. 392):

> By using the phrase 'substantial *risk*' the judge blurred the line between intention and recklessness, and hence between murder and manslaughter. The misdirection enlarged the scope of the mental element required for murder. It was a material misdirection.

Lord Steyn also took the opportunity to clarify the *Nedrick* direction and the effect of a jury finding that a defendant foresaw death or serious injury as a virtual certainty. While juries must consider all the evidence to determine what state of mind the defendant had when he acted, how that state of mind should be characterised is a matter of definition. Lord Steyn moved from treating the *Nedrick* direction as one relating purely to evidential matters to one relating to definition. He stated **first** (at p. 390) **that the 'effect of the critical direction is that a result foreseen as virtually certain is an intended result'** and, **secondly,** *Nedrick* **'stated what state of mind (in the absence of a purpose to kill or cause serious harm) is sufficient for murder'.** It seems clear from this that in Lord Steyn's view, where a jury is satisfied beyond reasonable doubt on the evidence that D foresaw death or serious injury as virtually certain to result from his actions, this amounts to an intention to bring about that consequence and thus satisfies the *mens rea* requirement for murder; no further step of drawing inferences from such a finding is required. This would seem to lay to rest the fiction that foresight of a virtually certain result is simply evidence from which the jury may infer intention.

Lord Steyn went on to reformulate the *Nedrick* direction and to abbreviate it to two crucial questions. The reformulation involved substituting for the word 'infer' the word 'find' so that the direction reads:

> Where the charge is murder and in the rare cases where the simple direction is not enough, the jury should be directed that they are not entitled to find the necessary intention unless they feel sure that death or serious bodily harm was a virtual certainty (barring some unforeseen intervention) as a result of the defendant's action and that the defendant appreciated that such was the case.

The only other statement a judge might choose to make is one reminding the jury that their decision must be made upon consideration of all of the evidence in the case. This is uncontroversial as this is the duty of the jury in any case whether the issue is one of intention or some other matter.

Undoubtedly the House of Lords could have been clearer in their decision. **There are three particular problems which may arise. First, the *Nedrick* direction is framed in the negative.** A better reworking of it would have been to state that if the jury are sure that the defendant foresaw death or serious bodily harm as a virtual certainty (barring some unforeseen intervention) as a result of his action, this amounts to an intention to bring about that result. This would have been in line with Lord Steyn's dictum that 'a result foreseen as virtually certain is an intended result' and would have made clear, beyond peradventure, that there is no discretion on the part of the jury once it has found that D foresaw death or serious bodily harm as a virtual certainty. When a trial judge adopted this approach, the Court of Appeal was presented with the opportunity to provide the necessary clarification. In *Matthews and Alleyne* [2003] EWCA Crim 192, however, they concluded that **'the law has not yet reached a *definition* of intent in murder in terms of appreciation of a virtual certainty'** (para. 43) retreating from the ground to which Lord Steyn had laid claim. Rix LJ went on to state (at paras. 43 and 45):

> [W]e do not regard *Woollin* as yet reaching or laying down a substantive rule of law. On the contrary, it is clear from the discussion in *Woollin* as a whole that *Nedrick* was derived from the existing law...and that the critical direction in *Nedrick* was approved, subject to the change of one word....
>
> [W]e think that, once what is required is an appreciation of virtual certainty of death, and not some lesser foresight of merely probable consequences, there is very little to choose between a rule of evidence and one of substantive law. It is probably this thought that led Lord Steyn to say that a result foreseen as virtually certain is an intended result.

So Lord Steyn, according to the Court of Appeal, has not provided a definition of intention. Foresight of death as a virtual certainty remains evidence from which intention (in the sense of aim, objective, or purpose) may be found. We are no closer to knowing what the elusive state of mind is that a jury has to find in order to conclude that D had the requisite intention. Perhaps it is simply a moral reaction providing the jury with sufficient leeway to decide, in an appropriate case, not to convict despite a conclusion that D foresaw death as a virtual certainty (see **3.2.3.5** *post*). In the instant case, where the defendants had killed the victim by throwing him from a bridge into a river 25 feet below, knowing that he could not swim, the Court of Appeal did not consider there could be any moral leeway once the jury concluded the appellants had foreseen death as a virtual certainty, Rix LJ stating (at para. 46):

> If the jury were sure that the appellants appreciated the virtual certainty of [V's] death and also that they then had no intention of saving him from such death, it is impossible to see how the jury could not have found that the appellants intended [V] to die.

A further problem which would have been resolved is that the test requires death or serious bodily harm to be a virtual certainty before consideration is given to D's appreciation of such. The issue should not be whether the result was a virtual certainty but rather whether when he acted D foresaw it to be such. D's culpability lies in acting with that degree of foresight. How should a jury determine a case where they conclude that D acted with a primary purpose having foreseen that if he achieved that purpose a secondary consequence (V's death) would be a virtual certainty, although the jury (with the benefit of hindsight) take the view that the secondary consequence was not, in fact, virtually certain to ensue from the achievement of D's primary purpose? Again, Lord Steyn's statement that 'a result foreseen as virtually certain is an intended result' suggests that the jury should find that D intended that result whereas the reworked *Nedrick* direction would suggest a finding of intention could not be made in these circumstances.

A final problem is the meaning of 'virtual certainty'. It is clear that Lord Steyn considered it to mean something which is as certain as things can be in this life as he described the test (at p. 391) as:

> very similar to the threshold of being aware 'that it *will* occur in the ordinary course of events' in the Law Commission's draft Criminal Code....

This led him to conclude, differently from Lord Bridge in *Moloney*, that:

> It may exclude a conviction of murder in the often cited terrorist example where a member of the bomb disposal team is killed. In such a case it may realistically be said that the terrorist did not foresee the killing of a member of the bomb disposal team as a virtual certainty. That may be a consequence of not framing the principle in terms of risk-taking....[But] I am satisfied that the *Nedrick* test, which was squarely based on the decision of the House in *Moloney*, is pitched at the right level of foresight.

Thus foresight of probability (of whatever degree) is not enough. A trial judge could not be faulted if, to avoid any confusion on the part of the jury, he sought to make it clear to them that foresight of a consequence as being highly probable does not equate to foresight of a virtual certainty.

While Lord Steyn specifically limited his comments to the crime of murder, it would be highly undesirable if courts were to adopt a different approach to the meaning of intention in other offences. They may soon have some statutory guidance as legislation may be forthcoming to deal with non-fatal offences against the person. In February 1998 the Home Office issued a Consultation Document, *Violence: Reforming the Offences Against the Person Act 1861* together with a draft Bill which is largely based on the Law Commission's Report, *Legislating the Criminal Code: Offences Against the Person and General Principles* (Law Com No. 218). The Bill provides in cl. 14 that:

> (1) A person acts intentionally with respect to a result if—
>   (a) it is his purpose to cause it, or
>   (b) although it is not his purpose to cause it, he knows that it would occur in the ordinary course of events if he were to succeed in his purpose of causing some other result.

This definition is largely consistent with *Woollin* except for one problem identified by Professor Smith, 'Offences Against the Person: The Home Office Consultation Paper' [1998] Crim LR 317, 318. If this definition is adopted for offences against the person, someone like Woollin could not be convicted of intentionally causing serious injury contrary to cl. 1(1) should the child not die as 'he had no other purpose—except to vent his anger, which is not a purpose to cause a result'. Professor Smith suggests that cl. 14(1)(b) should be amended to read:

> ...he knows *that it will occur in the ordinary course of events*, or that it would do so if he were to succeed in his purpose of causing some other result.

The debate has continued on how to define intention. The latest proposal by the Law Commission in Report No. 304, *Murder, Manslaughter and Infanticide* is:

> (1) A person should be taken to intend a result if he or she acts in order to bring it about.
>
> (2) In cases where the judge believes that justice may not be done unless an expanded understanding of intention is given, the jury may be directed as follows: an intention to bring about a result may be found if it is shown that the defendant thought that the result was a virtually certain consequence of his or her action.

This definition focuses on the defendant's belief and removes the requirement that the result should be a virtual certainty.

3.2.3.5 Good motives and oblique intent

An issue which was left unresolved in *Woollin* is whether a good motive may be a reason for a jury not finding intention where D acted realising that if he achieved his primary purpose the consequence prohibited by the offence (death in the case of murder) was virtually certain to ensue. Motive may, exceptionally, be made an element of an offence. For example, the Crime and Disorder Act 1998 provides for an enhanced penalty where certain offences are racially or religiously aggravated, such as assaults, criminal damage, or public order offences. An offence is racially or religiously aggravated where it 'is motivated (wholly or partly) by hostility towards members of a racial or religious group, based on their membership of that group' (see s. 28(1)(b)). But generally motive is irrelevant to liability, even where that motive may be good (see, for example, *Smith* [1960] 2 QB 423; *Chandler* v *DPP* [1964] AC 763). That a good motive does not absolve a person from criminal liability was affirmed by the Privy Council in *Yip Chiu-Cheung* v *R* [1994] 3 WLR 514 (see **8.3.3.3** *post*) where it was held that an undercover officer who agreed with others (in this case the appellant) to carry out a crime intending that crime to be committed (albeit so that he could obtain evidence to convict those others), had the *mens rea* for conspiracy. Similarly the House of Lords held in *Latif* [1996] 1 All ER 353 that a customs officer who brought heroin to England as part of an operation designed to catch a major trafficker (the appellant), had the necessary intention to evade the prohibition on the importation of heroin and, if charged, would have been guilty of an offence contrary to s. 50(3) of the Customs and Excise Management Act 1979.

In both *Yip Chiu-Cheung* and *Latif* the statements concerning motive and intention came in the context of appeals by what might be regarded as appellants for whom there would be little moral sympathy. The problem which remains, however, is those actors for whom there would be considerable moral sympathy but whose conduct may appear to fall within the strict letter of the law on intention if it is rigidly applied. For example, a doctor treating a terminally ill patient may use an analgesic to relieve pain knowing that a point will come when the increased doses necessary to relieve the pain will kill the patient. There are two antagonistic tensions at play: first, the logic of the *Nedrick/Woollin* test for oblique intention if applied without moderation could catch those whose motive for pursuing their primary purpose (pain relief in this example) is morally inconsistent with the *mens rea* for the offence, the *actus reus* of which was the side effect of achieving their primary purpose (cf. *Adams* **2.6.3.2** *ante*; *Steane* and *Gillick* v *West Norfolk and Wisbech*

AHA, **3.2.3.2** *ante*); and secondly, the reluctance of judges expressly to frame a defence (whether based in justification or excuse) to cover those who act from a good motive. This problem is set in even starker contrast when the virtually certain side effect of D achieving his morally commendable primary purpose is death, as in the pain relief case, and thus, prima facie, could amount to murder, whereas the accepted *mens rea* for murder does not cover, for example, the terrorist bomber who displays 'wicked recklessness' towards the bomb disposal team but does not foresee death as a virtual certainty.

If a prosecution for murder is brought against a doctor whose patient has died as a result of treatment prescribed by the doctor, several possibilities present themselves. First, the trial judge could adopt a *Gillick* approach and direct the jury that 'the bona fide exercise by a doctor of his clinical judgement [is a] complete negation of the [*mens rea* for murder]', i.e. there is no intention to kill. Secondly, (and perhaps operating in tandem with the first approach) he could direct the jury on intention without making any reference to the *Nedrick* direction on the basis that Lord Steyn recognised that the decision whether to give this direction is one for the trial judge to make on the basis of the circumstances of the case. Thirdly, and in contrast to the first two approaches, the trial judge could give the *Nedrick* direction but, in doing so, may emphasise the fact that whether the jury 'find' intention is entirely a matter for them and leave it to the jury to arrive at a decision based on their own view of the morality of the situation. Finally a judge may direct a jury that a finding of foresight of death as a virtual certainty is intention. In this latter situation, the doctor would be forced to rely on the somewhat ill-defined defence of necessity to avoid conviction (see **6.3.3** *post*).

In two cases the trial judges have adopted a similar approach. In *Cox*, Winchester Crown Court, 18 September 1992, 12 BMLR, D, a consultant rheumatologist, was charged with attempted murder of V, a patient who was terminally ill and in extreme pain. A short time before V's death D had administered an injection of potassium chloride in a quantity which could have no therapeutic purpose. The charge was attempted murder as V had been cremated and thus the actual cause of death could not be established. In directing the jury Ognall J adopted the *Gillick* position stating:

> If a doctor genuinely believes that a certain course is beneficial to his patient, either therapeutically or analgesically, then even though he recognises that that course carries with it a risk to life, he is fully entitled, nonetheless, to pursue it. If in those circumstances the patient dies, nobody could possibly suggest that in that situation the doctor was guilty of murder or attempted murder.

The problem in the instant case, however, was that the drug used had no therapeutic qualities and thus D's primary purpose may have been to kill rather than to alleviate pain. In directing the jury on this point Ognall J directed them that if D's primary purpose was to bring V's life to an end he was guilty of attempted murder. He also made it clear that if D's primary purpose was to kill V, his motive for doing so could afford him no defence. The jury convicted.

In *Moor*, Newcastle Crown Court, 11 May 1999, D, a GP, was charged with murdering V, a patient whom he believed to be terminally ill and in pain from cancer, by administering diamorphine to him. In directing the jury on the question of *mens rea*, Hooper J adopted a two stage approach. First, unless the prosecution satisfied them that the purpose of the injection of diamorphine was not to give treatment which D believed to be proper treatment to relieve pain and suffering, they should acquit. If, however, they were so satisfied, secondly, they had to consider whether D's intention in giving the injection was to kill. The jury acquitted. The approach in *Moor* is consistent with that in *Cox*: if D's purpose is proper medical treatment (pain relief would be such) his purpose is not to kill and he should be acquitted (even though he realises that death is a virtually certain consequence of the treatment). If, however, his purpose is not proper medical treatment, the question for the jury is whether his intention was to kill. By adopting this approach (the *Gillick* approach) these two trial judges have avoided giving the *Nedrick* direction. In effect a good motive is operating to negate findings of oblique intent.

> The problem of killing in order to save life arose in unusual and traumatic circumstances in the case *Re A (Children) (Conjoined Twins: Medical Treatment) (No. 1)* [2000] 4 All ER 961, involving the twins Jodie and Mary. The court had to consider whether it would be lawful for doctors to perform an operation to separate the twins the effect of which would be the inevitable death of Mary. The twins shared a common aorta which enabled Jodie's heart to pump the blood she oxygenated through Mary's body, as Mary's heart and lungs were deficient and incapable of sustaining her life. Mary's brain was also not fully developed. If an operation to separate them were not performed, both twins were expected to die within six months due to the strain being placed on Jodie's heart. If separated, the prospects for Jodie's survival were good albeit that she would suffer some disabilities and require further surgery. Mary was incapable of independent existence.
>
> The Court of Appeal was faced with three problems: **first, what was in the best interests of the children; secondly, if those interests were in conflict, could that conflict be resolved so as to allow one to prevail; and, thirdly, if the prevailing interest was in favour of the operation, could the operation be performed lawfully.** The first two questions raised family law issues, the third related to the criminal law. Ward LJ, with whom Brooke LJ agreed, concluded that while it was in Jodie's best interests for the operation to take place, this was not in Mary's best interests as it would mean her death. He stated that 'each life has inherent value in itself and the right to life, being universal, is equal for all of us'. Where the best interests of the children were in conflict, the court's task was to balance the welfare of each child against the other to find the 'least detrimental alternative'. This balancing exercise would not involve valuing each life but rather the 'worthwhileness' of the proposed treatment. For Mary the treatment was not worthwhile as she had always been 'designated for death' due to her disabilities. She was only alive because she was sucking 'the lifeblood out of Jodie' and by so doing would ultimately kill her. Only the doctors could save Jodie whereas Mary was beyond help. In those circumstances the balance weighed heavily in Jodie's favour, Ward LJ stating:
>
>> The best interests of the twins is to give the chance of life to the child whose actual bodily condition is capable of accepting the chance to her advantage even if that has to be at the cost of the sacrifice of the life which is so unnaturally supported.

Turning to the criminal law there were two main issues: **first, whether the operation to separate the twins would involve the intentional killing of Mary; and, secondly, if so whether this could be justified.** Both Ward LJ and Brooke LJ concluded that the doctors performing the operation would, following the decision of the House of Lords in *Woollin* [1998] 3 WLR 382, intend to kill Mary, however much they might not desire that result, as they would recognise her death as being the virtually certain consequence of their acts. (By contrast Walker LJ adopted the approach in *Gillick*.) The dilemma for the doctors, however, was not just a moral or social one but also a legal one as the failure to operate could amount to a breach of their duty to act in Jodie's best interests. This raised the crucial question in the case, originally framed by Lord Mackay in *Howe* [1987] 1 AC 417 (**6.2.7** *post*) whether 'the law should recognise in any individual in any circumstances, however extreme, the right to choose that one innocent person should be killed rather than another'?** As the doctors' duties to Jodie and Mary were in conflict Ward LJ concluded that '**the law must allow an escape through choosing the lesser of two evils**' in which case, the operation being justified would involve no unlawful act. Furthermore, as the reality of the situation was that Mary was slowly killing Jodie (even though this unique situation could not be classed as unlawful), the doctors were entitled to come to Jodie's defence to remove the threat of fatal harm Mary presented. This is, **in effect, a defence of necessity;** Brooke LJ expressly framed his solution in terms of a defence of necessity (see further **6.3.3** *post*). Walker LJ was also prepared, if necessary, to extend the defence of necessity to cover the instant case.

A problem which remained was the Human Rights Act 1998 and Art. 2 of the European Convention. The Court of Appeal was satisfied that the operation would not constitute a breach. Ward LJ took the view that with the rights of each child being in conflict and a solution being required, it was inconceivable that the court in Strasbourg would arrive at a different conclusion from the Court of Appeal. Brooke and Walker LJJ took the view that Art. 2(1) which protects individuals from being 'intentionally' deprived of life, was not infringed as 'intentionally' in this context had to be given its natural and ordinary meaning and thus applied 'only to cases where the purpose of the prohibited action is to cause death'. Thus as the doctors' purpose would be to save the life of Jodie rather than to cause the death of Mary, the operation would not constitute a violation of Art. 2.

3.2.4 Basic, specific, and ulterior intent

While there may be uncertainty regarding the meaning of the word 'intention' this is compounded by the fact that judges have created further confusion by the use of the word 'intent' in differing contexts. When reading judgments the terms 'basic intent', 'specific intent', and 'ulterior intent' will be encountered. It is important that the meaning of these terms is understood.

The term 'basic intent' is used to describe offences for which the mental element required is intention, knowledge, or recklessness. The phrase 'basic *mens rea*' would probably be more accurate as one of the ideas which the term seeks to convey is that the offence may be committed recklessly, in that there is no requirement that intention be proved.

The phrase 'basic intent' should be contrasted with both the phrases 'specific intent' and 'ulterior intent'. In *DPP* v *Morgan* [1976] AC 182, Lord Simon said that crimes of basic intent meant 'those crimes whose definition expresses (or, more often implies) a *mens rea* which does not go beyond the *actus reus*'. Here Lord Simon was drawing a distinction between crimes of 'basic intent' and crimes of 'ulterior intent'. **A crime of 'ulterior intent' is one where the definition of the *mens rea* requires proof of an intention to bring about a consequence beyond the actual *actus reus* of the offence.** This is best explained by examples. Burglary may be committed where a person enters a building as a trespasser with the intention of stealing, causing grievous bodily harm, or causing criminal damage. The *actus reus* is complete as soon as D enters the building as a trespasser, he need not go on to commit one of these further offences. The *mens rea* required is, first, that D knows he is a trespasser or is reckless as to this fact and, secondly, that he intends to commit one of the three further offences. This latter element of the *mens rea* is the 'ulterior intent' as it is a requirement beyond the *actus reus* which is satisfied by proof that D has entered as a trespasser. Other offences of 'ulterior intent' are, for example, wounding with intent to cause grievous bodily harm, wounding with intent to resist or prevent the lawful apprehension of any person, and assault with intent to rob.

The term 'specific intent' encompasses both crimes of 'ulterior intent' and other offences in respect of which D may plead that he lacked *mens rea* due to his intoxication at the time he committed the *actus reus*. If an offence is one of 'basic intent' D may not plead intoxication. Offences of 'basic intent' may be committed recklessly or with intent where the intent relates only to the act done (i.e. a conduct crime) and not to its consequences (see further *Heard* [2007] EWCA Crim 125, **5.6.3** *post*) whereas offences which the courts have classified as ones of 'specific intent' are either offences of 'ulterior intent' or offences for which proof of intention alone is required and the intention relates to the consequences as an aspect of the *actus reus*, for example, murder.

3.3 Knowledge

Where an act, omission, state of affairs, or event is unlawful where certain circumstances exist, and the offence is one requiring *mens rea*, knowledge of those circumstances on the part of the accused will establish *mens rea*. Many statutory offences impose this *mens rea* requirement by using the word 'knowing' or 'knowingly'. But, even where this word is not used, the courts have shown a willingness to imply it into statutory offences (see *Sweet* v *Parsley* [1970] AC 132). In *Roper* v *Taylor's Central Garages* [1951] 2 TLR 284, Devlin J stated that 'knowingly' only says expressly what is normally implied. Of course, the use of the word expressly in a statutory provision avoids all doubt. Often the word 'knowing' is used with the word 'believing' following as an alternative. In *Sherif and others* [2008] EWCA Crim 2653, the defendants were charged, *inter alia*, with offences contrary to s. 38B of the Terrorism Act 2000, of having information which they knew or believed might be of material assistance in preventing the commission by another of an act of terrorism. The 'others' were the bombers who bombed the London Underground and a bus on 21 July 2005. The Court of Appeal approved a direction from the trial judge that:

> Knowledge involves having seen, heard or experienced something yourself. Belief involves reaching a conclusion based on credible evidence, often from a number of sources.

The Court also confirmed that the test of knowledge or belief is a subjective one—whether the defendant himself knew or believed a particular state of affairs.

In *Roper* Devlin J stated that there were three degrees of knowledge. The first is **'actual knowledge'**, where the accused knows for a fact that the relevant circumstance exists. Actual knowledge is the equivalent of intention in that if the accused acts knowing the circumstance to exist he may be said to have acted intentionally in respect of it. Under s. 67 of the Sexual Offences Act 2003 the offence of voyeurism is committed where D, for the purpose of obtaining sexual gratification, observes V doing a private act (for example taking a shower), and he knows that V does not consent to being observed for his sexual gratification. The requirement here seems to be for actual knowledge. This is surprising in the context of this statute where for many more serious offences, such as rape, the absence of a reasonable belief in consent is sufficient to establish liability. One might have expected that absence of reasonable belief in consent would have been more appropriate in this offence where generally D will not know V and thus it will be impossible to prove actual knowledge on D's part of V's lack of consent.

The second degree of knowledge, according to Devlin J, is **'wilful blindness'** which is equivalent to subjective recklessness (discussed at **3.4.2.1** *post*). Where knowledge or belief is required proof of wilful blindness may provide the evidential basis for the tribunal of fact (magistrates or jury) to conclude that the defendant had the necessary knowledge or belief (see *Westminster City Council* v *Croyalgrange Ltd* [1986] 2 All ER 353). In this case the defendant company was convicted of knowingly permitting the use of premises as a sex establishment without a licence. Lord Bridge stated (at p. 359):

> it is always open to the tribunal of fact, when knowledge on the part of a defendant is required to be proved, to base a finding of knowledge on evidence that the defendant had deliberately shut his eyes to the obvious or refrained from inquiry because he suspected the truth but did not want to have his suspicion confirmed.

In *Sherif and others* the Court of Appeal confirmed this approach approving a direction to the jury where the judge indicated that:

> it was not sufficient for the prosecution to establish that a defendant had closed his eyes, but that the jury was entitled to conclude, if satisfied that he had deliberately closed his eyes to the obvious because he did not wish to be told the truth, that that fact was capable of being evidence to support a conclusion that that defendant either knew or believed the fact in question.

In cases of handling stolen goods, however, where the *mens rea* requirement is that the accused did so knowing or believing the goods to be stolen, the courts have held that wilful blindness is not sufficient (see **13.5.2.1** *post*).

The third degree of knowledge, according to Devlin J, is **'constructive knowledge'** which is really a species of negligence and rarely suffices to establish criminal liability. Phrases such as 'reasonable cause to believe', 'reason to believe', or 'reason to suspect' in the definitions of offences import this degree of knowledge. Liability is, in effect, incurred where the accused had the means of knowledge had he made the enquiries which a reasonable and prudent person would make or applied his mind to the situation in the way in which a reasonable person would have done. This variety of knowledge was adopted in the Protection from Harassment Act 1997, ss. 1 and 4 (see **4.1.2** *post*). In *Flintshire County Council* v *Reynolds* [2006] EWHC 195 (Admin) the respondent had been charged under s. 112 of the Social Security Administration Act 1992 with knowingly producing information which she knew to be false in a material particular for the purpose of obtaining a benefit. On a case stated, following her acquittal at the magistrates' court, the Divisional Court held that constructive knowledge is not enough to demonstrate that something has been done knowingly in the context of a criminal statute.

The amount of knowledge required to establish guilt need extend no further than the circumstance which the definition of the offence prescribes. For example, it is sufficient for a conviction of handling stolen goods that the accused knew the goods to be stolen although he was ignorant or mistaken as to the nature of the goods (*McCullum* (1973) 57 Cr App R 645). Where the offence involved is being knowingly concerned in the fraudulent evasion of a prohibition on the importation of various types of goods contrary to s. 170(2) of the Customs and Excise (Management) Act 1979, different penalties apply depending on the nature of the goods. However, a mistake as to the nature of the goods will not prevent the accused being convicted of a more serious offence than that which he believed he was committing. In *Ellis, Street and Smith* (1986) 84 Cr App R 235, the accused knew they were importing prohibited goods concealed in secret compartments in cars. They believed the goods were pornographic materials when they were, in fact, cannabis, a Class B controlled drug. The maximum penalty for importing Class B controlled drugs is 14 years' imprisonment whereas the maximum for importing pornographic goods is two years. The Court of Appeal held, however, that knowledge that the goods being imported were prohibited was all that was required. This contravenes the principle in *Courtie* [1984] AC 463 that the imposition of separate penalties in a statutory provision creates separate offences. Under the *Courtie* principle, importing pornographic goods is a separate offence from importing controlled drugs. The courts, however, are prepared to accept the *mens rea* of a lesser offence to establish guilt of a greater offence even though the greater offence may have been one which the accused would never have contemplated committing. The potential for injustice is considerable when it is realised that the maximum penalty for importing Class A controlled drugs, such as heroin or cocaine, is life imprisonment.

Where the *mens rea* requirement is knowledge, it must be proved that the accused had the requisite knowledge at the time of committing the offence. If the accused previously knew the prescribed fact but has forgotten it at the time he acted, this will not suffice (see *Russell* (1984) 81 Cr App R 315).

3.4 Recklessness

3.4.1 What might recklessness mean?

For some offences, such as murder or an attempt, only intention suffices to establish criminal liability. But for most crimes the *mens rea* required is intention or recklessness. Recklessness provides the baseline for liability in most offences and thus it is important to define clearly the parameters of this concept so that it is distinguishable from negligence which generally (subject to a few statutory exceptions and 'gross negligence manslaughter') does not suffice for criminal liability. A person may be reckless as to a consequence or as to a circumstance. **The notion that recklessness conveys is that of taking an unjustifiable risk.** This is reflected in the Draft Criminal Code where the Law Commission defines the term in cl. 18 as follows:

> a person acts—...
>
> (c) 'recklessly' with respect to—
> > (i) a circumstance when he is aware of a risk that it exists or will exist;
> > (ii) a result when he is aware of a risk that it will occur; and it is, in the circumstances known to him, unreasonable to take the risk.

Not all risk-taking is unreasonable; circumstances may exist which justify taking a risk. Whether taking a risk is justifiable depends on a balancing of the social utility or value of the activity involved against the probability and gravity of harm which might be caused. The Law Commission stated in its *Working Paper on the Mental Element in Crime* (Law Com No. 31 at p. 53):

> The operation of public transport, for example, is inevitably accompanied by risks of accident beyond the control of the operator, yet it is socially necessary that these risks be taken. Dangerous surgical operations must be carried out in the interests of the life and health of the patient, yet the taking of these risks is socially justifiable.

The tribunal of fact performs this balancing task using the objective test of whether a reasonable and prudent man would have taken the risk in the circumstances. Thus, if an act has no social utility but involves a slight possibility of the risk of harm, this would suffice to render the taking of that risk a reckless act.

 Question

If the tribunal of fact concludes that the accused has taken an unreasonable risk, is this sufficient to establish criminal liability? Or is awareness of the risk on the part of the accused

> necessary before criminal liability may be imposed? To put this another way, is it necessary for the accused to have foreseen the risk at the time he acted or is it sufficient that a reasonably prudent person would have foreseen the risk?

In most cases the accused is a reasonable person and will have foreseen what other reasonable persons would have foreseen. In some cases, however, the accused, because of mental deficiency, may be incapable of foreseeing what reasonable persons would have foreseen. In such a case is the accused to be found criminally liable for this failure or should criminal liability be limited to those who are, in some way, culpable because they are responsible actors? The views of the courts on this matter have changed over the years. The change was prophesised by Glanville Williams in *Criminal Law: The General Part*, para. 24, who identified the potential for the concept of recklessness to merge with that of carelessness due to three factors: first, 'the etymology of the word'; secondly, 'the constant pressure to extend the reach of the criminal law on account of the supposed policy of the individual case'; and thirdly, the need for a formula to be used to instruct juries because of the difficulty of proving recklessness. This third factor can cause a shift of emphasis from asking the jury 'to consider whether the defendant *must* have foreseen the consequence' to asking them 'whether the defendant *ought* as a reasonable man to have foreseen it'.

3.4.2 How have the courts defined recklessness?

3.4.2.1 Subjective recklessness

The courts originally gave recklessness a *subjective* meaning. **Thus an accused would be found to be reckless only where he had recognised the possibility of the prohibited consequence occurring (or the particular circumstance existing) and he had carried on regardless.** The leading authority on subjective recklessness is *Cunningham* [1957] 2 QB 396; as a result, this concept of recklessness is often referred to as '*Cunningham* recklessness'. In *Cunningham*:

> D removed a gas meter from an unoccupied house so that he could steal the money it contained. He left behind the fractured pipe from which gas was escaping. The gas seeped into the neighbouring house and P inhaled it. D was convicted of maliciously administering a noxious thing so as to endanger life contrary to s. 23 of the Offences Against the Person Act 1861. D's conviction was quashed as the judge had instructed the jury that 'maliciously' meant 'wickedly'. The Court of Criminal Appeal approved of the definition propounded by Kenny in *Outlines of Criminal Law* (1902) which stated:

> > In any statutory definition of a crime, 'malice' must be taken not in the old vague sense of wickedness in general but as requiring either (i) an actual intention to do the particular *kind* of harm that in fact was done or (ii) recklessness as to whether such harm should occur or not (i.e. the accused has foreseen that the particular kind of harm might be done, and yet has gone on to take the risk of it). It is neither limited to, nor does it indeed require, any ill-will towards the person injured.

> The issue which had not been clearly left to the jury was whether D had actually foreseen that removal of the gas meter might cause injury to someone but nevertheless had gone on to remove it.

In more recent statutory provisions the word 'maliciously' is not used; Parliament uses the words 'intentionally' or 'recklessly' expressly. In its Report, *The Mental Element in Crime* (Law Com No. 89), the Law Commission attributed this subjective meaning to recklessness. The Criminal Damage Act 1971 resulted from the work of the Law Commission who in their Report, *Offences of Damage to Property* (Law Com No. 29), approved the *Cunningham* definition of recklessness. Section 1 of the Act makes it an offence for a person to destroy or damage property belonging to another intentionally or recklessly. Several cases arose in the 1970s concerning the meaning of the word 'reckless' in this section (see *Briggs* [1977] 1 WLR 605; *Parker* [1977] 1 WLR 600; *Stephenson* [1979] 1 QB 695). In all of these cases the Court of Appeal confirmed that the test was subjective—it had to be proved that the accused recognised the risk even though, perhaps because of bad temper, he had suppressed it or driven it out.

In *Stephenson* the accused suffered from schizophrenia. He had crept into a hollow in a large straw stack and lit a fire to keep warm. The stack caught fire. The trial judge directed the jury that they could find the accused guilty if they were satisfied he had closed his mind to the obvious fact of risk from his act and that schizophrenia might be a reason which made a person close his mind to the obvious fact of risk. In effect he was directing the jury that if a reasonable prudent person would have recognised the risk as obvious they should convict the accused. The Court of Appeal quashed the conviction, Geoffrey Lane LJ stating (at p. 703):

> A man is reckless when he carries out the deliberate act appreciating that there is a risk that damage to property may result from his act. It is however not the taking of every risk which could properly be classed as reckless. The risk must be one which it is in all the circumstances unreasonable for him to take....We wish to make it clear that the test remains subjective, that the knowledge or appreciation of risk of some damage must have entered the defendant's mind even though he may have suppressed it or driven it out....The schizophrenia was on the evidence something which might have prevented the idea of danger entering the appellant's mind at all. If that was the truth of the matter, then the appellant was entitled to be acquitted. That was something which was never left clearly to the jury to decide.

3.4.2.2 *Caldwell* recklessness—an objective interlude

Unfortunately what seemed clear to the Court of Appeal was far from clear to the House of Lords. **Recklessness received radical redefinition in the 1980s in** *Caldwell* [1982] AC 341. The remainder of this section is, as a result of the House of Lords' decision in *G* [2003] UKHL 50, an historical narrative as their Lordships overruled their decision in *Caldwell* as 'offensive to principle and apt to cause injustice'; accordingly 'the need to correct it was compelling'. The fact that it took 22 years to correct this unjust decision is, however, a cause for concern. It indicates the extent to which the judiciary, at the highest levels, are capable of misunderstanding basic principles of criminal liability and of perpetuating error in the face of the most compelling arguments from the most distinguished commentators. Indeed, the error into which the House of Lords fell in *Caldwell* was exacerbated, rather than mitigated, by subsequent decisions in the Divisional Court, Court of Appeal, and House of Lords before enlightenment dawned on their Lordships in *G*.

3.4.2.2.1 *The test of recklessness*
In *Caldwell* D got drunk and set fire to a hotel in pursuit of a grievance he had against the owner. There were guests in the hotel at the time but the fire was discovered and extinguished before any serious damage was done. D was indicted on two counts of arson. He pleaded guilty to the first count of intentionally or recklessly damaging property belonging to another contrary to s. 1(1) of the Criminal Damage Act 1971 but pleaded not guilty to the second count of damaging property with intent to endanger life or being reckless whether life would be endangered contrary to s. 1(2) of the 1971 Act. He claimed that he was so drunk at the time that the thought that he might be endangering life had never crossed his mind. The trial judge directed the jury that drunkenness was not a defence to this charge and he was convicted. The House of Lords affirmed that where the prosecution indict the accused on the basis that he was reckless whether life was endangered, drunkenness is not a defence as this is an offence of 'basic intent' (see **5.6**, *post* for a discussion on intoxication). This should have been enough to dispose of the case. Their Lordships, however, took the opportunity to redefine recklessness. Lord Diplock, with whom Lords Keith of Kinkel and Roskill agreed, delivered the judgment of the majority. He stated his test of recklessness as follows (at p. 354):

> In my opinion, a person charged with an offence under s. 1(1) of the 1971 Act is 'reckless as to whether or not property would be destroyed or damaged' if (1) he does an act which in fact creates an obvious risk that property will be destroyed or damaged and (2) when he does the act he either has not given any thought to the possibility of there being any such risk or has recognised that there was some risk involved and has none the less gone on to do it.

3.4.2.2.2 *Reasons for the redefinition of recklessness*
Lord Diplock gave several reasons for this extension of the meaning of recklessness.

First, he considered that the word 'reckless' in a statute was not a term of art and thus should be given its dictionary meaning of 'careless, regardless, or heedless of the possible harmful consequences of one's acts'. This merged recklessness with negligence. **Secondly, Lord Diplock considered that the two states of mind in his test, of foresight of risk and failure to give thought to the possibility of there being any such risk, were equally blameworthy.** This, to say the least, is highly questionable as the person who deliberately takes a risk would appear to be much more culpable than the one who does not recognise the risk. It may be that Lord Diplock was concerned to prevent people relying on their own drunkenness as a reason for their failure to recognise a risk. However, such people would not escape liability as the House ruled they could not plead intoxication in respect of an offence for which 'recklessness is enough to constitute the necessary *mens rea*'; there was no need to extend the definition of recklessness to catch what had already been caught by the law relating to self-induced intoxication.

That the inadvertent accused who failed to give thought to an obvious risk was to be regarded as reckless, however, was confirmed by the House of Lords' decision in *Reid (ante)*.

The third reason was that the *Cunningham* test of recklessness called for a 'meticulous analysis by the jury of the thoughts that passed through the mind of the accused at or before the time he did the act that caused the damage'. He considered that the distinction between the advertent state of mind and the inadvertent state, for the purposes of a statutory offence of damage to property, 'would not be a practicable distinction for use in a trial by jury' and he could see no reason why Parliament, when it revised the law on offences of damage to property, 'should go out of its way to perpetuate fine and impracticable distinctions'. The whole history of the Criminal Damage Act 1971, from its genesis as a Draft Bill appended to the Law Commission's Report through its debate in Parliament to its enactment, revealed clear acceptance of the subjective meaning of recklessness. The distinction between advertent risk-taking and inadvertent risk-taking would seem to be fundamental to the distinction between the criminally culpable actor and the negligent actor. As this distinction is fundamental to criminal liability, it is extremely doubtful that Parliament considered it so fine that it should not be perpetuated. It is also highly questionable whether the distinction was impracticable. Juries are constantly faced with the task of deciding between two versions of events put forward by the prosecution and the defence. If the *mens rea* required for an offence is subjective recklessness, the jury will apply their common sense to this matter. If they would have foreseen the risk of damage or harm in the circumstances in which the accused acted, they may be satisfied that the accused must have foreseen the risk in the absence of some explanation or other evidence raising a reasonable doubt as to whether he foresaw that risk. If the accused is a person of normal intelligence, the inference that he foresaw what other people would have foreseen will, in most cases, be a proper one to draw and does not appear to require the meticulous analysis Lord Diplock envisaged. If for some reason the accused did not foresee the risk, he can always testify to this and seek to raise the doubt in the jury's mind by other evidence or cross-examination of prosecution witnesses. The task appears no more difficult than deciding whether the accused intended a result; in all cases where the accused does not admit to having the prescribed *mens rea* for an offence, the jury's task is one of drawing inferences from all the evidence in light of their own experience. Lord Diplock's approach in this case had a definite flavour of extending 'the reach of the criminal law on account of the supposed policy of the individual case'.

3.4.2.2.3 *To whom had the risk to be obvious?*

If an accused was to be convicted for failing to give thought to an obvious risk, an important issue to be decided would be to whom the risk had to be obvious; was it the reasonably prudent person or the accused himself had he bothered to consider the matter? Lord Diplock's views on this matter were expressed ambiguously. However, in *Lawrence* [1982] AC 510 Lord Diplock stated (at p. 526):

> Recklessness on the part of the doer of an act does presuppose that there is something in the circumstances that would have drawn the attention of an ordinary prudent individual to the possibility that his act was capable of causing the kind of serious harmful consequences that the section which creates the offence was intended to prevent....

This view was reluctantly accepted by the Divisional Court as the correct one in *Elliott* v *C* [1983] 1 WLR 939.

> D, who had been out all night without sleep, entered a garden shed where she found white spirit which she poured on to an old carpet and lit to keep warm. The fire spread to the shed which was destroyed. D was 14-years-old and of limited intelligence being in a remedial class at school. The magistrates acquitted her, finding that she had given no thought to the risk of the shed being destroyed, but that even if she had given thought to the matter the risk would not have been obvious to her. The Divisional Court directed the magistrates to convict as it was only necessary for the risk to have been obvious to the reasonably prudent man. The Court was not concerned with the reason for the accused's failure to give thought to an obvious risk. The Court felt bound to decide the case in this way because of Lord Diplock's statements in *Lawrence* and *Miller* [1983] 2 AC 161.

This case provoked considerable criticism at the time as the doctrine of *mens rea* derives from the idea of responsibility. A person is a responsible actor where he has the capacity to make conscious choices. If a person is incapable of foreseeing the consequences of his actions because of mental deficiency he cannot be considered blameworthy; unless, that is, he is to be blamed for being mentally deficient. It is hardly conceivable that people with inadequacies, for which they bear no responsibility and over which they have no control, merit the censure of the criminal law.

In *Stephen (Malcolm R)* (1984) 79 Cr App R 334, it was argued that the reasonably prudent person should at least be of the same age and sex as the accused and bear such of his characteristics as would have affected his ability to appreciate the risk involved in his conduct. The Court of Appeal rejected this argument and confirmed that the risk needed only to have been obvious to the reasonably prudent man who was a person of mature years and understanding. Thus the individual was to be judged against a standard which he may have been constitutionally incapable of attaining.

3.4.2.2.4 *Thinking about a risk and discounting it*

If a person gave thought to the possibility of his conduct involving the risk of damage but wrongly concluded that there was no risk, or that it was negligible in that it was one which a reasonable and prudent person might have taken in the circumstances, he would not appear to have been reckless as he had not failed to give thought to the possibility of risk nor had he recognised a risk and gone on to take it. In *Lawrence* [1982] AC 341, a case involving reckless driving, Lord Diplock stated (at p. 527):

> If satisfied that an obvious and serious risk was created by the manner of the defendant's driving, the jury are entitled to infer that he was in one or other of the states of mind required to constitute the offence and will probably do so; but regard must be had to any explanation he gives as to his state of mind which may displace the inference.

This was the one situation where *Caldwell* recklessness and negligence did not overlap. The concept of negligence includes the person who has given thought to the possibility of the risk existing and unreasonably concluded that it does not exist.

3.4.2.2.5 *To which crimes did the* Caldwell *test apply?*

In the years immediately following *Caldwell* there was considerable confusion as to whether the new test applied to all offences in which recklessness constituted the *mens rea*. After about 10 years of conflicting decisions in various cases dealing with various offences (see *Seymour* [1983] 2 AC 493; *Pigg* [1982] 1 WLR 762; *Satnam and Kewal* (1983) 78 Cr App R 149; *Large* v *Mainprize* [1989] Crim LR 213; *DPP* v *K (A Minor)* [1990] 1 WLR 1067; *Spratt* [1990] 1 WLR 1073; and *Savage* and *Parmenter* both reported at [1991] 4 All ER 698) matters resolved themselves and it became apparent that the *Caldwell* test was confined largely to offences under the Criminal Damage Act 1971.

3.4.2.2.6 *The final demise of* Caldwell *recklessness*

In *G* [2003] UKHL 50, two boys aged 11 and 12 entered the back yard of a shop and set fire to some newspapers they found there, throwing the papers under a large plastic wheelie-bin. The boys left, after which the bin caught fire, in turn setting another bin on fire, and the fire spread eventually causing £1 million worth of damage to the shop. The boys were charged with arson contrary to s. 1(1) and (3) of the Criminal Damage Act 1971. Their defence was that they had expected the paper fires to extinguish themselves. It was accepted that neither boy appreciated that there was any risk of the fire spreading in the way it had. The trial judge directed the jury in accordance with *Caldwell* that if the defendants had created a risk of the building being damaged by fire that would have been obvious to the ordinary reasonable adult bystander, they should convict them if either they had given no thought to the possibility of there being such a risk, or, having recognised that there was some risk involved they had nonetheless gone on and done the act. The jury had difficulty reaching a verdict and asked the judge why they should consider the test as perceived by a reasonable person. The trial judge expressed regret at the law he had to apply and counselled them that even if they found the law harsh, they had to apply it as it was. The jury convicted the boys and the Court of Appeal dismissed their appeal. The point of law of general public importance certified for consideration by the House of Lords was:

> Can a defendant properly be convicted under section 1 of the Criminal Damage Act 1971 on the basis that he was reckless as to whether property was destroyed or damaged when he gave no thought to the risk but, by reason of his age and/or personal characteristics the risk would not have been obvious to him, even if he had thought about it?

Their Lordships effectively answered the certified question in the negative but went further. Lord Bingham, with whom the other four Law Lords expressed their agreement, stated (at para. 41):

> I would answer the certified question obliquely, basing myself on clause 18(c) of the Criminal Code Bill annexed by the Law Commission to its Report 'A Criminal Code for England and Wales Volume 1: Report and Draft Criminal Code Bill' (Law Com No. 177, April 1989):

> 'A person acts recklessly within the meaning of section 1 of the Criminal Damage Act 1971 with respect to—
>> (i) a circumstance when he is aware of a risk that it exists or will exist;

(ii) a result when he is aware of a risk that it will occur; and it is, in the circumstances known to him, unreasonable to take the risk.'

There were several reasons for Lord Bingham's decision. His Lordship was of the view that **it could not be supposed that by 'reckless' Parliament, in legislating the Criminal Damage Act 1971, had meant anything different to the Law Commission in its Report** (Law Com No. 29) and its Working Paper No. 23 which had preceded it, wherein it was plain that in replacing the word 'maliciously' in the previous legislation with the word 'reckless' the intention was to retain the meaning of that word as defined in *Cunningham*. The decision of the majority in *Caldwell* was a misconstruction of the Act and amounted to a 'demonstrable error', or, as Lord Steyn put it, '*Caldwell* adopted an interpretation of section 1 which was **"beyond the range of feasible meanings"'**. This being so, Lord Bingham identified four reasons why the decision in *Caldwell* should be overruled despite its longevity and approval in other cases.

First, conviction of serious crime required not simply proof of causation by the defendant of the injurious result but also proof that when he so acted the defendant's state of mind was culpable. Intention and subjective recklessness (which included deliberate closing of the mind to an appreciated and unacceptable risk) were clearly culpable states of mind. But, his Lordship stated (at para. 32):

it is not clearly blameworthy to do something involving a risk of injury to another if (for reasons other than self-induced intoxication: *R v Majewski* [1977] AC 443) one genuinely does not perceive the risk. Such a person may fairly be accused of stupidity or lack of imagination, but neither of those failings should expose him to conviction of serious crime or the risk of punishment.

Secondly, Lord Bingham considered that the *Caldwell* direction could lead to obvious unfairness as the instant case demonstrated. His Lordship stated (at para. 33):

Here, the appellants could have been charged under section 1(1) with recklessly damaging one or both of the wheelie-bins, and they would have had little defence. As it was, the jury might have inferred that boys of the appellants' age would have appreciated the risk to the building of what they did, but it seems clear that such was not their conclusion (nor, it would appear, the judge's either). On that basis the jury thought it unfair to convict them. I share their sense of unease. It is neither moral nor just to convict a defendant (least of all a child) on the strength of what someone else would have apprehended if the defendant himself had no such apprehension. Nor, the defendant having been convicted, is the problem cured by the imposition of a nominal penalty.

Interestingly, even following this decision, had a person sleeping above the shop died as a result of the fire, the boys could still be convicted of manslaughter (on the basis of an unlawful act) even though they may have had no contemplation of the extent of the harm which could flow directly from their initial act of setting fire to newspaper belonging to another (see **9.3.3.1** *post*).

Thirdly, his Lordship was influenced by the reasoned and outspoken criticism of *Caldwell* expressed by leading academics, practitioners, and judges (including Lords Edmund-Davies and Wilberforce who dissented in *Caldwell*).

Finally, the majority's interpretation of 'recklessly' in s. 1 of the 1971 Act was a misinterpretation which was 'offensive to principle and…apt to cause injustice'. His Lordship rejected the suggestion of a simple modification of the *Caldwell* direction for the benefit of children as such would continue to offend the principle that conviction should depend upon proving a culpable state of mind; it would itself be anomalous unless also modified to take account of the limited understanding of those who are mentally handicapped; it would lead to further contentious argument about the qualities and characteristics which might be taken into account; and, to adopt such a modification would simply substitute one misinterpretation of s. 1 for another.

A further reason to support their Lordships' conclusion was expressed by Lord Steyn who recognised the general trend towards a subjective approach to liability, in respect of which s. 8 of the Criminal Justice Act 1967 (see **3.2.3.1** *ante*) was of central importance. This subjective approach was supported by a number of their Lordships' earlier decisions: *Morgan* [1976] AC 182 (see **3.6.1.1.1** *post*); *Beckford* [1988] AC 130 (see **3.6.1.1.2** *post*); *B (A Minor)* v *DPP* [2000] 2 AC 428 (see **3.6.1.1.3** and **4.2.3.1** *post*); and *K* [2002] 1 AC 462 (see **4.2.3.1** *post*). Contrary to the view of Lord Diplock that the subjective test of recklessness would not be practicable, Lord Steyn stated (at para. 58):

> One can trust the realism of trial judges, who direct juries, to guide juries to sensible verdicts and juries can in turn be relied on to apply robust common sense to the evaluation of ridiculous defences. Moreover, the endorsement by Parliament of the Law Commission proposals could not seriously have been regarded as a charter for the acquittal of wrongdoers.

While the decision of their Lordships is confined to the meaning of the word 'reckless' in the Criminal Damage Act 1971, it is difficult to see how the objective test could be revived in the context of any other statutory offence without Parliament expressly legislating for that interpretation. This is confirmed by the decision of the Court of Appeal in *Attorney-General's Reference (No. 3 of 2003)* [2004] EWCA Crim 868, where **the Court applied the subjective definition of recklessness to the offence of misfeasance in public office further intimating that it applies generally in the criminal law.** The Court considered how the House of Lords had interpreted 'wilful neglect' in the case of *Sheppard* [1981] AC 394 (see **3.5** *post*) taking the view that a subjective test was required whereby it was necessary for D to have a subjective awareness of the duty to act or a subjective recklessness as to the existence of the duty.

3.5 Wilfulness

The term 'wilfully' is often used in statutes. The cases are inconsistent regarding the question whether or not this imports a requirement of *mens rea*. In *Arrowsmith* v *Jenkins* [1963] 2 QB 561, on a charge of wilful obstruction of the highway contrary to s. 121(1) of the Highways Act 1959, the Divisional Court held that it was sufficient that the accused by an exercise of free will did an act which caused an obstruction. This seemed to import nothing more than a requirement of voluntariness. As such the word 'wilfully' is effectively otiose as the requirement of voluntariness is implied by the general principles of the criminal law. There is, however, a notable number of similar decisions relating to other statutory offences (see e.g. *Maidstone Borough Council* v *Mortimer* [1980] 3 All ER 552; *Hudson* v *MacRae* (1863) 4 B & S 585; *Cotterill* v *Penn* [1936] 1 KB 53).

By contrast, in the earlier case of *Eaton* v *Cobb* [1950] 1 All ER 1016, the Divisional Court held that the word 'wilfully' imported a requirement of *mens rea*. Humphreys J stated (at p. 1017):

> In my view 'wilfully obstruct' in a statute which makes such obstruction a criminal offence means wilfully to obstruct...the test...is whether or not the obstruction was intentional.

In this case D had opened his car door in the path of a cyclist after having checked his mirror and seeing the road apparently clear. The Divisional Court took the view that while he wilfully opened the door he did not 'wilfully obstruct' the highway as there was no intention so to do. This decision is similar to those of the offence of wilfully obstructing a police constable in the execution of his duty contrary to s. 51(3) of the Police Act 1964. In *Lewis* v *Cox* [1985] QB 509, Webster J stated (at p. 516):

> [T]he simple facts which the court has to find are whether the defendant's conduct in fact prevented the police from carrying out their duty, or made it more difficult for them to do so, and whether the defendant intended that conduct to prevent the police from carrying out their duty or to make it more difficult to do so.

In this case D had twice opened the rear door of a police van with the object of discovering from his friend who had been arrested where he was being taken. While D's ultimate aim may not have been obstruction, this was, in fact, a necessary precondition to the achievement of his ultimate aim. As he knew the van would be prevented from driving away by his opening of the door, he therefore intended the obstruction.

In *Sheppard* [1981] AC 394, the House of Lords imported a *mens rea* requirement into the offence of wilful neglect of a child contrary to s. 1 of the Children and Young Persons Act 1933. Section 1 provides:

> (1) If any person who has attained the age of sixteen years and has the custody, charge, or care of any child or young person under that age, wilfully assaults, ill-treats, neglects, abandons, or exposes him...in a manner likely to cause him unnecessary suffering or injury to health...that person shall be guilty of a misdemeanour....

The case arose from the failure of parents to procure medical aid for their child who died from malnutrition and hypothermia. In relation to the four positive acts which the section proscribes ('neglect' being a failure to act), Lord Diplock expressed the view that the word 'wilfully' imported *mens rea*. If the word was to be understood as simply requiring a voluntary act, this was not its natural meaning and it would be otiose. Regarding neglect, which in this case involved the failure to provide medical aid, Lord Diplock stated (at pp. 404, 405):

Such a failure...could not be properly described as 'wilful' unless the parent *either* (1)
had directed his mind to the question whether there was some risk...that the child's
health might suffer unless he were examined by a doctor and provided with such cura-
tive treatment as the examination might reveal as necessary, and had made a conscious
decision, for whatever reason, to refrain from arranging for such medical examination,
or (2) had so refrained because he did not care whether the child might be in need of
medical treatment or not.

While part (2) appears to suggest *Caldwell* recklessness, in *Attorney-General's
Reference (No. 3 of 2003)* [2004] EWCA Crim 868, the Court of Appeal concluded
that the test was one of subjective recklessness as Lord Diplock intended to exclude
from liability those parents who, through lack of intelligence or ignorance, are
genuinely unaware of the threat to their child's health. Following the decisions in
Sheppard and *Attorney-General's Reference (No. 3 of 2003)* earlier cases which suggest
that the word 'wilfully' simply imports the requirement for a voluntary act, rather
than subjective *mens rea*, must be of doubtful authority.

3.6 Mistake

 Question

If the accused makes a mistake will this affect his criminal liability?

The answer to this question will depend on the nature of the mistake he makes. His
mistake may be such as to negate his *mens rea* in respect of a circumstance which
is part of the *actus reus* of the offence.

 Example

D is charged with the theft of an umbrella which he took from an umbrella-stand in a restaurant. If D believed the umbrella was his own there would be no dishonesty (i.e. *mens rea*) in
respect of the appropriation of 'property belonging to another' (i.e. a circumstance in the
actus reus—see s. 1 of the Theft Act 1968). If, however, *mens rea* is not required in respect of
a particular circumstance, a mistake in respect of it may be of no relevance.

A mistake may also be made with regard to circumstances which justify or excuse
the commission of an offence such as pleas of self-defence or duress.

An **issue which has been problematical for many years is whether a mistake
must be a reasonable one** (i.e. such as a reasonable person might have made in the
circumstances) before it will relieve the accused of liability. Needless to say judicial
pronouncements on this issue have been contradictory.

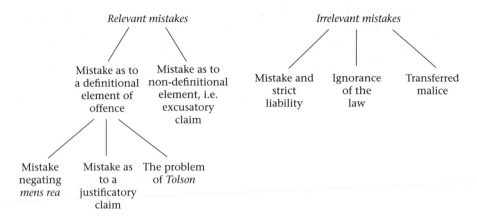

Figure 3.1 Mistakes

Mistakes may be divided into two categories, namely *relevant* mistakes and *irrelevant* mistakes. Figure 3.1 illustrates the different types of mistakes and the relationship between the various sub-categories. Most uncertainty and inconsistency has arisen in respect of relevant mistakes.

3.6.1 **Relevant mistakes**

A mistake may be relevant where it relates to either a definitional element of the offence or an excusatory claim (e.g. duress). The definitional elements of the offence are the *actus reus* and justificatory claims such as self-defence. The latter may be viewed as part of the *actus reus* (see **2.1.2 *ante***). At one time, only mistakes which were reasonable could operate to negate liability. In *DPP v Morgan* [1976] AC 182, the House of Lords removed this requirement in certain circumstances so that an honest mistake could suffice. Consequently relevant mistakes have to be divided into those relating to definitional elements of the offence and those relating to non-definitional elements.

3.6.1.1 Mistake as to a definitional element of the offence

There are three categories of mistake as to a definitional element of an offence.

3.6.1.1.1 *Mistake negating* mens rea

Where an offence is one requiring *mens rea* the accused must have *mens rea* in relation to every element of the *actus reus*. **If the accused's mistake is to operate to negate his liability it must relate to the existence of an element of the *actus reus*; it is not sufficient that his mistake is as to some quality of an element of the *actus reus*.** For example, D steals a Jaguar belonging to V believing it to be green. The car is red but D is colour-blind. His mistake is one of quality and will not affect his liability. He intended to appropriate property belonging to another and he did so. In *McCullum* (1973) 57 Cr App R 645, it was held that it was sufficient for a conviction of handling stolen goods that D knew the goods were stolen albeit that he was ignorant or mistaken as to the nature of the goods. Similarly, in *Ellis, Street and Smith* (1986) 84 Cr App R 235 (see **3.3 *ante***), it was sufficient that the accused knew the goods they were importing were prohibited goods, albeit they thought they were importing pornography rather than drugs. These examples should be contrasted with the example in **3.6** *ante* of taking the wrong umbrella, where the mistake relates to the existence of an element of the *actus reus*. If D believes that the property he is taking is his own he is not acting dishonestly as he does not believe he is appropriating property belonging to another; his mistake negates his *mens rea* (see further discussion of s. 2 of the Theft Act 1968, **11.2.2.2.1** *post*). The result would be the same if D had destroyed the umbrella believing it was his own and had been charged with criminal damage contrary to s. 1(1) of the Criminal Damage Act 1971 (see *Smith (David)* [1974] QB 354).

Formerly a mistake as to the existence of a definitional element would only operate to negate the accused's *mens rea* where the mistake was a reasonable one. The House of Lords considered this issue in *DPP* v *Morgan* [1976] AC 182.

> This was a case involving rape where the appellants claimed that they believed the victim was consenting. The trial judge had directed the jury that they should acquit only if they were satisfied that the appellants' mistake as to the victim's consent was reasonable. The House of Lords held this was a misdirection as the only requirement was that the belief in consent be an honest one. Lord Hailsham stated (at p. 214):
>
> > Once one has accepted...that the prohibited act in rape is non-consensual sexual intercourse, and that the guilty state of mind is an intention to commit it, it seems to me to follow as a matter of inexorable logic that there is no room either for a 'defence' of honest belief or mistake, or of a defence of honest and reasonable belief or mistake. Either the prosecution proves that the accused had the requisite intent, or it does not. In the former case it succeeds, and in the latter it fails.

Thus an honest belief in consent negates *mens rea*; a 'defence' of mistake is, in reality, a denial that the prosecution has proved its case. Of course, the more reasonable the mistake is, the more likely it is that the accused will be believed. Lord Hailsham recognised this when he went on to state (at p. 214):

> Since honest belief clearly negatives intent, the reasonableness or otherwise of that belief can only be evidence for or against the view that the belief and therefore the intent was actually held...

 Question

Does the principle in *Morgan* apply generally to all offences requiring *mens rea* or only to the offence of rape?

In *Phekoo* [1981] 1 WLR 1117, the Court of Appeal confined the decision to the offence of rape holding that mistakes as to definitional elements in other offences had to be reasonable if they were to negative *mens rea*. In *Kimber* [1983] 1 WLR 1118, the Court of Appeal held that the same inexorable logic which spawned the decision in *Morgan* also dictated that on a charge of indecent assault *mens rea* would be negatived by an honest belief in the victim's consent. This same logic dictates the same result in all offences requiring *mens rea*. That this is correct has been confirmed by the House of Lords in *B (A Minor)* v *DPP* [2000] 2 WLR 452 (see **3.6.1.1.3** *post*). **Where a particular offence requires only negligence in respect of an element of the *actus reus*, then the mistake must be a reasonable one if it is to negative negligence** (see **3.6.1.1.3** *post*). **If strict liability applies to an element of the *actus reus* a mistake, reasonable or not, will be irrelevant** (see **4.2.1** *post*).

While the principle in *Morgan*, that an honest mistake in respect of a definitional element negates *mens rea*, has become of general application, the law relating to consent in respect of sexual offences has been changed as from May 2004 when the Sexual Offences Act 2003 came into effect. For offences committed after this date belief in consent, to be effective, must be reasonable. (For further discussion of consent in respect of sexual offences see **10.2** *post*.)

3.6.1.1.2 *Mistake as to a justificatory claim*

 Question

D hits V in the belief that V was about to attack him when, in fact, V was simply performing an April Fools' Day prank. Will D's plea of self-defence succeed to negate his liability where it is an honestly held belief or must the belief be a reasonable one?

In *Albert* v *Lavin* [1982] AC 546, the Divisional Court held that an accused could rely on his mistaken belief only when pleading self-defence where that belief was based on reasonable grounds. This raises the question whether a justification is something separate from the definitional elements of an offence (see **2.1.2** *ante*). If it is there might be some reason in principle for requiring such mistakes to be reasonable. If, however, the absence of a justificatory claim is part of the definitional elements of the offence the inexorable logic of *Morgan* would seem to apply. In *Kimber*, Lawton LJ disagreed with the reasoning in *Albert* v *Lavin*. When the issue arose directly in *Williams (Gladstone)* (1984) 78 Cr App R 276, the Court of Appeal departed from *Albert* v *Lavin*. D was convicted of assault occasioning actual bodily harm. D had witnessed what he believed to be an assault by M on N. D intervened and punched M. D claimed he honestly believed that N was being unlawfully assaulted by M and that he was trying to rescue N. In fact M was acting lawfully, seeking to arrest N for a robbery he had seen him commit. The jury were directed that D's mistake would be relevant if it was honest and based on reasonable grounds. The Court of Appeal quashed D's conviction. The Court defined 'assault' as 'an act by which the defendant, intentionally or recklessly, applies unlawful force to the complainant'. Thus the force must be unlawful and D must intend to apply unlawful force to the victim. Lord Lane CJ stated that the mental element cannot be substantiated 'by simply showing an intent to apply force and no more'. He was of opinion that there are three situations where the use of force is lawful. First, in limited circumstances the victim may consent to the force (but see now *Brown*, **10.1.1.3.1** *post*); secondly, where the defendant is acting in self-defence; and thirdly, where the defendant is using reasonable force in the prevention of crime or to arrest offenders under s. 3 of the Criminal Law Act 1967. If the accused makes a mistake he is to be judged against the facts as he believed them to be. The Court stated (at p. 281):

the jury should be directed first of all that the prosecution have the burden or duty of proving the unlawfulness of the defendant's actions; secondly, if the defendant may have been labouring under a mistake as to the facts, he must be judged according to his mistaken view of the facts; thirdly, that is so whether the mistake was, on an objective view, a reasonable mistake or not.

In *Beckford* v *R* [1988] AC 130, the Privy Council approved the decision in *Williams* as correctly stating the law. Lord Griffiths stated (at p. 144):

If then a genuine belief, albeit without reasonable grounds, is a defence to rape because it negatives the necessary intention, so also must a genuine belief in facts which if true would justify self-defence be a defence to a crime of personal violence because the belief negates the intent to act unlawfully.

The element of unlawfulness is thus part of the definitional elements of the offence and requires *mens rea* to be proved in respect of it. If the accused mistakenly believes he is acting in self-defence he does not intend to act unlawfully (see further *Blackburn* v *Bowering* [1994] 3 All ER 380; *Faraj* [2007] EWCA Crim 1033).

Some statutory offences prohibit conduct where it is done 'without lawful excuse' (see, for example, ss. 1(1), 2, and 3 of the Criminal Damage Act 1971). In these offences the absence of lawful excuse is one of the definitional elements of the offence which the prosecution must prove. Section 5(3) expressly declares that it is sufficient that a belief in one of the circumstances which would constitute a lawful excuse is honest; there is no requirement that the belief be based on reasonable grounds (for a full discussion of s. 5 of the Criminal Damage Act 1971, see **14.2.2.2** *post*).

3.6.1.1.3 *The problem of* Tolson

The offence of bigamy under s. 57 of the Offences Against the Person Act 1861 is committed where a person 'being married, shall marry any other person during the life of the former husband or wife'. A proviso to the section provides that it shall not extend to second marriages where the first marriage has been dissolved or annulled, or where the husband or wife has been continually absent from the person who is remarrying for seven years, and has not been known by that person to be living within that time. In *Tolson* (1889) 23 QBD 168, a wife remarried five years after last seeing her husband whom she believed to have been lost at sea. She was charged with bigamy when it was discovered that he was still alive. She did not come within the proviso although the jury found that she believed on reasonable grounds and in good faith that he was dead. The Court for Crown Cases Reserved quashed her conviction. In *Gould* [1968] 2 QB 65, it was held that a reasonable belief that the first marriage had been dissolved was a defence. In *Morgan* the decision in *Tolson* was approved along with other bigamy cases which followed it (see *King* [1964] 1 QB 285 and *Gould*). Lord Fraser stated that 'bigamy does not involve any intention except the intention to go through a marriage ceremony'. It is a general principle that *mens rea* is required as to all the elements of the *actus reus* of an offence unless these are excluded expressly or by necessary implication. The approval of *Tolson* in *Morgan* can only be explained on the basis that *mens rea* was not required as to the element of 'being married', negligence being sufficient. If this is correct, there is nothing to distinguish the state of mind of the bigamist from that of every other person who marries. As bigamy is a serious offence it is disappointing that the House of Lords did not take the opportunity to disapprove of *Tolson* as the requirement of *mens rea* should not lightly be set aside.

Their Lordships confronted the problem again in *B (A Minor)* v *DPP* [2000] 2 WLR 452 (**4.2.3.1** *post*) where the requirement that a mistaken belief had to be based on reasonable grounds was described by Lord Nicholls (at pp. 457, 458) as a 'relic from the days before a defendant could give evidence in his own defence' which explained why juries would judge a defendant's state of mind 'by the conduct to be expected of a reasonable person'. In *Sweet* v *Parsley* [1970] AC 132 (**4.2.3.1** *post*) Lord Diplock had stated that (at p. 163):

> a general principle of construction of any enactment, which creates a criminal offence, [is] that, even where the words used to describe the prohibited conduct would not in any other context connote the necessity for any particular mental element, they are nevertheless to be read as subject to the implication that a necessary element in the offence is the absence of a belief, held honestly and upon reasonable grounds, in the existence of facts which, if true, would make the act innocent.

Lord Nicholls concluded that this presumption required modification to reflect the current state of the criminal law on mistakes of fact by omitting the reference to reasonable grounds. He did not, however, pass any comment to resolve the status of *Tolson* which remains an aberrant decision limited to bigamy and awaits a suitable opportunity for their Lordships to overrule it. The House of Lords did not take the opportunity offered in *R* v *K* [2001] UKHL 41, [2001] 3 WLR 471 (see **4.2.3.1** *post*) to resolve the uncertainty surrounding the status of *Tolson* but, by confirming that the presumption of *mens rea* is to apply unless excluded expressly or by necessary implication, it must be taken to have implicitly overruled *Tolson* such that if similar circumstances were to arise in the future an honest belief in the death of a spouse should be sufficient to defeat a charge of bigamy.

3.6.1.2 Mistake as to a non-definitional element

Where an accused seeks to rely on an excusatory defence (see **6.1** *post*) his plea involves an admission that he performed the *actus reus* of the offence with the requisite *mens rea*. If the defence is successful the accused is excused the normal consequences of conviction and sentencing which would otherwise ensue. If an accused makes a mistake in respect of an element of an excusatory defence, such as duress, the issue arises whether such a mistake must be a reasonable one. In *Graham* (1982) 74 Cr App R 235, Lord Lane CJ made it clear that an accused may only rely on the defence of duress where his belief that he would be killed or seriously injured if he did not commit the offence was a reasonable one. In *Howe* [1987] 1 AC 417, the House of Lords endorsed this view without further consideration. Subsequent cases have accepted that in duress or duress of circumstances the issue is one of reasonable belief (see, for example, *Abdul-Hussain et al* [1999] Crim LR 570; *Cairns* [1999] 2 Cr App R 137; *Safi* [2003] EWCA Crim 1809). While *Cairns* was misconstrued in *Martin* [2000] 2 Cr App R 42 as having held that the test in duress was subjective, thereby creating further uncertainty (see further **6.2.4.2** *post*), the

House of Lords in *Hasan* [2005] UKHL 22, has confirmed the objective nature of the test. Lord Bingham of Cornhill, whose reasoning was approved by Lords Steyn, Rodger, and Brown, stated (at para. 23):

> But the words used in *Graham* and approved in *Howe* were 'he reasonably believed'. It is, of course, essential that the defendant should genuinely, ie actually, believe in the efficacy of the threat by which he claims to have been compelled. But there is no warrant for relaxing the requirement that the belief must be reasonable as well as genuine.

This different treatment of mistakes, dependent on whether they relate to matters of justification or of excuse, has the potential for further anomalous consequences. In 'Necessity, duress and self-defence' [1989] Crim LR 611, Professor Elliott gives the example of a motorist, D, who unreasonably believes he is being attacked by V. If D drives away in a dangerous fashion and is charged with dangerous driving, he would not succeed if he raised a plea of duress of circumstances (see **6.3.2** *post*) because of his unreasonable mistake. By contrast, if he drove his car at V, on a charge of dangerous driving he could raise the defence of self-defence.

The Law Commission in its Draft Criminal Code removes this anomaly by cl. 41 which provides that 'a person who acts in the belief that a circumstance exists has any defence that he would have if the circumstance existed'; there is no requirement that the belief be reasonable.

3.6.2 Irrelevant mistakes

3.6.2.1 Mistake and offences of strict liability

An offence is one of strict liability where *mens rea* is not required in respect of an element of the *actus reus*; *mens rea* may be required in respect of other elements of the offence. If the accused makes a mistake in respect of an element for which liability is strict his mistake is irrelevant as his state of mind need not be established in respect of that element in order to determine guilt (see **Chapter 4**). If the mistake is in respect of an element for which *mens rea* is required, the mistake will operate in the normal way as regards liability (see *Blackburn v Bowering* [1994] 3 All ER 380). In *Prince* (1875) LR 2 CCR 154, D was convicted of an offence under s. 55 of the Offences Against the Person Act 1861 (since repealed). Under the 1861 provision it was an offence unlawfully to take an unmarried girl under the age of 16 out of the possession of her father against his will. D was convicted although he had reasonable grounds to believe the girl was over 16. The Court of Crown Cases Reserved affirmed his conviction holding that the offence was one of strict liability in respect of the circumstance of the girl's age. As knowledge of the girl's age was not required, a mistake thereto was irrelevant (on age-related offences and strict liability see *B (A Minor) v DPP* [2000] 2 AC 428, **4.2.3.1** *post*). Lord Bramwell stated, however, that had the accused mistakenly believed the girl's father had consented to her being taken, or if he believed she was not in anyone's possession, care or charge, his conviction would have been quashed as an intention to take the girl out of her father's possession against his will had to be proved.

? Question

Can a person be convicted even if he does not know the law or is mistaken about it?

In *Howells* [1977] QB 614, D was convicted of possession of a revolver without a firearm certificate, contrary to s. 1 of the Firearms Act 1968. D thought the gun was an antique which would have been covered by an exception under s. 58(2); in fact it was a modern reproduction. His appeal against conviction was dismissed by the Court of Appeal on the ground that 'to allow a defence of honest and reasonable belief that the firearm was an antique and therefore excluded would be likely to defeat the clear intention of the Act'.

In Australia and Canada there is a defence of honest and reasonable belief which may be raised to a charge of a strict liability offence. In *Proudman* v *Dayman* (1943) 67 CLR 536 (an Australian case), Dixon J stated (at p. 540):

> As a general rule an honest and reasonable belief in a state of facts which, if they existed, would make the defendant's act innocent affords an excuse for doing what would otherwise be an offence.

The legislature may expressly exclude this defence in any statutory offence, in which case the offence is one of absolute liability. L. H. Leigh, *Strict and Vicarious Liability* (1982) at pp. 58–61, points out that there are dicta in *Sweet* v *Parsley* [1970] AC 132 and *Morgan* which could be built upon to give recognition to such a defence in England and Wales but so far no court has sought to do so.

3.6.2.2 Ignorance of the law

As a general rule, ignorance of, or a mistake as to, the law is irrelevant as the citizen is presumed to know the law of the land. This presumption is applied even if it was impossible for the accused to know the law. In *Bailey* (1800) Russ & Ry 1, D was a sailor who, before the end of a voyage, committed an act which constituted an offence under a statute which had been passed after the voyage had commenced. D was convicted but the judges recommended a pardon. The prosecution have to prove only that an accused brought about the *actus reus* of the offence with which he is charged with the requisite *mens rea*; they do not have to prove that he knew that what he was doing was contrary to the law. For example, if the accused comes from a country where buggery is not an offence and commits an act of buggery with a man under the age of 16 in this country in the belief that it is not an offence here, this does not negate his liability as he intentionally did the act which constituted the *actus reus* of the offence (see *Esop* (1836) 7 C & P 456).

In *Lee*, *The Times*, 24 October 2001, D was charged with assault with intent to resist lawful arrest contrary to s. 38 of the Offences against the Person Act 1861. D had been driving his car when he was stopped by police officers for a roadside safety check. On smelling alcohol on D's breath one of the officers asked him to perform a breathalyser test. The officer concluded that the test was positive and told D that he was under arrest. D disputed the test and punched both officers. At his trial D claimed that he believed the arrest to be unlawful and thus had no intention to resist lawful arrest. In upholding his conviction the Court of Appeal held his mistake was one of law as to the authority of the officer to arrest him as compared to one of fact, e.g. whether the person seeking to arrest him was a police officer (cf. *Brightling* [1991] Crim LR 364; *Blackburn* v *Bowering* [1994] 3 All ER 380). Relying on *Bentley* (1850) 4 Cox CC 406 (see **10.1.3.2** *post*) the Court took the view that the lawfulness of the arrest was a question of law, not one of fact, and it depended on the officer's belief, not D's belief. The *mens rea* for the offence was an intention to resist arrest and knowledge that the person he assaulted was a person seeking to arrest him. Thus D's belief that he had not committed an offence was irrelevant.

There is an exception to the general rule stated earlier. In some cases the accused's mistake as to the civil law may negate his *mens rea* in respect of an element of the *actus reus* of the offence with which he is charged. In *Smith (David)* [1974] QB 354, D was charged with criminal damage to fixtures in a flat of which he was the tenant. D had installed the fixtures to cover wiring he had installed for his stereo equipment. When he was given notice to quit, D damaged the fixtures in removing the wiring. He claimed he believed he was damaging his own property as he had installed it. D's mistake was as to the civil law; in fact, fixtures become the property of the landlord. D's conviction was quashed as he did not intend to damage 'property belonging to another'. If D had removed the fixtures and taken them with him when he left he would not have been liable for theft as s. 2(1)(a) of the Theft Act 1968 specifically deals with mistakes as to the civil law. It provides that an appropriation of property is not to be regarded as dishonest if the appropriator believed that he had in law the right to deprive the other of it.

In *Secretary of State for Trade and Industry* v *Hart* [1982] 1 WLR 481, D acted as an auditor of two companies although he was disqualified from doing so by the Companies Acts because he was a director of each company. D was charged with the offence of acting as an auditor of a company knowing that he was disqualified for appointment to that office. D submitted that he did not know of the statutory provisions which disqualified him. The Divisional Court held it was not sufficient to know the relevant facts rendering him disqualified; it had to be proved that he knew he was disqualified by law from acting as an auditor. D's ignorance of company law meant that he did not have the requisite *mens rea* for the offence. If the accused had admitted that he knew that he was disqualified from acting as an auditor but did not know that this was an offence, he would have been convicted as he would have been in the same position as the accused in *Esop*.

In each case it is crucial to determine the *mens rea* required by the offence. If *mens rea* is not required as to the element of the *actus reus* in respect of which the accused is mistaken, his mistake will be irrelevant. If, however, negligence is required as to that element, the accused's mistake will negate his liability if it was a reasonable one. In the case of bigamy an accused will not be liable if he reasonably, but mistakenly, believed that his first marriage had been dissolved (a mistake of civil law) at the time he entered into the second marriage (see *Gould* [1968] 2 QB 65).

3.6.2.3 Transferred malice

> **? Question**
>
> D wishes to kill V. He sees a person whom he believes to be V and shoots at him, killing him. In fact he has killed V's twin brother. Can D avoid a conviction for murder because his mistake brought about an unintended result?

D will be liable as he intended to kill another person unlawfully and he killed the person at whom he was aiming. His mistake is as to a matter which the law treats as irrelevant, namely the identity of the victim. Likewise if D intends to burn down 10 Downing Street, but in the dark he mistakenly sets fire to No. 11, he will be guilty of arson as he has, without lawful excuse, intentionally damaged property belonging to another.

In this example would it make any difference if D had shot at V but at the moment D pulled the trigger V had bent over and the bullet had hit and killed a man behind him? In this situation D has not killed the person at whom he was aiming but he has caused the *actus reus* of murder and he did intend to kill.

> In *Latimer* (1886) 17 QBD 359, D's conviction of unlawfully and maliciously wounding P was upheld, although D had aimed the offending blow with his belt at Q and it had glanced off striking P and causing a severe wound. The Court applied the doctrine of 'transferred malice' Lord Coleridge CJ stating (at p. 361):

> > It is common knowledge that a man who has an unlawful and malicious intent against another, and, in attempting to carry it out, injures a third person, is guilty of what the law deems malice against the person injured, because the offender is doing an unlawful act, and has that which the judges call general malice, and that is enough.

If, in *Latimer*, the belt had glanced off Q and the buckle had connected with a valuable vase, breaking it, D would have brought about a different *actus reus* to that intended, namely criminal damage. In such a case if D was charged with criminal damage his intention to injure Q could not be combined with this *actus reus* to support a conviction as the *actus reus* he has caused and *mens rea* he had relate to different offences (see *Pembliton* (1874) LR 2 CCR 119). Of course, if it could be proved that D had foreseen this risk and gone on to take it, D could be convicted of criminal damage on the basis of recklessness. He might also be charged with attempting to wound Q. Professor A. J. Ashworth makes the point that in virtually all cases of transferred malice the accused could have been convicted of attempt and thus there is no need for the doctrine (see 'Transferred malice and punishment for unforeseen consequences' in *Reshaping the Criminal Law* (ed. P. Glazebrook (1978)). Professor Ashworth argues that charging attempt would be an improvement as then the accused would be prosecuted for the intended harm rather than the accidental result. The Law Commission in its Draft Criminal Code, however, opted to retain the doctrine of transferred fault (see also Law Com No. 218, paras. 42.1 to 42.6). In its *Commentary on Draft*

Criminal Code Bill (Law Com No. 177) it states its primary reason for this as follows (at para. 8.57):

> Where a person intends to affect one person or thing (X) and actually affects another (Y), he may be charged with an offence of attempt in relation to X; or it may be possible to satisfy a court or jury, without resort to the doctrine, that he was reckless with respect to Y. But an attempt charge may be impossible (where it is not known until trial that the defendant claims to have had X and not Y in contemplation); or inappropriate (as not describing the harm done adequately for labelling or sentencing purposes). Moreover, recklessness with respect to Y may be insufficient to establish the offence or incapable of being proved.

In *Attorney-General's Reference (No. 3 of 1994)* [1996] 2 WLR 412, the doctrine of transferred malice was affirmed and applied in a novel way by the Court of Appeal. B stabbed his pregnant girlfriend in the abdomen. No injury to the foetus was detected. The child was born prematurely and died subsequently due to complications arising from her premature birth. B was charged with murder. The trial judge directed an acquittal on the ground that no conviction for either murder or manslaughter was possible in law. Before the Court of Appeal three arguments were raised. Relying on Glanville Williams, *Criminal Law: The General Part* (paras. 44 and 48) it was argued, first, that an 'unexpected difference of mode [by which the relevant consequence occurs should] be regarded as severing the chain of causation if it is sufficiently far removed from the intended mode' and, secondly, that the doctrine of transferred malice 'should be limited to cases where the consequence was brought about by negligence in relation to the actual victim'. The Court of Appeal considered that it was neither right nor necessary 'to reintroduce any question of causation at the stage when *mens rea* falls to be considered' and that there was no justification for the proposed imposition of a requirement of negligence toward the intended victim. A further argument that malice could not be transferred to a person who was not in being at the time of the act causing death was also rejected. The Court of Appeal concluded that malice could be transferred in this situation. Lord Taylor CJ stated earlier in his judgment:

> In the eyes of the law the foetus is taken to be a part of the mother until it has an existence independent of the mother. Thus an intention to cause serious bodily injury to the foetus is an intention to cause serious bodily injury to a part of the mother just as an intention to injure her arm or her leg would be so viewed. Thus consideration of whether a charge of murder can arise where the focus of the defendant's intention is exclusively the foetus falls to be considered under the head of transferred malice, as is the case where the intention is focused exclusively or partially upon the mother herself.

On further appeal to the House of Lords [1997] 3 WLR 421, their Lordships held that B could be convicted of manslaughter but not of murder. An intention to harm the mother could not be equivalent to intent to harm the foetus or the child it would become, since they were two distinct organisms living symbiotically. There was no basis for extending the doctrine of transferred malice to a case where there had been no intention to injure the foetus. The *mens rea* for murder was not, therefore, present. Lord Mustill referred to the doctrine of transferred malice as a 'fiction' which lacked a 'sound intellectual basis'. He did not explain in what way the doctrine involved a fiction. When the doctrine is applied in the context of murder where D aimed to kill X but missed and killed Y, there is no fiction involved where he is charged with the murder of Y and it is proved that he had the intention to kill a person. The law would be deficient if it did not protect the public generally in circumstances such as these. Their Lordships, however, had no difficulty in concluding that B could be guilty of manslaughter resulting from an unlawful and dangerous act. They were of the view that it was unnecessary for the act to have been directed against the person who died as a result of it or for B to have known that his act was likely to injure that person. It was sufficient to prove that B intentionally stabbed the mother, that the act caused the death, and that reasonable people would have appreciated the risk that some harm would result to *a person*, not necessarily the foetus or person it would become. There was an argument that a foetus should not be regarded as being a potential victim of manslaughter. This was firmly rejected, Lord Hope of Craighead stating (at p. 443):

> For the foetus, life lies in the future, not the past. It is not sensible to say that it cannot ever be harmed, or that nothing can be done to it which can ever be dangerous. Once it is born it is exposed, like all other living persons, to the risk of injury. It may also carry with it the effects of things done to it before birth which, after birth, may prove to be harmful. It would seem not to be unreasonable therefore, on public policy grounds, to regard the child in this case, when she became a living person, as within the scope of the *mens rea* which B had when he stabbed her mother before she was born.

If the doctrine of transferred malice could not be applied to the foetus for the purposes of a conviction for murder, how could a conviction of manslaughter (which is also homicide) be possible? If a manslaughter verdict is possible, why not a murder verdict given that in the instant case B had the necessary *mens rea* for murder and his act caused the death of a person, the *actus reus* of murder? Their Lordships do not answer this question. Indeed, they do not appear to recognise that there is something incongruous about the decision they gave. The only consolation is that the facts are so unusual that it is unlikely that this decision will be the source of injustice in the future.

If D shoots at V because he believes that V is about to shoot him but he misses and kills W, D could plead self-defence if charged with W's murder. If he was justified in shooting V (this depends on using only such force as was reasonable in the circumstances), and thus did not intend *unlawfully* to kill another person, he cannot be convicted of murdering W as there is no *mens rea* to transfer. Where, however, P and D engage in a gunfight in the course of which P shoots at D, misses and kills V, neither P nor D having a justification for their actions, both would be guilty of murder by means of the doctrine of transferred malice, P as the principal and D as an accessory (see *Gnango* [2011] UKSC 59; see **7.1.2.1** *post*).

FURTHER READING

J. Chalmers and F. Laverick, 'Fair Labelling in Criminal Law' (2008) 71 *MLR* 217.
R. A. Duff, 'The Politics of Intention: A Response to Norrie' [1990] *Crim LR* 637.

E. Griew, 'States of Mind, Presumptions and Inferences', in *Criminal Law: Essays in Honour* of J. C. Smith (ed. P. Smith, 1987).

S. G. Griffin, 'Inferring the Requisite Intention to Kill' (1989) 139 *NLJ* 1637.

J. Horder, 'Transferred Malice and the Remoteness of Unexpected Outcomes from Intentions' [2006] *Crim LR* 383.

D. Kimel, 'Inadvertent Recklessness in the Criminal Law' (2004) 120 *LQR* 548.

I. Kugler, 'Conditional Oblique Intention' [2004] *Crim LR* 284.

W. Lucy, 'Controversy in the Criminal Law' (1988) 8 *LS* 317.

A. Norrie, 'Oblique Intention and Legal Politics' [1989] *Crim LR* 793; 'Intention: More Loose Talk' [1990] Crim LR 642.

A. Pedain, 'Intention and the Terrorist Example' [2003] *Crim LR* 579.

A. P. Simester, 'Moral Certainty and the Boundaries of Intention' (1996) 16 *OJLS* 445.

A. T. H. Smith, 'Error and Mistake of Law in Anglo-American Criminal Law' (1985) 14 *Anglo-Am LR* 3.

G. Williams, 'Convictions and Fair Labelling' [1983] *CLJ* 85.

G. Williams, 'Oblique Intention' [1987] *CLJ* 417; 'The Mens Rea for Murder: Leave it Alone' (1989) 105 LQR 387.

4

Negligence and strict liability

4.1 Negligence

4.1.1 The meaning of negligence

Mens rea, **as it has been traditionally understood, requires an advertent state of mind on the part of the accused.** Intention and recklessness are states of mind falling within the compass of *mens rea*. **Negligence has not been accepted as a *mens rea* term as it does not require advertence on the part of the accused to a particular risk.** Negligence is, however, a type of legal fault as it sets an objective standard to which a person's behaviour must conform. The standard set is that of the reasonable (or prudent) person. Thus if a reasonable person would have recognised the risk of a consequence occurring or a circumstance existing in the situation in which the accused acted (or omitted to act), the accused will be liable whether or not he gave any thought to the possibility of there being a risk involved in his conduct.

The *Caldwell* recklessness test overlapped to some degree with negligence as, under *Caldwell*, an accused could be liable where he failed to give thought to an obvious risk. Negligence, however, covers an area which *Caldwell* did not cover. If a person gives thought to a risk but concludes that there is no risk or that it is negligible he could not be liable under *Caldwell*. The concept of negligence, however, includes the person who has given thought to the possibility of the risk existing and unreasonably concluded that it does not exist. Negligence also covers the person who recognises the risk but takes steps which he believes would eliminate it, if the steps he takes fall below the standard of conduct to be expected from the reasonable person.

4.1.2 Criminal liability for negligence

Traditionally the common law did not impose liability for negligence with the exception of manslaughter where 'gross' negligence is a ground of liability (see **9.3.3.2** *post*). There are few crimes where negligence is the sole basis of liability. The most notable example is s. 3 of the Road Traffic Act 1988 (as substituted by s. 2 of the Road Traffic Act 1991), under which it is an offence to drive a motor vehicle on a road without due care and attention or without reasonable consideration for other persons using the road. This offence is generally referred to as careless driving. In *McCrone* v *Riding* [1938] 1 All ER 157, Lord Hewart CJ stated the standard of driving which is required as follows (at p. 158):

> That standard is an objective standard, impersonal and universal, fixed in relation to the safety of other users of the highway. It is in no way related to the degree of proficiency or degree of experience to be attained by the individual driver.

This standard applies to all drivers, even the inexperienced learner driver. The standard set is that of the reasonably prudent and skilful driver. If the accused drives in a way in which such a reasonable driver would not have driven, he will be liable.

Negligence as to the existence of a circumstance is sometimes sufficient to establish liability. This is sometimes referred to as 'constructive knowledge' (see **3.3** *ante*). For example, under s. 25 of the Firearms Act 1968 it is an offence 'for a person to sell or transfer any firearm or ammunition to...another person whom he knows or has reasonable cause for believing to be drunk or of unsound mind'. Constructive knowledge was resorted to as a basis of liability for the two offences created by the Protection from Harassment Act 1997 to deal with the problem of stalking; the term 'stalking' was not used in the Act as it was perceived to be simply an example of harassment and this term was preferred as it was wider. The Protection of Freedoms Act 2012, by s. 111 has created two new offences of stalking by inserting two sections, ss. 2A and 4A into the 1997 Act; stalking has thus been recognised as a particular form of harassment and the label 'stalker' is, perhaps, one which carries greater stigma. A person may be convicted of the summary offence, under s. 2, of pursuing a course of conduct, as defined in s. 1, which amounts to harassment of another if he knows or ought to know that it amounts to harassment, or the indictable offence, under s. 4, of engaging in a course of conduct which causes another to fear, on at least two occasions, that violence will be used against him, if he knows or ought to know that his course of conduct will cause the other so to fear. Where the course of conduct, in either case, amounts to stalking, the offence will be charged either under s. 2A as a summary offence or under s. 4A as an indictable offence. The justification for the imposition of liability based on constructive knowledge is the difficulty which might exist of proving *mens rea* on the part of those who engage in harassment or stalking who often suffer from mental or personality disorders (see further Allen, 'Look Who's Stalking: Seeking a Solution to the Problem of Stalking' [1996] 4 Web JCLI).

In the Sexual Offences Act 2003 there are a number of offences intended to protect children from sexual harm, abuse, and exploitation. For serious offences such as rape of a child under 13, assault by penetration of a child under 13, sexual assault of a child under 13, and causing or inciting a child under 13 to engage in sexual activity, a child under 13 is considered incapable of consenting (ss. 5, 6, 7, and 8 respectively). It is Parliament's intention that liability in respect of the circumstance of the child's age should be strict and it should not be a defence that the defendant believed the child to be over 13. For other offences, such as sexual activity with a child and causing or inciting a child to engage in sexual activity (ss. 9 and 10 respectively) the defendant will not be guilty where the child is over 13 but under 16 and he reasonably believes that the child is 16 or over. In *G* [2006] EWCA Crim 821 (affirmed by the House of Lords [2008] UKHL 37), the Court of Appeal found that the need for a mental element in respect of age for the s. 5 offence was negatived by necessary implication arising from the contrast between, for instance, the s. 9 offence with its reference to reasonable belief that the child was over 16, and the absence of any such reference in relation to children under 13. It is clear that for these offences liability is strict where the child is under 13 but negligence is required where the child is 13 or over.

Although liability is rarely imposed for negligence there are two other ways in which negligence may become relevant. In certain strict liability offences statute may provide that it is a defence for the accused to prove that he was not negligent. Under the Trade Descriptions Act 1968, which creates a number of offences which require no proof of *mens rea* or negligence by the prosecution, s. 24(1) provides that it is a defence for the person charged to prove:

(a) that the commission of the offence was due to a mistake or to reliance on informa-tion supplied to him or to the act or default of another person, an accident or some other cause beyond his control; and
(b) that he took all reasonable precautions and exercised all due diligence to avoid the commission of such an offence by himself or any person under his control.

The Food and Environment Protection Act 1985 contains a defence in s. 22(1) in similar terms to s. 24(1)(b). The second way in which negligence may be relevant is the converse of the first; negligence in respect of a subsidiary element of the *actus reus* of the offence with which he is charged may deprive the accused of a defence which would otherwise have been available to him. For example, bigamy is an offence where negligence in respect of the subsidiary element of 'being mar-ried' is sufficient. Thus if an accused goes through a second ceremony of marriage having made an unreasonable mistake that his former marriage has been annulled or dissolved or that his spouse is dead, he will be guilty of bigamy (see *King* [1964] 1 QB 285).

4.1.3 Does the reasonable person share any of the accused's characteristics?

While the standard against which the accused's conduct is measured is objective, that of the reasonable man, the question arises whether there are situations in which a subjective element may be imported into negligence so that the reasonable person shares any physical or mental limitations from which the accused might suffer. It is clear that if the accused had some special knowledge which the ordinary person would not possess, the standard against which he will be judged is that of the rea-sonable person possessing that special knowledge (see *Lamb* [1967] 2 QB 981).

The Misuse of Drugs Act 1971 contains various offences relating to the produc-tion, cultivation, possession, and supply of drugs. Section 28 provides a defence in relation to some of these offences:

(2)...it shall be a defence for the accused to prove that he neither knew of nor suspected nor had reason to suspect the existence of some fact alleged by the prosecution which it is necessary for the prosecution to prove if he is to be convicted of the offence charged.

In *Young* [1984] 1 WLR 654, the accused sought to rely on his intoxication as his reason for not suspecting that he was in possession of a controlled drug. The Courts-Martial Appeal Court held that this would not avail him as a defence based on the ground of 'no reason to suspect' involved the concept of objective rationality. There are many statutory defences based on 'reasonable cause' or 'reasonable grounds' to believe (see e.g. s. 1(5) of the Official Secrets Act 1989) and these have been interpreted as imposing an objective test of whether the reasonable person would have held the requisite belief (see *McArdle* v *Egan* (1933) 150 LT 412). It would appear that if there was an objective reason to suspect, it will not avail the accused that persons suffering from his mental or physical incapacities would not have been aware of it.

In the Sexual Offences Act 2003, however, the offences of rape, assault by penetration, sexual assault, and causing sexual activity without consent, are offences which may be committed where the defendant 'does not reasonably believe that B consents'. Whether a belief is reasonable is to be determined having regard to all the circumstances, including any steps the defendant has taken to ascertain whether the complainant consents. This is not, strictly speaking, an offence of pure negligence as the standard is not that of the 'reasonable person' (a standard to which a particular defendant might not be able to attain, where, for example he had learning difficulties or suffered from a mental disorder) but rather what is reasonable in all the circumstances (a test which is flexible enough to take into account the particular characteristics of the defendant).

4.2 Strict liability

4.2.1 The meaning of strict liability

> **Key Point**
>
> If *mens rea* or negligence need not be proved in respect of one or more elements of the *actus reus* of an offence, that offence is one of strict liability.

This must be contrasted with absolute liability. If an offence is one of absolute liability even the absence of voluntariness on the accused's part will not avail him. Very few offences involve absolute liability (see *Larsonneur* and *Winzar* v *Chief Constable of Kent*, **2.4.2** *ante*). **If an offence is one of strict liability the prosecution must prove the *actus reus* was committed by the accused; this involves establishing that the accused's conduct was voluntary.**

While an accused may not be found guilty of a strict liability offence where his conduct was involuntary, just as he could not be convicted of an offence requiring *mens rea* or negligence, he may be convicted even though he caused the prohibited consequence inadvertently and in a totally blameless way. For example, D, a butcher, asked a vet to examine a carcass to check that it was fit for human consumption, and, on receiving the vet's assurance that it was fit, he offered it for sale. D was convicted of the offence of exposing unsound meat for sale because the meat turned out to be unfit for human consumption, the vet having negligently performed his examination (see *Callow* v *Tillstone* (1900) 83 LT 411). D had exercised due care and taken reasonable steps to avoid committing the offence; his conduct was quite blameless. The offence, however, was one of strict liability as neither *mens rea* nor negligence were required in respect of the unsoundness of the meat. Short of not selling meat at all, there was no way for D to avoid liability. Similarly, if the accused is charged with driving a motor vehicle on a road either while unfit through drink contrary to s. 4 of the Road Traffic Act 1988, or with a level of alcohol in his blood, breath, or urine above prescribed limits contrary to s. 5, he will be convicted even though he was unaware of his condition and not responsible for it, as where it is due to his soft drink being surreptitiously laced with alcohol. When construing road traffic legislation, the courts have held that these offences are strict liability offences which impose liability on the blamelessly inadvertent driver in the previously mentioned situation, although the court may treat the 'laced drink' as a special reason for refraining from disqualifying the driver under s. 34(1) of the Road Traffic Offenders Act 1988 (see *Shippam* [1971] RTR 209; *Williams v Neale* [1971] RTR 149).

It should be noted that while liability may be strict in respect of one element of the *actus reus*, *mens rea* or negligence may be required in respect of other elements. In *Prince* (1875) LR 2 CCR 154, D was convicted of taking an unmarried girl under the age of 16 out of the possession of her father against his will, contrary to s. 55 of the Offences Against the Person Act 1861. D believed on reasonable grounds that the girl was 18 but he knew she was in the custody of her father. D was convicted as knowledge that the girl was under 16 was not required. By contrast, in *Hibbert* (1869) LR 1 CCR 184, D met a girl of 14 in the street and took her to another place where they had sexual intercourse. D was acquitted of the s. 55 offence as it was not proved that he knew the girl to be in the custody of her father; *mens rea* was required as to this element. Section 55 of the Offences Against the Person Act 1861 was replaced by s. 20 of the Sexual Offences Act 1956. Whether this was a strict liability offence was left in some doubt following the decision of the House of Lords in *B (A Minor) v DPP* [2000] 2 WLR 452 (see **4.2.3.2** *post*) where their Lordships cast doubt on the reasoning of the court in *Prince* in concluding that liability was strict in respect of the *actus reus* element of age. Their Lordships did not overrule *Prince*, however, as the correct construction of s. 20 was not an issue before them. The s. 20 offence has been repealed by the Sexual Offences Act 2003.

4.2.2 The origins of strict liability

It is a presumption of the common law that *mens rea* is required to be proved to establish guilt of a criminal offence. Strict liability invariably arises in respect of offences created by statute. The precursors to offences of strict liability are to be found in some eighteenth-century regulatory statutes relating to the adulteration of foodstuffs and tobacco, which created defences for merchants and others charged with such offences to prove that the adulteration took place without their knowledge and despite the exercise of due diligence to prevent it (see further L. H. Leigh, *Strict and Vicarious Liability* (1982)). In the nineteenth century there was an increase in regulatory legislation concerned with food and drugs, health, liquor, factories, pollution, and other public welfare matters. Faced with this welter of legislation and the difficulties of enforcement, the courts dispensed with the requirement of *mens rea* in many cases where there were no express words in the statute requiring proof of *mens rea*. This development could be justified on several grounds. First, earlier regulatory legislation requiring proof of *mens rea* made convictions difficult to secure. Secondly, later legislation either did not use words, such as 'maliciously', 'intentionally', 'knowingly', 'wilfully', or 'permitting', which would impose a requirement of *mens rea*, or these words were used in some sections of Acts and not in others. Thirdly, most of this regulatory legislation could be regarded as creating offences *mala prohibita* rather than *mala in se*. **Offences such as murder, rape, theft are *mala in se* because they are inherently immoral. Regulatory offences generally do not involve inherently immoral activities. Conduct becomes criminal simply because it is prohibited**. For example, many strict liability offences relate to driving vehicles and the safety and construction of vehicles. There is nothing inherently immoral in driving at 71 mph as opposed to 69 mph. Driving at 71 mph is an offence, however, because Parliament has decided that, in the interests of safety, a line has to be drawn somewhere between acceptable speed and unacceptable speed. Regulatory offences are created by Parliament for the better running of society and the penalty is imposed to encourage observance of the law. Those who break such laws, however, are not really thought of as criminals.

 Question

Is strict liability confined to regulatory offences?

Strict liability has not been confined to regulatory offences (see *Prince* **4.2.1** *ante*) and, indeed, it was not a necessary consequence of the difficulty of proving such offences. The legislation could have been interpreted to involve a reversal of the burden of proof so that the accused would be convicted unless he proved that he had not been at fault, i.e. a 'no negligence' or 'due diligence' defence could have been implied. While not going this far, courts in recent years have sought to reaffirm the presumption of *mens rea* and are, perhaps, less willing to find that an offence is one of strict liability. How do courts decide when construing a statute whether or not the offence it creates is one of strict liability? This question will be answered in the next section.

4.2.3 Identifying offences of strict liability

If Parliament did its job properly there should never be any room for doubt whether or not an offence is one of strict liability. If *mens rea* is required this could be expressly stated by using one of the long list of words (e.g. intentionally, knowingly, wilfully, permitting, etc.) which impose this requirement. Alternatively, if the offence is intended to be one of strict liability, this could be expressly stated as was the case with ss. 1 and 2 of the Contempt of Court Act 1981 which expressly stated that strict liability applied to certain offences under the Act. Unfortunately, many statutory provisions remain silent and the courts are left to divination, or, as they prefer to call it, statutory interpretation whereby they seek to discover the intention of Parliament. Certain factors or considerations may assist the courts in this quest.

4.2.3.1 The presumption of *mens rea*

 Key Point

The absence of express words imposing a requirement of proving *mens rea* is not conclusive that the offence is one of strict liability.

In the earlier part of the last century judges were, perhaps, more easily persuaded that strict liability was intended in such circumstances. In 1969, however, the House of Lords, in its decision in *Sweet* v *Parsley* [1970] AC 132, gave notice of a significant shift in position by reaffirming the presumption of *mens rea*. If it is clearly expressed that an offence is to be one of strict liability, the courts would carry out the will of Parliament. Where, however, the statute is silent, Lord Reid stated the position as follows (at p. 148):

> In such cases there has for centuries been a presumption that Parliament did not intend to make criminals of persons who were in no way blameworthy in what they did. That means that whenever a section is silent as to *mens rea* there is a presumption that, in order to give effect to the will of Parliament, we must read in words appropriate to require *mens rea*.... In the absence of a clear indication in the Act that an offence is intended to be an absolute offence, it is necessary to go outside the Act and examine all relevant circumstances in order to establish that this must have been the intention of Parliament. I say 'must have been' because it is a universal principle that if a penal provision is reasonably capable of two interpretations, that interpretation which is most favourable to the accused must be adopted.

Lord Pearce outlined the matters which the court would examine to determine whether Parliament's intention had been to impose strict liability (at p. 156):

> But the nature of the crime, the punishment, the absence of social obloquy, the particular mischief and the field of activity in which it occurs, and the wording of the particular section and its context, may show that Parliament intended that the act should be prevented by punishment regardless of intent or knowledge.

In the case before them the House of Lords concluded that the offence was not one of strict liability. Miss Sweet had been convicted of being concerned in the management of premises which were used for the purpose of smoking cannabis contrary to s. 5(b) of the Dangerous Drugs Act 1965. Miss Sweet had let rooms in a farmhouse to students. She had retained a bedroom for her own use on the occasions when she visited the property, but she resided elsewhere. The House of Lords held that knowledge that the premises were being used for the prohibited purpose was required. Section 8 of the Misuse of Drugs Act 1971, which replaced the 1965 Act, avoids ambiguity by expressly imposing the requirement of knowledge.

The Privy Council in *Gammon (Hong Kong) Ltd* v *A-G of Hong Kong* [1985] AC 1, reaffirmed the presumption of *mens rea*. Lord Scarman indicated in his speech the matters which a court should consider to determine whether that presumption had been rebutted by a particular statutory provision. He stated (at p. 14):

In their Lordships' opinion, the law…may be stated in the following propositions…:

(1) there is a presumption of law that *mens rea* is required before a person can be held guilty of a criminal offence; (2) the presumption is particularly strong where the offence is 'truly criminal' in character; (3) the presumption applies to statutory offences, and can be displaced only if it is clearly or by necessary implication the effect of the statute; (4) the only situation in which the presumption can be displaced is where the statute is concerned with an issue of social concern; public safety is such an issue; (5) even where a statute is concerned with such an issue, the presumption of *mens rea* stands unless it can also be shown that the creation of strict liability will be effective to promote the objects of the statute by encouraging greater vigilance to prevent the commission of the prohibited act.

In *B (A Minor)* v *DPP* [2000] 2 WLR 452 the House of Lords reaffirmed the common law presumption that *mens rea* would be required to be proved unless Parliament has indicated the contrary intention either expressly or by necessary implication.

Lord Steyn saw this presumption in constitutional terms as an aspect of the principle of legality, quoting with approval Lord Hoffmann's dictum in *R* v *Secretary of State for the Home Department, ex parte Simms* [1999] 3 WLR 328 at p. 341:

But the principle of legality means that Parliament must squarely confront what it is doing and accept the political cost. Fundamental rights cannot be overridden by general or ambiguous words. This is because there is too great a risk that the full implications of their unqualified meaning may have passed unnoticed in the democratic process. In the absence of express language or necessary implication to the contrary, the courts therefore presume that even the most general words were intended to be subject to the basic rights of the individual.

 Question

Does reference to constitutional principles not risk unduly complicating matters?

Raising the presumption of *mens rea* to the level of a constitutional principle has the impact that the presumption is greatly strengthened and thus will be less easy to rebut. This position was affirmed by the House of Lords in *R* v *K* [2001] UKHL 41, [2001] 3 WLR 471, in a case involving an alleged indecent assault by a man aged 26 on a 14-year-old girl contrary to s. 14 of the Sexual Offences Act 1956 (now replaced by s. 3 of the Sexual Offences Act 2003; see **10.2.3** *post*). The appellant claimed he believed the girl to be over the age of 16 at the time of the consensual sexual intimacy between them. In quashing the appellant's conviction the House of Lords concluded that the language of s. 14 did not, as a matter of necessary implication, exclude the presumption of *mens rea*. Indeed, reading the presumption into the section avoided absurdity and anomaly. Lord Steyn confirmed (at para. 32) that the applicability of the presumption was not dependent on there being an ambiguity in the text of the statute. Rather the presumption applies unless there is express language to the contrary or it is ruled out by necessary implication, that is, 'an implication which is compellingly clear' (*B* (*A Minor*) v *DPP* [2000] 2 WLR 452, 464, *per* Lord Nicholls of Birkenhead; see also *M and B* [2009] EWCA 2615).

The result of their Lordships' decisions in *B* and *K* is that the presumption of *mens rea* appears to be given greater force than previously. The full impact of the decisions will only become evident over time. It may be that some of the earlier authorities on strict liability may have to be reconsidered and some offences which have been treated as being offences of strict liability may, following reconsideration, be treated as offences requiring *mens rea*. In the realm of age-related sex offences, however, the impact of *B* and *K* is much more limited as the Sexual Offences Act 2003 has created a raft of age-related offences where liability is strict (see **10.2.5** *post*). Likewise if on analysis the court concludes that the offence is a regulatory one the force of the presumption of *mens rea* does not appear to be that great as a series of Court of Appeal decisions tends to indicate (see *Doring* [2002] Crim LR 817; *Muhamad* [2003] EWCA Crim 1852; *Matudi* [2004] EWCA Crim 697).

In the four sections which follow, the factors which courts consider in deciding whether the presumption of *mens rea* has been rebutted will be examined. A factor which was previously influential in displacing the presumption, the social context, will probably no longer be so in light of their Lordships' approach which appears to confine consideration to the words of the statute and whether they expressly, or by necessary implication, rebut the presumption. While a consideration of one factor may point to rebuttal of the presumption, consideration of the others may point to the presumption being upheld. The decision in respect of each particular offence may involve a balancing of competing factors.

4.2.3.2 The statutory context

? Question

If the section of an Act which creates an offence does not contain any of the usual *mens rea* words such as 'intentionally', 'knowingly' or 'recklessly', is that not the best indication that Parliament intended the offence to be one of strict liability?

If words which impose the requirement of *mens rea* are present in the section under consideration, there is no room for confusion as the intention of Parliament will have been clearly expressed. The absence of such words, however, is not conclusive that *mens rea* is not required as it is in this circumstance that the presumption of *mens rea* operates. Assistance may be sought from other sections in the statute. If *mens rea* words are used in other sections but not in the section under consideration, this may suggest that Parliament intended this section to create a strict liability offence. The perceived purpose of the provision may be of importance in arriving at a conclusion. In *Cundy* v *Le Cocq* (1884) 13 QBD 207, D, a publican, was convicted of selling intoxicating liquor to a person who was drunk contrary to s. 13 of the Licensing Act 1872. D did not know the person was drunk nor was there any evidence of negligence. D's conviction was upheld, however, by the Divisional Court which examined other sections of the Act and found that they contained the word 'knowingly' which s. 13 did not contain. Its view that the offence was one which did not require *mens rea* was confirmed by its examination of the purpose of the Act which it concluded was 'for the repression of drunkenness' and it was therefore right to place upon the publican the responsibility of determining whether his customer was sober and thus remove from him the temptation to sell liquor without regard to the sobriety of the customer.

In *Pharmaceutical Society of Great Britain* v *Storkwain Ltd* [1986] 1 WLR 903, the House of Lords adopted the same approach when construing s. 58(2)(a) of the Medicines Act 1968. D had been charged under this provision with supplying 'prescription only' drugs to customers who had presented forged prescriptions. D believed in good faith and on reasonable grounds that the prescriptions were valid. The presence of express requirements of *mens rea* in other sections of the Act and the absence of such a requirement in this section added to the fact that pharmacists were in a position to put illicit drugs on the market, led their Lordships to conclude that Parliament intended to impose strict liability.

The fact that one section of an Act is silent regarding *mens rea* when other sections are not is not, however, conclusive of the question whether that section creates an offence of strict liability. In *Sherras* v *De Rutzen* [1895] 1 QB 918, the Divisional Court had to consider another provision under the Licensing Act 1872. D, a publican, was convicted under s. 16(2) of having unlawfully supplied liquor to a constable on duty. D believed the officer was off duty as he was not wearing his armlet and thus made no enquiry of the officer as to his status. D regularly served officers in uniform if they were off duty and therefore not wearing their armlets. The Court noted that s. 16(1) made it an offence for a licensee 'knowingly' to harbour or suffer to remain on his premises any constable on duty. The Court, however, quashed D's conviction importing a requirement of knowledge into s. 16(2), Wright J stating (at p. 923) that:

> [I]f guilty knowledge is not necessary, no care on the part of the publican could save him from conviction…since it would be as easy for the constable to deny that he was on duty when asked, or to produce a forged permission from his superior officer as to remove his armlet before entering the public house.

Day J concluded that the effect of the absence of the word 'knowingly' from s. 16(2) was to shift the burden of proof on that issue to the accused. This approach, however, has not been generally adopted.

The statutory context may extend to other statutes. In *B (A Minor)* v *DPP* [2000] 2 WLR 452, B, aged 15, sat next to a girl aged 13 on a bus and asked her several times to perform oral sex with him which she refused to do. He was charged with inciting a girl under the age of 14 to commit an act of gross indecency with him, contrary to s. 1(1) of the Indecency with Children Act 1960 (replaced by ss. 8 and 10 of the Sexual Offences Act 2003). B honestly believed the girl was over 14 but when the justices ruled that this was no defence to the charge he changed his plea to guilty. On a case stated by the justices, the Divisional Court of the Queen's Bench Division dismissed B's appeal. The Divisional Court certified, *inter alia*, that the following point of law of general public importance was involved in its decision, namely, 'Is a defendant entitled to be acquitted of the offence of inciting a child aged under 14 to commit an act of gross indecency…if he may hold an honest belief that the child in question was aged 14 years or over?'. In arriving at an affirmative answer to this question, the House of Lords considered other sexual offences under the Sexual Offences Act 1956 involving an age ingredient. Lord Nicholls of Birkenhead stated (at p. 460):

> If the interpretation of section 1 of the Act of 1960 is to be gleaned from the contents of another statute, that other statute must give compelling guidance. The Act of 1956 as a whole falls short of this standard. So do the two sections, sections 14 and 15, which were the genesis of section 1 of the Act of 1960.

Other factors, such as the seriousness and breadth of the offence, also pointed against the presumption being rebutted.

4.2.3.3 The social context

Examining the statutory context of an offence may not be sufficient to resolve the question whether the presumption of *mens rea* has been rebutted; in such circumstances the social context of the offence is highly relevant. In *Gammon* (**4.2.3.1** *ante*) Lord Scarman stated that the presumption of *mens rea* was particularly strong where an offence was 'truly criminal' but this presumption could be displaced where the offence related to an issue of social concern. This seems to be suggesting that some offences are more 'criminal' than others and that offences relating to issues of social concern are not truly criminal. This raises the problem of how one is to distinguish a 'real crime' from a 'quasi-crime'. The distinction seems to be between offences which involve infractions of the moral code and those offences of a regulatory nature which involve a breach of the law but to which no social stigma attaches, that is those offences 'which are not criminal in any real sense but are acts which in the public interest are prohibited under a penalty' (*per* Wright J, in *Sherras* v *De Rutzen* [1895] 1 QB 918 at 922). The problem with this dichotomy is that public morality changes from one generation to the next. For example, offences relating to pollution may have been regarded as purely regulatory and not truly criminal when enacted. The present generation, however, is likely to regard those guilty of pollution as being criminals because of increased public awareness of environmental issues and the serious and long-term harm which may result from pollution. The distinction that should be made is perhaps between regulatory offences and other offences as some regulatory offences may involve moral stigma.

 Question

How do the courts distinguish between 'real' and 'quasi-'crimes?

In deciding if an offence is 'quasi-criminal' the courts pay attention to two particular factors. First, they consider whether the offence is one of general application to all members of the public or applies to a specific class of persons who are engaged in a particular activity, trade, or profession such as selling food, drugs, liquor, or engaging in industrial activities. If the offence is of the latter type the courts will more readily hold it to be one of strict liability. In *Sweet* v *Parsley* [1970] AC 132, Lord Diplock stated (at p. 163):

> Where penal provisions are of general application to the conduct of ordinary citizens in the course of their everyday life, the presumption is that the standard of care required of them in informing themselves of facts which would make their conduct unlawful is that of the familiar common law duty of care. But where the subject-matter of a statute is the regulation of a particular activity involving potential danger to public health, safety or morals, in which citizens have a choice whether they participate or not, the court may feel driven to infer an intention of Parliament to impose, by penal sanctions, a higher duty of care on those who choose to participate and to place on them an obligation to take whatever measures may be necessary to prevent the prohibited act, without regard to those considerations of cost or business practicability which play a part in the determination of what would be required of them in order to fulfil the ordinary common law duty of care.

This may help to explain the decision in *Pharmaceutical Society of Great Britain* v *Storkwain Ltd* as the prohibition was specific to pharmacists and the accused had chosen to engage in that profession. (See also *Harrow London Borough Council* v *Shah* [1999] 3 All ER 302 where the Divisional Court held that the offence of selling a lottery ticket to an under-age child was not 'truly criminal in character'.) It could be argued, however, that Parliament must be presumed to be legislating within the context of what is practicable in the real world. Pharmacists could only avoid dispensing drugs on a forged prescription if they checked every prescription with the doctor who appeared to have written it; such a practice could hardly be considered practicable. The imposition of strict liability thus appears to be harsh and unnecessary; the purpose of the legislation, to encourage pharmacists to take care when dispensing drugs, could have been achieved by the imposition of a requirement that the prosecution must prove negligence.

The second factor which the courts consider is the social danger which the offence is aimed at preventing. The greater the social danger the more likely it is that the presumption of *mens rea* will be found to be rebutted. Consequently many strict liability offences relate to the control of pollution, inflation, drugs, driving, the regulation of industrial activities, and hygiene and safety in respect of the production and sale of food. For example, many motoring offences impose strict liability. Motoring is an activity in which citizens generally engage and thus motoring offences might be expected to require proof of *mens rea* or negligence. However, as the potential danger to the public is grave, courts have found the presumption of *mens rea* to have been rebutted. In the field of pollution strict liability is imposed. In *Alphacell Ltd* v *Woodward* [1972] AC 824, the House of Lords held the accused company guilty of causing polluted matter to enter a river, contrary to s. 2(1)(a) of the Rivers (Prevention of Pollution) Act 1951 although there was no evidence that the company knew of the pollution or that they had been negligent. Lord Salmon stated (at p. 848):

> It is of the utmost public importance that rivers should not be polluted. The risk of pollution…is very great. The offences created by the Act of 1951 seem to me to be prototypes of offences which 'are not criminal in any real sense, but are acts which in the public interest are prohibited under a penalty.'…I can see no valid reason for reading the word 'intentionally', 'knowingly' or 'negligently' into section 2(1)(a)….This may be regarded as a not unfair hazard of carrying on a business which may cause pollution on the banks of a river. If…it were held…that no conviction could be obtained…unless

the prosecution could discharge the often impossible onus of proving that the pollution was caused intentionally or negligently, a great deal of pollution would go unpunished and undeterred...

The House of Lords was influenced by the devastating effects pollution can have, the assumption of responsibility by voluntarily choosing to conduct a business which may cause pollution and the need to deter others from causing pollution by encouraging greater vigilance. Similar considerations influenced the Privy Council in *Gammon Ltd* v *A-G of Hong Kong* [1985] AC 1. The appellants, who were respectively the registered contractor, the project manager, and the site agent for building works, were charged with deviating in a material way from work shown on an approved plan contrary to the Hong Kong Building Ordinance. Part of a temporary support system on the building site had collapsed. The issue to be decided was whether the appellants had to know that their deviation was *material* or whether liability was strict in relation to this element of the offence. The Privy Council held that the offence was one of strict liability. They were influenced by the threat to public safety which would arise from material deviations from plans, the need to deter the incompetent from engaging in building work, and the need to encourage greater vigilance on the part of those who do engage in such work.

4.2.3.4 The severity of the punishment

 Question

Does a heavy maximum sentence guarantee that the offence will not be found to be one of strict liability?

The decisions of the courts in this area vary considerably. On the one hand the provision of a low maximum punishment by Parliament may indicate that the offence is one which is not truly criminal, thereby giving support to a finding of strict liability. The assumption is that a high maximum penalty indicates that the offence is truly criminal and that an accused should only be convicted where he is shown to be blameworthy. On the other hand, however, the provision of a severe punishment, such as prison, may lend support to the contention that the offence deals with a matter of grave social danger for which strict liability is appropriate.

In the *Storkwain* decision the House of Lords were not persuaded by the argument that Parliament could not have intended to impose strict liability for an offence which carried a maximum sentence of two years' imprisonment as the other factors which they considered pointed to strict liability. In *Gammon* the Privy Council considered that the maximum penalty of a fine of $250,000 and imprisonment for three years indicated the 'seriousness with which the legislature viewed the offences'. While this was a 'formidable' argument against strict liability, viewed in light of the ordinance as a whole their Lordships concluded (at p. 17) that:

there is nothing inconsistent with the purpose of the ordinance in imposing severe penalties for offences of strict liability. The legislature could reasonably have intended

> severity to be a significant deterrent, bearing in mind the risks to public safety arising from some contraventions of the ordinance.

Similarly, in *Howells* [1977] QB 614, on a charge of possession of a firearm without a firearm certificate contrary to s. 1(1)(a) of the Firearms Act 1968, the Court of Appeal concluded that the fact that the maximum penalty was five years' imprisonment did not preclude the imposition of strict liability. The Court found that other factors such as the wording of the Act and the danger to the community resulting from possession of lethal firearms outweighed this factor.

By contrast, in *B (A Minor)* v *DPP* (see **4.2.3.2** *ante*) the House of Lords took the view that the more serious the offence the less likely it was that the presumption of *mens rea* would be rebutted. Lord Nicholls of Birkenhead stated:

> The more serious the offence, the greater is the weight to be attached to the presumption, because the more severe is the punishment and the graver the stigma which accompany a conviction.

In the instant case the maximum penalty was 10 years' imprisonment and, in addition, the notification requirements under Part I of the Sex Offenders Act 1997 applied indicating an offence of truly criminal character to which considerable stigma is attached. A further concern was the breadth of the offence as, according to Lord Nicholls, an act of gross indecency 'can embrace conduct ranging from predatory approaches by a much older paedophile to consensual sexual experimentation between precocious teenagers of whom the offender may be the younger of the two'. Lord Steyn pointed out that as the offence covers incitement to an act of gross indecency, verbal sexual overtures between teenagers where one was under the age of 14 would also be covered (as in the instant case). (For a discussion of age-related offences under the Sexual Offences Act 2003 see **4.1.2** *ante* and **10.2.5** *post*.)

4.2.3.5 Promoting the enforcement of the law

The fact that a statute deals with an issue of social concern is not sufficient to displace the presumption of *mens rea* unless strict liability will be effective in encouraging vigilance and observance of the law. In *Reynolds* v *G. H. Austin & Sons Ltd* [1951] 2 KB 135, the defendant company was charged with a contravention of the Road Traffic Acts. The company were a private hire coach company who had contracted to take members of a women's guild on an outing. The organiser of the outing advertised to the general public that there were spare tickets available. The company did not have a public service licence and performed the contract unaware that the trip had been advertised to the public. The Divisional Court held that the offence was not one of strict liability. Devlin J stated (at pp. 149, 150):

> if a man is punished because of an act done by another, whom he cannot reasonably be expected to influence or control, the law is engaged, not in punishing thoughtlessness or inefficiency, and thereby promoting the welfare of the community, but in pouncing on the most convenient victim....where the punishment of an individual will not promote the observance of the law either by that individual or by others whose conduct he may reasonably be expected to influence then, in the absence of clear and express words, such punishment is not intended.

In *Lim Chin Aik* v *The Queen* [1963] AC 160, the Privy Council quashed the appellant's conviction, under s. 6(2) of the Immigration Ordinance 1952 of the State of Singapore, of remaining in Singapore (after having entered) when he had been prohibited from entering by an order made by the Minister under s. 9. The Privy Council stated that it was not enough to label the statute as one dealing with a grave social evil and infer that strict liability is intended. It was important also to enquire whether strict liability would assist in the enforcement of the regulations. 'There must be something he can do, directly or indirectly, by supervision or inspection, by improvement of his business methods or by exhorting those whom he may be expected to influence or control, which will promote the observance of the regulations'. In the instant case the imposition of strict liability would simply serve to convict a 'luckless victim' as the prohibition had not been published or made known to the appellant. Thus strict liability will not be imposed where the accused either has no means of knowing the law or of taking action to ensure observance of the law (cf. *R* (*Grundy & Co Excavators Ltd and Parry*) v *Halton Division Magistrates' Court* [2003] EWHC 272 (Admin)).

4.2.4 Justifications for strict liability

The two justifications generally given for the creation of strict liability offences are that they encourage greater safety and improved standards of prevention, thereby offering the public better protection from the risks inherent in particular activities, and that they relieve the prosecution of the difficult task of proving *mens rea*, thereby increasing both administrative efficiency and the deterrent effect of conviction. Is strict liability necessary for the protection of the public and the enforcement of particular laws? A facile answer would be, 'Yes, it must be because Parliament has enacted so many offences which impose strict liability'. The fact that Parliament has created so many strict liability offences, however, does not establish the necessity of their existence. Strict liability offences are only necessary if there is no other means of achieving the ends of protecting the public and enforcing the law.

A distinguished social scientist, Baroness Wootton, argued ardently in favour of the extension of strict liability to cover all crimes. In *Crime and the Criminal Law* (2nd edn, 1981) she stated (at p. 46):

> If, however, the primary function of the courts is conceived as the prevention of forbidden acts, there is little cause to be disturbed by the multiplication of offences of strict liability. If the law says that certain things are not to be done, it is illogical to confine this prohibition to occasions on which they are done from malice aforethought; for at least the material consequences of an action, and the reasons for prohibiting it are the same whether it is the result of sinister malicious plotting, of negligence or of sheer accident.

This begs the very important question of what is a forbidden act? It could be argued that in murder the forbidden act is causing the death of another person. A surgeon who performs an operation on a patient could be found to have committed the forbidden act if his patient dies under anaesthetic even though the chances of success of the operation were low but the risk was taken as, without the operation, the patient would have died in a few weeks or months. To find such a surgeon guilty of murder would be ludicrous and would involve divorcing the law from the social and moral context in which it operates, not to mention deterring all other surgeons from performing operations involving any risk of death. Such an approach, far from protecting the public, would end up leaving them more at risk. What the law seeks to prevent is forbidden acts in the circumstances where the perpetrator of the act is morally culpable. Baroness Wootton would seek to distinguish the culpable from the blameless by leaving it to the judge to mete out an appropriate sentence. Such an approach, however, does not overcome the stigma attached to criminal conviction. Nor does it make for efficiency as the courts would be cluttered with prosecutions of blameless individuals who would ultimately be dealt with by means of an absolute discharge. It is not possible to protect people from all harm; the law's role, however, is to seek to protect them from the intentional or reckless infliction of harm and, in some circumstances, from the negligent infliction of harm. If harm could not have been prevented by the exercise of reasonable care, the prosecution of the blamelessly inadvertent will not prevent the occurrence of such harm in the future.

In the area of regulatory offences the social context is important. We need people to engage in industrial processes, to make and sell food, to dispense drugs, to drive motor vehicles. There may be risks involved in all these activities meriting the exercise of care on the part of those engaging in them. The law should encourage such care but not be so harsh as to discourage people from embarking upon these enterprises in the first place. Thus the blamelessly inadvertent pharmacist should not be punished for dispensing drugs on a forged prescription if he was exercising that degree of care to be expected of pharmacists consistent with considerations of economics and practicability. Similarly, the butcher selling meat should take reasonable precautions to avoid selling meat which is unfit. Punishing him where, despite such precautions, he has sold unfit meat serves no purpose unless it is to discourage the sale of meat altogether (see *Callow v Tillstone*, **4.2.1** *ante*). Alternatively, if the butcher is forced to employ an analyst to test every carcass this would raise his costs to the extent that meat would become too expensive for many people to afford, which in turn would have detrimental effects on the ordinary consumer, the farmer and all those involved in processing and selling meat. It is also highly questionable whether strict liability leads to a higher standard of care. In *R v City of Saulte Ste Marie* (1978) 85 DLR (3d) 161, before the Supreme Court of Canada, Dickson J stated (at p. 171):

> There is no evidence that a higher standard of care results from absolute liability. If a person is already taking every reasonable precautionary measure, is he likely to take additional measures, knowing that however much care he takes, it will not serve as a defence in the event of breach? If he has exercised care and skill, will conviction have a deterrent effect upon him or others?

By contrast, in *Alphacell*, Lord Salmon took the view that strict liability would encourage those who might be potential polluters 'not only to take reasonable steps to prevent pollution but to do everything possible to ensure that they do not cause it'. This may reflect a degree of commercial naivety on the part of Lord Salmon. If expenditure of thousands of pounds for preventive measures will not ultimately prevent the risk of pollution, the factory owner may prefer to save his money, keep his unit costs down, retain his competitiveness, increase his profits, and run the risk of being caught and fined several hundred pounds should his operations cause pollution at a time when an inspector is around.

? Question

Does strict liability make for efficient law enforcement and effective prevention/deterrence?

Clearly the task of the prosecution is facilitated as, in strict liability offences, it is only necessary to prove that the *actus reus* was committed and there is no need to prove the more difficult issue of *mens rea*. Indeed, if the prosecution seek to lead evidence that the defendant had *mens rea* or was negligent, this evidence must be excluded as it is irrelevant to the issues which they must prove to establish guilt of the offence charged (see *Sandhu* [1997] Crim LR 288). In the many regulatory offences that exist this makes for easier enforcement as it is only necessary for a pollution inspector to prove that the accused's factory is discharging effluent into the river, or a health inspector need only prove that meat sold was unfit. No enquiry need be made to discover if the accused knew that he was causing pollution or selling unfit meat. This, however, ignores a problem. How is a sentencer to sentence someone convicted of a strict liability offence if he does not know whether he committed the offence intentionally, recklessly, negligently, or inadvertently despite the most stringent precautions? The person who intentionally causes pollution deserves a very much heavier sentence than the one who has exercised reasonable care. As the prosecution only have to establish that pollution was caused by the accused, the facts which would disclose the level of the accused's culpability would not be proved in the trial. This may necessitate a further post-conviction hearing to determine the factual basis of the offence (see *Newton* (1982) 4 Cr App R (S) 388). This would seem to cancel out any efficiency benefits deriving from dispensing with the proof of *mens rea* for the purposes of conviction. It also may be difficult to establish the factual basis of the offence as the investigating official may not have inquired into, or obtained evidence relating to, the culpability of the accused as this was not necessary for the purposes of obtaining a conviction. If he does make such inquiries and acquire evidence he is performing the same task as an officer investigating a crime requiring proof of *mens rea* and this will defeat any claim of administrative efficiency. In addition, if there is any doubt as to the factual basis of the offence, this must be resolved in favour of the accused as the normal burden of proof applies (see *Newton* and *Gortat and Pirog* [1973] Crim LR 648). If efficiency is to be obtained and no evidence of culpability sought, all offenders will appear the same and thus will be treated as if they had been blamelessly inadvertent; i.e. culpability is reduced to the level of the lowest common denominator. If this occurs, sentences will not serve to deter the culpable. In addition, if a result arises from blameless inadvertence and could not, by the exercise of reasonable care, have been avoided, the imposition of a penalty will not prevent future infractions unless the offender desists entirely from the activity involved. If penalties which truly reflect the offender's culpability can only be determined by thorough investigation and proof to the same standard required for conviction, there would seem to be little reason for having strict liability offences.

If regulatory offences are seeking to encourage the exercise of reasonable care, strict liability would not appear to be necessary. If a person has exercised reasonable care and the forbidden harm still occurs, punishing him will not make the incidence of that harm any less likely in the future. The punishment appears unjust and serves no purpose. If punishment is not inflicted, as where an absolute discharge is given because the accused is blameless, the whole process of prosecution and trial appears pointless and militates against efficiency in respect of other cases relating to blameworthy offenders. The conclusion thus seems to be that strict liability achieves nothing which could not be achieved by means of a requirement of negligence. It may be that considerations of administrative efficiency might dictate that on proof of the *actus reus* a presumption of negligence is raised, subject to rebuttal by proof on the balance of probabilities by the accused that he was not negligent. This is not unacceptable as if the accused has been exercising reasonable care in respect of a particular activity in which he is engaged he should be able to prove this by evidence of the production system, supervision, checks, safety precautions, etc. involved.

4.2.5 Defences to strict liability

The High Court of Australia in *Proudman* v *Dayman* (1943) 67 CLR 536, and the Supreme Court of Canada in *R* v *City of Saulte Ste Marie* developed a general due diligence (or 'no-negligence') defence to offences of strict liability which places the burden of proof on the accused. In the latter case Dickson J stated (at p. 181):

> The correct approach...is to relieve the Crown of the burden of proving *mens rea*, having regard to...the virtual impossibility in most regulatory cases of proving wrongful intention. In a normal case, the accused alone will have knowledge of what he has done to avoid the breach and it is not improper to expect him to come forward with the evidence of due diligence...This involves consideration of what a reasonable man would have done in the circumstances. The defence will be available if the accused reasonably believed in a mistaken set of facts which, if true, would render the act or omission innocent, or if he took all reasonable steps to avoid the particular event.

While the recognition of strict liability offences in England and Wales was a judicial decision, no court has been prepared to import a common law 'due diligence' defence. Parliament, however, has sought to mitigate the worst effects of strict liability by including defences in some statutes. Due diligence defences have been provided in, for example, s. 67 of the Offices, Shops and Railway Premises Act 1963; s. 24(1) of the Trade Descriptions Act 1968; s. 34 of the Weights and Measures Act 1985; and s. 28 of the Misuse of Drugs Act 1971. In some statutes the due diligence defence has been combined with a 'third party' defence requiring the accused to prove both that he exercised due diligence and that the offence was due to the act or default of a third party (see e.g. Food Safety Act 1990, s. 21(2)). If successful such a defence leaves the third party liable to conviction on the basis of strict liability. If, for example, a shopkeeper was charged with an offence under s. 8 of the Food Safety Act based on his sale of a bottle of ginger ale to a customer which, when opened, was found to contain the decomposed remains of a snail, the shopkeeper might avoid conviction if he proved that he had exercised all due diligence and that the contravention was due to the act or default of the manufacturer. If the bottle was made of dark glass there would be nothing that the shopkeeper could do to check the contents other than open it and pour them out; this would not be reasonable. But if the bottle was made of clear glass, and the snail was visible, the shopkeeper would fail in his defence as, although not responsible for the contamination, he could have discovered it by a cursory inspection. If the third party responsible for the contravention is not identifiable, the third party defence is not available.

4.2.6 Strict liability and the ECHR

Article 6(2) of the European Convention on Human Rights provides that 'everyone charged with a criminal offence shall be presumed innocent until proved guilty according to law'. It has been argued that strict liability offences contravene this presumption as on proof of the act or conduct guilt is presumed. In *Salabiaku v France* (1998) EHRR 379, the European Court of Human Rights held that there was no contravention as:

> In principle the contracting States may, under certain conditions, penalise a simple or objective fact as such irrespective of whether it results from criminal intent or from negligence.

In essence the Art. 6(2) right is concerned with ensuring a fair trial in procedural terms and is not concerned with the fairness of the substantive law. This was affirmed by the Divisional Court in *Barnfather* v *Islington London Borough Council* [2003] EWHC 418 (Admin). However, in *Salabiaku* the European Court stated, somewhat obscurely, that 'presumptions of fact or law' in criminal proceedings should be confined within 'reasonable limits'. Reliance was sought to be placed on this proposition in *G* [2008] UKHL 37 where the appellant had been convicted of rape contrary to s. 5 of the Sexual Offences Act 2003 which is a strict liability offence where the complainant is under 13. The appellant (who was aged 15) pleaded guilty on the basis that he believed she was 15 and the intercourse was consensual (albeit that a child under 13 cannot consent to penetrative sex). The House of Lords unanimously held that strict liability did not violate Art. 6(1) or (2). The Art. 6(1) guarantee of a fair trial and the Art. 6(2) presumption of innocence had no bearing on the substantive law enacted by signatory states. Lord Hope of Craighead sought to explain *Salabiaku* on the basis that the contracting states are free to apply the criminal law to any act, so long as it is not one which is carried out in the exercise of one of the rights protected under the Convention. Thus, even if legislation creating a criminal offence might breach other Convention rights, it will not render the trial under which it is enforced unfair.

On the second question before the House, whether it is 'compatible with a child's rights under article 8…to convict him of rape…in circumstances where…his offence fell properly within the ambit of s.13?' Lord Hope and Lord Carswell dissented. They were of opinion that a conviction for rape was disproportionate and incompatible with Art. 8 as the act fell within the less serious offence of sexual activity with a child under ss. 9 and 13 of the Sexual Offences Act 2003 which was more than adequate to protect the rights of the girl. The majority disagreed taking the view that Art. 8 was not engaged and upheld the conviction. They further stated that even if Art. 8 was engaged, the prosecution was 'both rational and proportionate in pursuit of the legitimate aims of the protection of health and morals and of the rights and freedoms of others' (Baroness Hale at para. 55).

In *G v UK* [2011] ECHR 1308, the European Court of Human Rights, considering G's conviction for rape of a child under 13, did not consider that the absence of a defence based on reasonable belief that the complainant was aged 13 or over gave rise to any issue under Art. 6 as it was not the court's role to dictate the content of domestic criminal law. By a majority the Court also held that while the applicant's Art. 8(1) right to respect for private life was engaged, the margin of appreciation allowed to Member States while narrow where matters of intimacy were involved, nonetheless did provide for conviction of this offence as there was under Art. 8(2) a powerful countervailing public interest in the legitimate aim of protecting young and vulnerable children from premature sexual activity, exploitation, and abuse. The Court did not, however, consider whether prosecuting for this offence rather than the lesser alternative offence under ss. 9 and 13 of the Sexual Offences Act 2003 was 'necessary in a democratic society'. G was, after all, himself under 16 and the maximum sentence under s. 5 is life imprisonment (as compared to five years for the alternative); furthermore there was no evidence to suggest that the complainant was specifically exploited and abused.

FURTHER READING

B. Jackson, '*Storkwain*: A Case Study in Strict Liability and Self-regulation' [1991] Crim LR 892.

L. H. Leigh, *Strict and Vicarious Liability* (1982, Sweet & Maxwell).

C. Manchester, 'Knowledge, Due Diligence and Strict Liability in Regulatory Offences' [2006] Crim LR 213.

I. Paulus, 'Strict Liability: Its Place in Public Welfare Offences' (1978) 20 Crim LQ 445.

G. Richardson, 'Strict Liability for Regulatory Crime: The Empirical Research' [1987] Crim LR 295.

F. B. Sayre, 'Public Welfare Offences' (1933) 33 Col LR 55.

J. C. Smith, 'Responsibility in Criminal Law', in *Barbara Wootton, Essays in Her Honour* (1986, eds. Bean and Whynes) 141.

M. Smiths and A. Pearson, 'The Value of Strict Liability' [1969] Crim LR 5.

5

Capacity and incapacitating conditions

5.1 Introduction

A person should only be held criminally liable where he has the capacity to understand his actions, in the sense of being able to understand the nature of those actions and the circumstances in which they occur, and to recognise the consequences which may flow from them, and, having understood them, where he has the capacity to control them. Moral culpability should not attach to the person who at the time he acted (or omitted to act) was unable to understand what he was doing and/or unable to control what he was doing, as such a person is not a responsible actor and therefore is not deserving of blame or punishment. The criminal law has recognised this requirement of rational capacity by excepting persons who lack rational capacity from liability in certain circumstances. According to N. L. A. Barlow, 'Drug intoxication and the principle of *Capacitas Rationalis*' (1984) 100 LQR 639 (at p. 647), the principle or presumption of rational capacity operates as 'a precondition to punishment; as a standard, a criterion, for determining eligibility for and immunity from punishment'. In this chapter the issues of infancy, insanity, automatism, and intoxication will be examined. These conditions are often said to give rise to defences. They will be examined in this chapter, however, rather than **Chapter 6**, as they specifically relate to the issue of whether the accused had rational capacity at the time of his act. In the case of defences such as duress or self-defence, there is no question of the accused's rational capacity being in doubt; implicit in these defences is the idea that the accused did exercise rational judgement and chose to act as he did but his claim is that his acts were either justified or excusable because of the circumstances in which he found himself.

5.2 Age and criminal responsibility

For the purposes of criminal procedure, sentencing and criminal liability there are various terms applied to different age groups. A *child* is a person aged 10 years or more but under 14 years of age. A *young person* is aged 14 years or more but under 17 years of age. A *young offender* is aged 14 years or more but under 21 years. The procedures before the courts and the sentences available on conviction will vary according to the age of the offender. But before issues of sentencing arise the issue of criminal liability has to be considered. It is an irrebuttable presumption of the criminal law that a child under 10 years of age at the time an alleged offence was committed cannot be found guilty of that offence (see s. 50 of the Children and Young Persons Act 1933, as amended). A child under 10 is said to be *doli incapax*, that is, incapable of crime. This presumption derives from a recognition of the immaturity of children who will not have a fully developed understanding of what is right and wrong nor the ability to appreciate the consequences of their acts fully. If a child is charged with an offence and it is established that he was under 10 years of age at the time the alleged offence was committed, the case against him will be dismissed without any inquiry whether he understood what he was doing. This may mean that precocious children under 10 who are given to breaking the law escape liability because the presumption is irrebutable. The solution in the past to this problem was for a local authority or other authorised person to commence proceedings in the family proceedings court in respect of the child under s. 31 of the Children Act 1989 for an order placing the child in the care of a local authority or putting him under the supervision of a local authority. In proceedings under the 1989 Act the child's welfare is the paramount consideration of the court (s. 1(1) of the Children Act 1989) and under s. 31(2) an order may only be made if the court is satisfied:

(a) that the child concerned is suffering, or is likely to suffer, significant harm; and
(b) that harm, or the likelihood of harm, is attributable to—
    (i) the care given to the child, or likely to be given to him if the order were not made, not being what it would be reasonable to expect a parent to give to him; or
    (ii) the child's being beyond parental control.

These requirements are very stringent and will not be satisfied merely upon proof that the child has committed what would be a criminal offence but for the principle of *doli incapax*.

The Crime and Disorder Act 1998 provides further powers to deal with children under 10 who have committed acts which, in the case of those over 10, could have constituted criminal offences, or who are undisciplined or have engaged in anti-social behaviour. These powers stem from a belief on the part of the Government that timely intervention is necessary to prevent children developing patterns of criminal and anti-social behaviour. Under s. 11 a local authority may apply to a magistrates' family proceedings court for a child safety order to be made. If such an order is made the child is placed under the supervision of a responsible officer, *viz.* a social worker or a member of the youth offending team, for a period of up to three months and subjected to certain restrictions or conditions (in exceptional circumstances the period may be increased to a maximum of 12 months). Such an order may be made if one or more of the following conditions under s. 11(3) is satisfied:

(a) the child has committed an act which, if he had been aged 10 or over, would have constituted an offence;
(b) a child safety order is necessary for the purpose of preventing the commission by the child of an act which would have constituted an offence if committed by a child aged 10 or over;
(c) the child has contravened a ban imposed by a curfew notice under s. 14...;
(d) the child has acted in a manner that caused or was likely to cause harassment, alarm or distress to one or more persons not of the same household as himself.

Unlike the requirements of s. 31 of the 1989 Act these conditions are extremely wide. Leng, Taylor and Wasik, *Blackstone's Guide to the Crime and Disorder Act 1998*, comment (at p. 30):

Thus, taking sweets from a friend or even a risk that a child might do so would qualify under (a) and (b), a curfew contravention might involve 10 minutes innocent play after 9 pm by a child who did not understand the curfew and who was not wearing a watch, and condition (d) might be satisfied by raucous play to the annoyance of an elderly neighbour.

A consequence of the *doli incapax* principle is that not only is the child not guilty of the crime, but the child has not committed a crime. But, if the offence was instigated by another person, that person, rather than being a secondary party, becomes the principal acting through an innocent agent; he commits the crime. Where the offence is one such as rape, which cannot be committed through an innocent agent, the secondary party may be convicted where he or she has procured the *actus reus* with the requisite *mens rea* (see further *DPP* v *K and B* [1997] 1 Cr App R 36, *7.1.3.3 post*). The absence of a crime may also negate the criminal liability of others. For example, in *Walters* v *Lunt* [1951] 2 All ER 645, a mother and father were acquitted of the charge of receiving from their son a child's tricycle knowing it to be stolen. As the son was seven years of age he could not steal and thus the tricycle was not stolen. Had the parents instigated the taking of the tricycle by their son they would have stolen it through an innocent agent.

Where a child was 10 years of age or over and under the age of 14 at the time of the alleged offence, there used to be a rebuttable presumption at common law that the child was *doli incapax*. The presumption could be rebutted by proof that the child had 'mischievous discretion', that is he knew the act he was doing was seriously wrong; this was something additional to the *mens rea* for the offence. If evidence was brought which proved that the child had reached a stage of development whereby he understood the wrongfulness of his act, he would be convicted. The older the child and the more obviously wrong the act, the easier it would be to rebut the presumption. If the presumption was not rebutted it would still be open to the local authority to commence proceedings under s. 31 of the Children Act 1989 (*ante*). Over the years there were calls for the abolition of this presumption but when the last Conservative Government considered this issue in 1990 it rejected these calls stating in *Crime, Justice and Protecting the Public* (Cm 965) at para. 8.4:

The Government does not intend to change these arrangements which make proper allowance for the fact that children's understanding, knowledge and ability to reason are still developing.

In *C (A Minor)* v *DPP* [1995] 3 WLR 888 the Divisional Court expressed the view that the presumption did a serious disservice to the law and ruled that it was no longer part of the law of England. C appealed to the House of Lords. The point of law certified for their Lordships' consideration was:

Whether there continues to be a presumption that a child between the ages of 10 and 14 is *doli incapax* and if so, whether that presumption can only be rebutted by clear positive evidence that he knew that his act was seriously wrong, such evidence not consisting merely in the evidence of the acts amounting to the offence itself.

Their Lordships allowed the appeal answering both questions in the affirmative, considering that any change in the law was a matter within the exclusive remit of Parliament. Parliament received its chance to consider the presumption following the election of the Labour Government in May 1997. In a Home Office consultation paper, *Tackling Youth Crime*, September 1997, the Government argued that the presumption was archaic, illogical, and unfair and stood in the way of intervening at an early stage to seek to rehabilitate young offenders and prevent future offending (see Walsh, 'Irrational Presumptions of Rationality and Comprehension' [1998] 3 Web JCLI for a trenchant critique of these arguments). This begs the question as to whether criminal prosecution, conviction, and sentencing of young offenders can be rehabilitative. The consultation paper was followed by a White Paper ominously titled, *No More Excuses—a new approach to tackling youth crime in England and Wales* (Cm 3809) where the Government indicated its intention to abolish the presumption rejecting an alternative solution which was to reverse the presumption, i.e. a child between 10 and 14 would be presumed to have capacity subject to proof to the contrary being tendered by the defence. This solution would have provided the opportunity for children whose moral awareness had not fully developed to be able to establish this and thereby avoid being held criminally responsible for their acts. The Government, however, favoured speed of intervention and efficiency over such demands for fairness. The outcome was the abolition of the rebuttable presumption of *doli incapax* in respect of children aged over 10 by s. 34 of the Crime and Disorder Act 1998. To all intents and purposes all children over the age of 10 are assumed to have reached the same level of moral culpability as adults. If anything deserved to be labelled 'archaic, illogical, and unfair' it would be this provision rather than the presumption it abolished. There is something seriously troubling about a society which does not seek to protect its children from exposure to the full rigour of the criminal law and criminal justice system.

There was some doubt whether s. 34 merely abolished the presumption of *doli incapax* but left the possibility of a child defendant raising a defence to the effect that he did not know that what he was doing was seriously wrong. In *CPS v P* [2007] EWHC 946 (Admin) one member of the Administrative Court, Smith LJ, expressed *obiter* the opinion that a separate defence of *doli incapax* might continue to exist as all that s. 34 abolished was the universal presumption. In *T* [2008] EWCA Crim 815 the Court of Appeal decided that no defence of *doli incapax* survived the enactment of s. 34. The Court took the view that by the time s. 34 was enacted, whatever the position may have been historically, the presumption was coterminous with the concept (defence) of *doli incapax* such that when Parliament abolished the presumption it also abolished the defence. When this decision was appealed further to the House of Lords in *JTB* [2009] UKHL 20, it was confirmed. The upshot of this is that where a child between the age of 10 and 14 is prosecuted no issue as to his comprehension of the wrongness of his act may arise. However, this does not prevent such a child seeking to rely on his age as a factor relevant to *mens rea*; for example, whether he foresaw the consequences of his acts even though those consequences might have been obvious to an adult, or to defences, for example, the reasonableness of his acts under the defence of duress.

Boys under the age of 14 used to be irrebuttably presumed to be incapable of sexual intercourse and thus could not be convicted as perpetrators of rape (*Groombridge* (1836) 7 C & P 582), offences involving sexual intercourse (*Waite* [1892] 2 QB 600), or buggery whether as agent or as patient (*Tatam* (1921) 15 Cr App R 132). This presumption was abolished by the Sexual Offences Act 1993, s. 1.

5.3 Insanity

5.3.1 Introduction

The defence of insanity is concerned with the accused's mental state at the time when the alleged offence was committed. The accused's mental state may be relevant at two other times. First, in a criminal trial it is relevant at the time he is arraigned and called to plead to the charge against him. Under ss. 4 and 4A of the Criminal Procedure (Insanity) Act 1964 (as substituted by s. 2 of the Criminal Procedure (Insanity and Unfitness to Plead) Act 1991) an accused may be found 'unfit to plead' where it is established that because of his mental condition he is unable to understand the charge and the difference between a plea of guilty and a plea of not guilty, to challenge jurors, to instruct counsel, and to follow the proceedings.

The issue of the accused's fitness to plead (which prior to s. 22 of the Domestic Violence, Crime and Victims Act 2004 coming into force was tried by a jury specially empanelled) is determined by the judge as soon as it arises (s. 4(3) of the Criminal Procedure (Insanity) Act 1964). If the judge considers it expedient to do so, having regard to the supposed disability, and where it is in the accused's interests, he may postpone consideration of the issue up to the time of the opening of the case for the defence (s. 4(2)). This is appropriate where the prosecution case appears weak as they may not be able to establish a prima facie case to answer; the judge will then direct the jury to acquit.

An accused may not be found unfit to plead except on the written or oral evidence of two or more registered medical practitioners, at least one of whom is approved for the purposes of s. 12 of the Mental Health Act 1983 by the Secretary of State as having special experience in the diagnosis or treatment of mental disorder. If the accused is found unfit to plead the trial must not proceed or further proceed. A jury will then determine on the basis of evidence (if any) already adduced or on evidence adduced by the prosecution and/or a person appointed by the court under s. 4A of the 1964 Act to put the case for the defence (i.e. defence counsel), whether the accused did the act or made the omission constituting the *actus reus* of the offence charged against him (s. 4(2)). If the issue of unfitness to plead arose on the arraignment and the judge ruled that the accused was unfit to plead, a jury will be empanelled to determine whether the accused did the act or made the omission. If the issue of unfitness arose later in the course of the trial (or was postponed by the trial judge), the jury by whom the accused was being tried will determine this issue (s. 4A(5)). If not satisfied that the accused did the act or made the omission, the jury should acquit of the count in question (s. 4A(4)). If the jury are satisfied the accused did the act or made the omission, the judge decides on the correct disposal. He may make an order for admission to a hospital approved by the Secretary of State (with or without an order restricting the accused's discharge), a supervision and treatment order, or an absolute discharge (s. 5(2) of the 1964 Act; s. 24 of the Domestic Violence, Crime and Victims Act 2004 substituted a new s. 5 into the 1964 Act).

If the sentence for the offence is fixed by law (i.e. murder), and the accused has a mental disorder requiring specialist treatment under the Mental Health Act 1983, the court must order detention in hospital with restriction on discharge without limit of time (s. 5(3)). The Home Office Circular (24/2005) explains the effect of the new s. 5 thus (at para. 12):

> ...the court is only obliged to make a hospital order with a restriction order on a charge of murder if the conditions for making a hospital order are met. If the conditions are not met, for example if the reason for the finding of unfitness to plead relate to a physical disorder, the court's options are limited to a supervision order or absolute discharge.

The second time in a criminal trial when the mental condition of the accused will be relevant is when he has been convicted. His mental condition will be relevant to the question of the appropriate sentence to be imposed (see further M. Wasik, *Emmins on Sentencing* (4th edn, 2001)).

If an accused is found to have been insane at the time the *actus reus* was committed the verdict the jury return is 'not guilty by reason of insanity' (see s. 2(1) of the Trial of Lunatics Act 1883). This is generally referred to as the 'special verdict'. Prior to 1991 on such a verdict being returned the judge had to order the accused to be detained in a hospital to be selected by the Home Secretary (s. 5(1) of and sch. 1 to the Criminal Procedure (Insanity) Act 1964). The fact that the consequence of a special verdict was automatic committal to a mental hospital was one of the deterrents against pleading insanity or, in some cases, from running a line of defence which might have been interpreted by the court as an insanity defence (see *Sullivan* and *Hennessy*, **5.3.3.2.1** *post*). The prospect of indefinite detention in a mental hospital led some defendants to plead guilty and cast themselves upon the mercy of the judge when sentencing them, rather than rely on a defence which was technically available to them. The Criminal Procedure (Insanity and Unfitness to Plead) Act 1991 gives much greater discretion in disposing of an accused on a special verdict being returned. The court has the same powers of disposal as are available where an accused is found unfit to plead (see *ante*). This may result in the defence being pleaded more frequently.

While much ink is expended in textbooks and academic journals seeking to explain, analyse, and rationalise the defence of insanity, it is, in practice, a rarely used defence. Part of the reason for its infrequent use is that many of those accused of murder, who in the past might have raised the defence of insanity, now raise the defence of diminished responsibility under s. 2 of the Homicide Act 1957 (see **5.5** *post*). A study of the operation of the defence by R. D. Mackay, 'Fact and fiction about the insanity defence' [1990] Crim LR 247, reveals that in the 14 years from 1975 to 1988 there were only 49 verdicts of 'not guilty by reason of insanity'. Of these verdicts 14 were returned in murder cases, 23 in cases of non-fatal assaults, and the remainder were returned in a variety of cases involving arson, robbery, burglary, deception, and reckless driving.

In a further study covering the five years immediately following the coming into force of the Criminal Procedure (Insanity and Unfitness to Plead) Act 1991 there were 44 findings of 'not guilty by reason of insanity' (see Mackay and Kearns, 'More Fact(s) about the Insanity Defence' [1999] Crim LR 714, 716). The authors speculate that the reason for this increase is that 'the new legislation has started to become more widely known by lawyers and psychiatrists as it has permeated the body of medico-legal knowledge. This in turn may have led to an appreciation that the 1991 Act has removed the more glaring disincentives inherent within the 1964 Act of running a defence of [not guilty by reason of insanity]'. The vast majority of offences in respect of which the special verdict was returned were offences of violence. In 17 cases the disposal was as it would have been prior to the passage of the 1991 Act; a restriction order without limit of time. However, in 23 cases a community-based disposal was utilised. The authors speculate that this fact will, itself, stimulate greater use of the insanity defence. The fact remains, however, that the 1991 Act has not removed the stigmatising label of 'insane' which may still deter some defendants from raising the insanity defence. In addition, the Act did not address the problem of the legal definition of insanity which remains grossly outdated and fails to recognise developments in medical knowledge.

A further study by the same authors for the years 1997–2001 ('Yet More Facts about the Insanity Defence' [2006] Crim LR 399) records a continued but gradual increase in the use of the insanity defence with offences against the person being the most represented and only a small number of cases of murder. The most frequent diagnosis is that of schizophrenia. The majority of those found not guilty by reason of insanity receive supervision orders.

In July 2012 the Law Commission issued two papers concerned with insanity and automatism. In the first, *Insanity and Automatism: a Scoping Paper*, the Law Commission identified some possible problems with these defences and called for information from legal and medical practitioners on how they were operating in practice. They also published some statistics covering 2002–2011 indicating that insanity is successfully pleaded in over 20 cases per year. In the second paper, *Insanity and Automatism: Supplementary Material to the Scoping Paper*, they reviewed the law and examined its compatibility with the European Convention on Human Rights. Once information is acquired, the Commission will commence a review of the defences.

5.3.2 The rationale for a defence of insanity

 Key Point

There are five different ways in which a person's mental condition may affect his responsibility for his conduct. First, he may perform a prohibited act in a state of impaired consciousness due to some mental condition or internal cause. In such a condition his act is involuntary and he is referred to as an automaton. Secondly, he may be conscious and perform willed bodily movements which constitute the *actus reus* of an offence but due to his mental condition he may not know or understand what he is doing. Thirdly, he may be conscious and able to comprehend what he is doing but due to his mental condition be unaware that it is wrong. Fourthly, he may know what he is doing and that it is wrong but due to his mental condition he may not be able to control what he is doing. Fifthly, he may know what he is doing and that it is wrong but due to a delusional state he may believe that his act is appropriate. In each of these cases it could be said that the accused is not a responsible actor at the time of his act as he is not totally in touch with reality. The capacity for rational judgement has

➡

> →
>
> been impaired. As such he may not be an appropriate subject for punishment although, if he continues to be a danger to the community, it may be appropriate for the community to be protected from him.

These five states of impairment vary in their impact on the definitional elements of the offence. In the first state there is no *actus reus* as the act was not voluntary and, necessarily, if it was not voluntary there was no *mens rea* either. In the second state there is an *actus reus* but no *mens rea*. In the third, fourth, and fifth states there is an *actus reus* and *mens rea* but serious doubts arise with regard to the rational capacity, and thus responsibility, of the actor.

While it was stated earlier that the criminal law had recognised the principle of rational capacity by exempting persons from criminal liability who lack it, the recognition of this principle has been almost accidental rather than designed. This becomes evident from a study of the operation of the defence of insanity. The effect of this defence is that in certain circumstances individuals who lacked rational capacity at the time of the commission of the alleged offence are excused from criminal liability; the defence covers the first three conditions outlined earlier. The defence has developed, however, in the absence of a clearly articulated theoretical foundation and in isolation from modern medical opinion. As a result the defence is deficient in some cases as it does not cover a particular type of individual who clearly lacks rational capacity, namely those who fall within the fourth and fifth situations outlined earlier. In other circumstances, the defence of insanity itself works injustice as it brings within its ambit individuals who, in any other context, would not be considered insane, for example, the epileptic (*Sullivan*) or the diabetic (*Hennessy*) or the sleepwalker (*Burgess* [1991] 2 QB 92), who technically fall within the first situation outlined earlier. This problem highlights the difficulty in delineating the dividing line between automatism and insanity, or, as it is often termed non-insane automatism and insane automatism. Not all individuals who are reduced to an automatous condition are insane; some are insane, some are clearly sane and others fall in between because their condition technically fits the criminal law's definition of insanity but does not correspond to any medical definition of insanity. Indeed, psychiatrists do not talk of insanity but prefer to use terms such as mental illness or mental disorder.

While the Criminal Procedure (Insanity and Unfitness to Plead) Act 1991 has addressed the problem of the injustice of the automatic disposal to a mental hospital, it has not addressed the problem of the definition of insanity and the tendency of the defence to cover inappropriate conditions while failing to cover other conditions where rational capacity is absent. There are other problems with the defence in respect of the way in which it conflicts with other general principles of criminal liability which will be dealt with later.

5.3.3 **The law**

The law relating to the defence of insanity is to be found in the rules set out in *M'Naghten* (1843) 10 Cl & F 200, which delineate the circumstances in which an accused will be held not to have been legally responsible for his conduct. These rules are not concerned with medical definitions of insanity, and, indeed, these may bear little resemblance to the criminal definition. The origin of the M'Naghten Rules is interesting. Daniel M'Naghten was found to be insane and acquitted on a charge of murdering Sir Robert Peel's private secretary, it being his intention to kill Peel. He was committed to hospital but there was a public outcry at the perceived leniency of the verdict. The matter was debated in the House of Lords, where it was decided to seek the opinion of the judges on the legal principles relating to insanity. The joint answer given by 14 judges is not technically binding as a precedent as it is only an opinion rather than a judgment upon a case before a court. The rules, however, have been treated as authoritative ever since.

The principles stated by the judges are as follows:

(1) Everyone is presumed sane and to possess a sufficient degree of reason to be responsible for their crimes until the contrary is proved.
(2) To establish a defence of insanity it must be clearly proved that at the time of committing the act, the accused was labouring under such a defect of reason, from disease of the mind, as (a) not to know the nature and quality of the act he was doing; or (b) if he did know it, not to know he was doing what was wrong.

5.3.3.1 Procedural matters

Question

Who bears the burden of proving insanity?

The first principle stated earlier refers to the presumption of sanity. **If the accused is to raise the defence of insanity the burden of proving it is upon him**. Generally it is for the prosecution to prove the guilt of the accused beyond reasonable doubt and to disprove any defence he may raise. In the case of insanity it is not sufficient for the accused to raise the defence; he bears a burden of proving it. He is not required to prove it beyond reasonable doubt but need only do so on a balance of probabilities.

This raises a problem: if the accused is claiming that he did not know what he was doing, relying on ground 2(a) (see **5.3.3**), he is being asked to prove on the balance of probabilities something the contrary of which the prosecution have not proved. If the prosecution prove beyond reasonable doubt that he knew what he was doing, and thus had *mens rea* that would be an end to the matter. But if they fail to prove this it seems superfluous, and indeed illogical, to require the accused to prove the contrary on a balance of probabilities. The courts, however, have not recognised this problem although Glanville Williams has in *Criminal Law: The General Part* (2nd edn, 1961, para. 165), where he argues that on ground 2(a) it should only be necessary for the accused to introduce evidence of insanity which raises a reasonable doubt whether he had the necessary *mens rea*. Further support for this argument is gained by the fact that if the accused's defence is one of automatism due to some cause other than a disease of the mind, the burden of proof remains on the prosecution and the accused need only raise a doubt to succeed. In *Attorney-General's Reference (No. 3 of 1998)* [1999] 3 WLR 1994, the Court of Appeal confirmed that where the issue of insanity is raised during a trial, the prosecution are relieved of the duty of proving *mens rea* as s. 2(1) of the Trial of Lunatics Act 1883 only requires it to be proved that the accused 'did the act or made the omission charged'. The Court did not address the problem of the burden of proof on the accused.

> ### ? Question
>
> Does raising a defence such as automatism or diminished responsibility harbour risks for a defendant?

While an accused may not expressly raise the defence of insanity, the nature of his defence may, in effect, amount to an insanity defence as where, for example, he claims he was acting as an automaton or lacked *mens rea* and medical evidence points to this being due to a disease of the mind giving rise to a defect of reason of the appropriate kind outlined in the second principle stated earlier. In the past it was obviously in the accused's interests to claim that he was an automaton or lacked *mens rea* without expressly claiming he was insane, as he would hope to be acquitted without suffering committal to a mental hospital which was the automatic consequence of a special verdict being returned. **The question whether a defence amounts to one of insanity is one of law to be decided by the judge on the basis of the medical evidence** (see *Dickie* [1984] 3 All ER 173). In exceptional circumstances a judge may raise the issue of insanity and leave it to the jury providing there is evidence embracing all the relevant considerations in the M'Naghten Rules (see *Thomas* [1995] Crim LR 314). If the judge concludes that the medical evidence supports a defence of insanity he should leave it to the jury to decide if the accused was insane. In several of the cases discussed later the trial judge ruled that the accused's defence of automatism was, in effect, one of insanity as the medical evidence of his mental condition established that it was due to a disease of the mind. In the past in such cases the result was often that the accused changed his plea to guilty to avoid the consequences of a special verdict. It is also open to the prosecution to raise the issue of insanity. In *Bratty v Attorney-General for Northern Ireland* [1963] AC 386, Lord Denning stated (at p. 411):

> I think that Devlin J was quite right in *Kemp's* case in putting the question of insanity to the jury, even though it had not been raised by the defence. When it is asserted that the accused did an involuntary act in a state of automatism, the defence necessarily puts in issue the state of mind of the accused man: and thereupon it is open to the prosecution to show what his true state of mind was. The old notion that only the defence can raise a defence of insanity is now gone. The prosecution are entitled to raise it and it is their duty to do so rather than allow a dangerous person to be at large.

Where the defence raise a plea of diminished responsibility in response to a charge of murder, it is open to the prosecution to rebut this by adducing or eliciting evidence of insanity (see s. 6 of the Criminal Procedure (Insanity) Act 1964). In such circumstances the burden of proving insanity will be on the prosecution (see *Bastian* [1958] 1 WLR 413).

The ultimate question whether the accused was insane is for the jury to determine; although the medical evidence will be crucial to their decision, it is not for doctors to decide the issue but for the jury to decide it on the basis of their evidence. However, the jury must act on the evidence tendered; if this all points to the accused being insane but the jury convict, such a conviction may be overturned on appeal on the ground that no reasonable jury could have reached such a verdict (*Matheson* (1958) 42 Cr App R 145). But if there is other evidence to the contrary, a jury verdict will not be overturned simply because the medical evidence supported the defence (see *Rivett* (1950) 34 Cr App R 87; *Latham* [1965] Crim LR 434).

5.3.3.2 The constituents of the defence

There are three conditions to be satisfied in any case where a defence of insanity is raised: first that the accused was suffering from a disease of the mind; second, that this gave rise to a defect of reason; and third, that as a result he either did not know the nature and quality of his act or he did not know that what he was doing was wrong. These will be examined in turn.

5.3.3.2.1 *Disease of the mind*

? Question

Is this the language doctors use?

Disease of the mind is a legal term and not a medical term. The law is concerned with the question whether the accused is to be held legally responsible for his acts. This depends on his mental state and its cause complying with legally defined criteria. The issue for the court is whether the accused had a defect of reason arising from a disease of the mind. The problem, however, is that psychiatrists prefer to use terms such as psychoneurosis and psychosis rather than disease of the mind. The former comprises anxiety states, obsessional states, and hysteria; these conditions would not generally meet the criteria for insanity. Most psychoses, on the other hand, satisfy the legal criteria of insanity. Psychoses may be divided into two categories, organic or functional. Organic psychoses are due to a physical cause such as poisoning of the brain by alcohol or drugs, infections such as syphilis, degeneration of the brain due to poor blood supply or tumours, or brain diseases, including senile dementia, atherosclerosis, and chorea. Functional psychoses include conditions such as schizophrenia, paranoia, psychopathic personality traits, and manic depression. There are other conditions which may cause a malfunctioning of the mind which, while they may have an organic cause, are not neuroses or psychoses, for example, epilepsy or hyperglycaemia arising from diabetes. The problem for the medical witness is whether he should speak the language of the psychiatrist or convert these terms into what he believes they equate to in the legal terminology. This may not be considered a major problem in respect of the question whether the accused was suffering from a defect of reason due to a disease of the mind as this is for the judge to decide. The danger there, however, is in relation to the medical evidence regarding the effects of such a disease on the accused's mental faculties, as the jury ultimately have to decide if the other criteria of the defence of insanity have been satisfied. If the psychiatrist seeks to translate medical terms into legal terms there is a danger that he will subvert the role of the jury by answering questions which are for their consideration, whereas, if he does not and simply confines himself to the role of the expert witness giving evidence for the jury's evaluation, there is a danger that he will mystify the jury.

This does not answer the question, however, of what constitutes a disease of the mind.

In *Kemp* [1957] 1 QB 399, it was argued that 'disease of the mind' meant that there had to be an organic disease of the brain which had caused degeneration of the brain. The accused was charged with causing grievous bodily harm having made a motiveless attack on his wife with a hammer. He suffered from arteriosclerosis which affected the flow of blood in his brain and had caused a temporary loss of consciousness during which the attack was made. He did not suffer from general mental trouble nor had his brain degenerated. Devlin J rejected the arguments of the defence that this was simply a case of automatism and ruled that the defence being raised was one of insanity, stating (at p. 407):

> The law is not concerned with the brain but with the mind, in the sense that 'mind' is ordinarily used, the mental faculties of reason, memory and understanding. If one read for 'disease of the mind' 'disease of the brain', it would follow that in many cases pleas of insanity would not be established because it could not be proved that the brain had been affected in any way, either by degeneration of the cells or in any other way. In my judgment the condition of the brain is irrelevant and so is the question whether the condition of the mind is curable or incurable, transitory or permanent.

Devlin J went on to explain that the words 'disease of the mind' were included in the M'Naghten Rules to limit the words 'defect of reason' which were not intended to apply to defects of reason 'caused simply by brutish stupidity without rational power'. This sought to distinguish the untrained mind from the diseased mind.

In *Bratty* Devlin J's dicta in *Kemp* received the approval of Lord Denning in the House of Lords who added a further gloss, stating (at p. 412):

> any mental disorder which has manifested itself in violence and is prone to recur is a disease of the mind. At any rate it is the sort of disease for which a person should be detained in hospital rather than be given an unqualified acquittal.

This represents a particularly ill-considered dictum. Diseases of the mind may manifest themselves in other ways which do not involve violence, for example, pyromania or kleptomania. In addition there are conditions which manifest themselves in violence which do not fall within the definition of disease of the mind as the case of *Quick* [1973] QB 910 discloses.

> The appellant was a diabetic who committed an assault when suffering from hypoglycaemia. This condition was caused by taking insulin and failing to eat which gave rise to a deficiency of blood sugar causing the appellant to be unaware of what he was doing. The trial judge ruled that his defence of automatism amounted to a plea of insanity, whereupon he pleaded guilty to the charge rather than face the

prospect of the jury returning the special verdict. The Court of Appeal quashed his conviction ruling that the cause of his condition was not his diabetes but his use of insulin which was an external factor and his defence of automatism should have been left to the jury. Lawton LJ interpreted the phrase 'disease of the mind' to mean a 'malfunctioning of the mind caused by disease' whereas a 'malfunctioning of the mind of transitory effect caused by some external factor such as violence, drugs including anaesthetics, alcohol and hypnotic influences cannot fairly be said to be due to disease'.

The use of the criterion of internal/external causes to distinguish insanity from automatism is fatuous. Hypoglycaemic coma may be caused by overproduction of insulin by the pancreas. As this is an internal cause, it would be classed as a disease and result in a finding of insanity should the sufferer commit an offence while in hypoglycaemic coma due to an overactive pancreas. Is the person suffering from an overactive pancreas more deserving of the label 'criminally insane' than the diabetic who does not control his food and insulin intake? The current state of the law suggests an affirmative answer. To say that the law is an ass is to engage in understatement.

In *Sullivan* [1984] AC 156 the House of Lords had to grapple with the problem of the dividing line between insanity and automatism.

> The appellant had pleaded guilty to assault occasioning actual bodily harm after the trial judge ruled that his defence of automatism to a charge of inflicting griev- ous bodily harm was really a defence of insanity. The appellant who had attacked a friend and kicked him about the head and body, claimed that the attack was com- mitted in the course of an epileptic seizure and he was not aware of doing it. Lord Diplock expressed his approval of Devlin J's dictum in *Kemp* and went on to state (at p. 172):

> > If the effect of a disease is to impair [the faculties of reason, memory and understand- ing] so severely as to have either of the consequences referred to in the latter part of the Rules, it matters not whether the aetiology of the impairment is organic, as in epilepsy, or functional, or whether the impairment itself is permanent or is transient and intermit- tent, provided that it subsisted at the time of the commission of the act.

Lord Diplock did go on to state that automatism would be available as a defence where temporary impairment resulted from an external physical factor although he did not consider it necessary to examine in detail the possible causes of automatism.

Although Sullivan's attack on his friend appeared to be purposive, despite him being unconscious, a result of the decision in the case is that an epileptic who invol- untarily connects with someone while his arms and legs are thrashing about in the course of a seizure is insane for the purposes of criminal liability whereas a diabetic in hypoglycaemic coma, caused by a low blood-sugar level, is not. By contrast, however, a diabetic in hyperglycaemic coma, caused by a high blood-sugar level, is insane. This is the conclusion of the Court of Appeal in *Hennessy* [1989] 2 All ER 9.

> D, a diabetic, was charged with taking a conveyance without authority and driving whilst disqualified. He raised the defence of automatism claiming that due to stress,

anxiety, and depression he had failed to take his insulin which resulted in hyperglycaemic coma. The trial judge ruled that this was in reality a defence of insanity as
the condition was due to the disease of diabetes. D changed his plea to guilty and
appealed. The Court of Appeal took the view that in *Sullivan* Lord Diplock had sought
to distinguish between external factors giving rise to a malfunction of the mind and
inherent causes giving rise to such a malfunction. The Court upheld the trial judge's
ruling that diabetes constituted a disease of the mind as it was an inherent defect.
Counsel for D argued further that the stress, anxiety, and depression from which he
was suffering were external factors. The Court held, however, that while they may
be the result of the operation of external factors (*per* Lord Lane CJ, at p. 14):

> they are not separately or together external factors of the kind capable in law of causing
> or contributing to a state of automatism. They constitute a state of mind which is prone
> to recur. They lack the feature of novelty or accident, which is the basis of the distinction
> drawn by Lord Diplock in *R v Sullivan*.

In *Quick* Lawton LJ had said that **'the law should not give the words "defect
of reason from disease of the mind" a meaning which would be regarded
with incredulity outside the court'**. It is difficult to imagine that the ordinary
person would not regard these decisions with incredulity. Is it desirable that epileptics face the prospect of being labelled criminally insane if they are unfortunate enough to suffer a seizure during the course of which they thrash around
and involuntarily hit or kick a third party? Society may require protection from
epileptics who, in the course of an epileptic seizure, engage in purposive conduct
of a violent or dangerous nature (as appeared to be the case in *Bratty*) but no such
distinction has been drawn by the courts. Is the distinction between a diabetic
in hyperglycaemic coma and one in hypoglycaemic coma so marked in its dangers, consequences, and risk of recurrence that the former should be found insane
while the latter goes free? In the cases of *Quick* and *Hennessy* the conduct involved
appeared to be purposive rather than convulsive but the outcome in each case
differed. The fact that the judges in *Quick*, *Sullivan*, and *Hennessy* accepted guilty
pleas from the defendants tends to indicate dissatisfaction with the operation of
the insanity defence.

   Judicial dissatisfaction spilled over into open rebellion in Kingston Crown Court
on 10 September 1990 (see *The Independent*, 11 September 1990). In the case of
McFarlane Judge Bertram Wakely gave a direction to the jury in open and express
defiance of the decision of the House of Lords in *Sullivan*. D was charged with
inflicting actual bodily harm on a policeman during a search of her home for allegedly stolen property. D had suffered from epilepsy for 14 years. The defence case
was that she struck the officer during an epileptic fit brought on by the strain of a
dawn raid by several officers. Rather than directing the jury on the special verdict,
Judge Wakely directed them that if they believed that D might have been having an
epileptic fit they should return a verdict of not guilty. The jury acquitted D. While
Judge Wakely may not have applied the law (as authoritatively declared in *Sullivan*)
his judgment was an application of the spirit of Lawton LJ's dictum in *Quick*. One
can only hope that one day both law and spirit will be in step! (See further the
examples of *Bilton* and *Davies* and compare with *Lowe* all referred to by Mackay and
Mitchell in 'Sleepwalking, Automatism and Insanity' [2006] Crim LR 901.)

?   Question

Mackay and Reuber, 'Epilepsy and the Defence of Insanity—Time for Change?' [2007] Crim LR 782, point out that it is well known that flashing lights and flash photography may trigger epileptic seizures, sometimes even in people who would not otherwise have seizures. If Sullivan's seizure had been triggered by flashing lights, would this have been an 'external factor' meriting an acquittal on the basis of non-insane automatism?

It had been hoped that reform of the insanity defence might be prompted by the enactment of the Human Rights Act 1998. Article 5 of the European Convention of Human Rights provides:

1. Everyone has the right to liberty and security of person. No one shall be deprived of his liberty save in the following cases and in accordance with a procedure prescribed by law;…

   (e) the lawful detention…of persons of unsound mind…

In the leading case before the European Court of Human Rights, *Winterwerp* v *Netherlands* (1979) 2 EHRR 387, the Court stated (at para. 39):

In the Court's opinion, except in emergency cases, the individual concerned should not be deprived of his liberty unless he has been reliably shown to be of 'unsound mind'. The very nature of what has to be established before the competent national authority—that is, a true mental disorder—calls for objective medical expertise. Further, the mental disorder must be of a kind or degree warranting compulsory confinement. What is more, the validity of the continued confinement depends upon the persistence of such a disorder.

It is doubtful whether conditions such as diabetes, epilepsy, or somnambulism would be classified by objective medical experts as mental disorders. Certainly they would not fall within the definition of 'mental disorder' in s. 1 of the Mental Health Act 1983 which governs the conditions for civil commitment to a mental hospital and covers 'mental illness, arrested or incomplete development of mind, psychopathic disorder and any other disorder or disability of mind'.

Imagine that D, a diabetic in hyperglycaemic coma kills someone and is charged with murder. D's plea of automatism is rejected and the prosecution prove insanity, the jury return the special verdict and the judge commits D to a secure mental hospital with a restriction order. D appeals against the special verdict and the hospital committal claiming that they are incompatible with Art. 5. Detention of such a person who is not of 'unsound mind' would be a breach of Art. 5. This is what prompted the substitution of a new s. 5 into the Criminal Procedure (Insanity) Act 1964 by s. 24 of the Domestic Violence, Crime and Victims Act 2004. D now would not receive a hospital order with a restriction order as he does not have a mental disorder requiring specialist treatment under the Mental Health Act 1983. But, however much one might consider that a diabetic, epileptic or sleepwalker should not be labelled insane, no change has been made in the test for insanity. The change effected by the 2004 Act, accordingly, is only a half-measure as the incongruities of the insanity defence remain unaddressed.

5.3.3.2.2 *Defect of reason*

If the defence of insanity is to succeed, the disease of the mind must give rise to a defect of reason. This appears to mean that the powers of reasoning must be impaired. If the accused simply fails, because of confusion or absent-mindedness, to use the powers of reasoning which he has, this will not bring him within the M'Naghten Rules.

> In *Clarke* [1972] 1 All ER 219, D was charged with the theft of items from a supermarket. Her defence was that she had no intention of stealing but had absent-mindedly placed the items in her shopping basket. She called medical evidence to establish that her absent-mindedness was due to a combination of depression and diabetes. The trial judge ruled that this was a defence of insanity, whereupon she pleaded guilty and appealed. The Court of Appeal quashed the conviction as D was not someone deprived of her powers of reasoning but simply someone who was momentarily absent-minded or confused who thus lacked the necessary *mens rea* for the offence.

If the accused's defect of reason is to be effective in establishing the defence of insanity, it must affect his legal responsibility for his conduct in one of the two ways specified in the M'Naghten Rules. Thus he must prove that either he did not know the nature and quality of his act or, if he did know this, he did not know that what he was doing was wrong.

5.3.3.2.3 *Nature and quality of the act*

In *Codere* (1916) 12 Cr App R 21, it was argued that the word 'nature' referred to the physical character of the act whereas the word 'quality' referred to its moral character. The Court of Criminal Appeal rejected this contention holding that 'nature and quality' referred only to the physical character of the act. Thus it is necessary for the accused to prove that he did not know what he was doing, or did not appreciate the consequences of his act, or did not appreciate the circumstances in which he was acting. **In all of these situations the accused would lack *mens rea* but, because his defect of reason is due to a disease of the mind, he is liable to the special verdict rather than simple acquittal.** This limb of the defence will cover the automaton who does an act in a state of impaired consciousness (e.g. *Sullivan* and *Hennessy*). It will also cover the person who acts under a delusion, for example, he believes he is chopping down a tree when, in fact, it is a person. Similarly it covers the person who cuts off a sleeper's head because 'it would be great fun to see him looking for it when he woke up' (see Stephen, *History of the Criminal Law*, vol II, p. 166); such a person does not understand the consequences of his acts. By contrast if D, suffering from a pathological fear of women, kills V because he believes V is a woman, but V is, in fact, a man in drag, his mistake is immaterial and will not avail him as it does not affect his knowledge that he is killing another person.

5.3.3.2.4 *Knowledge that the act is wrong*

Under this limb of the Rules there is an implicit admission by the accused that he had the *mens rea* for the offence but that he was not a responsible actor as he did not know that what he was doing was wrong. The law in relation to this limb of the defence is not particularly clear. There are two possibilities: (1) that the accused must prove that he did not know that the act was contrary to the law; or (2) that the accused must prove that he did not know that the act was wrong according to the standard adopted by reasonable people. In *M'Naghten* the suggestion was that if the accused knew the act was wrong, in the sense of being one which he knew he ought not to do, this would be fatal to his defence whether or not he knew the actual law prohibiting it as 'the law is administered upon the principle that everyone must be taken conclusively to know it, without proof that he does know it'. This view was reinforced by *Codere* where the Court stated that 'the standard to be applied is whether according to the ordinary standard adopted by reasonable men the act was right or wrong'. Thus it appeared that the defence of insanity would fail if the accused knew either that his act was prohibited by the law or that it was regarded as wrong by reasonable people.

Doubt has been cast on this proposition by the case of *Windle* [1952] 2 QB 826. D killed his wife by giving her a fatal dose of aspirin. The wife was certifiably insane and had spoken of committing suicide on many occasions. On giving himself up to the police D said, 'I suppose they will hang me for this'. At his trial for murder, medical evidence was given that D suffered from a form of communicated insanity called *folie à deux*, although the experts on both sides agreed he knew that he was doing an act prohibited by the law. Devlin J withdrew the defence of insanity from the jury and D was convicted. The Court of Criminal Appeal upheld the conviction, Lord Goddard CJ stating *obiter* (at pp. 833, 834):

> Courts of law can only distinguish between that which is in accordance with law and that which is contrary to law.... The law cannot embark on the question, and it would be an unfortunate thing if it were left to juries to consider whether some particular act was morally right or wrong. The test must be whether it is contrary to law.... In the opinion of the court there is no doubt that in the M'Naghten Rules 'wrong' means contrary to law and not 'wrong' according to the opinion of one man or of a number of people on the question of whether a particular act might or might not be justified.

This judgment appears to widen the defence as an accused who knew his act was morally wrong may still raise the defence if his contention is that because of his defect of reason he did not know it was legally wrong to do what he did. *Windle* was confirmed by the Court of Appeal in *Johnson* [2007] EWCA Crim 1978 where it was held that knowledge of illegality was the sole criterion of what was wrong.

This limb of the M'Naghten Rules has been subjected to criticism. Glanville Williams, *Textbook of Criminal Law* (2nd edn, 1983) at p. 645, argues that 'unless very benevolently interpreted it adds almost nothing to the other questions'. The Butler Committee, *Report of the Committee on Mentally Abnormal Offenders* (Cmnd 6244, 1975) stated (at p. 218):

> Knowledge of the law is hardly an appropriate test on which to base ascription of responsibility to the mentally disordered. It is a very narrow ground of exemption since even persons who are grossly disturbed generally know that murder and arson are crimes.

This would suggest that this limb of the defence, if applied strictly, will be of little use. This discussion is academic as in practice it appears that almost half of the special verdicts returned in Mackay's 1990 study (see **5.3.1** *ante*) were based on this ground. His study also revealed that trial courts are effectively ignoring the dicta in the appellate cases and special verdicts are being returned in cases where the accused knew his act to be legally wrong but did it because of delusions which caused him to believe it to be morally right!

Mackay concluded (at p. 251):

> In many of these cases there seems to have been little attempt made to distinguish between lack of knowledge of legal wrong…and unawareness of moral wrong. Indeed, the general impression gained from reading the documentation in these cases was that the wrongness issue was being treated in a liberal fashion by all concerned, rather than in the strict manner regularly depicted by legal commentators.

The later research by Mackay and Kearns in 1999 confirms that this continues to be the case where the 'wrongness' limb was used in 25 out of the 44 cases studied. They state (at p. 723):

> [T]he overwhelming impression is that the question the majority of psychiatrists are addressing is: if the delusion that the defendant was experiencing at the time of the offence was in fact reality, then would the defendant's actions be morally justified? — rather than the narrow cognitive test of legal wrongness required by the M'Naghten Rules…In so doing, it may be argued that psychiatrists in many respects are adopting a common sense or folk psychology approach and that the courts by accepting this interpretation are, in reality, expanding the scope of the M'Naghten Rules.

(See also Mackay and Mitchell, 'Yet More Facts about the Insanity Defence' [2006] Crim LR 399.) One can only state again that it would be desirable for the law, practice, and theory to be in harmony.

5.3.3.2.5 *Insane delusions and irresistible impulses*

Although the jury acquitted M'Naghten, under the test the judges propounded he would have been convicted. He was suffering from paranoia which gave rise to a morbid delusion that he was being persecuted by 'Tories'. This delusion did not prevent him from knowing that he was killing another person and from knowing that it was wrong. It is an arguable point, however, whether he was a responsible actor deserving of punishment.

The judges dealt expressly with the issue of delusions stating:

> if [the accused] labours under [a] partial delusion only, and is not in other respects insane, we think he must be considered in the same situation as to responsibility as if the facts with respect to which the delusion exists were real. For example, if under the influence of his delusion he supposes another man to be in the act of attempting to take away his life, and he kills that man, as he supposes, in self-defence, he would be exempt from punishment. If his delusion was that the deceased had inflicted a serious injury to his character and fortune, and he killed him in revenge for such supposed injury, he would be liable to punishment.

This does not really add anything to the Rules as this situation is already covered by the test relating to the nature and quality of the act. In the example of self-defence the accused did not appreciate the circumstances in which he was acting and thus did not know the nature and quality of his act. In the second example the accused knows that he is killing a person and there is nothing to suggest that he did not know that this was wrong. The problem is that there are delusions which may call into question the responsibility of the accused for his acts but which do not fall within the Rules. For example, there are many cases where the accused kills his victim because he believes that the victim is possessed by the devil, or because he is in a paranoid state believing that the victim is persecuting him or plotting his death. In all these cases the accused would not fall within the Rules if he knows he is killing another person and that killing is wrong. His delusional state, however, would suggest that he is not a responsible actor deserving of punishment even though society deserves to be protected from him. These cases point to a deficiency of the Rules. In practice, however, this deficiency appears to be overlooked as Mackay (1990) cites examples of cases where the special verdict has been returned although the Rules do not appear to have been satisfied.

If the accused understands what he is doing and knows that it is wrong, the fact that he could not resist the impulse to do it will be of no avail. The Privy Council in *Sodeman* [1936] 2 All ER 1138 ruled that the defence could not be founded on uncontrollable impulse (see also *Kopsch* (1925) 19 Cr App R 50). However, medical evidence that in a particular case irresistible impulse was a symptom of the disease from which an accused was suffering, affecting his ability to know the nature and quality of his act or its wrongness, could be left to the jury (see *A-G for South Australia* v *Brown* [1960] AC 432). Thus irresistible impulse on its own will not found a defence, but it may be used to support the claim that the accused either did not know what he was doing or that it was wrong, where there is medical evidence to that effect. Irresistible impulse is relevant, however, to support a defence of diminished responsibility.

5.3.4 **Proposals for reform**

The M'Naghten Rules have been the subject of persistent criticism by lawyers and doctors on several grounds. First, they do not reflect current psychiatric thinking on mental disorder. The language used in the Rules is that of lawyers and has little congruence to the language of psychiatry. Secondly, the Rules lead to absurd distinctions such as those between diabetics suffering from hypoglycaemia and those suffering from hyperglycaemia. The distinctions do not reflect any substantial difference in the responsibility of such persons for their acts and are doubtless regarded with incredulity by ordinary members of the public. Thirdly, the Rules cover persons who normally would not be liable to civil committal to hospital under the Mental Health Act 1983, such as diabetics, epileptics, and sleepwalkers, while failing to cover others who are covered by that Act such as the defendant in *Windle*, those suffering from insane delusions which do not prevent them from knowing what they are doing, and those subject to uncontrollable impulses.

These criticisms have led to various calls for reform. The most significant report was that of the Butler Committee (Cmnd 6244, 1975). The Butler proposals form the basis for the mental disorder provisions in the Law Commission's Draft Criminal Code. The Draft Code abandons the language of the M'Naghten Rules and uses terms such as 'mental disorder', 'severe mental illness', and 'severe mental handicap' which reflect medical terminology. Clause 34 contains definitions which clarify the conditions which amount to a 'mental disorder' and greatly broaden the range of effects which such conditions must have to merit the return of a mental disorder verdict. The effect will be that those who are not responsible but who are not covered by the M'Naghten Rules will be covered under these provisions. Clause 34 of the Draft Code provides:

> 'mental disorder' means—
>
> (a) severe mental illness; or
> (b) a state of arrested or incomplete development of mind; or
> (c) a state of automatism...which is a feature of a disorder, whether organic or functional and whether continuing or recurring, that may cause a similar state on another occasion;...
>
> 'severe mental illness' means a mental illness which has one or more of the following characteristics—
>
> (a) lasting impairment of intellectual functions shown by failure of memory, orientation, comprehension and learning capacity;
> (b) lasting alteration of mood of such degree as to give rise to delusional appraisal of the defendant's situation, his past or his future, or that of others, or lack of any appraisal;
> (c) delusional beliefs, persecutory, jealous or grandiose;
> (d) abnormal perceptions associated with delusional misinterpretation of events;
> (e) thinking so disordered as to prevent reasonable appraisal of the defendant's situation or reasonable communication with others; 'severe mental handicap' means a state of arrested or incomplete development of mind which includes severe impairment of intelligence and social functioning.

The one possible deficiency in these definitions is that 'severe mental illness' does not cover cases where a characteristic of the illness is uncontrollable impulses. If the charge is murder the accused may plead diminished responsibility, but if the charge is attempted murder or causing grievous bodily harm, this defence is not available and conviction would result.

There are two bases upon which a mental disorder verdict should be returned. First, 'if the defendant is proved to have committed an offence but it is proved on the balance of probabilities (whether by the prosecution or the defendant) that he was at the time suffering from severe mental illness or severe mental handicap' (cl. 35(1)). This covers cases where the accused may have formed the *mens rea* for the offence but his mind was so disordered that he was not a responsible actor. It is open to the prosecution, however, to prove that 'the offence was not attributable to the severe mental illness or severe mental handicap' (cl. 35(1)). Secondly, cl. 36 provides:

> A mental disorder verdict shall be returned if—
>
> (a) the defendant is acquitted of an offence only because, by reason of evidence of mental disorder or a combination of mental disorder and intoxication, it is found that he acted or may have acted in a state of automatism, or without the fault required for the offence, or believing that an exempting circumstance existed; and
> (b) it is proved on the balance of probabilities (whether by the prosecution or by the defendant) that he was suffering from mental disorder at the time of the act.

This provision covers situations where the accused's mental disorder caused him to act as an automaton or it prevented him from knowing what he was doing so that he did not form the *mens rea* required for the offence, or it caused him to believe in a circumstance of defence as, for example, where under a delusional belief that he is under attack he kills in self-defence. In these three circumstances the definitional elements of the offence would not have been proved, or a defence disproved, and the accused would be entitled to an acquittal. The clause provides that, where mental disorder is the reason for the acquittal, a mental disorder verdict should be returned. This recognises that the accused was not a responsible actor but provides protection for the public in the form of the order of disposal which the court may make. Thus diabetics or epileptics will be liable to a mental disorder verdict if their condition reduces them to a state of automatism, but this verdict avoids the stigmatising effect of a finding of insanity and gives the judge discretion in choosing a disposal appropriate to the accused's case.

5.4 Automatism

5.4.1 Defining automatism

It was stated at **2.4.1** *ante* that where the *actus reus* of an offence requires conduct on the part of the accused, whether an act or omission, liability will only accrue where the conduct is willed. **Where a person acts while in a state of unconsciousness or impaired consciousness this is referred to as automatism.** In such a condition the movements of a person's body or limbs are involuntary (see *Watmore* v *Jenkins* [1962] 2 QB 572). In *Bratty* v *A-G for Northern Ireland* [1963] AC 386, 409, Lord Denning defined an involuntary act or automatism as:

> an act which is done by the muscles without any control by the mind, such as a spasm, a reflex action or a convulsion; or an act done by a person who is not conscious of what he is doing, such as an act done whilst suffering from concussion or whilst sleep-walking.

What is required is that the accused's mind is not controlling his limbs at all; it is not sufficient that the accused's mind is acting imperfectly if he is still reacting to stimuli and controlling his limbs in a purposive way (see *Broome* v *Perkins* [1987] Crim LR 271; *Roberts* v *Ramsbottom* [1980] 1 All ER 7; *A-G's Reference (No. 2 of 1992)* (1993) 97 Cr App R 429). Even a trance-like state will be insufficient if the accused is still performing some purposive acts. In *Isitt* (1978) 67 Cr App R 44, D was involved in a road accident and it appeared that he was drunk. He returned to his van and drove off at speed with a police car in pursuit. D evaded the pursuing vehicle, evaded a police road block, and finally came to a halt when he drove up a cul-de-sac only to run off through fields. When finally interviewed at home he claimed he could not remember the incident and, at his trial for dangerous driving, he called psychiatric evidence to the effect that the original accident had caused hysterical fugue leading to memory loss. It was claimed that his subconscious mind had taken over so that he did not appreciate what he was doing when he was driving, and although he knew he was trying to get away from the scene of an accident, he was totally unaware of legal restrictions and moral concern. He was convicted and the Court of Appeal dismissed his appeal, Lawton LJ stating (at p. 48):

> It is a matter of human experience that the mind does not always operate in top gear.
>
> There may be some difficulty in functioning. If the difficulty does not amount in law to either insanity or automatism, is the accused entitled to say 'I am not guilty because my mind was not working in top gear'? In our judgment he is not....
>
> In our judgment on the psychiatrist's evidence, it is clear that he was accepting that the appellant's mind was working to some extent. The driving was purposeful driving, which was to get away from the scene of the accident. It may well be that, because of panic or stress or alcohol, the appellant's mind was shut to the moral inhibitions which control the lives of most of us. But the fact that his moral inhibitions were not working properly, in our judgment, does not mean that the mind was not working at all.

It is an essential requirement of criminal liability that the accused's acts or omissions which constitute the *actus reus* of the offence were voluntary (see *Bratty, per* Lord Denning at p. 409). Thus, if the prosecution cannot prove beyond reasonable doubt that the accused's conduct was voluntary, he will be acquitted. Mental capacity, however, is presumed and the prosecution will only be required to negative an assertion of automatism where the defence have laid a proper evidential foundation for that assertion (*Bratty*). The accused's own evidence will rarely be sufficient and should be supported by medical evidence which points to the cause of the mental incapacity (*Bratty*). Where the cause of the automatism is a disease of the mind within the M'Naghten Rules, the acquittal will take the form of the special verdict of not guilty by reason of insanity resulting in committal to a mental hospital. It is therefore crucial to determine which causes of automatism will lead to an outright acquittal and which will lead to a finding of insanity.

5.4.2 The causes of automatism

Where the accused's state of impaired consciousness is due to self-induced intoxication by drink or drugs this will not avail him if the crime with which he is charged is one of 'basic intent', although it may negative *mens rea* for a crime of 'specific intent' (see **5.6.3** *post*). The distinction between automatism due to a disease of the mind and that due to other causes is a very important one. In *Bratty*, D was charged with murder having strangled a girl. He raised three defences: automatism, lack of intent for murder, and insanity. The medical evidence pointed to the attack occurring in the course of a psychomotor epileptic seizure. In such a condition the sufferer may perform complicated acts of a purposive, as opposed to convulsive, kind while in an unconscious or somnambulist state. The trial judge ruled that the defence case was one of insanity as the medical evidence pointed to the accused's automatous condition being due to a disease of the mind, and refused to leave the other two defences to the jury. The jury rejected the defence of insanity and convicted. This conviction was upheld by both the Court of Appeal and the House of Lords. Lord Denning accepted that the 'major mental diseases, which doctors call psychoses...are clearly diseases of the mind'. To these he added 'any mental disorder which has manifested itself in violence and is prone to recur'. This hardly provided a useful guide for distinguishing automatism from insanity. **The distinction which emerges from subsequent cases centres on classifying causes as being either internal or external**. In *Quick* [1973] QB 910, Lawton LJ, seeking to define 'disease of the mind' stated (at p. 922):

> the fundamental concept is a malfunctioning of the mind caused by disease. A malfunctioning of the mind of transitory effect caused by the application to the body of some external factor such as violence, drugs including anaesthetics, alcohol and hypnotic influences cannot fairly be said to be due to disease.

In *Sullivan* Lord Diplock implicitly accepted the distinction between internal and external causes. A verdict of not guilty would thus be acceptable in 'cases where temporary impairment…results from some external physical factor such as a blow on the head causing concussion or the administration of an anaesthetic for therapeutic purposes'. It would appear, therefore, that **automatism will not result in a finding of insanity where the cause is external and physical such as concussion resulting from a blow to the head, or impaired consciousness resulting from the administration of drugs (e.g. insulin leading to hypoglycaemia) or anaesthetics.** Stress, anxiety, or depression which lead to impaired consciousness are not themselves external physical factors (see *Hennessy* [1989] 2 All ER 9), but where they are due to an external physical factor and they lead to impaired consciousness, automatism may be successfully pleaded (see *R v T* [1990] Crim LR 256). In the latter case D was charged with robbery and causing actual bodily harm. In her defence she claimed she was acting as an automaton as a result of being raped three days prior to the alleged offences. Medical evidence supported her claim to being raped and a psychiatrist diagnosed that she was suffering from post traumatic stress disorder which brought about a dissociative state such that the offences had been committed during a psychogenic fugue and she was not acting with a conscious mind or will. Southan J, at Snaresbrook Crown Court, held that the issue of automatism should be allowed to go to the jury as the rape was an external factor and post traumatic stress was not a disease of the mind. In *Rabey* (1977) 37 CCC (2d) 461, where the accused sought to plead automatism based on a dissociative state caused by the psychological blow of rejection by a girl with whom he had become infatuated, the Supreme Court of Canada held that 'the ordinary stresses and disappointments of life which are the common lot of mankind do not constitute an external cause'. The Court was of the opinion that the impact of this ordinary event on the accused was primarily due to his psychological or emotional make-up. Rape can hardly be considered one of the 'ordinary stresses or disappointments of life'. Southan J considered that 'such an incident could have an appalling effect on any young woman, however well-balanced normally'. The case is consequently easily distinguishable from *Rabey*.

In *Roach* [2001] EWCA Crim 2698 the Court of Appeal highlighted the importance of taking into account the causative factors resulting in a state of automatism. D suffered from an underlying condition which could have led to a state of insane automatism. There was evidence, however, that external factors, namely the combination of alcohol and prescribed drugs, may have rendered D an automaton when he committed the offence. In quashing his conviction because of a misdirection by the trial judge, Potter LJ stated, (at para. 28) that;

> the legal definition of automatism allows for the fact that, if external factors are operative upon an underlying condition which would not otherwise produce a state of automatism, then a defence of (non-insane) automatism should be left to the jury.

While the distinction between internal and external causes may appear conceptually simple it has not always been strictly applied. The condition which causes a problem for the courts is that of somnambulism. There are numerous examples of people engaging in purposive conduct while apparently asleep who awake either remembering nothing at all or recalling the events as a dream. If an accused performs an act while asleep the cause for such unconscious conduct would appear to be internal. If, in response to a charge, he pleaded automatism based on somnambulism, the outcome should be a ruling that this was a defence of insanity. However, there are cases where such pleas have been accepted as simple automatism, as in *Lillienfield*, *The Times*, 17 October 1985. In this case, the Crown Court treated as automatism the actions of the accused who, in a state of somnambulism, had stabbed a friend 20 times. In *Bratty* Lord Denning blithely placed acts done while sleepwalking in the same category as those done while concussed. He cited with approval the dictum of Stephen J in *Tolson* (1889) 23 QBD 168, 187:

> Can anyone doubt that a man who, though he might be perfectly sane, committed what would otherwise be a crime in a state of somnambulism, would be entitled to be acquitted? And why is this? Simply because he would not know what he was doing.

The fatal flaw in this line of reasoning, however, is the assumption that because, in common parlance, such a person would not be described as insane, the law will treat him similarly. The same questions asked by Stephen J could be asked in respect of the diabetic in hyperglycaemic coma (*Hennessy*) and the epileptic (*Sullivan*); the law, however, regards these people as insane and the case of the sleepwalker is indistinguishable. The Court of Appeal came to this conclusion in *Burgess* [1991] 2 QB 92. D pleaded automatism due to sleepwalking in response to a charge of wounding with intent. The trial judge ruled that this was a case of insane automatism. On appeal against the jury's finding that D was not guilty by reason of insanity, the Court of Appeal upheld the trial judge's ruling; D's automatism was due to an internal cause. (See further the examples of *Bilton* and *Davies* and compare with *Lowe*: all referred to by Mackay and Mitchell in 'Sleepwalking, Automatism and Insanity' [2006] Crim LR 901.)

On 15 October 2008 Harry Cohen MP introduced a Private Members' Bill, the Rape (Defences) Bill, to amend the Sexual Offences Act 2008 to prohibit the defence of sleepwalking or non-insane automatism in proceedings relating to rape. Several cases which received media coverage prompted this move as it appeared that defendants, mostly following heavy drinking, raised sleepwalking in their defence to charges of rape and received acquittals without any ruling such as that made in *Burgess* being given by the trial judges. If alcohol induced the sleepwalking this could render it self-induced (see **5.4.3**) and, if it did not, it would arise from an internal cause and be a case of insane automatism. The Bill was not enacted, but it is clear that the issue of sleepwalking as a defence, and how it relates to that of insane automatism, requires clarification.

5.4.3 Self-induced automatism

Automatism is self-induced where it results from something which the accused has done or failed to do. The most frequent example of self-induced automatism is intoxication arising from the voluntary ingestion of alcohol or proscribed drugs. The effect of intoxication on criminal liability is discussed in detail later (see **5.6** *post*). For present purposes it is sufficient to state that self-induced intoxication is not a defence to offences of basic intent, although it may be relevant where the accused is charged with an offence of specific intent, as evidence of intoxication may help the accused to create a doubt as to whether he had formed the intent necessary to be convicted of the offence. **Where automatism is due to some cause other than intoxication by alcohol or proscribed drugs, the accused cannot be convicted of an offence of specific intent and it may provide a defence to crimes of basic intent** (*Bailey* [1983] 1 WLR 760).

> In *Bailey*, D raised automatism as his defence to charges under ss. 18 and 20 of the Offences Against the Person Act 1861 of unlawful wounding and wounding with intent. D was a diabetic and claimed he had failed to take sufficient food after taking insulin which caused a hypoglycaemic coma in the course of which he committed the offence. The jury convicted D of the s. 18 offence on the direction from the recorder that self-induced automatism was no defence to offences of specific or basic intent. The Court of Appeal ruled that the recorder's direction was clearly wrong in respect of the s. 18 offence which was one of specific intent. They also held that self-induced automatism, other than due to intoxication by alcohol or drugs, may provide a defence to crimes of basic intent. Griffiths LJ stated (at p. 765):
>
> > The question in each case will be whether the prosecution have proved the necessary element of recklessness. In cases of assault, if the accused knows that his actions or inaction are likely to make him aggressive, unpredictable or uncontrolled with the result that he may cause some injury to others and he persists in the action or takes no remedial action when he knows it is required, it will be open to the jury to find that he was reckless.

The Court based its ruling on the view that there was an absence of common knowledge amongst diabetics of the possible effects of failure to take food after insulin, whereas it is common knowledge that those who become intoxicated by alcohol or drugs may become aggressive or do dangerous or unpredictable things. If, however, a diabetic did appreciate the risk of becoming aggressive, unpredictable, or uncontrollable due to a failure to take food after taking insulin and he deliberately ran that risk, this would amount to recklessness and lead to liability for any offence of basic intent which he committed in that state.

5.5 Diminished responsibility

The defence of diminished responsibility was created by s. 2 of the Homicide Act 1957. Almost from the point of its enactment it was the subject of criticism and there have been various proposals for its reform. The Coroners and Justice Act 2009 has radically amended s. 2 of the Homicide Act 1957 recasting the defence. The new defence applies to all murders committed on or after 4 October 2010. For murders committed prior to that date the original version of the defence applies. In order to understand the new defence it is necessary to understand the original defence and the reform proposals which led to its replacement.

5.5.1 The original defence of diminished responsibility

5.5.1.1 The operation of the defence

The defence of diminished responsibility is not a general defence; it may only be pleaded in defence to a charge of murder. Its effect, if successfully raised, is in the nature of a partial excuse; the accused is acquitted of murder but is convicted of manslaughter. On a conviction of manslaughter the judge has discretion when sentencing the accused whereas, on conviction for murder, the mandatory sentence is life imprisonment. In sentencing for manslaughter, the judge may reflect in the sentence imposed the degree to which he considers the accused's responsibility for his act was impaired by his mental condition. The official statistics reveal that about 50% of those convicted of manslaughter due to diminished responsibility receive hospital orders under s. 37 of the Mental Health Act 1983, and the majority of these (about 80%) have a restriction order under s. 41 attached. Of the remainder, the sentences range from probation and suspended sentences to various terms of imprisonment. The defence has all but replaced the insanity defence on a charge of murder where the accused was suffering from a mental incapacity. The defence covers all cases which would fall within the M'Naghten Rules and many other conditions which these do not cover.

The defence was introduced in response to the Royal Commission on Capital Punishment (Cmnd 8932, 1949–1953), which had argued for an expanded insanity defence. The Government accepted that the defence of insanity was limited and that injustices could occur in murder cases but considered that an expanded defence of insanity would cause major difficulties. The defence was created by s. 2 of the Homicide Act 1957. As with insanity, **the accused bears the burden of proving the defence** (s. 2(2)) on a balance of probabilities (*Dunbar* [1958] 1 QB 1). The fact that a burden of proof is cast upon the accused does not, however, constitute a breach of Art. 6(2) of the European Convention for the Protection of Human Rights and Fundamental Freedoms which declares that 'everyone charged with a criminal offence shall be presumed innocent until proved guilty according to law', as a person charged with the offence of murder is not required to prove anything unless he seeks to rely on s. 2 which is to his benefit as it creates a defence (see *R v Ali; R v Jordan* [2001] 2 WLR 211). In practice the accused is rarely put to his proof as a plea of guilty of manslaughter is accepted in about 80% of the cases in which the defence of diminished responsibility is raised (see S. Dell, 'Diminished responsibility reconsidered' [1982] Crim LR 809). In *Vinagre* (1979) 69 Cr App R 104, the Court of Appeal stated that pleas to manslaughter on the grounds of diminished responsibility should only be accepted when there is clear evidence of mental imbalance. The defence will generally be put to their proof where there is disagreement between the psychiatric reports or where these reports do not wholeheartedly support the defence. Where the accused raises the defence of diminished responsibility, and the prosecution have evidence that he is insane, it may adduce or elicit evidence tending to prove this (see s. 6 of the Criminal Procedure (Insanity) Act 1964), but this power would appear to be rarely used. Section 6 also allows for the converse situation; the prosecution may, where the accused pleads insanity, contend that he was suffering from diminished responsibility. The trial judge has no power to raise the issue of diminished responsibility if the defence do not do so, but if he detects evidence of diminished responsibility he may point this out to defence counsel and leave it so that the defence can decide whether to raise this issue and seek to prove it before the jury (see *Campbell* (1987) 84 Cr App R 255).

5.5.1.2 Nature of the defence

Section 2 of the Homicide Act 1957 provides:

> (1) Where a person kills or is party to the killing of another, he shall not be convicted of murder if he was suffering from such abnormality of mind (whether arising from a condition of arrested or retarded development of mind or any inherent causes or induced by disease or injury) as substantially impaired his mental responsibility for his acts and omissions in doing or being a party to the killing.

There are three elements to the defence which will be examined in turn.

Medical evidence is crucial to the success of the defence (see *Dix* (1981) 74 Cr App R 306) and a jury may not return a verdict of manslaughter on the ground of diminished responsibility unless there is medical evidence of an abnormality of mind arising from one of the specified causes. While the decision is ultimately for the jury, they must act on the evidence and if the medical evidence supporting a finding of diminished responsibility is unchallenged, and there is nothing in the facts or circumstances to cast doubt on it, they must accept it (see *Matheson* (1958) 42 Cr App R 145; *Bailey* (1978) 66 Cr App R 31). However, as Lord Parker CJ stated in *Byrne* [1960] 2 QB 396, 403, the jury 'are not bound to accept the medical evidence if there is other material before them which, in their good judgment, conflicts with it and outweighs it' (see further *Eifinger* [2001] EWCA Crim 1855).

It is important to note that s. 2 **does not require proof that the abnormality of mind caused the killing** (although in many cases such a causal link may be apparent); the section is framed in such a way as to indicate that it is sufficient to establish the defence that D's mind was abnormal at the time of the killing such that his mental responsibility for his acts was substantially impaired. Obviously, if the defence claims that D's ability to control his acts was impaired by his mental abnormality, this condition has causal significance. However, if the focus of the defence is on D's moral culpability for his acts (which could be diminished due to mental illness or D's arrested or retarded development of mind), there may be no causal connection between D's condition and the killing, but it does bear directly on the question of the extent to which he should be held responsible for it (see further G. R. Sullivan, 'Intoxicants and Diminished Responsibility' [1994] Crim LR 156).

5.5.1.2.1 *Abnormality of mind*

It must be proved that the accused was suffering from an abnormality of mind at the material time. This is a question for the jury but medical evidence is important. The jury should weigh this up with all the other evidence 'including acts or statements of the accused and his demeanour' (see *Byrne* [1960] 2 QB 396). In *Byrne* Lord Parker CJ defined **'abnormality of mind'** (at p. 403) as:

> a state of mind so different from that of ordinary human beings that the reasonable man would term it abnormal. It appears to us to be wide enough to cover the mind's activities in all its aspects, not only the perception of physical acts and matters, and the ability to form a rational judgment as to whether an act is right or wrong, but also the ability to exercise will-power to control physical acts in accordance with that rational judgment.

In *Byrne* sexual psychopathy giving rise to violent perverted sexual desires which he found difficult, if not impossible, to control, amounted to an abnormality of mind. By contrast, in *Seers* (1984) 79 Cr App R 261, D was convicted of the murder of his wife when suffering from chronic reactive depression which constituted an abnormality of mind.

5.5.1.2.2 *Specified causes*

Unless the abnormality of mind from which the accused is alleged to suffer is shown to arise from one of the causes specified in parenthesis in s. 2(1), the defence will fail (see *King* [1965] 1 QB 443 at 450). **The aetiology of the abnormality of mind is a matter to be determined by medical evidence** (*Byrne*). There is little guidance, however, on what is meant by the causes specified in parenthesis. They were meant to rule out emotions such as hatred, rage, or jealousy and external factors such as alcohol or drugs. There are cases, however, where jealousy (see *Miller, The Times*, 16 May 1972; *Asher, The Times*, 9 June 1981) and rage (see *Coles* (1980) 144 JPN 528) have resulted in a s. 2 verdict. In the Northern Irish case of *McQuade* [2005] NICA 2, the Court of Appeal were faced with the question whether or not 'injury' (in this case psychological harm) resulting from years of sexual abuse was capable of amounting to an abnormality of the mind from one of the specified causes. The Court of Appeal, taking into account the decisions in *Ireland, Burstow*, and *Chan-Fook* which held that bodily harm or injury for the purposes of offences against the person included injury to the mind, held that the important question was whether the mind had been injured, not how it had been injured, i.e. by physical or psychological means.

Intoxication will not support a verdict of manslaughter but alcoholism (alcohol dependence syndrome) may give rise to an abnormality of mind arising from 'disease or injury'. There is no need to prove actual damage to the brain, although such damage may make it more likely to find there is an abnormality of the mind (*Wood* [2008] EWCA Crim 1305 where the Court of Appeal explained and limited the earlier decisions of *Tandy* (1988) 87 Cr App R 45 and *Inseal* [1992] Crim LR 35). The issue for the jury is whether the alcoholism has produced an abnormality of mind. It will only do so where there is gross impairment of judgement and emotional responses or the drinking was involuntary. Guidance in directing juries was provided in *Stewart (James)* [2009] EWCA Crim 593 where the Court of Appeal pointed out first, that the fact that D suffered from alcohol dependency syndrome did not necessarily mean he had an abnormality of mind. That depended on the jury's findings about the nature and extent of the syndrome and whether, looking at the matter broadly, his consumption of alcohol before the killing was fairly to be regarded as the involuntary result of an irresistible craving for, or compulsion to, drink. If D proved the necessary abnormality of mind, the second question was whether that was caused by disease or illness; the answer to this question would normally follow from the answer to the first question. Finally, if the first and second questions were answered affirmatively, the jury had to consider whether D's responsibility was substantially impaired and this should be considered in conventional terms. In deciding this the jury should take account of (a) the extent and seriousness of D's dependency; (b) the extent to which his ability to control his drinking, or to choose whether or not to drink, was reduced; (c) whether he was capable of abstinence from alcohol, and if so; (d) for how long; and (e) whether he was choosing for some particular reason to decide to get drunk or to drink even more than usual (for example, to celebrate his birthday).

Temporary mental impairment lasting for several hours resulting from ingestion of a medically prescribed drug does not constitute an 'injury' (*O'Connell* [1997] Crim LR 683). Where the evidence suggests more than one cause for the abnormality of the mind, one of which is intoxication (or some other cause not specified in s. 2), the judge should direct the jury to ignore the effect of the inadmissible causes and consider whether the effect of the admissible cause or causes was an abnormality of the mind such as to impair substantially the accused's mental responsibility (*Fenton* (1975) 61 Cr App R 261; *Gittens* [1984] QB 698). In *Atkinson* [1985] Crim LR 314, the Court of Appeal approved the following direction to juries in such cases:

> Have the defence satisfied you on the balance of probabilities—that if the defendant had not taken drink—(i) he would have killed as he in fact did? And (ii) he would have been under diminished responsibility when he did so?

This direction was approved in *Egan* [1993] Crim LR 131. These questions were speculative and hypothetical and highly problematic. In many cases the issue is not whether the drink caused the killing but whether it caused the impairment of mental responsibility. If it did, as where, for example, D's ability to control his acts was impaired by drinking, such an impairment, which could be construed as an abnormality of mind, would not have arisen from one of the specified causes. If, however, regardless of D's intoxication, his mental responsibility was impaired at the time of the killing due to a specified cause (in *Egan* there was psychiatric evidence to the effect that D was on the 'borderline of subnormality'), he should be entitled to succeed on the s. 2 defence. Thus, for example, if mental illness has substantially impaired D's 'ability to form a rational judgment as to whether an act is right or wrong', or if D is mentally retarded, these are constants which remain the case whether or not he was intoxicated and relate directly to the issue whether D is a person who should be held morally culpable for his acts and deserving of the mandatory life sentence.

In *Deitschmann* [2003] UKHL 10, the House of Lords was faced directly with this problem. The point of law of general importance certified by the Court of Appeal was:

> (1) Does a defendant seeking to prove a defence of diminished responsibility...in a case where he had taken drink prior to killing the victim, have to show that if he had not taken drink

(a) he would have killed as he in fact did; and

(b) he would have been under diminished responsibility when he did so?

(2) If not, what direction ought to be given to a jury as to the approach to be taken to self-induced intoxication which was present at the material time in conjunction with an abnormality of mind which falls within s. 2(1) of the 1957 Act?

The House of Lords, in answering the first question in the negative and over-ruling *Atkinson* and *Egan*, affirmed that the issue was not whether specified causes under s. 2(1) *or* intoxication caused the killing but whether the defendant suffered from an abnormality of mind which substantially impaired his responsibility for killing. There was no requirement that the abnormality of mind be the sole cause of a defendant's act of killing. Even if he would not have killed but for being intoxicated, this did not prevent an abnormality of mind from which he suffered from substantially impairing his mental responsibility for the killing. However, the effect of the intoxication was to be left out of account in so far as it may have exacerbated his abnormality of mind.

5.5.1.2.3 *Substantially impaired mental responsibility*

It should be noted that the term 'diminished responsibility' is not used in s. 2; it appears in the marginal note. Section 2 is hardly a paradigm of legislative clarity as it appears to conflate two ideas, namely, those of impaired capacity and reduced liability. If the accused is to be convicted only of manslaughter rather than murder it is because his impaired capacity diminishes his moral culpability for his act. **The question ultimately resolves itself into a moral one for the jury: whether they think that the accused deserves to be convicted of murder or manslaughter.** The jury's response, however, may vary greatly depending on the extent of their sympathy for the accused and the nature of his offence. Thus manslaughter verdicts have been returned on the basis of very little evidence of abnormality, such as in cases of reactive depression or hysterical dissociation where a person kills in response to extreme anxiety, grief, or stress (often in the context of a 'mercy killing'), whereas horrific killings by someone whom all the psychiatrists agreed suffered from a severe abnormality of the mind (paranoid schizophrenia) amounting to diminished responsibility, may result in a conviction of murder, as occurred in the case of Peter Sutcliffe (the 'Yorkshire Ripper').

The crucial question in a case where diminished responsibility is raised in defence, is whether the abnormality was such as to impair substantially the accused's mental responsibility for his acts. 'Substantial' mean 'less than total—more than trivial' (see *Lloyd* [1967] 1 QB 175). In *Byrne* the Court of Appeal stated that 'mental responsibility for his acts' pointed to 'a consideration of the extent to which the accused's mind is answerable for his physical acts which must include a consideration of the extent of his ability to exercise will-power to control his physical acts'. This was said to be a question of degree and essentially one for the jury. Lord Parker CJ stated (at p. 403):

> Medical evidence is, of course, relevant, but the question involves a decision not merely as to whether there was some impairment of the mental responsibility of the accused but whether such impairment can properly be called 'substantial', a matter upon which juries may quite legitimately differ from doctors.

Thus there is no absolute scientific measure; inability to resist impulses is clearly covered but where there is merely difficulty in resisting impulses, the issue of substantial impairment will depend on the degree of difficulty. While the question whether the accused's mental responsibility was substantially impaired is one for the jury to decide, in *Bailey* (1978) 66 Cr App R 31, the Court of Appeal stated (at p. 32) that juries must accept and act on medical evidence if there is nothing before them in terms of facts or circumstances to throw doubts on it (see also *Sanders* (1990) 93 Cr App R 245). If the medical evidence is weak or equivocal or if there is other evidence which tends to point to a contrary conclusion, the jury weigh that evidence and draw their own conclusions (see *Walton* [1978] AC 788). Griew, 'The future of diminished responsibility' [1988] Crim LR 75, points out that it is common practice for psychiatrists in their reports to state whether the accused's mental responsibility was substantially impaired. He states (at p. 84) that one of the reasons why judges have allowed and even encouraged this is 'the convenience of the expert opinion as a device for stretching the scope of the section—for humanely using it to produce a greater range of exemption from liability for murder than its terms really justify'. This helps to explain both the practice of accepting pleas of diminished responsibility and why mercy killings or those performed in conditions of reactive depression or dissociation have regularly resulted in s. 2 convictions.

5.5.2 Proposals for reform

Tracking reform proposals on diminished responsibility is like trying to map ever-shifting sandbanks. Both the Butler Committee and the Criminal Law Revision Committee, *Fourteenth Report: Offences Against the Person* (Cmnd 7844) recommended that the diminished responsibility defence should be revised. They agreed that s. 2 had created problems for doctors, judges, and juries. The section confuses issues of legal responsibility or liability and moral culpability. Doctors may be able to testify as to the accused's mental condition and its likely effects but they should not be required to testify as to legal or moral responsibility. Likewise, juries are asked to determine whether there was an abnormality of mind which is not a medical term, and then to determine if this affected his moral culpability to such an extent as to reduce his legal liability. These are difficult concepts for any jury and it is not surprising that counsel and judges prefer to settle these matters with a guilty plea wherever possible.

The Law Commission in its Draft Criminal Code largely adopted the Butler Committee's recommendations for a revised defence. Clause 56 of their Draft Code provided:

(1) A person who, but for this section, would be guilty of murder is not guilty of murder if, at the time of his act, he is suffering from such mental abnormality as is a substantial enough reason to reduce his offence to manslaughter.
(2) In this section 'mental abnormality' means mental illness, arrested or incomplete development of mind, psychopathic disorder, and any other disorder or disability of mind, except intoxication.
(3) Where a person suffering from mental abnormality is also intoxicated, this section applies only where it would apply if he were not intoxicated.

This defence is founded on the concept of 'mental abnormality' which is given a definition the same as that of mental disorder in s. 1(2) of the Mental Health Act 1983. There is no requirement, however, for the mental abnormality to arise from 'specified causes'. This, perhaps, recognises the fact that the parenthesis in s. 2 was of little relevance because many psychiatrists were prepared to give, and courts to accept, a very liberal interpretation of the term 'inherent causes'. Clause 56, therefore, if enacted, would simply have codified the practice which had grown up and legitimised it.

On finding the accused to be suffering from a mental abnormality, the jury would return a manslaughter verdict if they considered that the abnormality 'is a substantial enough reason to reduce his offence to manslaughter'. This would have involved a major change in practice. Psychiatrists have been prepared to testify that the accused's mental responsibility was substantially impaired and courts have engaged in the pretence that this is an expression of expert opinion which justifies their acceptance of a guilty plea to manslaughter. This pretence would not be possible under the proposed test as only a jury can answer the question whether the mental abnormality is a substantial enough reason to reduce the accused's offence to manslaughter. It would therefore be of crucial importance that the psychiatrists' description of the effects of the diagnosed mental abnormality on the accused's behaviour, in terms of his perceptions, comprehension, rationality, and will-power, provided the jury with information which would assist them in determining his mental responsibility. This could hardly be considered an improvement on s. 2. Unsurprisingly no progress was made in bringing this revised defence to the statute books. In their Report *Partial Defences to Murder* (Law Com No. 290), the Law Commission shifted their position recommending that for as long as the law of murder remains as it is, and conviction carries a mandatory sentence of life imprisonment, there should be no change to the law on diminished responsibility. The Law Commission considered that while the then current law had its faults, it did not cause injustice and none of the proposals for reform would sufficiently improve the law to make legislation worthwhile (see paras. 5.86–5.87).

In their most recent report, *Murder, Manslaughter and Infanticide* (Law Com No. 304), the Law Commission discovered a new sandbank and proposed a completely new formulation of the diminished responsibility defence. This reflects the fact that in this same report they also recommended the reform of homicide to create two offences of murder—first degree and second degree (see **9.2.2** *post*). The Law Commission recommended the following definition (para. 5.112):

(a) a person who would otherwise be guilty of first degree murder is guilty of second degree murder if, at the time he or she played his or her part in the killing, his or her capacity to:
   (i)   understand the nature of his or her conduct; or
   (ii) form a rational judgement; or
   (iii) control him or herself, was substantially impaired by an abnormality of mental functioning arising from a recognised medical condition, developmental immaturity in a defendant under the age of eighteen, or a combination of both; and

(b) the abnormality, the developmental immaturity, or the combination of both provides an explanation for the defendant's conduct in carrying out or taking part in the killing.

This recommendation is based on a desire for a clearer definition which is better able to accommodate developments in expert diagnostic practice. The focus of the defence is upon the defendant's capacity which must be impaired in one of three ways as a result of one of two causes or a combination of them. The first is an 'abnormality of mental functioning arising from a recognised medical condition'. Thus psychotic disorders and neurotic disorders (such as post traumatic stress disorder) would be covered. This terminology is favoured by psychiatrists who will be required to offer an opinion on (1) whether D was suffering from an abnormality of mental functioning stemming from a recognised medical condition; and (2) whether and in what way the abnormality had an impact on D's capacities (see para. 5.117). It is then for the jury to decide if, in light of that evidence, D's mental capacity, in terms of understanding, judgement, or control, has been substantially impaired. The second cause is that of developmental immaturity in a defendant under the age of 18. This is a new cause which has not featured in previous reform recommendations. This proposal recognises the very low age of criminal responsibility that exists in England and Wales. There is the potential for unfairness, and hence injustice, where owing to developmental immaturity, a defendant does not have the understanding, judgement, and control that might be expected of an adult. As children mature at different rates, and biological and social and environmental factors may impact upon that development, this recommendation has the virtue of seeking to make allowances for those different factors. The potential for impaired capacity to arise from a combination of an abnormality of mental functioning and developmental immaturity, is also catered for thereby relieving psychiatrists of the impossible responsibility of trying to disentangle the contribution of these complex causes to a juvenile defendant's impaired capacity.

In the Consultation Paper, *Murder, manslaughter and infanticide: proposals for reform of the law* CP19/08, the Ministry of Justice presented the Government's response to the Law Commission's proposals. The Government accepted the need for a new partial defence of diminished responsibility based on the concept of a 'recognised medical condition'. Rather than providing an explanation for the defendant's behaviour, the Government proposed that the abnormality of mind 'should cause, or be a significant contributory factor in causing, the defendant's conduct.' They rejected, however, the proposal for 'developmental immaturity' to be a cause of the abnormality of mental functioning. The Government did not consider that the absence of such a provision was causing significant problems in practice, and also considered that there was a risk that such a provision might catch inappropriate cases.

In January 2009 the Government published a summary of the responses to the consultation and outlined its position in *Summary of Responses and Government Position: Response to Consultation CP(R) 19/08*. The amended diminished responsibility defence was duly enacted by s. 52 of the Coroners and Justice Act 2009.

5.5.3 The new diminished responsibility defence

Section 52 of the Coroners and Justice Act 2009 replaces s. 2(1) of the Homicide Act 1957 with three new subsections, (1), (1A), and (1B). **The effect of a successful plea of diminished responsibility remains the same, a verdict of manslaughter rather than murder, and the burden remains on the defence to prove the**

defence on the balance of probabilities. The aim of the amendments is to modernise the defence so that it better fits with medical practice. The term 'abnormality of mind' has been replaced by '**abnormality of mental functioning**'. The abnormality of mental functioning must arise from '**a recognised medical condition**' rather than the causes specified in parenthesis in the original s. 2. Rather than having to show his mental responsibility was substantially impaired, D will now have to show that his ability to do one or more things, namely, **to understand the nature of his conduct, to form a rational judgement, or to exercise self-control**, were substantially impaired. The new defence will also be more restricted as D will have to show, in addition, that his abnormality of mental functioning **caused or was a significant contributory factor in causing, D's conduct in killing**. The overlap between insanity and diminished responsibility is now very marked; rather than diminished responsibility being the defence of choice it may be that greater reliance will be placed on the insanity defence. Only time will tell whether this becomes one of the unintended outcomes of the reform.

While the new defence reflects some of the proposals made by the Law Commission, the Government remained adamant that developmental immaturity would not be recognised as a ground for raising the defence. The Government was insistent that cases of abnormal immaturity on the part of a child would fall within general recognised medical conditions such as learning disabilities and autistic spectrum disorders. This, perhaps, is unduly optimistic and certainly does not address the problem of the 10-year-old who does not have the developmental maturity of an adult when it comes to considering his ability to exercise self-control, nor does it address the problem of the child who, perhaps as the result of extreme neglect and/or abuse, but not suffering any medical condition, simply has missed out on the normal socialising experiences of childhood which teach self-discipline, moral values, and self-control. The question also arises whether this omission leaves the developmentally immature adult at an advantage over the normal child as a 40-year-old with the mental age of 10 may raise the defence relying on a medical condition to explain his developmental immaturity whereas a normal 10-year-old will be accorded no such opportunity even though the self-control he may be expected to exercise is no different. When exercising their common sense, the jury, comparing the 40-year-old with other normal adults, may conclude that the impairment to his ability to exercise self-control is more than trivial.

Section 52(1) of the Coroners and Justice Act 2009 provides:

(1) In section 2 of the Homicide Act 1957 (c. 11) (persons suffering from diminished responsibility), for subsection (1) substitute—

"(1) A person ("D") who kills or is a party to the killing of another is not to be convicted of murder if D was suffering from an abnormality of mental functioning which—

(a) arose from a recognised medical condition,
(b) substantially impaired D's ability to do one or more of the things mentioned in subsection (1A), and
(c) provides an explanation for D's acts and omissions in doing or being a party to the killing.

(1A) Those things are—

(a) to understand the nature of D's conduct;
(b) to form a rational judgment;
(c) to exercise self-control.

(1B) For the purposes of subsection (1)(c), an abnormality of mental functioning provides an explanation for D's conduct if it causes, or is a significant contributory factor in
causing, D to carry out that conduct."

The elements of the defence are examined in the following paragraphs.

5.5.3.1 Abnormality of mental functioning

The term 'abnormality of mental functioning' is meant to be preferred by psychiatrists over the term 'abnormality of mind'. The hope is both that psychiatrists
will be more comfortable with the new terminology and also that conditions put
forward by defendants will be tied in more closely to accepted diagnostic criteria
thereby discouraging spurious pleas of diminished responsibility.

5.5.3.2 Recognised medical condition

The abnormality of mental functioning has to arise from a recognised medical
condition. This term is wider than the three specified causes in the old s. 2. **It
includes physical medical conditions as well as psychological and psychiatric conditions.** Thus conditions such as alcohol dependency syndrome, diabetes, and epilepsy which are not mental disorders but which may affect a person's
ability to do the things specified in s. 2(1A), are covered. Depressive illnesses will
be covered so the defence will remain potentially available to victims of prolonged domestic violence or sexual abuse. It is open to question whether some of
the more generous examples of accepted pleas under the old law involving mercy
killings will fall within the new law; there would have to be clear evidence of a
depressive illness having the necessary impact on D's ability to do the specified
things in s. 2(1A).

Psychiatrists and psychologists use one of the two internationally accepted classificatory systems when diagnosing mental conditions: either the World Health
Organisation: International Classification of Diseases (ICD-10); or the American
Psychiatric Association: Diagnostic and Statistical Manual of Mental Disorders
(DSM-IV). It is the hope of the legislators that the new terminology will lead to
claims of diminished responsibility being grounded in valid medical diagnoses
under these classificatory systems. While conditions not yet recognised in either
classificatory system are not expressly excluded, it will be difficult to raise a defence
based on a condition psychiatrists are just beginning to recognise until such condition is included in one of the classificatory systems.

 Question

Is there a danger that pleading diminished responsibility will become too easy if all that
D has to do is show he has a 'recognised medical condition'?

This is a potential problem with the new definition of the defence if the focus is placed on 'recognised medical condition' without paying adequate regard to the remainder of the section and the additional criteria laid down therein which have to be satisfied for the defence to succeed. In *Dowds* [2012] EWCA Crim 281 the Court of Appeal faced this problem head-on in the context of a claim that being intoxicated, intoxication being a recognised medical condition, entitled D to rely on the defence.

> D and his partner P were heavy drinkers with a history of violence to each other when drunk. D, having consumed a large quantity of vodka with P had an argument with her in the course of which he stabbed her about 60 times. At his trial for murder he sought to raise the defence of diminished responsibility claiming that he could not remember what happened as he was intoxicated and that intoxication was a recognised medical condition. He made no claim to being an alcoholic or to being clinically dependent on drink; rather he was electively drunk, his drinking being voluntary. At the outset of the trial His Honour Judge Wait was invited to rule whether or not simple voluntary and temporary drunkenness was capable of founding the partial defence of diminished responsibility. He ruled that as a matter of law it could not. On being convicted of murder D appealed and the Court of Appeal indicated their decision also applied to intoxication by all intoxicants. The Court referred to the general position in English law that voluntary intoxication could not provide an excuse. After examining the Law Commission recommendations for reform of diminished responsibility and the parliamentary history of the new section, the Court concluded that neither could have intended voluntary intoxication to satisfy the criteria for the reformulated defence. Thus, while voluntary intoxication might be a recognised medical condition for psychiatric purposes, it was not one for the purposes of the defence of diminished responsibility. The fact that psychiatrists or psychologists might be able to identify a condition and describe its causes and consequences does not mean that the condition will automatically have legal significance. Hughes LJ explained (at para. 31):

>> The 'imperfect fit' to which the authors of DSM-IV refer is nowhere more clearly demonstrated than in the breadth and kind of conditions which are included in both ICD-10 and DSM-IV. ICD-10 includes, for example, 'unhappiness' (R45.2), 'irritability and anger' (R45.4) 'suspiciousness and marked evasiveness' (R46.5), 'pyromania' (F63.1), 'paedophilia' (F65.4), 'sado-masochism' (F65.5) and 'kleptomania' (F63.2). DSM-IV includes similar conditions and also such as 'exhibitionism' (569) 'sexual sadism' (573) and 'intermittent explosive disorder' (663/667). The last of these is defined as 'discrete episodes of failure to resist aggressive impulses that result in serious assaultive acts or destruction of property, where the degree of aggression is grossly out of proportion to any precipitating psychosocial stressors'. Not all of these are treated by the classification systems as mental disorders, but all are, doubtless, 'recognised medical conditions' in the sense that they are perfectly sensibly included in guides for description of patients by doctors. It follows that a great many conditions thus included for medical purposes raise important additional legal questions when one is seeking to invoke them in a forensic context. 'Intermittent explosive disorder', for example, may well be a medically useful description of something which underlies the vast majority of violent offending, but any suggestion that it could give rise to a defence, whether because it amounted to an impairment of mental functioning or otherwise, would, to say the least, demand extremely careful attention. In other words, the medical classification begs the question whether the condition is simply a description of (often criminal) behaviour, or is capable of forming a defence to an allegation of such.

This is an important decision as it determines that while acute intoxication may substantially impair D's capacity, for policy reasons it is not acceptable as a 'recognised medical condition'. Accordingly, the fact that a condition appears in the internationally accepted classifications of diseases (ICD-10 and DSM-IV), is not of itself sufficient to satisfy s. 2(1)(a). However the Court did not provide any criteria for determining which recognised medical conditions would satisfy the statute and which would not. Clearly there will need to be further appellate decisions before this is resolved. The effect, however, is that the trial judge will rule whether or not the condition D is relying upon for the basis of his diminished responsibility defence is acceptable such that the defence will be left to the jury to determine whether or not the other conditions specified in the statute are met.

5.5.3.3 Substantially impaired ability

If D suffers from an abnormality of mental functioning, arising from a recognised medical condition, this may support his claim of diminished responsibility if it substantially impairs his ability to do one or more of the three things listed in s. 2(1A). This contrasts with the previous law which required that D's *mental responsibility* for acting as s/he did was substantially impaired. This test involved a moral question of degree for the jury to determine. The new law contains no reference to 'responsibility' in the new s. 2 leaving the jury with a factual question rather than a moral one.

As with the previous law, the impairment need not be total but it must be more than trivial. As the thing that must be impaired is D's ability to do any, or a combination, of the things listed in s. 2(1A), medical evidence detailing the nature and extent of any such impairment will be quite crucial in enabling the jury to make their assessment of whether or not that impairment is substantial. The three things listed in s. 2(1A) are considered in the following paragraphs.

5.5.3.3.1 *Ability to understand the nature of D's conduct*
This limb may overlap with the first limb of the M'Naghten Rules where the issue is whether D did not know the nature and quality of the act he was doing (see **5.3.3.2.3** *ante*). In the M'Naghten test the effect of the defect of reason is to rule out *mens rea*. The diminished responsibility defence operates where D has *mens rea* but his understanding is, in some way, impaired. Thus, if D is in a delusional state and stabs V believing V is a three-headed monster, D would not understand the nature and quality of his act such that he would not have the intent to kill another person. His appropriate defence, provided his defect of reason arose from a disease of the mind, would be insanity and not diminished responsibility. By contrast, however, if D suffers from a recognised medical condition which does not leave him delusional but as a result of which he does not fully understand cause and effect, and believing real life is like video games (to which he is addicted) and he stabs V in a fit of temper when V attempts to take a game from him not understanding that real people cannot be revived like the characters in the video game, V's appropriate defence would be diminished responsibility. He has intended serious injury and thus has the *mens rea* for murder. The issue for the jury would be whether there was a more than trivial impairment of his ability to understand the nature of his conduct.

5.5.3.3.2 *Ability to form a rational judgement*
Where D's perception of reality is to some extent impaired as a result of his medical condition, this will impact on his ability to form a rational judgement. For example,

a battered wife after years of abuse develops a severe depressive illness which distorts her perception of reality such that she believes that the only way to escape her hopeless situation is to kill V, her abusive husband. The issue for the jury would be whether her illness had impaired her ability to form a rational judgement in a more than trivial way. While outside observers might have been able to identify alternative strategies for D, medical evidence as to the effects of the abuse on her psychology and her reasoning abilities will be quite crucial in providing a basis for the jury's determination. To an extent, this limb will overlap with the first limb as if D does not fully understand the nature of his own conduct, he will have difficulty in making rational judgements on his own actions. It may be that this limb will provide the basis for future pleas of diminished responsibility in the context of mercy killings if the medical evidence can establish that D suffers from a medical condition (perhaps some form of depression) arising from the demands of continually caring for V in distressing circumstances, such that eventually D's perception of reality becomes distorted and D gives way to V's pleas and kills V.

5.5.3.3.3 *Ability to exercise self-control*

Many medical conditions may have effects upon individuals' abilities to control their tempers and to exercise self-restraint. This limb may operate in circumstances where the separate defence of loss of self-control would not succeed because D's loss of self-control is not linked to one of the required qualifying triggers (see **9.3.2.2** *post*).

 Example

D, a severely retarded adult with an intellectual age of that of an eight-year-old, suffers continual teasing from youths in the neighbourhood. D eventually snaps, losing his self-control and hits one of the youths with a brick, killing him. The teasing, while unkind, does not come close to constituting 'circumstances of an extremely grave character' such as would be required to raise the defence of loss of self-control. Medical evidence is presented, however, that D's ability to exercise self-control is not that of a normal adult and the effects of the teasing over a period of time have led to the onset of depression which had a further impairing impact on his ability to exercise self-control. The issue for the jury would be whether or not the impairment of his ability to exercise self-control is more than trivial.

5.5.3.4 An explanation for D's conduct in killing

The third requirement of the abnormality of mental functioning if the defence is to succeed, is that it provides an explanation for D's conduct in killing (or being a party to the killing) (s. 2(1)(c)). Section 2(1B) stipulates that such an explanation is provided where the abnormality of mental functioning 'causes, or is a significant contributory factor in causing, D to carry out that conduct'. Thus there must be a connection between D's abnormality and the killing; it is not enough that D has killed and that he does suffer from an abnormality of mental functioning. The abnormality need not be the sole cause—so other causes, such as provocation, may be at work—but it has to be at least a significant contributory factor such that, without that abnormality, the other cause(s) would not have operated on their own to bring about the killing. Thus, if the abnormality of mental functioning, in the circumstances, made no difference to D's behaviour (i.e. he would have killed as and when he did regardless of his abnormality), the defence will fail.

 Example

D suffers from an abnormality of mental functioning arising from a recognised medical condition (for example, a brain injury in childhood seriously impairing his mental develop-ment) which substantially impairs his ability to exercise self-control such that if annoyed he suffers severe fits of temper in which he becomes violent. If D kills in one of such temper fits, he could potentially satisfy the conditions for diminished responsibility if charged with murder. However, if the actual killing committed by D is carried out in a cold and calculated way where D planned it and executed it with his emotions under control, his abnormality of mental functioning would not have caused or been a significant contributory factor in caus-ing him to kill and his plea of diminished responsibility will fail.

Under the previous law D may have succeeded if the jury concluded that morally he should not be held responsible for the killing as no causal connection between the abnormality of mind and the killing was required. This is, perhaps, an extreme example, but others may arise, particularly where D is not the principal but is a participant in a joint enterprise where his abnormality of mental functioning may not play any contributory part in the killing by the principal.

5.6 **Intoxication**

5.6.1 **Intoxication and responsibility**

Intoxication may result from the consumption of alcohol or other drugs. As alcohol is the most widely available intoxicant it is not surprising that most cases in which the issue arises relate to alcohol induced intoxication. The principles which apply, however, are the same whether it is alcohol, amphetamines, barbiturates, hallucinogens, or other drugs which cause the intoxication. In an intoxicated state a person's mental powers of perception, reasoning, self-control, judgement and ability to foresee consequences may all be impaired as well as his physical reactions and coordination. In some circumstances, intoxication is the essence of a criminal offence as where, for example, D is found drunk in a public place, or is under the influence of drink or drugs when in charge of a motor vehicle in a public place. Other offences may be committed by D when intoxicated, in which case it is impor-tant to determine whether his intoxication is relevant to his criminal liability.

 Question

Is an accused to be acquitted of a criminal offence because he was, due to his voluntary intoxication, deprived of the capacity to control his conduct or to formulate the *mens rea* required for the offence?

A person who is insane or an automaton will be acquitted because he bears no responsibility for his condition and is not, therefore, responsible for, or culpable in respect of, acts he performed in that condition. By contrast, a voluntarily intoxicated person is responsible for his own impaired condition. If the criminal law treats intoxicated offenders differently from those suffering from other incapacitating conditions this may be justifiable on that basis. If the intoxicated offender is convicted of offences he committed whilst in that condition, conviction and punishment may deter him in future from becoming intoxicated, and hopefully, from reoffending.

5.6.2 The effect of voluntary intoxication on criminal liability

Intoxication is not a defence which may be pleaded in answer to a charge; it does not operate to excuse the accused's conduct. It is no excuse for the accused to say that had he been sober he would never have done as he did (see *DPP v Majewski* [1977] AC 443), nor may he raise a plea of automatism based on voluntary intoxication (see *Lipman* [1970] 1 QB 152). **The only relevance of intoxication is in respect of the question whether the accused had the *mens rea* required for the offence**; he may not have formed the *mens rea* because of his intoxication or he may have acted under a drunken mistake which negates his *mens rea*. If he did form the necessary *mens rea*, however, it matters not that he was intoxicated at the time or that he had done something which he would not have done if sober (*Bowden* [1993] Crim LR 380). If the offence is one of negligence or strict liability intoxication will be irrelevant to the accused's liability. **Where the offence is one requiring *mens rea*, however, voluntary intoxication is only relevant if the offence is one of 'specific intent' as opposed to one of 'basic intent'.**

5.6.3 Offences of specific and basic intent

The law relating to intoxication is essentially the result of policy decisions on the part of the courts. On occasion, however, judges engaged in the pretence that their decisions were, in fact, dictated by principle. Upon closer scrutiny the principles proved to be flawed thereby creating doubt and confusion. The flaws were not obvious when the principles were first articulated but became so as the doctrine of *mens rea* developed in a way which meant that it no longer fitted neatly alongside the principles relating to intoxication. Further developments in both areas have resulted in clarification of the principles although they still do not fit neatly side by side.

The early authorities treated drunkenness as an aggravating factor but during the nineteenth century the rigidity of this rule was gradually relaxed in a piecemeal fashion. As the doctrine of *mens rea* became more refined it was realised by judges that this had implications for criminal liability where reliance was placed on the accused's intoxication. These authorities were considered in *DPP v Beard* [1920] AC 479, where the term 'specific intent' was first coined by Lord Birkenhead. D raped a girl and, while doing so suffocated her. The House of Lords restored a conviction for murder on the basis of the 'felony murder rule' (which has since been abolished by s. 1 of the Homicide Act 1957). This rule stated that where a person killed in the course of committing a felony the accused would be convicted of murder without any need to prove malice aforethought. As it was not contested that Beard intended to rape his victim and death ensued from this, his drunkenness was irrelevant as it did not affect his formation of the *mens rea* for rape. In the course of his speech Lord Birkenhead, after examining the authorities, stated (at p. 499):

> these decisions establish that where a specific intent is an essential element in the offence, evidence of a state of drunkenness rendering the accused incapable of forming such an intent should be taken into consideration in order to determine whether he had in fact formed the intent necessary to constitute the particular crime.

It is far from clear what Lord Birkenhead meant by the word 'specific'; most probably he meant nothing more than the *mens rea* required by the particular crime in question. This view finds support in statements Lord Birkenhead made later in his speech to the effect that the general principle was that 'a person cannot be convicted of a crime unless the *mens* was *rea*' and thus 'drunkenness rendering a person incapable of the intent, would be an answer'. Subsequent cases, however, have placed the dicta of Lord Birkenhead in a different light. It is now clear that evidence of drunkenness is relevant for the purpose of considering whether or not the accused had the necessary intent; **it is not necessary that he be rendered incapable of forming the intent by his drunkenness** (see *Pordage* [1975] Crim LR 575; *Sheehan and Moore* (1974) 60 Cr App R 308). This is also consistent with the effect of s. 8 of the Criminal Justice Act 1967 (see **3.2.3.1** *ante*). But this principle has been limited in its ambit by judges who seized on the term 'specific intent' and gave it a specialised meaning which Lord Birkenhead probably never intended. They considered that it would be undesirable if those who reduced themselves into an aggressive, dangerous, or unpredictable condition escaped all criminal liability; if they did they would be undeterred from reducing themselves into that condition in the future. Thus after *Beard* judges started to speak of offences of 'specific intent' to which intoxication could be pleaded and those of 'basic intent' to which the question of intoxication was irrelevant. Lord Birkenhead had never mentioned the term 'basic intent' and thus had not sought to create any such distinction between offences. He had specifically referred to unlawful homicide stating that if intoxication rendered the accused incapable of forming the intent to kill or to do grievous bodily harm, he would not be guilty of murder but would be guilty of manslaughter. Lord Birkenhead was not sure what the justification for this was; perhaps principle or perhaps the policy that persons who killed when drunk deserved to be punished for their drunkenness. As the principles relating to 'unlawful act manslaughter' were far from clear at this stage his confusion was understandable; he did not say, however, that manslaughter was an offence of basic intent.

The leading case is now that of *DPP* v *Majewski* [1977] AC 443.

> D was intoxicated as a result of taking barbiturates, amphetamines, and alcohol. In this condition he struck a police officer and was charged with assault occasioning actual bodily harm and assaulting a police officer in the execution of his duty. He sought to rely on his intoxication to establish that he was so intoxicated that he did not form the appropriate *mens rea*. The House of Lords held that intoxication was only relevant where the offence charged was one of specific intent, but where, as in the case of assault, the offence was one of basic intent intoxication substituted for

mens rea. Thus an accused may be convicted of a basic intent offence even though, as a result of his voluntary intoxication, he did not have the *mens rea* normally required to be proved, and even if his intoxication rendered him an automaton. Lord Elwyn Jones LC described this as a substantive rule of the common law unaffected by s. 8 of the Criminal Justice Act 1967. He explained how intoxication operated in an offence of basic intent as follows (at pp. 474, 475):

> If a man of his own volition takes a substance which causes him to cast off the restraints of reason and conscience, no wrong is done to him by holding him answerable criminally for any injury he may do while in that condition. His course of conduct in reducing himself by drugs and drink to that condition in my view supplies the evidence of *mens rea*, of guilty mind certainly sufficient for crimes of basic intent. It is a reckless course of conduct and recklessness is enough to constitute the necessary *mens rea* in assault cases.

As a statement of principle, this is open to criticism on two grounds. First, a presumption of recklessness conflicts with s. 8 of the Criminal Justice Act 1967, which requires a jury to examine all the evidence before deciding whether the accused did foresee the result which his conduct brought about. Secondly, if becoming intoxicated is reckless, this recklessness arises at a time prior to the commission of the *actus reus* of the offence and thus there is no coincidence of *actus reus* and *mens rea*. In addition, recklessness involves a recognition of the risk which eventuates in the commission of the *actus reus*. At the time the accused becomes intoxicated it is only general or unspecified risks which may exist; there was no suggestion that when Majewski became intoxicated he foresaw the actual risk which eventuated. Thus the recklessness arising from intoxication relates to a time prior to the commission of the *actus reus* and a risk of an unspecified nature unconnected to any specific *actus reus*. If intoxication is to give rise to this irrebuttable presumption of recklessness which will provide the *mens rea* element for offences of basic intent, it can only be supported as a decision based on policy considerations; it is not one which is derived from the principles of the criminal law. Lord Salmon was prepared to admit to this as he stated that the decision was not one which could be supported by logic but was one which accorded with 'justice, ethics, and common sense' as it sought to preserve individual liberty, an important aspect of which is the protection of citizens against physical violence.

The problem which remains, however, is how to distinguish crimes of basic intent from those of specific intent. One suggestion was that crimes of specific intent were those of ulterior intent (see **3.2.4** *ante*). Lord Simon recognised a problem with this as murder, an offence universally accepted as being one of specific intent, was not one of ulterior intent. He suggested that the crucial factor is that 'the *mens rea* in a crime of specific intent requires proof of a purposive element'. This suggestion, however, is equally flawed as the *mens rea* of murder does not necessarily involve a purpose equivalent to the result caused, for example, where the accused intends to cause grievous bodily harm but his victim dies. In Lord Elwyn Jones' view, the crucial factor in offences of assault, dictating that they were offences of basic intent, was that they could be committed recklessly. Thus, following *Majewski*, there was considerable doubt in relation to the factor which distinguished offences of specific intent from those of basic intent. The only way to be sure was to await a judicial decision in respect of each offence to discover into which category an offence was to be placed.

In *Caldwell* [1982] AC 341, Lord Diplock stated that *Majewski* is authority for the proposition that **'self-induced intoxication is no defence to a crime in which recklessness** is enough to constitute the necessary *mens rea'* (see also *Hardie* [1985] 1 WLR 64). This dictum in itself, however, does not precisely determine whether an offence is one of specific intent; rather it indicates that offences which may be committed recklessly are not. In the recent case of *Heard* [2007] EWCA Crim 125 the Court of Appeal addressed the point.

> D was heavily intoxicated and exposed his penis, took it in his hand and rubbed it against the thigh of a police officer who arrested him for sexual assault contrary to s. 3(1) of the Sexual Offences Act 2003. At his trial D claimed to have no recollection of the event owing to his intoxication. He further sought to plead in his defence that his voluntary intoxication was a complete defence as it prevented him from having the intent to touch the officer which had to be proved under s. 3(1). The trial judge ruled that the s. 3(1) offence was one of basic intent and that consequently voluntary intoxication was not a defence. The Court of Appeal held first that the fact that he was disinhibited and did something he would not have done when sober, and the fact he could not recall the incident, did not lead to the conclusion that the touching was not intentional. A drunken intent was still an intent. If it could be said that the mind of the person charged with sexual assault had gone with his deliberate physical act of touching, the intoxication was irrelevant. Secondly, and *obiter*, they were satisfied that the fact that the offence could not be committed recklessly did not conclude the question whether this was an offence of specific intent. Crimes of specific intent are those where the offence requires proof of purpose or consequence, which includes crimes of ulterior intent. Sexual assault required no more than proof of a basic intent with the result that voluntary intoxication could not be relied upon to negate that intent.

The Court of Appeal placed reliance on Lord Simon in *DPP v Majewski* who drew a distinction between **'(i) intention as applied to acts considered in relation to their purposes and (ii) intention as applied to acts apart from their purposes'**. It would appear that evidence of voluntary intoxication is only relevant and admissible where the offence is one of 'ulterior' intent (e.g. burglary—see **13.2** *post*) or where the required intention relates to a prohibited consequence (e.g. murder—see **9.2** *post*). If the requirement of intention relates only to the performance of the prohibited act, in this case touching, then the offence remains one of basic intent for the purposes of intoxication. Thus basic intent is not limited to those offences where recklessness suffices. The Court, however, recognised that there is no universally logical test for distinguishing between crimes in which voluntary intoxication can be advanced as a defence and those where it cannot; there is a large element of policy and categorisation will be conducted on a case-by-case basis. Any suggestion, therefore, that voluntary intoxication supplies the *mens rea* for an offence of basic intent cannot be sustained; rather intoxication amounts to 'broadly equivalent culpability'.

Proof in the instant case that the touching was voluntary (i.e. deliberate as opposed to accidental) was sufficient to establish liability. It follows that if the word 'intention' appears in the definition of an offence, it is necessary to carefully determine what needs to be 'intended' as notwithstanding the appearance of the word 'intention', the offence may be one of basic intent. If the required intention relates to a prohibited consequence or if the required intention is 'ulterior' then the offence would appear to be one of 'specific intent'. If, however, the word 'intention' relates only to the performance of the prohibited act itself then the offence is one of basic intent. The offence of attempt falls within specific intent as although this is a conduct crime (the intended substantive offence not having been committed) the more than merely preparatory act is carried out purposively—i.e. with the purpose of committing the substantive offence. It is probable also that if *Heard* is followed criminal damage/arson being reckless whether life is endangered will be categorised as an offence of specific intent as the state of mind goes to an ulterior or purposive element of the offence.

The approach adopted by the Court of Appeal in *Heard* is very much a policy one; prior to the enactment of the Sexual Offences Act 2003 the offence of indecent assault, which could be committed recklessly, was one of basic intent. The replacement offence of sexual assault under s. 3 of the 2003 Act requires proof of intention. If the previous understanding of *Majewski* had been applied, this would be an offence of specific intent. As many sexual assaults are committed by persons who have consumed drink or drugs, such a change would have presented the possibility of intoxication being raised as a defence in many such cases. The Court of Appeal's re-interpretation of *Majewski* closes off that avenue of defence.

In cases of offences against the person where the accused successfully pleads intoxication in respect of an offence of specific intent, he will not avoid criminal liability as generally there will be an alternative offence of basic intent of which he may be convicted. For example, if he is charged with murder, he may be convicted of manslaughter; if he is charged with wounding with intent to cause grievous bodily harm contrary to s. 18 of the Offences Against the Person Act 1861, he may be convicted of malicious wounding contrary to s. 20. If, however, he is charged with a property offence of specific intent (e.g. theft), there will generally be no alternative basic intent offence with which he may be charged. In some cases of burglary the accused may have committed criminal damage to gain entry to the premises but many burglaries do not involve any damage.

The effect of the rules relating to voluntary intoxication is that if the accused is charged with an offence of basic intent a plea of intoxication will be fatal as it will relieve the prosecution of the duty of proving *mens rea*. It is still unclear whether the prosecution may seek to prove the accused's intoxication at the outset. There is nothing in the speeches in *Majewski* which would rule this out; as their Lordships treated intoxication as the equivalent of *mens rea* it could be argued that they implicitly accepted the propriety of the prosecution proving it. There is no reason of policy to object to this; if the reason for the intoxication rule is the desire to protect the public, that protection would be effectuated by permitting the prosecution to prove intoxication.

5.6.4 Degree of intoxication and jury direction

When intoxication is raised in defence to a crime of specific intent the question in issue is not whether the defendant was *incapable* of forming the intent, but whether, even if still capable, he did form that intent (see *Pordage* [1975] Crim LR 575; *Garlick* [1981] Crim LR 178). The onus of proof remains on the prosecution to prove beyond reasonable doubt that regardless of the alleged intoxication, D formed the requisite intent (see *Sheehan and Moore* (1974) 60 Cr App R 308; *Pordage* [1975] Crim LR 575). In *Sheehan and Moore* the Court of Appeal made it clear that a direction based on

Beard was not appropriate and was inconsistent with s. 8 of the Criminal Justice Act 1967 (see **3.2.3.1** *ante*). Geoffrey Lane LJ stated (at p. 312):

> The jury should…be instructed to have regard to all the evidence, including that relating to drink, to draw such inferences as they think proper from the evidence, and on that basis to ask themselves whether they feel sure that at the material time the defendant had the requisite intent.

Consistent with this position is the principle that where on a charge of an offence of specific intent evidence of intoxication emerges during the trial which might lead a reasonable jury to conclude that there is a reasonable possibility that D did not form the intent, whether or not D expressly raises it, the judge is under an obligation to direct the jury on this matter as intent is an essential element of the offence which the Crown has to prove (see *Bennett* [1995] Crim LR 877; *Brown and Stratton* [1998] Crim LR 485; cf. *Groark* [1999] Crim LR 669).

Unfortunately a line of cases has developed which is undermining the clarity of this position largely due to two mistakes which are becoming prevalent in judicial reasoning. The first is the assertion (with *Beard* [1920] AC 479 being cited as the authority) that evidence of intoxication must be to the effect that it rendered D incapable of forming the requisite intent. This ignores *Garlick, Sheehan and Moore,* and *Pordage*. Secondly, there is a tendency to regard intoxication as a defence requiring proof by the accused (again due to reliance on dicta in *Beard* which were made before the leading case on the burden of proof, *Woolmington* [1935] AC 462, was decided) when, in fact, it is simply a denial that the Crown has discharged its burden of proving beyond reasonable doubt that D had the requisite intent. Both these mistakes were made by the Court of Appeal in *McKnight, The Times,* 5 May 2000 where Henry LJ placed considerable reliance on the Privy Council case of *Sooklal* v *The State of Trinidad and Tobago* [1999] 1 WLR 2011, where both mistakes were also made. In *McKnight*, a murder case, the Court of Appeal held that the trial judge is obliged to direct the jury to consider the question of the accused's claim that she was intoxicated and did not form the necessary intent only where there is a sufficient factual basis established in the evidence for the claim that D was so drunk as to be incapable of forming the intent or was so drunk as not to know what she was doing. Henry LJ cited with approval the speech of Lord Hope of Craighead in *Sooklal* where he stated (at p. 2017):

> Whenever reduction of a charge of murder on the ground of self-induced intoxication is in issue, the ultimate question is whether the defendant formed the *mens rea* for the crime charged…What is required is specific evidence that the defendant was so intoxicated that he lacked the specific intent which is essential for murder: that is the intent to kill or to inflict grievous bodily harm upon the victim…
>
> This test is not satisfied by evidence that the defendant had consumed so much alcohol that he was intoxicated. Nor is it satisfied by evidence that he could not remember what he was doing because he was drunk. The essence of the defence is that the defendant did not have the guilty intent because his mind was so affected by drink that he did not know what he was doing at the time when he did the act with which he was charged. The intoxication must have been of such a degree that it prevented him from foreseeing or knowing what he would have foreseen or known had he been sober.

Henry LJ then went on to conclude that the test is 'whether drunkenness had rendered her *incapable* of forming an intention to kill or cause grievous bodily harm' (emphasis added). The Court of Appeal appears to have followed this approach in *Porceddu* [2004] EWCA Crim 1043. In an area of the law already beset by uncertainty, contradictions, and strained logic, the two previously discussed decisions have the unfortunate effect of leaving the law in a state of greater uncertainty. If there is any evidence that D may not have formed the necessary intent due to intoxication this should be left to the jury as it relates to the crucial issue which the prosecution are under a burden to prove beyond reasonable doubt, namely, *mens rea*. It is submitted that the earlier decisions of the Court of Appeal are correct in principle and the decision in *McKnight* and the Privy Council decision in *Sooklal* are in error.

5.6.5 Intoxication and defences

 Question

We all know that when people are drunk they may misunderstand or misperceive things and then react in this light. Does this mean they could rely on their drunken mistakes to raise a defence which would not have been available to them if they had been sober?

If an accused is relying on a defence of duress and claims that he made a mistake because of his intoxicated condition so that, for example, he believed he was under threat when in fact there was no threat, his drunken mistake will not avail him as it will necessarily be unreasonable. Similarly, if the accused sought to plead provocation in response to a charge of murder he could not rely on his intoxication as a reason for his loss of self-control; he was expected to exercise the self-control of a sober and reasonable person (see *Newell* (1980) 71 Cr App R 331). Under the new defence of loss of self-control intoxication will also be irrelevant along with all other circumstances whose only effect is to reduce D's capacity for tolerance or self-restraint (see s. 54(3) Coroners and Justice Act 2009; *9.3.2.2.3 post*).

Where a defence is one of justification, such as self-defence, a mistaken belief in respect of the circumstances upon which the defence is founded, will not deprive the accused of the right to rely on that defence provided the belief was honestly held; there is no requirement that it also be reasonable (see *Williams (Gladstone)* (1984) 78 Cr App R 276, *3.6.1.1.2 ante*). The effect of mistake in such a case is to negate the *mens rea* for the offence as the definition of the offence (whether it be murder, malicious wounding, assault, etc.) requires that the act be done *unlawfully*; if the accused believes he is acting in self-defence he does not intend to act *unlawfully*. Thus if D, believing that V is about to kill him, defends himself from the anticipated attack and kills V, he would not be guilty of murder as he did not intend unlawfully to kill or cause grievous bodily harm. If D's mistake was a drunken one, one would expect that he should still be able to rely upon it as the offence of murder is one requiring a specific intent. In *O'Grady* [1987] 3 WLR 321, however, the Court of Appeal took a different view. Lord Lane CJ considered that in such cases there was no difference between offences of basic intent and those of specific intent. Contradicting his own judgment in *Williams* (although he did not appear to realise this), he stated that the issue of mistake should be considered separately from that of intent. This is, to say the least, a novel idea; it is also fatuous as if a person is mistaken he does not have the requisite intent, mistake and intent being simply two sides of the same coin. In Lord Lane's view, however, where the jury are satisfied that the defendant was mistaken in his belief that any force, or the force which he in fact used, was necessary to defend himself and are further satisfied that the mistake was caused by voluntarily induced intoxication, the defence must fail. The anomalous result of this decision, however, is that if D, when drunk, shoots at what he believes to be a stag but it turns out to be a person, he may plead intoxication in response to a charge of murder as this will be relevant in considering whether he had the specific intent to kill or seriously injure a person whereas, if D, when drunk, mistakenly believes that V is about to kill him and he shoots and kills V, he will be found guilty of murder. *O'Grady* was followed by the Court of Appeal in *O'Connor* [1991] Crim LR 135, where the Court held that intoxication was irrelevant on the question whether D believed he was acting in self-defence. The conviction for murder was quashed, however, as the trial judge had not directed the jury to take account of D's intoxication when considering whether he had formed the specific intent to cause grievous bodily harm. What better illustration of the illogicality of the *O'Grady* decision could there be? A jury might be forgiven for thinking that a trial judge had taken leave of his senses following a direction that they must ignore the accused's intoxication when considering whether he believed he was acting in self-defence, but that his intoxication must be taken into account in deciding whether he intended to kill or cause grievous bodily harm. In *Hatton* [2005] EWCA Crim 2951, the Court of Appeal confirmed that the conclusion in *O'Grady* was a general one and it is not open to a defendant to rely on a mistake induced by voluntary intoxication as a basis for raising self-defence whether the charge was murder or manslaughter.

While Lord Lane's judgment in *O'Grady* is unsupportable in terms of principle it was, in fact, a policy decision. Lord Lane considered that where a victim has, through no fault of his own, been injured or killed because of a drunken mistake, '[r]eason recoils from the conclusion that in such circumstances a defendant is entitled to leave the Court without a stain on his character'. In fact, a defendant would not leave the court without a conviction as he could be convicted of an offence of basic intent. In *O'Grady*, the accused was convicted of manslaughter at first instance. In such circumstances a manslaughter verdict could be returned either because manslaughter is an offence of basic intent and thus intoxication supplies the *mens rea* for unlawful act manslaughter, or on the basis that the accused's mistake was grossly negligent, thereby founding a charge of gross negligence manslaughter.

Confusion in this area is compounded by the Court of Appeal decision in *Richardson and Irwin* [1999] 1 Cr App R 392.

D and E as a drunken prank seized V, their friend whom they claimed they believed was consenting, and held him over a balcony. V fell sustaining several broken bones and D and E were charged with unlawfully and maliciously inflicting GBH contrary to s. 20 of the Offences Against the Person Act 1861. Unbelievably the Court of Appeal held that D's and E's convictions should be quashed as the trial judge should have directed the jury that, when considering the question of consent, they should have taken account of evidence that the defendants' minds were affected by alcohol.

Section 20 is an offence of basic intent and one would have expected the Court to rule that intoxication is irrelevant on such a charge. This decision, however, gives rise to the strange anomaly that D's intoxication relieves the prosecution of the need to prove foresight of some harm but does not relieve them of the need to prove absence of a belief in consent. This decision is consistent with the questionable authority of *Aitken* [1992] 1 WLR 1006 (see **10.1.1.3.1** *post*) but the Court of Appeal did not consider the cases of *O'Grady* [1987] 3 WLR 321 or *O'Connor* [1991] Crim LR 135. The authority of *Richardson and Irwin*, accordingly must be open to doubt. It is certainly difficult to find any policy reason to support the decision particularly when one considers that, had D and E not been drunk, they would not have made the mistake regarding V's consent and most probably would not have engaged in such potentially dangerous horseplay.

To add further to the confusion in the area of intoxication and defences, the courts apply different principles to specific statutory defences which provide that a particular belief provides a defence to the charge.

> In *Jaggard* v *Dickinson* [1980] 3 All ER 716, D went to a house which she believed belonged to a friend. She believed, correctly, that her friend would not object to her breaking into his house. D was drunk, however, and had gone to the wrong house. D was convicted of criminal damage and appealed, contending that, despite her intoxication, she was entitled to rely on the defence of lawful excuse in s. 5(2) and (3) of the Criminal Damage Act 1971. This provides that a person has a lawful excuse if he believes that the person entitled to consent to the damage would have done so had he known of the circumstances, and that it is immaterial whether a belief is justified or not if it is honestly held. As criminal damage is an offence of basic intent D could not have relied on her intoxication to negative her *mens rea*. The Divisional Court, however, held that she could rely on her intoxication as Parliament had 'specifically required the Court to consider the defendant's actual state of belief, not the state of belief which ought to have existed'. The Court considered a belief may be honestly held whether it stems from intoxication, stupidity, forgetfulness, or inattention. Thus D's intoxication was relevant to the defence of lawful excuse for 'it helped to explain what would otherwise have been inexplicable, and hence lent colour to her evidence about the state of her belief'.

The anomalous result of this decision is that if D damages A's property believing, because of a drunken mistake, that it is his own, he will be guilty of criminal damage as this is an offence of basic intent and his drunkenness will substitute for *mens rea*, whereas, if he damages A's property believing, because of a drunken mistake, that it is B's and that B would consent to him doing so, he will have a defence.

5.6.6 The problem of Dutch courage

Question

If D, having decided to commit a particular offence of specific intent, takes drink or drugs to give himself the courage to do so, may he rely on his intoxication at the time he committed the offence to establish that he did not have the *mens rea* required?

In *A-G for Northern Ireland* v *Gallagher* [1963] AC 349, D decided to kill his wife and bought a knife and a bottle of whiskey. He drank the whiskey and killed his wife. He sought to argue in the alternative that he either was insane at the time he killed her or he was so drunk that he was incapable of forming the intent to do so. He was convicted of murder. In the House of Lords Lord Denning stated (at p. 382):

> If a man, whilst sane and sober, forms an intention to kill and makes preparation for it, knowing it is a wrong thing to do, and then gets himself drunk so as to give himself Dutch courage to do the killing, and whilst drunk carries out his intention, he cannot rely on this self-induced drunkenness as a defence to a charge of murder, nor even as reducing it to manslaughter. He cannot say that he got himself into such a stupid state that he was incapable of an intent to kill....The wickedness of his mind before he got drunk is enough to condemn him, coupled with the act which he intended to do and did do.

While this may conflict with the requirement of contemporaneity between *actus reus* and *mens rea*, it is an exception justifiable on grounds of policy. As Smith and Hogan argue, *Criminal Law* at p. 309, if the accused had used an innocent agent to commit the murder he would have been liable and thus the accused in his responsible state should be liable for the acts he intended should be done in his irresponsible state.

5.6.7 Intoxication causing insanity or an abnormality of mental functioning

If the accused's drinking or drug-taking produces a disease of the mind, such as delirium tremens, he may be found insane under the M'Naghten Rules. In *Davis* (1881) 14 Cox CC 563, D raised the defence of insanity based on delirium tremens arising from a history of excessive drinking, although he was sober at the time of the offence. In directing the jury Stephen J stated (at p. 564):

> drunkenness is one thing and diseases to which drunkenness leads are different things; and if a man by drunkenness brings on a state of disease which causes such a degree of madness, even for a time, which would have relieved him from responsibility if it had been caused in any other way, then he would not be criminally responsible.

This direction was approved in *Beard* and *Gallagher*. In *Gallagher* there was evidence that the accused was suffering from psychopathy. The effect of this disease of the mind was to weaken the sufferer's powers of self-control, and this would be aggravated by drink. An impairment of the power of self-control does not fall within the M'Naghten Rules although it is relevant to a defence of diminished responsibility (see *Byrne*). The House of Lords made it clear that if the accused's disease of the mind did not bring him within the M'Naghten Rules, this defect could not be rectified by taking into account the aggravating effect of alcohol. It is necessary for the alcohol to cause the disease of the mind and for this to result in the accused either not knowing what he is doing or not knowing that it is wrong.

If an accused pleads diminished responsibility based on an abnormality of mental functioning due to some cause other than intoxication, the jury must ignore the effects of the accused's intoxication when seeking to decide whether the abnormality of mental functioning substantially impaired his ability to understand the nature of his conduct, to form a rational judgement, or to exercise self-control. Alcohol dependency syndrome may amount to an abnormality of mental functioning arising from a medical condition if it, itself, substantially impairs D's ability to do one of those three things.

5.6.8 Involuntary intoxication

> **? Question**
>
> What happens when D becomes intoxicated involuntarily?

Involuntary intoxication may arise in three different ways. It may arise where the accused is drugged by others or his drink is laced with alcohol. Secondly, it may arise from him taking drugs which have been medically prescribed, provided he has taken these drugs in accordance with the instructions. In both these cases he may, in his defence, rely on his intoxication to negative *mens rea* whether the offence be one of specific or basic intent. **If however, the accused is proved to have formed the requisite *mens rea* for the offence, he will be convicted and the issue of involuntary intoxication will be a mitigating factor in relation to his sentence** (see *Kingston* (1994) 99 Cr App R 286). It is no defence to plead that he would never have committed the offence when sober if he nonetheless formed the requisite *mens rea* in his intoxicated state (see *Davies* [1983] Crim LR 741). If the accused knows he is drinking alcohol but is mistaken as to its strength, this does not render his intoxication involuntary (see *Allen* [1988] Crim LR 698).

The third situation where intoxication may be treated as involuntary is where the accused takes a non-dangerous drug, provided he was not reckless in taking the drug.

> In *Hardie* [1985] 1 WLR 64, D was charged with criminal damage with intent to endanger life or being reckless whether life was endangered contrary to s. 1(2) of the Criminal Damage Act 1971. In his defence he claimed he did not have the requisite *mens rea* due to intoxication arising from taking Valium. D took the Valium tablets, which belonged to another person, to calm his nerves having been told by that person that they would do him no harm. On D's appeal against conviction the Court of Appeal held that *Majewski* did not apply. Unlike alcohol and other dangerous drugs which are liable to cause unpredictability or aggressiveness and thus give rise to the conclusive presumption of recklessness, it was not generally known that taking Valium 'would be liable to render a person aggressive or incapable of appreciating risks or have other side effects such that its self-administration would itself have an element of recklessness'. The correct direction to the jury would have been 'that if they came to the conclusion that, as a result of the Valium, the appellant was, at the time, unable to appreciate the risks to property and persons from his actions they should then consider whether the taking of the Valium was itself reckless'.

The Court derived support from *Bailey* (see **5.4.3** *ante*). The test of recklessness would thus appear to require subjective awareness, at the time of taking the drug, of the risk of becoming unpredictable, dangerous, aggressive, or incapable of appreciating risks to others; there is no need to prove foresight of the particular risk which eventuates. The Court did say, however, that the taking of a soporific or sedative drug would not be an answer to a charge of, for example, reckless driving (and, presumably, dangerous driving contrary to s. 2 of the Road Traffic Act 1988).

5.6.9 Proposals for reform

The Butler Committee (Cmnd 6244, 1975) proposed the creation of a new offence of dangerous intoxication. Where an accused was acquitted of a 'dangerous offence' because he lacked the requisite *mens rea* due to voluntary intoxication, a jury would be able to convict him of dangerous intoxication. This alternative offence would be available where the accused was charged with any offence involving injury to the person or death or consisting of a sexual attack on another, or involving the destruction of, or causing damage to, property so as to endanger life. The maximum sentence on such a conviction would be one year's imprisonment on a first offence and three years for a subsequent offence. The problem with such a conviction, however, is that it does not distinguish between the types of dangerous offences which the accused may have committed. A minority of the Criminal Law Revision Committee in its Fourteenth Report, *Offences Against the Person*, proposed a modification of the Butler Committee proposal. They proposed that the jury should return a special verdict that the accused had done the act alleged in a state of intoxication, in effect, 'Guilty but intoxicated'. The court would have the same sentencing powers as are available on conviction of the alleged offence but would be able to reflect the culpability of the accused in the sentence it pronounces. This verdict would also reflect the actual harm done by the accused.

The Law Commission in its Consultation Paper No. 127, *Intoxication and Criminal Liability* (HMSO, 1993) recommended the abolition of the *Majewski* rule and the creation of a new offence of criminal intoxication. In its final Report, *Legislating the Criminal Code: Intoxication and Criminal Liability* (Law Com No. 229 (HMSO, 1995)), the Law Commission retreated from this position following the consultation process in which the majority of the judges of the Queen's Bench Division opposed the proposal expressing the view that abolition of the *Majewski* rule would be perceived by the public as unacceptable (para. 1.27) and they, along with others, asserted that the present law did not, in fact, present difficulties to juries and that it worked fairly and without any undue difficulty (para. 1.28). The Law Commission, accordingly, recommended codifying the common law with minor modifications. The Draft Bill which accompanied the report was, however, unnecessarily complex and thus could hardly be promoted as an improvement on the existing state of the law. The Government duly rejected it in its Consultation Paper, *Violence: Reforming the Offences Against the Person Act 1861* (February 1998 (see **10.1.5** *post*)).

After an interval of 14 years, the Law Commission has returned to the subject of intoxication in a new report, *Intoxication and Criminal Liability* (Law Com No. 314, Cm 7526) which again seeks to codify the main principles of the common law but seeks to do so in a more straightforward way. Essentially the Law Commission proposes the retention of the distinction between specific and basic intent offences but it changes the terminology. Where D is voluntarily intoxicated when he commits the external elements of an offence, his intoxication may be relevant to his liability depending upon whether or not the offence is one requiring a fault element greater than subjective recklessness. Five subjective fault elements are specified which the prosecution would have to prove regardless of D's state of intoxication.

These are:

- intention as to a consequence;
- knowledge as to something;
- belief as to something (where the belief is equivalent to knowledge as to something);
- fraud; and
- dishonesty.

For offences for which a lesser fault element is required, D's intoxication at the material time will mean that he will be treated as having been aware of anything of which he would have been aware but for his intoxication. Thus proof of intoxication at the material time substitutes for proof of *mens rea*, that is, the fault element. This is justified on the basis that by becoming voluntarily intoxicated D has made himself dangerous in disregard of public safety, which is:

> morally equivalent to having the fault element of recklessness as to others' safety. Consequently D is to be regarded as having acted with a sufficient fault element to warrant a conviction for the offence. (para. 2.45)

The Commission proposes no change to the common law as regards drunken mistakes and defences despite the criticisms that have been levelled at the cases relating to self-defence. Likewise no change is proposed in respect of involuntary intoxication. The Report does venture into new territory, however, in seeking to place on a statutory basis the law where D is a secondary party, or involved in a joint enterprise, or where he is charged with an offence of encouraging or assisting another person to commit a crime. Here the recommendations descend into complexity with the prospect that the criticisms of the Law Commission's previous Report could apply equally here and greatly damage their chances of ever being enacted into legislation.

FURTHER READING

N. L. A. Barlow, 'Drug Intoxication and the Principle of *Capacitas Rationalis*' (1984) 100 LQR 639.

J. Child, 'Drink, Drugs and Law Reform: A Review of the Law Commission Report No. 314' [2009] Crim LR 488.

S. Dell, 'Wanted: An Insanity Defence that Can Be Used' [1984] Crim LR 431.

S. Gardner, 'The Importance of *Majewski*' [1984] OJLS 279.

M. Gibson, 'Intoxicants and Diminished Responsibility: The Impact of the Coroners and Justice Act 2009' [2011] Crim LR 909.

R. D. Mackay, 'Fact and Fiction about the Insanity Defence' [1990] Crim LR 247; 'Post-Hinckley Insanity in the USA' [1988] Crim LR 88; 'The Abnormality of Mind Factor in Diminished Responsibility' [1999] Crim LR 117; 'Righting the Wrong?— Some Observations on the Second Limb of the M'Naghten Rules' [2009] Crim LR 80; 'Ten More Years of the Insanity Defence' [2012] Crim LR 946.

R. D. Mackay and G. Kearns, 'More Fact(s) about the Insanity Defence' [1999] Crim LR 714; 'The Coroners and Justice Act 2009 – Partial Defences to Murder: (2) The New Diminished Responsibility Plea' [2010] Crim LR 290.

R. D. Mackay and B. J. Mitchell, 'Provoking Diminished Responsibility: Two Pleas Merging into One' [2003] Crim LR 745; 'Yet More Facts about the Insanity Defence' [2006] Crim LR 399; 'Sleepwalking, Automatism and Insanity' [2006] Crim LR 901.

R. D. Mackay and M. Reuber, 'Epilepsy and the Defence of Insanity—Time for Change? [2007] Crim LR 782.

J. Miles, 'The Coroners and Justice Act 2009: a "dog's breakfast" of homicide reform' [2009] Archbold News 5.

E. Paton, 'Reformulating the Intoxication Rules: The Law Commission's Report' [1995] Crim LR 382.

J. Peay, 'Insanity and Automatism: Questions from and about the Law Commission's Scoping Paper' [2012] Crim LR 927.

J. Rumbold and M. Wasik, 'Diabetic Drivers, Hypoglycaemic Unawareness, and Automatism' [2011] Crim LR 863.

G. R. Sullivan, 'Intoxicants and Diminished Responsibility' [1994] Crim LR 156.

C. Walsh, 'Irrational Presumptions of Rationality and Comprehension' [1998] 3 Web JCLI.

C. Wells, 'Whither Insanity?' [1983] Crim LR 787.

S. White, 'The Criminal Procedure (Insanity and Unfitness to Plead) Act' [1992] Crim LR 4.

W. Wilson *et al*, 'Violence, Sleepwalking and the Criminal Law: (1) The Medical Aspects' [2005] Crim LR 601; 'Violence, Sleepwalking and the Criminal Law: (2) The Legal Aspects' [2005] Crim LR 614.

6

General defences

6.1 Introduction

When an accused is being tried for an offence and the prosecution have sought to prove that he committed the *actus reus* with the requisite *mens rea*, he may respond by giving an explanation; for example, that he acted under an honest mistake or that he brought about the prohibited consequence accidentally. In common parlance such explanations are referred to as defences. This is, however, inaccurate as such explanations are simply assertions that the prosecution have failed to establish an element of the *actus reus* or the *mens rea* of the offence. By contrast, general defences, such as duress, involve the defendant in conceding that he did commit the *actus reus* and that he intended to bring it about but assert that he should be excused for so doing. **Where a defence operates as an excuse the culpability of the accused is negated and he is excused from the normal consequences of conviction and sentencing which would flow from commission of the prohibited act with the requisite *mens rea*.** Thus an excuse operates as a shield protecting the accused from conviction and sentence.

Self-defence and prevention of crime are also usually classified as general defences. If raised successfully such a plea provides a justification for the accused's use of force. **Where a defence operates as a justification the wrongfulness of the accused's conduct is negated as his conduct is considered to have been an appropriate course of action in the circumstances in which he found himself.** Thus a plea of justification operates to cancel the unlawfulness of the accused's conduct; there being no unlawful act, there is thus no crime of which to convict him. Such assertions, accordingly, are not strictly speaking defences but they will be dealt with in this chapter for convenience.

 Question

Does it matter whether a defence operates as a justification or an excuse?

Whether the defence acts as an excuse or a justification is, from the point of view of the accused, irrelevant; in either case he is acquitted. It may, however, be important to others that the nature of the defence be determined as it is possible to be convicted of aiding and abetting an accused who is acquitted by reason of an excuse but not one who is acquitted by reason of a justification. In the latter case there is no offence to aid and abet. It is also thought that conduct which is merely excusable may be resisted by a person threatened by it whereas if the conduct is justifiable it is thought that, in some circumstances, it may not be resisted. This is phrased so tentatively because of the complexities which may arise, as the following example illustrates.

Example

PC, a plainclothes police officer, has reasonable grounds for suspecting that an offence has been committed and he has reasonable grounds for suspecting that D is guilty of it. He seeks to arrest D as he believes he has reasonable grounds to do so under s. 24(5) of the Police and Criminal Evidence Act 1984 (a new s. 24 was substituted by s. 110 of the Serious Organised Crime and Police Act 2005). D has not committed any offence and when he sees PC approach him he fears he is about to be assaulted and tries to run off. PC performs a rugby tackle on D seeking to use reasonable force to arrest an offender under s. 3(1) of the Criminal Law Act 1967. D, believing he is being unlawfully attacked, punches PC breaking his nose. If D is charged with unlawfully and maliciously inflicting grievous bodily harm on PC contrary to s. 20 of the Offences Against the Person Act 1861 he could plead self-defence, as he was unaware of PC's identity, but if PC had been in uniform it is thought that he could not resist arrest even though he had not committed any offence.

Classifying defences is important for another reason; it is possible to limit the scope of defences which operate as excuses by limiting their operation to certain offences. In effect the courts are saying that certain types of conduct are excusable in certain circumstances but other types of conduct are not excusable in any circumstances.

When the accused pleads one of these general defences there is a burden on him to lay a proper foundation for the defence, making it a fit and proper issue for the jury to consider. In some cases the facts from which the defence might reasonably be inferred may have emerged in the testimony of prosecution witnesses. If not, the accused must discharge this evidential burden by testifying himself and/ or calling witnesses to testify with regard to the defence, thereby making it a live issue in the trial. If this burden is discharged (which is a decision for the judge), the prosecution are given the burden of disproving the defence. If the prosecution fail to discharge this burden by satisfying the jury beyond reasonable doubt that the accused was not acting, for example, under duress, the jury must acquit him.

The defences considered in this chapter have in common the feature that the accused claims he acted as he did because of some compelling circumstance which forced him to choose between so acting or suffering some other form of harm to occur.

6.2 Duress

6.2.1 General

When an accused pleads duress he is claiming that he committed the *actus reus* of the offence with which he is charged, with the relevant *mens rea* but that he did so because his will had been overborne by the wrongful threats of another to inflict harm on himself and/or his family. Judicial statements to the effect that duress operates to render the accused's act involuntary are incorrect (see e.g. Widgery LJ in *Hudson and Taylor* [1971] 2 QB 202, 206). Duress does not operate in the way that automatism operates (see **5.4** *ante*). The correct explanation of the way in which duress operates was stated by Lord Wilberforce in *DPP for Northern Ireland* v *Lynch* [1975] AC 653, at pp. 679, 680:

> At the present time, whatever the ultimate analysis in jurisprudence may be, the best opinion...seems to be that duress...is something which is superimposed on the other ingredients which by themselves would make up an offence, i.e. on the act and intention. *Coactus volui* sums up the combination: the victim completes the act and knows that he is doing so; but the addition of the element of duress prevents the law from treating what he has done as a crime.

The reason for allowing a defence of duress is that it is a concession to human frailty when faced with the choice of suffering harm or breaking the criminal law; in such a situation there is no real choice. Professor G. P. Fletcher describes this as 'moral involuntariness' (*Rethinking Criminal Law* (1978) p. 803) undeserving of punishment, a view which echoes Lord Morris in *DPP* v *Lynch* (at p. 670):

> it is proper that any rational system of law should take fully into account the standards of honest and reasonable men. By those standards it is fair that actions and reactions may be tested. If then someone is really threatened with death or serious injury unless he does what he is told to do is the law to pay no heed to the miserable, agonising plight of such a person? For the law to understand not only how the timid but also the stalwart may in a moment of crisis behave is not to make the law weak but to make it just. In the calm of the court-room measures of fortitude or of heroic behaviour are surely not to be demanded when they could not in moments for decision reasonably have been expected even of the resolute and the well disposed.

If then it is accepted that there are circumstances in which an accused should be excused from criminal liability because his act was a response to threats made to him, what are those circumstances? The House of Lords provides a detailed analysis of the authorities in *Hasan* [2005] UKHL 22.

6.2.2 The nature of the threat

For a defence of duress to succeed it is not sufficient for the accused to claim that his will was overborne by threats. The threats must be of a particular kind if they are to provide the foundation for duress. In *Hudson and Taylor* [1971] 2 QB 202, Lord Widgery CJ stated that **the threats must be of death or serious personal injury** (see also *DPP* v *Lynch*) however minor the offence D commits might be (see *Eden D.C.* v *Braid* [1998] COD 259). For these purposes the Court of Appeal has stated **that the injury anticipated must be physical**—a fear of serious psychological harm will not suffice (see *Baker and Wilkins* [1997] Crim LR 497). It is difficult to explain this limitation particularly when the Court of Appeal had recently confirmed that 'grievous bodily harm' includes serious psychological injury for the purposes of s. 20 of the Offences Against the Person Act 1861 (see *Burstow* [1997] 1

Cr App R 144 which has been confirmed by the House of Lords in *Burstow* [1998] AC 147, **10.1.2.1** *post*). In *Quayle and others: Attorney-General's Reference (No. 2 of 2004)* [2005] EWCA Crim 1415, the Court of Appeal held that a threat of severe pain would not suffice, even if that might lead to psychological injury. The Court appears to have come to this view because of the large element of subjectivity in the assessment of pain where it is not directly associated with any physical injury. While not having to make a final determination on the matter, the Court of Appeal indicated in *Dao and others* [2012] EWCA Crim 1717 that a threat of false imprisonment would not be sufficient on its own to support a defence of duress. **A threat to damage or destroy property is also not sufficient** (*M'Growther* (1746) Fost 13) as 'the law must draw a line somewhere; and, as a result of experience and human valuation, the law draws it between threats to property and threats to the person' (*per* Lord Simon in *Lynch* [1975] AC 653, 687). **Threats to expose sexual immorality will also not suffice** (*Singh* [1973] 1 WLR 1600; *Valderrama-Vega* [1985] Crim LR 220). If the accused committed the offence of which he stands charged because of some threat less than death or serious personal injury, while this will not excuse him, it may be considered as a factor mitigating sentence. The Court of Appeal reaffirmed the previously stated points in *A* [2012] EWCA Crim 434, while also indicating that a threat to cause serious injury would include a threat to rape, Lord Judge CJ stating:

> 64. ...Duress cannot and should not be confused with pressure. The circumstances in which different individuals are subject to pressures, or perceive that they are under pressure, are virtually infinite. Such pressures may indeed provide powerful mitigation.... Dealing with it very broadly duress involves pressure which arises in extreme circumstances, the threat of death or serious injury, which for the avoidance of any misunderstanding, we have no doubt would also include rape, and which cannot reasonably be evaded.

While the **threats of death or serious injury** must be a *sine qua non* of the accused's decision to commit the offence, they **need not be the sole reason for so acting** (*Valderrama-Vega* [1985] Crim LR 220). In this case the accused claimed that he had imported cocaine because of death threats from a Mafia-type organisation. In addition he said he needed the money which he stood to earn as he was under severe financial pressure due to a large debt he owed his bank. Furthermore he had been threatened with the disclosure of his homosexual propensities. The jury had been directed that duress was available as a defence only if the accused acted *solely* because of the death threats; they should have been left to decide whether the accused would not have acted as he did but for the death threats.

D may rely on duress even though the threat to kill or injure is made in respect of others. In *Ortiz* (1986) 83 Cr App R 173, the Court of Appeal assumed that a threat to injure the accused's wife or family could do so (see also *Valderrama-Vega*). This is confirmed by the 'duress of circumstances' case of *Martin* [1989] 1 All ER 652 (see **6.3.2** *post*). In *Hurley and Murray* [1967] VR 526, the Supreme Court of Victoria held that threats to kill or seriously injure the accused's common law wife could amount to duress. In *Conway* [1988] 3 All ER 1025 (**6.3.2** *post*) the defence of duress of circumstances was accorded to the accused where the threat of injury had been made to a passenger in his car. In *Wright* [2000] Crim LR 510 the Court of Appeal

approved the Judicial Studies Board specimen direction in which it specifies that
**the threat must be directed against D, a member of his immediate family, or
a person 'for whose safety the defendant would reasonably regard himself
as responsible'** (see also *Hasan* [2005] UKHL 22, where *obiter* the House of Lords
approved this at para. 21).

? Question

Is responsibility limited to that arising from relationship or that deriving from the situation
in which D finds himself?

In *Abdul-Hussain and Others* [1999] Crim LR 570 (see **6.2.5** *post*) Rose LJ, in listing 11
propositions relating to duress and duress of circumstances (see **6.3.2** *post*) stated
that '**Imminent peril of death or serious injury to the defendant, or those to
whom he has responsibility, is an essential element of both types of duress**'.
This proposition was reiterated and expanded upon by Lord Woolf CJ in *Shayler*
[2001] 1 WLR 2206, where he stated (at para. 49):

> ...(ii) the evil must be directed towards the defendant or a person or persons for whom
> he has responsibility or, we would add, persons for whom the situation makes him
> responsible;....We make the addition to (ii) to cover, by way of example, the situation
> where the threat is made to set off a bomb unless the defendant performs the unlawful
> act. The defendant may not have had any previous connection with those who would be
> injured by the bomb but the threat itself creates the defendant's responsibility for those
> who will be at risk if he does not give way to the threat.

? Question

To take a duress by threats example, could D, a passer-by, rely on the defence of duress to a
charge of aiding or harbouring an escaped prisoner where D did so solely as a result of the
prisoner's threats to kill the prison warders whom he was holding at knife-point, if D would
not drive the prison van?

It is clear from Lord Woolf CJ's dictum (quoted earlier) that D would be permitted
to rely on the defence of duress in this instance because of the responsibility placed
upon him by the situation in which he finds himself. Lord Woolf CJ made it clear
later in his judgment that **if an issue arose as to whether 'situational responsibility' actually existed, the matter be resolved by applying the reasonable person
test.** He stated (at para. 63):

> [The defence is to be regarded] as being available when a defendant commits an other-
> wise criminal act to avoid an imminent peril of danger to life or serious injury to him-
> self or towards somebody for whom he reasonably regards himself as being responsible.
> That person may not be ascertained and may not be identifiable. However, if it is not

possible to name the individuals beforehand, it has at least to be possible to describe the individuals by reference to the action which is threatened would be taken which would make them victims absent avoiding action being taken by the defendant. The defendant has responsibility for them because he is placed in a position where he is required to make a choice whether to take or not to take the action which it is said will avoid them being injured. Thus if the threat is to explode a bomb in a building if the defendant does not accede to what is demanded the defendant owes responsibility to those who would be in the building if the bomb exploded.

6.2.3 The threat/offence nexus

Duress by threats may only be relied on as a defence where there is a nexus between the threats made to the accused and the offence he commits in response to those threats. In *Cole* [1994] Crim LR 582, the accused's conviction of robbery was upheld on appeal although he, his girlfriend, and child had been threatened with violence by money lenders if he failed to pay the money he owed them. Simon Brown LJ, relying on dicta in *Hudson and Taylor* [1971] 2 QB 202, *DPP for Northern Ireland* v *Lynch* [1975] AC 653, and *Dawson* [1978] VR 536, stated:

> [I]t is plain that the defence of duress by threats can only apply when the offence charged (the offence which the accused asserts he was constrained to commit) is the very offence which was nominated by the person making the threat, i.e. when the accused was required by the threat to commit the offence charged.

As the money lenders had not nominated any offence as a means by which the accused should acquire the money to pay them, the defence of duress failed.

It is not clear from *Cole* how specific the instructions from the duressor must be. In Cole's case he robbed a building society. If the money lender had told him to 'steal it or else...' would that have been a sufficiently specific nomination of the offence? As robbery involves stealing, presumably it would. But if the money lender had said 'How you choose to get it is up to you; but you had better get it', this, presumably, would not suffice as there is no direction to commit any offence, even though the pressure the accused is under to get the money is no different. In the latter case the accused may seek to raise duress of circumstances as his defence (see **6.3.2**, *post*), but in such a case the issue of the imminence of the peril facing the accused will be crucial; as the peril facing Cole would only eventuate later if he failed to pay the money, he could not rely on duress of circumstances.

6.2.4 The test for duress

Because the defence of duress is founded on the notion that morally involuntary conduct is not blameworthy, some standard is necessary against which to measure the accused's conduct. It is not sufficient that he acted because of a threat; if the ordinary person in that situation would have shown greater fortitude and resisted the threat the accused is morally blameworthy for acceding to the threat. Accordingly, **the test for duress involves both subjective and objective elements.** These were clearly stated by Lord Lane CJ in *Graham* (1982) 74 Cr App R 235, as two questions to be considered by the jury and have since been affirmed by the House of Lords in *Howe* [1987] 1 AC 417:

(1) Was the defendant, or may he have been, impelled to act as he did because, as a result of what he reasonably believed [the person issuing the threat] had said or done, he had good cause to fear that if he did not so act [that person] would kill him or...cause him serious personal injury?

(2) If so, have the prosecution made the jury sure that a sober person of reasonable firmness, sharing the characteristics of the defendant, would not have responded to whatever he reasonably believed [the person making the threat] said or did by [doing as the defendant did]? The fact that a defendant's will to resist has been eroded by the voluntary consumption of drink or drugs or both is not relevant to this test.

There are several points to note about these questions.

6.2.4.1 Burden of proof

The questions are framed so as to **cast the burden of proof on the prosecution** to disprove the defence once it is made a live issue in the trial. Thus, if the jury, while not being convinced that the accused was threatened and committed the offence charged in response to the threat, feel that he may have been threatened and may have acted as he did in response to the threat, they must give him the benefit of the doubt and pass on to consider the next question. Similarly, if they conclude that a reasonable person might have responded to the threat in the same way as the accused, the benefit of the doubt again would have to be given to the accused. It is not for the accused to prove duress but for the prosecution to disprove it.

6.2.4.2 Subjective and objective standards

The first question as framed by Lord Lane CJ in *Graham* focuses on the subjective issue of whether the accused did (or may have done) as he did because of the threats he believed had been made. Although framed as a subjective question, the question also contained an objective element, namely, that the accused's belief could only avail him where it is a reasonable one and it gives rise to *good cause* to fear death or serious personal injury. In determining the first question in duress it was believed that any condition from which D suffered which may have affected his perception should not be taken into account in determining the reasonableness of his belief. Thus **if D's belief was irrational, he could not rely on it and the defence of duress would fail at this stage without the jury having to proceed to the second question in Lord Lane CJ's test.**

The first chink in this position was created by the Divisional Court in *DPP* v *Rogers* [1998] Crim LR 202 where *obiter* there is a suggestion by Brooke LJ that references in the first question to the defendant's 'reasonable belief' were mistaken. In *Martin* [2000] 2 Cr App R 42, D suffered from schizoid-affective disorder which meant that he was more likely than others to regard things said to him as threatening and to believe that such threats would be carried out. The trial judge ruled that evidence of this condition was irrelevant in relation to the first question. The Court of Appeal held that duress and self-defence being analogous (relying on Lord Lane's dictum to this effect in *Graham*), the same subjective approach should be taken in respect of the accused's belief. In other words,

D's psychiatric conditions may provide the explanation for his mistaken belief and thus were relevant to the jury's consideration of the first question. While this may be seen by some as a welcome development, the reasoning of the Court of Appeal is difficult to support. Lord Lane's dictum in *Graham* pre-dated his decision in *Williams (Gladstone)* (1984) 78 Cr App R 276, (see **3.6.1.1.2** *ante*) which established the subjective approach for self-defence. At the time *Graham* was decided D could only rely on a mistaken belief in the need to use force in self-defence where that belief was based on reasonable grounds. Secondly, the Court of Appeal placed reliance on the duress of circumstances case of *Cairns* [1999] 2 Cr App R 137 reading this as having established a subjective test for duress of circumstances. However, that case did not establish such a test; the case concerned a direction by the trial judge that the defence could only be availed of where the perceived threat was 'an actual or real threat'. The Court of Appeal held this to be a misdirection, the issue being whether the accused reasonably perceived a threat of serious injury or death. In *Safi* [2003] EWCA Crim 1809 the Court of Appeal confirmed that **it is not necessary to establish that there actually was a threat, it being sufficient that the defendant believed there was a threat.** The Court, however, did not find it necessary to resolve the issue of whether D's belief must be reasonable or whether it was sufficient that it was genuinely held. In *Hasan* [2005] UKHL 22, Lord Bingham of Cornhill categorically stated (at para. 23):

> But the words used in *R v Graham* and approved in *R v Howe* were 'he reasonably believed'. It is of course essential that the defendant should genuinely, i.e. actually, believe in the efficacy of the threat by which he claims to have been compelled. But there is no warrant for relaxing the requirement that the belief must be reasonable as well as genuine.

Consequently it is unclear whether *Martin* has amended the first question to dispense with the requirement that D's belief be a reasonable one or whether the test remains as it was but D's mental condition is to be treated as relevant to the question, that is, whether his belief was reasonable or not is to be judged against the reasonable man having that particular condition.

The **second question to be considered by the jury sets a purely objective standard.** Lord Lane stated (at p. 300):

> As a matter of public policy, it seems to us essential to limit the defence of duress by means of an objective criterion formulated in terms of reasonableness....Provocation and duress are analogous. In provocation the words or actions of one person break the self-control of another. In duress the words or actions of one person break the will of another. The law requires a defendant to have the self-control reasonably to be expected of the ordinary citizen in his situation. It should likewise require him to have the steadfastness reasonably to be expected of the ordinary citizen in his situation.

Thus, if an ordinary person sharing the characteristics of the accused would have resisted the threats, the accused will be convicted as he is blameworthy for failing to show the degree of fortitude which the criminal law demands of all citizens. If the ordinary person would have responded to the threat in the way the accused did, the accused will be acquitted.

Which of D's characteristics are attributed to the reasonable person?

There has been uncertainty as to which characteristics of the defendant should be attributed to the reasonable person. Some characteristics, such as age, may be relevant to the degree of fortitude to be expected of a defendant; characteristics such as physical illness or disability may affect a person's ability to protect themselves or render the threat more grave to them than to a person without that characteristic; mental characteristics may affect a person's fortitude making that person more timid or pliable. In *Bowen* [1996] 2 Cr App R 157 evidence was called to indicate that D had a low IQ and was abnormally vulnerable and suggestible. The judge refused to allow these matters to go to the jury. On appeal against this ruling it was also argued that evidence of D's low IQ was relevant to the question of whether D had taken reasonable steps to escape from the threat as he had failed to seek the help of the police. The Court of Appeal dismissed the appeal and stated the principles which could be derived from the cases. First, 'the mere fact that the accused is more pliable, vulnerable, timid or susceptible to threats than a normal person' does not amount to a characteristic to attribute to the reasonable person, and psychiatric evidence is not admissible on this matter (see *Horne* [1994] Crim LR 584; *Hurst* [1995] 1 Cr App R 82). Secondly, 'characteristics due to self-induced abuse, such as alcohol, drugs or glue-sniffing' are not relevant (see also *Flatt* [1996] Crim LR 576). Thirdly, any characteristic to be attributed to the reasonable person must be such as makes the defendant less able to resist the threats than persons without that characteristic. Stuart-Smith LJ stated (at p. 166):

> Obvious examples are age, where a young person may well not be so robust as a mature one; possibly sex, though many women would doubtless consider they had as much moral courage to resist pressure as men; pregnancy, where there is added fear for the unborn child; serious physical disability, which may inhibit self-protection; recognised mental illness or psychiatric conditions, such as post traumatic stress disorder leading to learned helplessness.

Stuart-Smith LJ went on to state that psychiatric evidence may be admitted to show that the accused is suffering from some mental illness, mental impairment, or recognised psychiatric condition, provided persons generally suffering from such a condition may be more susceptible to pressure and threats (see also *Walker* [2003] EWCA Crim 1837; *Antar* [2004] EWCA Crim 2708). At what point a low IQ constitutes a 'mental impairment' is not clear, as an IQ of 68 was not regarded as low enough to amount to a characteristic such that it 'makes those who have it less courageous and less able to withstand threats and pressure'. The Court of Appeal, however, largely skipped over the question whether a low IQ might impair a person's ability to recognise or take an avenue of escape which a person of average IQ would have recognised or taken.

In *Rogers*, unreported, 15 June 1999 (Case No: 99/2314/W4) the Court of Appeal quashed D's conviction and ordered a retrial where evidence of his mental condition, not available at his trial, came to light when the case was adjourned for reports prior to sentencing. The reports of a consultant psychiatrist and chartered psychologist revealed that he suffered from Asperger's syndrome, a developmental disorder of autistic personality which renders sufferers from the syndrome vulnerable and easily exploited and more susceptible to threats than others not so afflicted. The Court was satisfied that if the trial jury had heard this evidence it might have altered their view of D's plea of duress.

The difficulty *Bowen* leaves unresolved is distinguishing cases where timidity or pliability result from a mental illness or psychiatric condition from those where it is simply part of the defendant's character or nature to be such. **Provided the mental characteristic results from a recognised illness or condition it is relevant to the objective question.** The reference to post traumatic stress disorder as an example of a recognised psychiatric condition arises from the earlier case of *Emery* (1993) 14 Cr App R (S) 394.

> D, who claimed to be suffering from 'dependent helplessness' (battered wife syndrome), had been convicted of cruelty to a child on the basis that she had failed to protect it from the father (her partner) who, over a period of several weeks, had battered it resulting in its death. The trial judge had admitted evidence from expert medical witnesses which supported D's claim that she was so intimidated by her partner's previous violence to her that she was coerced into taking no steps to obtain help. Lord Taylor CJ, although holding that the medical witnesses had been allowed to go too far, expressed the view that it would have been permissible for them to give an 'account of the causes of the condition of dependent helplessness, the circumstances in which it might arise and what level of abuse would be required to produce it'. Such evidence is relevant to the first subjective question whether the defendant may have been acting as she did because she feared that if she did not so act the person issuing the threat would kill or seriously injure her. In a case of dependent helplessness, the background is crucial and forms part of the duress as it helps to explain the later actions of the person suffering from abuse leading to this condition. Lord Taylor CJ went on to state (at p. 398):

> > The issue the jury had to decide in regard to Miss Emery was, whether or not the prosecution had negatived duress, and therefore the question for the doctors was whether a woman of reasonable firmness with the characteristics of Miss Emery, if abused in the manner which she said, would have had her will crushed so that she could not have protected her child.

In this case the history of violence is all part of the duress so that the jury would be asked to envisage its impact on a woman who, prior to the onset of violence, was a person of reasonable firmness. In the instant case the jury rejected the defence of duress. In each case it will ultimately be for the jury to decide whether an alleged characteristic may have had a bearing on the defendant's response to the threat and what effect such a characteristic might have had on a reasonable person similarly positioned.

The increasing recognition of characteristics to attribute to the reasonable person is diluting the objective nature of the second question which juries have to consider. For over 20 years the Law Commission has argued for the reformulation of the test for duress (see Law Com No. 83, para. 228) most recently stating its position in *Legislating the Criminal Code: Offences Against the Person and General Principles* (Law Com No. 218). Duress is defined in cl. 25(2):

> A person does an act under duress by threats if he does it because he knows or believes—
> (a) that a threat has been made to cause death or serious injury to himself or another if the act is not done, and
> (b) that the threat will be carried out immediately if he does not do the act or, if not immediately, before he or that other can obtain effective official protection, and
> (c) that there is no other way of preventing the threat being carried out, and the threat is one which in all the circumstances (including any of his personal characteristics that affect its gravity) he cannot reasonably be expected to resist.

This makes it clear that with regard to the second question for the jury to consider in duress, the Law Commission is of the opinion that the focus should not be on whether a reasonable person would have resisted the threat, but rather on the accused's ability to resist it. It states at para. 29.14:

> On consultation, there was strong support for our view that the defence should apply where *the particular defendant in question* could not reasonably have been expected to resist the threat. We do not accept the contrary view, for which there was very little support, that the defence should be withheld from the 'objectively weak'. First, such an approach would be ineffectual as a means of law enforcement. If a person is in a condition that makes it unreasonable to expect him to resist, then he will not resist, and the fact that a different person in those circumstances might have resisted will not affect the matter. Second, the purpose of the defence is not to enforce unrealistically high standards of behaviour. Rather, the defence acknowledges that where the defendant could not reasonably have been expected to act otherwise he should not be convicted of a crime.

This approach is consistent with the Law Commission's generally subjectivist position in respect of criminal liability. Those who favour a more objectivist approach support the current position as it sets an objective standard of steadfastness which is considered appropriate in the context of an excusatory defence.

6.2.4.3 Intoxication and duress

If the accused, because he is intoxicated, mistakenly believes he is being threatened, his mistake will not avail him as such a mistake is necessarily unreasonable. If, rather, he claims that his will to resist was eroded as a result of his intoxication, he will likewise not benefit from this as he is to be judged against the sober person's standard of reasonable firmness. Lord Lane CJ did not advert to the situation where the accused was involuntarily intoxicated. It is submitted that in such a case the accused's case should be considered in the light of his honest beliefs and his response should be measured against the standard of the ordinary person similarly suffering from involuntary intoxication.

6.2.5 **Imminence of the threat and opportunities to escape**

If an accused is to be able to plead duress successfully the threat must have been operative at the time he committed the offence. **The issue is not whether the** threat could be put into effect immediately if the accused did not commit the crime but whether the threat was operating on his mind at the time he committed the crime such that he feared death or serious injury would ensue imminently. In *Hudson and Taylor* [1971] 2 QB 202, Widgery LJ made it clear that what was required was for the offence to be committed under 'immediate and unavoidable pressure' stating (at p. 206):

> It is essential to the defence of duress that the threat shall be effective at the moment when the crime is committed. The threat must be a 'present' threat in the sense that it is effective to neutralise the will of the accused at that time. Hence an accused who joins a rebellion under the compulsion of threats cannot plead duress if he remains with the rebels after the threats have lost their effect and his own will has had a chance to re-assert itself: *Rex v M'Growther* (1746) Fost. 13.

In *Hurley and Murray* [1967] VR 526, the Court held that the defence of duress could be relied on by D even though he was out of range of those issuing the threats, as his common law wife was being held hostage and the threats against her were operating on his mind at the time he committed the offence. In *Hudson and Taylor* the appellants were teenage girls who were convicted of perjury having been denied the defence of duress by the recorder as the threat of harm to them could not be put immediately into effect in the courtroom when they were testifying. The girls claimed that they had been threatened with violence by a gang if they did not give false evidence at the trial of one of its members. While testifying the girls had seen one of the gang members in the gallery of the Court. In allowing their appeals and quashing their convictions Widgery LJ stated (at p. 207):

> When…there is no opportunity for delaying tactics, and the person threatened must make up his mind whether he is to commit the criminal act or not, the existence at that moment of threats sufficient to destroy his will ought to provide him with a defence even though the threatened injury may not follow instantly, but after an interval.… [T]he threats…were likely to be no less compelling, because their execution could not be effected in the court room, if they could be carried out in the streets of Salford the same night.

In *Abdul-Hussain and Others* [1999] Crim LR 570, the Court of Appeal followed the approach adopted in *Hudson and Taylor*. In this case the appellants had sought to rely on the defence of duress of circumstances in answer to a charge of hijacking contrary to s. 1(1) of the Aviation Security Act 1982. The appellants were Shiite Muslims from Southern Iraq who had fled to Sudan. They were overstayers in Sudan and feared being arrested and returned to Iraq where they expected to be tortured and executed. To avoid this eventuality they hijacked a plane at Khartoum Airport and forced the pilot to fly to London where they sought political asylum. At their trial the judge ruled that the defence of duress of circumstances would not be left to the jury as death or injury would not have immediately followed had they not hijacked the plane. The Court of Appeal quashed their convictions as the issue for the jury is whether the threat of imminent death or injury operated on the mind of the defendant at the time he committed the crime with which he is charged, so as to over-bear his will, there being no need for the execution of that threat to be immediately in prospect. Rose LJ stated:

> [I]f Anne Frank had stolen a car to escape from Amsterdam and been charged with theft, the tenets of English law would not, in our judgment, have denied her a defence of duress of circumstances, on the ground that she should have waited for the Gestapo's knock on the door.

As duress is an excuse, the fact that there is a threat operating on the defendant's mind will not automatically result in acquittal. The threat and the defendant's response to it must be set in the context of any opportunity of avoiding the threat whether through escape or seeking official protection. In *Hudson and Taylor* Widgery LJ stated (at p. 207):

> In the opinion of this court it is always open to the Crown to prove that the accused failed to avail himself of some opportunity which was reasonably open to him to render the threat ineffective, and that upon this being established the threat in question can no longer be relied upon by the defence. In deciding whether such an opportunity was reasonably open to the accused the jury should have regard to his age and circumstances, and to any risks to him which may be involved in the course of action relied upon.

It is not enough that there was, in fact, an opportunity for the defendant to escape the threat; to defeat a claim of duress it is necessary for the prosecution to prove that the defendant both appreciated the opportunity to escape and rejected it, it being one which a reasonable person in a like situation would have taken (see *McDonald* [2003] EWCA Crim 1170).

This said, however, in *Hasan* [2005] UKHL 22, Lord Bingham of Cornhill expressed doubts over the decision in *Hudson and Taylor* stating (at paras. 27 and 28):

> I can understand that the Court of Appeal . . . had sympathy with the predicament of the young appellants but I cannot, consistently with principle, accept that a witness testifying in the Crown Court at Manchester has no opportunity to avoid complying with a threat incapable of execution then or there. . . .
>
> It should . . . be made clear to juries that if the retribution threatened against the defendant or his family or a person for whom he reasonably feels responsible is not such as he reasonably expects to follow immediately or almost immediately on his failure to comply with the threat, there may be little if any room for doubt that he could have taken evasive action, whether by going to the police or in some other way, to avoid the crime with which he is charged.

This position reflects the excusatory nature of the defence as a concession to human frailty—but a limited one. While D can always avoid committing the crime in question, the issue of concern for D is whether he can avoid the implementation of the threat. When it is directed at his family, as in *Hurley and Murray*, D may have no confidence that even a police armed response unit could save his family. In weighing these competing factors in the balance, Lord Bingham places priority on the need to prevent crime; D's concern for his family is subsidiary. Its relevance would arise in sentencing when it would be a strong mitigating factor. If the accused is extremely timorous and fears taking an avenue of escape of which the reasonable person would have availed, he will be denied the defence.

6.2.6 Duress arising from voluntary association with criminals

? Question

Is the defence of duress available to an accused who has voluntarily associated with criminals who use violence, thereby exposing himself to the risk of compulsion?

In *Sharp* [1987] 1 QB 853, D had joined a gang which had carried out a series of armed robberies of sub-post offices culminating in the murder of a sub-postmaster. He claimed he only took part in this last robbery because a gun had been pointed at his head by another gang member who threatened to blow it off if he did not participate. He was convicted of manslaughter when the trial judge rejected duress as a possible defence. The Court of Appeal, relying on codes in other common law jurisdictions, dicta in *Lynch*, and the decision of the Northern Ireland Court of Appeal in *Fitzpatrick* [1977] NI 20, dismissed the appeal. Lord Lane CJ stated (at p. 861):

> where a person has voluntarily, and with knowledge of its nature, joined a criminal organisation or gang which he knew might bring pressure on him to commit an offence and was an active member when he was put under such pressure, he cannot avail himself of the defence of duress.

Thus as the defence of duress is a concession to human frailty which will be denied where the accused has failed to avail himself of an opportunity to escape from the duress, so too it is denied to the accused who freely undertakes the risk of being subjected to duress. Several questions arise, however, in this situation of voluntary association. First, must D be aware of the risk of those with whom he is associating subjecting him to coercion, or is it sufficient that he ought to have been so aware? Secondly, must D join the gang or organisation or is it sufficient that he voluntarily associates with them? Thirdly, must D be aware of simply the risk of coercion or must he be aware of the risk of being coerced into committing offences of the type with which he is being tried? Initially the answers to these questions deriving from several Court of Appeal cases were not entirely consistent. In *Baker and Ward* [1999] 2 Cr App R 335, the Court expressed the view that voluntary association does not require joining a gang or organisation, it being sufficient that D has involved himself in criminal activities which bring him into contact with other criminals in circumstances where he could be subjected to compulsion; drug-dealing on a scale which is significant could be such a case. The Court of Appeal in this case also made it clear that when associating with the criminals, the defendant has to be aware of the risk that they might try to coerce him into committing offences *'of the type for which he is being tried'*. By contrast, in *Heath* [2000] Crim LR 109 and *Harmer* [2000] Crim LR 401, the Court of Appeal upheld convictions holding that it was enough to exclude duress that indebted drug users realised that if they became indebted to their suppliers they might be subjected to violence. The Court appeared to dispense with the requirement that the defendant be aware of the risk of the violence being used to coerce him into committing a crime of the type for which he was being tried. In *Z* [2003] EWCA Crim 12, the Court of Appeal recognised the conflict between *Heath* and *Harmer*, on the one hand, and *Baker and Ward* on the other. Referring to *Lynch v DPP for Northern Ireland, Fitzpatrick*, and *Sharp*, the Court of Appeal affirmed that the position as expressed in *Baker and Ward* was the correct one and declined to follow *Heath* and *Harmer*. When *Z* was appealed further to the House of Lords as *Hasan* [2005] UKHL 22 (the House of Lords lifting the order for anonymity accorded the appellants by the Court of Appeal), their Lordships adopted a contrary position. Lord Bingham of Cornhill stated (at paras. 37–38):

> The defendant is seeking to be wholly exonerated from the consequences of a crime deliberately committed. The prosecution must negative his defence of duress, if raised by the evidence, beyond reasonable doubt. The defendant is, *ex hypothesi*, a person who has voluntarily surrendered his will to the domination of another. Nothing should turn on the foresight of the manner in which, in the event, the dominant party chooses to exploit the defendant's subservience. There need not be foresight of coercion to commit crimes, although it is not easy to envisage circumstances in which a party might be coerced to act lawfully. In holding that there must be foresight of coercion to commit crimes of the kind with which the defendant is charged, *R v Baker and Ward* mis-stated the law.
>
>   There remains the question…whether the defendant's foresight must be judged by a subjective or an objective test….The practical importance of the distinction in this context may not be very great, since if a jury concluded that a person voluntarily associating with known criminals ought reasonably to have foreseen the risk of future coercion they would not, I think, be very likely to accept that he did not in fact do so. But since there is a choice to be made, policy in my view points towards an objective test….The policy of the law must be to discourage association with known criminals, and it should be slow to excuse the criminal conduct of those who do so. If a person voluntarily becomes or remains associated with others engaged in criminal activity in a situation where he knows or ought reasonably to know that he may be subject to compulsion by them or their associates, he cannot rely on the defence of duress to excuse any act which he is thereafter compelled to do by them.

This statement of principle by Lord Bingham is quite sweeping. Effectively D will be denied the defence of duress if he associated with others involved in criminal activity whom he *ought* to have foreseen might subject him to compulsion by threats or violence. (In *Ali* [2008] EWCA Crim 716 the Court of Appeal accepted the very broad nature of this test as including in that case a person who D knew carried a knife and with whom D had been warned against associating.) There is no requirement for foreseeable consequences of the compulsion to be offences of the same type as that charged. The exclusion from reliance on duress, however, is limited to the situation where D remains associated with those who have subjected him to coercion. Presumably D's reasonable attempts to extricate himself from their clutches will restore his entitlement to raise duress as a defence if coercion is subsequently exercised over him.

6.2.7 **Limits to the defence**

Because duress is a defence developed by the common law there has been uncertainty relating to its limits.

Question

Should a person be required to sacrifice his own life rather than escape by killing another?

This question has been asked and answered differently by the courts over the last 30 years. In *Kray* [1970] 1 QB 125, Widgery LJ stated *obiter* that duress was available to a person charged with being an accessory before the fact to murder. In *DPP for Northern Ireland* v *Lynch* [1975] AC 653, the House of Lords, by a majority of three to two, held that duress was available to a person charged with aiding and abetting murder.

> Lynch drove a car which contained members of the IRA in Northern Ireland on an expedition in which they shot and killed a police officer. He claimed he was not a member of the IRA and that he believed he would be shot if he did not obey the leader of the group. The trial judge had held that duress was not available to a person charged with aiding and abetting murder. The House of Lords ordered his retrial in which he pleaded duress but he was obviously disbelieved by the jury as he was convicted.

In *Abbott* v *The Queen* [1977] AC 755, the Privy Council drew a distinction between principals and secondary parties, holding that duress was not available to a principal charged with murder. While there may be a difference in the mode of participation it is difficult to see that there is necessarily any distinction in the degree of culpability between principal and secondary offenders; is the maker of a bomb necessarily less blameworthy than the one who plants it?

The need to draw this distinction between principal and secondary parties charged with murder has been removed by the decision of the House of Lords in *Howe* [1987] 1 AC 417. Unfortunately their Lordships did so by ruling that **duress is not a defence to murder whether as a principal or secondary** party thereby reversing their decision in *Lynch*. The reasons put forward by their Lordships at times verge on the fatuous. Lord Hailsham, knowing of many acts of heroism by ordinary people, was of opinion that a law which protected the 'coward and the poltroon' could not be regarded as either 'just or humane'; accordingly the ordinary man, rather than kill another, might be expected to sacrifice his own life. However, there is no general duty to heroism in the criminal law and the standard against which the accused is generally measured is that of the reasonable man who might be considered neither heroic (or foolhardy) nor cowardly being a 'sober person of reasonable firmness'. How would Lord Hailsham characterise the ordinary man whose wife and family are held hostage under threat of death by terrorists if he does not plant a bomb intended to cause injury? If he resists the threat at the expense of the lives of his wife and children is he a hero? or if he complies with the threat at the expense of a third party's life is he a poltroon? This scenario, unfortunately, is all too realistic: there were three car bomb attacks on security forces in Northern Ireland in October 1990 where terrorists held families hostage while the husbands were forced to drive the cars containing bombs to police or army installations.

Lords Hailsham, Griffiths, and Mackay expressed the view that to allow duress as a defence to murder would involve overruling *Dudley and Stephens* (1884) 14 QBD 273, which they took to have decided that necessity was not a defence to a charge of murder. Lord Griffiths stated that this decision was based on 'the special sanctity that the law attaches to human life and which denies to a man the right to take an innocent life even at the price of his own or another's life'. This ignores the fact that the taking of one life may lead to a net saving of lives. Their Lordships also ignored the fact that *Dudley and Stephens* is a case whose ratio is far from clear (see **6.3.3** *post*).

Lord Griffiths was of opinion that the defence should not be afforded to a murderer as the 'defence of duress is so easy to raise and may be so difficult for the prosecution to disprove'. If this is so it is an argument for disallowing all defences. It also ignores the fact that in *Graham* the jury convicted where the accused pleaded duress on a charge of murder and, on the retrial of Lynch for murder, the jury in Northern Ireland convicted. Further it contradicts Lord Hailsham who stated that 'juries have been commendably robust' in rejecting the defence where appropriate.

Lords Hailsham and Griffiths expressed the view that the issue of duress in murder would best be dealt with by the executive through the agency of the Parole Board or Royal Pardon. Their views should be contrasted with that of Lord Wilberforce in *Lynch* who stated (at p. 685):

> A law which requires innocent victims of terrorist threats to be tried and convicted as murderers, is an unjust law even if the executive, resisting political pressures, may decide, after all, and within the permissible limits of the prerogative to release them. Moreover, if the defence is excluded in law, much of the evidence which would prove the duress would be inadmissible at the trial, not brought out in court, and not tested by cross-examination.

Lord Bridge was of opinion that it was by legislation alone that the scope of the defence of duress could be defined, while Lord Mackay believed the defence was too uncertain for it to be extended to cover an actual killer. As duress is a common law defence one would have expected their Lordships to accept the responsibility placed on judges to develop and clarify the common law. Once again Lord Wilberforce recognised this in *Lynch* where he stated (at pp. 684, 685):

> We are here in the domain of the common law: our task is to fit what we can see as principle and authority to the facts before us, and it is no obstacle that these facts are new. The judges have always assumed responsibility for deciding questions of principle relating to criminal liability and guilt, and particularly for setting the standards by which the law expects normal men to act....The House is not inventing a new defence: on the contrary, it would not discharge its judicial duty if it failed to define the law's attitude to this particular defence in particular circumstances.

The rule that duress is not available as a defence to murder is absolute and applies even to a child of the age of criminal responsibility no matter how susceptible he might be to the duress (see *W* [2007] EWCA Crim 1251).

Following the decision in *Howe* there was uncertainty whether duress would be available as a defence on a charge of attempted murder, although Lord Griffiths stated *obiter* that it was not. The issue arose before the House of Lords in *Gotts* [1992] 2 WLR 284.

> D, aged 16, was threatened with death by his father unless he killed his mother who had fled to a women's refuge with the other two children to escape the violence, depravity, and abuse inflicted upon her and the children by the husband. Subsequently D stabbed his mother but was restrained by bystanders so that, although she sustained serious injuries, she did not die. He was charged with attempted murder and sought to plead duress. The trial judge ruled that duress was not available on a charge of attempted murder whereupon D pleaded guilty and appealed. The Court of Appeal upheld the trial judge's ruling and the House of Lords, by a majority of three to two, dismissed D's further appeal. Lord Jauncey of Tullichettle stated (at p. 293):
>
> > It is of course true that withholding the defence in any circumstances will create anomalies but . . . nothing should be done to undermine in any way the highest duty of the law to protect the freedom and lives of those who live under it. I can therefore see no justification in logic, morality or law in affording to an attempted murderer the defence which is withheld from a murderer. The intent required of an attempted murderer is more evil than that required of a murderer and the line which divides the two offences is seldom, if ever, of the deliberate making of the criminal.

The Court of Appeal had been concerned to avoid an anomaly between murder and attempted murder and, in addition, was influenced by the fact that the sentence for attempt was in the discretion of the court. In the instant case the sentence imposed was probation for three years which reflected the mitigating effect duress had in the circumstances. While the Court of Appeal may have been satisfied that no injustice was done to Gotts, they totally ignored the fact that, had his mother died, a matter totally depending on chance and in no way altering D's culpability, there would have been no discretion in sentencing D as the sentence for murder is life imprisonment for an adult and detention at Her Majesty's pleasure for a juvenile. If duress is not to be available as a complete defence on a charge of murder perhaps it should be made a partial defence in the way that loss of self-control (previously provocation) operates reducing the offence to manslaughter. On a conviction of manslaughter the sentence is in the discretion of the court, thereby providing the judge with the flexibility required so that he can reflect the mitigating nature of the circumstances in the sentence he imposes.

While *Gotts* dealt with the problem of attempted murder, further anomalies remain unresolved. In *Gotts* Lord Lane CJ opined that duress would be available on a charge of conspiracy to murder or incitement to murder as they are one stage further away from the completed offence than is attempt. In *Ness and Awan* [2011] Crim LR 645, McCombe J left the defence of duress to the jury for their consideration in a case of conspiracy to murder. This approach seems to ignore the fact that for D to be convicted of conspiracy to murder it must be proved he had an intention that V be killed; this is the same *mens rea* that was used by the House of Lords in *Gotts* to justify denying the defence in attempted murder. It also appears that duress may be pleaded as a defence to a charge under s. 18 of the Offences Against the Person Act 1861. Thus an accused may be acquitted of wounding with intent to cause grievous bodily harm following a defence of duress, but if his victim dies subsequently he may be convicted of murder. The *mens rea* of murder is intention to kill or intention to cause serious bodily injury. In both cases D's culpability is the same and the gravity of the threats is no different but the outcome hangs on chance—whether the victim lives or dies. **Is the logical conclusion therefore that duress should not be available on a charge under s. 18? Or is it conceivable that the House of Lords were right in *Lynch* but wrong in *Howe*?** In *Gotts* in the Court of Appeal Lord Lane CJ stated, somewhat dismissively, that there would be anomalies wherever the line was drawn. Lord Jauncey, in the House of Lords, was of the same opinion. It is a sad day when the Lord Chief Justice of England and a Law Lord are not perturbed by anomalies in the criminal law which are the creation of the judges and which are capable of wreaking gross injustices.

The other offence over which there is uncertainty is treason. In *Steane* [1947] KB 997, Lord Goddard CJ took the view that duress was not available on such a charge before doing considerable violence to the definition of intention to permit the quashing of the appellant's conviction (see **3.2.3.2** ante). This decision must be considered *per incuriam*; in *Purdy* (1945) 10 JCL 182, Oliver J directed the jury that on a charge of treason based on assisting with German propaganda while a prisoner of war, fear of death would be a defence. In *Lynch* their Lordships cited this case along with *Oldcastle* (1419) 1 Hale PC 50, *M'Growther* (1746) Fost 13, and *Stratton* (1779) 1 Doug KB 239, which all recognised the availability of duress on certain charges of treason but it would not be available as a defence to treason involving the death of the Sovereign (see *Axtell* (1660) Kel 13, cited by Lord Simon at 697).

When duress arises in a new situation, the courts adopt the approach articulated by the Court of Appeal in *R v Abdul-Hussain* [1999] Crim LR 570 and the proposition that:

> Unless and until Parliament provides otherwise, the defence of duress, whether by threats or from circumstances, is generally available in relation to all substantive crimes, except murder, attempted murder and some forms of treason (*R v Pommell* [1995] 2 Cr App R 607, 615C).

This approach was affirmed by the Court of Appeal in *Shayler* [2001] 1 WLR 2206 when holding that the defence was available to charges under the Official Secrets Act 1989.

6.3 Necessity

6.3.1 General

The question whether there is a general defence of necessity in English law has long taxed criminal lawyers. Duress relates to the situation where a person commits an offence to avoid the greater evil of death or serious injury to himself or another threatened by a third party. **Necessity relates to the situation where a person commits an offence to avoid the greater evil to himself or another**

**which would ensue from objective dangers arising from the circumstances
in which he or that other are placed.** While duress operates as an excuse it was
thought that necessity, if it existed as a defence, operated as a justification rendering the accused's conduct lawful. But is there such a defence?

Early writers on English law such as Bracton, Coke, and Hale all quoted maxims
which conceded that necessity might justify conduct which would otherwise be
unlawful. In *Moore* v *Hussey* (1609) Hob 96, Hobart J stated 'All laws admit certain
cases of just excuse, when they are offended in the letter, and where the offender is
under necessity, either of compulsion or inconvenience'. Examples given by these
writers of necessity were: pulling down a house to prevent a fire spreading; a prisoner escaping from a burning jail although statute made prison-breach a felony;
jettisoning cargo to save a vessel in a storm (see *Mouse's Case* (1620) 12 Co Rep 63).

In several traffic cases there are *obiter dicta* to the effect that there is a defence
of necessity. In *Johnson* v *Phillips* [1976] 1 WLR 65, Wien J stated that a constable
would be entitled to direct motorists to disobey traffic regulations if this was reasonably necessary for the protection of life or property. In *Woods* v *Richards* [1977]
RTR 201, Eveleigh J stated that the defence of necessity depended on the degree of
emergency which existed or the alternative danger to be averted.

Despite these authorities and dicta there was still uncertainty in the law as there
were other *obiter dicta* which suggested there was no defence of necessity. In *Buckoke*
v *GLC* [1971] Ch 655, Lord Denning stated (at p. 668):

> A driver of a fire engine with ladders approaches the traffic lights. He sees 200 yards
> down the road a blazing house with a man at an upstairs window in extreme peril. The
> road is clear in all directions. At that moment the lights turn red. Is the driver to wait for
> 60 seconds, or more, for the lights to turn to green? If the driver waits for that time, the
> man's life will be lost. I suggested to both counsel that the driver might be excused in
> crossing the lights to save the man. He might have the defence of necessity. Both coun-
> sel denied it. They would not allow him any defence in law. The circumstances went
> to mitigation, they said, and did not take away his guilt. If counsel are correct—and
> I accept that they are—nevertheless such a man should not be prosecuted. He should
> be congratulated.

It seems strange that the law should operate in a way such as to discourage appropriate conduct; but this it seems to do and little reliance can be placed on the good
sense of prosecuting authorities not to prosecute in such circumstances as the following case illustrates. In *Kitson* (1955) 39 Cr App R 66, D, who had been drinking
and had fallen asleep in a car in which he was the passenger, woke to find the driver
gone and the car careering down a hill. He took control of the vehicle and steered
it to safety. He was prosecuted and convicted of driving under the influence of
drink. Obviously he should have preferred to die himself or allow the car to kill
others rather than take control of it while under the influence of alcohol! Would
Lord Denning have congratulated Mr Kitson if he had shown great fortitude and
restraint and, rather than be labelled a criminal, he had permitted the car to continue on its course at the expense of the lives of several pedestrians? Presumably he
would as in *London Borough of Southwark* v *Williams* [1971] 2 All ER 175 he stated (at
p. 179) 'Necessity would open a door which no man could shut.... The plea would
be an excuse for all sorts of wrongdoing. So the courts must, for the sake of law and
order, take a firm stand'.

A counter argument to this position is that the criminal law should not only be used to discourage inappropriate conduct but should, by means of exceptions to criminal liability, also encourage appropriate conduct.

Statute may effectively incorporate a defence of necessity. In *DPP* v *Harris* [1995] 1 Cr App R 170, D, a police officer, was charged with driving without due care and attention, contrary to s. 3 of the Road Traffic Act 1988, having collided with another vehicle after driving through a red traffic light in pursuit of a vehicle believed to contain armed robbers. Regulation 34(1)(b) of the Traffic Signs Regulations 1981 permits police vehicles to cross traffic lights showing red provided that to do so does not involve the likelihood of danger to the driver of any other vehicle. The Divisional Court took the view that this regulation provided the only defence available to a charge of careless driving in these circumstances and therefore excluded any general defence of necessity.

By contrast, in *Cichon* v *DPP* [1994] Crim LR 918, the Divisional Court held that the offence of allowing a pit bull terrier to be in a public place without being muzzled, contrary to s. 1(2)(d) of the Dangerous Dogs Act 1991, was an absolute offence and Parliament could not have intended any defence of necessity to apply. In the instant case the owner had removed the dog's muzzle because the dog had kennel cough and the owner considered it cruel to keep it muzzled while it was coughing. Schiemann J, while being prepared to assume that in some circumstances a defence of necessity could be raised by a defendant, stated:

> The Act does not in terms (and nor in my judgment does the common law) allow the person in control of the dog to make a value judgment as between what is good for the dog and what is good for the rest of mankind. We have here an absolute prohibition and a breach of that prohibition is to be followed by an order for the dog's destruction, however blameless the dog and its owner....No doubt the justification for this hard law was thought to be a desire to protect the public from such dogs....

Schiemann J's position, therefore, is to hold that in no circumstances can the anticipated harm to the dog (property) outweigh the potential harm to persons which such an unmuzzled dog might cause. This does leave open the possibility that a defence of necessity might avail where removal of the muzzle is for the purpose of avoiding harm to persons.

 Example

D, while taking his pit bull terrier for a walk, sees E entering a bank armed with a gun. D follows E and observes him threatening the cashier with the gun. D removes the muzzle from the dog which then attacks E, biting the arm which is holding the gun and as a result of which D arrests E. In this case the value judgement would be between harm to the robber and the potential harm to the cashier. It would be difficult to believe that the courts would deny a defence of necessity in these circumstances.

In several twentieth-century cases the defence of necessity was implicitly recognised. In *Bourne* [1938] 3 All ER 615, an obstetric surgeon was charged with unlawfully using an instrument with intent to procure a miscarriage, contrary to

s. 58 of the Offences Against the Person Act 1861, having performed an abortion on a 14-year-old girl who was the victim of a violent rape. MacNaghten J dealt with the matter from the point of view of the meaning of 'unlawfully' in s. 58 avoiding express mention of necessity. The jury acquitted after being directed that the accused would not have been acting unlawfully if he acted in good faith to save the girl's life. He stated (at p. 620) that 'the unborn child in the womb must not be destroyed unless the destruction of that child is for the purpose of preserving the yet more precious life of the mother'. If what was done was not unlawful it was justified; the only justification which covers this choice between evils is necessity. A similar approach was adopted in *Gillick* v *West Norfolk and Wisbech AHA* [1986] AC 112, where the House of Lords stated that a doctor who prescribed contraceptives for a girl under 16 would not be guilty of aiding, abetting, counselling, or procuring the offence of unlawful sexual intercourse committed by her with a man, provided he honestly believed his action to be necessary for the physical, mental, and emotional health of the girl. Lord Scarman stated (at p. 190):

> The bona fide exercise by a doctor of his clinical judgment must be a complete negation of the guilty mind which is an essential ingredient of the criminal offence of aiding and abetting the commission of unlawful sexual intercourse.

The doctor's motive for prescribing contraceptives was, however, irrelevant if he knew that this would have encouraged an underage girl to engage in sexual intercourse (see **3.2.3.2** *ante*). Would it not have been more honest for the House of Lords to state openly that necessity would be a defence instead of further confusing intention by declaring that motive may negate guilty mind? (See now s. 73 of the Sexual Offences Act 2003 which expressly legislates that a doctor, in these circumstances, is not guilty of aiding, abetting, or counselling the commission of a sexual offence against the child.)

In *In re F (Mental Patient: Sterilisation)* [1990] 2 AC 1, a House of Lords' decision referring to necessity, it was held to be lawful to carry out a sterilisation operation on a mental patient who lacked the capacity to consent as there was a grave risk that she would become pregnant which would have had disastrous psychiatric consequences for her. Lord Brandon of Oakbrook considered that operations on patients incapable of consenting would be lawful provided they were carried out to save life or to ensure improvement or prevent deterioration in the patient's physical or mental health. While Lord Brandon did not expressly mention necessity it is implicit in his speech.

By contrast Lord Goff of Chieveley did mention necessity expressly. He stated that **the common law principle of necessity could justify action which would otherwise be unlawful in three groups of cases: first, cases of public necessity where D interferes with another's property in the public interest** (e.g. destroying his house to prevent the spread of a fire); **secondly, cases of private necessity where D interferes with another's property to save his own person or property from imminent peril** (e.g. where he enters upon V's land without his consent in order to prevent the spread of fire on to his own land); **and thirdly, 'action taken as a matter of necessity to assist another person without his consent'** (e.g. there is no assault where D seizes V and forcibly drags him from the path of an oncoming vehicle thereby saving him from injury or death). Lord Goff stated that there were many emanations of the third principle and that it was 'concerned not only with the preservation of the life or health of the assisted person, but also with the preservation of his property...and even with certain conduct on his behalf in the administration of his affairs'. His Lordship considered that the instant case concerned action taken to preserve the life, health, or well-being of another who is unable to consent to it. In such a situation two conditions must be satisfied to bring the action within the bounds of necessity:

(a) there must be a necessity to act when it is not practicable to communicate with the assisted person, [and]

(b) the action taken must be such as a reasonable person would in all the circumstances take, acting in the best interests of the assisted person.

Lord Goff's three categories are very narrow and appear to be a long way from providing for a general defence of necessity based on a test of balancing harms (i.e. that D commits an offence to avoid a greater evil to himself or another) (see further **6.3.3** *post*).

In *R v Bournewood Community and Mental Health NHS Trust* [1998] 3 All ER 289, the defence of necessity was recognised and applied by the House of Lords to justify the informal detention and treatment of a mentally incompetent person who had become a danger to himself. The formal procedures under the Mental Health Act 1983 had not been invoked but the House of Lords held that the common law doctrine of necessity applied, Lord Goff of Chieveley stating (at p. 300):

I have no doubt that all the steps in fact taken...were in fact taken in the best interests of Mr L and, in so far as they might otherwise have constituted an invasion of his civil rights, were justified on the basis of the common law doctrine of necessity.

While this case is an example of the defence of necessity being applied, the reasoning of their Lordships does not supply any further explanation of the rationale underpinning the defence nor any further guidance on its ambit and operation.

In *R (Nicklinson) v Ministry of Justice* [2012] EWHC 2381 (Admin), the Divisional Court ruled that the defence of necessity would not be available to any person who might assist the claimant, a sufferer of 'locked-in' syndrome, to end his life. The Court recognised the difference between a doctor not seeking to prolong life and positively acting to end life; the former would not involve any criminal liability as was recognised in *Airedale NHS Trust v Bland* (see **2.5.2.2.3** *ante*) but extending the law to cover the latter would involve a major change, rather than an incremental development, involving controversial matters of social policy which it was for Parliament to resolve rather than the courts.

6.3.2 Duress of circumstances: necessity by any other name?

Perhaps some judicial reluctance to recognising a defence of necessity was due to the general belief that it operated as a justification. In Canada in *Perka et al v The Queen* (1984) 13 DLR (4th) 1, the Supreme Court of Canada held that necessity should be recognised in Canada as an excuse thereby implying 'no vindication of the deeds of the actor'. Thus the defence was seen as a concession to human frailty and was based on 'society's expectation of appropriate and normal resistance to pressure'. In *Lynch* Lord Simon expressed the view that there was no sustainable distinction in principle between necessity and duress, the latter being 'merely a particular application of the doctrine of necessity'. Might it be possible, therefore, to incorporate some forms of necessity within an extended defence of duress without opening 'a door which no man could shut'? This is what appears to have happened almost by sleight of hand in several cases before the Court of Appeal. It is a development which was facilitated by Lord Lane's formulation of the test for duress in *Graham*, which did not require that the person from whom the threat emanated should have specified that the accused commit a particular crime; the issue is simply whether the accused may have acted as he did because he feared that if he did not so act he would suffer death or serious injury.

In the first case, *Willer* (1986) 83 Cr App R 225, D was charged with reckless driving. He had been confronted by a gang of youths who threatened to kill him and a passenger in his car. To escape he drove his car over the pavement and into a shopping precinct. When the assistant recorder ruled that the defence of necessity was not available to him he changed his plea to guilty. The Court of Appeal quashed his conviction. While they appeared to accept that the defence of necessity may have been available, they held that the appropriate defence was one of duress. Watkins LJ stated (at p. 227):

> the assistant recorder upon those facts should have directed that he would leave to the jury the question as to whether or not...the appellant was wholly driven by force of circumstance into doing what he did and did not drive the car otherwise than under that form of compulsion, i.e. under duress.

In the second case, *Conway* [1988] 3 All ER 1025, D was charged with reckless driving and pleaded necessity on the basis that he drove as he did because his passenger feared an attack from two men who were approaching the car. The two men were, in fact, plainclothes police officers who were approaching the car to arrest the passenger. At the trial the judge did not leave the defence of duress of circumstances or necessity to the jury. The Court of Appeal felt constrained to quash the conviction, regarding the decision in *Willer* as binding on it. **It saw the defence of necessity/duress of circumstances as a 'logical consequence of the existence of the defence of duress as that term is ordinarily understood, i.e. "do this or else"'; thus it would be subject to the same limitations, namely that the harm sought to be avoided must be death or serious injury.** The Court found support for this position in the speech of Lord Hailsham LC in *Howe* [1987] 1 AC 417, where he said (at p. 429):

> Duress is only that species of the genus of necessity which is caused by wrongful threats. I cannot see that there is any way in which a person of ordinary fortitude can be excused from the one type of pressure on his will rather than the other.

In the third case, *Martin* [1989] 1 All ER 652, D drove a car while disqualified from driving after threats from his wife that she would commit suicide if he did not do so. D had pleaded guilty to the charge of driving while disqualified when the trial judge ruled that this was an absolute offence to which necessity was not a defence.

The Court of Appeal quashed the conviction and Simon Brown J took the opportunity to summarise the principles governing necessity stating (at p. 653):

> [F]irst, English law does, in extreme circumstances, recognise a defence of necessity. Most commonly this defence arises as duress, that is pressure on the accused's will from the wrongful threats or violence of another. Equally however it can arise from objective dangers threatening the accused or others. Arising thus it is conveniently called 'duress of circumstances'.

By formulating the defence of necessity as a form of duress it is clear that English courts regard it as an excuse rather than a justification.

Secondly, Simon Brown J went on to say (at p. 653) '**the defence is available only if, from an objective standpoint, the accused can be said to be acting reasonably and proportionately in order to avoid a threat of death or serious injury**'. This acts as a limitation on the circumstances in which necessity may be pleaded. It is not a mere matter of balancing harms so that the defence would be available if the harm committed is less than the harm the accused feared would otherwise occur. The defence is only available if the harm the accused seeks to avoid is that of death or serious injury to himself or another (see further *Pipe v DPP* [2012] EWHC 1821 (Admin)). By comparison in *Perka* the Supreme Court of Canada formulated the defence on the basis of a balancing of harms stating that there had to be proportionality in that the harm caused must be a lesser evil to the harm averted.

Thirdly, Simon Brown J stated (at pp. 653, 654):

> [A]ssuming the defence to be open to the accused on his account of the facts, the issue should be left to the jury, who should be directed to determine these two questions: first, was the accused, or may he have been, impelled to act as he did because as a result of what he reasonably believed to be the situation he had good cause to fear that otherwise death or serious physical injury would result; second, if so, would a sober person of reasonable firmness, sharing the characteristics of the accused, have responded to that situation by acting as the accused acted? If the answer to both those questions was Yes, then the jury would acquit: the defence of necessity would have been established.

The test for necessity is thus exactly the same as for duress with the exception of the source from which the threat emanates. The test as stated by Simon Brown J is consistent with that stated by Lord Lane CJ in *Graham*, *ante*, as confirmed by the House of Lords in *Howe*, *ante*, and it has been further affirmed by the Court of Appeal in *Abdul-Hussain*, *ante*. In the last-mentioned case the Court of Appeal did draw attention to one issue which may have greater significance in the context of duress of circumstances where the offence committed by the defendant is chosen by him in response to the perceived threat rather than in duress by threats being specified by the person who is issuing the threats, namely that of proportionality. The jury will have to consider whether the offence which the defendant committed was a reasonable and proportionate response to the threat perceived in the circumstances. This is part of the objective question whether a reasonable person would have done as the defendant did.

An interesting attempt to plead duress of circumstances was made in *Rodger and Rose* [1998] 1 Cr App R 143, where the appellants sought to raise the defence on charges of breaking prison. They claimed they had escaped as they had become suicidal in prison. The trial judge declined to leave the defence to the jury which decision was confirmed by the Court of Appeal. Sir Patrick Russell, having reviewed the decisions in *Willer, Conway, Martin,* and *Pommell* stated:

> All these authorities had one feature in common which is not present in the instant appeals. The feature which was causative of the defendants committing the offence was in all the authorities extraneous to the offender himself. In contrast, in these appeals it was solely the suicidal tendencies, the thought processes and the emotions of the offenders themselves which operated as duress. That factor introduced an entirely sub-jective element not present in the authorities....
>
> We do not think that such a development of the law would be justified, nor do we think that such an extension would be in the public interest. If allowed it could amount to a licence to commit crime dependent on the personal characteristics and vulnerabil-ity of the offender. As a matter of policy that is undesirable and in our view it is not the law and should not be the law.

In *Quayle and others: Attorney-General's Reference (No. 2 of 2004)* [2005] EWCA Crim 1415, the Court of Appeal, approving of *Rodger and Rose*, held that duress of circum-stances was not available as a defence to several defendants charged with various offences of possession, cultivation, and supply of cannabis which they genuinely and reasonably believed were necessary to avoid pain arising from a medical condi-tion. One of the reasons to support the decision was the absence of an extraneous circumstance capable of objective scrutiny by judge and jury. Following considera-tion of *Rodger and Rose, Abdul-Hussain,* and *Shayler*, the Court stated (at para. 75):

> [T]he requirement of an objectively ascertainable extraneous cause has a considerable, and in our view understandable, basis. It rests on the pragmatic consideration that the defence of necessity, which the Crown would carry the onus to disprove, must be con-fined within narrowly defined limits or it will become an opportunity for almost untri-able and certainly peculiarly difficult issues, not to mention abusive defences.

The requirements of imminence and immediacy apply equally to duress of circum-stances. In *Quayle and others: Attorney-General's Reference (No. 2 of 2004)* the Court held that the defence could not succeed where 'the defendant was taking a delib-erately considered course of conduct over a substantial period of time, involving continuous and regular breaches of the law.' Expanding on this the Court stated (at para. 81):

> Where there is not imminent or immediate threat or peril, but only a general assertion of an internal motivation to engage in prohibited activities in order to prevent or allevi-ate pain, it is also difficult to identify any extraneous or objective factors by reference to which a jury could be expected to measure whether the motivation was such as to override the defendant's will or to force him to act as he did.

As with the defence of duress, D may only rely on the defence of duress of circum-stances so long as the threat continues (see *Pommell* (1995) 2 Cr App R 607). While initial driving with excess alcohol to escape assailants may have been excusable due to duress of circumstances, it would not be necessary for D to continue to drive a further two and a half miles home (see *DPP* v *Jones* [1990] RTR 34). If D drives off with excess alcohol to escape a threat he will be guilty of the driving offence if the prosecution prove that he continued to drive after the threat had ceased to operate (see *DPP* v *Bell* [1992] Crim LR 176; *DPP* v *Mullally* [2006] EWHC 3448 (Admin)).

6.3.3 The limits of duress of circumstances

The defence of necessity recognised as duress of circumstances is subject to the same limitations as the defence of duress (see *Pommell* (1995) 2 Cr App R 607). The positive result of this is that it implies that necessity could be pleaded by a thief if he stole food to save himself from starvation thereby refuting the dictum of Lord Denning in *London Borough of Southwark* v *Williams* [1971] 2 All ER 175 at 179, that 'if hunger were once allowed to be an excuse for stealing, it would open a door through which all kinds of lawlessness and disorder would pass'. The negative results, however, are that necessity in this form is an excuse and is not available on a charge of murder or attempted murder. Things have thus come full circle; in *Howe* their Lordships used the case of *Dudley and Stephens* as authority that necessity was not a defence to murder and thus duress should not be a defence to murder. *Howe* was one of the authorities used in *Conway* to develop the defence of duress of circumstances/necessity. The case of *Dudley and Stephens* however is open to several interpretations. In *Lynch* Lord Simon took the ratio to be that there was no defence of necessity known to English law. In *Howe* three of their Lordships interpreted it to mean that necessity was not a defence to murder. The decision in *Dudley and Stephens* could as easily be interpreted as holding there was no necessity to kill in the situation in which the two accused found themselves. They were adrift in an open boat with another man and a boy after being shipwrecked. After several days without food and water they decided to kill the boy who was very weak and they fed on his body. Four days later they were rescued. On their trial for murder the jury returned a special verdict finding that the men would have died before rescue had they not eaten the boy who, because of his weak state, would have died sooner, and that there was no reasonable prospect of relief and no appreciable chance of saving life except by killing. However, there was no greater necessity for killing the boy than any of the three men. Lord Coleridge CJ agreed with this last point. Indeed, as the mariners' peril was due to them being adrift, killing any one of them was not going to assure their rescue and thus it could be argued that there was no necessity to kill anyone. The outcome for the two mariners, however, was that they were convicted of murder but the death sentence was commuted to six months' imprisonment.

As *Dudley and Stephens* is such an unsatisfactory authority it would have been possible and more desirable for their Lordships in *Howe* to ignore it and decide the issue *de novo*. There are situations in which killing another may be an appropriate action and even commendable but the criminal law would now discourage such action. Professor J. C. Smith in *Justification and Excuse in the Criminal Law* gives two illustrations. At the inquest into the deaths arising from the *Herald of Free Enterprise* disaster in Zeebrugge harbour an army corporal gave evidence that he led dozens of people to safety up a rope ladder. On the ladder was a petrified passenger who was refusing to move. When persuasion failed the corporal instructed another passenger below this man to push him off the ladder which he did and he was never seen again. If such a situation were to arise again the criminal law now clearly indicates that a person should die and allow many others to die rather than risk killing the person obstructing their avenue of escape. Should not the criminal law promote the net saving of human life? To quote Professor Smith (at p. 77) 'The law has lost touch with reality if it condemns as murder conduct which right-thinking people regard as praiseworthy'.

The second illustration is related by Simpson in *Touching the Void* (1988). One climber slipped off a 19,000-foot cliff in the Andes and was left dangling on a rope attached to his partner. When the partner reached the point of exhaustion and realised that his life was in peril he cut the rope. Miraculously the other climber survived as he fell on to a snow-covered ice bridge below. Again, if a climber was to seek guidance from the criminal law before going on an expedition, he would discover that it would direct him in such a situation that he should die along with his partner rather than cut the rope to save himself.

Perhaps the defence of necessity is available to the passengers on the sinking ship and to the climber. While the narrow defence of necessity recognised by Lord Goff in *In re F, ante*, does not touch on these situations, there are indications in *Re A (Children) (Conjoined Twins: Medical Treatment) (No. 1)* [2000] 4 All ER 961 (see **3.2.3.5** *ante*) that necessity may be a broader defence than previously conceded and that it may apply to killing. *Re A* raised the crucial question, originally framed by Lord Mackay in *Howe* [1987] 1 AC 417, whether 'the law should recognise in any individual in any circumstances, however extreme, the right to choose that one innocent person should be killed rather than another'? As the doctors' duties to Jodie and Mary were in conflict, Ward LJ concluded that 'the law must allow an escape through choosing the lesser of two evils', in which case the operation being justified would involve no unlawful act even though it would inevitably result in Mary's death. This was, in effect, a defence of necessity but there was no clear agreement between the three Lord Justices of Appeal on the limits of this defence. The narrowest approach was that of Ward LJ who was concerned to point out the very limited extent to which this decision should be regarded as a precedent emphasising the uniqueness of the case. He stated (at p. 1018):

> Lest it be thought that this decision could become authority for wider propositions, such as that a doctor, once he has determined that a patient cannot survive, can kill the patient, it is important to restate the unique circumstances for which this case is authority. They are that it must be impossible to preserve the life of X without bringing about the death of Y, that Y by his or her very continued existence will inevitably bring about the death of X within a short period of time, and that X is capable of living an independent life but Y is incapable under any circumstances (including all forms of medical intervention) of viable independent existence.

His judgment offers no hope for the drowning passengers or the tiring climber. Brooke LJ, however, expressly framed the issue in the case as one of necessity. He conducted a comprehensive review of the history and case law relating to this defence concluding that there was no need for an emergency to exist and the threat which constitutes the harm need not be unlawful or constitute 'unjust aggression'. He overcame the problem of *Dudley and Stephens* and *Howe* which would render necessity unavailable as a defence to murder stating (at p. 1051):

> I have considered very carefully the policy reasons for the decision in *R v Dudley and Stephens*, supported as it was by the House of Lords in *R v Howe*. These are, in short,

that there were two insuperable objections to the proposition that necessity might be available as a defence for the *Mignonette* sailors. The first objection was evident in the court's questions: Who is to be the judge of this sort of necessity? By what measure is the comparative value of lives to be measured? The second objection was that to permit such a defence would mark an absolute divorce of law from morality.

In my judgment, neither of these objections are dispositive of the present case. Mary is, sadly, self-designated for a very early death. Nobody can extend her life beyond a very short span.... It is true that there are those who believe most sincerely...that it would be an immoral act to save Jodie, if by saving Jodie one must end Mary's life.... But there are also those who believe with equal sincerity that it would be immoral not to assist Jodie if there is a good prospect that she might live a happy and fulfilled life if this operation is performed. The court is not equipped to choose between these competing philosophies. All that a court can say is that it is not at all obvious that this is the sort of clear-cut case, marking an absolute divorce from law and morality, which was of such concern to Lord Coleridge and his fellow judges.

Brooke LJ adopted the tests for necessity which Sir James Stephen provided in his *Digest of Criminal Law* (1887):

(i) the act is needed to avoid inevitable and irreparable evil;

(ii) no more should be done than is reasonably necessary for the purpose to be achieved;

(iii) the evil inflicted must not be disproportionate to the evil avoided.

He concluded that as the principles of family law 'point irresistibly to the conclusion that the interests of Jodie must be preferred to the interests of Mary, I consider that all these requirements are satisfied in this case'. This amounts to a general defence of necessity based on a balancing of harms and, as such, would apply to the passengers on the sinking ship and the tiring climber.

Walker LJ had concluded that performing the operation would not involve the commission of the offence of murder in respect of Mary as, applying the principle in *Gillick*, 'the bona fide exercise by a doctor of his clinical judgement [is a] complete negation of the [*mens rea* for murder]' (see **3.2.3.2** and **3.2.3.5** *ante*). Speaking *obiter*, he stated that he was also prepared, if necessary, to extend the defence of necessity to cover the instant case.

Re A, accordingly, does not finally resolve the question whether there is a general defence of necessity based on a balancing of harms test. Ward LJ's judgment points against this; Brooke LJ's judgment is strongly in favour; and Walker LJ's judgment has *obiter dicta* supportive only of an extension of the defence of necessity to cover the instant case but no more and thus aligns itself more closely to the position of Ward LJ.

When the opportunity arose in *Shayler* [2001] 1 WLR 2206, for the Court of Appeal to indicate whether necessity existed as a defence distinct from duress, it eschewed it retreating to the comfort zone of duress of circumstances. Lord Woolf CJ even went so far as to state (at para. 55):

[T]he distinction between duress of circumstances and necessity has, *correctly*, been by and large ignored or blurred by the courts. Apart from some of the medical cases like *In re F (Mental Patient: Sterilisation)* [1990] 2 AC 1 the law has tended to treat duress of circumstances and necessity as one and the same. (emphasis added)

It is mind-boggling to hear the Lord Chief Justice commending the neglect or confusion of his judicial colleagues in failing to recognise differences between duress of circumstances and necessity. The two cannot be the same if, as *Re A* establishes, necessity may be a defence to murder, at least in medical situations. In referring to *Gillick* and *Re F* Lord Woolf CJ went on to state (at para. 59) that 'any extension of the defence here is slight: protection of the physical and mental well-being of a person from serious harm is still being required'. This ignores the fact, however, that there was no imminent risk of death or serious injury in either case, a requirement which his Lordship considered to be central to the defence. In addition Lord Woolf CJ stated (at para. 58):

> it is insufficient for the defendant to believe that at some uncertain point in the future harm will occur if he does not act to avoid it; he must reasonably believe he has to act now to avert harm in the imminent future. He must believe the harm he seeks to prevent would otherwise happen, if not immediately, then at least before it could be prevented by his or others' legal action.

Gillick and *Re F* were both cases where the doctors anticipated harm at 'some uncertain point in the future'. Likewise, in both cases, as in *Re A*, there is no suggestion that the will of the doctors was overborne by the threat of harm to their patients if they did not act. Rather, in performing their duty to act in their patients' best interests, the doctors were doing that which was appropriate and justified and, therefore, legal. In duress, however, the accused is excused because of his or her will being overborne, resulting in the doing of something which is not consistent with his or her duty (to obey the law) and not appropriate (it being illegal) albeit understandable as something which any other reasonable person might do if placed in the same situation. Duress and necessity are not the same; blurring the distinctions between them can only lead to confusion and injustice. It is to be hoped that when next the Court of Appeal is confronted with this problem it will abandon languor and endeavour to provide a clear and workable statement of the law on necessity. In the post September 11, 2001 world, such a statement is necessary if, for example, those who might have to deal with a hijacked plane in the air and heading for central London are to know whether the law permits them to shoot it down over the North Sea killing the crew and passengers, this being the only way of avoiding the loss of thousands of lives if the plane is allowed to continue flying to its target.

6.4 Marital coercion

There is nothing to prevent a spouse pleading duress on the basis of threats from the other spouse. A further defence is available to wives under s. 47 of the Criminal Justice Act 1925 which provides that 'on a charge against a wife for any offence other than treason or murder it shall be a good defence to prove that the offence was committed in the presence of, and under the coercion of, the husband'. This defence is rarely pleaded but several points should be noted. The burden of proving coercion lies on the accused. This is less favourable than the defence of duress but coercion would appear to include threats or intimidation of a lesser degree than required for duress. In *Lynch* [1975] AC 653, 693, Lord Simon stated that 'coercion in its popular sense denotes an external force which cannot be resisted and which impels its subject to act otherwise than he would wish'. While duress suggested threats, he considered that coercion 'extends to any force overbearing the wish' (at p. 694). At first instance in *Richman* [1982] Crim LR 507, Hutton J directed the jury that coercion could be physical or moral. A wife had to prove that her will was overborne by the wishes of her husband. Coercion, however, differed from trying to persuade someone out of loyalty but involved proof that the wife was forced unwillingly to participate in the crime. Judge Hutton's direction was approved by the Court of Appeal in *Shortland* [1996] 1 Cr App R 116. It would seem, therefore, that a wife could not plead coercion on the basis that she committed the offence out of love or a sense of duty; there must be some pressure from the husband.

When duress is pleaded there is no need to show that the person who issued the threats was present at the time the offence was committed; it is sufficient that the threats were imminent. In coercion, however, the husband must be shown to be present when the offence was committed. Duress may be pleaded even though the accused acted under a mistaken belief, provided this mistake was a reasonable one. In coercion a mistaken belief in marriage, albeit a reasonable one, will not avail as the statute is interpreted strictly (see *Ditta, Hussain and Kara* [1988] Crim LR 42).

The need for this defence is highly questionable as it is doubtful whether a woman coerced to commit an offence would give evidence in court which could be used to establish the guilt of her husband as her accomplice. The Law Commission (Law Com No. 83) recommended the abolition of the defence and it is not included in the Draft Criminal Code (Law Com No. 177).

6.5 **Private defence and prevention of crime**

6.5.1 **General**

An accused charged with an offence may seek to plead that he acted as he did to protect himself, or his property, or others from attack, or to prevent crime, or to effect a lawful arrest. In strict terms such pleas are not 'defences' in the sense in which duress is a defence as, if raised successfully, they provide a justification for the accused's conduct thereby rendering it lawful.

 Example

It is an offence under s. 20 of the Offences Against the Person Act 1861 to wound another person unlawfully and maliciously. If D is charged with this offence but pleads that he inflicted the wound on V who was attacking him with an axe, his use of reasonable force in the circumstances would be justified and thus lawful. As the use of lawful force is not an offence D would be acquitted of the s. 20 offence as an element of the *actus reus* was missing.

Where the accused pleads one of these justifications the onus is on the prosecution to disprove it beyond reasonable doubt. These principles were stated by Lord Griffiths in *Beckford* v *R* [1988] AC 130, as follows (at p. 144):

> It is because it is an essential element of all crimes of violence that the violence or the threat of violence should be unlawful that self-defence, if raised as an issue in a criminal trial, must be disproved by the prosecution. If the prosecution fail to do so the accused is entitled to be acquitted because the prosecution will have failed to prove an essential element of the crime namely that the violence used by the accused was unlawful.

Self-defence is a justification recognised by the common law. It is a general defence which applies not only to offences of violence but is also available to the accused where, for example, he threatens to use violence (see *Cousins* [1982] QB 526; *Afzal* [1993] Crim LR 791). It covers not only defence of oneself but also of others (see *Rose* (1884) 15 Cox CC 540; *Duffy* [1967] 1 QB 63); the term private defence is thus more appropriate and less confusing. Private defence overlaps with s. 3 of the Criminal Law Act 1967 which provides:

> (1) A person may use such force as is reasonable in the circumstances in the prevention of crime, or in effecting or assisting in the lawful arrest of offenders or suspected offenders or of persons unlawfully at large.
>
> (2) Subsection (1) above shall replace the rules of common law on the question when force used for a purpose mentioned in the subsection is justified by that purpose.

Both the common law and s. 3 impose the same requirement that the force used is such as is reasonable in the circumstances (see *Devlin* v *Armstrong* [1971] NI 13; *McInnes* [1971] 1 WLR 1600). If D uses force to defend himself or another from an unlawful attack by P he will usually also be acting to prevent a crime. In most cases it will not matter whether the plea is based in private defence or in prevention of crime. But if s. 3 were interpreted as having superseded the common law on private defence, D would be left defenceless where P, in attacking him, is not committing a crime (as where P is under 10 years of age, insane, in a state of automatism, or under a material mistake of fact) and D knows this. In such a case D could not claim to be acting to prevent a crime; he could, however, claim to be defending himself from an unjustified attack and therefore rely on private defence. It appears that the courts accept that private defence and prevention of crime under s. 3(1) co-exist as justifications (see *Cousins* [1982] QB 526). Under s. 3(1) 'crime' means an offence under domestic law and does not cover something which is only a crime under international law (see *Jones and others* [2006] UKHL 16).

In one of the worst examples of gesture politics resulting in pointless legislation, the Government, honouring a pledge made by the Secretary of State for Justice to the Labour Party Conference in 2007 to introduce new legislation on the use of force in self-defence and the prevention of crime, enacted s. 76 of the Criminal Justice and Immigration Act 2008 (CJIA). The concern underlying the legislation was that people were not doing enough to help each other on the streets and that confusion over the law on self-defence and the use of force in prevention of crime might underlie this. Section 76 was enacted to clarify the operation of the common law on the use of reasonable force in self-defence, in prevention of crime, or in the arrest of offenders. The section does not codify all of the law relating to these defences but seeks to put into statutory form four principles derived from the case law. To the extent that it simply legislates for what case law had already established, it was pointless. Further, as it does not provide any different answer to the question 'How much force may I use?' than the law already provided, it will not provide any different outcome in situations where 'have a go heroes' find themselves arrested and even prosecuted when, for example, they use force in their own home against a burglar or intervene on the street to assist another when attacked. While tabloid stories about the arrest and prosecution of 'have a go heroes' generated much of the public disquiet, s. 76 will not in any way resolve the problem police officers face when such situations arise and when there may be contradictory or inconsistent eye-witness accounts of events. The question of what is 'reasonable force' is inevitably context-specific and that context includes not only the external circumstances but also D's perception and belief in relation to those circumstances. Sometimes the only way to determine whether the 'have a go hero' was acting reasonably in self-defence or to prevent a crime, rather than unreasonably to exact revenge or as a vigilante, may be to prosecute him for an offence against the person and leave the jury to determine the issue. This may be particularly so where D was operating under some mistake, as in this situation the external circumstances provide no justification for the use of force whereas D's perception and belief may do so. But the enactment of s. 76 could not stem the problems which arise from context. The use of force by several householders on burglars raised particular problems; not so much to do with self-defence but to do with policing as the response of the police often appeared heavy-handed and more concerned with the rights of burglars than the fear they might engender in householders awakened late at night. Following further tabloid newspaper stories and public disquiet s. 148 of the Legal Aid, Sentencing and Punishment of Offenders Act 2012 makes (when it comes into force) amendments to s. 76.

Section 76 only comes into play where D is charged with an offence and seeks to raise the common law defences of self-defence or defence of property or the statutory defence under s. 3(1) of the Criminal Law Act and the question arises whether the force used against V was reasonable in the circumstances (s. 76(1) and (2)). Currently the four (but when the 2012 Act amendment comes into force, five) principles put into statutory form in s. 76 are:

(1) the question whether D's use of force was reasonable in the circumstances is to be decided on the basis of the circumstances D believed to exist (s. 76(3)), even if his belief was mistaken and unreasonable (s. 76(4));

(2) D cannot rely on any mistaken belief attributable to intoxication that was voluntarily induced (s. 76(5));

(3) the degree of force used by D is not to be regarded as having been reasonable in the circumstances as D believed them to be if it was disproportionate in those circumstances (s. 76(6));

(4) in deciding the question in (1) above, a possibility that D could have retreated is to be considered (so far as relevant) as a factor to be taken into account, rather than as giving rise to a duty to retreat (s. 76(6A) as inserted by s. 148 of the 2012 Act);

(5) a person acting for a 'legitimate purpose' (i.e. self-defence, prevention of crime, or lawful arrest) may not be able to weigh to a nicety the exact measure of any necessary action (s. 76(7)(a)) and evidence of his only having done what he honestly and instinctively thought was necessary for a legitimate purpose constitutes strong evidence that only reasonable action was taken by him for that purpose (s. 76(7)(b)).

The provision provides no guidance on how other problem areas, such as the use of pre-emptive force and unknown circumstances of justification, should be resolved. It also stands in stark contrast to s. 110 of the Serious Organised Crime and Police Act 2005 which the same Government introduced and which limited the powers of a citizen to effect an arrest. This provision seemed to be aimed at discouraging citizens from 'having a go' whereas the rhetoric preceding the enactment of s. 76 appeared to be the opposite. Section 76, accordingly, does not 'do what it says on the tin'; it provides no clarification of the law as all it does is state in statutory form principles which the case law has long established.

6.5.2 The necessity of force

The use of force is not justified if it is not necessary. Certain factors will be relevant in considering whether the prosecution have proved beyond reasonable doubt that force was not necessary in the circumstances which existed or which the accused believed to exist. It is not necessary, however, for there to be an actual attack in progress before the accused may use force in private defence; it is sufficient if he apprehends an attack and uses force to prevent it. In *Beckford* Lord Griffiths stated (at p. 144) **'a man about to be attacked does not have to wait for his assailant to strike the first blow or fire the first shot; circumstances may justify a pre-emptive strike'.** The danger the accused apprehends, however, must be sufficiently specific or imminent to justify the actions he takes (see *Devlin* v *Armstrong*), and must be of a nature which could not reasonably be met by more pacific means (*Fegan* [1972] NI 80). Where the accused's apprehension may justify his response in using force to defend himself, it does not, however, justify him in inciting others to use force. In such circumstances their use of force would be unlawful unless each individually apprehended the unlawful use of violence on himself and acted in response to this apprehension rather than in response to the accused's incitement (see *Devlin* v *Armstrong*).

6.5.2.1 Preparing for an attack

 Question

Where a person apprehends an unlawful attack on himself, may he make preparations to defend himself where those preparations may involve breaches of the criminal law?

This issue arose in *Attorney-General's Reference (No. 2 of 1983)* [1984] QB 456. D's shop had been attacked and damaged by rioters. Fearing further attacks he made some petrol bombs which he intended to use to protect himself and his property.

He was charged with making an explosive substance in such circumstances as to give rise to a reasonable suspicion that he had not made it for a lawful object contrary to s. 4 of the Explosive Substances Act 1883. He pleaded that his lawful object was self-defence and the jury acquitted. The Attorney-General referred the case to the Court of Appeal. Lord Lane CJ stated (at p. 470):

> The fact that in manufacturing and storing the petrol bombs the respondent committed offences under [the Explosives Act 1875 which prohibits the manufacture and storage of explosives without a licence] did not necessarily involve that when he made them his object in doing so was not lawful. The means by which he sought to fulfil that object were unlawful, but the fact that he could never without committing offences reach the point where he used them in self-defence did not render his object in making them for that purpose unlawful. The object or purpose or end for which the petrol bombs were made was not itself rendered unlawful by the fact that it could not be fulfilled except by unlawful means.

The case is not totally satisfactory as, while it decided in relation to the offence under the 1883 Act that the respondent had made the petrol bombs for a lawful object, it seemed to suggest that he would have been liable for an offence under the 1875 Act. Lord Lane CJ stated (at p. 471):

> ...a defendant is not left in the paradoxical position of being able to justify acts carried out in self-defence but not acts immediately preparatory to it. There is no warrant for the submission...that acts of self-defence will only avail a defendant when they have been done spontaneously. There is no question of a person in danger of attack 'writing his own immunity' for violent future acts of his.... He may still arm himself for his own protection, if the exigency arises, although in so doing he may commit other offences. That he may be guilty of other offences will avoid the risk of anarchy contemplated by the reference.

In relation to a charge under s. 1 of the Prevention of Crime Act 1953 of carrying an offensive weapon in a public place, a person could rely on the defence provided in the section of proving that he had lawful authority or reasonable excuse for carrying it. In *Evans* v *Hughes* [1972] 1 WLR 1452, the Divisional Court stated that only 'an imminent particular threat affecting the particular circumstances in which the weapon was carried' could ground a reasonable excuse. Section 139 of the Criminal Justice Act 1988 creates an additional offence of having an article with a blade or point in a public place without 'good reason or lawful authority'. This is aimed at those in the habit of carrying knives and similar articles.

Professor J. C. Smith criticised the *Attorney-General's Reference* decision in *Justification and Excuse in the Criminal Law* (at pp. 122, 123) arguing that, if an act is justifiable because done in self-defence or prevention of crime, this ought to be a sufficient answer to a charge of any crime alleged to be involved in the doing of the act. He provided the following illustration:

> If I happen upon a bank robbery and, being shot at by one of the robbers, I pick up the revolver which has been dropped by a wounded policeman and, quite reasonably, fire it in self-defence, I am surely not guilty of an offence under the Firearms Act 1968, s. 1, of being in possession of a firearm without holding a firearm certificate.

As private defence or prevention of crime may only be pleaded in response to offences involving the use of force the answer to Professor Smith's rhetorical question is that he would be guilty of the offence under s. 1 of the 1968 Act (see Elliott, 'Necessity, duress and self-defence' [1989] Crim LR 611, 618), although a charge under s. 1 of the Prevention of Crime Act 1953 could be met by the specific defence provided by that section as interpreted in *Evans* v *Hughes*. Smith and Hogan, in *Criminal Law* (at p. 262), argue that the courts should develop the law so that 'where contravention of *any* law is (i) necessary to enable the right of public or private defence to be exercised, and (ii) reasonable in the circumstances, it ought to be excused'. It is submitted that this is what has partially happened by accident through the development of duress of circumstances. In the robbery example given earlier, on a charge under s. 1 of the Firearms Act 1968, duress of circumstances could be pleaded as an excusatory defence. The issue of imminence of the threat necessary for a successful plea of duress/duress of circumstances obviates the use of the defence by a person who arms himself with a gun because he anticipates that one day he may be attacked; the defence would only be available to the person who arms himself immediately prior to what he believes to be an imminent attack. However, duress/duress of circumstances is only available where the accused fears death or serious physical injury whereas private defence may be pleaded in justification where a lesser degree of harm is anticipated. Thus Smith and Hogan's plea for further development of the law still requires further judicial action if all anomalies are to be removed, particularly as Parliament chose to take no action in s. 76 of the CJIA.

6.5.2.2 Duty to retreat?

Formerly it was believed that the common law imposed a requirement that a person could only plead private defence where he had retreated as far as he could before resorting to the use of force. In *Bird* [1985] 1 WLR 816, the Court of Appeal made it clear that there is no such requirement but rather it is a factor to be considered in deciding whether it was necessary to use force, and whether the force used was reasonable (see s. 76(6A) of the CJIA which gives statutory force to this common law principle). Lord Lane CJ stated (at p. 820) what should have been obvious:

> If the defendant is proved to have been attacking or retaliating or revenging himself, then he was not truly acting in self-defence. Evidence that the defendant tried to retreat or tried to call off the fight may be a cast-iron method of casting doubt on the suggestion that he was the attacker or retaliator or the person trying to revenge himself. But it is not by any means the only method of doing that.

If there were a duty to retreat a person would never be able to use pre-emptive force. Similarly a person is under no duty to refrain from going where he may lawfully go because he knows he is likely to be attacked (see *Field* [1972] Crim LR 435). A distinction must be drawn between the situation where a person acts lawfully but in the realisation that he may be subjected to violence as a result (cf. *Beatty* v *Gillbanks* (1882) 9 QBD 308), and the situation where he deliberately engineers or provokes an attack on himself so that he may respond with force and seek to plead self-defence. In the latter situation the justification of self-defence will not be open to him where V uses only reasonable force to rebuff D's attack (see *Balogun*

[1999] 98/6762/X2 and *Browne* [1973] NI 96). But where D starts out as the aggressor, self-defence may be available to him in respect of V's retaliation if V uses violence out of all proportion to that used by D. In such circumstances, D's claim of self-defence will depend on whether he reasonably apprehended that he was in immediate danger from which he had no other means of escape, and whether he used no more force than was necessary (see *Rashford* [2005] EWCA Crim 3377; see also *Keane and McGrath* [2010] EWCA 2514). The insertion of a requirement of 'reasonable apprehension' on the part of D rather than simple honest belief, is probably unintentional on the part of the Court of Appeal and derives from its uncritical reliance upon Scottish authority in *Burns v HM Advocate* [1995] SLT 1090.

6.5.2.3 Mistake

If the prosecution can prove beyond reasonable doubt that there was no necessity to use force this will be an end of the matter, unless the accused can bring forward some evidence that he was operating under a mistake. First, if D makes a mistake as to the need to use force, the force used is necessarily *objectively* unreasonable, i.e. no force being necessary, any force used would be unreasonable. For example, V, D's friend, as an April Fools' Day prank disguises himself and pretends to be a robber. D, believing V is a real robber about to rob him, assaults V. The reasonableness of the force used by the accused, however, is to be judged in light of the circumstances as he believed them to be (see *Williams* (1984) 78 Cr App R 276; *Beckford* [1988] AC 130, **3.6.1.1.2**; s. 76(3) and (4) of the CJIA *ante*). Lord Griffiths stated in *Beckford* (at p. 144) that 'it is an essential of all crimes of violence that the violence or threat of violence should be unlawful'. In such circumstances, if D uses only such force as was reasonable *in the circumstances as he believed them to be*, the effect of his mistake is that he did not intend to use unlawful force and thus lacked the *mens rea* for any offence of violence against V. **Secondly, where the accused's mistake relates not to the need to use force but to the extent of that necessity, i.e. the gravity of the threat he is facing, the force D uses in response to the perceived threat will, again, be *objectively* unreasonable.** For example, in a dark alley V confronts D pointing a toy pistol at D demanding that he hand over his money or be shot. D, believing the gun to be real, uses his karate skills and aims a fatal blow to V's head. There was an assault on D which would have justified the use of some force by D to defend himself. The problem is that D anticipated greater danger to himself than existed and used force which may have been appropriate in those anticipated circumstances. Again the reasonableness of the force used by D will be judged according to the circumstances as he believed them to be, not according to the circumstances as they actually were (see *Scarlett* (1994) 98 Cr App R 290 as clarified by *Owino* [1996] 2 Cr App R 128; s. 76(3) and (4) of the CJIA).

In each of these examples it will not matter whether the mistake made is unreasonable (see *Williams*, **3.6.1.1.2** *ante*); but obviously the more reasonable the mistake is the more likely it is that the jury will believe D. If, however, the accused's mistake, whether as to the need to use any force or as to the degree of force necessary, was caused by his voluntary intoxication, the defence will fail (s. 76(5) of the CJIA) whether or not the offence with which he is charged is one of specific or basic intent (see *O'Grady* [1987] 3 WLR 321; *O'Connor* [1991] Crim LR 135, see **5.6.5** *ante*).

In determining the circumstances as D *believed them to be* one would have thought that psychiatric evidence might, in some cases, be relevant where D's psychiatric condition might affect the way in which he perceives the world around him. For example, if D suffers from a psychiatric condition which causes him to perceive a greater threat of danger from a situation than the ordinary person would, one would expect this to be taken into account by the jury when considering what D's honest belief might have been. The reasonableness of the force D used can only be judged in light of the circumstances as he honestly believed them to be and if his psychiatric condition affected his perception and, therefore, his belief, that condition must be relevant to this issue. However, when the Court of Appeal was confronted with this very situation in the case of *Martin (Anthony)* [2001] EWCA Crim 2245, [2002] 1 Cr App R 27, it ruled that psychiatric evidence relating to D's perception of his circumstances was not admissible. There was medical evidence to the effect that Martin suffered from a personality disorder which would have caused him to perceive a much greater danger to his physical safety than the average person when he disturbed burglars in his lonely farmhouse and fired at them with his shotgun, killing one and severely wounding the other. The Court of Appeal arrived at its decision on policy grounds distinguishing self-defence from provocation on the basis that self-defence is both a complete defence and one which applies to all assaults. Neither of these facts seems pertinent to the issue of what D's honest belief was when he fired his shotgun. The Court of Appeal also ignored its own previously declared position in relation to duress (a complete defence to all crimes bar murder and attempted murder) where in *Martin (DP)* [2000] 2 Cr App R 42, treating duress as analogous to self-defence, it held that psychiatric evidence was admissible to explain D's mistaken belief that things said were threatening when they would not have been perceived as such by the average person (see **6.2.4.2** *ante*).

A further reason for the decision supplied by Lord Woolf CJ in *Martin (Anthony)* (at para. 66) was 'the undoubted fact that self-defence is raised in a great many cases resulting from minor assaults and it would be wholly disproportionate to encourage medical disputes in cases of that sort'. Martin, however, stood convicted of murder; it could hardly be considered disproportionate to the gravity of that offence to permit an exploration of medical evidence. Lord Woolf CJ went on to state (*Martin (Anthony)* (at para. 66)):

> Lord Hobhouse...in *Smith* [see **9.3.2.2.1** *post*] recognised that in relation to self-defence, too generous an approach as to what is reasonable could result in 'exorbitant defence'....
>
> As a matter of principle we would reject the suggestion that the approach of the majority in *Smith* in relation to provocation should be applied directly to the different issue of self-defence.

With respect, this confuses several issues. The issue in *Smith* related to the objective question on a plea of provocation of whether the accused exercised the degree of self-control to be expected of the reasonable man; the issue in the current case relates to the subjective question of what was D's honest belief, a matter very different and totally unrelated to any issue before the House of Lords in *Smith*. Secondly, the argument raised on the appeal in the instant case was not for a more generous approach to the question of what degree of force might be considered reasonable in response to a particular perceived threat, but rather that relevant evidence as to what was the threat which D perceived should be admitted and then the reasonableness of the force he used in response to that perceived threat be determined in the normal way. But Lord Woolf CJ further confused matters when he stated that evidence that D is suffering from a psychiatric condition might be admitted 'in exceptional cases' where that evidence is 'especially probative'. Firstly, the admissibility of evidence does not depend on whether it is probative but whether it is relevant to an issue in the case. What weight should be attributed to it, i.e. whether it is probative of any particular fact, is a matter for the jury to determine. Secondly, his Lordship did not explain what cases might be considered exceptional nor what he meant by 'especially probative'. If the suggestion is that medical evidence will be admitted only where it relates to a very serious psychiatric condition which greatly impairs D's powers of perception, the Court misunderstands the nature of the defence of self-defence and the effect of mistake on such a plea (see **3.6.1.1.2** *ante*). If, as Lord Griffiths stated in *Beckford* v *R* [1988] AC 130 (at p. 144) 'a genuine belief in facts which if true would justify self-defence...negates the intent to act unlawfully' the genuineness of that belief does not depend on the seriousness of the psychiatric condition which might have given rise to it. Furthermore, in *Shaw* v *R* [2001] UKPC 26; [2002] 1 Cr App R 10, Lord Bingham of Cornhill, delivering the opinion of the Privy Council, stated (at para. 19) that an essential question for the jury's consideration in a case involving a plea of self-defence is, 'taking the circumstances *and the danger* as the [accused] honestly believed them to be, was the amount of force which he used reasonable?' (emphasis added) This makes it clear that D's honest belief comprises not just his perception of the objective circumstances in which he was placed but also his perception of the danger to which those circumstances gave rise. Lord Woolf's dicta suggests that the danger to which a situation gives rise is something to be assessed objectively rather than from the subjective perspective of the accused. This runs contrary to every authority in the Court of Appeal and the Privy Council since the Court of Appeal decided *Williams (Gladstone)* (1984) 78 Cr App R 276. Section 76(8) of the CJIA provides that sub-s. (7) (see **6.5.1** *ante*) 'is not to be read as preventing other matters from being taken into account where they are relevant to deciding' whether D's use of force was reasonable in the circumstances. This would seem to leave the door open to the courts to resile from the position articulated in *Martin (Anthony)* and adopt one consistent with *Martin (DP)* and *Shaw*.

6.5.2.4 Unknown circumstances of justification

While the use of force must have been necessary in the circumstances for the accused to be able to rely on one of the justifications under consideration, a problem which has arisen is whether the accused must know or believe that circumstances exist which would justify his use of force even though those circumstances actually do exist. The answer was originally in the affirmative.

> In *Dadson* (1850) 4 Cox CC 358, D, a constable, was on duty watching a copse from which wood had been stolen. P emerged carrying wood which he had stolen. He ran away when D called to him and D shot him so that he could arrest him. D was convicted of shooting at P with intent to cause him grievous bodily harm. D raised the justification that he was shooting to arrest an escaping felon. Stealing wood was only a felony where the thief had two previous convictions for that offence. In fact

P had several such convictions and thus was a felon but D did not know this. D's conviction was upheld as he was not justified in shooting P as the fact that P was committing a felony was not known to him at the time.

When the Criminal Law Act 1967 was passed it was argued by some that s. 2 (now replaced by s. 24 of the Police and Criminal Evidence Act 1984) and s. 3 had the effect of reversing *Dadson*. Thus it was argued that if a person actually had committed an arrestable offence an arrest of him would be lawful even though the arresting officer did not know nor suspect on reasonable grounds that he had committed that offence. The Law Commission in its reports on *Codification of the Criminal Law* (Law Com Nos. 143 and 177) has recommended that an accused should be able to rely on unknown circumstances of justification in any case where the use of force was necessary and reasonable. Professor Brian Hogan argued strongly against this view in 'The *Dadson* principle' [1989] Crim LR 679. In *Chapman* (1988) 89 Cr App R 190, the Divisional Court effectively reaffirmed *Dadson* (and thus the principle for which it is authority) pointing out that if a person is unaware of circumstances justifying an arrest he cannot perform a lawful arrest as he will not be able to comply with s. 28(3) of the Police and Criminal Evidence Act 1984 which requires that he inform the suspect of the grounds for the arrest. Thus if the arrest is unlawful any force used to effect it is likewise unlawful.

6.5.3 The reasonableness of the force

Although the prosecution may be unable to prove that the accused did not honestly believe force to be necessary in the circumstances (as he believed them to be), they may still defeat a plea of private defence if the accused used more force than was reasonable in the circumstances as he believed them to be, i.e. 'disproportionate' force (see s. 76(6) of the CJIA). It is for the jury to determine what degree of force was reasonable in the circumstances.

6.5.3.1 Assessing the reasonableness of the force used

Adapting the test laid down by Lord Diplock in *Attorney-General for Northern Ireland's Reference (No. 1 of 1975)* [1977] AC 105, 137, the jury, when considering the reasonableness of the force used, should be directed to ask themselves:

> Are we satisfied that no reasonable man (a) with knowledge of the facts as were known to the accused or…believed by him to exist (b) in the circumstances and time available to him for reflection (c) could be of the opinion that the prevention of the risk of harm to which others might be exposed if the suspect were allowed to escape [or the defence of himself or others, or the prevention of crime, or the defence of property] justified exposing [the accused's victim] to the risk of harm to him that might result from the kind of force that the accused contemplated using?

While the jury are carrying out this exercise of balancing harms in the 'calm analytical atmosphere of the court-room…with the benefit of hindsight' (*per* Lord Diplock at p. 138) it is important that they seek to place themselves in the position in which the accused found himself, under all the stresses to which he was exposed and with the time which he had available to him in which to make his decision whether to use force and the degree of force to use. Lord Morris in *Palmer v The Queen* [1971] AC 814, stated (at p. 832):

> There are no prescribed words which must be employed in or adopted in summing up. All that is needed is a clear exposition, in relation to the particular facts of the case, of the conception of necessary self-defence....If there has been an attack so that defence is reasonably necessary it will be recognised that a person defending himself cannot weigh to a nicety the exact measure of his necessary defensive action.

The accused's own beliefs in the situation are also pertinent to the issue. *Shannon* (1980) 71 Cr App R 192 and *Whyte* [1987] 3 All ER 416, affirmed Lord Morris's view (at p. 832) that:

> If a jury thought that in a moment of unexpected anguish a person attacked had only done what he honestly and instinctively thought was necessary that would be most potent evidence that only reasonable defensive action had been taken. (See s. 76(7)(b) of the CJIA.)

In *Owino* [1996] 2 Cr App R 128, it was argued by counsel for the appellant, on the basis of a potentially ambiguous dictum in *Scarlett* (1994) 98 Cr App R 290, that, if an accused uses more force than is reasonable, his belief that the degree of force he is using is reasonable should result in an acquittal as he would not be intending to use unlawful force. If this was so D would be entitled to an acquittal where, for example, he was charged with murder having taken a gun and shot a shoplifter who ran off from his shop when D sought to arrest him, D asserting in his defence that he honestly believed that it was reasonable to shoot shoplifters to arrest them. D's mistake, however, in this situation is not one of fact but one of law, i.e. the degree of force which the law permits to be used for the purpose of arresting an offender. Counsel's argument in *Owino* was rejected, Collins J stating (at p. 134):

> What [Beldam LJ] was not saying [in *Scarlett*], in our view (and indeed if he had said it, it would be contrary to authority) was that the belief, however ill-founded, of the defendant that the degree of force he was using was reasonable, will enable him to do what he did. As Kay J indicated in argument, if that argument was correct, then it would justify, for example, the shooting of someone who was merely threatening to throw a punch, on the basis that the defendant honestly believed, although unreasonably and mistakenly, that it was justifiable for him to use that degree of force. That clearly is not, and cannot be, the law.

In *Legislating the Criminal Code: Offences Against the Person and General Principles* (Law Com No. 218), the Law Commission states at para. 36.9:

> It is not for the defendant himself to adjudicate upon the reasonableness of the steps that he takes to prevent the offence.

This position is endorsed by s. 76(7)(b) of the CJIA. While the fact that D claims that what he did was what he honestly and instinctively thought was necessary in the circumstances is 'strong evidence that only reasonable action was taken by D', this is not a trump card; D is still subject to s. 76(6) which stipulates that the force D uses is not to be regarded as reasonable in the circumstances if it is dispropor-tionate. Determining at what point force becomes disproportionate is for the jury bearing in mind that D 'may not be able to weigh to a nicety the precise measure of any necessary action' (s. 76(7)(a) of the CJIA).

Question

Where a person intervenes to prevent a crime or to arrest an offender, as opposed to acting in self-defence, should he be afforded the same margin of overreaction as the person acting in self-defence?

6.5.3.2 Excessive force

If the jury conclude that the degree of force which the accused used in the circumstances as he believed them to be was excessive, i.e. such that no reason-able person, making all due allowance for the pressure under which the accused was operating, could consider justified, **that use of force will be unlawful.** If the accused is charged with a non-fatal offence against the person, a distinction may be made between the accused who mistakenly uses unreasonable force and the one who deliberately does so; allowance may be made for the former's incorrect assessment of the appropriate degree of force to use when sentencing him. Where the accused, however, is charged with murder, no such allowance may be made in choosing the nature of the penalty to impose as the sentence for murder is manda-tory life imprisonment. It has been argued that where excessive force is used, and the charge is one of murder, an excusatory defence of excessive force should be recognised which would operate to reduce the conviction to one of manslaughter, thereby giving the court discretion in sentencing the offender where the accused makes a mistake as to the degree of force which it would be reasonable to use in the circumstances. Such a defence was recognised in Australia in *McKay* [1957] ALR 648 and affirmed in *Howe* (1958) 100 CLR 448. In *Palmer* [1971] AC 814 the Privy Council rejected an argument for the recognition of a defence of excessive force and this was affirmed in *Attorney-General for Northern Ireland's Reference (No. 1 of 1975)* [1977] AC 105 where Lord Diplock stated (at p. 148):

> If a plea of self-defence is put forward in answer to a charge of murder and fails because excessive force was used though some force was justifiable, as the law now stands the accused cannot be convicted of manslaughter. It may be that a strong case can be made for an alteration of the law to enable a verdict of manslaughter to be returned where the use of some force was justifiable but that is a matter for legislation not for judicial decision.

Subsequently the High Court of Australia overruled its previous decisions and adopted the position stated by the Privy Council in *Palmer* (see *Zekevic* v *DPP* (1987) 61 ALJR 375). The Criminal Law Revision Committee (Fourteenth Report, Cmnd 7844, para. 28), the Law Commission (Law Com No. 177, Draft Criminal Code Bill, cl. 59), and the *Report of the Select Committee of the House of Lords on Murder and*

Life Imprisonment (HL Paper 78–1, session 1988–89, para. 83) all recommended a defence similar to the Australian qualified defence. In *Clegg* [1995] 1 AC 482, the House of Lords revisited the authorities on excessive force. Their Lordships confirmed the existing position but expressed their regret that this was the law; any change in the law, however, was a matter for Parliament to consider. Following this decision the then Home Secretary, Michael Howard, announced a review of the law in this area on 24 January 1995. The *Report of the Inter-Departmental Review of the Law on the Use of Lethal Force in Self-Defence or the Prevention of Crime* (Home Office, 1996) expressed the view (at para. 83) that a verdict of manslaughter on a charge of murder where excessive force was used 'might assist in a comparatively small number of cases' but did not consider that the availability of such an option:

> would enable the court or jury to achieve a result which would necessarily always be seen as just. More options required finer distinctions and judgements to be made. With more borders between cases, there could be more cases that were seen to fall unfairly on the wrong side of the borderline, this time between acquittal and conviction for manslaughter, and between conviction for murder and manslaughter.

The Report concluded (at para. 84) that a change in this area alone would be difficult to make 'without taking a more fundamental look at the scope and operation of the law on, and the penalty for, murder'.

In *Murder, manslaughter and infanticide: proposals for reform of the law* (CP 19/08) the Government accepted the analysis the Law Commission made in their Report *Partial Defences to Murder* (Law Com No. 290) as to the problems with provocation, and subsequently reproduced in their Report *Murder, Manslaughter and Infanticide* (Law Com No. 304). The Government, however, proposed a different approach to reform through the creation of two partial defences to replace provocation, one of which is 'killing in response to a fear of serious violence' (this has been enacted by ss. 54–56 of the Coroners and Justice Act 2009—see **9.3.2.2** *post*). The defence, however, requires a loss of self-control and thus would not seem to fully address the cases discussed earlier where the problem is not loss of self-control but an error in assessing the degree of force that would be considered reasonable in defending oneself, preventing crime, or arresting an offender. The defence is also limited to circumstances where there is a fear of violence by D and this has to derive from V and be targeted at D or specified others; this would appear to rule out excessive force in arresting an offender.

6.5.4 Extent of the justifications

While the justifications under consideration are generally raised in response to charges of offences against the person, they are not confined to such offences. In *Renouf* [1986] 1 WLR 522, D was charged with reckless driving. He had driven his car in pursuit of another vehicle, the occupants of which had assaulted him and damaged his car. D forced the vehicle off the road and rammed it. He sought to rely on s. 3(1) of the Criminal Law Act 1967 but was convicted when the trial judge ruled that it was incapable of affording a defence to a charge of reckless driving. The Court of Appeal quashed his conviction as the acts alleged to amount to reckless driving constituted the use of force for the purpose of assisting in the lawful arrest of offenders and thus it should have been left to the jury to consider whether it was reasonable (see also *Symonds* [1998] Crim LR 280).

It would appear, however, that these justifications may be pleaded only in relation to offences which are not offences against the person where the circumstances constituting the offence amount to using force. The justifications may not be pleaded in respect of other offences committed incidentally (see **6.5.2.1** *ante*). Had Mr Renouf driven recklessly in pursuit of his assailants and then, drawing alongside their vehicle he had pointed a gun at the driver threatening to shoot if he did not stop, he may have been able to plead that he was using reasonable force to arrest an offender had he been charged with assault. By contrast, if he had been charged with driving recklessly he would have failed in a plea of justification in relation to this charge as his reckless driving did not constitute the force in this situation but rather was incidental to his use of force or, as Lawton LJ put it in *Renouf*, it amounted to a reckless act 'antecedent to the use of force'.

6.5.5 Resisting justifiable conduct

In **6.1** *ante* the example was given of D seeking to resist his arrest by PC. In the first case, where he did not know that PC was a police officer, D thought he was about to be attacked. In the circumstances as he believed them to be he would have been justified in using force; the only question would be whether the force he used was reasonable (see *Williams* (**6.5.2.3** *ante*); cf. *Kenlin* v *Gardner* (1967) 2 QB 510). In the second case, where he knew PC was a police officer, and the officer was acting lawfully, he would not be justified in resisting arrest even though he had not committed any crime; if D has made a mistake it is not one of fact but rather one of law relating to the circumstances in which a person may be arrested (cf. *Fennell* [1971] 1 QB 428). If PC, making a lawful arrest, uses more force than is reasonably necessary, D could use force in self-defence as, in this circumstance, the officer would be acting unlawfully in using unjustifiable force. The problematical case would be the situation where PC mistakes D for a dangerous criminal and seeks to use force either to arrest him or to defend himself or others. For example, PC sees D walking along the street and hides in a doorway until D walks past and then tackles him from behind seeking to restrain him. In this circumstance the officer is acting lawfully both in seeking to arrest D and with regard to the use of force, provided he honestly believed that force was necessary either to effect an arrest or to defend himself or others and he used no more force than he believed was reasonably necessary. (The amount of force that may be used to effect an arrest may be less than that which may be necessary in self-defence as it is inconceivable that deadly force would be reasonable to effect an arrest whereas it may be reasonable in self-defence.) Is D, however, obliged to submit to the infliction of this force on him? The case law provides no clear answer, but it is submitted that, if he uses force in return, it is arguable that his force is not being used to resist arrest but to resist what he believes to be an unlawful assault. If Williams could use reasonable force to defend someone whom he believed was being assaulted, who was in fact being lawfully arrested, it would be strange if D, believing he was being assaulted, could not use force to defend himself.

6.5.6 **Fatal force and the European Convention on Human Rights**

Article 2 of the European Convention for the Protection on Human Rights and Fundamental Freedoms provides:

1 Everyone's right to life shall be protected by law. No one shall be deprived of his life intentionally save in the execution of a sentence of a court following his conviction of a crime for which this penalty is provided by law.

2 Deprivation of life shall not be regarded as inflicted in contravention of this Article when it results from the use of force which is no more than absolutely necessary:

    (a) in the defence of any person from unlawful violence;

    (b) in order to effect a lawful arrest or to prevent the escape of a person lawfully detained;

    (c) in action lawfully taken for the purpose of quelling a riot or insurrection.

The State could be in contravention of Art. 2 where a state official, for example a police officer or a soldier, uses force in circumstances not covered by the exceptions listed in Art. 2(2). These exceptions amount to an exhaustive list and in each case the degree of force permitted to be used must be 'no more than absolutely necessary in the circumstances'. In contrast s. 3 of the Criminal Law Act 1967 provides for force being used *inter alia* 'in the prevention of crime' and both this provision and the common law on self-defence permit the use of 'such force as is reasonable in the circumstances'. It is this latter test which may have to be reconsidered by domestic courts following the enactment of the Human Rights Act 1998 when considering fatal force used by state officials. The English case law on the use of force does not distinguish between force used by state officials and that used by private individuals. This will have to reconsidered in several respects in light of European Convention case law.

In *McCann and Others* v *United Kingdom* (1996) 21 EHRR 97, the United Kingdom was found to be in breach of Art. 2. Following intelligence information received that a Provisional IRA active service unit was planning a terrorist bomb attack on Gibraltar, SAS soldiers were sent to assist the Gibraltar authorities to arrest them. Three members of the unit were intercepted after they had crossed from Spain into Gibraltar and parked a car. They were shot and killed by the SAS soldiers who believed that they had planted a car bomb which could be detonated by a radio controlled trigger and thus shot them repeatedly to ensure they were unable to trigger the bomb. In fact there was no bomb (although explosives were subsequently discovered in Spain at a property they had rented) nor any radio controlled trigger, nor were they armed. The Court emphasised that Art. 2 was one of the most fundamental provisions in the Convention. They stated that Art. 2(2) did not provide exceptions where it is permissible intentionally to kill but rather instances where it is permissible to use force which may result in the deprivation of life. The crucial point, however, was that the use of force must be no more than 'absolutely necessary' for the achievement of one of the purposes set out in Art. 2(2). This test would be applied strictly and the Court would scrutinise not only the actions of the individuals who use that force but also all the surrounding circumstances including such matters as the planning and control of the operation to see whether it was organised so as 'to minimise, to the greatest extent possible, recourse to lethal force'. On the issue of compatibility of the law on self-defence with Art. 2 the Court

concluded (at para. 155) that 'the difference between the two standards is not sufficiently great that a violation of Article 2(1) could be found on this ground alone'.
The Court concluded generally, that in light of the information they had and the
instructions they had received, the soldiers did honestly believe, for good reasons,
that lethal force was necessary (para. 200). The Court stated (at para. 200):

> It considers that the use of force by agents of the State in pursuit of one of the aims delin-
> eated in Article 2(2) of the Convention may be justified under this provision where it is
> based on an honest belief which is perceived, for good reasons, to be valid at the time
> but which subsequently turns out to be mistaken. To hold otherwise would be to impose
> an unrealistic burden on the State and its law-enforcement personnel in the execution
> of their duty, perhaps to the detriment of their lives and those of others.
>   It follows that, having regard to the dilemma confronting the authorities in the cir-
> cumstances of the case, the actions of the soldiers do not, in themselves, give rise to a
> violation of this provision.

However, the Court went on to conclude that the planning and control of the operation amounted to a breach of Art. 2 as there were errors in the intelligence gathering and the assumptions made about the attack, insufficient allowance had been
made for alternative possibilities, and the training of the soldiers giving rise to
immediate reflex actions which necessarily did not involve assessments of whether
less force might be sufficient, 'lacks the degree of caution in the use of firearms to
be expected from law enforcement personnel in a democratic society, even when
dealing with dangerous terrorists'.

Following *McCann* argument persisted that the Convention requirement that
force be 'absolutely necessary' is arguably more exacting than the domestic test
of 'reasonable in the circumstances' and that where the official using force makes
a mistake, the beliefs on which the official acted must be based on 'good reason'
which again is arguably more exacting than the subjective test of honest belief
required by *Gladstone Williams* and *Beckford* and now s. 76 of the CJIA (see **6.5.2.3**
ante). In *R (Bennett)* v *HM Coroner for Inner London* [2006] EWHC Admin 196, Mr
Bennett had been shot and killed by a Metropolitan police officer. The Coroner's
direction to the jury on self-defence was challenged where she directed them in
accordance with English law that they had to determine 'whether the force used
was reasonable, having regard to the circumstances which were believed to exist'.

It was claimed that the test of reasonableness did not comply with Art. 2 which
it was argued requires that the use of force be 'absolutely necessary'. Collins J, after
considering the European case law, concluded (at para. 25):

> the European Court of Human Rights has considered what English law requires for
> self-defence, and has not suggested that there is any incompatibility with Article 2. In
> truth, if any officer reasonably decides that he must use lethal force, it will inevitably be
> because it is absolutely necessary to do so. To kill when it is not absolutely necessary to
> do so is surely to act unreasonably. Thus, the reasonableness test does not in truth dif-
> fer from the Article 2 test as applied in *McCann*. There is no support for the submission
> that the court has with hindsight to decide whether there was in fact absolute necessity.
> That would be to ignore reality and to produce what the court in *McCann* indicated was
> an inappropriate fetter upon the actions of the police which would be detrimental not
> only to their own lives but to the lives of others.

Collins J has squared the circle quite cleverly—the use of fatal force can only be reasonable in all the circumstances where it is absolutely necessary. The court will not make a hindsight assessment whether force was, in fact, absolutely necessary. The police officer on the ground is only able to make his assessment based on his perception of the circumstances that exist. If he is mistaken, fatal force is not actually necessary. But to constrain him by such concerns would, as the European Court recognised in *McCann*, harbour the potential to be to the detriment of their lives and those of others. The circumstances, therefore, against which his decision to use fatal force must be assessed are those as he perceived them to be at the time; an honest but mistaken belief, therefore, can provide a 'good reason'. In effect, the European Convention is a document for application in the real world not the perfect world of hindsight. This would appear to draw a line under the matter.

6.6 Reform

In *Legislating the Criminal Code: Offences Against the Person and General Principles* (Law Com No. 218), the Law Commission includes a draft Criminal Law Bill which seeks, *inter alia*, to place duress and duress of circumstances on a statutory footing. The main changes which the Law Commission recommends are that the burden of proving the defence should be placed on the accused on a balance of probabilities, and that the defence should be available in respect of a charge of murder or attempted murder, thereby reversing the House of Lords' decisions in *Howe* and *Gotts*. The change in the burden of proof is presented partly as a trade-off to make the availability of the defence to murder more acceptable (see paras. 33.2 and 33.3). In addition, the Law Commission regards the defence of duress by threats as 'wholly exceptional, depending on factors unique to that defence which distinguish it from all others' (para. 33.5) as 'it is much more likely than any other defence to depend on assertions which are peculiarly difficult for the prosecution to investigate or disprove' (para. 33.6). In particular, in duress 'the circumstances on which the defence is founded will characteristically have occurred well before, and quite separately from, the actual commission of the offence' (para. 33.7). This is a very sweeping generalisation which is questionable. But if the problem is the surprise element wrong-footing the prosecution, it could be resolved by requiring the defence to give notice of their intention to rely on the defence of duress.

Problems of proof or disproof arise in relation to all defences whether the defence raised is self-defence or duress. In some cases there may be independent witnesses who can support the accused's account whereas in others there may not. It is difficult to see how duress requires different treatment nor how shifting the burden of proof is any more likely to result in the truth of the claim being established. The Law Commission, however, considers that the plausibility of the accused's story is important and relevant to the decision (on the reversed burden of proof) 'whether it was more likely than not that what the defendant claimed in fact occurred' (para. 33.10). While plausibility is relevant to the issue of whether or not a story is true it should not be regarded as determinative of that issue as often highly implausible stories are true. On these terms defendants who tell true but implausible stories face the prospect of a miscarriage of justice. The Law Commission, however, supports its proposal further on the basis of the risk that members of a criminal gang may concoct a story which the prosecution would have difficulty in refuting (para. 33.12). There is a risk of concoction in all defences which shifting the burden of proof will not redress but it will make it more difficult for all honest defendants to rely on the defence.

In their latest Report, *Murder, Manslaughter and Infanticide* (Law Com No. 304), the Law Commission recommend that:

(1) Duress should be a full defence to first degree murder, second degree murder and attempted murder.

(2) For duress to be a defence to first degree murder, second degree murder and attempted murder, the threat must be one of death or life-threatening harm.

(3) The defendant should bear the legal burden of proving the qualifying conditions of the defence on a balance of probabilities.

At paras. 6.43 and 6.44 the Law Commission provide the following explanation for this recommendation:

6.43 The argument that duress should be a full defence to first degree murder has a moral basis. It is that the law should not stigmatise a person who, on the basis of a genuine and reasonably held belief, intentionally killed in fear of death or life-threatening injury in circumstances where a jury is satisfied that an ordinary person of reasonable fortitude might have acted in the same way. If a reasonable person might have acted as D did, then the argument for withholding a complete defence is undermined. In the words of Professor Ormerod, 'if the jury find that the defendant has, within the terms of the defence, acted reasonably, it seems unfair to treat him as a second degree murderer or even a manslaughterer'.

6.44 Further, the option also accords with the way that duress operates as a complete defence in relation to other offences and it is, therefore, conducive to coherence and consistency....

The Law Commission, however, reaffirm their commitment to the burden of proof resting upon the defendant where duress is pleaded in respect of murder, adopting the position of Lord Bingham of Cornhill in *Hasan* that duress is 'peculiarly difficult for the prosecution to investigate and disprove beyond reasonable doubt'.

FURTHER READING

M. Bohlander, '*In Extremis*—Hijacked Airplanes, "Collateral Damage" and the Limits of the Criminal Law' [2006] Crim LR 579.

A. Buchanan and G. Virgo, 'Duress and Mental Abnormality' [1999] Crim LR 517.

E. Colvin, 'Exculpatory Defences in Criminal Law' (1990) 10 OJLS 381.

D. W. Elliott, 'Necessity, Duress and Self-defence' [1989] Crim LR 611.

S. Gardner, 'Direct Action and the Defence of Necessity' [2005] Crim LR 371.

B. Hogan, 'The *Dadson* Principle' [1989] Crim LR 679.

J. Horder, 'Occupying the Moral High Ground: The Law Commission on Duress' [1994] Crim LR 334.

D. Lanham, 'Offensive Weapons and Self-defence' [2005] Crim LR 85.

F. Leverick, 'Is English Self-defence Law incompatible with Article 2 of the ECHR?' [2002] Crim LR 347.

J. Loveless, 'Domestic Violence, Coercion and Duress' [2010] Crim LR 93.

H. P. Milgate, 'Duress and the Criminal Law: Another About Turn by the House of Lords' [1988] CLJ 61.

S. Ost, 'Euthanasia and the Defence of Necessity' [2005] Crim LR 355.

N. M. Padfield, 'Duress, Necessity and the Law Commission' [1992] Crim LR 778.

J. C. Smith, *Justification and Excuse in the Criminal Law* (1989, Sweet & Maxwell).

K. J. M. Smith, 'Duress and Steadfastness: In Pursuit of the Unintelligible' [1999] Crim LR 363.

G. R. Sullivan, 'Bad Thoughts and Bad Acts' [1990] Crim LR 559.

P. A. J. Waddington, '"Overkill" or "Minimum Force"?' [1990] Crim LR 695.

G. Williams, 'The Theory of Excuses' [1982] Crim LR 732.

W. Wilson, 'The Structure of Criminal Defences' [2005] Crim LR 108.

S. Yeo, 'Killing in Defence of Property' (2000) NLJ 730.

7

Parties to crime

7.1 Accomplices

7.1.1 Principals and accessories

All the parties to a crime are accomplices.

 Example

A decides that he wants V killed. He encourages D to perform the murder. B supplies D with
a knife to perform the murder, C supplies A with information regarding V's movements,
E drives D and F to V's home and acts as lookout, F assists D to kill V by holding him while
D stabs him and G, V's discontented butler, shouts encouragement at D and F as they attack
V. All seven parties are accomplices to the murder of V but only D is the perpetrator of the
offence; the others are accessories.

**The person who perpetrates the crime is referred to as the principal. A person
is the perpetrator if his act is the most immediate cause of the *actus reus* of
the offence;** in the earlier example D's act is clearly the immediate cause of V's
death. Had two people, D and G, stabbed V, they would each be principals. In
some cases D may be liable as principal even though the *actus reus* was brought
about by another. **D will be liable where he has used another person to procure
the commission of the offence and that person is not guilty of the offence
due to, for example, infancy, lack of *mens rea* or insanity. Such a person is
generally referred to as an 'innocent agent'.** For example, D gives E a parcel
telling him it is a birthday present and asks him to deliver it to V. The parcel
contains a bomb and V is killed when it explodes. D would be guilty of murder
as the principal because E, not knowing the nature of the parcel, lacked *mens rea*
and was an innocent agent. Similarly, if D employs E, his eight-year-old son, to
climb through windows of houses to steal items, D would be guilty of burglary as
principal because E, being an infant, is not criminally liable and is an innocent
agent. Problems arise where E is found to be an innocent agent but D is personally
incapable of committing the offence as a principal (see **7.1.3** *post*).

Others, **not being principals, who participate in the commission of an
offence are referred to as accessories or secondary parties and will be liable to
conviction if it is proved that they aided, abetted, counselled, or procured the**

commission of the crime by the principal. The law is to be found in s. 8 of the Accessories and Abettors Act 1861, as amended by the Criminal Law Act 1977:

> Whosoever shall aid, abet, counsel or procure the commission of any indictable offence whether the same be an offence at common law or by virtue of any act passed or to be passed, shall be liable to be tried, indicted and punished as a principal offender.

Section 44 of the Magistrates' Courts Act 1980 contains a similar provision for summary offences.

While the consequence of conviction as a principal or an accessory is the same, it is important in some circumstances to be able to distinguish between them. **The *mens rea* required of the accessory differs from that of a principal and *mens rea* must always be proved even where the principal's offence is one of strict liability.** In some cases an offence may only be committed by persons of a specified class or may not be committed as a principal by persons of a specified class, for example, only a licensee can commit an offence involving a breach of the conditions of the licence (see *Morris* v *Tolman* [1923] 1 KB 166). Where vicarious liability is in issue it is important to identify the principal and the accessory as vicarious liability may only be imposed in respect of the act of a principal (see **7.2** *post*).

The courts have struggled on many occasions to understand the very principles they have declared in respect of principals and accessories. The problem became particularly acute in the context of deaths arising from drug-taking. In their efforts to ensure that drug-suppliers should be held culpable for deaths ensuing from their supply of illicit drugs, the courts distorted the principles of accessorial liability. Where V self-administers an illegal drug as a result of which he dies, he is the immediate cause of his own death, his act being 'free, deliberate and informed'; his act involves the commission of no offence. In *Rogers* [2003] EWCA 945 the Court of Appeal held that D had played a part in the mechanics of the injection of heroin which caused death where he applied the tourniquet to V's arm while V injected himself. By this device the Court concluded that D had committed the *actus reus* of the offence of administering a noxious thing contrary to s. 23 of the Offences Against the Person Act 1861. But how could D be a principal where V's act of self-injection was the most immediate cause of his death? Of course, if the Court had accepted this, then V, as principal would have been committing no offence as it is a requirement of the s. 23 offence that the noxious thing be administered to another; and if V committed no offence, D could not be convicted as an accessory. (see further **2.6.3.5.4** *ante*)

In *Kennedy (No. 2)* [2005] EWCA Crim 685, the Court of Appeal added further to the confusion by affirming a conviction of manslaughter where D had supplied the heroin-filled syringe but played no part in its administration by V to himself as a result of which he died. The Court considered that D was acting in concert with the deceased and thus there was no breach in the chain of causation. This reasoning ignored the fact that D and V could not be joint principals as V was not committing any offence. Further, as V was also the immediate cause of the *actus reus* this meant that D could not be a principal. In addition, as V was fully aware of what was going on, he could not be said to be an innocent agent. Nonetheless the Court concluded that D and V were acting in concert in committing the s. 23 offence which formed the unlawful act upon which D's conviction of manslaughter could be founded. These problems were only finally resolved when *Kennedy (No 2)* [2007] UKHL 38 was decided in the House of Lords and overturned Kennedy's conviction of manslaughter; it also declared that the decision in *Rogers* was wrong, reaffirming the principle of *novus actus interveniens* and its intimate connection to the principles underpinning secondary liability. (see further **2.6.3.5.4** *ante*)

Occasionally it is not possible for the prosecution to determine prior to the trial whether more than one person was involved in the offence, and if so, what D's role was. In such circumstances they may allege, in a single count, the alternative allegations that D was principal in the first degree or that he aided and abetted, counselled, or procured the offence (see *Gaughan* [1990] Crim LR 880). A problem which may arise, however, was identified by Lamer J in a murder case before the Supreme Court of Canada, *Thatcher* (1987) 39 DLR (4) 275, who stated (at p. 313):

> if the Crown presents evidence which tends to inculpate the accused under one theory and exculpate him under the other, then the trial judge must instruct the jury that if they wish to rely on such evidence, then they must be unanimous as to the theory they adopt.

If the evidence is consistent with both theories then it would not matter, particularly if the jury were split as to the basis for conviction provided they were all satisfied that he had committed the offence either as principal or accessory (see *Gianetto* [1997] 1 Cr App R 1).

In most cases there will be no problem identifying the principal and the accessory but in some circumstances, while it may be clear an offence has been committed, and that two or more accomplices were involved, it may be unclear who was the principal and who was the accessory. Thus if A and B were involved in the commission of an offence both may be convicted where it is proved that each of them must have been guilty in one capacity or the other (see *Swindall and Osborne* (1846) 2 Car & Kir 230; and *Chan Wing-Siu* v *The Queen* [1985] 1 AC 168). Both may be principals as where, for example, A and B in pursuance of a joint enterprise attack V, raining blows on him and he dies (see *Macklin and Murphy's Case* (1838) 2 Lew CC 225), or A and B act in concert to rob a bank, A threatening the staff with a gun while B appropriates the money; provided each had the requisite *mens rea* they could be convicted as principals to murder and robbery.

 Key Point

The term 'joint enterprise' is used regularly in the cases. The parties to an offence, principals, and accessories, will be engaged in a joint enterprise where they have a common purpose. For example, A and B agree to burgle a factory. Their common purpose is to steal from the factory. In the course of the burglary, they may carry out many different actions which may raise issues regarding the extent of the common purpose. In the course of the burglary A encounters a security guard and hits him over the head with a cosh killing him; B encounters a cleaner and rapes her. A and B, while each being liable individually for murder and rape respectively, and jointly for burglary on the basis of their intent to steal, may further be liable as accessory to the other's murder or rape depending on the extent of their contemplation of the other's actions. See further **7.1.4.3** and **7.1.4.4** *post*. Joint enterprise is not a separate form of liability but rather is simply an example of secondary liability and is subject to the same principles (see *Mendez and Thompson* [2010] EWCA Crim 516; and *Stringer* [2011] EWCA Crim 1396).

The cases tend to talk in terms of there being a joint enterprise, or pre-arranged plan or talk of the accused 'acting in concert'. This is not a prerequisite of liability. If A and B independently embark on an attack on V at the same time and he dies, both may be convicted of murder provided each had the requisite *mens rea* even though there is no pre-arranged plan or agreement between them (see *Mohan v R* [1967] 2 AC 187).

> In *Mohan* A and B attacked V with cutlasses killing him. The evidence indicated that only one wound proved fatal but it could not be established who inflicted that wound. A and B appealed against convictions of murder arguing that as there was no pre-arranged plan to attack V the Crown had to show which of them struck the fatal blow. The Privy Council dismissed the appeals on the basis that as A and B were attacking the same man at the same time with similar weapons and with the common intention that he should suffer grievous bodily harm, each of them was present aiding and abetting the other and thus there was no need to prove any pre-arranged plan.

But if the evidence does not establish a common purpose such that each is intending to assist or encourage the other to cause harm (i.e. it only establishes an independent intention to cause harm), neither will be liable for the other's acts. In *Petters and Parfitt* [1995] Crim LR 501, the appellants had been charged with murder and convicted of manslaughter. There was evidence that each had punched the deceased and that one had kicked him causing his death. As the evidence did not establish who had delivered the fatal kick, and the jury had been inadequately directed on the question whether the appellants had been acting independently or whether they had shared a common purpose, the Court of Appeal quashed the convictions. **It should be noted that 'joint enterprise' can also cover a situation where A is the accessory who counsels the offence or assists in its commission and B perpetrates it; 'joint enterprise' is not confined to the situation where each participant in the offence is a principal** (see *Wan and Chan* [1995] Crim LR 297).

Where the offence is one of strict liability, and it is unclear which of the accused was the principal, each may be convicted only where the prosecution prove that each had *mens rea*. In *Smith v Mellors and Soar* [1987] RTR 210, both M and S were over the blood-alcohol limit when seen running away from a car which had been driven on the road. Driving with a blood-alcohol level above the prescribed limit is a strict liability offence. As it could not be proved who was driving neither could be convicted unless he had the *mens rea* required for conviction as an accessory. Thus the prosecution had to prove that each accused knew that the other had had too much to drink to be fit to drive.

In some cases it may be clear that an offence has been committed and that either A or B committed it, but it is not clear who did it nor is it clear whether the other was an accessory. In such circumstances if the prosecution cannot bring forward prima facie evidence that each of them is guilty in one capacity or another, the charges against both will be dismissed (see *Uddin* [1998] 2 All ER 744). In *Lane and Lane* (1986) 82 Cr App R 5, the evidence showed that the child of the accused had been fatally injured between noon and 8.30pm. Each parent had been present for some of the time and absent for some of it but throughout the period the child had always been in the presence of a parent. As it could not be proved who had injured the child nor that each had been involved as principal or accessory, there was no case to answer on the charges of manslaughter against each (see now Domestic Violence, Crime and Victims Act 2004, s. 5, **9.3.5.3** *post*). If, however, the prosecution can prove that one of the accused committed the offence and the other aided or abetted him in doing so, then both may be convicted. In such circumstances it does not matter that the principal offender cannot be identified as s. 8 of the Accessories and Abettors Act 1861 states that those who aid, abet, counsel, or procure an offence are 'liable to be indicted, tried and punished as a principal offender' (see *Forman and Ford* [1988] Crim LR 677, **7.1.2.2** *post*).

7.1.2 Aiding, abetting, counselling, or procuring

7.1.2.1 Defining terms

If an accused is charged as an accessory he will be charged with aiding, abetting, counselling, or procuring the particular offence and he is liable to conviction if it is proved that he participated in any one of these four ways (see *Smith, Re* (1858) 3 H & N 227; *Ferguson* v *Weaving* [1951] 1 KB 814). There has been much argument regarding the meaning of each individual term and 'aiding and abetting' have generally been paired together as if they were synonymous. In *Attorney-General's Reference (No. 1 of 1975)* [1975] QB 773, Lord Widgery CJ took the view that each word probably had a different meaning. **'Aiding' suggests helping or assisting** the principal to commit the offence whether before its commission or at the time of its commission. In the scenario given at the beginning of **7.1.1** *ante*, B, C, and E all assist D prior to the commission of the murder (see *Thambiah* v *R* [1966] AC 37); F is present assisting him at the time of the offence (see *Clarkson* [1971] 1 WLR 1402) and E also assists at that time by keeping watch (see *Betts and Ridley* (1930) 22 Cr App R 148). **'Abetting' suggests the activity of one who incites, instigates, or encourages** the principal to commit the offence (see *Wilcox* v *Jeffery* [1951] 1 All ER 464). **'Counselling' also suggests advising or encouraging** the commission of the offence. In *National Coal Board* v *Gamble* [1959] 1 QB 11, Devlin J expressed the opinion that 'abetting' involved presence at the scene of the crime offering encouragement. At common law 'abetting' denoted encouragement at the time of the offence and 'counselling' encouragement given previously. In the scenario in **7.1.1** *ante*, A would be liable for counselling the commission of the offence and G for abetting it; F, by his presence and assistance, is also offering encouragement and thus is also an abettor.

In *Attorney-General's Reference (ante)*, Lord Widgery CJ considered that in most cases of aiding, abetting, or counselling the parties would have met and discussed the offence they had in mind. While this may be generally true, it is not a requirement for liability as an accessory. The principal may have met with the accessories separately or there may have been no discussion at all. For example, in the scenario in **7.1.1** *ante*, G abetted the offence but he never discussed it or planned it with D or any of the other parties. **What seems to be necessary is some meeting of minds or consensus, namely that the offence committed is the one encouraged and the principal is aware of that encouragement even if he would have committed it without encouragement** (see *Calhaem* [1985] 1 QB 808). The amount of encouragement offered need not be particularly great for liability to arise. In

Gianetto [1997] 1 Cr App R 1, the Court of Appeal agreed that A could be convicted of murder where, in response to D stating 'I am going to kill your wife', he said 'Oh goody', and D then went ahead and killed A's wife. In the case of aiding, however, there need not be a meeting of minds. For example, in the scenario in **7.1.1** *ante*, if H, the maid, restrained W, V's wife, and prevented her from phoning the police or from trying to rescue V, H would have assisted D in committing the offence although D was totally unaware of H's intervention.

An unusual example of aiding and abetting is provided by the case of *Gnango* [2011] UKSC 59. G, armed with a gun, was searching for B at a residential car park; B apparently, owed him some money. Upon B appearing he shot at G who took cover behind a car and fired several shots in return. B continued shooting and one of his shots hit V, a passer-by, killing him. The Supreme Court restored G's conviction for murder (which the Court of Appeal had quashed) on the basis that G and B had agreed to shoot and be shot at by the other, each having an intent to kill the other. The intent B had was transferred (see **3.6.2.3** *ante*) when B killed V having done so with encouragement from G (through his shooting at B thereby encouraging him to shoot back at G). G, accordingly, had encouraged B's act of murdering V.

It is not necessary to prove any causal link between the assistance or encouragement and the commission of the offence (see *A-G's Reference; Calhaem*; and *Stringer* [2011] EWCA Crim 1396). By contrast 'procuring' involves a different concept altogether. In *A-G's Reference* (*ante*), Lord Widgery CJ stated **that procuring required a causal link to be established between what the procurer did and what the principal did. Procuring, Lord Widgery said, means 'to produce by endeavour'** (see also *Luffman* [2008] EWCA Crim 1379).

> The facts of the case giving rise to the Reference were that A surreptitiously added alcohol to D's drink knowing that he would shortly be driving his car home. D was convicted of the strict liability offence of driving with an excessive quantity of alcohol in his body contrary to s. 6(1) of the Road Traffic Act 1972. The Court of Appeal held that this amounted to procuring as A had set out to see that a particular state of affairs happened and had taken appropriate steps to produce it. The addition of the alcohol to D's drink was a direct cause of the excess alcohol level in his blood. Thus Lord Widgery stated (at p. 780) that the offence had been procured 'because, unknown to the driver and without his collaboration, he has been put in a position in which in fact he has committed an offence which he never would have committed otherwise'.

The suggestion in *A-G's Reference* is that it must be the procurer's purpose to produce the *actus reus*. In *Millward* [1994] Crim LR 527, M instructed H to drive a tractor and trailer. M knew, but H did not know, that the hitch mechanism was dangerously defective. As H was driving, the trailer became detached causing a fatal accident. H was acquitted of causing death by reckless driving but M was convicted as he had procured the offence. While it was clear that it was M's purpose to bring about the reckless driving, it was not his purpose to bring about the death. This issue was not discussed in the case but perhaps the principle is that the purpose requirement is confined to the initiating cause of a consequence. This may be justified on two bases: (1) *mens rea* is not required as to death in the offence of causing death by reckless driving, proof of causation being sufficient, and (2) a secondary party is liable for the unforeseen consequences of an enterprise to the same extent as the principal offender.

7.1.2.2 Presence, activity, and inactivity

Mere presence at the scene of an offence and failure to intervene or prevent it is generally not sufficient to render such a person liable as an accessory, although it may provide prima facie (but not conclusive) evidence of an intention to encourage the perpetrator (see *Coney* (1882) 8 QBD 534). If a person is to be convicted in such circumstances **it must be proved that there was encouragement in fact and that there was an intention to encourage** (see *Clarkson* [1971] 1 WLR 1402; and *Bland* [1988] Crim LR 41). This may be established by proving that the accused was present as a result of a prior agreement that the offence be committed (see *Smith v Reynolds* [1986] Crim LR 559) or that he did some positive act of assistance or encouragement knowing the circumstances which constitute the offence. It is not necessary to establish that commission of the crime was the accessory's purpose in the latter situation (see *National Coal Board* v *Gamble* [1959] 1 QB 11).

Voluntary presence at the scene of a crime, without more, may amount to actual encouragement. In *Wilcox* v *Jeffery* [1951] 1 All ER 464, A's presence, as a paying member of the audience at a concert given by D, amounted to aiding and abetting D to contravene the Aliens Order 1920. D had been permitted to enter the United Kingdom only on condition that he take no employment. Further evidence of A's intention to encourage D was derived from A's behaviour in that he had met D at the airport and, after the concert, he wrote and published a laudatory review of the concert in the periodical of which he was the proprietor. In this case there would clearly have been no performance if there had been no audience so the presence of each member of the audience was an encouragement to D to perform (see also *Coney, ante*). But presence is not always sufficient to amount to encouragement. In *Allan* [1965] 1 QB 130, A was present at the scene of an affray. He was totally passive doing nothing to offer encouragement to those involved in the fighting, although he harboured a secret intention to join in if help was needed by the side which he favoured. The Court of Criminal Appeal stated (at p. 138):

> In our judgment, before a jury can properly convict an accused person of being a principal in the second degree to an affray, they must be convinced by the evidence that, at the very least, he by some means or other encouraged the participants. To hold otherwise would be, in effect, ...to convict a man on his thoughts, unaccompanied by any physical act other than the fact of his mere presence.

This case is distinguishable from *Wilcox* v *Jeffery* as, without spectators, the affray would still have occurred so mere presence, without more, did not amount to encouragement.

Where A has the right to control the actions of another and deliberately refrains from doing so, his inactivity may amount to actual encouragement. For example, a publican who takes no steps to make his customers leave his premises after closing time, may be convicted of aiding and abetting their consumption of alcohol outside hours (*Tuck* v *Robson* [1970] 1 WLR 741). Likewise if the owner of a car sits as a passenger in it while it is driven dangerously and does nothing to prevent or discourage this, at a time when there was opportunity to intervene, he may be guilty of aiding and abetting the dangerous driving (see *Webster* [2006] EWCA Crim 415). His failure to exercise his right of control is evidence of encouragement (see *Du Cros* v *Lambourne* [1907] 1 KB 40; *Cassady* v *Reg. Morris* [1975] RTR 470; *J. F. Alford Transport Ltd and Others* [1997] 2 Cr App R 326). Indeed, actual presence is not necessary if it can be proved that A knows of D's illegal activity and deliberately turns a blind eye to it, and D is thereby encouraged to continue this illegal activity, and A knows his inaction is encouraging D so to do (see *J. F. Alford Transport Ltd, ante*).

If A is under a duty to act, his omission to do so may give rise to liability as an accessory just as it may as a principal. While A may not have a right to control D, his omission to fulfil his duty may amount to encouragement of D. For example, if one parent ill-treats his child in the presence of the other parent, the latter's failure to fulfil his or her duty to protect the child may amount to encouragement of the former (see *Russell and Russell* (1987) 85 Cr App R 388). The conclusion of encouragement is not automatic as there may not have been time to intervene or the parent may have been in terror of the other. In *Forman and Ford* [1988] Crim LR 677, a suspect was assaulted while in a cell with two officers. It was not possible to establish which was the assailant and there was no evidence that they were acting in concert. The Court held that both officers could be convicted if the jury are satisfied in respect of each of them that if he himself did not commit the assault he encouraged the other to do so by failing to intervene or report the offence and the other relied on him neither to intervene to prevent nor afterwards to report the offence. In this situation each officer is under a duty to prevent crime and to keep the peace so his inactivity can amount to positive encouragement.

7.1.3 **Proving the principal offence**

> **? Question**
>
> Is it possible to convict A as an accessory without convicting D as the principal?

The fact that D has been acquitted in a separate trial does not preclude a court from convicting A as the evidence against D may have been weak. What is necessary is that it be proved beyond reasonable doubt that the principal offence was committed. Several situations may arise.

7.1.3.1 Absence of an *actus reus*

A person cannot be convicted as an accessory unless there was an *actus reus*.

> In *Thornton* v *Mitchell* [1940] 1 All ER 339, a bus driver reversed his bus relying on the signals of his conductor as he was unable to see behind the bus. Two pedestrians behind the bus were knocked down and injured. The driver was charged with careless driving and the conductor with aiding and abetting that offence. The justices dismissed the charge against the driver as he had done nothing which he should not have done and had not been careless, but they convicted the conductor. The Divisional Court held the conductor could not be convicted as there was no *actus*

reus of careless driving. The Court quoted with approval the dictum of Avory J in *Morris* v *Tolman* [1923] 1 KB 166 (at p. 171) 'in order to convict, it would be necessary to show that the respondent was aiding and abetting the principal, but a person cannot aid another in doing something which that other has not done'. As there was no *actus reus* it was not possible to regard the conductor as the principal working through an innocent agent.

This principle was applied in two cases of causing death by dangerous driving (see *Loukes* [1996] Crim LR 341 and *Roberts and George* [1997] Crim LR 209). The *actus reus* of this offence involves death being caused by the driving of a vehicle in a dangerous condition. A driver will be liable where 'it would be obvious to a competent and careful driver that driving the vehicle in its current state would be dangerous'. In both cases drivers of tipper trucks were acquitted of the offence, where defects in their vehicles had caused the deaths of other road users, as there was no evidence that the defects were, or would have been, obvious to them. In each case their employers, who had been convicted on the basis of procuring the offences, had their convictions quashed as the acquittals of the drivers meant that in both cases the *actus reus* of the offence had not been established.

7.1.3.2 Perpetrator exempt from prosecution

If the perpetrator of the principal offence is, for some special reason, exempt from prosecution, this does not preclude the conviction of another as an accessory for encouraging or assisting the commission of the offence. In *Austin* [1981] 1 All ER 374, the father of a child, assisted by A, snatched the child from the lawful custody of his estranged wife. A was convicted of child stealing contrary to s. 56 of the Offences Against the Person Act 1861 (since repealed). The Court of Appeal held that while the proviso to the section exempted the father from liability to prosecution, he had committed the offence of child stealing. Accordingly, the proviso provided no obstacle to the conviction of A as an accessory to that offence.

7.1.3.3 Perpetrator not liable to conviction

Where the principal offence has been committed a person who has encouraged or assisted the principal to commit it will be liable as an accessory even though the offence is one which the accessory could not commit as a principal. Thus a woman may be convicted of rape as an accessory (see *Ram and Ram* (1893) 17 Cox CC 609). What would happen in such a case, however, if the principal was not liable to conviction because he lacked the requisite *mens rea* or had a defence, but the accomplice had the requisite *mens rea* and did encourage or assist in the commission of the *actus reus*? For example, A, a woman, encourages E to have sexual intercourse with V, against V's will, and she restrains V while E has intercourse. If E successfully raises a plea of insanity, the special verdict of 'not guilty by reason of insanity' will be returned. A could not be convicted as a principal acting through an innocent agent as she is not capable of committing rape as a principal. The law would appear to be deficient if A was to escape criminal liability for rape because of these technicalities. A possible solution would be to hold that the *actus reus* of rape had been committed in that sexual intercourse occurred to which V did not consent, and that A had aided and abetted the commission of that *actus reus*.

In *Bourne* (1952) 36 Cr App R 125, A forced his wife to commit buggery with a dog. His conviction of aiding and abetting the commission of the offence was upheld on appeal as, although the wife would not have been guilty as principal because of the defence of duress, the *actus reus* of buggery had been committed. It would also have been true to say that the wife had the *mens rea* for the offence as duress acts merely as an excuse which exempts the accused from conviction where she has committed an offence as a result of the threats of another (see **6.2.1** *ante*). In *Cogan and Leak* [1976] QB 217, Leak compelled his wife to have sexual intercourse with Cogan. Cogan's conviction was quashed following the House of Lords' decision in *Morgan* (see **3.6.1.1.1** *ante*) as his defence of honest belief in Mrs Leak's consent had not been left to the jury. Leak's conviction was upheld as he had procured the commission of the offence. Lawton LJ stated (at p. 223):

> the act of sexual intercourse without the wife's consent was the *actus reus*; it had been procured by Leak who had the appropriate *mens rea*, namely his intention that Cogan should have sexual intercourse with her without her consent. . . . it is irrelevant that the man whom Leak had procured to do the physical act himself did not intend to have sexual intercourse with the wife without her consent. Leak was using him as a means to procure a criminal purpose.

This accords with the decision in *Bourne*. Unfortunately Lawton LJ went on to state that Leak could have been indicted as the principal working through an innocent agent. This creates several difficulties. At that time Leak could not commit rape as a principal as he was cohabiting with his wife (but see **10.2.1** *post*). Further, it is difficult to see how it could be said that 'Leak had sexual intercourse with V without her consent'. While there is no intellectual difficulty in affirming, for example, that D stole, killed, or committed arson through an innocent agent as personal action on the part of the accused is not implicit in the definition of the offence, rape does appear to presume personal action on the part of the perpetrator; Leak most clearly did not have intercourse with his wife at that time. If this basis of the decision is followed it leads to the even more ludicrous conclusion that A, in the scenario at the beginning of this section, could be charged as the principal to the offence of rape even though as a woman she is incapable of performing the *actus reus*; according to s. 1(1) of the Sexual Offences Act 2003 only a man may commit rape! The only conclusion one can arrive at is that this part of the decision in *Cogan and Leak* is wrong and that only the part of the decision which accords with *Bourne* should be followed. **Thus A will be liable as an accessory where he has encouraged, assisted, or procured the commission of an *actus reus* albeit that the perpetrator is not liable as a principal.** The Court of Appeal in *Millward* [1994] Crim LR 527 (see **7.1.2.1** *ante*) expressly confirmed this principle and it was applied in *DPP v K and B* [1997] 1 Cr App R 36. In this case the Divisional Court allowed an appeal by the DPP and remitted the case to the magistrate with a direction to convict the respondents who were girls aged 14 and 11. They had procured a boy, who was never apprehended, to rape a girl, W, whom they had falsely imprisoned. The evidence established that the boy was over 10 but the prosecution had been unable to rebut the presumption of *doli incapax* (see **5.2** *ante*). The Divisional Court held that this did not preclude the conviction of the respondents as procurers as the *actus reus* of rape had been proved and they had 'had the requisite *mens rea*, namely, the desire that rape should take place and the procuring of it'.

7.1.3.4 Perpetrator and accessory liable but for different offences

The same facts may supply the *actus reus* of several offences. For example, unlawful homicide includes murder and manslaughter, for which the *actus reus* is the same, conviction of either depending on the *mens rea* of the accused or the availability of the mitigating defences of diminished responsibility or loss of control. Accordingly **there is nothing wrong in principle with D being convicted of murder as a principal and A being convicted of manslaughter as an accessory if A lacked the *mens rea* for murder.**

 Example

A and D embark on a joint enterprise to burgle a factory agreeing to knock out V the watchman with a cosh. D knows that V has an eggshell skull and that such an assault will cause at least grievous bodily harm to him. A is unaware of this and does not contemplate any injury to V beyond actual bodily harm. If D coshes V and he dies, D would be liable for murder as he intended to cause grievous bodily harm but A would only be liable for manslaughter on the basis of an unlawful and dangerous act. (See *Yemoh* [2009] EWCA Crim 930; and *Carpenter* [2011] EWCA Crim 2568).

The converse also applies (and is consistent with the principle in *Bourne*) so that A may be convicted of the greater offence whereas D is convicted of the lesser as the *actus reus* has been committed and the accessory's liability depends on his own *mens rea*. In *Howe* [1987] 1 AC 417, Lord Mackay (with whom Lords Bridge, Brandon, and Griffiths agreed) considered the following hypothetical situation (at p. 458):

> A hands a gun to D informing him that it is loaded with blank ammunition only and telling him to go and scare X by discharging it. The ammunition is in fact live, as A knows, and X is killed. D is convicted only of manslaughter, as he might be on those facts.

Lord Mackay agreed with the Court of Appeal that it would be absurd if A should thereby escape conviction for murder and that the previous authority of *Richards* [1974] QB 776 was wrongly decided. He stated (at p. 458):

> where a person has been killed and that result is the result intended by another participant, the mere fact that the actual killer may be convicted only of the reduced charge of manslaughter for some reason special to himself does not, in my opinion in any way, result in a compulsory reduction for the other participant.

If the perpetrator, D, intentionally kills in pursuance of a joint enterprise where he and A had agreed only to inflict some minor injury on the victim, the fact that D's act was beyond the common design and uncontemplated by A would absolve A from liability for manslaughter (see **7.1.4.4** *post*).

The examples so far have involved a difference in *mens rea* between A and D. Where murder is charged an accused may be convicted of manslaughter if he successfully raises a defence of diminished responsibility or loss of self-control. Section

2(4) of the Homicide Act 1957 specifically provides that the fact that one party to a killing is not liable to be convicted of murder because of diminished responsibility does not affect the question whether the killing amounted to murder in the case of any other party to it. Section 55(8) of the Coroners and Justice Act 2009 makes similar provision in respect of the defence of loss of self-control.

7.1.4 *Mens rea* of an accessory

The *mens rea* required of an accessory may be simply stated as an **intention to assist or encourage the commission of the principal offence combined with knowledge of the circumstances which constitute the offence.** This statement requires elucidation; this will reveal the problems associated with the *mens rea* of accessories.

7.1.4.1 Intention to assist or encourage the principal

Defining the *mens rea* required of accessories has presented major difficulties for the courts. The principal is the one whose act has caused the *actus reus* of the offence and the *mens rea* required of him generally relates to the doing of that act and the bringing about of its causally connected consequences. **As the acts of the accessory do not cause the *actus reus* the *mens rea* required cannot equate exactly to that of the principal.**

 Example

> D shoots at V intending to kill him and succeeds. D's *mens rea* directly mirrors the *actus reus* he has brought about. A supplied D with the gun knowing that D wished to kill V, although he hoped D would fail. It can be seen that A's act assists D but the *actus reus* of murder does not directly mirror his state of mind. If A is to be liable for murder it will be because he has intended to assist D knowing that D intends to kill rather than on the basis that he, himself, intended to kill V.

In *National Coal Board* v *Gamble* [1959] 1 QB 11, the Divisional Court held that intention to assist or encourage had to be proved in addition to knowledge of the circumstances. **The commission of the principal offence may not be the accused's desire, motive, or purpose.** Devlin J stated (at p. 23):

> But an indifference to the result of the crime does not of itself negative abetting. If one man deliberately sells to another a gun to be used for murdering a third, he may be indifferent about whether the third man lives or dies and interested only in the cash profit to be made out of the sale, but he can still be an aider and abettor. To hold otherwise would be to negative the rule that *mens rea* is a matter of intent only and does not depend on desire or motive.

In *NCB* v *Gamble*, A's servant B operated the weighbridge at a colliery. B informed D that his lorry was overladen; driving an overladen lorry on the road was an offence. D said that he was prepared to take the risk whereupon B gave him the weighbridge ticket and the property in (i.e. ownership of) the coal passed to D. Without this ticket D could not have left the colliery. A was charged with aiding, abetting, counselling, or procuring D's offence of driving an overladen lorry on the road. For the purposes of the appeal it was assumed that B knew he had the right to prevent the lorry leaving the colliery. A, through its servant B, supplied D with an essential item for the commission of the offence, namely the weighbridge ticket, and did so knowing the circumstances which would render D's act of driving on the road an offence. A's indifference to this consequence was irrelevant to liability as A, through its servant, had voluntarily done an act which assisted D knowing the circumstances which constituted the offence. **The intention required, therefore, is the voluntary performance of an act with the realisation that this assists or encourages D in his course of conduct** (see further *J. F. Alford Transport Ltd and Others* [1997] 2 Cr App R 326; see also *Bryce* [2004] EWCA Crim 1231).

There was much discussion in *NCB v Gamble* about whether ownership of the coal had passed prior to, or only after, the weighbridge ticket had been handed over. The suggestion was that if A only became aware of D's illegal purpose after ownership in the property had passed, but before delivery, he could not be liable as an accessory when he delivered what was D's property to him. This is unsatisfactory and not required by the law of contract. A contract for an illegal purpose is unenforceable regardless of when the seller learns of that purpose. No distinction should be made between the situation where A sells a gun to D knowing from the outset that D intends to use it to kill someone and the situation where D has paid for the gun (and ownership of it has passed) but before A delivers it to him he tells A that he intends to use it to kill someone (cf. *Garrett v Arthur Churchill (Glass) Ltd* [1970] 1 QB 92).

A problem with *NCB v Gamble* is that it provides the potential for extensive liability for accessories. For example, A sees D, a motorist, standing beside a vehicle which has a punctured tyre. He offers to change the tyre. When performing this act of charity he notices that one of the other tyres is partially bald, and therefore illegal. If A completes the task, will he be liable for aiding and abetting D's offence of driving a vehicle on the road with a defective tyre? Or, similarly, if he had noticed that one of the rear light panels was damaged before he changed the wheel, would he be liable for aiding and abetting D's offence of driving with defective lights? If intention does not require proof of a purpose, motive, or desire that the offence be committed, A's voluntary act of assistance with knowledge of the circumstances which constitute the principal offence, would seem to be sufficient for liability as an accessory.

7.1.4.2 Knowledge of the circumstances constituting the offence

In *Johnson v Youden* [1950] 1 KB 544, Lord Goddard CJ stated (at p. 546):

> Before a person can be convicted of aiding and abetting the commission of an offence he must at least know the essential matters which constitute that offence. He need not actually know that an offence has been committed, because he may not know that the facts constitute an offence and ignorance of the law is not a defence.

The 'essential matters which constitute that offence' refers to the circumstances of the *actus reus*, its consequences (in the case of a result crime) and, in certain circumstances, the *mens rea* of the principal. **A cannot be liable as an accessory if**

he is unaware of the circumstances which constitute the offence. In *Ferguson* v *Weaving* [1951] 1 KB 814, A, the licensee of a public house, was charged with aiding and abetting customers to commit the offence of consuming intoxicating liquor on licensed premises outside the permitted hours. A did not know that customers were still drinking after closing time. The Divisional Court held she could not be convicted if she did not know that customers were committing the principal offence.

Some matters, however, cannot be known although they may be foreseen, for example, the consequences of the perpetrator's act or his *mens rea*. Thus **where A gives assistance prior to the commission of the offence, it is more accurate to refer to his 'contemplation' rather than his knowledge.** 'Knowledge' for these purposes includes wilful blindness and subjective recklessness (see *Carter* v *Richardson* [1974] RTR 314 and *Blakely, Sutton* v *DPP* [1991] Crim LR 763) but it does not include constructive knowledge, a species of negligence. In *J. F. Alford Transport Ltd and Others* [1997] 2 Cr App R 326, the appellants' convictions of aiding and abetting the making of a false entry on a record sheet (i.e. a tachograph) contrary to s. 99(5) of the Transport Act 1968 were quashed by the Court of Appeal. Nineteen of the company's drivers had pleaded guilty to this offence as principals and the case against the appellants, as managers of a small company, was that they must have known and accepted, if not encouraged, what the drivers had done. Kennedy LJ, giving the judgment of the Court, stated that they accepted that knowledge may be inferred if a defendant shuts his eyes to the obvious, but went on to emphasise that Lord Goddard CJ's dictum in *Johnson* v *Youden* needs to be understood. He placed reliance on Gibbs CJ in the Australian case of *Giorgianni* v *The Queen* (1985) 156 CLR 473 at 483, stating:

> Gibbs CJ accepted that it would be sufficient to infer knowledge if a defendant deliberately refrained from making enquiries the results of which he did not care to have, but, he continued:
>
>> 'The failure to make such enquiries as a reasonable person would have made is not equivalent to knowledge; it is not enough to render a person liable as a secondary party that he ought to have known all the facts and would have done so if he acted with reasonable care and diligence. That is so even when the offence is one of strict liability, so that the actual perpetrator may be convicted in the absence of knowledge.'

As knowledge could not be proved the convictions had to be quashed.

Where the principal offence is one of strict liability, while the principal may be convicted without proof of *mens rea*, **an accessory may be convicted only where *mens rea* is proved.** In *Callow* v *Tillstone* (1900) 83 LT 411, A, a veterinary surgeon, was charged with aiding and abetting the exposure for sale by D, a butcher, of unsound meat. A had examined a carcass at D's request and certified it sound. A had performed the examination negligently and the meat was unsound. D was convicted of the strict liability offence of exposing the meat for sale. A's conviction, however, was quashed as he did not know the meat was unsound.

7.1.4.3 Knowledge of the type of offence

Where A counsels or procures D to commit a particular crime, A necessarily knows the type of offence involved as the commission of the offence is A's

purpose. For example, if A writes to D encouraging him to kill V, A will know that if D does so he will commit murder as he will have done so with the necessary *mens rea*.

Where A aids or abets D to commit an offence, commission of that offence may not be A's purpose or object.

 Example

A may sell D a gun to make a profit indifferent to the fact that D intends to use it to kill V. A may not intend for D to kill V, but he gives assistance intentionally knowing that D has the intention to kill. Several problems may arise, however, in cases of aiding and abetting: (i) A may not know the exact details of the crime D has in mind although he knows D intends to kill; (ii) A may not know the exact crime D intends to commit although he knows D is going to commit one of a range of offences; (iii) A knows that if particular circumstances arise D *will* commit a particular offence; and (iv) A knows that if particular circumstances arise D *may* commit a particular crime.

It is crucial, therefore, to determine how precise A's knowledge must be if he is to be convicted as an accessory.

In *Bainbridge* [1960] 1 QB 129, the Court of Criminal Appeal had to consider situation (i) stated in the previous example.

> A supplied oxygen-cutting equipment to D who used it to break into a branch of the Midland Bank and steal £18,000. A appealed his conviction as an accessory claiming that it had to be proved that he knew the precise details of the intended offence. The Court held it was sufficient that A knew the particular type of offence intended which was later committed.

Mere knowledge that the equipment was going to be used for some illegal venture, however, would not be sufficient. In *Bainbridge* the equipment had been used for only one offence. The Court left unresolved the question whether A would have been liable for breaking and entering offences committed on other banks. If A need not know the precise details of the offence the logical answer to this question is that he would be liable for each breaking and entering offence committed by using the equipment he had supplied.

In *Maxwell* v *DPP for Northern Ireland* (1979) 68 Cr App R 128, the House of Lords approved of, and extended, the principle in *Bainbridge* to cover situation (ii) in the earlier example.

> A drove his car guiding members of the UVF (an illegal organisation) in another car to a public house where he knew a terrorist attack was to be carried out whether by guns or bombs or otherwise. A pipe bomb was thrown into the pub. A was charged with (1) doing an act with intent to cause an explosion likely to endanger life or cause serious injury to property and (2) possession of explosive substances with intent to endanger life or cause serious injury to property. A was convicted and his conviction upheld as, although he did not know the precise type of offence intended to be committed, he knew that one of a limited number of serious crimes was intended and was, in fact, committed.

Thus an accessory will be liable where he contemplates the commission of one or more of a range of crimes by the principal and he intentionally lends

assistance to the principal who then commits one or more of these offences.
Lord Scarman stated (at p. 153) 'An accessory who leaves it to his principal to choose
is liable, provided always the choice is made from the range of offences from which
the accessory contemplates the choice will be made'. Thus if A gives D a jemmy
contemplating only that he will use it to break into houses to steal therein or break
open crates to steal their contents, he would be liable for any such offences, but he
would not be liable if D used the jemmy to injure a night-watchman who disturbed
him as he was attempting to enter the building. A problem which is unresolved,
however, is that burglary is an offence of ulterior intent. The ulterior intent specified under s. 9(2) of the Theft Act 1968 which must be proved for conviction under
s. 9(1)(a) is intention to steal, or inflict grievous bodily harm, or cause criminal
damage (see **13.2** *post*).

 Question

If D entered a house as a trespasser with the intention of inflicting grievous bodily harm on
the occupant, V, could A be convicted as an accessory to burglary?

The answer depends on whether burglary is a 'type' of crime or the different varie-
ties of burglary are different 'types' of crime. It is arguable that D's *mens rea* is one
of 'the essential matters which constitute the offence'. If A only contemplated D
stealing, D's intention to inflict GBH would appear to render the offence D committed a different type from the offence A contemplated. The contrary argument
is that the *actus reus* of burglary is the same regardless of the intent with which it is
committed and that A's assistance related to the effecting of the *actus reus*. Perhaps
assistance in resolving this conflict may be sought from the cases on deliberate
departure by the perpetrator from the joint enterprise. Breaking into a house with
intention to inflict GBH could be considered a substantial variation from the joint
enterprise which envisaged breaking into a house with intent to steal (see **7.1.4.4**
post). What is not in doubt is that if D does inflict GBH on the occupant A is not an
accessory to the offence of inflicting GBH.

   If A and D decide to rob a bank and agree that D will carry a gun to shoot anyone
who offers resistance, A will be liable for wounding or murder if D does shoot a
bank clerk or customer who resists. This is situation (iii) in the earlier example and
A will be liable even though he fervently hoped that no one would resist or if he
believed that resistance was only a remote possibility on the basis that 50 robberies
had been carried out successfully without any resistance being offered. It matters
not that A may have foreseen only a small risk of resistance being offered as he has
intentionally participated in an enterprise contemplating wounding or killing if
necessary; an intention is no less so because it is conditional on the occurrence of
other events (see *Betts and Ridley* (1930) 22 Cr App R 148).

   In **some cases the agreement between the parties to use force is not express
but implied** or, as it is referred to in some cases, 'tacit'. If it is a tacit understanding
of the parties before the enterprise is embarked upon that violence will be used if
certain circumstances arise, A will be liable. For example, A notices D is carrying

a gun, which they had not previously discussed. A asks D what it is for to which D replies 'Just in case!'. If A still goes ahead with the robbery he will be liable to the extent of his contemplation as he is tacitly agreeing to its use for whatever purpose he contemplates D intends. If he contemplated that D would use it to kill or wound he will be liable for murder if D does kill. If A only contemplated that D would use the gun to frighten but D used it to kill, A will not be liable for homicide (see further **7.1.4.4** *post*).

In situation (iv) A does not know that D will wound or kill if certain circumstances arise but he contemplates that he might. Is this situation distinguishable from situation (iii) discussed earlier?

Question

Is liability limited to tacit agreement or is contemplation of the possibility that D might commit the offence sufficient?

In *Chan Wing-Siu* [1985] 1 AC 168, the Privy Council gave the leading judgment on joint enterprises.

> A, D, and E, armed with knives, went to a flat intending to steal from V the occupant. V refused to hand over any money whereupon he was stabbed to death. A, D, and E were charged with murder. A claimed he was not involved in the killing as he was restraining V's wife in another room when D and E killed V. A argued at the trial and again on appeal that it had to be proved that he foresaw that death or grievous bodily harm would probably result from the joint enterprise if a contingency in which a weapon might be used by one of his companions eventuated. The jury were directed that each was guilty if proved to have contemplated that a knife might be used on the occasion by one of his accomplices with the intention of inflicting serious bodily injury. All three were convicted and appealed. The Privy Council dismissed their appeals. Sir Robin Cooke stated (at p. 175):

> > ...a secondary party is criminally liable for acts by the primary offender of a type which the former foresees but does not necessarily intend....[This principle] turns on contemplation or, putting the same idea in other words, authorisation, which may be express but is more usually implied. It meets the case of a crime foreseen as a possible incident of the common unlawful enterprise. The criminal culpability lies in participating in the venture with that foresight.

This statement is not entirely clear as Sir Robin equates contemplation with authorisation. The latter is more in line with the idea of joint conditional intent whereas the former relates to foresight of possible future *mens rea* which the perpetrator may form. Sir Robin appeared to accept later in his judgment that contemplation of the risk that another party to the offence might inflict harm with an intention adequate for murder would be sufficient. This has been affirmed as the correct basis for liability in subsequent Court of Appeal decisions after a period of some doubt. In *Hyde* [1990] 3 All ER 892, the Court of Appeal reviewed the authorities and concluded that the factor crucial to liability was contemplation rather than tacit agreement. Lord Lane CJ stated (at p. 896):

> If [A] realises (without agreeing to such conduct being used) that [D] may kill or intentionally inflict serious injury, but nevertheless continues to participate with [D] in the venture, that will amount to a sufficient mental element for [A] to be guilty of murder if [D], with the requisite intent, kills in the course of the venture.... [A] has in those circumstances lent himself to the enterprise which [A] realises may involve murder.

Hyde was approved by the Privy Council in *Hui Chi-ming* v *R* [1992] 1 AC 34 where Lord Lowry explained Sir Robin Cooke's ambiguous use of the word 'authorisation' (at p. 53):

> Their Lordships consider that [he] used this word...to emphasise the fact that mere foresight is not enough: the accessory in order to be guilty, must have foreseen the relevant offence which the principal may commit *as a possible incident of the common unlawful enterprise* and must, with such foresight, still have participated in the enterprise. The word 'authorisation' explains what is meant by contemplation but does not add a new ingredient.

In *R* v *Powell and Another*; *R* v *English* [1997] 3 WLR 959, the House of Lords confirmed that the test is one of 'contemplation', Lord Hutton stating (at p. 969) that:

> there is a strong line of authority that where two parties embark on a joint enterprise to commit a crime, and one party foresees that in the course of the enterprise the other party may carry out, with the requisite *mens rea*, an act constituting another crime, the former is liable for that crime if committed by the latter in the course of the enterprise.

The principle is a general one although the cases in which it has been developed have involved murder.

It may appear that an accessory is more harshly treated than the principal as the latter can only be convicted of murder where he intended to kill or cause grievous bodily harm, whereas the accessory will be liable if he foresaw this as a possible incident of the joint enterprise. In the appeal in *Powell* it was argued that this was an unacceptable anomaly. The *mens rea* of the accessory, however, relates not to the *actus reus* of the offence but to his own participation; he is liable because of his intentional participation in the contemplated offence(s), namely he has assisted or encouraged another to carry out an enterprise realising that it may result in that other committing murder. In such circumstances, according to Lord Hutton (at p. 976):

> the rules of the common law are not based solely on logic but relate to practical concerns and, in relation to crimes committed in the course of joint enterprises, to the need to give effective protection to the public against criminals operating in gangs.

Problems of remoteness may arise where the risk A contemplates is highly improbable. In *Chan Wing-Siu* Sir Robin Cooke confined an accessory's liability to situations where he had foreseen 'a substantial risk, a real risk, a risk that something might well happen'. In *Hui Chi-ming* Lord Lowry referred to foresight of 'possible incidents'. This issue did not receive detailed consideration in *Powell* although Lord Hutton did quote Sir Robin Cooke in *Chan Wing-Siu* who stated (at p. 177):

> Where a man lends himself to a criminal enterprise knowing that potentially murderous weapons are to be carried, and in the event they are in fact used by his partner with an intent sufficient for murder, he should not escape the consequences by his reliance upon a nuance of prior assessment, only too likely to have been optimistic.

He then went on to answer the certified question in *Powell* by stating (at p. 978):

> It is sufficient to found a conviction for murder for a secondary party to have realised that in the course of the joint enterprise the primary party *might* kill with intent to do so or with intent to cause grievous bodily harm. (emphasis added)

The House of Lords did not seek in any way to quantify the degree of risk which the secondary party must foresee for liability to arise. It is submitted that this is correct as the taking of even a slight risk cannot be justified where the enterprise in which the party is engaging is criminal. In relation to English's appeal Lord Hutton went on to state his agreement with the Privy Council in *Chan Wing-Siu* that (at p. 981):

> The secondary party is subject to criminal liability if he contemplated the act causing the death as a possible incident of the joint venture, unless the risk was so remote that the jury take the view that [he] genuinely dismissed it as altogether negligible.

7.1.4.4 Liability for acts beyond the common design

 Key Point

Three situations may arise and the liability of an accessory differs between them:

(1) D accidentally commits a different offence in performing the common design or commits the contemplated offence in a different but non relevant context;

(2) D commits the contemplated offence in unforeseen circumstances; and

(3) D deliberately commits an offence outside the scope of the parties' common design.

In situation (1) for example, if A encourages D to assault V and D does so but V dies, both A and D will be liable for manslaughter. Death may have been unforeseen but each party to a joint unlawful enterprise is equally liable for the consequences of acts done in pursuance thereof (see *Baldessare* (1930) 22 Cr App R 70). In *Anderson and Morris* [1966] 2 QB 110, Lord Parker stated the principle as follows (at p. 118):

> [W]here two persons embark on a joint enterprise, each is liable for the acts done in pursuance of that joint enterprise, [and]...that includes liability for unusual consequences if they arise from the execution of the agreed joint enterprise.

Similarly the doctrine of transferred malice applies to the liability of accessories. If D, endeavouring to assault V, had accidentally assaulted W, or assaulted W mistaking him for V, both A and D would be liable for the assault; the context of the offence differs from the common design in a non-relevant way (see *Gnango* [2011] UKSC 59, **7.1.2.1** *ante*). By contrast, if D had deliberately assaulted W, this would fall within situation (3) and A would not be liable as the execution varies from the common design in a matter of substance. Hawkins stated the principle as follows (2 PC c29, s. 21):

> But if a man command another to commit a felony on a particular person or thing and he do it on another; as to kill A and he kill B or to burn the house of A and he burn the house of B or to steal an ox and he steal a horse; or to steal such an horse and he steal another; or to commit a felony of one kind and he commit another of a quite different nature; as to rob JS of his plate as he is going to market, and he break open his house in the night and there steal the plate; it is said that the commander is not an accessory because the act done varies in substance from that which was commanded.

What amounts to a variation in substance will not always be easy to define. In the examples Hawkins gives the perpetrator departs from the plan in each case in a significant way. An insignificant variation would be the case of robbing JS; if the principal had robbed him on the way back from market the accessory would remain liable for robbery. A variation from the common design, however, will not relieve an accessory of all liability. He may remain liable for incitement or conspiracy or he may be liable for a necessarily included lesser offence. In the example of stealing JS's plate (which falls within situation (3) *ante*) the accessory would not be liable for burglary but he would be liable for simple theft as the counselled offence was robbery which involves theft and the offence committed was burglary which in this instance also involved theft. Similarly, if A had encouraged D to indecently assault V and D had raped V, A would not be liable for rape but would still be liable for indecent assault as rape necessarily involves indecent assault.

In *Saunders and Archer* (1573) 2 Plowd 473, S desired to kill his wife and sought the assistance of A who supplied him with poison. S put this poison in an apple and gave it to his wife who ate a little but gave the remainder to their daughter. S watched this without intervening and the daughter died of poisoning. S was held guilty of murder; his failure to intervene amounted to a deliberate variation in substance from the common design and thus A was acquitted. If S had not been present when the wife gave the apple to the daughter the doctrine of transferred malice would have applied. If the facts of *Saunders and Archer* occurred today, A could be convicted of conspiracy to murder or of aiding, abetting, counselling, or procuring S's attempt to kill his wife (see *Hapgood and Wyatt* (1870) LR 1 CCR 221).

Where the common design involves a conditional intention, the accessory will only be liable where the condition is fulfilled. For example, A and D suspect that V, their accomplice in crimes of robbery, is cheating them out of their fair share of the loot. A suggests to D that he should kill V if this happens again. After V divides the loot following the next robbery D shoots him although he has not cheated as D wants a bigger share. A would not be liable as an accessory as the condition had not been fulfilled but he could be liable for conspiracy to kill.

A problem which sometimes arises is that of the contemplated offence being committed by different means. If A contemplates that D might kill V with a gun but nonetheless continues with the enterprise, he cannot hope to evade liability if D kills V with some other weapon. In *English* [1997] 3 WLR 959, Lord Hutton stated (at p. 981):

> [I]f the weapon used by the primary party is different to, but as dangerous as, the weapon which the secondary party contemplated he might use, the secondary party should not escape liability for murder because of the difference in the weapon, for example, if he foresaw that the primary party might use a gun to kill and the latter used a knife to kill, or vice versa.

In each case it will be for the jury to decide whether the use of a particular weapon went beyond the common design of the parties (see further *Uddin* [1998] 2 All ER 744; *Greatrex* [1999] 1 Cr App R 126). **Where, however, situation (3) arises D does not merely commit the contemplated offence in circumstances which depart from the common design in an immaterial way but he goes beyond the common design and commits an offence different from that contemplated.** This situation seems to arise most often in spontaneous attacks by a group on another or others. The problem for the jury will be to determine what the intentions of the individual assailants were and what possible offences by their fellow assailants they contemplated. Following the decisions of the House of Lords in *R v Powell; R v English* [1997] 3 WLR 959, the Court of Appeal in *Uddin* stated the principles as follows (p. 751):

> (i) Where several persons join to attack a victim in circumstances which show that they intend to inflict serious harm and as a result of the attack the victim sustains fatal injury, they are jointly liable for murder; but if such injury inflicted with that intent is shown to have been caused solely by the actions of one participant of a type entirely different from the actions which the others foresaw as part of the attack, only that participant is guilty of murder.

An example endorsed by Lord Hutton in *English* occurred in the case of *Gamble* [1989] NI 268. A and B were parties to what they thought was going to be a punishment beating and contemplated that it might involve at the worst 'knee-capping' the victim. The other two participants, however, murdered the victim in the course of an attack which involved multiple stab wounds, gunshot wounds, and blows to the head and body. Two of the gunshot wounds would have been fatal had death not been caused by cutting the victim's throat. Carswell J, sitting without a jury in the Crown Court of Northern Ireland, convicted A and B of wounding with intent to inflict grievous bodily harm. Counsel for the Crown had argued that as A and B had both intended GBH and that this was sufficient *mens rea* for murder, they should be convicted of murder. In response to this argument Carswell J stated (at p. 284):

> Although the rule remains well entrenched that an intention to inflict grievous bodily harm qualifies as the *mens rea* of murder, it is not in my opinion necessary to apply it in such a way as to fix an accessory with liability for a consequence which he did not intend and which stems from an act which he did not have within his contemplation.

In *Uddin* the second principle stated is:

> (ii) In deciding whether the actions are of such a different type the use by that party of a weapon is a significant factor. If the character of the weapon, e.g. its propensity to cause death is different from any weapon used or contemplated by the others and if it is used with a specific intent to kill, the others are not responsible for the death unless it is proved that they knew or foresaw the likelihood of the use of such a weapon.

In *English* A and D attacked a police officer using wooden posts. Unknown to A, D carried a knife and drew it stabbing the officer who died from the stab wounds. A's conviction for murder was quashed as D's action went beyond the common design. Furthermore, Lord Hutton made it clear in *English* that in such circumstances because the unforeseen use of the knife took the killing outside the scope of the joint enterprise (which was to injure V using wooden posts), the jury should also have been directed that A was not guilty of manslaughter. A participant such as A would, however, be guilty of the offences he had committed such as assault occasioning actual bodily harm, or inflicting grievous bodily harm (see also *Uddin*; cf. *Webb* [2006] EWCA Crim 962).

In *O'Flaherty and Others* [2004] EWCA Crim 526, the Court of Appeal emphasised that the principles set out in *Uddin* are not principles of law but matters of evidence. The question whether the use, for example, of a knife is fundamentally different from any act which the defendant realised the principal might do was a question of fact for the jury. The Court made it clear that what they wished to avoid was 'the creation of a complex body of doctrine as to whether one weapon (for instance a knife) differs in character from another (for example a claw hammer) and which weapons are more likely to inflict fatal injury.' Of course, if A acquires knowledge during the course of a concerted assault on V that D has a lethal weapon and A continues with the assault, this will alter the outcome. Beldam LJ stated the principle in *Uddin* (at p. 752):

> (v) If in the course of the concerted attack a weapon is produced by one of the participants and the others knowing that he has it in circumstances where he may use it in the course of the attack participate or continue to participate in the attack, they will be guilty of murder if the weapon is used to inflict a fatal wound.

In the previously discussed cases of *English*, *Gamble*, and *Uddin* the principal, D, has departed from the scope of the joint enterprise by committing a crime of a different type from that contemplated by the secondary party, A, or in a different manner from that foreseen by A.

At this point, the law appeared to be reasonably clear and one would have hoped that new situations that might arise would be readily fitted into this framework. But a problem which the cases did not directly address was that of the principal doing the act contemplated but with a more serious intent than the accessory foresaw. For example, A and D agree to attack V to cause him serious harm but D carries out the attack intending to kill V and does so. The intent to cause serious harm is sufficient for murder. In these circumstances, if A only contemplated D acting with this intent, could he nonetheless be convicted as an accessory to murder? If D has not used a more dangerous weapon than was contemplated, one would expect the answer to be in the affirmative. The House of Lords addressed this problem in *Rahman* [2008] UKHL 45.

> A group of Asian youths, including the appellants A and B, armed with baseball bats, a metal bar and a table leg, engaged in a fight with another group of youths, including V, armed with pieces of wood. V was killed, the cause of death being three knife wounds inflicted by one of the group of Asian youths. A and B were arrested at the scene, the others having escaped, and were charged with murder. The Crown case was that A and B involved themselves in the attack either with the deliberate intent to inflict serious physical harm or, by their conduct, intentionally encouraged others to do so; each had the common intention that serious bodily harm be inflicted; and the circumstances of the attack were such that each of them knew that weapons such as baseball bats, and a knife or knives might be used to inflict such harm. A and B contended that they had joined the enterprise with at most the intent to cause serious harm but had no knowledge or foresight that anyone else intended to kill. They contended that they neither had knives nor foresaw anyone else using a knife. Further, they contended that the nature of the knife wounds demonstrated an intent to kill and thus the acts of the principal were outside the scope of the joint enterprise to inflict serious harm. The judge directed the jury to convict a particular defendant only if they were sure that he realised that 'one or more of the attackers might produce and use a knife in the attack and that such attacker might kill with the intention of killing [V] or causing him really serious injury'. A and B were convicted and had their appeals to the Court of Appeal dismissed.

The case should not have given rise to any difficulty as the jury could only convict if satisfied that that defendant realised a fellow attacker might produce a knife and use it with the *mens rea* for murder. The Court of Appeal certified that a point of law of general public importance was involved in its decision as follows:

> If in the course of a joint enterprise to inflict unlawful violence the principal party kills with an intention to kill which is unknown to and unforeseen by a secondary party, is the principal's intention relevant,
>
> (1) to whether the killing was within the scope of a common purpose to which the secondary party was an accessory?
>
> (2) to whether the principal's act was fundamentally different from the act or acts which the secondary party foresaw as part of the joint enterprise?

Their Lordships answered both questions in the negative. The essence of their answer is that **if D kills with intent to kill and all that A foresaw was that D might intentionally cause serious injury, D's greater *mens rea* does not serve to make his act fundamentally different so as to bring the situation within** *English*. Lord Bingham gave two reasons for this response. The first was to avoid making an already complex area of the law any more complex. He stated (at paras. 24 and 25):

> ... Given the fluid, fast-moving course of events in incidents such as that which culminated in the killing of the deceased, incidents which are unhappily not rare, it must often be very hard for jurors to make a reliable assessment of what a particular defendant

foresaw as likely or possible acts on the part of his associates. It would be even harder, and would border on speculation, to judge what a particular defendant foresaw as the intention with which his associates might perform such acts. It is safer to focus on the defendant's foresight of what an associate might do, an issue to which knowledge of the associate's possession of an obviously lethal weapon such as a gun or a knife would usually be very relevant.

Secondly, the appellants' submission...undermines the principle on which...our law of murder is based. In the prosecution of a principal offender for murder, it is not necessary for the prosecution to prove or the jury to consider whether the defendant intended on the one hand to kill or on the other to cause really serious injury. That is legally irrelevant to guilt. The rationale of that principle plainly is that if a person unlawfully assaults another with intent to cause him really serious injury, and death results, he should be held criminally responsible for that fatality, even though he did not intend it. If he had not embarked on a course of deliberate violence, the fatality would not have occurred....To rule that an undisclosed and unforeseen intention to kill on the part of the primary offender may take a killing outside the scope of a common purpose to cause really serious injury, calling for a distinction irrelevant in the case of the primary offender, is in my view to subvert the rationale which underlies our law of murder.'

Of course, the jury do have to consider already whether A foresaw that D would act with the *mens rea* which the offence requires; what their Lordships wished to avoid is any closer analysis of the type of intent D had in a murder case where either of two states of mind will suffice. This position merits no criticism. The problem, however, is when one moves to the second element of the certified question and consideration has to be given to what 'fundamentally different' means and when reliance may be placed upon this principle. Their Lordships endorsed the principles set out in *Chan Wing-Siu*, *Hyde* and *Powell and English*, Lord Rodger of Earlsferry stating (para. 33):

If A and D agree to kill their victim and proceed to attack him with that intention, they are both guilty of murder irrespective of who struck the fatal blow....It can...make no difference if A and D agree to kill their victim by beating him to death with baseball bats, but in the course of the attack D pulls out a gun and shoots him. A must still be guilty of murder: since he intended to bring about the death of the victim, A cannot escape guilt on the ground that he did not foresee that D would kill him by using a gun instead of a baseball bat. The unforeseen nature of the weapon is immaterial.

Lords Bingham and Rodger suggested no change to the 'fundamental difference' principle; Lord Bingham was of the view that 'fundamentally different' had a 'plain meaning' and was not a term of art. In the context of the instant case, a change in D's intent did not make his act of stabbing fundamentally different from that contemplated by A and D. If matters had stopped here, there would have been no difficulty. Lord Brown of Eaton-under-Heywood, however, decided to go further in his exposition of the 'fundamental difference' principle and Lords Neuberger of Abbotsbury and Scott of Foscote expressed their agreement. As the convictions were based on a clear finding by the jury that A and D had foreseen the use of a knife with the *mens rea* for murder, anything further is strictly *obiter*. Lord Brown stated (at para. 68):

If A realizes (without agreeing to such conduct being used) that D may kill or intentionally inflict serious injury, but nevertheless continues to participate with D in the venture, that will amount to a sufficient mental element for A to be guilty of murder if D, with the requisite intent, kills in the course of the venture *unless (i) D suddenly produces and uses a weapon of which A knows nothing and which is more lethal than any weapon which A contemplates that D or any other participant may be carrying and (ii) for that reason D's act is to be regarded as fundamentally different from anything foreseen by A.* [The italicised words are designed to reflect the *English* qualification].

With respect, this statement of principle bears little resemblance to the *English* principle. It would permit A to rely on 'fundamental difference' where he recognised that D might kill with intent. The restatement by Lord Brown seems to contradict the position endorsed by Lord Rodger quoted earlier to the effect that 'the unforeseen nature of the weapon is immaterial'. It also seems to conflict with *Chan Wing-Siu* which Lords Bingham and Rodger endorsed. In particular, if A lends himself to a venture foreseeing that D might kill with the necessary intent, why should it matter a jot what weapon D chooses to use to kill V? In *English* the fundamental difference related not just to the weapon D used but the purpose (intent) for which he used it. The joint venture was to beat up V. While A could have been liable for murder had the joint beating of V with sticks resulted in his death, he was not to be convicted where D stabbed V killing him. A had not foreseen a killing, and certainly not one with a different weapon and with intent to kill. Both the use of the different weapon, and the intent with which it was used, seemed to be equally significant in making D's act something fundamentally different to that which A had contemplated and which had constituted the limits of the common purpose to their joint enterprise.

Lord Brown's restatement of the 'fundamental difference' principle also involves a requirement that A be unaware of the weapon which D uses to kill V. In *English* the House of Lords endorsed the decision in *Gamble* where V was killed by D by having his throat slit, A having contemplated only a knee-capping. This was a consequence which A did not foresee, desire, or intend. In *Gamble* V had also been shot three times and would have died of those wounds (which were not wounds to his knees) had his throat not first been slit. Their Lordships in *English* did not resolve the issue whether A should have been convicted had the death in *Gamble* been caused by the other bullet wounds which A had not foreseen. In *Rahman*, however, Lords Scott, Brown, and Neuberger doubted the correctness of *Gamble* on its facts as under the restated 'fundamental difference' principle, a knife would not be considered more lethal than a gun. It is difficult to see, however, how such a killing could fall within A's contemplation. Rarified debates will doubtless ensue in some courtrooms over the 'lethal' relativities of various weapons. The answer to such questions is very far removed from the issue of what did A contemplate and in what way did D do an act beyond that which was contemplated. Limiting 'fundamental difference' of an act, to 'fundamental difference of the lethal qualities of a weapon' may be considered by some of their Lordships to be an easier issue for a jury to determine. This shift of focus, however, does not make the law either clearer or more just if it involves losing sight of the need to identify the common purpose between A and D which is at the heart of joint enterprise. Why should A not be entitled to an acquittal for murder in circumstances similar to those in *Gamble* where, for example, the agreed knee-capping (the common purpose) becomes an execution where D shoots V in the head—an act (and an intent) completely outwith A's contemplation and outwith their common purpose? D's act here is fundamentally different to that which A and D agreed even though the weapon used is the one A contemplated being used.

It has been left to the Court of Appeal to try to resolve some of the problems left by *Rahman*. In *Mendez and Thompson* [2010] EWCA Crim 516, the Court of Appeal sought to state some clear principles (after engaging in a very confused exposition of the principles of secondary liability erroneously stating that they are founded on the principle of causation). The following propositions may, however, usefully be drawn from their judgment:

1. If the common purpose is to kill and D does so, it should not alter A's liability for murder whether D used a different and possibly surer way of achieving the objective than they had planned.

2. In cases where the common purpose is not to kill but to cause serious harm, A is not liable for the murder of V if the direct cause of V's death was a deliberate act by D which was of a kind (a) unforeseen by A and (b) likely to be altogether more life-threatening than acts of the kind intended or foreseen by A. The reference to 'a deliberate act' is to the quality of the act— deliberate and not by chance—rather than to any consideration of D's intention as to the consequences.

(See also *A, B, C and D* [2010] EWCA Crim 1622).

 Question

Where D performs the very acts which A foresaw, but does so with the *mens rea* for a more serious crime than any contemplated or foreseen by A, will A be acquitted or be liable to the extent of his contemplation?

For example, A contemplates that D might hit V over the head intending ABH but D does the act intending GBH or death, may A be convicted of manslaughter if D is convicted of murder? In *Lovesey and Peterson* [1970] 1 QB 352 Lord Widgery CJ stated (at p. 356):

> It is clear that a common design to use unlawful violence, short of the infliction of grievous bodily harm, renders all co-adventurers guilty of manslaughter if the victim's death is an unexpected consequence of the carrying out of that design. Where, however, the victim's death is not the product of the common design but is attributable to one of the co-adventurers going beyond the scope of that design, by using violence which is intended to cause grievous bodily harm, the others are not responsible for that unauthorised act.

This decision was followed in *Dunbar* [1988] Crim LR 693 and *Wan and Chan* [1995] Crim LR 296. By contrast in *Stewart and Schofield* [1995] 1 Cr App R 441 the Court of Appeal took the view that each party to a contemplated unlawful act which caused death should be liable to the extent of their *mens rea*. This decision was followed by the Northern Ireland Court of Appeal in *Gilmour* [2000] 2 Cr App R 407.

A drove D and E to a house where they threw a petrol bomb resulting in the death of three children in the ensuing fire. A had remained in the car throughout but knew that a petrol bomb was to be thrown into the house. He was tried before a judge sitting alone and convicted of three counts of murder and appealed. The Court of Appeal concluded that the trial judge was wrong to conclude that he appreciated that the principals intended to inflict grievous bodily harm and quashed his convictions of murder. It was further argued that as A did not share the intention of the principals he should not be guilty of manslaughter. The Northern Ireland Court of Appeal rejected this argument drawing a distinction between the situation where a principal departs from the contemplated joint enterprise committing a more serious act of a different kind from that foreseen by the accessory, and that where the principal carries out the very act contemplated by the accessory, though the latter does not realise that the principal intends a more serious consequence from the act. Carswell LCJ stated (at p. 415):

> We do not, however, see any convincing policy reason why a person acting as an accessory to a principal who carries out the very deed contemplated by both should not be guilty of the degree of offence appropriate to the intent with which he so acted.

A verdict of manslaughter on each of the three counts was substituted. (see also *R v Day (M) and Others* [2001] Crim LR 984; *A-G's Reference (No. 3 of 2004)* [2005] EWCA Crim 1882; *Yemoh* [2009] EWCA Crim 930; and *Carpenter* [2011] EWCA Crim 2568).

7.1.5 Withdrawal from the joint enterprise

 Question

If A has encouraged D to commit an offence, or is present assisting D to commit an offence, is it possible for him to escape liability by withdrawing from the enterprise before the offence is committed?

Withdrawal will clearly not affect A's liability for incitement or conspiracy or attempt where the principal has reached the stage of performing a 'more than merely preparatory act' (see **8.4.3** *post*) before A withdraws. Actual withdrawal from the enterprise must be effective if A is to escape liability for the completed offence; a mere change of heart without more is not sufficient (see *Becerra* (1975) 62 Cr App R 212; *Rook* (1993) 97 Cr App R 327). What is required will depend on the assistance or encouragement A has given. If A has counselled D to commit the offence he may withdraw by expressly countermanding or revoking his encouragement (see *Saunders and Archer* (1573) 2 Plowd 473; *Croft* [1944] 1 KB 295) although he may still be liable for incitement. The communication must, where practicable and reasonable, be timely and 'serve unequivocal notice upon the other party to the common unlawful cause that if he proceeds upon it he does so without the further aid and assistance of those who withdraw' (*per* Sloan JA in *Whitehouse* (1941) 1 WWR 112, quoted with approval in *Becerra*).

In *Mitchell* [1999] Crim LR 496, the Court of Appeal ruled that a direction based on *Whitehouse* requiring communication of withdrawal by the accessory to the principal was not necessary when violence was spontaneous rather than pre-planned. A, B, and D had engaged in a fight with U, V, and W, the owner of a restaurant and his two sons after D had assaulted other customers in the restaurant and caused damage to the restaurant. There was some evidence that after leaving V prostrate on the ground having been the recipient of a concerted attack involving beating with a stick, kicking, and stamping on his head, D had returned to administer a further beating to V's head with the stick. The Court of Appeal quashed A and B's convictions for murder and ordered a retrial as if the fatal blows were those which D administered at a time when A and B had desisted from the attack and walked away, their desistance may have been sufficient to constitute withdrawal from the joint enterprise leaving D solely responsible for the murder of V. As this possibility had not been clearly left to the jury the Court of Appeal considered the convictions unsafe. It is submitted that this ruling is too favourable to accessories. If A has participated in a violent attack upon V in which he has intended GBH to V and has contemplated that D may at least intend the same, A should remain liable to conviction for murder even though he has ceased his attack on V if D persists with the attack resulting in V's death. A's simple desistance does not in any way countermand the encouragement or assistance he has already rendered to D, nor does it serve any kind of notice on D that the prior encouragement is countermanded. To seek to distinguish pre-planned violence from spontaneous violence will give rise to inane discussions as to the relative meanings of 'spontaneous' and 'pre-planned' which are irrelevant to the question of accessorial liability. There are no degrees of joint enterprise which depend on spontaneity or pre-planning.

Fortunately the Court of Appeal has moved quickly to limit *Mitchell*. In *Robinson*, 3 February 2000 (Case No: 9903443Y3), D and a group of youths had followed V taunting him. The group looked to D for leadership and called on him to hit V. D did so, whereupon the group joined in the attack. D stood back while they did so but when the attack appeared to be going further than he intended, he intervened and the attack ceased. The Court of Appeal followed *Becerra* holding that, in the instant case where violence was not spontaneous, communication of withdrawal was necessary. Furthermore, Otton LJ stated:

> There is a clear line of authority that where a party has given encouragement to others to commit an offence it cannot be withdrawn once the offence has commenced. (See *R v Whitefield* (1983) 79 Cr App R 36, *R v Rook* (1993) 97 Cr App R 327 and *R v Pearman* [1996] 1 Cr App R 24.)

His Lordship, who also gave the judgment of the Court in *Mitchell*, quoted from Professor Smith's *Commentary to Mitchell* [1999] Crim LR 496 with approval, and made it clear that *Mitchell* was an exceptional case stating:

> it can only be in exceptional circumstances that a person can withdraw from a crime he has initiated. Similarly in those rare circumstances communication of withdrawal must be given in order to give the principal offenders the opportunity to desist rather than complete the crime. This must be so even in situations of spontaneous violence unless

it is not practicable or reasonable so to communicate as in the exceptional circumstances pertaining in *Mitchell* where the accused threw down his weapon and moved away before the final and fatal blows were inflicted.

This appears to be treating *Mitchell* as a very exceptional case and shifting the emphasis away from the spontaneous nature of the violence to the fact that the original violence had clearly ceased and A and B had withdrawn before D returned to inflict further violence. Had the attack been continuing when they withdrew, the suggestion in *Robinson* is that this would not have been effective. The effect of this judgment appears to limit withdrawal where encouragement has been offered to the period prior to the commencement of the offence. If the attack on the victim which D has initiated commences, it will be too late for him to withdraw and avoid liability. Unfortunately, in *O'Flaherty and Others* [2004] EWCA Crim 526, the Court of Appeal in *obiter* comments not having had the benefit of being referred to *Robinson* expressed approval of the decision in *Mitchell and King* that 'while communication of withdrawal is a necessary precondition for disassociation from pre-planned violence it is not necessary when violence is spontaneous.' The Court of Appeal's ability to propagate confusion is depressing.

Where A has supplied the means of committing the crime, a change of heart and quitting of the scene prior to the offence being committed would not be sufficient (*Whitehouse*). In *Becerra*, A, D, and E broke into a house intending to steal. A gave D a knife to use if necessary on anyone interrupting them. When V came downstairs to investigate the noise, A said, 'There's a bloke coming. Let's go,' and jumped out of the window. D stabbed V with the knife, killing him. A's conviction of murder was upheld by the Court of Appeal as he had not effectively withdrawn from the joint enterprise. What amounts to effective withdrawal will vary with the circumstances of each case. It was believed that sometimes nothing less than physical intervention would suffice. The Court did not state if this would have been necessary in the instant case; it was sufficient for the purposes of disposing of the appeal to state that what A had done was not enough. The Northern Ireland Court of Appeal adopted a similar approach in *Graham* [1996] NI 157 in upholding A's conviction for murder. A had taken a terrorist kidnap victim, V, from a house in which he had hidden following his escape to a house where A knew the kidnappers would be, realising that they would likely kill V. A refused to render any further assistance to the kidnappers and asked them not to harm V. The kidnappers took V to waste ground and shot him in the head. Carswell LJ stated (at p. 169):

> We consider that at the late stage which the murder plan had reached, and after the appellant had played such a significant part in assisting the killers to accomplish their aim, it could not be a sufficient withdrawal to indicate to them that he no longer supported their enterprise. Something more was required, and the judge was amply justified in holding that what the appellant did was not enough. His pleas were useless and the withholding of co-operation…was of minimal effect. We do not find it necessary to attempt to specify what acts would have been required of the appellant in the circumstances. It is sufficient for present purposes for us to say that the steps which he did take cannot be regarded as sufficient for withdrawal.

In *Grundy* [1977] Crim LR 543, A gave burglars information about premises and the habits of the occupants six weeks before the burglary took place. Four weeks later A tried to dissuade them from committing the offence. His conviction was quashed as this evidence of effective withdrawal had not been left to the jury. In *Whitefield* (1983) 79 Cr App R 36, A gave D similar information and agreed to break into the premises with D. Later he withdrew but D went on alone and A took no steps to stop him. The Court of Appeal held that there was evidence that A had served unequivocal notice on D that if he proceeded with the burglary he would do so without A's aid and assistance, and the judge's ruling that this was not enough and that notification of the police or other steps to prevent the burglary was required, was wrong. Both these cases appear to be unduly liberal towards the accessory. The information supplied remained of use to the burglars and was not negated by the suppliers' subsequent efforts to dissuade the burglars. If the appellants in *Grundy* and *Whitefield* had only counselled the commission of burglary without supplying information which assisted the burglars, verbal communication of withdrawal would suffice. Where something more is done, it is submitted that the withdrawal should not be considered effective if the accessory has not notified the police or warned the owners of the premises. The Court of Appeal in *Rook* (1993) 97 Cr App R 327, found it unnecessary to, and thus was not prepared to, decide whether, in cases where aid has been given prior to the commission of the crime, steps would be necessary to neutralise such aid for withdrawal to be effective. Unfortunately, in *O'Flaherty and Others* [2004] EWCA Crim 526, the Court of Appeal, once again, in *obiter* comments expressed its approval of the decisions in *Grundy* and *Whitefield*. Mantell LJ stated (at para. 60):

> In cases of assistance it has sometimes been suggested that, for there to be an effective withdrawal, reasonable steps must have been taken to prevent the crime. It is clear, however, this is not necessary.

The failure of the Court of Appeal to distinguish between the situation where a person participates only by verbally inciting or encouraging and that where he participates by providing something of continuing use or assistance to the principal (whether it be a weapon or information) is, to say the least, disappointing. In light of the confusion propagated by the Court of Appeal in its various judgments, however, it is not surprising. It is this author's view, as it is of many other commentators, that withdrawal should not, as a matter of principle, be considered effective where it does not neutralise the effect of any assistance already given or, at least, endeavour to do so by taking other reasonable steps.

7.1.6 Victims as accessories

The fact that A is a victim of the offence does not, of itself, prevent him being convicted as an aider and abettor. For example, consent is a limited defence to offences against the person operating only where the action can be positively justified by some public interest. If A is a masochist and he permits D, a sadist, to wound him for his sexual gratification, A would be an aider and abettor to D's offence of unlawful wounding as there is no public interest justifying D's action (see further

10.1.1.3.1 *post*). Similarly, if A permits D to perform an unlawful abortion on her she can be convicted as an aider and abettor to that offence (see *Sockett* (1908) 1 Cr App R 101). Where a statute is designed to protect a certain class of persons, however, a member of that class who is the victim of the offence cannot be convicted as an accessory. In *Tyrrell* [1894] 1 QB 710, A, a girl between the ages of 13 and 16, was convicted of aiding and abetting D to have unlawful sexual intercourse with her contrary to s. 5 of the Criminal Law Amendment Act 1885 (see now Sexual Offences Act 2003, s. 9). Her conviction was quashed on appeal, Lord Coleridge CJ stating (at p. 712) that 'it is impossible to say that the Act…can have intended that the girls for whose protection it was passed should be punishable under it for the offences committed upon themselves' (see also *Whitehouse* [1977] QB 868).

In *Gnango* [2011] UKSC 59 the Supreme Court made it clear that the victim rule only operates where an offence is created specifically to protect the victim; it does not operate generally where a person happens to be an actual or intended victim of the offence. In this case the fact that G was engaged in a gunfight with B and could have been murdered by him did not serve to shield G from conviction for murder as an accessory when V, a passer-by, was accidentally shot by B who was liable to conviction as principal on the basis of the doctrine of transferred malice (see **3.6.2.3** and **7.1.2.1** *ante*).

7.1.7 Entrapment and accessorial liability

Many offences are only detected because of proactive policing. For example, undercover drugs officers infiltrating a smuggling operation or drugs dealing enterprise to obtain evidence against the participants, or an undercover officer or informer infiltrating a gang of robbers to obtain information leading to their apprehension *in flagrante delicto*, or undercover officers lingering in public toilets to arrest any person who solicits them for homosexual purposes. Is such an officer ever liable to conviction as an accessory?

 Key Point

The situations and persons involved may be divided into four types:

(1) those who merely observe the crime but play no part in the instigation of the offence, namely spies;

(2) those decoys who accede to the accused's suggestions and thereby help provide the opportunity for the commission of the offence, namely collaborators;

(3) those decoys who expose the accused to temptation and thereby facilitate the commission of the offence by the accused, namely tempters; and

(4) those decoys who actively entice, encourage, or persuade the accused to commit an offence, which he would not otherwise commit, for the purpose of entrapping him, namely *agents provocateurs*.

The aim of the spy or decoy in all cases is to obtain evidence of the commission of an offence by the accused which will be sufficient for, or necessary to, a prosecution. The propriety of the behaviour of the spy or decoy in so doing varies from one category to another. The courts appear to approve of the behaviour in the first three categories but consider that the behaviour involved in the fourth situation goes too far and involves the *agent provocateur* in complicity in the offence which the accused ultimately commits. In *Mullins* (1848) 3 Cox CC 526, Maule J stated (at p. 531) that a person acting as a spy does not deserve to be blamed 'if he instigates offences no further than by pretending to concur with the perpetrators'. In *Birtles* (1969) 53 Cr App R 469, Lord Parker CJ stated (at p. 473):

> [I]t is vitally important to ensure so far as possible that the informer does not create an offence, that is to say, incite others to commit an offence which those others would not otherwise have committed. It is one thing for the police to make use of information concerning an offence that is already laid on.... But it is quite another thing, and something of which this court thoroughly disapproves, to use an informer to encourage another to commit an offence, or indeed an offence of a more serious character, which he would not otherwise commit, still more so if the police themselves take part in carrying it out.

This view has been echoed in subsequent cases such as *McCann* (1971) 56 Cr App R 359; *Mealey and Sheridan* (1975) 60 Cr App R 59; *McEvilly and Lee* (1973) 60 Cr App R 150.

In *Edwards* [1991] Crim LR 45, undercover officers were introduced to E, a suspected drugs dealer. E agreed to supply them with drugs and agreed a discount on future deals. It was clear that this particular conspiracy to supply drugs to the officers would not have taken place but for the officers' enticement of E. E, however, was prosecuted for conspiracy to supply controlled drugs to persons unknown; the officers' evidence was treated as evidence of this wider, established conspiracy which they clearly had not instigated, and thus they had not acted as *agents provocateurs*.

In *Sang* [1979] 2 All ER 1222, Lord Salmon suggested that police officers and informers involved in improper instances of entrapment should be prosecuted. He stated (at p. 1236):

> I would now refer to what is, I believe, and hope, the unusual case in which a dishonest policeman, anxious to improve his detection record, tries very hard with the help of an *agent provocateur* to induce a young man with no criminal tendencies to commit a serious crime, and ultimately the young man succumbs to the inducement....The policeman and the informer who acted together in inciting him to commit the crime should...both be prosecuted and suitably punished.

Lord Diplock also accepted that a police officer or informer would be liable as accessories (at p. 1226). Lord Salmon includes several superfluous requirements such that the police officer be dishonest, the accused be young, and the crime serious. These add nothing to the basic criterion which is that the accused is encouraged to commit an offence which would not otherwise have been committed, that is, to use Lord Parker's words, an offence which was not 'laid on'. The fact that the officer's or informer's motive may have been the detection of crime is irrelevant (see further *Yip Chiu-Cheung v R* [1994] 3 WLR 514 and **8.3.3.3** *post*).

In *Smith* [1960] 2 QB 423, D, a private individual seeking to expose corruption in local government, offered a bribe to the mayor of Castleford. D was convicted of corruption contrary to s. 1(2) of the Public Bodies Corrupt Practices Act 1889, the Court of Appeal holding that the purity of his motives provided him with no defence. Where an offence is 'laid on', however, it may be appropriate in some circumstances for a police officer or informer to participate in the offence. In *Birtles* Lord Parker CJ stated (at p. 473):

> In such a case the police are clearly entitled, indeed it is their duty, to mitigate the consequences of the proposed offence, for example, to protect the proposed victim, and to that end it may be perfectly proper for them to encourage the informer to take part in the offence or indeed for a police officer himself to do so.

If an officer or informer does participate his behaviour will be lawful. In *Clarke* (1984) 80 Cr App R 344, Macpherson J enlarged upon Lord Parker's dicta stating (at p. 348):

> In using the expression 'it may be perfectly proper' the Lord Chief Justice was, in our judgment, contemplating that in such exceptional cases where an informer (and/or a policeman) took part in a 'laid on' case there should be no finding that it was unlawful so to do.

For example, D tells A that he is going to commit a burglary. A is unable to dissuade him from so doing but agrees to drive D to the scene of the offence. A then telephones the police and D is caught *in flagrante delicto*. The decision in *Clarke* would suggest that A's assistance was justified. There must be limits to this, however, as offences involving injury to people or irreparable damage to property should not be assisted in any way. This limited defence obviously requires considerable clarification.

Where D commits an offence as a result of improper entrapment this used to be treated as a mitigating factor to be taken into account in sentencing (see *Sang, ante*; *Underhill* (1979) 1 Cr App R (S) 270). In *Sang* the House of Lords declared that there was no defence of entrapment nor could evidence obtained as a result of the activities of an *agent provocateur* be excluded by the trial judge in exercise of his discretion on ground of unfairness as this would let in a defence of entrapment by the back door. The Police and Criminal Evidence Act 1984, s. 78, reversed the effect of *Sang* in respect of the discretion to exclude evidence which had been obtained unfairly. Evidence obtained as a result of entrapment could be excluded where its admission would have such an adverse effect on the fairness of the proceedings that the court ought not to admit it (see further *Smurthwaite and Gill* (1994) 98 Cr App R 437). Of course, if there is other independent evidence sufficient to prove the charge against D, exclusion of the evidence of an *agent provocateur* will have little effect. This problem will largely be obviated by reliance on the doctrine of abuse of process recognised by the House of Lords in *R v Horseferry Road Magistrates' Court, ex parte Bennett* [1994] 1 AC 42. In this case their Lordships held that a court has jurisdiction to stay proceedings and order the release of the accused when the court becomes aware that there has been a serious abuse of power on the part of the executive. To permit the prosecuting authority to take advantage of such an abuse of power would be contrary to the rule of law as the State should not be seen to be instigating criminal offences in order to prosecute them. In *Latif and Shafzad*

[1996] 1 WLR 104 the House of Lords confirmed that this doctrine was applicable in entrapment cases.

In the most recent cases before the House of Lords, *R v Looseley* and *A-G's Reference (No. 3 of 2000)* [2001] UKHL 53, [2002] 1 Cr App R 29, the circumstances in which entrapment would amount to an abuse of process were further elucidated. Police conduct would not amount to improper entrapment where it 'did no more than present the defendant with an unexceptional opportunity to commit a crime' (*per* Lord Nicholls, para. 23). By contrast there would be a violation of the concept of fairness 'if a defendant were to be convicted and punished for committing a crime which he only committed because he had been incited, instigated, persuaded, pressurised or wheedled into committing it by a law enforcement officer' (*per* Lord Bingham of Cornhill, *Nottingham City Council* v *Amin* [2000] 1 Cr App R 426, 431, cited with approval by Lord Hutton at para. 109). Thus, if the police do no more than might have been expected from others in the circumstances, there is no abuse of process. The courts will be engaged in a balancing exercise in determining whether in any particular case the conduct of the police is so seriously improper as to bring the administration of justice into disrepute. In determining where the balance lies the court will take account of several factors. First, the nature of the offence may be relevant as proactive techniques are more appropriate for offences where there is no victim, such as drug-dealing, or offences where victims are reluctant to report the offence, for example, corruption. In these cases the secrecy surrounding the activity and the difficulty of detection by conventional means would weigh in favour of using proactive methods. Secondly, the reason for the particular operation will be of relevance. Wholesale 'virtue-testing' without good reason would not be acceptable, nor would the conduct of a vendetta against an individual or a group. What is required is reasonable suspicion either that a particular individual is engaged in criminal activity or that criminal activity of a particular kind is prevalent in a particular location. In addition the officers carrying out the operation should be duly authorised to do so in compliance with *Undercover Operations Code of Practice* issued jointly by the UK police authorities and HM Customs and Excise (now HM Revenue and Customs) in response to the Human Rights Act 1998. Thirdly, the nature and extent of police participation in the crime is an important consideration as 'the greater the inducement held out by the police, and the more forceful or persistent the police overtures, the more readily may a court conclude that the police overstepped the boundary: their conduct might well have brought about the commission of a crime by a person who would normally avoid crime of that kind' (*per* Lord Nicholls, para. 29). A relevant factor may also be the vulnerability of the defendant. For example, persistent importuning of a drug addict to supply drugs would overstep the boundary whereas persistent requests of a suspected drug dealer would not, as drug dealers display a degree of cautious reluctance when approached by a new customer. Thus behaving in the manner of an ordinary customer of a trade being carried on by the defendant would not normally transgress the boundary. Finally, the fact that the defendant has a criminal record will not of itself justify targeting him unless there is evidence to ground reasonable suspicion that he is currently engaged in criminal activity.

The House of Lords concluded that the position in England and Wales, as it had developed over recent years, was consistent with the requirements of Art. 6 of the European Convention on Human Rights as explained in *Teixeira de Castro* v *Portugal* (1999) 28 EHRR 101.

7.1.8 **Reform**

In its Report *Participating in Crime* (Law Com No. 305) the Law Commission accepts that secondary liability for participation in an offence committed by a principal offender should be retained. It does, however, recommend a series of reforms designed to make the law more rational and fair. The Report is intended to be read in tandem with its earlier Report *Inchoate Liability for Assisting and Encouraging Crime* (Law Com No. 300) which has resulted in fairly rapid reform by the enactment of ss. 44–67 of the Serious Crime Act 2007 (see **8.2** *post*). The Law Commission propose that D should be liable for aiding and abetting (which will be called under the new scheme 'assisting and encouraging') the commission of an offence by P only if D does his act of assistance or encouragement with the intention that P will thereby commit the offence. Foresight/contemplation will not be enough. Separate provision for joint venture cases is also proposed which will be based on foresight on the part of D of what P might do when, for example, they embark on a joint criminal venture, such as burglary, in the course of which P kills V.

In its Consultation Paper *Murder, manslaughter and infanticide: proposals for reform of the law* (CP 19/08) the Government sets out its proposals for reform of the law on complicity in homicide accepting much of the Law Commission's analysis and recommendations. Clauses 1 to 4 are quoted in the following section. The proposal is to create a new statutory offence of intentionally assisting or encouraging murder (cl. 1) and a statutory offence of murder where P is guilty of manslaughter owing to a lack of *mens rea* and D assisted or encouraged intending P to kill or cause serious injury (cl. 2). The Law Commission's recommendation to retain a broad offence of murder in the context of a joint criminal venture is also adopted (cl. 3). Reform to the 'fundamental difference' principle is also proposed seeking greater flexibility based on whether P's act was within the scope of the joint criminal venture: it would be where the act did not go far beyond that which was planned, agreed to, or foreseen by the secondary party. The fundamental difference principle may only be relied on where D has not foreseen death of V as a possibility, but unlike the current situation, even when successfully raised, it will only result in a reduction of D's liability to manslaughter (cl. 4).

1 Assisting or encouraging the offence of murder

Where a person ('P') has committed the offence of murder, another person ('D') is guilty of the offence if—

(a) D did an act which assisted or encouraged one or more other acts to be done by another person,

(b) P's criminal act was that act or one of those acts, and

(c) D's act was intended to assist or encourage a person to kill, or cause serious injury to, another person.

2 Assisting or encouraging the offence of manslaughter

(1) This section applies where a person ('P') commits the offence of manslaughter in circumstances where P acts without the state of mind required for conviction of the offence of murder.

(2) Another person ('D') is guilty of the offence of murder if—

(a) D did an act which assisted or encouraged one or more other acts to be done by another person,

(b) P's criminal act was that act or one of those acts, and

(c) D's act was intended to assist or encourage a person to kill, or cause serious injury to, another person.

3 Murder in the context of a joint criminal venture

(1) Where—

    (a) two or more persons participate in a joint criminal venture, and

    (b) one of them ('P') commits the offence of murder in the context of the venture, another participant ('D') is guilty of the offence of murder if subsection (2) or (3) applies.

(2) This subsection applies if D foresaw that in the context of the venture a person might be killed by a participant acting with intent to kill, or to cause serious injury to, a person.

(3) This subsection applies if—

    (a) D foresaw that, in the context of the venture, serious injury might be caused to a person by a participant acting with intent to cause such injury, and

    (b) P's criminal act was within the scope of the venture.

(4) P's criminal act was within the scope of the venture if it did not go far beyond that which was planned or agreed to, or which was foreseen, by D.

(5) The existence of a joint criminal venture, and that which was planned, agreed or foreseen as part of such a venture, may be inferred from the conduct of the participants (whether or not there is an express agreement).

(6) D does not escape liability under this section for an offence of murder committed by P at a time when D is a participant merely because D is at that time—

    (a) absent,

    (b) against the venture's being carried out, or

    (c) indifferent as to whether it is carried out.

(7) 'Participant' means a participant in the joint criminal venture.

4 Manslaughter in the context of a joint criminal venture

(1) Where—

    (a) two or more other persons participate in a joint criminal venture, and

    (b) one of them ('P') commits the offence of murder in the context of the venture, another participant ('D') is guilty of the offence of manslaughter if subsection (2) or (3) applies.

(2) This subsection applies if D foresaw that, in the context of the venture, serious injury might be caused to a person by a participant acting with intent to cause such injury.

(3) This subsection applies if—

    (a) D foresaw that in the context of the joint criminal venture harm (other than serious harm), or the fear of harm, might be caused to a person by a participant, and

    (b) a reasonable person in D's position with D's knowledge of the relevant facts would have foreseen an obvious risk of serious injury being caused to a person, or of a person being killed, by a participant in the context of the venture.

(4) The existence of a joint criminal venture may be inferred from the conduct of the participants (whether or not there is an express agreement).

(5) D does not escape liability for manslaughter under this section in relation to an offence of murder committed by P at a time when D is a participant merely because D is at that time—

    (a) absent,

    (b) against the venture's being carried out, or

    (c) indifferent as to whether it is carried out.

(6) 'Participant' means a participant in the joint criminal venture.

7.2 Vicarious liability

In the law of tort an employer is responsible for the torts of his employees acting in the course of their employment. This is known as 'vicarious liability' which is a form of strict liability arising from the master-servant relationship, without reference to any fault of the employer. There is no such general rule in criminal law; generally if the master is to be liable it will be on the basis of being an accessory under the principles outlined earlier. The principle was stated by Raymond CJ in *Huggins* (1730) 2 Strange 883 (at p. 885):

> It is a point not to be disputed but that in criminal cases the principal is not answerable for the act of the deputy, as he is in civil cases; they must each answer for their own acts and stand or fall by their own behaviour. All the authors that treat of criminal proceedings, proceed on the foundation of this distinction; that to affect the superior by the act of the deputy, there must be command of the superior which is not found in this case.

Huggins was the warden of Fleet prison who was charged with aiding and abetting B, a turnkey, to murder a prisoner who had died as a result of the turnkey's neglect. As this occurred without Huggins's knowledge he was not guilty.

While this is the general rule, it is subject to exceptions. At common law there were two offences for which an employer could be liable for the acts of his employees even if these had not been authorised and he remained ignorant of them, namely **public nuisance** (see *Stephens* (1866) LR 1 QB 702) and criminal libel (this was modified by s. 7 of the Libel Act 1843). Occasionally statute expressly imposes vicarious liability. For example, s. 59(1) of the Licensing Act 1964 provides:

> Subject to the provisions of this Act, no person shall, except during the permitted hours—
>
> (a) himself or by his servant or agent sell or supply to any person in licensed premises... any intoxicating liquor...

More usually, however, vicarious liability is the result of judicial interpretation of statutory offences of a regulatory nature. Various reasons are put forward to support such interpretations. Imposing liability on the employer for contraventions of legislation by his employees may be a more effective way of encouraging compliance with the legislation; the employer, after all, is the one who has overall control of the business and can regulate the conduct of his employees. It may also be considered unjust to punish an employee for the breach of some regulation as he may not have had the means of detecting the breach or of preventing it. A further justification is that vicarious liability is necessary to make certain provisions effective where some *mens rea* offences may only be committed by persons of a particular status, such as licensees. Such legislation would be rendered nugatory if the licensee could claim that the act had been performed without his knowledge by his servant; the response of the courts has been to create the 'delegation principle'. While these justifications have some force, they do represent an attempt by the judges to come to the rescue of the legislature as all these problems could have been met by means of better drafting of the legislation.

7.2.1 Vicarious liability by implication

The approach of the courts to statutory interpretation for the purpose of determining whether a provision imposed vicarious liability was stated by Atkin J in *Mousell Bros* v *London and North Western Ry* [1917] 2 KB 836 (at p. 845):

> [W]hile prima facie a principal is not to be made criminally responsible for the acts of his servants, yet the legislature may prohibit an act or enforce a duty in such words as to make the prohibition or the duty absolute; in which case the principal is in fact liable if the act is in fact done by his servants. To ascertain whether a particular Act of Parliament has that effect or not, regard must be had to the words used, the nature of the duty laid down, the person upon whom it is imposed, the person by whom it would in ordinary circumstances be performed, and the person upon whom the penalty is imposed.

In many statutes it is unclear upon whom the duty is imposed; in such cases the courts generally conclude that it is imposed on the employer as he is the one who has control of the enterprise. **Where the performance of the duty requires positive acts the doctrine of vicarious liability is necessary. But where the offence is one of strict liability, consisting of an omission to perform a duty imposed on the employer, he will be personally liable as the perpetrator (without resort to the doctrine of vicarious liability) as, the duty being unfulfilled, the omission is as much his as that of any servant to whom he assigned the task.** In *Hodge* v *Higgins* [1980] 2 Lloyd's Rep 589, a vessel was observed in the River Humber at night without a forward light. The master had retired to bed ill leaving the vessel in the charge of the mate. The master was convicted of neglect of duty contrary to s. 27 of the Merchant Shipping Act 1970, which made it an offence for the master of a ship to omit to do anything required to preserve the ship from loss, destruction, or serious damage. The magistrate found, and the Divisional Court upheld his finding, that there was a breach of this duty and the master could not evade his responsibility as the duty was his alone.

Where the offence requires a positive act the courts have to decide if the act of the employee can be attributed to the employer. If it can, without undue strain to the wording of the legislation, and the offence is one of strict liability, the employer will be held to be a joint principal with his employee. Thus words such as 'sell', 'supply', and 'use' have frequently been given this extended meaning. In *Coppen* v *Moore (No. 2)* [1898] 2 QB 306, D, the owner of several shops, instructed his managers to sell American ham under the description 'breakfast ham'. A shop assistant in one shop, without the knowledge of her manager or D, sold some ham as 'Scotch ham'. It was an offence under s. 2(2) of the Merchandise Marks Act 1887 to sell any goods 'to which any...false trade description is applied'. The assistant had done the physical act of selling and committed this offence, but the Divisional Court held that D was also liable as, property in the ham being vested in him, he had in law sold the ham. Had D not been convicted as a principal by means of the implication of vicarious liability, it would not have been possible to convict him as an accessory due to his lack of knowledge.

Other cases establish that an employer is 'in possession' of goods which his employee possesses (*Melias Ltd* v *Preston* [1957] 2 QB 380), 'uses' a vehicle which his employee uses (*Green* v *Burnett* [1955] 1 QB 78), and 'presents' a play which his employee presents (*Grade* v *DPP* [1942] 2 All ER 118). By contrast, however, only the actual driver of a vehicle can be said to be 'driving' (cf. *Thornton* v *Mitchell* [1940] 1 All ER 339). Likewise, where words which import *mens rea* are used, such as 'knowingly', 'maliciously', 'fraudulently', 'permitting', 'suffering', or 'allowing', the employer can only be liable where he had *mens rea* himself (see *James & Son* v *Smee* [1955] 1 QB 78); his employee's *mens rea* cannot be imputed to him, unless the case falls within the bounds of the 'delegation principle' (see **7.2.2** *post*).

This approach of extending the meaning of words has been used to impose liability not only in the employer/employee situation but also to impose liability on a principal for the act of his agent or independent contractor (see *Quality Dairies (York) Ltd* v *Pedley* [1952] 1 KB 275; and *F. E. Charman Ltd* v *Clow* [1974] 1 WLR 1384), on a partner for the act of his fellow partner (see *Clode* v *Barnes* [1974] 1 All ER 1166), and on a licensee for unlawful sales by the bar staff even though they were not his employees but employees of the owner of the bar (see *Goodfellow* v *Johnson* [1966] 1 QB 83). **The issue is whether there is a sufficient nexus between the parties so that it can be said that the accused had some control over the actions of the other.** A further consideration is whether the imposition of liability would serve to encourage stricter supervision to ensure compliance with regulatory legislation. Ultimately the matter is one for judicial interpretation. The Law Commission, when considering vicarious liability for the acts of independent contractors, stated (Law Com No. 177) at para. 9.49:

> It is one thing to hold that a person carrying on a business of supplying milk or heavy building materials 'uses' a vehicle if he employs an independent contractor to supply those things in the contractor's vehicle. It would be quite another thing to hold that a householder 'uses' the removal van owned by a firm of removers whom he engages to carry his furniture to a new residence.

7.2.2 The delegation principle

Where the offence is not one of strict liability but requires proof of *mens rea* or negligence, the general rule is that an employer cannot be convicted on the basis of vicarious liability without it being proved that he knew what was going on or was negligent. **The delegation principle forms an exception to this rule. Under this principle the *mens rea* of the employee may be imputed to the employer**

where it is established that the latter had delegated his responsibilities to the former.

The creation of this principle proved necessary to deal with cases where *mens rea* offences could only be committed by persons of a particular status, such as licensees of licensed premises. If the employee performed the act constituting the *actus reus* of the offence with *mens rea* he could not be convicted as a principal as he was not a person of the requisite status. The licensee, lacking knowledge, could not be a principal and thus the employee could not be convicted as an accessory. The outcome would be that the purpose of the statute in regulating the conditions under which alcohol could be sold would be defeated where the licensee had handed over management responsibilities to his employee.

In *Somerset* v *Hart* (1884) 12 QBD 360, Lord Coleridge CJ suggested that a man could put another in his position so as to represent him for the purpose of knowledge. This was built upon in *Allen* v *Whitehead* [1930] 1 KB 211. Under s. 44 of the Metropolitan Police Act 1839 it was an offence for the owner or keeper of a refreshment house knowingly to permit or suffer prostitutes to meet there. D owned a cafe which was run by a manager. The manager knowingly permitted prostitutes to meet there unknown to D. D was convicted as to hold otherwise would be to render the provision nugatory; the manager's knowledge was imputed to him. In *Linnett* v *Metropolitan Police Commissioner* [1946] KB 290, Lord Goddard CJ indicated the nature of the delegation principle (at p. 294):

> The principle underlying these decisions does not depend upon the legal relationship existing between master and servant or between principal and agent; it depends on the fact that the person who is responsible in law, as for example, a licensee under the Licensing Acts, has chosen to delegate his duties, powers and authority to another.

In this case, accordingly, one of two co-licensees, who was absent, was held liable for the acts of the other who had knowingly permitted disorderly conduct in the licensed premises contrary to s. 44 of the Metropolitan Police Act 1839.

What constitutes delegation is not totally clear. In *Vane* v *Yiannopoullos* [1965] AC 486, D, the licensee of a restaurant was on another floor when a waitress in the restaurant, contrary to instructions, served drinks to two youths who did not order a meal. The magistrate dismissed an information charging him with knowingly selling intoxicating liquor to persons to whom he was not permitted to sell, contrary to s. 22(1)(a) of the Licensing Act 1961. The House of Lords dismissed the prosecutor's appeal. Lord Evershed stated that delegation required the handing over of all effective management of the premises. Lord Hodson stated that it did not cover cases of partial transfer of authority. Lord Reid did not believe there could be delegation where the licensee remained on the premises. In the course of their speeches some of their Lordships expressed disquiet about the doctrine. Lord Donovan stated that 'if a decision that "knowingly" means "knowingly" will make the provision difficult to enforce, the remedy lies with the legislature'. Lord Reid found difficulty justifying the principle but considered that it was too long established to overturn it. It appeared, therefore, that what was required was a complete transfer of authority and responsibilities to another person and the absence of the licensee from the premises.

In *Winson* [1969] 1 QB 371, the Court of Appeal confirmed that partial delegation was insufficient to impute knowledge to the licensee (see also *Bradshaw* v *Ewart-James* [1983] QB 671). In *Howker* v *Robinson* [1973] 1 QB 178, however, the Divisional Court upheld a conviction of a licensee for selling alcohol to a person under the age of 18 where this had been done by a barman in the lounge while the licensee was in the public bar. The Divisional Court treated the question of delegation as one of fact and accepted the magistrates finding that there had been delegation. The decision appears unsupportable on two grounds. First, this was not a case of the licensee taking no part in managing the business; if there was any delegation of authority it was only partial. Indeed it is difficult to discover even partial delegation of the licensee's proprietary or managerial functions. Secondly, the justification for the delegation principle is that it is necessary to avoid rendering certain statutory provisions nugatory. In this case, however, a failure to find delegation would not have had this effect as the relevant provision, s. 169(1) of the Licensing Act 1964, specifically prohibited 'the holder of the licence or his servant' from selling alcohol to a person under 18. Thus the barman could have been prosecuted for the offence as liability was not limited to persons with the status of licensees. It is submitted, therefore, that *Howker* v *Robinson* was wrongly decided.

The Law Commission's Draft Criminal Code (Law Com No. 177) excludes the delegation principle from Code offences (see cl. 29) proposing instead that if Parliament intends vicarious liability to be imposed on the basis of the fault of another it must do so expressly. Clause 29(2) provides that 'a fault element of an offence may be attributed to a person by reason of the fault of another only if the terms of the enactment creating the offence so provide'.

7.2.3 Limitations on vicarious liability

There are three limitations on vicarious liability. **First, vicarious liability can only arise where the person who did the act did so within the scope of his employment or, if not an employee but acting as the accused's agent, within the scope of his authority.** For example, if an employee does an authorised activity in an unauthorised way he remains within the scope of his employment (see *Coppen* v *Moore (No. 2)*, **7.2.1** *ante*). By contrast, if the sales assistant had started to sell stolen goods under a false description the employer would not be liable as he would have been performing a wholly unauthorised activity. Similarly, if an employee uses his employer's vehicle to deliver goods, his use of the vehicle is also his employer's use, but, if he uses it as a get-away vehicle for a robbery, his use, being a wholly unauthorised activity, would not be his employer's use. In *Adams* v *Camfoni* [1929] 1 KB 95, D was a licensee charged with selling alcohol outside the permitted hours. The sale had been effected by a messenger boy who had no authority to sell liquor or anything else. Accordingly D was acquitted.

Secondly, where the employee's acts amount to the aiding and abetting of an offence, the employer cannot be held vicariously liable for such aiding and abetting on the basis of imputed knowledge, even though the offence was one which he could have personally aided and abetted (see *Ferguson* v *Weaving*, **7.1.4.2** *ante*).

Thirdly, it was held in *Gardner* v *Akeroyd* [1952] 2 QB 743, that **vicarious liability cannot be imposed in respect of an attempt to commit an offence**, even though vicarious liability could have been imposed for the completed offence.

7.2.4 Statutory defences

There is no general defence of due diligence which an employer may plead in respect of an offence committed by his employee for which he is vicariously liable. Some statutes do contain express provision for due diligence defences; others combine the due diligence defence with a 'third party' defence (see **4.2.5** *ante*). Where the offence is a strict liability offence which may only be committed by a person of a particular status, the employee cannot be a principal. If he is not a principal there is no 'third party' whom the employer can bring before the court as the actual offender. A third party defence can only operate where the offence is one of strict liability and not limited to persons of a particular status, in which case both employer and employee are joint principals.

7.3 Corporate liability

A corporation is a legal person and therefore may be criminally liable even though it has no physical existence and cannot act or think except through its directors or servants. A corporation is, for example, a limited company, a public corporation like those formed to run nationalised industries, or a local authority. At common law an unincorporated association is not a legal person and therefore not subject to criminal liability. Section 5 of and sch. 1 to the Interpretation Act 1978 provide that in every Act, unless the contrary intention appears, 'person' includes a body of persons corporate or unincorporate. This definition applies prospectively in respect of unincorporated associations so that these bodies may be criminally liable for offences created after 1 January 1979 (the commencement date for the 1978 Act) where the word 'person' is used in the definition of the offence.

A corporation is vicariously liable for strict liability offences to exactly the same extent as a natural person. A corporation will also be criminally liable for the breach of any statutory duty imposed upon it in a particular capacity such as an occupier or keeper (see *Evans & Co Ltd* v *LCC* [1914] 3 KB 315). **Its criminal liability extends further than this, however, to cover direct liability for acts performed by natural persons who are identified with it, i.e. the principle of identification** (see **7.3.1** *post*). There are **two limitations**, however, to corporate liability identified in *R* v *ICR Haulage Ltd* [1944] KB 551. **First, there are certain offences which, from their very nature, cannot be committed by corporations,** for example, bigamy, rape, incest, and perjury. In all these cases, if suitable circumstances arose, a corporation could be liable as an accessory. *Obiter dicta* in some old cases suggested that a corporation could not be convicted of an offence of violence. These were acted on in *Cory Bros & Co* [1927] 1 KB 810 but doubted in *ICR Haulage Ltd*. In *R* v *HM Coroner for East Kent, ex parte Spooner* (1989) 88 Cr App R 10, where an application for judicial review of the decision of the coroner at the inquest into the deaths resulting from the sinking of the *Herald of Free Enterprise* off Zeebrugge was refused, Bingham LJ, in the Divisional Court, stated *obiter* that a corporation could be convicted of manslaughter on appropriate facts. This was subsequently confirmed by Turner J when P & O European Ferries (Dover) Ltd, two directors, and a senior manager were tried for manslaughter in respect of the deaths resulting from the Zeebrugge disaster (see *R v P & O European Ferries (Dover) Ltd* (1990) 93 Cr App R 72). Turner J held that a company is 'properly indictable for the crime of manslaughter' through 'the controlling mind of one of its agents' who 'does an act which fulfils the prerequisites of the crime of manslaughter'. The prosecution ended in failure, however, when Turner J withdrew from the jury consideration of the charges as there was no evidence that anyone who constituted 'the controlling mind' of the company had the requisite *mens rea* to support a conviction of manslaughter. In 1994, however, OLL Ltd, and its managing director, Peter Kite, were both convicted of manslaughter following the deaths of four teenagers in a canoeing tragedy at an outdoor pursuits centre run by OLL Ltd. The success of this prosecution was probably due to the fact that OLL Ltd was a small company and Peter Kite was aware of the dangers of canoe expeditions in Lyme Bay following a letter from two former instructors at the centre complaining of inadequate safety precautions.

Secondly, a corporation will not be convicted of an offence where the only punishment which may be imposed is physical. In *ICR Haulage Ltd*, Stable J stated (at p. 554) that 'the court will not stultify itself by embarking on a trial in which, if a verdict of guilty is returned, no effective order by way of sentence can be made'. Thus a corporation cannot be tried for murder or treason as the only punishments available to the court on conviction are life imprisonment or death. Where a corporation is convicted of an offence it will be punished by the imposition of a fine and/or compensation order.

7.3.1 The principle of identification

In vicarious liability an employer is held liable for the acts of his employee; in corporate liability a corporation is liable for its own acts. **As a company has no physical existence and cannot think or act, a fiction has to be applied to convert the acts and thoughts of a human person into those of the corporation thereby attributing personality to it.** This fiction is the principle of identification which was explained by Lord Reid in *Tesco Supermarkets Ltd* v *Nattrass* [1972] AC 153 (at p. 170) as follows:

> A living person has a mind which can have knowledge or intention or be negligent and he has hands to carry out his intentions. A corporation has none of these: it must act through living persons, though not always one or the same person. Then the person who acts is not speaking or acting for the company. He is speaking as the company and his mind which directs his acts is the mind of the company. There is no question of the company being vicariously liable. He is not acting as a servant, representative, agent or delegate. He is an embodiment of the company, one could say, he hears and speaks through the persona of the company, within his appropriate sphere, and his mind is the mind of the company. If it is a guilty mind then that guilt is the guilt of the company.

It is a question of law for the judge whether a person is to be regarded as the company or simply its employee or agent. The judge when directing the jury must tell them the facts which they must find if a person is to be regarded as having acted as the company. If those facts are proved and the jury are satisfied that that person did the act (or omitted to act) with the requisite *mens rea*, the company can be convicted of the offence. The corporation will only be liable where the person identified with it was acting within the scope of his office; it will not be liable for acts which he did in his personal capacity (see *DPP v Kent and Sussex Contractors Ltd* [1944] KB 146). In determining whether a person acted as the company or simply as its servant or agent, a distinction has to be drawn between those who represent the mind of the company and those who represent its hands. In *H. L. Bolton, (Engineering) Co Ltd v T. J. Graham & Sons Ltd* [1957] 1 QB 159, Denning LJ stated (at p. 172):

> A company may in many ways be likened to a human body. It has a brain and a nerve centre which controls what it does. It also has hands which hold the tools and act in accordance with directions from the centre. Some of the people in the company are mere servants and agents who are nothing more than hands to do the work and cannot be said to represent the mind or will. Others are directors and managers who represent the directing mind and will of the company, and control what it does. The state of mind of these managers is the state of mind of the company and is treated by the law as such.

The fact that a person is involved in 'brain' work rather than manual work is not the test; **what is required is that such persons 'represent the directing mind and will of the company and control what it does'** (*per* Lord Reid, *Tesco Supermarkets Ltd v Nattrass* [1972] AC 153 at 171). This covers directors, the managing director, the company secretary, and other superior officers responsible for managing the affairs of the corporation. If one of these persons delegated some part of his management functions, giving the delegate full discretion to act independently, the delegate would also fall within the class of persons whose acts are those of the corporation (see *Lennard's Carrying Co Ltd v Asiatic Petroleum Co Ltd* [1915] AC 705 and *Worthy v Gordon Plant (Services) Ltd* [1985] CLY 624). Who exactly is covered will vary from case to case but the memorandum and articles of association of the company may provide some guidance.

In the *Tesco* case, the company was charged with an offence under the Trade Descriptions Act 1968. Tesco sought to raise a defence under s. 24(1) of the Act on the grounds that the commission of the offence was due to the act or default of another person, the branch manager of the store, and it had exercised all due diligence to avoid the commission of the offence. The magistrates found that the company had set up a proper system, so it had exercised all due diligence, but they found that the branch manager was not 'another person' as his acts were those of the company. On appeal to the House of Lords the conviction was quashed. The House held that the defence was available as the branch manager was another person being the 'hands' and not the 'brains' of the company; there had been no delegation by the board of directors of any of their managerial functions in respect of the affairs of the company to the branch manager. He had to obey general directions from the company and take orders from his regional and district supervisors. Accordingly, his acts or omissions were not those of the company.

The *Tesco* case indicated that the principle of identification operates not only to establish liability but it can excuse liability for certain regulatory offences where a third party defence is available. As the branch manager did not act as the company, his act was that of a third party. The company, through its superior officers, had established a proper system of supervision and thus had exercised all due diligence (see also *St Regis Paper Co. Ltd* [2011] EWCA Crim 2527).

There are several problems arising from the principle of identification (these have been identified by C. Wells, see Further reading *post*). **First, the larger and more diverse a company is, the more likely it is that it will be able to avoid liability.** Tesco had over 800 branches; a branch manager would have no control over the company's affairs. In a small company the controlling officers are much closer to the action which may involve the commission of offences.

Secondly, the principle in *Tesco* does not fit well with many regulatory offences (including the offence involved in that case) which do not require *mens rea* but for which defences (e.g. due diligence or the 'third party' defence; see **4.2.5** *ante*) exist to mitigate the harshness of strict liability. Should such offences (Wells refers to them as 'hybrid' offences) fall under the identification principle or would they be more appropriately dealt with under the vicarious liability approach? In another case involving Tesco, *Tesco Stores Ltd* v *Brent LBC* [1993] 2 All ER 718, T was convicted of supplying an '18' classified video to a person under that age contrary to s. 11(1) of the Video Recordings Act 1984. Under s. 11(1)(b) it was a defence for the accused to prove that he 'neither knew nor had reasonable grounds to believe that the person concerned had not attained that age'. T argued that the directing minds of the company (who would be directors in the London headquarters) had no means of knowing the age of the purchaser. The justices found that the cashier had reasonable grounds to believe that the purchaser was under 18 and convicted T. The Divisional Court dismissed T's appeal holding that it was impracticable to suppose that those who controlled a large company would have knowledge or information about the age of the purchaser, but that as the person who supplied the video was under T's control and she had such knowledge or information, the defence was not available to the company. This effectively meant that the offence was one of vicarious liability (see also *R* v *British Steel plc* [1995] ICR 587).

Thirdly, the identification principle has also been diluted by the decision of the Privy Council in *Meridian Global Funds Management Asia Ltd* v *Securities Commission* [1995] 3 All ER 918. In this case the Privy Council attributed knowledge to the company for the purposes of determining their liability for the offence of failing to make a disclosure under the New Zealand Securities Act 1988 where the facts required to be disclosed were known to the senior investment team. This team did not constitute the 'directing mind' of the company. The Privy Council upheld the company's conviction on the basis of its interpretation of the statute, taking into account the statutory language, its contents and the underlying policy which would be defeated if knowledge on the part of those who constituted the 'directing mind' of the company was required to be proved. This special rule of attribution would apply where a court considers that a statute was intended to apply to companies and application of the identification principle would defeat the purpose of the statute.

The fourth problem is that the company will only be liable if the person identified with it is, himself, individually liable in that he had the *mens rea* for the offence. Where there are several superior officers involved, each may not have the requisite degree of knowledge to constitute the *mens rea* of the offence. In the area of safety, for example, there may be many failures within a corporation at different levels which may coalesce to result in a major disaster resulting in loss of life. Different individuals may know, or do, or fail to do, different things. But, if a company is a legal person, and the knowledge of its officials is its knowledge, can that knowledge be aggregated and, in the aggregate, constitute the *mens rea* for a crime? This particular question has been considered in the context of manslaughter. For a time it was thought that manslaughter was an offence of which a corporation could not be convicted. This view was rejected in *P & O European Ferries Ltd* (1990) 93 Cr App R 72. In *Armstrong v Strain* [1952] 1 KB 232, Devlin J stated, 'You cannot add an innocent state of mind to an innocent state of mind and get as a result a dishonest state of mind'. If an offence is one demanding proof of *mens rea* this suggests that it is not possible to aggregate the states of mind of several individuals which individually do not fully satisfy the *mens rea* requirement to conclude that in aggregate they do. Following the decision of the House of Lords in *Seymour* [1983] 2 AC 493, manslaughter demanded proof of recklessness in the *Caldwell/Lawrence* sense (see **3.4.2.2** *ante*). In this context the aggregation principle was rejected in *R v HM Coroner for East Kent, ex parte Spooner* (1989) 88 Cr App R 10 and *P & O European Ferries Ltd*. Since the decision of the House of Lords in *Adomako* [1995] 1 AC 171 (see **9.3.3.2** *post*), however, manslaughter by gross negligence is not an offence requiring *mens rea*. This being so, is it possible to aggregate the negligence of individuals within a corporation to arrive at a finding of gross negligence on the part of the corporation? In *Kite and OLL Ltd* (Winchester Crown Court, 8 December 1994, unreported) the company was convicted of manslaughter but this followed on the conviction of its managing director, the company being a one-man concern. In *A-G's Reference (No. 2 of 1999)* [2000] 1 Cr App R 207, the issue of aggregation was directly addressed. A high speed train crashed into a freight train at Southall killing seven people and injuring many others. The company operating the high speed train was indicted for manslaughter but the trial judge ruled that a non-human defendant could only be convicted where guilt of a human being with whom it could be identified was also established. As no such individual was indicted the charges against the company were dismissed. Two questions were referred to the Court of Appeal by the Attorney-General:

(a) Can a defendant be properly convicted of manslaughter by gross negligence in the absence of evidence as to that defendant's state of mind?

(b) Can a non-human defendant be convicted of the crime of manslaughter by gross negligence in the absence of evidence establishing the guilt of an identified human individual for the same crime?

The Court of Appeal answered the questions 'Yes' and 'No' respectively, rejecting an argument by the Attorney-General that the reasoning in the *Meridian* case should be applied. Relying on *ex parte Spooner* and *P & O European Ferries*, Rose LJ concluded:

> unless an identified individual's conduct, characterisable as gross criminal negligence, can be attributed to the company the company is not...liable for manslaughter. Civil negligence rules...are not apt to confer criminal liability on a company.

Rose LJ missed the point, however, that the cases on which he relied related to manslaughter when it was considered to be an offence requiring proof of recklessness, whereas following *Adomako* it is an offence of negligence. In addition, in *Adomako* Lord Mackay stated that 'the ordinary principles of the law of negligence apply to ascertain whether or not the defendant has been in breach of a duty of care towards the victim who has died'. Next the jury has to consider causation and then whether the breach was gross enough to constitute a crime. If the operation system was not safe (and there was considerable evidence to this effect as the driver had passed three signals at danger before the crash and both the Automatic Warning System and the Automatic Train Protection System had been switched off), is Rose LJ suggesting that this could not amount to civil negligence unless an actual individual was proved to be negligent? This would, indeed, be novel as negligence is concerned with conduct rather than states of mind. Why should the failures of those in the company concerned with safety not be aggregated to establish negligence overall on the part of the company? While discussions about the liability of a company for manslaughter may no longer excite the same feelings because of the enactment of the Corporate Homicide and Corporate Manslaughter Act 2007 (see **7.3.3.2** *post*) the previously discussed cases remain authorities on the issue of aggregation. Whether the courts will see fit to revisit them in the context of other offences remains to be seen.

So far *Tesco* v *Nattrass* has not been overruled but there clearly are limitations to its applicability such that it would be wrong to treat it as having established an absolute principle. The problem which remains, however, is identifying those circumstances in which the identification principle applies and those in which it does not.

7.3.2 Liability of officers

Apart from their liability as perpetrators or accomplices of the offences for which a corporation may be held criminally liable, the **officers of a company may be made liable by statutory provision.** Many statutes, such as the Betting, Gaming and Lotteries Act 1963 (s. 53) and the Trade Description Act 1968 (s. 20) contain the following provision:

> Where an offence under this Act which has been committed by a body corporate is proved to have been committed with the consent or connivance of, or to be attributable to any neglect on the part of, any director, manager, secretary or other similar officer of the body corporate or any person who was purporting to act in any such capacity, he as well as the body corporate shall be guilty of that offence.

While this largely duplicates the liability imposed by the criminal law on perpetrators or accomplices, it does extend it and it may also make the task of the prosecution easier where proving liability under the normal principles would be difficult. 'Consent' and 'connivance' largely overlap with 'aiding, abetting, counselling or procuring', but they may be easier to prove. In particular 'connivance' may be established by proving wilful blindness to the commission of the offence and acquiescence in it (see *Somerset* v *Hart* (1884) 12 QBD 360). The main extension of liability is effected by the words 'attributable to any neglect on the part of' which imposes liability for negligence where the officer has failed to prevent the commission of an offence by the corporation. Section 18 of the Theft Act 1968 contains a similar provision but it omits any reference to 'attributable to any neglect'.

An offence will not be attributable to the neglect of all directors because it is attributable to the neglect of one or of some other official of the company as there is no general duty upon a director to 'supervise his co-directors or to acquaint himself with all the details of the running of the company' (*per* Lord Parker CJ in *Huckerby* v *Elliott* [1970] 1 All ER 189). Lord Parker went on to state (at p. 194):

> [I]t is perfectly proper for a director to leave matters to another director or to an official of the company, and . . . he is under no obligation to test the accuracy of anything that he is told by such person, or even to make certain that he is complying with the law.

Similarly, where an officer of a company has delegated work to his senior staff it is reasonable for him to expect that work to be completed in accordance with the instructions given, so that he will not be guilty of neglect if he does not check such work (see *Lewin* v *Bland* [1985] RTR 171). However, if a director has reason to distrust another director or official or person to whom work has been delegated, or reason to suspect that that person was not carrying out his duty, and he does nothing, this could amount to neglect. In *R* v *McMillan Aviation Ltd* [1981] Crim LR 785, the company was charged with selling goods to which a false trade description had been applied contrary to s. 1 of the Trade Descriptions Act 1968, and a director was charged with the same offence on the basis of attributable neglect. Judge Rubin, in directing the jury in Kingston-upon-Thames Crown Court, stated that he would be liable where it was proved 'that he knew the trade description was false, in which case quite clearly he had a duty to prevent the offence, or that he had reasonable cause to suspect that the company was applying a false trade description, in which case he would have a duty to take steps to see if it was false or not and if he failed to do so he was guilty'.

7.3.3 Reform and the Corporate Manslaughter and Corporate Homicide Act 2007

7.3.3.1 Background

Under the previous law, based on the identification principle, a company could be convicted of manslaughter only where a 'directing mind' of the organisation was also guilty of the offence, that is some senior individual who embodies the company in his actions and decisions. Where no such senior individual was liable, it was not possible to convict the company even though a series of errors by individuals within the company, when aggregated together, might be sufficient to establish gross breach of duty on the part of the company. In 1996 the Law Commission in its Report *Legislating the Criminal Code: Involuntary Manslaughter* (Law Com No. 237) proposed a new offence of 'corporate killing'. Following this Report the Government published a Consultation Paper, *Reforming the Law on Involuntary Manslaughter: the Government's Proposals* (2000) which endorsed the proposal for a new offence. In March 2005 a draft Corporate Manslaughter Bill (Cm 6497) was published setting out the Government's proposals for reform. The draft Bill was subject to pre-legislative scrutiny by the Home Affairs and Work and Pensions Committees whose Report was published in December 2005 (HC 540 I–III). In

March 2006 the Government responded in *The Government Reply to the First Joint Report from the Home Affairs and Work and Pensions Committees Session 2005–06 HC 540* (Cm 6755).

In July 2006 the Corporate Manslaughter Bill received its First Reading in the House of Commons. It did not complete its stages in the 2005–06 session and was re-introduced in November 2006. This became the Corporate Manslaughter and Corporate Homicide Act 2007 which largely came into force on 6 April 2008. This is a highly technical piece of legislation which will doubtless create numerous practical difficulties and generate considerable appellate work.

7.3.3.2 Corporate Manslaughter and Corporate Homicide Act 2007

The important aspects of the new Act are that it dispenses with the need to find a controlling or directing mind that is also personally guilty of manslaughter (the identification principle) and it also greatly reduces the scope for Crown immunity which previously existed. The offence applies (see s. 1(2)) to bodies corporate which covers companies and public bodies such as NHS trusts and local authorities. It also applies to Government departments and the police (albeit that certain exclusions apply to public policy decisions, military activities, policing and law enforcement, emergencies, child protection, and probation functions). The offence also applies to a partnership, a trade union or employers' association, which is an employer.

7.3.3.2.1 *The offence*

The new offence is defined in s. 1 as follows:

> (1) An organisation to which this section applies is guilty of an offence if the way in which its activities are managed or organised—
>
> (a) causes a person's death, and
>
> (b) amounts to a gross breach of a relevant duty of care owed by the organisation to the deceased.
>
> (3) An organisation is guilty of an offence under this section only if the way in which its activities are managed or organised by its senior management is a substantial element in the breach referred to in subsection (1).

The offence builds on key aspects of the offence of gross negligence manslaughter. The important development, however, is that liability for the new offence is dependent upon a finding of gross negligence in the way in which the activities of the organisation are run rather than being contingent upon the guilt of an individual 'directing mind'. The offence is committed where, in particular circumstances, an organisation owes a relevant duty of care and the way in which the activities of the organisation have been managed or organised amounts to a gross breach of that duty and causes a person's death. A substantial element of the gross breach must be the way in which the activities were managed or organised by the senior management. A breach is gross if it falls far below what could reasonably have been expected of the organisation in the circumstances (s. 2(4)(b)). Senior management comprises those who play a significant role in the management of the whole or a substantial part of the organisation's activities. This covers those in the direct chain of management at an operational level and those with strategic or regulatory compliance roles. This approach allows for collective rather than just individual failure to be assessed, unlike the current offence.

7.3.3.2.2 *Relevant duty of care*

Section 2(1) defines the 'relevant duty of care' to mean any of the following duties owed by the organisation under the law of negligence:

(a) a duty owed to its employees or to other persons working for the organisation or performing services for it;

(b) a duty owed as occupier of premises;

(c) a duty owed in connection with—

    (i)   the supply by the organisation of goods or services (whether for consideration or not),

    (ii) the carrying on by the organisation of any construction or maintenance operations,

    (iii) the carrying on by the organisation of any other activity on a commercial basis, or

    (iv) the use or keeping by the organisation of any plant, vehicle or other thing;

(d) a duty owed to a person who, by reason of being a person within subsection (2), is someone for whose safety the organisation is responsible.

The duties are fault based as they must be duties 'under the law of negligence'. Thus the new offence does not impose new duties which are not already part of the civil law. Doubtless the duties which will most often lead to prosecutions under the new Act will be those of employers and occupiers.

Paragraph (d) relates to persons in custody whether as arrested suspects, prisoners (convicted or on remand), asylum/immigration detainees, and detained mental patients. This was a very contentious amendment to the Bill introduced in the Lords by the former Chief Inspector of Prisons, Lord Ramsbotham, because of concerns over deaths in custody. At one point it looked as if the whole Bill might fail owing to Government objections to this amendment. The compromise negotiated was that the commencement for this part of the Act would require approval of both Houses of Parliament under the affirmative resolution procedure. At the time of writing s. 2(1)(d) has not commenced.

Whether a duty of care is owed in a particular situation is a matter of law for the judge to decide (s. 2(5)). It is then for the jury to determine whether death was caused by a gross breach of duty. The common law rules preventing a duty of care being owed (a) by one person to another because they are both engaged in unlawful conduct, and (b) to a person by reason of his acceptance of a risk of harm, are to be disregarded (s. 2(6)).

7.3.3.2.3 *Gross breach*

Unusually the Act includes fairly detailed provision for the issues which a jury should consider in arriving at the decision whether the death was caused by a gross breach of duty. Section 8 provides:

(1) This section applies where—

    (a) it is established that an organisation owed a relevant duty of care to a person, and

    (b) it falls to the jury to decide whether there was a gross breach of that duty.

(2) The jury must consider whether the evidence shows that the organisation failed to comply with any health and safety legislation that relates to the alleged breach, and if so—

   (a) how serious that failure was;

   (b) how much of a risk of death it posed.

(3) The jury may also—

   (a) consider the extent to which the evidence shows that there were attitudes, policies, systems or accepted practices within the organisation that were likely to have encouraged any such failure as is mentioned in subsection (2), or to have produced tolerance of it;

   (b) have regard to any health and safety guidance that relates to the alleged breach.

(4) This section does not prevent the jury from having regard to any other matters they consider relevant.

Consideration of the these matters is obligatory. The task for a jury in any trial for the new offence will not be an easy one; nor will it be easy for the prosecution to jump through all the hoops which the Act sets up in order to reach the point where there could be a reasonable prospect of securing a conviction. It is unlikely that there will be many more prosecutions under the new Act than under the old law. Trials, if they take place, will undoubtedly be lengthy and complex. At the end, if convicted, the only penalty the court will be able to impose is that of a fine (as well as a possible order under s. 9 to take specified steps to remedy the breach and under s. 10 to publicise their conviction). Whether this Act will be the remedy sought for the ills of the previous law must remain, for some time, an open question.

FURTHER READING

M. Allen, 'Entrapment: Time for Reconsideration' (1984) 13 Anglo-Am LR 57.

A. Ashworth, 'Testing Fidelity to Legal Values: Official Involvement and Criminal Justice' (2000) 63 MLR 633.

A. Ashworth, 'Re-drawing the Boundaries of Entrapment' [2002] Crim LR 161.

D. Bergman, 'Recklessness in the Boardroom' (1990) 140 New LJ 1496.

M. Bohlander, 'The Sexual Offences Act 2003 and the *Tyrrell* Principle— Criminalising the Victims?' [2005] Crim LR 701.

R. Buxton, 'Being an Accessory to One's Own Murder' [2012] Crim LR 275.

C. M. V. Clarkson, 'Kicking Corporate Bodies and Damning Their Souls' (1996) 59 MLR 557; 'Corporate Culpability' [1998] 2 Web JCLI.

I. H. Dennis, 'The Mental Element for Accessories', in *Criminal Law: Essays in Honour of J. C. Smith* (1987, ed. P. Smith).

M. Giles, 'Complicity—the Problems of Joint Enterprise' [1990] Crim LR 383.

J. Gobert, 'Corporate Criminality: New Crimes for the Times' [1994] Crim LR 722.

J. Gobert, 'The Corporate Manslaughter and Corporate Homicide Act 2007—Thirteen years in the making but was it worth the wait?' (2008) 71 MLR 413.

M. Jefferson, 'Corporate Criminal Liability in the 1990s' (2000) 64 JCL 106.

D. Lanham, 'Accomplices and Transferred Malice' (1980) 96 LQR 110; 'Accomplices and Withdrawal' (1981) 97 LQR 575.

L. H. Leigh, *Strict and Vicarious Liability* (1982, Sweet & Maxwell).

D. Ormerod and R. Taylor, 'The Corporate Manslaughter and Corporate Homicide Act 2007' [2008] Crim LR 589.

P. J. Pace, 'Delegation—a Doctrine in Search of a Definition' [1982] Crim LR 627.

J. C. Smith, 'Aid, Abet, Counsel and Procure', in *Reshaping the Criminal Law* (1978, ed. P. Glazebrook); 'Criminal Liability of Accessories: Law and Law Reform' (1997) 113 LQR 453.

K. J. M. Smith, 'Withdrawal and Complicity' [2001] Crim LR 769.

R. Sullivan, 'Corporate Killing—Some Government Proposals' [2001] Crim LR 31.

G. Virgo, 'Making Sense of Accessorial Liability' [2006] Archbold News Issue 6; 'Joint Enterprise Liability is Dead: Long Live Accessorial Liability' [2012] Crim LR 850.

R. S. Welch, 'The Criminal Liability of Corporations' (1946) 62 LQR 345.

C. Wells, 'The Decline and Rise of English Murder: Corporate Crime and Individual Responsibility' [1988] Crim LR 788; 'Manslaughter and Corporate Crime' (1989) 139 New LJ 931; 'Corporations: Culture, Risk and Criminal Liability' [1993] Crim LR 551; 'Corporate Liability for Crime—*Tesco* v *Nattrass* on the Danger List?' (1996) 1 Archbold News 5.

G. Williams, 'Which of You Did It?' (1989) 52 MLR 179; 'Complicity, Purpose and the Draft Code' [1990] Crim LR 4 and 98; 'Victims and Other Exempt Parties in Crime' (1990) 10 LS 245.

8

Inchoate offences

8.1 Introduction

A person does not break the criminal law simply by having evil thoughts (*Higgins* (1801) 2 East 5). To plan and scheme in one's mind to commit an offence is not, in itself, unlawful. Where, however, a person takes steps towards effecting that plan to commit a substantive offence, he may in the process commit one of the inchoate crimes of attempt, conspiracy, or encouraging or assisting the commission of an offence. At common law the offence of incitement would have been the third in this list. The Serious Crime Act 2007 abolished the offence of incitement and replaced it with three offences based on encouragement or assistance which came into effect on 1 October 2008.

The law would be seriously deficient as a means of protecting persons or property from harm if it could only intervene after a substantive offence had been committed and the harm done. The inchoate offences permit intervention at an earlier stage before any harm has been done but at a time when the accused has moved from mere mental planning to the stage of performing overt acts which manifest his intention that a particular substantive offence be committed. 'Inchoate' means 'just begun or undeveloped'. This accurately reflects the nature of these crimes as they are committed when the accused begins to manifest his criminal intention overtly and at a stage prior to the consummation of that intention in the commission of the substantive offence.

Example

(i) A bears a grudge against V and decides to set fire to his house; (ii) A tells B of his decision and encourages B to assist him; (iii) B agrees to help and they formulate a plan to effect their purpose; (iv) A and B go to V's house, having first telephoned to check he is not at home, and douse it with paraffin; (v) they set light to the paraffin at different points around the house. At (i) A commits no offence as he is merely thinking evil thoughts. In (ii) his initial recounting of his decision involves no offence but when he encourages B to participate he commits the offence of encouraging the commission of an offence. B commits no offence by listening to A but when he agrees to participate he and A commit the offence of conspiracy (iii). When they set fire to the house (v) they commit the offence of arson. However, at (iv) A and B are guilty of attempted arson.

It is important to note that these inchoate offences are steps on the way to the commission of a substantive offence (but see common law conspiracy, **8.3.4** *post*);

they are not crimes existing in the abstract. Thus the indictment would charge A with encouraging B to commit arson, and A and B with conspiracy to commit arson, and attempt to commit arson. An indictment which simply charged the accused with 'encouragement' or 'conspiracy' or 'attempt' in the abstract would be defective.

Note that a number of the cases in this chapter involve conspiracy, or attempt to commit one of several deception offences, such as obtaining property or services by deception. On 15 January 2007 the Fraud Act 2006 came into force sweeping away a range of offences under the Theft Acts and replacing them with new offences under the Fraud Act (see further **Chapter 12** *post*).

8.2 Encouraging or assisting offences

In cl. 47 of the Draft Criminal Code (LC 177), which would have codified the existing common law, the Law Commission defined **incitement** as follows:

> A person is guilty of incitement to commit an offence or offences if—
>
> (a) he incites another to do or cause to be done an act or acts which, if done, will involve the commission of the offence or offences by the other; and
>
> (b) he intends or believes that the other, if he acts as incited, shall, or will do so with the fault required for the offence or offences.

This would have been a fairly brief and simple definition of the offence of incitement involving little complexity. In their Report, *Inchoate Liability for Assisting and Encouraging Crime* (Law Com No. 300, 2006), the Law Commission proposed the abolition of the common law offence of incitement and its replacement with two new statutory inchoate offences which would prohibit assisting and encouraging crime. Clause 1 to the draft Bill contained the offence of intentionally encouraging or assisting a criminal act. This offence would be committed if D did an act capable of encouraging or assisting P's commission of a criminal act and D did so intending to encourage or assist the doing of that criminal act. Clause 2 contained a separate offence of encouraging or assisting criminal acts believing that one or more of them will be done. This offence would be committed where D did an act capable of encouraging or assisting the doing of a criminal act and D believed that the criminal act would be done and that his act would encourage or assist the doing of that act. This offence was proposed to deal with the lacuna in the law on inchoate offences and complicity whereby if D rendered assistance to P to commit an offence (without entering into an agreement such that he could be charged with conspiracy or without uttering words of encouragement such that he could be charged with incitement) but P did not go ahead and commit the offence, D could not be convicted either of aiding or abetting the principal offence (as it had not been committed) or of any inchoate offence. An example the Law Commission give is that of D, in return for payment, lending a van to P believing that P would use it to commit a robbery. P, however, is arrested by the police in connection with another matter before he can attempt to commit the robbery. D would not be guilty of any offence whereas if he had uttered words of encouragement to P to commit a robbery he would be guilty of incitement even if he provided no assistance. The Law Commission considered that this lacuna (facilitation without encouragement) inhibited the police from being able to intervene at an early stage in criminal enterprises particularly where they had the intelligence gathering capability to enable them to identify preliminary acts of assistance before P attempted to commit any offence.

For once the ink had hardly dried on the Law Commission Report when the Government decided to enact legislation based largely upon the Law Commission's recommendations. In January 2007 the Serious Crime Bill was introduced in the House of Lords and the Serious Crime Act (SCA) was enacted on 30 October 2007. The SCA does not adopt verbatim the Law Commission draft Bill although it does replicate its complexity; the Government will be most undeserving of any criticism which accuses them of having *simplified* the law. Part 1 of the SCA, which came into force on 6 April 2008, creates Serious Crime Prevention Orders (dubbed super ASBOs) designed to restrict or disrupt those involved in serious crime. Part 2, which came into force on 1 October 2008, abolishes the common law offence of incitement and replaces it with three new offences which will also deal with the lacuna (facilitation without encouragement) identified by the Law Commission. The Act also includes a defence and an exemption from liability.

D's liability relates to the (hypothetical) offence he intended or believed would be committed by P. If the offence is committed D will be an accessory to it and additionally liable under the law on secondary liability. It is unfortunate that this provision has the effect of creating an extensive overlap with the law on secondary participation dealt with in **Chapter 7**. Some of the confusion and overlap might have been mitigated had the Government enacted the Law Commission's recommendations in *Participating in Crime* (Law Com No. 305). The two Reports were meant to form a package for the reform of incitement and secondary liability and would have led to the creation of a total of eight offences. The widening of liability under the offences of encouraging and assisting crime was to be counterbalanced by a narrowing of secondary liability. The piecemeal approach to reform adopted by the Government, however, is hardly desirable and will only lead to confusion in an area of law which is already confused. It is seriously disappointing that an enactment which seeks to reform and clarify one area of the law, incitement, should lead to confusion in another, secondary participation.

The main provisions of the offences and defences are outlined later. Sections 47 and 65–67 apply to all three offences but will be examined in detail only in relation to the s. 44 offence. When considering the offences under ss. 45 and 46, refer back to the analysis under s. 44.

8.2.1 Intentionally encouraging or assisting an offence

Section 44 provides:

> (1) A person commits an offence if—
>
>   (a) he does an act capable of encouraging or assisting the commission of an offence; and
>
>   (b) he intends to encourage or assist its commission.

(2) But he is not to be taken to have intended to encourage or assist the commission
of an offence merely because such encouragement or assistance was a foreseeable
consequence of his act.

8.2.1.1 *Actus reus*

Whether or not D's act was 'capable' of encouraging or assisting P to commit a
crime, is a question of fact. What 'encouraging or assisting' means will be a matter
for the jury or magistrates to determine but s. 65(1) makes it clear that encouraging
includes threatening or putting pressure on another person to commit an offence.
The focus of the offence is on D's act or acts as **the offence is committed when D
does the relevant act which is capable of encouraging or assisting the commission of an offence** with the necessary intent. There is no need for P to be aware of
the encouragement or assistance or to have acted in response to it as liability arises
where D's act is **capable** of encouraging or assisting. This extends the liability
beyond that which the law of incitement covered as this offence required that the
incitement be communicated to someone.

For the purposes of this, and the next two offences, 'act' includes a course of conduct (s. 67). An act 'capable of assisting or encouraging the commission of an offence'
includes 'taking steps to reduce the possibility of criminal proceedings being brought
in respect of that offence' (s. 65(2)(a)) which, although the statute is silent on the
matter, logic dictates must be an act done before the relevant offence is committed.

 Example

If D being aware that P is going to rob a bank, arranges for a getaway car to be available
for him and lets him know this before D enters the bank, this would be an act capable of
encouraging or assisting P in the commission of the robbery. By contrast if D comes out of
the bank having robbed it, and D assists him at that point in making his getaway by lending
him his car, this act, having occurred after the robbery took place, could not be capable of
encouraging or assisting P in the commission of the robbery.

The 'act' requirement may also be satisfied by D 'failing to take reasonable steps to
discharge a duty' (s. 65(2)(b)). An example given by the Law Commission is that of a
disgruntled security guard, D, who omits to turn on a burglar alarm with the intention of assisting P to burgle the premises of D's employer. The fact that the offence
requires proof of an ulterior intent means that mere inadvertence; for example simply forgetting to switch the alarm on, will not give rise to liability on the part of D.

D may indirectly encourage or assist the commission of an offence where D
arranges for another, E, to do an act capable of encouraging or assisting P to commit an offence, and E does so, then D will be treated as having done E's act (s. 66).
The Explanatory Notes give the example of a gang leader D who instructs a member of his gang E to encourage another person P to kill V.

D may encourage or assist the commission of another inchoate offence, for example D encourages E to solicit P to commit murder (soliciting murder is an offence
under s. 4 of the Offences Against the Person Act 1861).

8.2.1.2 *Mens rea*

This is an offence which requires direct intent; oblique intent will not suffice. Section 44(2) provides that D is not to be taken to have 'intended to encourage or assist the commission of an offence merely because such encouragement or assistance was a foreseeable consequence of his act'. D's act must be capable of encouraging or assisting the commission of an offence. For example, D's act might be the supply of a weapon with the intent that P use it to kill or injure another. Alternatively he might simply offer verbal encouragement to P to commit a particular offence. Where the offence D assists or encourages is an offence requiring proof of fault it must be proved that D either (i) intended or believed that P would have the necessary fault, or (ii) was reckless whether or not P would have the necessary fault, or (iii) if D were to do the act himself he would have the necessary fault (s. 47(5)(a)). Paragraph (iii) is designed to cover the situation where P may lack the requisite *mens rea* for the offence D has assisted or encouraged but D would have had the *mens rea* had he done the act himself. Where this limb is relied upon D is to be assumed to be able to do the relevant act (i.e. there is no defence of impossibility—see s.47(6)). The Explanatory Notes provide an example of these very particular circumstances which are designed to prevent D from evading liability purely because it is impossible for him/her to commit the offence:

Example

D (a woman) encourages P to penetrate V with his penis (rape) and believes that if P were to do so, it would be without V's consent. P reasonably believes that V does consent so does not have the mental element required for conviction of rape. Therefore, D's fault is determined under s. 47(5)(a)(iii) in that if she were to commit the act, she would do it with the fault required. However it is not possible for a woman to commit the act of penetration with a penis so were it not for this subsection, D would escape liability.

Where the offence D assists or encourages requires proof of particular consequences or circumstances, it must be proved that D either intended or believed that were the act to be done, it would be done in those circumstances or with those consequences, or was reckless thereto (s. 47(5)(b)). The Explanatory Notes to the Act further explain that requiring some degree of belief in relation to the circumstances ensures that D will not be guilty of an offence of encouraging or assisting a strict liability offence unless he believes or is reckless as to whether those circumstances exist. The following example is provided (para. 156):

D asks P to drive him home from the pub as he has had too much to drink. P is insured to drive D's car but unknown to D and P, P was disqualified from driving the day before. P is committing the principal offence of driving whilst disqualified, despite the fact he is not aware that he is disqualified, as this is an offence of strict liability. However it would not be fair to hold D liable in such circumstances.

In respect of consequences, the Explanatory Notes provide the following example (para. 157):

> D gives P a baseball bat and intends P to use it to inflict minor bodily harm on V. P however uses the bat to attack V and intentionally kills V. It would not be fair to hold D liable for encouraging and assisting murder, unless he also believes or is reckless as to whether V will be killed.

If D's act is capable of encouraging or assisting the commission of a number of offences, D can be charged with the s. 44 offence in respect of each offence he intends to encourage or assist to be committed (s. 49(2)).

8.2.2 Encouraging or assisting an offence believing it will be committed

Section 45 provides:

> A person commits an offence if—
> (a) he does an act capable of encouraging or assisting the commission of an offence; and
> (b) he believes—
>   (i) that the offence will be committed; and
>   (ii) that his act will encourage or assist its commission.

This offence covers the situation where D may not intend that a particular offence be committed but **he believes both that it will be committed and that his act will encourage or assist its commission**. This would cover the situation where D supplies a weapon to P believing he is going to use it to commit murder but being quite indifferent whether or not he does as his sole concern is to make a profit from the sale.

If D's act is capable of encouraging or assisting the commission of a number of offences, D can be charged with the s. 45 offence in respect of each offence he believes will be encouraged or assisted to be committed (s. 49(2)). Thus where D lends P a crowbar believing D will use it to break into houses to steal, D could be liable for each separate burglary P commits.

D will not be liable for the s. 45 offence where he does an act believing it will encourage or assist P to commit another inchoate offence (as listed in sch. 3; see s. 49(4)).

8.2.3 Encouraging or assisting offences believing one or more will be committed

Section 46 provides:

> (1) A person commits an offence if—
>   (a) he does an act capable of encouraging or assisting the commission of one or more of a number of offences; and

(b) he believes—

    (i) that one or more of those offences will be committed (but has no belief as to which); and

    (ii) that his act will encourage or assist the commission of one or more of them.

(2) It is immaterial for the purposes of subsection 1(b)(ii) whether the person has any belief as to which offence will be encouraged or assisted.

This offence covers the situation where D may not intend that a particular offence be committed but he believes both that one or more offences **will** be committed and that his act will assist or encourage the commission or one or more of them. It does not matter whether he has any belief as to which offence his act will assist or encourage (s. 46(2)). This offence covers the situation where D provides assistance or encouragement believing that one of a range of offences will be committed, for example, where D drives P to V's house knowing that P is going to wreak revenge on V but not knowing whether he is going to beat up V, kill him, or burn his house (cf. *Maxwell* v *DPP for Northern Ireland* **7.1.4.3** *ante*). The difference, however, from the *Maxwell* situation is that there a substantive offence is committed and D is charged as an accessory to it whereas for this offence no substantive offence is committed. The focus is upon D's *mens rea*—the offences he believed would be committed.

In *S* [2011] EWCA Crim 2872 (where D had supplied various chemical cutting agents knowing they would assist the recipient drug dealers in supplying Class A or Class B drugs) the Court of Appeal provided guidance on drafting indictments in respect of this complicated offence. The prosecution need to identify each offence D's act was capable of encouraging or assisting and charge a separate count in respect of each. For D to be convicted of any particular count it must be proved that he believed that that particular offence would be committed with the relevant fault; or that one or more of the specified offences would be committed but he had no belief as to which.

D will not be liable for the s. 46 offence where he does an act believing it will encourage or assist P to commit one or more other inchoate offences (as listed in sch. 3; see s. 49(4)).

8.2.4 Defence of acting reasonably

Section 50 provides:

(1) A person is not guilty of an offence under this Part if he proves—

    (a) that he knew certain circumstances existed; and

    (b) that it was reasonable for him to act as he did in those circumstances.

(2) A person is not guilty of an offence under this Part if he proves—

    (a) that he believed certain circumstances to exist;

    (b) that his belief was reasonable; and

    (c) that it was reasonable for him to act as he did in the circumstances as he believed them to be.

(3) Factors to be considered in determining whether it was reasonable for a person to act as he did include—

    (a) the seriousness of the anticipated offence (or, in the case of an offence under section 46, the offences specified in the indictment);

    (b) any purpose for which he claims to have been acting;

    (c) any authority by which he claims to have been acting.

It is difficult to conceive of circumstances where D charged with the s. 44 offence, which requires intention, could rely on this defence. It is notable that the Explanatory Notes to the Act provide no examples of when the defence could be raised. The Law Commission did not recommend the defence to be available for the s. 44 offence. The Law Commission provided three examples (at para. A.63) of when reliance might be placed on the defence, only one of which merits reproduction, the other two being bizarre:

> D, a motorist, changes motorway lanes to allow a following motorist (P) to overtake, even though D knows that P is speeding

8.2.5 Protective offences: victims not liable

Section 51 provides:

(1) In the case of protective offences, a person does not commit an offence under this Part by reference to such an offence if—

    (a) he falls within the protected category; and

    (b) he is the person in respect of whom the protective offence was committed or would have been if it had been committed.

(2) 'Protective offence' means an offence that exists (wholly or in part) for the protection of a particular category of persons ('the protected category').

This provision puts on a statutory footing the '*Tyrrell* principle' (see **7.1.6** *ante*). The Explanatory Notes provide the following example:

> D is a 12-year-old girl and encourages P, a 40-year-old man to have sex with her. P does not attempt to have sex with D. D cannot be liable of encouraging or assisting child rape despite the fact it is her intent that P have sexual intercourse with a child under 13 (child rape) because she would be considered the 'victim' of that offence had it taken place and the offence of child rape was enacted to protect children under the age of 13.

8.2.6 Jurisdiction

D may be found guilty of an offence under ss. 44, 45, or 46 if he anticipates that the conduct he encourages or assists will take place wholly or partly in England and Wales regardless of where D is at the time (s. 52(1)). The Explanatory Notes provide the following example:

> D in Belgium sends a number of emails to P in London, encouraging him to plant a bomb on the tube. D can be prosecuted in England and Wales...despite the fact he was outside the jurisdiction when he did his act.

The opposite situation, of D being in England and Wales but encouraging or assisting the commission of an offence outside England and Wales, may give rise to liability (see s. 52(2) and sch. 4). There are three situations specified. The first covers offences for which P could be tried in England and Wales (sch. 4, para. 1). For example, D in England, communicates with P who is a British citizen living abroad, encouraging P to kill V living in the same country. Under English law (see s. 9 of the OAPA 1861) murder committed by a British citizen is punishable in English courts wherever it is committed. The second situation applies where D acts wholly or partly in England and Wales and although the offence he encourages or assists might take place outside England and Wales, it is an offence under the law of that place (sch. 14, para. 2). For example, D in England sends an email to P in Spain containing details of how to disarm an alarm system used by a bank in Madrid. D intends to assist P to rob the bank. The third situation arises where D, outside England and Wales, encourages or assists P to commit an offence (also outside England and Wales), but the courts in England and Wales would have jurisdiction if D had himself committed the anticipated offence (sch. 14, para. 3).

The Explanatory Notes give the following example:

> D (a British citizen) in Canada sends a parcel of poison to P in France encouraging him to use it to murder V (also in France). It would be possible to try D in England because he is a British citizen and the anticipated principal offence (murder) is one which could be tried in England, Wales or Northern Ireland as it would be committed by a British citizen.

8.3 Conspiracy

8.3.1 Introduction

At common law the offence of conspiracy was committed where two or more persons agreed 'to do an unlawful act, or to do a lawful act by unlawful means' (*Mulcahy* (1868) LR 3 HL 306). This definition did not limit liability to agreements to commit crimes but also included agreements to commit some torts, to defraud, to corrupt public morals, or to outrage public decency. In *Kamara* v *DPP* [1974] AC 104, the House of Lords held that an agreement to commit the tort of trespass to land, if accompanied by an intention to inflict more than merely nominal damage, amounted to a criminal conspiracy. The Law Commission (Law Com No. 76, para. 1.113) expressed the view that conspiracy should be confined to agreements to commit criminal offences and it is its aim that legislation should ultimately achieve this result. The Criminal Law Act 1977, which resulted from the work of the Law Commission and created the offence of statutory conspiracy, has only partially achieved this result. Pending a comprehensive review of offences of fraud and of the law relating to obscenity and indecency, s. 5 of the 1977 Act preserved the offence of conspiracy to defraud and, possibly, the offence of conspiracy to corrupt public morals or outrage public decency. Agreements to commit torts, however, are no longer indictable as conspiracy. In its Report, *Fraud* (Law Com No. 276) the Law Commission recommended the abolition of conspiracy to defraud as a separate offence. The Fraud Act 2006, whilst radically altering the law on fraud, did not abolish common law conspiracy to defraud.

8.3.2 **Common elements**

Certain elements are common to both statutory conspiracies and common law conspiracies.

8.3.2.1 Agreement

The essence of conspiracy is an agreement between two or more persons to effect the particular prohibited purpose. The agreement may be express or implied, but whatever form it takes, the offence of conspiracy is complete as soon as the parties agree. There is no requirement that they begin to put the agreement into effect, nor need all the details of the agreement be settled. Thus A and B would be guilty of conspiracy to rob where they had agreed to rob a bank even though they had not settled the time or place where the robbery was to take place. While conspiracy is complete as soon as two parties agree to effect an unlawful purpose, the conspiracy will continue to subsist as long as they agree and will only terminate on its completion by performance or by abandonment or frustration (see *DPP v Doot* [1973] AC 807). **As conspiracy is a continuing offence, other persons may join an existing conspiracy and become parties to it.** For example, if A approaches C and asks him to join him and B in robbing a bank, when C agrees he becomes guilty of conspiracy to rob. This illustrates a further point that it is not necessary for all the parties to a conspiracy to be in contact with each other. What is necessary is that all the parties to the conspiracy have a common purpose communicated to at least one other party to the conspiracy (see *Ardalan* [1972] 2 All ER 257; *Scott* (1979) 68 Cr App R 164).

8.3.2.2 Parties

While it must be proved that there was an agreement between D and another, that other need not be identified (*Phillips* (1987) 86 Cr App R 18). However, **there must be at least two parties to the agreement;** agreements with certain persons may not suffice to establish the offence of conspiracy. For example, where the director of a company who is solely responsible for the conduct of the company's business decides to commit an offence in the company's name, he cannot be convicted of conspiring with the company as only one mind was involved albeit that the company has a separate legal personality (see *McDonnell* [1966] 1 QB 233). But where a director conspires in the course of the company's business with other persons or companies, the company may be indicted as a party to that conspiracy (see *R v ICR Haulage Ltd* [1944] KB 551).

Where the only parties to an agreement are husband and wife they cannot be guilty of conspiracy, whether statutory (s. 2(2) of the Criminal Law Act 1977) or common law (*Mawji v R* [1957] AC 126). However, a husband and wife can be convicted of conspiracy where a third party is also involved (*Whitehouse* (1852) 6 Cox CC 38; *Chrastny* [1991] 1 WLR 1381), or where the agreement was entered into before they married (*R v Robinson* (1746) 1 Leach 37).

Where the only other party to an agreement to commit an offence is a child under the age of criminal responsibility, D will not be guilty of conspiracy (s. 2(2)). Where the only other party to an agreement to commit an offence is an intended victim of that offence, D will not be guilty of conspiracy (s. 2(2)). The intended victim of the offence will not be guilty of conspiracy regardless of the number of persons involved in the conspiracy (s. 2(1)). The 1977 Act does not define 'victim'. Smith and Hogan, *Criminal Law*, (at p. 301) suggest that the meaning of 'victim' is confined to offences which exist for his protection so that he would not be convicted of that offence as an accessory when it is committed by another with his full knowledge and cooperation (see **7.1.6** *ante*). This may have been the legislature's intention but it is expressed ambiguously. In *Gnango* [2011] UKSC 59, Lord Phillips adverted, *obiter*, to this issue stating (at para. 49):

> If ['victim'] is given the wide meaning it would seem to produce the surprising result that a conspiracy by two persons that one will commit a terrorist atrocity as a suicide bomber, or to set fire to a house owned by one of them in furtherance of some ulterior motive, would appear not to subject either to criminal liability. There is a case for confining the meaning of 'victim' to persons of a class that the relevant Act is intended to protect....

If the issue arises in practice it is a fair assumption that this *obiter dictum* will be followed. There is no common law authority in respect of victims as parties to conspiracies, but the issue is unlikely to arise as it is difficult to imagine an agreement with the proposed victim of a fraud to defraud him.

We have seen that where a person cannot commit an offence as a principal this does not prevent him being liable as an accessory (see **7.1.3.3** *ante*). His exemption from liability as a principal will likewise not protect him from liability for conspiracy. Thus, for example, a woman may be convicted of conspiracy to rape. Where a person is exempt from liability for an offence, whether as principal or accessory, he will not necessarily be exempt from conviction for conspiracy with another to commit that offence. There is a paucity of authority in this area. The Law Commission recommended that the exemption should extend to liability for conspiracy (see Law Com No. 76, para. 1.56) disapproving of the only authority in favour of liability, *Whitchurch* (1890) 24 QBD 420, where a woman was convicted of conspiring to procure her own abortion though she was not pregnant and could not commit the substantive offence under s. 58 of the Offences Against the Person Act 1861. Parliament did not adopt this recommendation as it was considered that the provision to implement it would unduly complicate the 1977 Act and, in practice, non-pregnant women would not now be prosecuted. It appears that in practice the court will determine the question of liability by considering the purpose of the statute and whether it would be defeated by holding an exempt person liable for conspiracy or whether its purpose requires the extension of the exemption to cover conspiracy.

> In *Burns* (1984) 79 Cr App R 173, the question arose directly. The Court of Appeal upheld the conviction of a father of a child of conspiracy with others to steal it from the mother, although he was exempt from prosecution for the substantive offence under s. 56 of the Offences Against the Person Act 1861 (s. 56 has since been repealed by the Child Abduction Act 1984). Watkins LJ stated the considerations which influenced the court in its decision as follows (at p. 179):
>
> > We find [no authority] that leads us to say that it is in any way wrong or unjust for a person who is exempt, in the sense that James Burns was, from prosecution for the substantive offence to be proceeded against for the crime of conspiracy.

> The dangers of permitting a father of children to collect a posse of men and suddenly launch a siege of the home of his erstwhile wife, to break in and then snatch away sleeping children are surely self-evident. The criminal law does not in our view permit that sort of conduct. When a father who is exempt under s. 56 behaves in that way, it is, in our judgment, not only lawful but right and just that the prosecution should be free to bring a charge of conspiracy against him.

A person who agrees with another who is exempt from prosecution for the substantive offence to commit that offence may be convicted of conspiracy (see *Duguid* (1906) 21 Cox CC 200).

8.3.2.3 Acquittal of the other alleged conspirators

There must be at least two parties to a conspiracy. If A is charged with conspiracy with B and B is acquitted, can A be convicted? If other parties, not charged, are alleged to have been involved, the acquittal of B has no consequences for A provided that the prosecution prove that A agreed with at least one other person (see *Anthony* [1965] 2 QB 189). Where A and B are the only alleged conspirators the conviction of one and acquittal of the other need not necessarily involve any inconsistency as the evidence against one may have been much stronger than the evidence against the other; for example, A may have confessed to the conspiracy, such confession being highly probative evidence against A but being of no evidential value against B. If A and B are tried separately the inconsistent verdicts again may be due to the different evidence presented at each trial, or the way in which the case was conducted or simply the different view which different juries take of the witnesses (see *DPP v Shannon* [1975] AC 717). There was some doubt, however, at common law whether a jury trying several conspirators together could convict one and acquit the others, there being no other alleged conspirators. To avoid all doubt s. 5(8) and (9) of the Criminal Law Act 1977 provide:

> (8) The fact that the person or persons who, so far as appears from the indictment on which any person has been convicted of conspiracy, were the only other parties to the agreement on which his conviction was based have been acquitted of conspiracy by reference to that agreement (whether after being tried with the person convicted or separately) shall not be a ground for quashing his conviction unless under all the circumstances of the case his conviction is inconsistent with the acquittal of the other person or persons in question.

> (9) Any rule of law or practice inconsistent with the provisions of subsection (8) above is hereby abolished.

The effect of this provision is that where all the alleged conspirators are tried together and the evidence against each is of roughly equal weight, the judge should direct the jury that they must either convict all or none, and the judge should make it clear that if they are unsure about the guilt of one of the conspirators, they must acquit all (see *Longman and Cribben* (1980) 72 Cr App R 121; *Testouri* [2003] EWCA Crim 3735). But where the judge considers that the weight of the evidence against each conspirator is markedly different, he must direct them to consider each case separately and that they may convict or acquit as is appropriate according to the evidence (see *Roberts* (1983) 78 Cr App R 41).

8.3.3 **Statutory conspiracy**

The offence of statutory conspiracy is defined by s. 1(1) and (2) of the Criminal Law Act 1977, as amended by s. 5 of the Criminal Attempts Act 1981, as follows:

> (1) Subject to the following provisions of this Part of this Act, if a person agrees with any other person or persons that a course of conduct shall be pursued which, if the agreement is carried out in accordance with their intentions, either—
>
>   (a) will necessarily amount to or involve the commission of any offence or offences by one or more parties to the agreement, or
>
>   (b) would do so but for the existence of facts which render the commission of the offence or any offences impossible, he is guilty of conspiracy to commit the offence or offences in question.
>
> (2) Where liability for any offence may be incurred without knowledge on the part of the person committing it of any particular fact or circumstance necessary for the commission of the offence, a person shall nevertheless not be guilty of conspiracy to commit that offence by virtue of subsection (1) above unless he and at least one other party to the agreement intend or know that that fact or circumstance shall or will exist at the time when the conduct constituting the offence is to take place.

As conspiracy is an offence which centres on the agreement between the parties, which involves a meeting of minds, it is difficult to divide the offence into *actus reus* and *mens rea*. It is proposed, therefore, to analyse the separate ingredients contained in s. 1(1) which go to make up the offence.

8.3.3.1 Course of conduct

The essence of conspiracy is that the parties agree upon a course of conduct to be pursued. **For the parties to be liable for conspiracy the agreed course of conduct, if pursued in accordance with their intentions, must necessarily amount to or involve the commission of an offence by one or more of the conspirators.** Where the agreement is to commit a 'result crime' the phrase 'course of conduct' would be meaningless if confined to their actions divorced from the consequences of those actions. For example, if A and B agree to kill V by placing poison in a bottle of milk in his fridge, this will not necessarily result in murder as V may not drink the milk. If the phrase 'course of conduct' covered only the parties' physical acts, A and B would not be guilty of conspiracy to murder. This phrase must therefore include the intended consequences of those actions which, in this case, are the death of V. Thus the course of conduct agreed includes not only the actions intended to be taken but also the consequences of those actions.

If 'course of conduct' includes intended consequences, it is important to determine what consequences the parties intended as their liability will be limited to these. In *Siracusa* (1990) 90 Cr App R 340, O'Connor LJ stated (at p. 350):

> The *mens rea* sufficient to support the commission of a substantive offence will not necessarily be sufficient to support a charge of conspiracy to commit that offence. An intent to cause grievous bodily harm is sufficient to support the charge of murder, but is not sufficient to support a charge of conspiracy to murder or of attempt to murder.

In *Siracusa* the accused were charged, *inter alia*, with conspiracy to import heroin contrary to s. 170(2)(b) of the Customs and Excise Management Act 1979. The jury were directed that if they agreed on a course of conduct to be pursued which, if carried out in accordance with their intentions, would necessarily amount to the offence of being concerned in the fraudulent evasion of the prohibition either on the importation of cannabis or heroin, by one or more of the parties to the agreement, then they were guilty of conspiracy. Case law has established that a person may be convicted of the substantive offence of importing heroin where he believed that cannabis was being imported (see **3.3** *ante*). Where conspiracy is charged, however, this will not suffice. O'Connor LJ stated (at p. 350):

> [I]f the prosecution charge a conspiracy to contravene s. 170(2) of the Customs and Excise Management Act by the importation of heroin, then the prosecution must prove that the agreed course of conduct was the importation of heroin. This is because the essence of the crime of conspiracy is the agreement and in simple terms, you do not prove an agreement to import heroin by proving an agreement to import cannabis.

The course of conduct agreed also includes any facts or circumstance necessary for the commission of the substantive offence. A person cannot be convicted of conspiracy unless he and at least one other party to the agreement intend or know that such fact or circumstance shall or will exist at the time when the conduct constituting the offence is to take place. This is implicit in s. 1(2) which is not particularly clearly expressed. The substance of this provision is that, where recklessness or negligence suffice with respect to a fact or circumstance of the substantive offence or strict liability applies thereto, a person can be convicted of conspiracy to commit such an offence only where he and another party to the agreement intend that the circumstance shall exist or know that it will exist at the time the offence is to take place. This position has been confirmed by the House of Lords in *Saik* [2006] UKHL 18 after a series of decisions in the Court of Appeal relating to money-laundering offences had held that it was sufficient for the offence of conspiracy to be established that D had the *mens rea* of the substantive offence, which in these cases was satisfied by proof that he suspected, or had reasonable grounds to suspect, that the property was the proceeds of crime; i.e. recklessness or negligence sufficed as to the crucial fact or circumstance in the *actus reus* of the substantive offence. Lord Hope of Craighead stated (at para. 58):

> There is no doubt that the requirement [that the defendant and at least one other party to the agreement must 'intend or know' that the fact or circumstance 'shall or will exist' at the time when the conduct constituting the offence is to take place] was designed to eliminate the risk that someone could be guilty of conspiracy just because he was reckless as to the existence or otherwise of the circumstances that would make the conduct criminal.

A problem with s. 1(2) however, is that the words 'intend or know' are not entirely apposite. It is not strictly accurate to state that A intends a fact or circumstance to exist if he has no control over whether or not it exists, nor may it be possible for A, at the time of the agreement, to know that a particular fact or circumstance will exist at some future time. But in examining the constituents of conspiracy an important consideration, which the courts have not always understood or taken into account, is the point in time when the offence of conspiracy is complete. Lord Hope of Craighead highlighted this (at para. 75):

> A conspiracy is complete when the agreement to enter into it is formed, even if nothing is done to implement it. Implementation gives effect to the conspiracy, but it does not alter its essential elements. The statutory language adopts this approach. It assumes that implementation of the agreement lies in the future. The question whether its requirements are fulfilled is directed to the stage when the agreement is formed, not to the stage when it is implemented.

Example

A and B agree to handle particular goods. Several situations may arise: (i) they know at the time of their agreement that the goods are stolen; or (ii) the goods may not yet be stolen but it is their intention that when they are stolen they will handle them; or (iii) they may not know the provenance of the goods but their agreement is to handle them whether they be stolen goods or goods from a legitimate source.

In situations (i) and (ii) there should generally not be a problem; in (i) A and B know the provenance of the goods at the time they enter into their agreement while in (ii) the purpose of their agreement is to handle stolen goods. In respect of (i) Lord Brown of Eaton-under-Heywood stated (at para. 119):

> But if an agreement is made to handle goods believed to be stolen I for my part would have little difficulty in concluding for the purposes of section 1(2)...that the conspirators intended or knew that they would be stolen. Section 1(2) looks to the future so that the putative conspirator's state of mind is in any event better described as belief than as knowledge....One can never be certain that goods that are to come into one's possession at a future time will be stolen but a firm belief can be held and that is sufficient.

In *Saik* the House confirmed that knowledge could not be satisfied by proof only of belief or suspicion. Lord Nicholls of Birkenhead explained (at para. 20):

> Thus on a charge of conspiracy to handle stolen property where the property has not been identified when the agreement is made, the prosecution must prove that the conspirator *intended* that the property which was the subject of the conspiracy *would* be stolen property.

Situation (iii), however, is a little more problematic as it involves conditional intention; A and B have agreed to pursue a course of conduct which, if carried out *in accordance with their intentions*, may, or may not, depending on the provenance of the goods they ultimately handle, involve the commission of the substantive offence of handling. The issue did not strictly arise in *Saik* and the majority do not provide a clear answer. Baroness Hale of Richmond, who dissented, does, however, provide an answer to the conditional intent problem. She uses an example of A and

B considering having sex with a woman and agreeing that they will do so *even if* it turns out that she does not consent. Baroness Hale states (at para. 99):

> [I]t is important to distinguish between what happens when the substantive offence is committed—when the men have intercourse with the woman whether or not she consents—and what happens when they agree to do so. When they agree, they have thought about the possibility that she may not consent. They have agreed that they will go ahead *even if at the time when they go ahead they know that she is not consenting*. If so, that will not be recklessness; that will be intent to rape. Hence they are guilty of conspiracy to rape.

How lower courts may resolve the problem of situation (iii) whenever it arises remains to be seen. It is suggested that the approach of Baroness Hale would be consistent with that of the courts in the cases outlined later (**8.3.3.2** *post*).

If only one of the parties to the agreement has the relevant knowledge or intention there is no conspiracy. For example, if A and B agree to purchase a particular consignment of goods from C, A knowing them to be stolen and B having no such knowledge or belief, neither will be liable for conspiracy to handle stolen goods even though the agreed course of action, if pursued, would necessarily have involved the offence of handling stolen goods by A. Likewise, where the parties differ as to the intended consequences, this will affect their liability for conspiracy. For example, if A and B agree to wound V and A intends that V should die but B only intends that he should sustain grievous bodily harm, there is no conspiracy to kill but there is a conspiracy to cause grievous bodily harm.

8.3.3.2 If the agreement is carried out

Sometimes the agreement the parties make is a conditional one, for example, to beat up V on his way home from the pub if he is alone. Have they agreed on a course of conduct which, if it is carried out in accordance with their intentions, will necessarily amount to or involve the commission of an offence?

> In *Jackson* [1985] Crim LR 444, the appellants' convictions of conspiracy to pervert the course of justice were upheld by the Court of Appeal. The appellants had agreed with W, then on trial for burglary, that if he was convicted they would shoot him in the leg as they considered that the court would then deal with him more leniently. The Court of Appeal held that:
>
> > Planning was taking place for a contingency and if that contingency occurred the conspiracy would necessarily involve the commission of an offence. 'Necessarily' is not to be held to mean that there must inevitably be the carrying out of the offence; it means, if the agreement is carried out in accordance with the plan, there must be the commission of the offence referred to in the conspiracy count.

The object of the agreement was the commission of the offence; if the contingency did not occur no action would be taken. In *O'Hadhmaill* [1996] Crim LR 509 a conviction of conspiracy to cause an explosion was upheld where, during the IRA ceasefire, members of the IRA agreed to make bombs to be used if the ceasefire came to an end. If the ceasefire continued the bombs would not be used.

These situations should be contrasted with the situation where the object of the agreement is not the commission of that offence but the attainment of some other object, although the parties may contemplate the commission of an offence to attain that object. The following example was given in *Reed* [1982] Crim LR 819, and approved in *Jackson*:

> A and B agree to drive from London to Edinburgh in a time which can be achieved without exceeding the speed limits, but only if the traffic which they encounter is exceptionally light. Their agreement will not necessarily involve the commission of any offence, even if it is carried out in accordance with their intentions, and they do drive from London to Edinburgh within the agreed time. Accordingly the agreement does not constitute the offence of statutory conspiracy or indeed of any offence.

Driving from London to Edinburgh within a particular time was an object which could be attained without the commission of any offence; if the speed limit was broken, this was incidental to the main object of the agreement. In *Reed* the Court of Appeal contrasted the driving example with that of A and B who agree to rob a bank, if when they arrive at the bank it seems safe to do so. 'Their agreement will necessarily involve the commission of the offence of robbery if it is carried out in accordance with their intentions. Accordingly, they are guilty of the statutory offence of conspiracy'. The object of their agreement was robbery; the commission of the offence was not incidental to any other object.

One situation remains. What if A and B agree to rob the bank and to kill anyone who seeks to prevent their escape. Are they guilty of conspiracy to murder? The driving example might appear to suggest that they are not, as the main object of their agreement is to rob the bank and this can be attained without necessarily killing anyone. But if this agreement to kill is isolated from the agreement to rob, there is little to distinguish it from *Jackson* as it is an agreement to kill subject to a condition precedent. If no one seeks to prevent their escape the course of conduct will not be pursued, but if anyone does seek to prevent their escape, the agreed course of conduct will necessarily involve the commission of murder. Perhaps the correct approach to this problem is to separate the elements of the agreement from each other. The result is two separate agreements to pursue two courses of conduct: first, the agreement to rob the bank, and secondly the agreement, if a particular contingency occurs, to kill. The driving example is not severable in this way; there is one agreement to pursue one course of conduct which may or may not involve the commission of an offence.

8.3.3.3 In accordance with their intentions

At common law the prosecution had to prove not only an agreement to carry out an unlawful purpose but also an intention on the part of any alleged conspirator to carry out the unlawful purpose (see *Thomson* (1965) 50 Cr App R 1). The Law Commission did not recommend any change in the law. In Law Com No. 76, it stated (at para. 7.2):

> A person should be guilty of conspiracy if he agrees with another person that an offence shall be committed. Both must intend that any consequence specified in the definition

of the offence will result and both must know of the existence of any state of affairs which it is necessary for them to know in order to be aware that the course of conduct agreed upon will amount to the offence.

The implication of this view was that if A did not intend the substantive offence to be committed he could not be liable for conspiracy, and if there were only two parties to the alleged agreement, the other party likewise could not be guilty of conspiracy. In *Anderson* [1986] AC 27, the House of Lords was faced with the problem of an alleged conspirator who claimed he did not intend the substantive offence to be committed. D agreed for a fee to supply diamond wire to cut through prison bars to enable a prisoner to escape. He was convicted of conspiracy to effect the escape of a prisoner and appealed claiming that he intended only to supply the wire, receive his fee, and then go abroad but that he neither intended nor expected the plan to be carried out. The House of Lords could have upheld D's conviction on the basis that he had aided and abetted the conspiracy as the others involved clearly had the intention that the substantive offence be committed. Their Lordships chose, however, to uphold his conviction as a principal to the conspiracy. Lord Bridge, in a speech with which all the House agreed, stated (at p. 38):

> I am clearly driven by consideration of the diversity of roles which parties may agree to play in criminal conspiracies to reject any construction of the statutory language which would require the prosecution to prove an intention on the part of each conspirator that the criminal offence or offences which will necessarily be committed by one or more of the conspirators if the agreed course of conduct is fully carried out should in fact be committed.

Too great a concern for easing the task of the prosecution has once again led to a distortion of the substantive principles of the criminal law. If it is not necessary to prove an intention on the part of one of the parties to an agreement that the course of conduct be pursued, it would appear to be unnecessary to prove such an intention in relation to any other party. The absurd outcome is that a person may be guilty of conspiracy where no party to the alleged agreement intended the substantive offence to be committed. In such a case there is no agreement to commit a crime, and no statutory conspiracy according to s. 1(1), but yet Lord Bridge would permit the conviction of conspiracy of all the parties to this non-existent agreement!

 Question

If a person may be convicted of conspiracy 'irrespective of his intention', what is the *mens rea* of conspiracy?

Lord Bridge's answer to this question was distorted by his concern to render immune from liability 'respectable citizens' who enter into agreements for the purpose of 'exposing and frustrating the criminal purpose of the other parties to the agreement'. His concern would have been unnecessary had he adopted the Law Commission's view, as such a person would not intend the offence to be committed. Lord Bridge's abandonment of the requirement of proof of such an intention prima facie rendered such persons involved in entrapping offenders liable for conspiracy. In order to return them to the realms of innocence Lord Bridge invented a new *mens rea* requirement unsupported by the legislation, the Law Commission, or any common law authority. He stated (at p. 39):

> [T]he necessary *mens rea* of the crime is, in my opinion, established if, and only if, it is shown that the accused when he entered into the agreement, intended to play some part in the agreed course of conduct in furtherance of the criminal purpose which the agreed course of conduct was intended to achieve. Nothing less will suffice; nothing more is required.

This dictum itself contradicts Lord Bridge's earlier dicta as, if the intention of any alleged conspirator is irrelevant, it is impossible to determine the 'criminal purpose which the agreed course of conduct was intended to achieve'. Ignoring this absurdity, this dictum appears to require proof of an intention on the part of an alleged conspirator to play some part in the agreed course of conduct. Anderson's part was to be the supplier of the cutting wire and thus their Lordships confirmed his conviction of conspiracy. But it had always been understood that a person could be guilty of conspiracy even though he was to play no active role in the commission of the substantive offence. Lord Bridge's dictum would appear to remove such a person from the realms of liability. For example, A approaches B and asks him to kill C. If B agrees this would have amounted to conspiracy prior to *Anderson*. Now, however, A and B will only be liable for conspiracy to kill where A intended to play some part in the agreed course of conduct, namely the killing of C. Furthermore, far from rendering all persons involved in acceptable entrapment (see **7.1.7** *ante*) immune from criminal liability, Lord Bridge's dictum brings some such persons within the realms of criminal liablity if they intend to play some part in the agreed course of conduct—such action perhaps being necessary either to maintain their credibility as conspirators or to obtain the evidence necessary for a prosecution. Lord Bridge's good intentions only seem to have served to create more problems than he was seeking to resolve.

In *Siracusa* (1990) 90 Cr App R 340, the Court of Appeal sought to effect a damage limitation exercise by 'clarifying' Lord Bridge's dictum that it must be shown that 'the accused, when he entered into the agreement, intended to play some part in the agreed course of conduct...'. O'Connor LJ (a judicial clairvoyant if ever there was one!) stated (at p. 349):

> We think it obvious that Lord Bridge cannot have been intending that the organiser of a crime who recruited others to carry it out would not himself be guilty of conspiracy unless it could be proved that he intended to play some active part himself thereafter.

Thus, in the earlier example where A asks B to kill C, both A and B are, in the opinion of the Court of Appeal, guilty of conspiracy. O'Connor LJ went on to state (at p. 349):

> Participation in a conspiracy is infinitely variable: it can be active or passive. If the majority shareholder and director of a company consents to the company being used for drug smuggling carried out in the company's name by a fellow director and minority shareholder, he is guilty of conspiracy. Consent, that is the agreement or adherence to the agreement, can be inferred if it is proved that he knew what was going on and the intention to participate in the furtherance of the criminal purpose is also established by his failure to stop the unlawful activity. Lord Bridge's dictum does not require anything more.

So 'play some part in' means no more than continuing to concur in the activity of another or failure to stop the unlawful activity. It is hard to believe that this is what Lord Bridge meant. A problem with this interpretation, however, is that it presumes activity on the part of other parties in furtherance of the criminal purpose. It had always been accepted that a conspiracy was complete when the parties agree and there was no requirement of activity in furtherance of the agreement. Doubtless, in many cases, it is only possible to prove the existence of the agreement by inference from the overt acts of the parties, but matters of proof should not be confused with substantive principles. In addition, the real problem with Lord Bridge's speech, that of the abandonment of the requirement that a conspirator intend the substantive offence to be committed, remains.

The authority of *Anderson* has been thrown further into doubt by the Privy Council decision in *Yip Chiu-Cheung* v *R* [1994] 3 WLR 514 which, although not binding on English courts, is highly persuasive particularly as the committee comprised Lords Griffiths, Browne-Wilkinson, Mustill, Jauncey of Tullichettle, and Slynn of Hadley. *Siracusa* was not cited but their Lordships addressed issues raised in *Anderson*. In the case before them the appellant had been convicted of conspiracy to traffic in heroin contrary to common law (conspiracy being a common law offence in Hong Kong) and to s. 4 of the Dangerous Drugs Ordinance. The conspiracy concerned an agreement between the appellant and an American undercover drug enforcement agent that he would meet the appellant in Hong Kong where he would receive from him the supply of heroin which the agent would take to Australia. The Hong Kong authorities were aware of the plan and had agreed not to prevent the agent from proceeding to Australia as his aim was to identify others in the drugs ring. The agent, however, missed his flight to Hong Kong and the plan was abandoned. The appellant argued on appeal that the agent could not be a co-conspirator as he lacked the necessary *mens rea* for conspiracy. The Privy Council distinguished the situation relating to 'respectable citizens' involved in entrapment referred to by Lord Bridge on the basis that a person who enters into an agreement with the purpose of frustrating the crime does not have the *mens rea* to be a conspirator. Lord Griffiths stated (at p. 518):

> The crime of conspiracy requires an agreement between two or more persons to commit an unlawful act with the intention of carrying it out. It is the intention to carry out the crime that constitutes the necessary *mens rea* for the offence.

On this basis, even though the agent was 'acting courageously and with the best of motives', he intended to commit the offence of drug trafficking. Furthermore, Lord Griffiths added (at pp. 518, 519):

> Neither the police, nor customs, nor any other member of the executive have any power to alter the terms of the Ordinance forbidding the export of heroin, and the fact that they may turn a blind eye when the heroin is exported does not prevent it from being a criminal offence.

The fact that the agent would not be prosecuted does not mean that he would not have committed a crime and thus he had the necessary *mens rea* for conspiracy and therefore was the appellant's co-conspirator.

Although *Yip Chiu-Cheung* concerned common law conspiracy, it is difficult to see any distinction between this and statutory conspiracy. The signs clearly are that if the issue comes before the Supreme Court *Anderson* will not be followed; that much has been hinted at by the Court of Appeal in *King* [2012] EWCA Crim 805. Where there appears to be an agreement between parties to commit an offence but, in fact, none of them intend to carry the agreement out and it is nothing more than a fantasy, there is not a conspiracy; there needs to be some credible evidence of 'executory intent' for the case to be left to the jury (see *Goddard* [2012] EWCA Crim 1756).

In its Draft Criminal Code the Law Commission reasserts the traditional view of conspiracy in cl. 48 which specifically requires proof that a person charged with conspiracy, and at least one other party to the agreement, must have intended the offence to be committed.

8.3.3.4 Necessarily amount to or involve the commission of any offence

If the course of conduct agreed upon is carried out in accordance with the parties' intentions, will it necessarily amount to or involve the commission of an offence? **If A and B agree upon a course of conduct which they believe will amount to an offence but it is not an offence, their belief will not convert their agreement into the offence of conspiracy.** For example, believing that it is illegal to import lace into England, A and B agree to smuggle some lace into the country. In fact, there is no restriction on the importation of lace, so the agreement, if executed, will not involve the commission of any offence.

The agreement, when executed, must involve one or more of the parties to the agreement in the commission of an offence. Will participation as an aider, abettor, counsellor, or procurer of an offence suffice? In *Hollinshead* [1985] 1 All ER 850, the Court of Appeal held that an agreement to aid and abet an offence was not sufficient; a charge of conspiracy would only be sustainable where the agreement envisaged the commission of the offence as a principal by one or more of the parties. On the appeal hearing of that case in the House of Lords [1985] AC 975, their Lordships did not address this question; they upheld the convictions of the accused for common law conspiracy to defraud and considered it unnecessary to decide whether a statutory conspiracy to aid and abet an offence was possible. The wording of s. 1(1) and the fact that their Lordships did not decide that there was a statutory conspiracy seem to imply that a conspiracy to aid and abet is not possible (see also *Kenning* [2008] EWCA 1534). It should be noted, however, that there are a few statutory offences, whose *actus reus* consists of aiding and abetting or procuring something, for example aiding, abetting, counselling, or procuring another's suicide. In these cases the aider and abettor is the principal so that it is possible to conspire to aid and abet a suicide (see *Reed* [1982] Crim LR 819).

8.3.3.5 Impossibility

Section 1(1)(b) (inserted by s. 5 of the Criminal Attempts Act 1981) deals with the problem of impossibility where facts exist which render the commission of the agreed offence impossible. To some extent this provision is unnecessary as the situation is covered by the phrase 'carried out in accordance with their intentions'. For example, A and B agree to kill C by shooting him. Unknown to them he is already dead so commission of the substantive offence of murder is impossible. However, had the agreement been carried out in accordance with their intentions this would necessarily have involved the commission of the offence of murder. The inclusion of s. 1(1)(b), however, is useful as it serves to avoid all doubt.

Key Point

Thus A and B will be liable for conspiracy in the following circumstances:

(1) they agree to pick V's pocket which, unknown to them, is empty (the offence of theft is impossible in the circumstances);

(2) they agree to break into a safe to steal the contents using a jemmy which, unknown to them, is incapable of effecting their purpose (the offence of theft is impossible because of the inadequacy of the means chosen to commit it);

(3) they agree to have consensual intercourse with V whom they believe to be 15 but who has just celebrated her 16th birthday (the offence of having sexual intercourse with a girl under 16 is impossible as V lacks the necessary quality of being under 16).

These examples illustrate three types of impossibility: impossibility due to the circumstances (often referred to as physical impossibility), impossibility due to inadequacy of means, and impossibility due to the absence of a quality on the part of a person or subject-matter (e.g. goods being stolen to support a charge of handling stolen goods) necessary for the commission of the offence (this may also be referred to as legal impossibility). At common law, following the decisions in *Haughton* v *Smith* [1975] AC 476 and *DPP* v *Nock* [1978] AC 979, impossibility was a defence except where it arose from inadequacy of means.

8.3.4 **Common law conspiracies**

These are limited to conspiracy to defraud and possibly conspiracy to corrupt public morals or outrage public decency.

8.3.4.1 Conspiracy to defraud

Statutory conspiracy involves an agreement to commit an offence. Many frauds are crimes but some are not. Conspiracy to defraud was preserved by s. 5(2) of the Criminal Law Act 1977 to cover those frauds which are not crimes. For some time, however, there was confusion whether a conspiracy to defraud which would involve the commission of an offence could be charged as common law conspiracy. The problem was resolved by s. 12 of the Criminal Justice Act 1987:

(1) If—

    (a) a person agrees with any other person or persons that a course of conduct shall be pursued; and

    (b) that course of conduct will necessarily amount to or involve the commission of any offence or offences by one or more of the parties to the agreement if the agreement is carried out in accordance with their intentions,

the fact that it will do so shall not preclude a charge of conspiracy to defraud being brought against any of them in respect of the agreement.

The effect of this provision is to recognise the overlap between the two forms of conspiracy—they are not mutually exclusive. This leaves to prosecutors a choice as to how to charge a particular conspiracy, but this choice should be exercised in accordance with guidance issued by the Director of Public Prosecutions under s. 10 of the Prosecution of Offences Act 1985, which indicates the circumstances in which a charge of conspiracy to defraud is appropriate.

8.3.4.1.1 *The meaning of 'defraud'*

A conspiracy to defraud 'is an agreement to practise a fraud on somebody' (*Wai Yu-tsang* v *R* [1991] 4 All ER 664, 671, *per* Lord Goff). There is no need for anyone to be deceived if the course of conduct agreed by the parties is carried out. In *Scott* v *Metropolitan Police Commissioner* [1975] AC 819, D was convicted of conspiracy to defraud the copyright owners of films. D agreed with the employees of cinema owners to remove the films temporarily and to make copies of them without the knowledge or consent of the copyright owners. The copies were then to be distributed on a commercial basis accruing for the conspirators' profits which might otherwise have been secured by the copyright owners. Viscount Dilhorne stated (at p. 840):

[A]n agreement by two or more by dishonesty to deprive a person of something which is his or to which he is or would or might be entitled and an agreement by two or more to injure some proprietary right of his, suffices to constitute the offence of conspiracy to defraud.

In this case the copyright owners suffered a loss in either of two ways: (i) the sales of the unauthorised copies would affect the sales of legitimate copies of their films; and (ii) under *Reading* v *Attorney-General* [1951] AC 507, the accused were bound to account to the copyright owners for any profits they made, which they clearly did not intend to do.

In *Adams* v *The Queen* [1995] 1 WLR 52, D, a director of EHL, agreed with his five co-defendants, who comprised the investment team, to conduct a series of share transactions through a series of overseas companies and banks thereby making for themselves a profit which they concealed from EHL. The Privy Council upheld D's conviction of conspiracy to defraud. In this case the fraud consisted of the dishonest concealment of information from the company which D was under a duty to disclose to it, namely information concerning the secret profits made. Lord Jauncey of Tullichettle stated (at p. 65):

> Since a company is entitled to recover from directors secret profits made by them at the company's expense, it would follow that any dishonest agreement by directors to impede a company in the exercise of its right of recovery would constitute a conspiracy to defraud.

The victim of the conspiracy to defraud, however, may not suffer economic loss if the agreement is carried out. This will not prevent a conviction for conspiracy to defraud where a deception was involved and the victim was dishonestly deceived into taking an economic risk which he would not otherwise have taken as 'interests which are imperilled are less valuable in terms of money than those same interests when they are secure and protected' (*Allsop* (1976) 64 Cr App R 29, 32, *per* Shaw LJ). In this case the appellant, a sub-broker for a hire purchase company, in collusion with others entered false particulars on application forms in order to induce the company to accept applications which they might otherwise have rejected. The Court of Appeal upheld his conviction of conspiracy to defraud the company. If the creditors fulfilled the terms of the hire purchase agreements the company would suffer no loss but would, in fact, make a profit. The creditors, however, fell into higher risk categories than those with whom the company generally contracted.

Where a person is a public official there may be a conspiracy to defraud where he is dishonestly induced by deception to act contrary to his public duty (*Welham v DPP* [1961] AC 103).

In *Wai Yu-tsang v R*, the Privy Council affirmed the decisions in *Allsop* and *Welham*. A was the chief accountant of a bank in Hong Kong. He was charged with conspiracy with others to defraud the bank and its shareholders, creditors, and depositors by dishonestly concealing in the accounts of the bank the dishonouring of cheques the bank had purchased to the sum of US $124m. This sum exceeded the assets of the bank and A concealed this fact to prevent a run on the bank. The agreement to conceal this fact amounted to a conspiracy to defraud as it would or might deceive the victims into acting or failing to act so that they suffered economic loss or their economic interests would be put at risk. Delivering the decision of the Board, Lord Goff of Chieveley quoted with approval from Lord Denning's speech in *Welham* (at p. 133):

> The important thing about [the definition of defraud] is that it is not limited to the idea of economic loss, nor to the idea of depriving someone of something of value. It extends generally to the purpose of the fraud and deceit. Put shortly, 'with intent to defraud' means 'with intent to practise a fraud' on someone or other…If anyone may be prejudiced in any way by the fraud, that is enough.

Lord Goff considered that this was confirmed by the cases concerned with persons performing public duties, which were not to be regarded as a special category but rather illustrated the principle that conspiracies to defraud are not restricted to cases of intention to cause the victim economic loss. Thus a person may be defrauded when he is 'prejudiced in any way'. This provides the potential for greatly widening the ambit of this offence, an offence, it must be said, which already is extremely wide in that it criminalises behaviour which would not be criminal where it is performed by one person, but becomes so when agreed to be performed by two or more persons. It is a very curious law which renders criminal agreements to pursue courses of conduct which Parliament, in the Theft Acts 1968 and 1978 and the Forgery and Counterfeiting Act 1981, deliberately chose not to criminalise when performed by an individual. The Law Commission, however, in its Report, *Criminal Law: Conspiracy to Defraud* (Law Com No. 228, HMSO, 1994) recommends the continued existence of the offence pending its 'comprehensive review of dishonesty offences'.

8.3.4.1.2 *The* mens rea *of conspiracy to defraud*

The *mens rea* of conspiracy to defraud involves an intention to defraud and dishonesty. The problem which arises is determining what is meant by intention. The dicta in the cases are contradictory and confusing; much of the confusion deriving from the fact that there was equal uncertainty as to the meaning of 'defraud' when many of them were decided. The decision in *Wai Yu-tsang* (*ante*) may provide a means of rationalising the decisions. In *Scott* (*ante*) Lord Diplock stated that the 'purpose of the conspirators must be to cause the victim economic loss'. In most cases, however, the aim or purpose of the conspirators is to make a profit for themselves; it is rarely their direct purpose to cause a loss to some other person albeit that this might be the inevitable consequence of the performance of the agreed course of conduct. Indeed in *Scott* it would appear that the purpose of the conspirators was to make a profit for themselves, the lost profits to the copyright owners of the films being an inevitable consequence of their enterprise. In truth, therefore, they only had an oblique intent in respect of this loss.

In *Attorney-General's Reference (No. 1 of 1982)* [1983] QB 751, the Court of Appeal referred to the **'true object of the agreement'** as opposed to side effects or incidental consequences of the conspiracy. In this case loss would have been caused to X Ltd, the makers of whisky, if the defendants' agreement to sell in Lebanon whisky falsely labelled as being made by X Ltd had been put into effect. The Court of Appeal held, however, that this agreement only involved fraud in respect of the Lebanese purchasers who would have been deceived, but would not have involved an agreement to defraud X Ltd as any loss they might have suffered was only incidental to the true object of the agreement. Consequently, the parties could not be charged with conspiracy as it was not the object of the agreement to cause loss to anyone within the jurisdiction. This decision must be contrasted with that of the House of Lords in *Cooke* [1986] AC 909, where this refined and artificial analysis of 'true object' and 'incidental consequences' was not alluded to by their Lordships.

The House upheld the convictions of British Rail stewards of conspiracy to defraud British Rail where they had dishonestly sold to passengers their own food, rather than British Rail food, intending to keep the proceeds. Their object was doubtless to make a profit rather than to cause a loss to British Rail, although this was the inevitable consequence of their actions. Their convictions, therefore, could only be upheld on the basis that they had an oblique intent with respect to causing such loss.

In *Allsop* (**8.3.4.1.1** *ante*), the Court of Appeal were of the opinion that it did not matter that the appellant did not desire to cause loss to the company as the deceit he employed deceived the company and imperilled its economic interests. Shaw LJ stated (at p. 32):

> Where a person intends by deceit to induce a course of conduct in another which puts that other's economic interests in jeopardy he is guilty of fraud even though he does not intend or desire that actual loss should ultimately be suffered by that other in this context.

This is in line with the approach of the House of Lords in *Welham* (**8.3.4.1.1** *ante*) which established that 'intent to defraud' should not be given a narrow meaning, involving an intention to cause economic loss to another, but rather meant an intention to practise a fraud on another, or an intention to act to the prejudice of another man's right.

In *Wai Yu-tsang* the Privy Council affirmed *Allsop*, doubted Lord Diplock's dictum in *Scott*, approved *Welham* and did not refer to either the *Attorney-General's Reference (No. 1 of 1982)* or *Cooke*. It would appear, however, that the continuing authority of the *Attorney-General's Reference (No. 1 of 1982)* is questionable in light of the decisions in *Cooke* and the instant case. Lord Goff stated (at pp. 671, 672):

> The question whether particular facts reveal a conspiracy to defraud depends upon what the conspirators have dishonestly agreed to do, and in particular whether they have agreed to practise a fraud on somebody. For this purpose it is enough for example that…the conspirators have dishonestly agreed to bring about a state of affairs which they realise will or may deceive the victim into so acting, or failing to act, that he will suffer economic loss or his economic interests will be put at risk. It is however important in such a case…to distinguish a conspirator's intention (or immediate purpose) dishonestly to bring about such a state of affairs from his motive (or underlying purpose). The latter may be benign to the extent that he does not wish the victim or potential victim to suffer harm; but the mere fact that it is benign will not of itself prevent the agreement from constituting a conspiracy to defraud.

It would appear, therefore, that an intention to bring about a state of affairs which amounts to defrauding another, whether because he will suffer economic loss, or he is deceived into taking an economic risk, or he is deceived into acting contrary to his public duty, or his rights are placed at risk of prejudice, is sufficient. The dictum of Lord Goff quoted earlier uses the words 'will or may deceive the victim' suggesting that recklessness is sufficient. This was both unnecessary to the decision before the Privy Council and goes beyond what was decided in *Allsop*.

It must also be proved that the accused was dishonest. A person is dishonest if he realises that he is acting contrary to the standards of honesty of ordinary decent people (see *Ghosh* [1982] QB 1053, discussed at **11.2.2.2.2** *post*).

8.3.4.1.3 *Who is to be the perpetrator of the fraud?*

Statutory conspiracy is only committed where it is intended that at least one of the parties to the agreement perpetrate the offence. It appears, however, that **conspiracy to defraud may be committed even though the fraud is ultimately to be perpetrated by persons who were not parties to the agreement.** This is the purport of the decision in *Hollinshead* [1985] AC 975. The House of Lords upheld the convictions of the accused of conspiracy to defraud one or more electricity boards where they had manufactured and sold to a supposed middleman (in fact a police officer seeking to entrap them) devices designed to alter readings of electricity meters. The fraud on the electricty boards would be perpetrated by the ultimate purchasers of the devices when they used them to alter their meter readings. The course of conduct agreed upon by the accused would not have brought them into contact with the perpetrators of the frauds. Completion of their agreed course of conduct, by selling the devices, did not involve fraud on anyone. Nevertheless, the House of Lords held that their purpose was to cause economic loss to the electricity boards. It is clear, however, that their purpose was to make a profit from selling the devices to the middleman; this they would do regardless of what happened to the devices thereafter. Sense may only be made of the decision of their Lordships if 'purpose' is interpreted to mean 'intention'. Conspiracy to defraud, therefore, may be committed where the ultimate fraud is to be perpetrated by a person not a party to the agreement. In *Hollinshead*, however, it would not be correct to state that it was an inevitable consequence that the electricity boards sustain economic loss (the middleman may not have sold the devices or they may have been destroyed in a fire); it would be more accurate to state that this was virtually certain to result. If the parties to the agreement foresaw this, then it would be open to the jury to infer that they intended that result (see **3.2.3.3** *ante*).

8.3.4.2 Conspiracy to corrupt public morals or to outrage public decency

Section 5 of the Criminal Law Act 1977 provides:

> (1) Subject to the following provisions of this section, the offence of conspiracy at common law is hereby abolished...
>
> (3) Subsection (1) above shall not affect the offence of conspiracy at common law if and in so far as it may be committed by entering into an agreement to engage in conduct which—
>
>   (a) tends to corrupt public morals or outrages public decency; but
>
>   (b) would not amount to involve the commission of an offence if carried out by a single person otherwise than in pursuance of an agreement.

Subsection (3) is expressed in very tentative terms for two reasons. First, it was not clear whether there were substantive offences of corrupting public morals or outraging public decency. Secondly, even if there were such substantive offences, paragraph (b) gives expression to the uncertainty whether corrupting public morals or outraging public decency as the object of a conspiracy perhaps had a wider meaning. If so, action which, if done by a person acting alone, would not constitute either substantive offence might, if agreed to be done by two or more persons, constitute common law conspiracy to corrupt public morals or outrage public decency. The outcome of all this is uncertainty. If the meaning of corrupting public morals or outraging public decency is the same whether charged as substantive offences (if such exist) or as a conspiracy, then conspiracy to corrupt public morals or outrage public decency will be statutory conspiracies if these activities constitute substantive offences. It would obviously have been much more desirable if Parliament had taken the initiative and decided whether corrupting public morals or outraging public decency were substantive offences and, if so, had provided definitions. The

Law Commission had recommended the abolition of common law conspiracies to corrupt public morals or outrage public decency, along with substantive common law offences relating to morals and decency (Law Com No. 76, paras. 3.136–3.142), but its recommendations were ignored.

Are there substantive offences of corrupting public morals or outraging public decency and are the definitions of these activities the same whether charged as substantive offences or conspiracy? In *Shaw v DPP* [1962] AC 220, the accused was convicted of conspiracy to corrupt public morals arising from his publication of the 'Ladies Directory' advertising the names and addresses of prostitutes, together with photographs and details of the 'services' they were prepared to offer. The House of Lords upheld his conviction without deciding whether corrupting public morals was a substantive offence although the Court of Criminal Appeal had held that it was. In *Knuller v DPP* [1973] AC 435, the accused were charged with conspiracy to corrupt public morals and to outrage public decency arising from an agreement to publish, in a magazine called *IT*, advertisements soliciting homosexual acts in private between consenting adults. The conviction of conspiracy to corrupt public morals was upheld. Lord Simon expressed the view that 'corrupt' was a strong word meaning more than 'lead morally astray' suggesting 'conduct which a jury might find to be destructive of the very fabric of society'. Lord Reid considered that 'corrupt' was synonymous with 'deprave'. The conviction of conspiracy to outrage public decency was quashed as the direction to the jury was defective, although Lords Reid and Diplock thought that this was not an offence known to the law. Lords Simon, Kilbrandon, and Morris held that there was a substantive offence of outraging public decency and thus there could be a conspiracy to do so. The Court of Appeal in *Mayling* [1963] 2 QB 717 had likewise held that it was an offence to outrage public decency. In defining the offence Lord Simon in *Knuller* stated (at pp. 494, 495):

> *R v Mayling* shows that the substantive offence (and therefore the conduct the subject of the conspiracy) must be committed in public, in the sense that the circumstances must be such that the alleged outrageously indecent matter could have been seen by more than one person, even though in fact no more than one did see it. If it is capable of being seen by one person only, no offence is committed.…
>
>   I do not think that it would necessarily negative the offence that the act or exhibit is superficially hid from view, if the public is expressly or impliedly invited to penetrate the cover. Thus, the public touting for an outrageously indecent exhibition in private would not escape.… Another obvious example is an outrageously indecent exhibit with a cover entitled 'Lift in order to see…'. This sort of instance could be applied to a book or newspaper.… The conduct must at least in some way be so projected as to have an impact in public.

The jury must also consider whether public decency is outraged by the conduct involved. Lord Simon went on to state (at p. 495):

> It should be emphasised that 'outrage'…is a very strong word. 'Outraging public decency' goes considerably beyond offending the susceptibilities of, or even shocking, reasonable people. Moreover the offence is, in my view, concerned with recognised minimum standards of decency, which are likely to vary from time to time. Finally,

notwithstanding that 'public' in the offence is used in a locative sense, public decency must be viewed as a whole; and I think the jury should be invited, where appropriate, to remember that they live in a plural society, with a tradition of tolerance towards minorities, and that this atmosphere of toleration is itself part of public decency.

In a series of cases the Court of Appeal confirmed the continued existence of the substantive offence of outraging public decency (see *Gibson* [1990] 2 QB 619; *May* (1989) 91 Cr App R 157; *Lunderbech* [1991] Crim LR 784; *Rowley* [1991] 4 All ER 649; and most recently *Hamilton* [2007] EWCA Crim 2062). It is difficult to envisage conduct which, when done alone, would not amount to the substantive offence of outraging public decency but which, if done in concert, would amount to conspiracy to outrage public decency. It would seem that there is nothing left for the common law offence of conspiracy to cover so that a conspiracy to outrage public decency should be charged as a statutory conspiracy. It is submitted that the same should apply to conspiracy to corrupt public morals albeit the authorities on the existence of the substantive offence are not so clear cut.

One final point relates to the wording of s. 5(3)(b). **If the conduct agreed to be engaged in would 'amount to or involve the commission of an offence', the agreement cannot be charged as common law conspiracy** (if this continues to exist). The word 'offence' in para. (b) is unqualified; it is not confined to the substantive offences of corrupting public morals or outraging public decency.

8.3.4.3 Impossibility in common law conspiracy

The substance of the decision of the House of Lords in *DPP v Nock* [1978] AC 979 is that impossibility is generally an answer to a charge of common law conspiracy unless the impossibility arises from the inadequacy of the means to be used to effect the agreed course of conduct. It should be noted, however, that if at the time of the agreement, the object of the agreement was capable of being achieved, the fact that achievement subsequently becomes impossible due to some supervening event will not provide the accused with a defence as the offence of conspiracy is complete upon conclusion of an agreement without proof of any further steps to effect it being necessary.

8.4 Attempt

8.4.1 Statutory definition and scope

The common law offence of attempt to commit an indictable offence was abolished by the Criminal Attempts Act 1981 which created a new statutory offence of attempt. The Act was largely the result of the work of the Law Commission (see Law Com No. 102). Section 1(1) of the Act provides.

(1) If, with intent to commit an offence to which this section applies, a person does an act which is more than merely preparatory to the commission of the offence, he is guilty of attempting to commit the offence.

By s. 1(4), liability for attempts is confined to offences which, if completed, would be triable in England and Wales as indictable offences. Thus, generally, there is no liability for an attempt to commit a summary offence. Section 1(4) goes on to exclude from liability attempts to commit the following offences: conspiracy, aiding, abetting, counselling, procuring or suborning the commission of an offence, and assisting an offender who has committed an arrestable offence or compounding an arrestable offence contrary to ss. 4(1) and 5(1) of the Criminal Law Act 1967.

The definition in s. 1(1) implicitly excludes the possibility of convictions for attempt to commit some other crimes. For example, **the requirement of 'an act' means that a person cannot attempt to commit an offence which can only be committed by an omission. Similarly a person cannot be convicted of an attempt to commit a result crime, such as murder, on the basis solely of an omission where he was under a duty to act.** Where an offence may not be committed intentionally, as is the case with involuntary manslaughter where the killing is unintentional, there cannot be an attempt to commit that offence. If a person intends to kill he will be liable for attempted murder. It would also appear to be the case that a charge of attempted murder is appropriate even though a verdict of voluntary manslaughter (arising from diminished responsibility, provocation, or suicide pact) could have been returned had the intended victim died (see *Bruzas* [1972] Crim LR 367) or if a verdict of infanticide would have been available (but cf. *Smith* [1983] Crim LR 739).

Section 1(4) also adverts to jurisdictional issues. If D is to be liable for attempt to commit an offence, the offence, if completed, must be one for which he could have been indicted in England and Wales. For example, murder by a British citizen is indictable regardless of where it is committed. Thus if D sends a box of chocolates laced with poison to V who is in France, intending to kill him, D will be liable for attempted murder as soon as the chocolates are posted. If D's intention is only that V be made ill by the chocolates he is not liable for an attempt to administer poison contrary to s. 24 of the Offences Against the Person Act 1861 as such an offence committed abroad is not triable in England. If D is in France and gives the chocolates to V intending to kill him, he could, in theory, be prosecuted in England for attempted murder unless the courts take the view that there is no need for such extra-territorial jurisdiction. If so, they could give a restrictive meaning to the words 'does an act' construing them to require that the acts which constitute the attempt either be done within the jurisdiction or be intended to have some effect within the jurisdiction. If D is outside the jurisdiction when he does the acts which may constitute an attempt, he will be liable to conviction where the acts are designed to have an effect within the jurisdiction (see *DPP* v *Stonehouse* [1978] AC 55). Thus, if D, in France, sends poisoned chocolates to V, in England, intending to make V ill, he will be guilty of an attempt to administer poison (see further **8.5** *post*).

8.4.2 *Mens rea*

The essence of the offence of attempt is intention. While it must be proved that the accused did an act which was 'more than merely preparatory to the commission of the offence', the acts which may amount to the *actus reus* derive their significance from the accused's intention. **The acts, in themselves, may appear to be innocent but when added to the accused's intention they constitute a crime.** For example, if D lights a cigarette lighter beside some curtains in a restaurant this may or may not constitute attempted arson, depending on whether he does so intending to set fire to the curtains or to light a cigarette. Similarly, if D offers V a chocolate this may be a perfectly innocent act of generosity or it may constitute attempted murder if D offers it intending to kill V believing, mistakenly, that the chocolate contains poison. In both cases the act of offering the chocolate is exactly the same but it is D's intention which colours the act and converts the second situation into the *actus reus* of attempted murder.

It is important, therefore, to determine what the meaning of 'intent to commit an offence' is in the context of attempt. The Court of Appeal held in *Pearman* (1984) 80 Cr App R 259, that **the word 'intent' in s. 1(1) has the same meaning as at common law.** In *Whybrow* (1951) 35 Cr App R 141, the Court of Appeal held that although on a charge of murder proof of an intention to cause grievous bodily harm would suffice to establish *mens rea*, **on a charge of attempted murder 'the intent becomes the principal ingredient of the crime'.** Accordingly, it had to be proved that the accused intended to kill. **Thus where an accused is charged with attempt it must be proved that he had the intention to commit the substantive offence he is alleged to have attempted.** Similarly, if recklessness with regard to causing a consequence will suffice for the substantive offence, only intention with regard to that consequence will suffice where attempt is charged (see *O'Toole* [1987] Crim LR 759 where D's conviction of attempted arson was quashed). This is logical as a person cannot be said to be trying to bring about a result where that result is not his aim or object but is merely foreseen as a possible consequence of the achievement of his aim or object.

At common law the word 'intent' was defined by the Court of Appeal in *Mohan* [1976] QB 1, 11, as 'a decision to bring about, in so far as it lies within the accused's power, the commission of the offence which it is alleged the accused attempted to commit, no matter whether the accused desired that consequence of his act or not'. This definition encompassed direct intent and oblique intent (see **3.2.1** *ante*). In *Pearman* the Court of Appeal approved this definition and explained the meaning of the phrase 'no matter whether the accused desired that consequence of his act or not' as follows (at p. 263):

> [These words] are probably designed to deal with a case where the accused has, as a primary purpose, some other object, for example, a man who plants a bomb in an aeroplane, which he knows is going to take off, it being his primary intention that he should claim the insurance on the aeroplane when the freight goes down into the sea. The jury would not be put off from saying that he intended to murder the crew simply by saying that he did not want or desire to kill the crew, but that was something that he inevitably intended to do. Similarly, for example, a man who is cornered by the police when he is in a car may have the primary purpose of simply escaping from that situation. If he drives straight at the police officers at high speed, a jury is likely to conclude that he intended to injure a police officer and maybe cause him serious grievous bodily harm.

Some confusion as to the degree of foresight required where oblique intent is involved was caused by the Court of Appeal decision in *Walker and Hayles* (1990) 90 Cr App R 226 (see **3.2.3.3** *ante*). In this case W and H threw V from a third floor balcony after banging his head against a wall, threatening him with a knife, and declaring that they were going to kill him. V survived and W and H were charged with attempted murder. This was not a case involving oblique intent so the only issue should have been as to their intention in throwing him from the balcony: did they intend to kill him? If they intended some lesser degree of harm, this would not suffice for attempted murder. The jury were confused and sought clarification from the judge. Unfortunately the judge directed the jury in terms of inferring intention from the probability of death ensuing: if the accused knew there was a high probability of death the jury were entitled to infer they intended to kill. The Court of Appeal did not disapprove of using 'high probability' as the measure although they expressed a preference for the phrase 'virtual certainty'. This, however, is not the issue. If direct intention is involved, that is the accused has no other aim or purpose in committing the alleged offence than the result involved in that offence, it matters not that achievement of that result is possible, probable, or certain. If achievement of that result is his aim or purpose then he intends it whether or not he is likely to achieve it. For example, D aims a gun at V and fires intending to kill V but misses. D is guilty of attempted murder whether he had a 10% chance of succeeding in his purpose or a 99% chance. If there is doubt as to what D's purpose was (was it only to frighten, to wound, or to kill) this is a different issue. In this case it may be legitimate to point out that the more probable the result the more likely it is that D intended it, but it must be made clear that this is not conclusive of the matter as all the evidence in the case must be taken into account. It is only where there is evidence that D's aim or purpose was something other than to kill that a direction based on *Nedrick* [1986] 1 WLR 1025 as modified by *Woollin* [1998] 3 WLR 382 (see **3.2.3.3** and **3.2.3.4** *ante*), should be considered; there did not appear to be any such evidence in *Walker and Hayles*. However, if a jury are satisfied that D's direct intent was to cause grievous bodily harm they may (but need not necessarily) convict of attempted murder if satisfied that D knew that death was virtually certain to ensue. For example, if D throws V off a hundred metre high cliff (V miraculously surviving by catching hold of a protruding ledge) and claims 'I only wanted to break his legs', a jury should acquit of attempted murder if they believe D. But if they are satisfied that D realised that death was virtually certain to ensue they could infer the intention to kill from that foresight and convict of attempted murder. The example illustrates the very limited application of the *Nedrick* direction where attempted murder is charged and D claims he only intended to cause grievous bodily harm.

The focus so far has been upon consequences; what *mens rea* is required with regard to the material circumstances of the offence? In rape the material circumstance is that V does not consent to penetration of their vagina, anus, or mouth by D's penis (see s. 1 of the Sexual Offences Act 2003).

 Question

If D is charged with attempted rape, having failed to penetrate V, is it sufficient that he intended to penetrate V's vagina, anus, or mouth not reasonably believing that V consented, or must it be proved that he intended non-consensual penetration?

The Law Commission, in its Report which preceded the passage of the Act (Law Com No. 102, para. 2.15) took the view that intention as to every element of the offence was required; knowledge as to surrounding circumstances equating with intention as to consequences. The Court of Appeal, however, has decided that **if recklessness in respect of a circumstance will suffice for commission of the substantive offence, it will suffice on a charge of attempt to commit that offence.**

> In *Khan* [1990] 2 All ER 783, on a charge of attempted rape, the trial judge directed the jury that the accused were guilty if they were reckless as to whether the victim consented. At this time rape was defined as having sexual intercourse with a person who did not consent, either knowing they did not consent or being reckless as to whether they consented (s. 1(2) of the Sexual Offences Act 1956). Dismissing appeals against conviction, Russell LJ stated (at p. 788):

>> The only difference between the [offences of rape and attempted rape] is that in rape sexual intercourse takes place whereas in attempted rape it does not, although there has to be some act which is more than preparatory to sexual intercourse. Considered in that way, the intent of the defendant is precisely the same in rape and in attempted rape and the *mens rea* is identical, namely an intention to have intercourse plus a knowledge of or recklessness as to the woman's absence of consent.... Recklessness in rape and attempted rape arises not in relation to the physical act of the accused but only in his state of mind when engaged in the activity of having or attempting to have sexual intercourse.... The only 'intent'... of the rapist is to have sexual intercourse. He commits the offence because of the circumstances in which he manifests that intent, i.e. when the woman is not consenting and he either knows it or could not care less about the absence of consent.

The decision in *Khan* was affirmed by the Court of Appeal in *Attorney-General's Reference (No. 3 of 1992)* [1994] 2 All ER 121 where it was held that on a charge of attempted arson contrary to s. 1(2) of the Criminal Damage Act 1971, it was sufficient that the accused intended to damage the property by fire and was reckless whether life would thereby be endangered. This stretched the realms of liability for attempt further than *Khan* as criminal damage at this time involved *Caldwell* recklessness (see **3.4.2.2** *ante*). The Court of Appeal analysed the policy of attempt as requiring the punishment of those who have done their best to supply the element missing from the completed offence. Schiemann J stated (at p. 127):

> If, on a charge of attempting to commit the offence, the prosecution can show not only the state of mind required for the completed offence but also that the defendant intended to supply the missing physical element of the completed offence, that suffices for a conviction...The defendant must intend to damage property, but there is no need for a graver mental state than is required for the full offence.

This dictum is problematic. First, in *Khan*, the recklessness related to a circumstance—the absence of consent on the part of the victim. In aggravated criminal damage, however, the element of endangerment is not a circumstance or state of affairs but part of D's state of mind as to what must be proved as *mens rea* for the substantive offence is intention to endanger life or recklessness thereto.

There is no need for actual endangerment to be established (see *Sangha* [1988] 2 All ER 385, **14.3.2** *post*).

Secondly, the dictum presented the possibility of an accused being guilty of attempting an offence, not only of *Caldwell* recklessness, but also of strict liability where he is neither intentional nor reckless (in either sense) in respect of the circumstance of the *actus reus* to which strict liability attaches. This is an expansion of the law and one, it is submitted, which is undesirable. The Court of Appeal, it is submitted, has failed to construe the exact wording of s. 1(1) of the 1981 Act. While strict liability may be supportable where the substantive offence has been committed, it is difficult to argue that a person has 'intended to commit an offence' where it is one of strict liability and he has failed to perform the *actus reus* and had not adverted to a circumstance of that *actus reus*. The most that can be said is that he 'intended to commit an act' which forms part of the definition of the substantive offence but he did not intend to commit the offence. The arguments for or against this expansion of liability, however, were not addressed by the Court of Appeal. There may be policy arguments to support such an expansion of liability for attempt, but any such expansion is for Parliament to perform in an amendment to the 1981 Act and not for the Court of Appeal to perform by sleight of hand. For present purposes, however, it would appear that for attempted rape it will be sufficient to prove that D intended to penetrate V not reasonably believing that V consented as it is likely that the Court of Appeal's sleight of hand will continue being applied.

A final problem to be disposed of is that of conditional intention (cf. **8.3.3.2** *ante*). **A person has conditional intent where he intends to commit an offence if a particular condition is satisfied;** for example, D intends to steal from V's car if he finds any items of value in the car. In such a case there will be an attempted theft where D, with this intent, does an act which is more than merely preparatory to the commission of the offence, for example, opening the door of the car. Provided the prosecution do not charge D with attempting to steal specific items, there is no obstacle to a conviction. If the prosecution specify particular items they would have to prove that D would have stolen these had he discovered them. To avoid such difficulties of proof the prosecution need only charge D with 'attempting to steal from a car'. On such an indictment there is no need to prove that the car contained any items worth stealing, or even any items at all. If the car is completely empty so that theft from it is impossible, this will not prevent a conviction for attempt as the Criminal Attempts Act reversed the decision in *Haughton v Smith* [1975] AC 476 relating to impossible attempts (see **8.4.4** *post*).

8.4.3 *Actus reus*

The *actus reus* of attempt is the doing of 'an act which is more than merely preparatory to the commission of the offence' the accused intends to commit. This is a question of fact for the jury. Section 4(3) provides:

> Where, in proceedings against a person for an offence under s. 1 above, there is evidence sufficient in law to support a finding that he did an act falling within subsection (1) of that section, the question whether or not his act fell within that subsection is a question of fact.

The trial judge must decide whether there is sufficient evidence to support a finding that the accused did such an act. If there is not, he will direct an acquittal and, if there is, the jury will be left with the task of deciding what acts the accused did and whether these were more than merely preparatory to the commission of the offence. At some point D's acts will cross over from being *merely preparatory* to being *more than merely preparatory*. The Criminal Attempts Act provides no more guidance than the common law for determining the precise point when an attempt is committed.

The test generally settled at common law was known as the 'proximity' test formulated in *Eagleton* (1855) 6 Cox CC 559, 571 by Parke B:

> The mere intention to commit a misdemeanour is not criminal. Some act is required and we do not think that all acts towards committing a misdemeanour are indictable. Acts remotely leading towards the commission of the offence are not to be considered as attempts to commit it, but acts immediately connected with it are.

This test was very vague as there was no indication when acts passed over from being remote to being immediately connected with the intended offence. But, to some extent, this is inevitable as there is an infinite variety of methods of committing offences and an infinite variety of situations will arise. When examining the common law, the Law Commission recognised this (Law Com No. 102) stating (at para. 2.45):

> [I]n our view there is no magic formula which can now be produced to define what precisely constitutes an attempt.... Of the various approaches, only the 'proximity' test has produced results which may be thought broadly acceptable. Its disadvantages are that hitherto it has not worked well in some cases, and that it is imprecise. It shares the latter disadvantage with all other approaches but its flexibility does enable difficult cases to be reconsidered and their authority questioned. Further, where cases are so dependent on what are sometimes fine differences of degree, we think it is eminently appropriate for the question whether the conduct in a particular case amounts to an attempt to be left to the jury.

This led the Law Commission to propose a test which did not differ greatly from the proximity test but which was designed to avoid a problem identified in the proximity test. Proximity suggested that an act had to be immediately connected with the commission of the offence. There was a danger that this would be construed very restrictively limiting liability to situations where the accused had performed the last act necessary to commit the offence. Thus the Law Commission changed the terminology to indicate that the parameters of attempt were broader than might be suggested by the proximity test. The difference between the tests is essentially one of perspective. The proximity test looked backwards from the commission of the full offence to see if the acts the accused had performed were close enough to that point. The new test looks forwards from the point of preparatory acts to see whether the acts of the accused have gone beyond the preparatory stage.

From one point of view, all acts, apart from the last one necessary to bring about the commission of the offence, are preparatory acts. The inclusion of the word 'merely', however, suggests a grey area of ill-defined proportions between acts which are purely preparatory and the last act of commission. This grey area covers those acts performed by the accused when he might be described as being 'on the job' as opposed to preparing for it or, as the Court of Appeal put it in *Gullefer* [1987] Crim LR 195, when the accused has 'embarked on the crime proper'. This will obviously vary from case to case. An example may help to illustrate the position.

Example

D decides to kill V and with this intention he performs the following acts: (1) he spends several days observing V's movements in order to choose a good place and time for performing the killing; (2) he buys a gun and ammunition; (3) he visits a wood on several occasions for target practice; (4) on the day the offence is to be committed he loads the gun; (5) he drives to the scene of the proposed killing and hides in some bushes awaiting V's arrival; (6) he observes the road watching for V; (7) he sees V and takes aim; (8) he places his finger on the trigger; (9) he squeezes the trigger and fires the gun.

Point (9) is the last act to be performed by D in order to bring about commission of the offence of murder. If a police officer had been observing D, however, could he have intervened at some earlier point to prevent the killing while being sure that D would be convicted of attempted murder? To some extent points (1) to (8) were all acts preparatory to the last act but at some stage D moved from performing *merely preparatory* acts to performing *more than merely preparatory* acts. This would appear to be at some stage after point (4) and before point (9) when he might be described as being 'on the job' or as having 'embarked on the crime proper'. Whether a jury would be prepared to convict of attempted murder (assuming the judge leaves the issue to them) if the officer intervened at point (6) or (7) is highly questionable. Some juries might not even convict where D had reached point (8) if they paid undue attention to the fact that D could still relent and withdraw from committing the offence at that stage. What is clear, however, is that the jury's task does not simply involve applying the declared law to the facts as they find them but, in addition, involves them determining what the law is, that is, defining the meaning of 'more than merely preparatory'. This creates a risk of perverse and inconsistent verdicts.

There have been several decisions of the Court of Appeal which have sought to clarify the new test. In *Widdowson* (1985) 82 Cr App R 314, D wishing to obtain a van on hire-purchase terms but realising that he would not be accepted as creditworthy, filled in a credit enquiries form in the name of another person and was convicted of attempting to obtain services (the hire-purchase of the van) by deception. If the finance company had responded favourably to D's enquiry, it still remained for D to make a formal application for a hire-purchase deal. The Court of Appeal quashed the conviction, referring to common law tests which indicated that this would not be considered an attempt. The Court considered that D had not performed every act necessary to achieve the consequence of obtaining services by deception; his acts were not immediately but only remotely connected with the offence alleged to have been attempted; and, using the words of Lord Diplock in *DPP v Stonehouse* [1978] AC 55, 68, he had not 'crossed the Rubicon and burned his boats', that is he had not reached the point of no return but could still have withdrawn from commission of the offence. These tests would greatly reduce the ambit of attempt which the Law Commission had hoped to increase.

In *Boyle and Boyle* (1987) 84 Cr App R 270, the appellants were convicted of attempted burglary having been found by a policeman standing by a door, of which the lock and one hinge were broken. The Court of Appeal upheld their convictions being satisfied that the only thing left for them to do to commit the full offence was for one of them to step over the threshold of the property and enter as a trespasser, there being ample evidence of an intention to steal. The Court also referred to another test which had been approved at common law. This had been propounded in Stephen's *Digest of the Criminal Law* (9th edn) as follows 'An attempt to commit a crime is an act done with intent to commit that crime and forming part of a series of acts which would constitute its actual commission, if it were not interrupted'. This is a very vague test as it would appear to encompass all acts of preparation and those which are more than merely preparatory.

In *Jones* [1990] 1 WLR 1057, the Court of Appeal disapproved of the approach to construction of s. 1(1) of the Act which referred to previous conflicting case law. Taylor LJ stated that the correct approach was 'to look first at the natural meaning of the statutory words, not to turn back to earlier case law and seek to fit some previous test to the words of the section'. He cited with approval the judgment of Lord Lane CJ in *Gullefer* [1987] Crim LR 195 (reported also at [1990] 1 WLR 1063) where he stated (at p. 1066):

> It seems to us that the words of the Act of 1981 seek to steer a midway course. They do not provide, as they might have done, that the...*Eagleton* test is to be followed, or that, as Lord Diplock suggested, the defendant must have reached a point from which it was impossible for him to retreat before the *actus reus* of an attempt is proved. On the other hand, the words give perhaps as clear a guidance as is possible in the circumstances on the point of time at which *Stephen's* 'series of acts' begins. It begins when the merely preparatory acts have come to an end and the defendant embarks upon the crime proper. When that is will depend of course upon the facts in any particular case.

Jones had been convicted of the attempted murder of his former girlfriend's new boyfriend, F. Jones bought a gun, shortened the barrel, disguised himself, jumped into the rear seat of F's car as he left his daughter at school, pointed the gun at F and said 'You are not going to like this'. F managed to grab the gun and escape with it from the car. It was not established whether Jones had his finger on the trigger of the gun when he pointed it at F. The Court of Appeal dismissed Jones's appeal, Taylor LJ stating (at pp. 1062, 1063):

> Looking at the plain natural meaning of s. 1(1) in the way indicated by the Lord Chief Justice, the question for the judge in the present case was whether there was evidence from which a reasonable jury, properly directed, could conclude that the appellant had done acts which were more than merely preparatory. Clearly his actions in obtaining the gun, in shortening it, in loading it, in putting on his disguise, and in going to the school could only be regarded as preparatory acts. But, in our judgment, once he had got into the car, taken out the loaded gun and pointed it at the victim with the intention of killing him, there was sufficient evidence for the consideration of the jury on the charge of attempted murder. It was a matter for them to decide whether they were sure those acts were more than merely preparatory. In our judgment, therefore, the judge was right to allow the case to go to the jury.

In *Geddes* [1996] Crim LR 894, D's conviction of attempted false imprisonment was quashed by the Court of Appeal. D, equipped with a rucksack in which there was a kitchen knife, rope, and masking tape, had gained access to the boys' lavatory in a school. The Court of Appeal held that while there was no doubting D's intentions, his actions had not advanced sufficiently to merit a finding that he had performed a more than merely preparatory act (see also *Campbell* [1991] Crim LR 268 which was cited with approval). Lord Bingham CJ stated:

> It is, we think, an accurate paraphrase of the statutory test…to ask whether the available evidence, if accepted, could show that a defendant has done an act which shows that he has actually tried to commit the offence in question, or whether he has only got ready or put himself in a position or equipped himself to do so.

Professor J. C. Smith in his commentary to *Geddes* observes (at p. 896) that, while D was equipped to perform a kidnapping, there is no offence of going equipped to commit an offence against the person. There is, however, an offence under the Theft Act 1968, s. 25 of going equipped to commit any burglary, theft, or cheat which covers conduct which has not advanced beyond the preparatory stages towards commission of a crime. While the accused need not have performed the last act nor reached the point of no return to be liable for an attempt (see further *A-G's Reference (No. 1 of 1992)* [1993] Crim LR 274), the instant case, along with *Jones* and *Campbell*, tends to indicate that everything required to commit the offence must be in place, including the intended victim and that the accused must have commenced to commit the crime. In *Geddes*, had a child entered the lavatories when D was there and D had approached him, he would then have embarked on the crime proper. In terms of the example (p. 306 *ante*), this suggests that point (7) in that example would have to be reached before the judge would be entitled to leave the case to the jury. If this is so, there may be a need to consider creating an offence similar to the Theft Act 1968, s. 25 of going equipped to perform a sexual or violent offence against a person.

The facts in *Geddes* might now fall within the offence of trespass with intent to commit a sexual offence contrary to s. 63 of the Sexual Offences Act 2003, provided D's ultimate intent was to commit a sexual offence, he already being a trespasser. This offence would not cover a situation where, although D intended falsely to imprison V, he had no intent to commit a sexual offence. The s. 63 offence would also not cover a situation where, although D has the intent, and is equipped to put that intent into effect, he does not commit a trespass. Of course, if he was arrested attempting to gain access to premises where, if he did so, he would be a trespasser, he could be charged with attempting to commit the s. 63 offence.

While the decisions of the Court of Appeal discussed earlier adhere to a view that a distinction may be drawn between acts which fall within the 'preparation phase' of the intended crime from those which fall within the 'commission phase', it is clear that courts have difficulty in identifying where the line between the two is to be drawn. In *Tosti* [1997] Crim LR 746 Beldam LJ stated that 'there may be actions which are preparatory which are not merely so and which are essentially first steps in the commission of the offence'. The appellants had been convicted of attempted burglary and appealed. Beldam LJ stated:

> The short question for the court today is whether, having carried out a number of merely preparatory acts, that is to say providing themselves with oxyacetylene equipment, having driven to the scene, having concealed the oxyacetylene equipment in a hedge nearby, but having then approached the door of the barn, and bent down to examine how best to go about the job of breaking into the barn, they had committed acts which were preparatory, but not merely so—so that it could be said the acts of preparation amount to acts done in the commission of the offence. Essentially the question is one of degree: how close to, and necessary for, the commission of the offences were the acts which it was proved that they had done?

The Court of Appeal concluded that the judge's decision to leave the case to the jury had been correct. In the instant case the activity of the appellants could be characterised as 'casing the joint'—they had not yet begun to try to force an entry to the premises. If the quashing of the conviction in *Campbell* of attempted robbery was right (where the appellant was arrested outside the door of a post office which he intended to rob in possession of an imitation firearm and a threatening note), it is difficult to see how the instant decision can be correct.

It is doubtful whether the distinction sought to be drawn by the Court of Appeal in *Qadir and Khan*, unreported, 24 July 1997, Case No. 9602311X4, will produce any greater clarity. In this case the appellants had been convicted of being knowingly concerned in the attempted fraudulent evasion of the prohibition on exportation of a controlled drug. Potter LJ emphasised that a judge when ruling whether something was capable of constituting a more than merely preparatory act, should keep in mind the nature of the crime attempted, distinguishing between offences where the focus is upon an act and those where it is upon a transaction. He was of the view that for a crime such as killing or wounding the focus is upon an act at a particular time and acts substantially anterior to the moment of completion of the crime would be merely preparatory. By contrast for an offence of deception or evasion which involves a stratagem carried out over a period of time, as the *actus reus* may take place over an extended period of time, 'the moment of embarkation upon it may be quite remote in time from the point of its anticipated successful outcome'. But as a poisoner may administer poison over a protracted period and a deceiver may practise a deception on the spur of the moment, everything will depend on the individual case!

The only conclusion one can draw from the cases discussed in this section is, perhaps, that courts are becoming more prepared to look further back in time to define the point when mere preparation ceases and commission of the offence begins.

One final point to note in respect of the *actus reus* of attempt is that the fact that the accused is interrupted or desists prior to doing the last act necessary to commit the substantive offence he intended to commit does not prevent his conviction for attempt if he has performed a more than merely preparatory act. Thus there is no defence of withdrawal if the point has been reached where a more than merely preparatory act has been performed.

8.4.4 Impossibility

If D makes a mistake as to the law, believing that it prohibits what he intends to do, he will not be guilty of attempt if he endeavours to carry out his intention. What he is attempting to do is not a crime and the offence of attempt applies only to attempts to commit indictable offences.

Example

D comes from a country where adultery is a crime and he believes it is also a crime in England. He attempts to have consensual intercourse with E, a married woman, but fails. Had he succeeded he would have committed no offence; the fact that he fails does not render him liable for attempt as what he attempted to do is not a crime.

Key Point

There are three situations, however, where D may fail to commit an offence because it is impossible to commit it in the circumstances (cf. **8.3.3.5** *ante*). For example:

(1) D attempts to steal from V's pocket which, unknown to him, is empty (physical impossibility);

(2) D attempts to break into a safe to steal the contents using a jemmy which, unknown to him, is incapable of effecting his purpose (impossibility arising from inadequacy of means);

(3) D attempts to handle stolen goods but, unknown to him, the goods are not stolen (legal impossibility as the goods lack a quality essential for the commission of the offence).

At common law D would have been convicted of attempt only in the second situation (see *Haughton* v *Smith* [1975] AC 476) as it was considered that in this situation the crime was not really impossible as it could have been committed if D had used different or more adequate means. Thus, in *White* [1910] 2 KB 124, the accused was convicted of attempted murder where he tried to kill his mother using an insufficient dose of poison. Had he given her sugar, mistaking it for poison, he would not have been convicted as this would have been a case of physical impossibility. The distinctions which the common law made were considered refined and artificial. The Law Commission recommended that the law should be changed (Law Com No. 102, para. 2.96) placing the emphasis on the intention of the accused provided there was proof of a more than merely preparatory act. This recommendation was put into effect by s. 1(2) and (3) of the Criminal Attempts Act 1981 which provide:

(2) A person may be guilty of attempting to commit an offence to which this section applies even though the facts are such that the commission of the offence is impossible.

(3) In any case where—

  (a) apart from this subsection a person's intention would not be regarded as having amounted to an intent to commit an offence: but

  (b) if the facts of the case had been as he believed them to be, his intention would be so regarded,

then, for the purposes of subsection (1) above, he shall be regarded as having had an intent to commit that offence.

The purport of s. 1(2) is to render a person liable to conviction regardless of the category of impossibility which prevented commission of the intended substantive offence. Section 1(3) is, essentially, superfluous but it was included as a precaution to deal with the particular situation of legal impossibility. If D intended to handle a particular video, believing it to be stolen, when, in fact, it was not, he might claim that, as he intended to handle only that particular video, he did not intend to handle stolen goods but intended to handle a 'non-stolen video'. Simply to frame the argument exposes its ludicrous nature as D's subjective state of mind was to handle goods he believed to be stolen, that is, an intention to handle stolen goods. The fact that the objective status of the goods was that they were not stolen does not, in any way, impinge upon D's state of mind, just as the fact that a pocket is empty does not alter D's intention to steal from that pocket; if he were to claim that he intended to take nothing as there was nothing to take, he would be laughed out of court. But, to be doubly sure, Parliament enacted s. 1(3) which simply states that if the facts had been as he believed them to be (if the video had been stolen) he shall be regarded as having an intent to commit that offence (handling stolen goods).

But, be prepared for two surprises. In *Anderton v Ryan* [1985] AC 560, the House of Lords held that the Act had not affected cases of legal impossibility so that the appellant's conviction of attempting to handle stolen goods was quashed as the video she sought to handle was not stolen, or, as their Lordships put it, her acts **were 'objectively innocent'**. The next surprise is that just over a year later the House of Lords in *Shivpuri* [1987] AC 1 overruled this decision, Lord Bridge declaring (at pp. 21, 22) that:

the concept of 'objective innocence' is incapable of sensible application in relation to the law of criminal attempts. The reason for this is that any attempt to commit an offence which involves 'an act which is more than merely preparatory to the commission of the offence' but which for any reason fails, so that in the event no offence is committed, must *ex hypothesi*, from the point of view of the criminal law, be 'objectively innocent'. What turns what would otherwise, from the point of view of the criminal law, be an innocent act into a crime is the intent of the actor to commit an offence....A puts his hand into B's pocket. Whether or not there is anything in the pocket capable of being stolen, if A intends to steal his act is a criminal attempt; if he does not so intend his act is innocent....These considerations lead me to the conclusion that the distinction sought to be drawn in *Anderton v Ryan* between innocent and guilty acts considered 'objectively' and independently of the state of mind of the actor cannot be sensibly maintained.

As a result, their Lordships dismissed the appellant's appeal from a conviction of attempting to be knowingly concerned in dealing with prohibited drugs. Shivpuri was arrested in possession of a suitcase which he believed contained either heroin or cannabis. He admitted that he intended to receive the drugs and deal in them. In fact the case contained snuff which was not a prohibited drug. Shivpuri had the intention to commit the offence and he had done acts which were more than merely preparatory to the commission of the *intended* offence.

8.5 Jurisdiction

The general rule relating to territorial jurisdiction is that English courts are unable to try persons for offences committed outside England and Wales even if committed by a British citizen (see *Harden* [1963] 1 QB 8). A limited exception to this rule is that a British citizen who commits murder or bigamy abroad may be tried in England and Wales. The jurisdiction of English courts has, however, been extended in recent years through legislation and case law. As originally enacted, s. 1(4) of the Criminal Law Act 1977 gave the courts in England and Wales jurisdiction to try conspiracies where the court would have had jurisdiction to try the parties for the substantive offence if they had committed it in accordance with their intentions. Thus if A and B, being British citizens, agree in England to murder V in France, they could be tried in England for conspiracy to murder. If, by contrast, A and B had agreed merely to wound V in France they could not be tried for conspiracy as the English courts have no jurisdiction to try the substantive offence of wounding if committed in France.

Jurisdiction to try conspirators where their agreement is entered into in England and Wales to commit the substantive offence abroad has been extended by legislation. The original extension was introduced by the Sexual Offences (Conspiracy and Incitement) Act 1996 (SO(CAI)A) which created criminal offences to deal with the problem of 'sex tourism' where sexual activity is engaged in abroad with children under the age of 16. The SO(CAI)A adapted the existing offences of conspiracy and incitement to cover conspiracy to commit, or incitement to commit, sexual offences against children where those offences are committed outside the jurisdiction. (References to incitement are now to be treated as references to the offences under ss. 44–46 of the Serious Crime Act 2007 (s. 63(1) of the SCA).) The listed offences, which are confined to instances where the victim is under the age of 16, are those contrary to ss. 1–12, 14, and 15 to 26 of the Sexual Offences Act 2003. The agreement or assistance or encouragement to commit such an offence is punishable in England and Wales provided the conduct also amounts to a crime in the country where it was to be committed. The provisions of the SO(CAI)A relating to conspiracy have been repealed by the Criminal Justice (Terrorism and Conspiracy) Act 1998 (CJ(TAC)A) but the provisions relating to encouraging or assisting an offence remain in force. In the Sex Offenders Act 1997, Part II, Parliament extended jurisdiction to cover a range of substantive sexual offences where they were committed against children under 16 outside the jurisdiction by a British citizen or person resident in the United Kingdom. The 1997 Act has been repealed and replaced by s. 72 of the Sexual Offences Act 2003 (see **10.2.5.2.7** *post*).

The CJ(TAC)A was enacted in the aftermath of the Omagh bombing on 25 August 1998 when Parliament was recalled during its summer recess to consider new anti-terrorism legislation. While the primary focus of the Act was terrorist groups which might undermine the peace process in Northern Ireland, the opportunity was also taken to deal with a long-standing problem of terrorist groups within the United Kingdom who plotted terrorist activities here which were to be carried out abroad. The provisions in the SO(CAI)A relating to conspiracy have effectively been reworked so as to cover all offences. Section 5(1) of the CJ(TAC)A inserts a new s. 1A into the Criminal Law Act 1977 which makes it an offence to conspire within England and Wales to commit an offence outside the United Kingdom. This greatly expands the jurisdiction of English courts as an agreement to commit any offence is covered, not just agreements to commit the sexual offences specified in SO(CAI)A. There are four conditions which must be satisfied. First, that in pursuit of the agreed course of conduct an act or some other event must be intended to take place in a country or territory outside England and Wales (s.1A(2) as amended by s. 72 of the Coroners and Justice Act 2009). Secondly, that the act or event would constitute an offence in the other country or territory (s.1A(3)). Because of the difficulty of proving the law of foreign jurisdictions, s. 1A(8) creates a presumption that the conduct in question is also contrary to the law of the country where it was to be performed unless the defence serve a notice on the prosecution denying this, giving grounds for their opinion, and requiring the prosecution to prove that the conduct is contrary to law. Thirdly, the agreement to act in that way would be an offence in England and Wales if the act or event were to take place there (s. 1A(4)). Thus the act or event the parties agree to commit or cause to take place must amount to an offence in both England and Wales and the foreign country or territory. Fourthly, there must be some activity by a party to the agreement (or his agent) in England and Wales in relation to the agreement before its formation, or in pursuance of the agreement, or the party became a party to the agreement in England and Wales. Thus, for example, D would be liable to conviction where he agrees with E in England to steal property in France, or where in pursuit of an agreement between himself and E to steal property in France (entered into elsewhere) he comes to England to acquire equipment needed to carry out the theft.

The Criminal Law Act 1977 originally made no provision for the case of an agreement abroad to commit an offence in England. In *DPP* v *Doot* [1973] AC 807, the House of Lords held that such a conspiracy could be prosecuted in England if the parties acted in England in concert and in pursuance of the agreement. Lord Wilberforce was prepared to hold that acts by one conspirator in England should be sufficient to establish liability on the part of all the parties to the agreement. In *Somchai Liangsiriprasert* v *United States* [1990] AC 607, the Privy Council held that in Hong Kong, where the law on conspiracy was the same as the common law in England, an agreement abroad to commit an offence within the jursidiction was triable as conspiracy even though no overt acts had been performed within the jurisdiction. Lord Griffiths stated (at p. 620):

> But why should an overt act be necessary to found jurisdiction? In the case of conspiracy in England the crime is complete once the agreement is made and no further overt act need be proved as an ingredient of the crime. The only purpose of looking for an overt act in England in the case of a conspiracy entered into abroad can be to establish

the link between the conspiracy and England or possibly to show the conspiracy is continuing. But if this can be established by other evidence…it defeats the preventative purpose of the crime of conspiracy to have to wait until some overt act is performed in pursuance of the conspiracy….Crime is now established on an international scale and the common law must face this new reality. Their Lordships can find nothing in precedent, comity or good sense that should inhibit the common law from regarding as justiciable in England inchoate crimes committed abroad which are intended to result in the commission of criminal offences in England.

In *Sansom* (1991) 92 Cr App R 115, the Court of Appeal held that the principle enunciated in *Somchai* applied to statutory conspiracies (see also *Naini* [1999] 2 Cr App R 398).

Further provision has been made for the expansion of the territorial jurisdiction of English courts as a response to the growing concern over international crime involving fraud and dishonesty. Part 1 of the Criminal Justice Act 1993 provides courts in England and Wales with jurisdiction over various dishonesty offences and associated inchoate offences related thereto where the offence has an international aspect to it. The jurisdictional provisions apply to 'Group A' and 'Group B' offences which are defined in s. 1. Group A offences include, *inter alia*, theft, various offences under the Fraud Act 2006 (including fraud and obtaining services dishonestly), blackmail, handling stolen goods, and a range of offences under the Forgery and Counterfeiting Act 1981. Group B offences are encouraging or assisting offences under ss. 44–46 of the SCA, conspiracy or attempt to commit a Group A offence or conspiracy to defraud.

A court in England and Wales has jurisdiction to try a person for a Group A offence where any 'relevant event' occurs in England and Wales. A 'relevant event' is 'any act or omission or other event (including any result of one or more acts or omissions) proof of which is required for conviction of the offence' (s. 2(1)). Thus, for example, if D, in England, by a false representation persuades V to give him property in France, and V does so, D would be guilty of fraud, as a relevant event, the false representation, took place in England (see further s. 4).

By s. 3(2) an accused may be convicted of conspiracy to commit a Group A offence, or conspiracy to defraud, whether or not (a) he became a party to the conspiracy in England and Wales; or (b) any act or omission or other event in relation to the conspiracy occurred in England and Wales. What is required is that the substantive Group A offence, if committed, would have involved a 'relevant event' in England and Wales or, in the case of conspiracy to defraud, that the fraud would have been effected in England and Wales. Similarly, on a charge of attempt to commit a Group A offence, the accused may be guilty of the offence whether or not (a) the attempt was made in England and Wales; or (b) it had an effect in England and Wales. For example, D and E in France agree to seek to obtain property from V in England by false representation. If the agreement were to be carried out in accordance with their intentions, a relevant event would take place in England. If D posts the letter containing the false representation in France, an attempt will have occurred even though the letter never arrives at its destination.

Section 5(3) of the 1993 Act gives the courts jurisdiction over conspiracies to defraud where the fraud will take place abroad, provided either (a) a party to the conspiracy (or his agent) did anything in England and Wales in relation to it before

its formation, or (b) a party to it became a party in England and Wales (by joining it either in person or through an agent), or (c) a party to it (or his agent) did or
omitted anything in England and Wales in pursuance of it. Section 5(2) amends
the Criminal Attempts Act 1981 to cover acts done in England and Wales which
are more than merely preparatory to the commission of a Group A offence but the
offence, if completed, would have occurred in a foreign jurisdiction. Section 5(4)
covers encouraging or assisting the commission of Group A offences where the
offence encouraged, if committed, would occur in a foreign jurisdiction. In all
these cases under s. 5 a person may be convicted only if (1) in the case of conspiracy
to defraud 'the agreed course of conduct would at some stage involve (a) an act or
omission by one or more of the parties, or (b) the happening of some other event,
constituting an offence' in the foreign jurisdiction (see s. 6(1)), or (2) in the case of
attempt or encouragement or assistance 'what he had in view would involve the
commission of an offence under the law in force where the whole or any part of it
was intended to take place' (see s. 6(2)).

FURTHER READING

P. Alldridge, 'The Sexual Offences (Conspiracy and Incitement) Act 1996' [1997] Crim
    LR 30.

M. Cohen, 'Inciting the Impossible' [1979] Crim LR 239.

I. Dennis, 'The Rationale of Criminal Conspiracy' (1977) 93 LQR 39; 'The Elements of
    Attempt' [1980] Crim LR 758.

A. T. H. Smith, 'Conspiracy to Defraud: The Law Commission's Working Paper No.
    104' [1988] Crim LR 508.

J. C. Smith, 'Conspiracy to Defraud: Some Comments on the Law Commission Report'
    [1995] Crim LR 209.

K. J. M. Smith, 'Proximity in Attempt: Lord Lane's Midway Course' [1991] Crim LR
    576.

G. R. Sullivan, 'Inchoate Liability for Assisting and Encouraging Crime—the Law
    Commission Report' [2006] Crim LR 1047.

G. Virgo, 'Encouraging or Assisting more than one offence' [2012] 2 Arch Rev 6.

M. Wasik, 'Abandoning Criminal Intent' [1980] Crim LR 785.

G. Williams, 'The Lords and Impossible Attempts, or *Quis Custodiet Ipsos Custodes*'
    (1986) 45 CLJ 33.

9

Homicide

9.1 Introduction

There are several offences of unlawful homicide: murder, manslaughter, infanticide, and causing death by dangerous driving. There are other offences closely approximating to homicide such as child destruction and abortion. The common element to homicide offences, however, is the *actus reus*.

9.1.1 *Actus reus*

Coke described the *actus reus* of homicide as '**Unlawfully killing a reasonable person who is in being and under the King's Peace, the death following within a year and a day**' (Coke, 3 Inst 47). A killing is unlawful where it is not justified (see *Williams* (1984) 78 Cr App R 276; *Beckford* v *R* [1988] AC 130, **3.6.1.1.2** *ante*).

To be the victim of homicide a person must be 'in being'. A baby still in the womb cannot be the victim of homicide. It is important therefore to determine when a child being born becomes an independent 'person in being'. It appears that the child must be wholly expelled from the mother (*Poulton* (1832) 5 C & P 329) and be alive having an existence independent of the mother (*Enoch* (1833) 5 C & P 539). It is not necessary for the umbilical cord to have been severed. However, what constitutes an independent existence is problematical. Some cases suggested that the child must have breathed and others added the requirement of having an independent circulation. Medical science now establishes that foetuses have an independent circulation within a couple of months of conception. A further problem is that a child may be born alive but not breathe for several minutes. In *Brain* (1834) 6 C & P 349, Park J stated that breathing was not essential if the child was born alive. The problem of determining the point at which a child acquires an independent existence, however, does not appear to be a major one as the last reported case dealing with the matter was *Handley* (1874) 13 Cox CC 79. Where a child has been poisoned or injured while in the womb, is born alive but dies thereafter from the poison or injury, this may amount to murder or manslaughter depending on the state of mind of the person who administered the poison or inflicted the injury (see *West* (1848) 2 Car & Kir 784; *Senior* (1832) 1 Mood CC 346). In *A-G's Reference (No. 3 of 1994)* [1997] 3 WLR 421, the House of Lords held that for a conviction of murder D must intend for his act to injure or kill the child that the foetus would become. In the absence of such an intention a conviction for unlawful act manslaughter is possible. If his intention relates solely to the mother and the foetus is born alive but dies from injuries sustained in the womb, the doctrine of transferred malice is not applicable (see **3.6.2.3** *ante*).

If a person is dead he cannot be the victim of homicide. But what if V's heart has stopped and while a doctor is seeking to resuscitate him D shoots V through the head; can D be convicted of homicide? If the prosecution could not establish that V was alive D could be convicted of attempted murder. In *Malcherek and Steel* [1981] 1 WLR 690, the Court of Appeal adverted to the test of 'brain death', although they did not have to decide whether this was the legal definition of death they accepted that it was the test which the medical profession used. In *Airedale NHS Trust* v *Bland* there are dicta to the effect that brain-stem death is the legal test of death. If a person is 'brain dead' at the time of D's act, even though being artificially kept alive by mechanical means (perhaps so that vital organs may be used for transplant purposes), it is submitted that he cannot be the victim of homicide.

The phrase **'the King's Peace'** is a strange one as it appears that everyone in the world is under the King's or Queen's Peace, except an enemy alien who is killed in the course of war. If an enemy alien is a prisoner of war he is under the Queen's Peace. Murder and manslaughter are exceptional in that an English court may try a British citizen for these offences if committed in any country (see s. 9 of the Offences Against the Person Act 1861 and s. 3 of the British Nationality Act 1948). If the offence takes place on a British ship or aircraft it can be tried here whether the perpetrator is a British subject or an alien, but English courts have no jurisdiction if the offence occurs on a foreign ship outside territorial waters.

For homicides where the act (or omission) causing death was committed after 17 June 1996, **the rule that death must occur within a year and a day of such act or omission has been abolished.** The rule had become increasingly anachronistic as, with the development of medical knowledge, it is now possible to determine the cause of a person's death even though it may occur a long time after the original injury was inflicted by the defendant. In addition the use of life-support machines in hospitals has meant that patients who might otherwise have died relatively quickly may be kept alive for a considerable length of time in the hope of recovery. In such a case, however, a prosecution for homicide would be precluded if death occurred more than a year and a day after the act which caused it. The Criminal Law Revision Committee's Fourteenth Report on Offences Against the Person (Cmnd 7844, 1980) suggested that 'it would be wrong for a person to remain almost indefinitely at risk for prosecution for murder. A line has to be drawn somewhere and in our opinion the present law operates satisfactorily' (section 39). In *The Year and a Day Rule in Homicide* (Consultation Paper No. 136) the Law Commission carried out a review of the rule highlighting both the advantages and disadvantages of its retention. The Law Commission recommended its abolition in its report, *Legislating the Criminal Code: The Year and a Day Rule in Homicide* (Consultation Paper No. 230). Parliament acted promptly in response to its recommendations and the Law Reform (Year and a Day Rule) Act 1996 was passed into law on 17 June 1996. To safeguard against oppressive prosecutions any prosecution brought more than three years after the original act causing death was performed, or after the perpetrator has already been convicted of an offence committed in circumstances alleged to be connected with the death, requires the consent of the Attorney-General (see s. 2). In the latter circumstance the offence of which D has previously been convicted will most likely be a non-fatal offence against the person such as wounding or inflicting grievous bodily harm but it need not be such; the cause of the deceased's death may have arisen from, for example, the commission of a burglary, criminal damage, or dangerous driving.

9.2 **Murder**

9.2.1 **Definition**

Murder is unlawful homicide committed with 'malice aforethought'. The penalty for murder is mandatory life imprisonment. **'Malice aforethought'** describes the *mens rea* **required for a conviction of murder.** If malice aforethought is lacking the unlawful homicide will be manslaughter. It should be noted, however, that 'malice aforethought' is a technical term whose meaning implies neither ill-will nor premeditation. Thus a person who kills out of motives of mercy or compassion to alleviate suffering may, nevertheless, be guilty of murder, just as a person who kills in the 'heat of the moment' without prior planning may be guilty of murder. In *Inglis* [2010] EWCA Crim 2637 the Court of Appeal upheld the conviction for murder of a mother who killed her son by a heroin injection as he lay in a hospital bed seriously ill. She regarded the act as a mercy killing but the Court dismissed her appeal reiterating the position that all 'mercy killings' are unlawful and any change in the law is a matter for Parliament, Lord Judge CJ stating (at para. 37):

> [W]e must underline that the law of murder does not distinguish between murder committed for malevolent reasons and murder motivated by familial love. Subject to well established partial defences, like provocation or diminished responsibility, mercy killing is murder.

This was not a case of voluntary euthanasia as there was no evidence that the victim requested an assisted suicide; but even if he had, this would also have amounted to unlawful homicide (see also *R (Nicklinson)* v *Ministry of Justice* [2012] EWHC 2381 (Admin)).

It is important, therefore, to determine the meaning of 'malice aforethought'. Prior to 1957 it appeared that an accused could be convicted of murder where (1) he intended to kill ('express malice'), or (2) he intended to cause grievous bodily harm ('implied malice'), or (3) he killed in the furtherance of a felony (for example, rape or robbery) or when resisting or preventing a lawful arrest, even though there was no intent to kill or to cause grievous bodily harm ('constructive malice'). The courts had not been consistent in their use of the terms 'express' or 'implied' malice. Precise definition of 'implied malice' was not necessary as this appeared to overlap with 'constructive malice' as causing grievous bodily harm was a felony. In 1957 the Homicide Act abolished 'constructive malice'. Section 1 provides:

(1) Where a person kills another in the course or furtherance of some other offence, the killing shall not amount to murder unless done with the same malice aforethought (express or implied) as is required for a killing to amount to murder when not done in the course or furtherance of another offence.

(2) For the purposes of the foregoing subsection, a killing done in the course or for the purpose of resisting an officer of justice, or of resisting or avoiding or preventing a lawful arrest, or of effecting or assisting an escape or rescue from legal custody, shall be treated as a killing in the course or furtherance of an offence.

The question arose whether, by abolishing 'constructive malice', the Act had abolished liability where an accused intended to cause grievous bodily harm but not to kill. As s. 1(1) reserved liability where an accused had 'express malice' or 'implied malice' it had to be determined whether 'implied malice' meant something other than an intention to cause grievous bodily harm. In *Vickers* [1957] 2 QB 664, the Court of Criminal Appeal held that **'implied malice' meant an intention to cause grievous bodily harm**. In *Hyam* [1975] AC 55 the House of Lords failed to arrive at a decision on this issue. In *Cunningham* [1982] AC 566, the House finally decided that an intention to cause grievous bodily harm was 'implied malice' and was something separate from 'constructive malice'. The *mens rea* **of murder, therefore, is an intention to kill or an intention to cause grievous bodily harm** (as to the meaning of intention see **3.2** *ante*). In *A-G's Reference (No. 3 of 1994)* [1997] 3 WLR 421, Lord Mustill described 'implied malice' as a 'conspicuous anomaly'. In *Powell (Anthony)* [1999] AC 1 (**7.1.4.3** *ante*), Lord Steyn said of the rule (at p. 15) that it turned 'murder into a constructive crime...[resulting] in defendants being classified as murderers who are not in truth murderers....It results in the imposition of mandatory life sentences when neither justice nor the needs of society require the classification of the case as murder and the imposition of the mandatory life sentence'. He went on to recommend that 'a killing should be classified as murder if there is an intention to kill or an intention to cause really serious harm coupled with awareness of the risk of death'. Their Lordships accepted, however, that the problem was one which only Parliament could resolve.

'Grievous bodily harm' is a phrase which is to be given its natural meaning (*DPP v Smith* [1961] AC 290). In *Smith*, Viscount Kilmuir stated that 'bodily harm' requires no explanation and **'grievous' means 'really serious'**, although a direction to a jury which omitted the word 'really' would not be a misdirection (*Saunders* [1985] Crim LR 230). Thus a person may be convicted of murder even though he did not intend to kill nor even foresee death as a possibility. For example, D, a member of a terrorist group, performs a 'knee-capping' on V, a member who has broken the rules of the group. D has performed many such 'knee-cappings' in the past and no victim has ever died and he foresees no risk of V dying. V, however, fears hospitals and does not receive medical treatment and dies from septicaemia caused by the wound. As D intended to cause grievous bodily harm he would be convicted of murder. In *Rahman* [2008] UKHL 45 Lord Bingham of Cornhill explained the rationale behind the principle of constructive malice (at para. 25):

> The rationale of that principle plainly is that if a person unlawfully assaults another with intent to cause him really serious injury, and death results, he should be held criminally responsible for that fatality, even though he did not intend it. If he had not embarked on a course of deliberate violence, the fatality would not have occurred. This rationale may lack logical purity, but it is underpinned by a quality of earthy realism.

In their Draft Criminal Code (Law Com No. 177), the Law Commission recommend a change in the law. Clause 54 provides:

> (1) A person is guilty of murder if he causes the death of another—
>
>   (a) intending to cause death; or
>
>   (b) intending to cause serious personal harm and being aware that he may cause death...

The *Report of the Select Committee of the House of Lords on Murder and Life Imprisonment* (HL Paper 78–1, 1989) supports this recommendation stating (at para. 68):

> A person is not generally liable to conviction of a serious crime where the prohibited result was not only unintended but also unforeseen. This seems to the Committee to be a good rule of moral responsibility which should certainly apply to the most serious crime of all, murder. While the law continues to have two categories of homicide, unforeseen but unlawful killings are properly left to the law of manslaughter.

9.2.2 Reform

In 2005 the Home Office announced a review of the law of murder by the Law Commission. The review, however, was to some extent undermined from the outset as the Home Office reaffirmed their commitment to the mandatory life sentence for murder. The Law Commission published a Consultation Paper (No. 177) in December 2005, *A New Homicide Act for England and Wales?* It sought to negotiate the obstacle of the mandatory life sentence by constructing a framework of offences reflecting different degrees of culpability. In their final Report, *Murder, Manslaughter and Infanticide* (Law Com No. 304) the Law Commission retain this framework but with some modification following views expressed in the consultation.

(1) **First degree murder** (mandatory life penalty)
   (a) Killing intentionally.
   (b) Killing where there was an intention to do serious injury, coupled with an awareness of a serious risk of causing death.

(2) **Second degree murder** (discretionary life maximum penalty)
   (a) Killing where the offender intended to do serious injury.
   (b) Killing where the offender intended to cause some injury or a fear or risk of injury, and was aware of a serious risk of causing death.
   (c) Killing in which there is a partial defence to what would otherwise be first degree murder.

(3) **Manslaughter** (discretionary life maximum penalty)
   (a) Killing through gross negligence as to a risk of causing death.
   (b) Killing through a criminal act:
      (i) intended to cause injury; or
      (ii) where there was an awareness that the act involved a serious risk of causing injury.
   (c) Participating in a joint criminal venture in the course of which another participant commits first or second degree murder, in circumstances where it should have been obvious that first or second degree murder might be committed by another participant.

The Government responded to these proposals with its own Consultation Paper, *Murder, manslaughter and infanticide: proposal for reform of the law* (CP19/08). The Government rejected the redefinition of the basic offence of murder but proposed to proceed with legislation in the areas of provocation, diminished responsibility, complicity, and infanticide. The Government appeared oblivious to the fact that the Law Commission's proposals in respect of these matters were posited upon its key proposal to reform murder and manslaughter as set out earlier. As one commentator observed, 'The resulting structure, unfortunately, looks rather like a wheel without a hub' (J. R. Spencer, 'Messing up Murder' [2008] 8 Arch. News 5). The Coroners and Justice Act 2009 duly enacted changes to those four areas without effecting any change to the law of murder.

9.3 Manslaughter

9.3.1 Introduction

The offence of manslaughter generally covers all unlawful homicides which are not murder. The punishment for this offence is in the discretion of the court and therefore ranges from absolute discharge to life imprisonment, reflecting the immense range of circumstances which may fall within the compass of this offence.

   The offence of manslaughter may be divided into two generic types—voluntary and involuntary. Voluntary manslaughter is committed where the accused has killed with malice aforethought, and thus could be convicted of murder, but there are mitigating circumstances present reducing his culpability. As the sentence for murder is mandatory life imprisonment, a judge sentencing such an accused for murder would not be able to reflect these mitigating circumstances in the sentence. Accordingly, where an accused kills while suffering from diminished responsibility, or the killing is done under a loss of self-control or in pursuance of a suicide pact, he will be convicted of manslaughter. Involuntary manslaughter is an unlawful killing committed by an accused who did not have malice aforethought but who, nevertheless, had a state of mind which the law treats as culpable.

9.3.2 Voluntary manslaughter

9.3.2.1 Diminished responsibility

A full discussion of the provisions relating to diminished responsibility is to be found in **5.5** *ante.*

9.3.2.2 Loss of self-control

This is a new defence enacted by ss. 54–55 of the Coroners and Justice Act 2009. It replaces the defence of provocation which existed at common law and was modified by s. 3 of the Homicide Act 1957. Section 56 abolishes the defence of provocation with the new defence applying to any murder which occurred on or after 4 October 2010. For murders prior to this date, the defence of provocation continues to apply. For a full exposition of this defence see the Online Resource Centre.

   In order to understand the changes that have been made by ss. 54–56, a brief outline of the law of provocation is provided in the following paragraphs.

9.3.2.2.1 *Provocation*

Provocation is only a defence to a charge of murder reducing to manslaughter what, in the absence of provocation, would have been murder. If the jury are satisfied D killed with the requisite intent for murder they must convict of man-slaughter if the accused may have been provoked. The burden of proof in respect of provocation is upon the prosecution (*Cascoe* [1970] 2 All ER 833); if there is evidence raising the possibility of provocation the burden is upon the prosecution to prove beyond reasonable doubt that the accused was not provoked. If there is any evidence of provocation, the judge must leave the defence to the jury. Section 3 of the Homicide Act 1957, provides:

> Where on a charge of murder there is evidence on which the jury can find that the person charged was provoked (whether by things done or by things said or by both together) to lose his self-control, the question whether the provocation was enough to make a reasonable man do as he did shall be left to be determined by the jury; and in determining that question the jury shall take into account everything both done and said according to the effect which, in their opinion, it would have on a reasonable man.

There are two elements to the defence of provocation: **first, the subjective question whether the accused was provoked to lose his self-control; and, second, the objective question whether a reasonable man would have been provoked to lose his self-control and do as he did.** Because of the burden of proof being on the prosecution, the defence will succeed if the jury feel the accused may possibly have been provoked to lose his self-control and a reasonable man may possibly have lost his self-control and done as he did.

At common law words alone, except 'in circumstances of a most extreme and exceptional character' could not amount to provocation (*Holmes* v *DPP* [1946] AC 588). With two exceptions, actual violence by the deceased upon the accused was required. The exceptions were discovery by a husband of his wife in the act of committing adultery and discovery by a father of someone committing sodomy on his son. The Act removed all such restrictions. The provocation need not be illegal or wrongful (see *Doughty* (1986) 83 Cr App R 319) and **may emanate from third parties** (*Davies* [1975] QB 691) **or be directed at third parties** (*Pearson* [1992] Crim LR 193). What is crucial is that there is evidence that D was provoked to lose his self-control.

Loss of self-control does not have to be 'complete' to the extent that the accused did not know what he was doing; it is sufficient that he may not have been able to restrain himself from doing what he did (*Richens* [1993] Crim LR 384). In *Ibrams* (1981) 74 Cr App R 154 and *Thornton* [1992] 1 All ER 306, the Court of Appeal approved the dictum of Devlin J in *Duffy* [1949] 1 All ER 932 that there must be 'a sudden and temporary loss of self-control, rendering the accused so subject to passion as to make him or her for the moment not master of his mind'. While there may have been a history of provocative acts or words, if at the time of the killing, D was not provoked to lose his self-control, he cannot rely on past provocation. In *Ahluwalia* [1992] 4 All ER 889 where D killed her husband after a long history of domestic violence by him, it was argued that in domestic violence 'slow-burn' cases, where the accused only loses self-control after a prolonged period of provocation from the deceased, the *Duffy* test was inappropriate as a delay or 'cooling-off period' between the last act of provocation and the killing might, in fact, cause the accused to react more strongly. While only Parliament could change the law, the

Court accepted that delay would not as a matter of law negate provocation, provided that there was a 'sudden and temporary loss of self-control'.

The fact that D lost his self-control does not mean that his defence of provocation will succeed; the jury have then to consider the objective question. If the jury conclude that there is a reasonable possibility that the reasonable man might have done as D did, they must return a verdict of manslaughter. **The purpose of the objective question is to set a standard of self-control against which D's actions are to be measured**. The reasonable man standard was well established in the common law before s. 3 of the 1957 Act was passed and was a purely objective standard. The reasonable man was an adult person with normal physical and mental attributes and not having any characteristics which would single him out from ordinary people. This was consistent with the common law rule that provocation was limited to acts of violence by the deceased upon the accused. Thus, if the accused was disfigured or impotent, taunts about these matters could not constitute provocation so there was no need to attribute these characteristics to the reasonable man.

Section 3 of the Homicide Act 1957 changed this by allowing words alone to constitute provocation. Taunts or insults might acquire a seriousness deriving from the fact that they focused on a particular characteristic of the accused. That this might necessitate a redefinition of the reasonable man was intimated by the requirement in s. 3, that, in seeking to answer the objective question, the jury must 'consider everything both done and said according to the effect which, in their opinion, it would have on a reasonable man'. It would seem to be crucial, therefore, for the reasonable man to be placed in the same situation as the accused and thus to share such of the accused's characteristics, circumstances, history, or conditions as are pertinent to the provocation. Two particular problems presented themselves: first, D, due to his characteristics, history, or circumstances, may be particularly sensitive to the alleged provocative words or conduct; and secondly, D, due to his youthfulness or some mental impairment, may not be able to exercise the self-control to be expected of the ordinary adult. At a time before any appellate decisions were made on these issues, Professor Ashworth in 'The Doctrine of Provocation' (1976) 35 CLJ 292, expressed the view (at p. 312) that the defence of provocation was for those who were mentally normal, whereas those suffering from a mental abnormality should rely on the defence of diminished responsibility under s. 2 of the 1957 Act (see **5.5** *ante*). In seeking to apply the objective test, Ashworth concluded (at p. 300) that a distinction had to be drawn between those 'individual peculiarities which bear on the gravity of the provocation [which] should be taken into account, whereas individual peculiarities bearing on the accused's level of self-control should not'.

In *Camplin* [1978] AC 705 Lord Diplock stated (at p. 717) that the reasonable man is:

> an ordinary person of either sex, not exceptionally excitable or pugnacious, but possessed of such powers of self-control as everyone is entitled to expect that his fellow citizens will exercise in society as it is today.

He accepted (at p. 714) that the reasonable man was the 'embodiment of the standard of self-control required by the criminal law' but, following the 1957 Act, he could be attributed with those characteristics, or placed in those circumstances which would affect the gravity of the taunts or insults directed at the accused. In addition, age, which may be taken into account in assessing the gravity of the provocation (for example, a physical threat or assault may be graver due to the less developed physique of a young person), was also relevant when considering powers of self-control as 'to require old heads upon young shoulders is inconsistent with the law's compassion to human infirmity'. **But other factors which might reduce or impair the accused's powers of self-control were not attributable.** In *Morhall* [1996] AC 90 the House of Lords **emphasised that the reasonable man test is not concerned with ratiocination nor with reasonable conduct; rather it represents a standard of self-control.**

When directing a jury the judge should refer them to the hypothetical person:

> having the power of self-control to be expected of an ordinary person of the age and sex of the defendant, but in other respects sharing such of the defendant's characteristics as [the jury] think would affect the gravity of the provocation to him.

Things relevant to the gravity of the provocation should not be confined to characteristics but could include 'the defendant's history or the circumstances in which he was placed at the time', and the characteristics, history, or circumstances did not cease to be relevant because they were discreditable (in the instant case D's addiction, which formed the focus for taunts, was the relevant characteristic). Furthermore, a characteristic could be something temporary or transitory if the subject of taunts or insults.

Despite these clear pronouncements in the House of Lords, the Court of Appeal throughout the 1980s and 1990s continued to intimate that the standard of self-control to be expected of the reasonable person might be modified to take account of the defendant's psychiatric idiosyncrasies. The Privy Council considered those decisions in *Luc Thiet Thuan* v *R* [1996] 3 WLR 45, concluding that a mental infirmity which impairs an accused's power of self-control was not to be taken into account as it is inconsistent with a person having the power of self-control of an ordinary person who features in the objective test. The mental infirmity of the accused could be taken into account if it was the subject of taunts by the deceased as this would go to the gravity of the provocation but otherwise it would be irrelevant. Lord Goff reasoned that this position preserved the distinction between diminished responsibility and provocation which it must have been the intention of the legislature in passing the Homicide Act 1957 to maintain. Lord Steyn, who had concurred in *Morhall*, dissented expressing the view that mental characteristics which gave rise to impaired self-control should be taken into account when considering whether a reasonable person might have done as the accused did. Lord Steyn's reading of the Court of Appeal decisions was endorsed, *obiter*, by Lord Bingham CJ in *Campbell* [1997] 1 Cr App R 199. Lord Bingham's reasoning was itself adopted by the Court of Appeal in *Parker* [1997] Crim LR 760 where the accused was a chronic alcoholic with some brain damage which made him more susceptible to provocation.

The House of Lords reconsidered the issue in *Smith (Morgan)* [2000] 3 WLR 654, another case involving an alcoholic suffering from a depressive illness which impaired his ability to exercise self-control reducing his threshold for erupting with violence. The trial judge accepted the Crown's argument that this evidence was not relevant to the question whether a reasonable man might have lost his self-control. D was convicted of murder and appealed. The Court of Appeal allowed his appeal, substituting a verdict of manslaughter on the ground that his mental impairment was a characteristic to be attributed to the reasonable man not only in assessing the gravity of the provocation but also his reaction to it. The Crown appealed. The Court of Appeal granted leave to appeal and certified the following point of law of general public importance: 'Are characteristics other than age and sex, attributable to the reasonable man, for the purpose of section 3 of the Homicide Act 1957, relevant not only to the gravity of the provocation to him but also to the standard of self-control to be expected?' Unbelievably their Lordships by a majority of three to two answered the question in the affirmative. The majority concluded that Lord Diplock did not intend to draw any distinction between 'characteristics relevant to the gravity of the provocation and characteristics relevant to the power of self-control'. In Lord Hoffmann's view it would be to trespass on the jury's territory to tell them to ignore any factor or characteristic as it is the right of the jury 'to act upon its own opinion of whether the objective element of provocation has been satisfied'.

Following *Smith*, the jury when considering the objective question had to take into account any condition from which the accused suffered which impaired his ability to exercise self-control. The test was 'whether he has exercised the degree of self-control to be expected of someone in his situation' (*per* Lord Slynn at p. 661) i.e. someone with the same impaired powers of self-control; or whether his behaviour 'fell below the standard which should reasonably have been expected of him' (*per* Lord Hoffmann at p. 677); or whether the accused had 'made reasonable efforts to control himself within the limits of what he [was] reasonably able to do' (*per* Lord Clyde at p. 684). When one bears in mind the burden of proof on the prosecution to disprove provocation beyond reasonable doubt, there would be little chance of a jury scrupulously following a judge's direction in a case such as *Smith*, not returning a verdict of manslaughter if satisfied that the accused may have been provoked to lose his self-control: if the accused may have been provoked to act as he did, who could doubt that someone else suffering the same illness or condition which impaired his powers of self-control might not have done the same?

Following the decision of the House of Lords in *Smith* the Court of Appeal struggled to make sense of it. Their struggle, however, was short-lived as in a completely unprecedented judgment, *A-G for Jersey v Holley* [2005] UKPC 23, the Privy Council, sitting as a Board made up of nine serving Lords of Appeal in Ordinary, by a majority of six to three followed *Luc Thiet Thuan* and declared that *Morgan Smith* could not be regarded as an accurate statement of English law. The majority held that s. 3 of the Homicide Act 1957 had altered the common law defence of provocation. The statutory reference to the 'reasonable man' was intended to refer to the ordinary person, i.e. a person of ordinary self-control, and thereby it set an external standard of self-control. Lord Nicholls of Birkenhead, delivering the judgment of the majority, stated (at para. 22):

> Whether the provocative act or words and the defendant's response met the 'ordinary person' standard prescribed by the statute is the question the jury must consider, not

> the altogether looser question of whether, having regard to all the circumstances, the jury consider the loss of self-control was sufficiently excusable. The statute does not leave each jury free to set whatever standard they consider appropriate in the circumstances by which to judge whether the defendant's conduct is 'excusable'.

The majority recognised that inherent in the use of a uniform standard applicable to all defendants is 'the possibility that an individual defendant may be temperamentally unable to achieve this standard'. While sex and age are relevant to the application of this standard, other abnormalities not found in a person having ordinary powers of self-control, are not. The majority considered that s. 2, diminished responsibility, reflected Parliament's recognition of the potential harshness of s. 3 if it stood alone. It would be wrong for the courts to distort s. 3 to accommodate cases for which Parliament had expressly provided in enacting s. 2.

While in terms of strict precedent the Privy Council cannot overrule a decision of the House of Lords, the nine person panel in *Holley* declared it as their purpose to resolve the conflict in the authorities and clarify definitively the present state of English law. In *James and Karimi* [2006] EWCA Crim 14, the Court of Appeal unusually sitting in a five-strong panel, held that in the exceptional circumstances which pertained as a result of the decision in *Holley*, the principle of law was to be found in the decision of the Privy Council.

9.3.2.2.2 *The pressure for reform*

In their Report *Partial Defences to Murder* (Law Com No. 290), published in 2004 before the Privy Council decision in *Holley*, the Law Commission made a number of recommendations for the reform of the defence of provocation which were intended to recast the defence in a way consistent with the pre-*Smith (Morgan)* law by restoring an objective standard of self-control. The Law Commission eschewed use of the term 'self-control' and appeared to have recast the defence within a new and ill-defined set of moral parameters avoiding reference to the 'reasonable man' by using, instead, 'a person of the defendant's age and of ordinary temperament'. The defence would succeed if this person (of 'ordinary tolerance and self-restraint') might, in the circumstances in which the defendant was placed, have reacted in the same or a similar way. In making this assessment account may be taken of 'all the circumstances of the defendant other than matters whose only relevance to the defendant's conduct is that they bear simply on his or her general capacity for self-control'. The Law Commission's expressed preference was for the minority position in *Morgan Smith*.

If a person suffers from some retarded development of mind or is a psychopath, things which might have a bearing on cognitive and emotional development and, in turn, temperament, the Law Commission considered that such should not be taken into account in respect of provocation being more appropriate for consideration in relation to the defence of diminished responsibility (para. 3.130). The Law Commission also recognised that many of the wrong turnings in provocation were well-intentioned responses to the problem of battered women who kill. They explained how their reformed defence would apply in such cases (para. 3.111):

> This is not to deny a defence to an abused person whose temperament may have changed as a result of the provocation [i.e. the history of abuse], for that would be a matter which

bore not simply on the defendant's general temperament independent of the provocation but on the effect of the provocation itself. As Lord Millett said in *Smith (Morgan)* about such a case:

> 'The question for the jury is whether a woman with normal powers of self-control, subjected to the treatment which the accused received, would or might finally react as she did....It does not involve an inquiry whether the accused was capable of displaying the powers of self-control of an ordinary person, but whether a person with the power of self-control of an ordinary person would or might have reacted in the same way to the cumulative effect of the treatment which she endured.'

A more significant change proposed by the Law Commission related to the subjective test. The Law Commission wished to change the focus of the defence away from the issue of loss of self-control and to provide for the situation where excessive force is used in self-defence which does not provide a defence to murder. In consequence the subjective test was to be significantly reframed so that a defendant would be able to rely on provocation where he acted in response to:

i. gross provocation (meaning words or conduct or a combination of words and conduct) which caused the defendant to have a justifiable sense of being seriously wronged; or

ii. fear of serious violence towards the defendant or another; or

iii. a combination of [(i) and (ii)].

Lest a person with a justifiable sense of grievance seeks to use this in a calculated way as a means of wreaking revenge, the proposals excluded reliance on the defence where the defendant 'acted in considered desire for revenge'. However, as the defence would not rely on a loss of self-control but on the defendant having a 'justifiable sense of being seriously wronged' it is difficult to see how such a response is distinguishable from a desire for vengeance. Many may feel seriously wronged, but should the law be condoning the administration of retribution by the person wronged? The use of the adjective 'gross' to qualify the provocation to which the defendant is responding may avoid a defendant relying on minor slights to which he accords undue significance, but what constitutes 'gross' is lacking in definitional exactitude.

To accommodate situations where defendants act owing to a fear of serious violence, a person should not be treated as having acted in considered desire for revenge if he or she acted in fear of serious violence, merely because he or she was also angry towards the deceased for the conduct which engendered that fear. A further limitation on the defence was that it would not apply where the provocation was incited by the defendant for the purpose of providing an excuse to use violence.

One final proposal of significance was that the trial judge should not be required to leave the defence to the jury 'unless there is evidence on which a reasonable jury, properly directed, could conclude that it might apply'. This reflected the position in Australia and would help to address the problem of bizarre claims of provocation being accepted by an 'out of touch' jury. The one question which the Law Commission did not address is whether there should be a defence of provocation at all. Might not a better value to inculcate be that of self-discipline rather than self-righteous indignation?

In their Consultation Paper, No. 177, *A New Homicide Act for England and Wales?* published in 2005, the Law Commission made no changes to those initial recommendations except to propose that provocation should only be a defence to 'first degree murder' with the effect of reducing it to 'second degree murder' (see **9.2.2** *ante*). In their Report *Murder, Manslaughter and Infanticide* (Law Com No. 304) the Law Commission affirmed these recommendations.

The Government responded to these proposals with its own Consultation Paper, *Murder, manslaughter and infanticide: proposal for reform of the law* (CP19/08). While accepting the Law Commission's analysis of the problems, it proposed a different response, namely to abolish the defence of provocation and replace it with a new partial defence based on a loss of self-control. The Government rejected the proposals in respect of murder with the result that its new defence will operate to reduce the offence to manslaughter rather than second degree murder. In January 2009 the Government published a summary of the responses to the consultation and outlined its position in *Summary of Responses and Government Position: Response to Consultation CP(R) 19/08*. The new defence was duly enacted by ss. 54–56 of the Coroners and Justice Act 2009.

9.3.2.2.3 *Loss of Control*

Section 54(1) sets out the main elements of the defence and provides:

> (1) Where a person ('D') kills or is a party to the killing of another (V'), D is not to be convicted of murder if—
>
> (a) D's acts and omissions in doing or being a party to the killing resulted from D's loss of self-control,
>
> (b) the loss of self-control had a qualifying trigger, and
>
> (c) a person of D's sex and age, with a normal degree of tolerance and self-restraint and in the circumstances of D, might have reacted in the same or in a similar way to D.

Before examining these elements, it should be noted that **the burden of proof in respect of the defence of loss of control rests on the prosecution** to disprove the defence beyond reasonable doubt (s. 54(5)). This burden arises once 'sufficient evidence is adduced to raise an issue with respect to the defence'. It is for the judge to determine whether or not this evidential threshold has been satisfied which it will be if 'evidence is adduced on which, in the opinion of the trial judge, a jury, properly directed, could reasonably conclude that the defence might apply' (s. 54(6)). If the prosecution do not disprove the defence 'the jury must assume that the defence is satisfied' (s. 54(5)) which means that the judge's determination of whether or not to leave the defence to the jury acquires a degree of significance.

As with provocation there are subjective and objective elements to the defence; (a) and (b) (quoted earlier) represent the subjective elements and (c) the objective element. In construing the statute, however, courts should treat the old law of provocation as irrelevant as this is a new defence; nor are the Law Commission papers especially helpful (see *Clinton* [2012] EWCA Crim 2).

(a) *Loss of self-control* Unlike under provocation, the **loss of self-control need not be sudden** (s. 54(2)). Thus situations, as in cases of domestic violence, where D's reaction builds up over a period of time are not excluded. However, **the** defence may not be relied upon where 'D acted in a considered desire for revenge' (s. 54(4)); and 'a considered act of revenge, whether performed calmly or in anger, is not a loss of self control' (*per* Lord Judge CJ, *Clinton* [2012] EWCA Crim 2, para 128). But there may be problems with the new defence. It may be difficult to establish that there was a loss of self-control if D has not suddenly reacted by killing V. The longer the delay between the qualifying trigger and the act of killing, the more difficult it will be evidentially to establish actual loss of self-control. Further, how this interacts with s. 54(1)(c) may be problematic; for a person of normal tolerance and self-restraint, a delay between the trigger and the killing may provide a period for cooling-off and reflecting on other ways to deal with the situation. Whether these provisions amply accommodate the problems of killings in the context of domestic violence will only be known once the new defence has been in operation for a sufficient period.

(b) *Qualifying trigger* **Loss of self-control may only be relied upon where it is attributable to one or both of the two specified 'qualifying triggers'** set out in s. 55:

(i) D's fear of serious violence from V against D or another identified person (s. 55(3); and /or

(ii) a thing or things done or said (or both) which

    (a) constituted circumstances of an extremely grave character, and

    (b) caused D to have a justifiable sense of being seriously wronged (s. 55(4)).

Before examining these 'triggers' it is important to note that **D cannot rely on either if he has incited the situation to provide himself with an excuse** to use violence in response (see s. 55(6)). Thus if D goes looking for a fight by inciting V or insults V in order to provoke V to insult him, he will be denied the defence. This is perfectly logical as the defence is of an excusatory nature and D's behaviour in such circumstances is hardly to be excused or condoned.

Note also that D may rely on both qualifying triggers. For example, D, a domestic violence victim, may kill her abusive partner, V, having lost self-control both fearing serious violence and also feeling a justifiable sense of being seriously wronged as a result of the abuse to which she has been subjected.

(i) *Fear of serious violence* The first qualifying trigger is **fear of serious violence from V against D or another resulting in D's loss of self-control**. It was perceived that women who killed their abusive partners were ill-served by the defence of provocation because of the requirement for loss of self-control to be sudden and temporary. The new defence imposes no requirement of imminence with regard to the anticipated violence; it is enough that D anticipates an attack, loses her self-control, and kills V. The stereotypical situation intended to be covered would be where V returns home drunk and D, anticipating a further violent and/or sexual attack from V (consistent with his past behaviour) loses her self-control, and while he is dozing on the sofa, stabs him. The trigger would also cover, for example, the situation where V's violence is directed towards the children of the relationship and D kills him to protect them. A general fear for unspecified others, will not suffice.

The qualifying trigger may also operate where D, fearing serious violence, loses his self-control, over-reacts and kills V in circumstances where use of a lesser degree of force would have been justifiable and supported a defence of self-defence.

(ii) *Justifiable sense of being seriously wronged* Under provocation anything said or done might amount to provocation whether wrongful of not (see *Doughty*) and whether trivial or serious. The new defence seeks to set a higher threshold before D may rely on things said or done to excuse his loss of self-control. Thus the **things done or said have to amount to 'circumstances of an extremely grave character'.** The issue is not whether D perceives them as such but whether objectively they are such. Where D seeks to rely on things done or said which do not give rise to a fear of serious violence, the focus will generally be on V's behaviour and language (although the statute does not limit the focus to V's words or conduct). Often the situation will be one where insults or taunts are traded by V with D. In the past, under provocation, any evidence of provocative words or conduct had to be left to the jury. Now the provision in s. 54(6) means that the judge will play a crucial role in determining whether a jury, properly directed, could reasonably conclude that the words or conduct constituted circumstances of an extremely grave character.

Example

It is anticipated that the judicial filter will operate where, for example, V, D's daughter, refuses to enter a marriage arranged for her by D and runs off with her boyfriend, W, whom D does not consider suitable. If D, in the context of so-called 'honour killing' were to kill V or W, it is likely that a judge would not leave the defence of loss of self-control to the jury on the basis that no jury, properly directed, could reasonably conclude that the conduct of V and/or W constituted 'circumstances of an extremely grave character'. The basis for this determination is an objective one taking account of the society in which V and W live where human rights under the ECHR are enacted into law by the Human Rights Act 1998, and where the rights of V and W to self-determination are valued over and above any interest D might have in the maintenance of family honour.

Even if the threshold of things done or said amounting to circumstances of an extremely grave character is satisfied, D's loss of self-control will not satisfy the subjective limb of the defence unless, in addition, these circumstances caused D to have a justifiable sense of being seriously wronged. **Whether or not D's sense of being seriously wronged is justifiable, is an objective question** to be determined initially by the judge on the basis of whether or not a jury properly directed could reasonably conclude that it was and, if so, the jury will then be left to consider this question. Again, in the context of so-called 'honour killing' D would not get past the judge as any sense of grievance he might have could not be considered justifiable in England and Wales. The upshot of these provisions, accordingly, is that the defence of loss of self-control will be left to juries to consider in a much more limited range of situations than pertained with the defence of provocation.

At common law provocation could only be relied on if the deceased used actual violence on the defendant unless one of two exceptions applied, the relevant one here being D discovering V, his wife, in the act of committing adultery. With the

passage of s. 3 of the Homicide Act 1957 permitting words alone to constitute provocation, a confession by V to D of her adultery could be sufficient. For many years
critics of the defence of provocation used these two examples, along with the problems facing victims of domestic violence in raising the defence, to contend that the
defence of provocation was gender-based and favoured men over women. While
there was little evidence to support the contention that jealous husbands were
'getting away with murder' by successfully raising the defence of provocation (see
Impact Assessment, pp. 11–12 which accompanied the Government's Consultation
Paper), and under the new loss of self-control defence the judge would apply the
filter to any such pleas having to be satisfied that adultery is both 'extremely grave'
and could cause D to have a justifiable sense of being seriously wronged, s. 55(6)(c)
nonetheless expressly provides that 'the fact that a thing done or said constituted
sexual infidelity is to be disregarded'. Thus if V, spouse one, is caught in the act of
adultery by, or confesses adultery to, D, spouse two, D cannot rely on that sexual
infidelity to contend that the consequential loss of self-control causing D to kill V,
had a qualifying trigger. This has the potential to lead to some hair-splitting on the
part of judges and juries.

Example

In the course of a heated argument V confesses her adultery to D and then taunts D that she
had to find someone else to satisfy her as he was always a useless lover and now is impotent. In deciding if D's loss of self-control was due to a qualifying trigger, the confession
of adultery would have to be ignored but the subsequent taunts of being a useless lover
and of impotence would have to be taken into account as things said. Whether the taunts
would constitute circumstances of an extremely grave character or cause a justifiable sense
of being seriously wronged may be open to question when considered in isolation from the
confession of adultery.

In the Explanatory Notes accompanying the Coroners and Justice Act 2009, the
following example is given of a situation involving sexual infidelity where the
defence of loss of self-control might nonetheless still be raised:

> [W]here a person discovers their partner sexually abusing their young child (an act that
> amounts to sexual infidelity) and loses self-control and kills[, t]he fact that the partner's
> act amounted to sexual infidelity must be discounted but that act may still potentially
> be claimed to amount to the qualifying trigger in section 55(4) on the basis of the other
> aspects of the case (namely the child abuse).

In *Clinton* [2012] EWCA Crim 2 the Court of Appeal has sought to provide some
clarification regarding the prohibition on having regard to sexual infidelity holding that it applies only where sexual infidelity is the *sole* potential qualifying trigger. In the first example given earlier the sexual infidelity is an essential part of
the context in which the loss of self-control occurred and as such would not be
excluded in determining whether the other matters were grave and serious enough
to constitute a qualifying trigger. In the second example, in reality, it is highly
unlikely that a parent discovering the other abusing their child would lose their

self-control because of the infidelity rather than because of the commission of an offence against the child.

Perhaps it would have been better to have desisted from enacting s. 55(6)(c) and simply left it to the good sense of judges and of juries to assess sexual infidelity, where relevant, in the context of determining whether it amounts to extremely grave circumstances and whether it could be a justification for D's sense of being seriously wronged. As the *Impact Assessment* did not highlight any real problem with the more broadly based defence of provocation, it could be anticipated that there would not be a problem with the more narrowly based defence of loss of self-control thus making this provision unnecessary. The legislative history of this provision indicates it was re-inserted in the Bill at a late stage in the parliamentary process suggesting that its enactment was the worst kind of gesture politics.

(c) *Reaction of person with normal degree of tolerance and self-restraint* If D has killed and sufficient evidence has been adduced to raise the defence of loss of self-control, that is, that D may have lost his self-control and killed, and that loss of self-control may have had a qualifying trigger, he will be entitled to succeed in his defence unless the prosecution disprove that 'a person of D's sex and age, with a normal degree of tolerance and self-restraint and in the circumstances of D, might have reacted in the same or a similar way to D' (s. 54(1)(c)). This is the objective test and has similarities with the test under the Homicide Act 1957 as understood following the decision of the Privy Council in *A-G for Jersey* v *Holley* but it is notable that the word 'tolerance' is used in addition to 'self-restraint' indicating that this is something additional to the old concept of self-control. The statute avoids any use of the terms 'reasonable' or 'ordinary' to describe the person against whom D's reaction is to be measured. This person requires some designation, however, for the purposes of exposition, so s/he will be referred to as the 'normal person'. The normal person shares D's sex and age. Age clearly may have a relevance to the degree of self-control to be expected of a person; although, perhaps, maturity would be a better factor to consider as people mature at different rates and some never reach full maturity. However, the statute seeks to avoid this kind of complexity and adopts the simple approach of factoring in age and sex (whatever its relevance might be) for the purposes of determining whether the normal person may have reacted as D did. **It is enough that he may have reacted in 'the same or in a similar way to D'.** However, anything in D's circumstances which impairs his capacity to exercise the normal degree of tolerance and self-restraint to be expected of people living in England and Wales today, will not be attributed to the normal person (see s. 54(3)). If D has extreme views colouring his tolerance for others whether based on their race, religion, gender, or sexual orientation, those views will not be attributed to the normal person. Similarly if D's capacity for exercising self-restraint is impaired by, for example, mental illness or retarded development, these circumstances are not attributed to the normal person. If D's ability to exercise self-control is substantially impaired, he may be able to rely on the defence of diminished responsibility (see **5.5** *ante*).

In making the assessment of whether the normal person would have reacted in the same or a similar way to D, the normal person will be located in the same circumstances as D. This means that he will have the same history and characteristics as D insofar as these are relevant to the qualifying triggers which prompted the loss of self-control. Thus if D is being taunted about his sexual orientation, the normal person will have the same sexual orientation; if D is placed in fear of serious violence from V, her violent partner, the normal person will have that same history of living in a relationship involving domestic violence. This reflects the law on provocation as it was understood in *Camplin, Morhall* and *Luc Thiet Thuan*. But, in some ways the new defence is narrower again as circumstances that might impact upon D's fear of violence, or his sense of being seriously wronged have to have sufficient seriousness or gravity to pass the filter of the judge in s. 54(6). Furthermore, that same filter operates with regard to the objective test as well. If the judge does not consider that a jury, properly directed, could reasonably conclude that the person of normal tolerance and self-restraint might have reacted in the same way as D, the issue will not be left to the jury. Doubtless much case law will be generated in seeking to locate the parameters within which the new defence of loss of self-control operates. The judicial view of what is reasonable will be particularly important in this context. It is to be hoped that the Court of Appeal does not demonstrate the inconsistency which beset the defence of provocation over the past three decades when it comes to consider the new defence.

9.3.2.3 Suicide pacts

Section 4(1) of the Homicide Act 1957 (as amended by the Suicide Act 1961) provides: 'It shall be manslaughter and shall not be murder for a person acting in pursuance of a suicide pact between him and another to kill the other or be party to the other being killed by a third person'. Section 4(3) defines 'suicide pact' as follows:

> a common agreement between two or more persons having for its object the death of all of them, whether or not each is to take his own life, but nothing done by a person who enters into a suicide pact shall be treated as done by him in pursuance of the pact unless it is done while he has the settled intention of dying in pursuance of the pact.

If, for example, D enters into an agreement to kill V and then himself, and having killed V he relents or is prevented from killing himself, he may, on a charge of murder, raise the defence of suicide pact. In this case the burden of proof is upon the defence (s. 4(2)) to prove the facts grounding the defence on the balance of probabilities (*Woolmington* v *DPP* [1935] AC 462).

In their Consultation Paper, No. 177, *A New Homicide Act for England and Wales?* published in 2005, the Law Commission recommended the repeal of the defence of suicide pact; deserving cases should be covered by a reformed defence of diminished responsibility. In their Report, *Murder, Manslaughter and Infanticide* (Law Com No. 304) the Law Commission reconsidered this recommendation now taking the view that the defence should be retained pending a review of the broader question of whether there should be a partial defence of 'mercy' killing.

9.3.3 **Involuntary manslaughter**

Involuntary manslaughter is an offence of ill-defined boundaries covering the middle ground between murder and accidental death. If D did not have the *mens rea* for murder he may be guilty of manslaughter if the killing was 'unlawful'. Seeking to define this element of unlawfulness has taxed judicial minds for most of this century; and even now there remain areas of uncertainty. Involuntary manslaughter takes two forms.

The first form is constructive manslaughter and the second is gross negligence manslaughter. Gross negligence manslaughter is sometimes referred to as 'reckless manslaughter'. The two concepts clearly overlap but gross negligence is the broader term covering a greater range of conduct.

Sometimes the facts of a case may fall within the compass of both constructive and gross negligence manslaughter so that a verdict of manslaughter may be available on either of those grounds.

9.3.3.1 Constructive manslaughter

Prior to the Homicide Act 1957, the doctrine of constructive malice meant that an accused could be convicted of murder where he killed in the course of committing a felony albeit that he lacked the *mens rea* of murder. A parallel doctrine existed that if an accused killed in the course of doing an unlawful act, which was not a felony, he was guilty of manslaughter. The Homicide Act, by s. 1(1), abolished the doctrine of constructive murder, but constructive manslaughter remains. **This is often referred to as 'unlawful act' manslaughter.** The fact that death is caused by D's unlawful act, however, is not sufficient to lead to a manslaughter verdict. The term 'unlawful act' is qualified in several ways.

9.3.3.1.1 *A crime of commission*

In the nineteenth century there was some uncertainty in respect of the nature of the unlawfulness required. In *Fenton* (1830) 1 Lew CC 179, Tindal CJ directed the jury that it was sufficient if the accused did a wrongful act which was a tort. In *Franklin* (1883) 15 Cox CC 163, Field J doubted *Fenton* finding it abhorrent to construct a crime from a civil wrong. The doubts have since been resolved. In *Andrews* v *DPP* [1937] AC 576, Lord Atkin confirmed that **something more than negligence (which suffices for civil liability) is required.** In this case the accused had been driving dangerously when he killed the deceased. Driving is a lawful act which becomes unlawful when performed negligently. Lord Atkin sought to distinguish between acts which become unlawful when performed negligently and acts which are unlawful for some other reason stating (at p. 585):

> There is an obvious difference in the law of manslaughter between doing an unlawful act and doing a lawful act with a degree of carelessness which the legislature makes criminal. If it were otherwise a man who killed another while driving without due care and attention would *ex necessitate* commit manslaughter.

An act can only be unlawful in these terms, therefore, if it is done with *mens rea* (see *Lamb* [1967] 2 QB 981). In *Lamb*, D, in fun, pointed a revolver at a friend. He knew that there were two bullets in the chambers, but neither was opposite the barrel. He did not appreciate that the cylinder rotated automatically when the trigger was pulled. He pulled the trigger, a bullet was fired and his friend died. D was convicted of manslaughter following a direction from the judge that pointing the revolver and pulling the trigger was an unlawful act even if there was no intent to injure or alarm and that they need not consider whether the pointing of the gun was an assault. (For the definition of assault see **10.1.1** *post*.) The Court of Appeal quashed the conviction; if there was no assault there was no unlawful act. Sachs J stated (at p. 988):

> *mens rea*, being now an essential ingredient in manslaughter…that could not in the present case be established in relation to the first ground except by proving that element of intent without which there can be no assault.

There was also no *actus reus* of assault in this case as the friend, being a willing participant in the prank, did not apprehend any injury; the *actus reus* of assault is causing the victim to apprehend immediate application of unlawful force to his body.

In *Andrews* [2002] EWCA Crim 3021, the Court of Appeal appears to have ignored this requirement for the basic offence to be one requiring *mens rea* in confirming a conviction where D had injected V with insulin, with V's consent, resulting in V's death. The drug was administered in order to give V a 'rush'. The appeal focused on the issue of consent, the Court of Appeal affirming that consent made no difference to the unlawfulness of D's act. This is consistent with the authorities on consent (see **10.1.1.3.1** *post*). The unlawful act in the immediate case was alleged to have been supplying a prescription-only medicine without a prescription contrary to ss. 58 and 67 of the Medicines Act 1968. This is a strict liability offence. It is doubtful whether the Court intended any modification of the principle in *Andrews v DPP* as there was no argument on this point and thus no express statement to that effect. If similar facts arise any such difficulty may be avoided by charging on the basis that the unlawful act was administering a noxious thing contrary to s. 23 of the Offences Against the Person Act 1861 (see **10.1.4** *post*).

A problem decision in this area was that of *Cato* [1976] 1 WLR 110, where the Court of Appeal appeared to extend the ambit of unlawful acts. D injected V with heroin which V had supplied to D for this purpose. V died from respiratory failure caused by the heroin. D was convicted of manslaughter and of administering a noxious thing so as to endanger life contrary to s. 23 of the Offences Against the Person Act 1861. In upholding the manslaughter conviction, the Court of Appeal stated that, even if they had not upheld the conviction for the s. 23 offence (which they did), they would still have upheld the manslaughter conviction on the basis that by injecting the deceased with heroin which D had unlawfully taken into his possession, he had done an unlawful act. This appears to be wrong as injecting heroin is not an offence contrary to the Misuse of Drugs Act 1971. Possession of heroin is an offence but V did not die as a result of D's possession of the drug. However, the Court of Appeal elaborated further on the error in *Cato* in *Kennedy* [1999] Crim LR 65, where D supplied a syringe filled with heroin to V who injected it and died. In upholding D's conviction for manslaughter the Court of Appeal did so on the basis either that D was guilty of the s. 23 offence or that the self-injection by V was unlawful and D had assisted and wilfully encouraged this. As to the latter point, D could not be a secondary party to manslaughter, as V's self-injection could not amount to an unlawful act. This position was subsequently adopted by the Court of Appeal in *Dias* [2001] EWCA Crim 2986 (see **2.6.3.5.4** *ante*) which doubted whether *Kennedy* could have been decided correctly on this point as it conflicted with *Dalby* [1982] 1 All ER 916 (see **9.3.3.1.2** *post*). The Court of Appeal concluded that there was no offence of self-injection and thus V was not a principal, with the consequence that D could not be a secondary party. When the Criminal Cases Review Commission referred the case of *Kennedy* back to the Court of Appeal on the basis that there was a real possibility that the Court of Appeal would find the conviction unsafe in light of the doubts expressed in *Dias*, the Court of Appeal upheld the conviction on the basis that D had acted in concert with V to commit the s. 23 offence which amounted to the unlawful act (*Kennedy* [2005] EWCA Crim 685). The Court eschewed any notion that the question of an intervening act on the part of V arose on the basis that D's supply of the heroin-filled syringe to V for immediate use amounted to their acting in concert to commit the s. 23 offence. Somehow 'acting in concert' means something different to a joint enterprise involving a principal and secondary party. While D's act of supplying the heroin-filled syringe could not satisfy the requirement of dangerousness (nor the requirement of causation) as the syringe harboured no risk in itself (it was only when a further act was performed to the syringe, that of injection, that harm could ensue), the Court of Appeal ignored this issue satisfying itself that the whole enterprise of acting in concert to administer a noxious thing is dangerous. This was not the last word on the issue, however, as the case went to the House of Lords on the following question of general public importance:

> When is it appropriate to find someone guilty of manslaughter where that person has been involved in the supply of a class A controlled drug, which is then freely and voluntarily self-administered by the person to whom it was supplied, and the administration of the drug then causes his death?

In *Kennedy (No. 2)* [2007] UKHL 38, their Lordships answered the question in one word, 'Never'. They confirmed that the unlawful act on which a conviction of constructive manslaughter is based must itself be a crime and that act must be a significant cause of death. Their Lordships recognised that it is the injection which harbours the danger; it is performed by V as a free, deliberate, and informed act; it is not unlawful for V to do so; and D is not liable as an accessory as V is not the principal; and D's prior acts must be nothing more than 'but for' causes (see further **2.6.3.5.4** *ante*). Their Lordships further indicated that many difficulties would be avoided if the prosecutor clearly specified on the indictment where constructive manslaughter is charged, the unlawful act on which the count is based.

Of course, **there will be no unlawful act if the accused had a lawful excuse or justification for doing what he did**. For example, if D punches V in self-defence, using no more force than he believes to be reasonable in the circumstances, but V stumbles and falls on a stone fracturing his skull and dies, D will not be liable for manslaughter as there is no unlawful act (see *Scarlett* at **6.5.3.1** *ante*). Similarly if a parent uses only moderate and reasonable force to chastise his child and the child unexpectedly dies, the parent will not be guilty of manslaughter as the force used was lawful. In either case if the force used was excessive and the accused knew it to be so there would be no justification and the force would be unlawful providing a foundation for a manslaughter verdict.

Where D has committed an unlawful act of basic intent, the fact that he was intoxicated and lacked *mens rea*, will not avail him. In *Lipman* [1970] 1 QB 152, the Court of Appeal upheld D's conviction of manslaughter although the offence had been committed when he was on an hallucinatory trip due to taking LSD. The unlawful act he performed was a battery which was an offence of basic intent. If the unlawful act alleged is an offence of specific intent, D may rely on his intoxication as evidence that he lacked *mens rea* (*O'Driscoll* (1977) 65 Cr App R 50), but it is difficult to envisage an offence of specific intent which does not necessarily encompass a lesser offence of basic intent.

It should be noted that **constructive manslaughter requires the commission of an unlawful 'act'**. It appears that **an omission will not suffice** (but an omission will suffice for gross negligence manslaughter where there is a duty to act; see **2.5** *ante*). In *Lowe* [1973] QB 702, the Court of Appeal quashed D's conviction of manslaughter founded on the offence of wilful neglect of the child so as to cause unnecessary suffering or injury to its health contrary to s. 1(1) of the Children and Young Persons Act 1933. The trial judge had directed the jury that there was no difference between an omission likely to cause harm and an act likely to cause harm. The Court of Appeal, disapproving of *Senior* [1899] 1 QB 283 where, on similar facts, a conviction of manslaughter had been upheld, distinguished between acts and omissions, Phillimore LJ stating (at p. 707):

> [I]f I strike a child in a manner likely to cause harm it is right that if the child dies I may be charged with manslaughter. If, however, I omit to do something with the result that it suffers injury to its health which results in its death, we think that a charge of manslaughter should not be an inevitable consequence even if the omission is deliberate.

Obviously, if the omission was merely negligent, no liability for manslaughter should arise. But there is a great difference between neglect which is due to a lack of thought and that which is wilful, in the sense that there is a deliberate decision not to give food or liquids or to seek medical attention. Such conduct is just as reprehensible as positive acts which are likely to cause harm. *Lowe* is a decision which clearly requires reconsideration.

Whether the accused has done an unlawful act is a question for the jury to decide; even if all the evidence points to there being an unlawful act, the judge may not decide this issue himself but must leave it to the jury to determine (see *Jennings* [1990] Crim LR 588). If there is no unlawful act, an accused may still be convicted of manslaughter if the judge also directs the jury on gross negligence manslaughter and the requirements of this offence are satisfied (see **9.3.3.2** *post*).

9.3.3.1.2 *The unlawful act must be dangerous*

While it must be established that the accused had the *mens rea* for the offence which constitutes the unlawful act, this is not sufficient to lead to a conviction of manslaughter. An objective condition must also be satisfied, that is that the act was dangerous. In *Church* [1966] 1 QB 59, Edmund-Davies LJ explained that '**dangerous' meant that the unlawful act 'must be such as all sober and reasonable people would inevitably recognise must subject the other person to, at least, the risk of some harm resulting therefrom, albeit not serious harm'.** The degree of harm likely to be caused need not be serious, but it must be physical harm rather than a risk of emotional disturbance (*Dawson* (1985) 81 Cr App R 150). However, shock produced by fright may fall within the definition of harm where it produces some physical injury, such as a heart attack.

Several issues relating to the 'dangerousness' test require clarification. First, must the defendant have any awareness of the danger arising from his unlawful act? Secondly, must the actual form of harm which ensued have been foreseeable by the sober and reasonable person? Thirdly, must that danger or risk of harm be perceived in respect of the actual victim (to put this another way, would a perceived risk of harm to someone else be sufficient to satisfy this objective criterion)? Fourthly, and linked to the third question, must the act of the defendant be directed at the victim? Over the years these and a number of other issues have received clarification.

> In *DPP* v *Newbury* [1977] AC 500, two boys pushed a paving stone off the parapet of a railway bridge into the path of an oncoming train, hitting the train and killing the guard who was sitting next to the driver. The question for the House of Lords was whether a defendant could be convicted of manslaughter if he did not foresee that his act might cause harm to another. Their Lordships answered the question in the affirmative. Lord Salmon stated (at p. 506):

>> In Larkin (1942) 29 Cr App R 18, Humphreys J said, at p. 23:
>> Where the act which a person is engaged in performing is unlawful, then if at the same time it is a dangerous act, that is, an act which is likely to injure another person, and quite inadvertently the doer of the act causes the death of that other person by that act, then he is guilty of manslaughter.
>> I agree entirely…that that is an admirably clear statement of the law which has been applied many times. It makes it plain (a) that an accused is guilty of manslaughter if it is proved that he intentionally did an act which was unlawful and dangerous and that that act inadvertently caused death and (b) that it is unnecessary to prove that the accused knew that the act was unlawful or dangerous.

In *JM and SM* [2012] EWCA Crim 2293 the Court of Appeal dealt with the second question.

> JM and SM were ejected from a nightclub by the doormen. They returned and began to assault the doormen. In the course of this affray Mr Jopling, an experienced and apparently healthy doorman, went to the assistance of his colleagues. Shortly after the affray had been subdued, Mr Jopling collapsed and died. A post-mortem established that Mr Jopling had been suffering from a renal artery aneurysm; he died from blood loss arising from a rupture to the renal artery. This was highly unlikely to have occurred spontaneously but would have been consequent on shock and a sudden surge in blood pressure due to the release of adrenalin into the circulation during the attack by the defendants and the rupture occurred either while the affray was in progress or in its immediate aftermath. The trial judge ruled that, on this evidence, it would not be open to the jury to convict of manslaughter as they could not be sure that a sober and reasonable person would inevitably recognise the risk that the deceased would die in the way he did as this was a completely different form of harm from the harm recognisable in an affray, such as the danger of being hit or suffering injuries in a fall in the course of dealing with the defendants. On appeal by the prosecution, the Court of Appeal overturned that ruling concluding that there was evidence from which a jury properly directed could conclude that sober and reasonable people observing

the affray 'would readily have recognised that all the doormen involved in the effort to control the defendants were at the risk of some harm, and that the fatal injury occurred while it was in progress or in its immediate aftermath while Mr Jopling was still subject to its effects.' Lord Judge CJ explained (at para. 20):

> In our judgment, certainly since *Church* and *Newbury*, it has never been a requirement that the defendant personally should foresee any specific harm at all, or that the reasonable bystander should recognise the precise form or 'sort' of harm which did ensue. What matters is whether reasonable and sober people would recognise that the unlawful activities of the defendant inevitably subjected the deceased to the risk of some harm resulting from them.

The answers to the third and fourth questions stated earlier were provided in *A-G's Reference (No. 3 of 1994)* [1997] 3 WLR 421. The problem raised in the fourth question derives from some dicta in the case of *Dalby* [1982] 1 All ER 916 (cf. *Kennedy* [1999] Crim LR 65, **2.6.3.5.4** and **9.3.3.1.1** *ante*). D unlawfully supplied a drug to V which V took intravenously and he later died. On appeal against conviction for manslaughter D argued that the supply of the drug was not an act 'directed at the victim' and as V administered the drug to himself in too great a quantity this broke the chain of causation between the unlawful act of supply and the death. The Court of Appeal quashed the conviction stating that supplying the drug was not an act which caused direct harm. All the previous cases involved unlawful acts which 'inevitably would subject the other person to the risk of some harm from the act itself' whereas, in the present case, 'the supply of the drugs would itself have caused no harm unless the deceased had subsequently used the drugs in a form and quantity which was dangerous'. Thus the Court held that the supply of the drug was not an act directed against the victim and the supply did not cause any direct injury to him. Waller LJ concluded (at p. 919), 'In the judgment of this court, where the charge of manslaughter is based on an unlawful and dangerous act, it must be an act directed at the victim and likely to cause immediate injury however slight'. **What the Court appeared to be stating was that the unlawful act was not a cause of death and, incidentally (as this issue did not require decision if causation could not be proved), the act was not dangerous** (see *Kennedy (No. 2)* [2007] UKHL 38 *ante*). Unfortunately, in some subsequent cases, the concluding comment of Waller LJ was taken out of context and taken to require that an 'unlawful act', if it was to support a conviction of manslaughter, had to be directed against the victim, rather than meaning that the harm had to flow causally directly from the act.

In *Goodfellow* (1986) 83 Cr App R 23, D was convicted of manslaughter having set fire to the council house in which he lived as he wished to be rehoused. D rescued two of his children but his wife, another child, and another woman died as the fire spread more quickly than he had anticipated. On appeal it was contended that D's unlawful act was not an act directed at the victims. The Court of Appeal dismissed the appeal holding that the decision in *Dalby* only intended to stipulate that 'there must be no fresh intervening cause between the act and the death'. D's act may not have been directed at the victims but it was a direct cause of their deaths and it was, objectively, dangerous.

That the decision in *Goodfellow* is correct is confirmed by the decision in *A-G's Reference (No. 3 of 1994)* where Lord Hope of Craighead effectively answered the third and fourth questions stated earlier in the negative although he did not overrule *Dalby* but simply distinguished it. **It is enough that the unlawful act creates a risk of harm to someone and there is no need for the unlawful act to be directed at the person who ultimately dies as a result of it.** Lord Hope cited with approval the decision in *Mitchell* [1983] QB 741 where D hit E who was standing in a queue in a post office. E fell against V, an elderly lady, who fell breaking her leg and died thereafter as a result of a pulmonary embolism linked to her fall. The Court of Appeal affirmed D's conviction of manslaughter. Lord Hope also cited with approval *Larkin* and *Newbury* before concluding that D should have been convicted of manslaughter in the instant case where he had stabbed M, a pregnant woman which resulted in the premature birth of her child who in turn died some time later due to problems linked to her premature birth. Lord Hope was satisfied that the stabbing of the mother was an unlawful and dangerous act. Lord Hope stated (at p. 446):

> There can be no doubt that all sober and reasonable people would regard that act, within the appropriate meaning of this term, as dangerous. It is plain that it was unlawful as it was done with the intention of causing her injury. As B intended to commit that act, all the ingredients necessary for *mens rea* in regard to the crime of manslaughter were established, irrespective of who was the ultimate victim of it. The fact that the child whom the mother was carrying at the time was born alive and then died as a result of the stabbing is all that was needed for the offence of manslaughter when *actus reus* for that crime was completed by the child's death. The question, once all the other elements are satisfied, is simply one of causation. The defendant must accept all the consequences of his act, so long as the jury are satisfied that he did what he did intentionally, that what he did was unlawful and that, applying the correct test, it was also dangerous....In my opinion that is sufficient for the offence of manslaughter.

9.3.3.1.3 *What information is credited to the sober and reasonable person for the purpose of determining whether the unlawful act was dangerous?*
In deciding whether the act was such as all sober and reasonable people would recognise involved the risk of harm, **the sober and reasonable person is credited with the same knowledge as the accused had at the time of the offence.** In *Dawson* Watkins LJ stated (at p. 157) that the objective test 'can only be undertaken upon the basis of the knowledge gained by the sober and reasonable man as though he were present at the scene of and watched the unlawful act being performed'. It is the responsibility of the judge to inform the jury which facts are relevant for this purpose (*Dawson*). In *Dawson*, D and E robbed V's filling station wearing masks and armed with a pickaxe handle and replica gun. Shortly afterwards V died of a heart attack. It was not known to the accused, nor would it have been apparent, that V suffered from heart disease. The convictions of manslaughter were quashed for several reasons, one being that the trial judge had not made it clear that the jury could not take into account the fact that V suffered from heart disease when deciding if the unlawful act was dangerous. However, **the jury may take into account facts of which the accused became aware during the course**

of committing the unlawful act (*Watson* [1989] 2 All ER 865). In this case D and E threw a brick through the window of V's house and entered it. They confronted V, who was 87, frail, and suffering from a serious heart condition. After abusing V verbally they left and V died 90 minutes later from a heart attack. Although quashing the convictions of manslaughter on another ground, the Court of Appeal held that the sober and reasonable person could be credited with knowledge of the facts of which the appellants became aware after entering the house, namely, the victim's age and frailty. While the offence of burglary was complete upon crossing the threshold, the Court held that the unlawful act comprised the whole of the burglarious intrusion.

The sober and reasonable man will also be aware of the background to the unlawful act which includes preparatory acts done by the accused as this sets the act in context for the purpose of determining its objective dangerousness. In *Ball* [1989] Crim LR 730:

> D loaded a shotgun with two cartridges taken from his pocket which contained live and blank cartridges. He fired the gun at V claiming he only intended to frighten her. The cartridge in the chamber was a live one and V died. On appeal against his conviction of manslaughter it was argued that the objective assessment of the danger of D's act should be based on his mistaken belief that he was firing a blank cartridge and not on the actual fact that he was firing a live cartridge. The Court of Appeal rejected this submission, Lord Lane CJ stating:

> > [Once it is] established...that the act was both unlawful and that he intended to commit the assaults, the question whether the act is a dangerous one is to be judged not by the appellant's appreciation but by that of the sober and reasonable man, and it is impossible to impute into his appreciation the mistaken belief of the appellant that what he was doing was not dangerous because he thought he had a blank cartridge in the chamber. At that stage the appellant's intention, foresight or knowledge is irrelevant.

9.3.3.2 Gross negligence manslaughter

The second basis on which a person may be convicted of involuntary manslaughter is that of gross negligence. **This head of liability will be relied on where the act of the accused is not otherwise unlawful or where death results from the accused's omission to act** (for examples of such duties see **2.5.2.2** *ante*). Gross negligence was recognised as the test for manslaughter in *Bateman* (1925) 19 Cr App R 8 and approved by the House of Lords in *Andrews v DPP* [1937] AC 576. In *Bateman* Lord Hewart CJ held that in order to secure a conviction of A for manslaughter the prosecution had to prove that (at p. 11):

> A owed a duty to B to take care, that that duty was not discharged,...that the default caused the death of B...and that A's negligence amounted to a crime... [I]n order to establish criminal liability the facts must be such that, in the opinion of the jury, the negligence of the accused went beyond a mere matter of compensation between subjects and showed such disregard for the life and safety of others as to amount to a crime against the state and conduct deserving of punishment.

This test required there to be a duty of care owed by D to the victim, breach of which caused the victim's death (see **2.6** *ante*) and left it to the jury to determine whether the negligence of the accused was so gross that it demanded punishment as a crime rather than merely the imposition of civil liability and the payment of compensation. It is a very high degree of negligence which has to be established before criminal liability should ensue. This was confirmed by Lord Atkin in *Andrews* where he stated (at p. 583):

> [F]or the purposes of the criminal law there are degrees of negligence: and a very high degree of negligence is required to be proved before the felony is established. Probably of all the epithets that can be applied 'reckless' most nearly covers the case...but it is probably not all-embracing, for 'reckless' suggests an indifference to risk whereas the accused may have appreciated the risk and intended to avoid it and yet shown such a high degree of negligence in the means adopted to avoid the risk as would justify a conviction.

For many years the courts have used the terms 'recklessness' and 'gross negligence' interchangeably so that it was not clear whether these two concepts were exactly co-extensive. Following the House of Lords' decisions in *Caldwell* and *Lawrence* there was a shift in favour of recklessness. In *Seymour* [1983] 2 AC 493, a case of manslaughter arising from the reckless driving of a vehicle, the House of Lords declared that the test for manslaughter was the same as for the statutory offence of causing death by reckless driving contrary to s. 1(1) of the Road Traffic Act 1972. Thus a person would be guilty of manslaughter where he did an act (in the instant case drove a vehicle) which created an obvious and serious risk of causing physical injury to another person and either he was conscious of the risk or he gave no thought to it. Their Lordships declared that it would no longer be appropriate to refer to negligence. (The offence of reckless driving was replaced by that of dangerous driving: see the Road Traffic Act 1991, s. 1.)

In *Adomako* [1995] 1 AC 171 their Lordships reverted to the test of gross negligence as the correct basis upon which to establish liability for manslaughter. In this case the appellant, an anaesthetist, failed to notice for six minutes during an operation that the oxygen supply to the patient had become disconnected from the ventilator. As a result the patient suffered a cardiac arrest and died. The House of Lords affirmed the appellant's conviction. Lord Mackay of Clashfern LC stated (at p. 187) that 'the law as stated in...*Seymour*...should no longer apply since the underlying statutory provisions on which it rested have now been repealed by the Road Traffic Act 1991'. **His Lordship affirmed the continuing authority of *Andrews* which focused on breach of duty.** He stated (at p. 187):

> The jury will have to consider whether the extent to which the defendant's conduct departed from the proper standard of care incumbent upon him, involving as it must have done a risk of death to the patient, was such that it should be judged criminal....The essence of the matter...is whether having regard to the risk of death involved, the conduct of the defendant was so bad in all the circumstances as to amount in their judgment to a criminal act or omission.

Key Point

Following *Adomako*, therefore, the elements of the offence could be specified as follows:

- D owed V a duty of care;
- D breached that duty;
- the breach caused V's death; and
- the breach was grossly negligent.

9.3.3.2.1 *Duty of care*

Gross negligence manslaughter is the criminal offspring of the civil law of negligence. Duty of care has its ordinary civil law meaning—a person owes a duty of care to another where it is reasonably foreseeable that their acts or omissions will cause harm to another. In *Singh (Gurphal)* [1999] Crim LR 582 the Court of Appeal held that whether D owed a duty of care was a question of law for the judge to determine. This has been confirmed in subsequent decisions; see *Wacker* [2002] EWCA Crim 1944; *Evans* [2009] EWCA Crim 650. If the facts are in dispute (which will often be the case), it will be for the jury to determine whether, in light of the judge's directions on the law, a duty did exist (see *Willoughby* [2004] EWCA Crim 3365). For example, in the normal doctor/patient situation as pertained in *Adomako* there will not be any dispute over whether or not a duty of care existed; but if, for example, the doctor is on holiday and is asked by V, another holiday-maker, casually over a drink for advice, there could be serious dispute over whether any doctor/patient relationship existed and thus whether any duty of care arose if this turned out to be poor advice and V, acting upon it, died as a result.

The situations in which duties of care may arise are fairly limitless. The courts will apply the ordinary principles of negligence but necessarily, it may not be entirely clear in advance of a trial what situations are covered by these principles. Further complications arise where omissions are involved as, in addition to the duty of care, there must be a duty to act. In *Evans (Gemma)* [2009] EWCA Crim 650 (see **2.6.3.5.4** *ante*) D found herself convicted of manslaughter, along with her mother, T, where she had supplied heroin to her younger step-sister, C, who had taken it and overdosed. D and T kept her under observation overnight but did not seek medical assistance fearing that both they and C would get into trouble (C had recently been released under licence from a period of detention and was subject to recall). There was no question over the liability of T as her duty of care arose from her parental responsibility for her child (see **2.5.2.2.2** *ante*) but D owed no such duty arising out of relationship. The Court of Appeal, however, upheld her conviction on the basis that she was under a duty to take reasonable steps for the safety of C once she realised that the heroin she had supplied her was having a potentially fatal impact on her health. Lord Judge CJ relied on the case of *Miller* [1983] 2 AC 161 HL (see **2.5.2.2.4** *ante*) as a basis for the duty to act in the present case which he defined as follows (at para. 31):

> when a person has created or contributed to the creation of a state of affairs which he knows, or ought reasonably to know, has become life threatening, a consequent duty on him to act by taking reasonable steps to save the other's life will normally arise.

The duty of care derived from the normal principles of negligence, Lord Judge CJ relying upon their most recent exposition by Lord Scott of Foscote in *Mitchell* v *Glasgow City Council* [2009] 2 WLR 481, at para. 40, where he said:

> If a defendant has played some causative part in the train of events that have led to the risk of injury, a duty to take reasonable steps to avert or lessen the risk may arise.

In D's case, she had played a causative part in the train of events by supplying the heroin; but for this, V could not have self-administered and overdosed. Accordingly, this gave rise to the duty of care and her duty to act arose upon becoming aware of V's condition. Her failure to take reasonable steps to save V, such as summoning medical assistance, provided the basis upon which the jury could conclude that she had been grossly negligent.

While the civil law of negligence will provide guidance on the recognition of a duty of care, the wider principles of the civil law of negligence are not to be imported into the criminal law. In *Wacker* [2002] EWCA Crim 1944, the defendant sought to place reliance on the principle *ex turpi causa non oritur actio* to argue that as he had been involved in a criminal enterprise with those who died, there was no duty of care in negligence and thus there could not be any liability for gross negligence manslaughter. In a civil action for negligence *ex turpi causa* would provide a defence to a claim. The issue for the Court of Appeal was whether this principle applied in respect of criminal proceedings. In the instant case the defendant drove his refrigerated lorry, loaded with 60 illegal Chinese immigrants hidden behind a cargo of tomatoes, on to a channel ferry which disembarked at Dover. Customs and Excise officers, doing a spot check on his vehicle, discovered the immigrants, 58 of whom had died of suffocation on the crossing due to an air vent having been sealed by the defendant to reduce the risk of discovery. The Court of Appeal rejected the argument based on *ex turpi causa* on the basis that the civil law and criminal law served different functions. The criminal law's function was to protect individuals and might step in at the very point where the civil law is powerless to assist. Furthermore, the criminal law will act to prevent serious injury or death even where those subject to the risk of such had consented to it (see *Brown* **10.1.1.3.1** *post*). On this basis there was no justification in public policy for concluding that the criminal law would not apply where the person responsible for the death and the deceased were involved in some joint criminal venture which involved an element of acceptance of a degree of risk in order to further that venture (see further *Willoughby* [2004] EWCA Crim 3365). It was clear that a claim that keeping the vent shut increased the chances of evading detection was an argument which the Court, unsurprisingly, found singularly unattractive.

9.3.3.2.2 *Grossly negligent breach of duty*

It is important to recognise in relation to this variety of manslaughter that the central focus is not on the accused's state of mind but rather on his conduct which fails, to a gross degree, to measure up to an objective standard determined by the jury. The courts will not attempt to specify the degree of negligence required with any greater precision, as they recognise it is not possible to do so. **The reach of the criminal law, therefore, in this area of homicide is left to be determined by the jury who have to assess whether the negligence was gross.** The problem that results is that the law is unpredictable, because of the infinite variety of circumstances that may arise, and its application will necessarily be inconsistent. If the arbiter of fact was the same each time, the problem would not appear to be so grave, as one could hope for consistent application of the test in different cases. Not only will cases differ, however, but the arbiter of fact, the jury, will be different for each case. If precision in the definition of the offence is not possible, should the offence exist at all? It is worth noting that had the patient in *Adomako* survived but only in a persistent vegetative state due to brain damage arising from the lack of oxygen, the appellant would not have been guilty of a criminal offence in the absence of proof of *mens rea*, i.e. intention or recklessness; negligence of whatever degree would not suffice to found liability for a non-fatal offence against the person. In either case the appellant is equally culpable. Why should the chance occurrence of death, something outside his control, result in liability for one of the most serious offences in the criminal calendar, whereas survival of the patient in a condition which many would characterise as a 'living death' results in no criminal liability if *mens rea* cannot be proved?

Negligence presumes that a reasonable person would have foreseen the risk of a particular consequence occurring as a result of the conduct in question. For gross negligence manslaughter, what is the risk which D should have foreseen? In *Adomako* Lord Mackay referred to 'the risk of death involved'. In *Bateman* the negligence had to display 'a disregard for life and safety' before it could lead to liability. In *Singh (Gurphal)* [1999] Crim LR 582 the Court of Appeal held that on a charge of gross negligence manslaughter 'the circumstances must be such that a reasonably prudent person would have foreseen a serious and obvious risk not merely of injury or even serious injury but of death'.

While it is not possible to determine what factors influence a jury in concluding that the defendant's negligence was so serious as to merit the description 'gross' and be deserving of criminal sanction, some insight into the factors considered by the Crown Prosecution Service in deciding whether to charge a defendant with manslaughter may be gleaned from *R (On the application of Rowley) v DPP* [2003] EWHC 693 (Admin). The claimant sought judicial review of the decision by the CPS not to prosecute Salford City Council or its employees for manslaughter following the death of the claimant's handicapped son who had drowned when carers had left him alone for a few minutes in his bath. One factor which influenced the CPS was the absence of any evidence to suggest subjective recklessness on the part of the possible defendants. The Court considered this to be a valid approach, Kennedy LJ stating (at paras. 33–34):

> The issue raised in the present case...is whether the state of mind of the defendant is a factor which the jury may take into account in the defendant's favour when considering whether his conduct is so bad as to amount to a criminal offence. Mr Hunt [counsel for the claimant] submitted that subjective recklessness may help to establish a prosecution case, but that otherwise the state of mind of the proposed defendant is irrelevant.
>
> That seems to us to be an unrealistic approach which the authorities do not require, which no judge would enforce, and which no jury would adopt. Once it can be shown that there was ordinary common law negligence causative of death and a serious risk of death, what remains to be established is criminality or badness. In considering whether there is criminality or badness, Lord Mackay [in *Adomako*] makes it clear that all the circumstances are to be taken into account.

The Court of Appeal in *Misra; Srivastava* [2004] EWCA Crim 2375, while holding that the offence of gross negligence manslaughter did not offend the requirement of legal certainty under Art. 7 of the European Convention on Human Rights, confirmed, however, that **only a risk of death will be sufficient to establish the offence; a risk of bodily injury or injury to health was not sufficient.** On the issue of the circularity of the test, Judge LJ stated (at para. 62):

> The decision whether the conduct was criminal is described [in *Adomako*] not as 'the' test, but as 'a' test as to how far the conduct in question must depart from accepted standards to be 'characterised as criminal'. On proper analysis, therefore, the jury is not deciding whether the particular defendant ought to be convicted on some unprincipled basis. The question for the jury is not whether the defendant's negligence was gross, and whether, additionally, it was a crime, but whether his behaviour was grossly negligent and consequently criminal. This is not a question of law, but one of fact, for decision in the individual case.

One cannot help feeling that this explanation verges on sophistry and fails adequately to address the issues of unpredictability and inconsistency.

9.3.4 Reform

In its report, *Legislating the Criminal Code: Involuntary Manslaughter* (Law Com No. 237, 1996) the Law Commission identified two major problems relating to the wide range of conduct covered by involuntary manslaughter (at para. 3.1):

> [First] the offence encompasses, first, cases involving conduct that falls only just short of murder, where the accused was *aware* of a risk of causing death or serious injury, although he did not *intend* to cause either; second, cases where the accused is a professional person who makes a very serious mistake that results in death; and third, cases where a relatively minor assault ends in death. [Secondly] this leads to problems in sentencing and labelling, including the fundamental problem that many cases currently amounting to unlawful act manslaughter involve only minor fault on the part of the perpetrator, and therefore ought not, perhaps, to be described as manslaughter at all.

The Law Commission specifically highlighted the uncertainty in the current law arising from the terminology used in gross negligence manslaughter, the circular nature of the test the jury is required to apply, and the lack of any clear definition of the extent of liability for omissions. On unlawful act manslaughter it stated (at para. 3.6):

> [W]e consider that it is wrong in principle for the law to hold a person responsible for causing a result that he did not intend or foresee, and which would not even have been *foreseeable* by a reasonable person observing his conduct. Unlawful act manslaughter is therefore, we believe, unprincipled because it requires only that a foreseeable risk of causing *some* harm should have been inherent in the accused's conduct, whereas he is convicted of actually causing death, and also to some extent punished for doing so.

The Law Commission in its work has traditionally adopted a subjectivist approach, seeking to impose criminal liability on the basis of three principles (para. 4.5):

> The first of these is the 'mens rea principle', which imposes liability only for outcomes which were *intended* or *knowingly risked* by the alleged wrongdoer. The second principle, the 'belief principle', judges a defendant according only to what *she* believed she was doing or risking. Thirdly, according to the 'principle of correspondence', subjectivists insist that the fault element of a crime *correspond* to the conduct element; for example, if the conduct element is 'causing serious injury', the fault element ought to be 'intention or recklessness as to causing serious injury'. This ensures that the defendant is punished only for causing a harm which she *chose* to risk or to bring about.

On this basis the Law Commission recommended the creation of an offence of recklessly causing death for which the maximum penalty should be life imprisonment. Clause 1(1) of the Draft Involuntary Homicide Bill (appended to the report) defined this offence as follows:

> A person who by his conduct causes the death of another is guilty of reckless killing if—
>
> (a) he is aware of a risk that his conduct will cause death or serious injury; and
>
> (b) it is unreasonable for him to take that risk having regard to the circumstances as he knows or believes them to be.

This definition did not strictly comply with the 'correspondence principle' but the Law Commission explained this away on the basis that only a thin line divides behaviour that risks serious injury from that which risks death and it is frequently a matter of chance whether serious injury leads to death. This is consistent with the position regarding the *mens rea* of murder (see **9.2.1** *ante*).

In their 1996 Report the Law Commission also recognised that there may be circumstances in which liability based on *inadvertence* may be justified. Such liability should arise where the actor's inadvertence is *culpable*. The Law Commission took the view that culpability depends on two factors: first that the harm to which the actor failed to advert is obviously foreseeable; and secondly, that the actor would have been capable of perceiving the risk had she directed her mind to it. If the accused is an ordinary person she will be measured against the standard of what would have been reasonably foreseeable by the ordinary person in her situation. But if the accused is holding herself out as an expert, for example a doctor, the standard will be set higher, namely what would have been obvious to the average doctor in her position (see para. 4.18). In addition, the actor should only be held liable for a death which flows from inadvertent conduct where the conduct inherently involved a risk of death or serious injury. On this basis the Law Commission recommended the abolition of unlawful act manslaughter and the replacement of gross negligence manslaughter with a new offence of killing by gross carelessness.

In May 2000 the Home Office published a Consultation Paper, *Reforming the Law on Involuntary Manslaughter: The Government's Proposals* based on the Law Commission Report No. 237 which the Government largely accepted. The Home Office endorsed the Law Commission's recommendations of an offence of reckless killing, the abolition of unlawful act manslaughter and its replacement by an offence of killing by gross carelessness but also sought views on whether an additional homicide offence should be created to cover the situation where a death which was unforeseeable occurs and the following requirements apply (para. 2.11):

- a person by his or her conduct causes the death of another;
- he or she intended to [cause some injury] or was reckless as to whether some injury was caused; and
- the conduct causing, or intended to cause, the injury constitutes an offence.

This offence would be slightly narrower than unlawful act manslaughter as at least subjective recklessness as to the risk of some injury is required but liability would still be derived from the consequence of death ensuing. A case such as *Mitchell* [1983] QB 741 (**9.3.3.1.2** *ante*) could still arise. The Home Office provided no justification for basing liability on an accidental outcome rather than intention or foresight.

In its Consultation Paper No. 177, *A New Homicide Act for England and Wales?* published in 2005, the Law Commission revisited its proposals for manslaughter and modified them in light of its recommendation for the creation of two degrees of murder (see **9.2.2** *ante*). In their final Report *Murder, Manslaughter and Infanticide* (Law Com No. 304) the Law Commission recommends an offence of manslaughter that could be committed in three ways;

(1) killing another person through gross negligence ('gross negligence manslaughter'); or

(2) killing another person:

   (a) through the commission of a criminal act intended by the defendant to cause injury, or

   (b) through the commission of a criminal act that the defendant was aware involved a serious risk of causing some injury ('criminal act manslaughter').

The recommendation for gross negligence simply reflects the current position. The recommendation regarding criminal act manslaughter is almost identical to the proposal put forward by the Government for replacing 'unlawful and dangerous act' manslaughter in its Consultation Paper of 2000. In their Consultation Paper, No. 177, the Law Commission recommended that the offence of reckless killing, with some modification, be incorporated into the provisional recommendation for 'second degree murder'. In their final Report, *Murder, Manslaughter and Infanticide* (Law Com No. 304) the Law Commission confirm this recommendation expressing the view that any separate offence of reckless manslaughter to cover foresight of a lesser degree of harm than that required for second degree murder would be very narrow, overlapping with gross negligence manslaughter and would make the law unduly complicated (see **9.2.2** *ante*). With regard to gross negligence manslaughter, the Law Commission recommend that the prosecution be required to prove that there was gross negligence as to the risk of causing death, not merely as to causing serious injury. Consequently their recommendations on gross negligence manslaughter are a restatement of the current law. The Law Commission indicate that this reflects the views of the vast majority of consultees. They give their reasons for this recommendation as being (para. 3.59):

> Gross negligence manslaughter can be committed even when D was unaware that his or her conduct might cause death, or even injury. This is because negligence, however gross, does not necessarily involve any actual realisation that one is posing a risk of harm: it is a question of how glaringly obvious the risk would have been to a reasonable person. If liability for an offence as serious as manslaughter is to be justified in the absence of an awareness that one is posing a risk, D's negligence must relate to the risk of bringing about the very harm he or she has caused: the risk of causing death. Otherwise, the crime of manslaughter becomes unduly wide and a misleading label for what the offender has done.

The definition they give for this offence is as follows (para. 3.60):

(1) a person by his or her conduct causes the death of another;
(2) a risk that his or her conduct will cause death would be obvious to a reasonable person in his or her position;
(3) he or she is capable of appreciating that risk at the material time; and
(4) his or her conduct falls far below what can reasonably be expected of him or her in the circumstances.

When Parliament enacted the Coroners and Justice Act 2009, no change was made to involuntary manslaughter, the reforms being confined to voluntary manslaughter. It is unlikely that any further reform of homicide will take place in the foreseeable future.

9.3.5 Other unlawful homicides

9.3.5.1 Causing death by dangerous driving
The Road Traffic Act 1991 abolished the offence of causing death by reckless driving contrary to s. 1 of the Road Traffic Act 1988 (see further S. Cooper, *Blackstone's Guide to the Road Traffic Act 1991*). By s. 1 of the Act, a new s. 1 is substituted into the 1988 Act which provides that 'a person who causes the death of another person by driving a mechanically propelled vehicle dangerously on a road or other public place is guilty of an offence'. The offence of reckless driving in s. 2 of the 1988 Act was abolished and replaced by a new s. 2 offence of dangerous driving. 'Dangerous driving' is defined in a new s. 2A to the 1988 Act as follows:

(1) For the purposes of sections 1 and 2 above a person is to be regarded as driving dangerously if (and, subject to subsection (2) below, only if)—
(a) the way he drives falls far below what would be expected of a competent and careful driver, and
(b) it would be obvious to a competent and careful driver that driving in that way would be dangerous.

(2) A person is also to be regarded as driving dangerously for the purposes of sections 1 and 2 above if it would be obvious to a competent and careful driver that driving the vehicle in its current state would be dangerous.

(3) In subsections (1) and (2) above 'dangerous' refers to a danger either of injury to any person or of serious damage to property; and in determining for the purposes of those subsections what would be expected of, or obvious to, a competent and careful driver in a particular case, regard shall be had not only to the circumstances of which he could be expected to be aware, but also to any circumstances shown to have been within the knowledge of the accused.

The Act resulted from the Report of the North Committee set up by the Home Office and the Department of Transport—*Road Traffic Law Review* (HMSO, 1988). The North Committee identified a number of problems with the offences of reckless driving and causing death by reckless driving. The new offences are of an objective nature and require no advertence on the part of a jury to the accused's state of mind except for 'any circumstances shown to have been within the knowledge of the accused' (s. 2A(3)). He may have recognised that his driving was dangerous or given no thought to the manner of his driving, or have given thought to it and wrongly concluded that it was not dangerous. The focus, rather, is on the quality of the accused's driving. If a jury decide that the accused's driving fell far below the objective standard expected of a competent and careful driver under s. 2A(1)(a), they will convict if satisfied that it would be obvious to the competent and careful driver that driving in that way would be dangerous (s. 2A(1)(b)), in that it created a risk 'either of injury to any person or of serious damage to property' (s. 2A(3)).

Section 2A(2) is designed to deal with the situation where D drives a vehicle which is in a dangerous condition. He may drive very carefully but the vehicle itself is dangerous, that is, driving that vehicle on a road in its current state creates a risk either of injury to a person or of serious damage to property. There are two possible problems with this provision. First, if D is a lorry driver and overloads his vehicle or loads it in such a way that the load is unstable, this may not be obvious to the competent and careful driver although obvious to the competent and careful lorry driver. Section 2A(3) provides for this situation in that the competent and careful driver is expected to be aware of 'any circumstances shown to have been within the knowledge of the accused' which would cover any specialist skill or knowledge which D had. Secondly, the facts about the vehicle's condition may indicate that driving it would be dangerous but s. 2A(2) does not impose any requirement that D have knowledge of those facts. For example, D leaves his vehicle in a garage to be serviced and an inexperienced mechanic drains the brake fluid and forgets to refill the brake fluid reservoir. If a competent and careful driver knew of the vehicle's 'current state' it would be obvious to him that to drive a vehicle which has no working brakes is dangerous. If D drives the vehicle from the garage and kills V on a zebra crossing when the vehicle fails to stop, would he be liable for causing death by dangerous driving? The wording of s. 2A(3) suggests that the competent and careful driver is only taken to be aware of circumstances of which he could be expected to be aware. Thus, on those facts, the competent and careful driver would be someone who did not know that the brakes were not working. In *Strong* [1995] Crim LR 428 the Court of Appeal stated that something would be obvious to the competent and careful driver only if it could be 'seen or realised at first glance, evident to him'. If, for example, a fault could only have been discovered by crawling under the vehicle, this would not satisfy the 'obvious' test. If, however, in our example, D on trying the brakes found they did not work but dismissed that from his mind as a fluke, believing that the brakes must be working as the car had just come from the garage, and drove on killing V on a zebra crossing, he would be guilty of the s. 1 offence if the jury concluded that, in such circumstances, it would have been obvious to the competent and careful driver that the vehicle was dangerous.

A problem which remains following the creation of the s. 1 offence is whether some cases of causing death by dangerous driving may also amount to gross negligence manslaughter. In *Adomako* [1995] 1 AC 171 Lord Mackay LC expressed the view that the use of a manslaughter charge in respect of a road death would be rare. It might be appropriate, however, where the way in which the accused drove fell so far below what would be expected of a competent and careful driver and it would have been obvious to such a driver that driving in that way created a risk of death. As prosecutors must opt which offence to charge, and as the maximum sentence for the s. 1 offence is 14 years' imprisonment, it is unlikely that many will be tempted to prosecute for gross negligence manslaughter unless the risk of death was very high (see *Pimm* [1994] RTR 391; *Brown v The Queen* [2005] UKPC 18).

It should be noted that the Road Traffic Act 1991 created a new offence in s. 3 of causing death by careless driving when under the influence of drink or drugs to such an extent that the driver is unfit to drive or the proportion of alcohol in his breath, blood, or urine at the time exceeds the prescribed limits. Such a person may be driving a vehicle in a way which is not dangerous, although careless. However, he will be liable to conviction of this offence and on conviction will be liable to imprisonment for up to 10 years.

The Road Safety Act 2006, s. 20(1) inserted a new s. 2B into the Road Traffic Act 1988 creating a new offence of causing death by careless or inconsiderate driving which is punishable with up to five years' imprisonment. An offence, careless driving, which would not otherwise be punishable by imprisonment, becomes so where death results provided a causal link is proven between the driving and the death. No *mens rea* need be proved as regards the risk of death. The happenstance of death thereby converts a minor crime into a very serious one without there being any concomitant rise in the culpability of the defendant.

9.3.5.2 Infanticide

Section 1(1) of the Infanticide Act 1938, as originally enacted, provided:

> Where a woman by any wilful act or omission causes the death of her child being a child under the age of twelve months, but at the time of the act or omission the balance of her mind was disturbed by reason of her not having fully recovered from the effect of giving birth to the child or by reason of the effect of lactation consequent upon the birth of the child, then, notwithstanding that the circumstances were such that but for this Act the offence would have amounted to murder, she shall be guilty of [an offence], to wit of infanticide, and may for such offence be dealt with and punished as if she had been guilty of the offence of manslaughter of the child.

Section 1(2) provided for a defence of infanticide where the prosecution charge murder. This enactment replaced a 1922 provision which confined the defence of infanticide to 'newly-born' children. The impetus for the original provision was the difficulty of obtaining convictions for murder where mothers killed their babies. Where convictions were obtained, the death sentence would be duly pronounced but would inevitably be commuted by the Home Secretary of the day. The existence of the death penalty, therefore, played a considerable part in the creation of this offence/defence and its further reform in 1938. The principal effect of conviction for infanticide, rather than murder, was to give the judge discretion in sentencing.

The offence/defence is limited to the mother, and the child must be under 12 months when killed. Where the Crown charge murder, there is an evidential burden on the accused to tender some evidence pointing to the balance of her mind being disturbed; it is then for the Crown to disprove this. If the Crown charge infanticide they bear the burden of proving that the balance of the accused's mind was disturbed, but this is unlikely to be contested.

For a long time there has been considerable debate about whether women who kill their babies in the first year of life do so because of mental imbalance resulting from childbirth. The Butler Committee on Mentally Abnormal Offenders (Cmnd 6244) found that in most cases there is only a remote relationship between the effects of childbirth or lactation and the killing of the child. The Committee considered that the defence of diminished responsibility, which was created by the Homicide Act of 1957, would now cover all cases of mental imbalance. In practice the real reason for child-killing may be stress arising from caring for a child in an unfavourable social environment due to poor housing, poor family support, and poverty, or simply the stress of having to care for a difficult and demanding or unwanted infant. These are factors which affect fathers and mothers whether the child is under or over one year of age and manifest themselves in the problem of 'baby-battering'. The Criminal Law Revision Committee in its *Fourteenth Report: Offences Against the Person* (Cmnd 7844) recommended the retention of the defence but its amendment to reflect modern medical knowledge. Its recommendations were adopted by the Law Commission in its Draft Criminal Code (Law Com No. 177), cl. 64(1) of which provides:

> A woman who, but for this section, would be guilty of murder or manslaughter of her child is not guilty of murder or manslaughter, but is guilty of infanticide, if her act is done when the child is under the age of twelve months and when the balance of her mind is disturbed by reason of the effect of giving birth or of circumstances consequent upon the birth.

The reference to 'murder or manslaughter' in this provision is due to the earlier recommendations of the Law Commission which reduced the scope of the offence of murder. The new definition would be wide enough to encompass difficult circumstances of a social or environmental nature which may ensue from the birth of the child, although only the mother may be convicted of infanticide. If the father (with the *mens rea* for murder) kills his child, or if the mother (with the *mens rea* for murder) kills her child over the age of 12 months, he or she must rely on the defences of provocation or diminished responsibility if the offence is to be reduced from murder to manslaughter.

In *Kai-Whitewind* [2005] EWCA Crim 1092, the Court of Appeal added its voice to the calls for reform of the law of infanticide identifying two particular concerns: first, the fact that the 1938 definition does not cover circumstances subsequent to the birth, which are connected with it but not consequent upon it, for example, the stresses imposed on a mother by the absence of natural bonding with her child; and, secondly, the problem of mothers who have killed their children but who are unable to admit to it thereby rendering it difficult, or impossible, to obtain the psychiatric evidence necessary to demonstrate the disturbance to the balance of her mind. In their Consultation Paper, No. 177, *A New Homicide Act for England and Wales?* published in 2005, the Law Commission provisionally proposed raising the age of the child to two years which would catch most instances of child-killing where post-natal depression plays a part. In addition, the Law Commission recommended the removal of the reference to lactation as the theory that lactation is linked to post-natal depression is erroneous. In their final Report, *Murder, Manslaughter and Infanticide* (Law Com No. 304) the Law Commission recommended the retention of the defence having received further scientific research following their consultation which led them to conclude that while:

> no psychiatric disorders (perhaps, bar one) are specific to childbirth, the incidence of certain disorders is higher following childbirth. This temporal connection indicates that some women are more vulnerable to psychiatric disorder in the postpartum period.

With regard to the lactation theory the Law Commission received further research which suggested that lactation may increase dopamine sensitivity in some women, which may trigger psychosis. This led the Law Commission to recommend the retention of the reference to lactation in the statute. The Law Commission made one recommendation of a procedural nature to deal with the second problem raised in *Kai-Whitewind*. They recommended that:

> in circumstances where infanticide is not raised as an issue at trial and the defendant (biological mother of a child aged 12 months or less) is convicted by the jury of murder [first degree murder or second degree murder], the trial judge should have the power to order a medical examination of the defendant with a view to establishing whether or not there is evidence that at the time of the killing the requisite elements of a charge of infanticide were present. If such evidence is produced and the defendant wishes to appeal, the judge should be able to refer the application to the Court of Appeal and to postpone sentence pending the determination of the application.

Before any reform of the offence could occur, however, the Court of Appeal in *Gore* [2007] EWCA Crim 2789 delivered a judgment which tore to shreds most of the previous understanding of this offence.

> G gave birth to a child at home unattended. Several hours later the body of the child was found in sand dunes near G's home. Pathology experts suggested the child may have died from neonatal anoxia due to blocked airways which may have arisen from lack of attention following delivery. The time of death was put at between five

minutes after delivery and several hours. G was charged with infanticide on the basis that she had caused the death of the child by wilfully omitting to attend to the child or to seek medical attention following birth. G pleaded guilty albeit there was psychiatric evidence that she suffered from a hysterical dissociative state that might have founded a defence based on her mental state. The case was referred to the Criminal Cases Review Commission by the Attorney-General's Interdepartmental Group set up following the decision of the Court of Appeal in *R v Cannings* [2004] EWCA Crim 01 to consider homicide convictions where the victim was less than two-years-old. Concerns were expressed over (1) whether the child had been born alive; (2) what caused the blockage of its airways; and (3) the lack of evidence that G had wilfully omitted to care for the child. The case was, in turn, referred by the Commission to the Court of Appeal on the basis that (1) it was unlikely in light of new psychiatric evidence that G appreciated the nature of the charge; (2) G was prejudiced by the drafting of the indictment which made no mention of an intent to kill or cause GBH with consequential impact on the legal advice she received; (3) there was no evidence of an intent to kill; and (4) there were serious doubts over whether the omissions caused the death of the child. The appeal largely focused on the mental element in infanticide. The Court of Appeal held that the offence of infanticide was not confined to killings that would otherwise be murder and the *mens rea* of the offence was not intent to kill or cause GBH but simply that the act or omission which caused the death was wilful. Parliament had intended to create a new offence which covered situations much wider than those which would otherwise be murder. This being so, there was no defect in the indictment, G was not prejudiced and it was clear that she had wished to plead guilty.

This was a surprising decision. When the Court of Appeal had expressed concerns over infanticide in *Kai-Whitewind* the contention was that the offence should be expanded to embrace a wider range of mental/psychiatric conditions. In *Gore* the Court expanded the offence to embrace a wider range of offences, or even circumstances in which an infant might die. Despite the suggestion by Hallett LJ that infanticide carries less moral opprobrium than homicide, infanticide is a homicide offence. It had been understood to be one which arose in very limited circumstances which would otherwise amount to murder. All the debates at the time of the original 1922 Act and the 1938 Act suggested that the mischief which the offence/defence was designed to address was that of women being convicted of murder, sentenced to death, and experiencing that trauma only for the sentence subsequently to be commuted. The death penalty only applied to murder; a conviction of manslaughter always left the sentence at large. The Court of Appeal's construction of the statute ignored this mischief. It ignored also the fact that when originally enacted in 1922, the *mens rea* for murder was far from clear and, indeed, the general understanding of *mens rea* was still developing. The suggestion by Hallett LJ that this new approach is a humane one as a young mother would feel she could plead guilty to infanticide without having to accept that she had killed with the *mens rea* for murder, strikes this author as a novel, if not idiosyncratic, view of what is humane. The new interpretation meant that all that would be necessary for conviction would be proof of a wilful act or omission which causes death even though the mother who acted or omitted had no intent in respect of, or foresight of, the consequences of her act or omission. In G's case it was enough

that in the immediate aftermath of childbirth (with all that goes with that, emotionally and physically) she failed to seek medical attention for the child such that,
on one reading of the pathology evidence, the child died within five minutes of
birth. That wilful omission—which means no more than voluntary—was, however, sufficient for proof of an offence of homicide. In the Court's view this outcome was more humane than the alternative—the alternative being no homicide
charge at all! Remember, an omission cannot supply the unlawful and dangerous
act required for unlawful act manslaughter. Further, an omission may only suffice
to prove gross negligence manslaughter where the risk in respect of which a person
is grossly negligent is the risk of death. It is doubtful whether a prosecution for
gross negligence manslaughter based on a mother's failure to obtain medical assistance for her newborn child in the minutes immediately following its unattended
birth could get off the ground.

Following the decision in *Gore* the Government in its Consultation Paper,
Murder, manslaughter and infanticide: proposals for reform of the law (CP 19/08) proposed amendments to the Infanticide Act, the purpose of those amendments
being 'to make clear that infanticide cannot be charged in cases that would not
currently be homicide at all'. The Government recognised that the *Gore* interpretation of 'wilful act or omission' could include negligence below the level of
gross negligence.

These proposals were quickly enacted by the Coroners and Justice Act 2009,
s. 57, gaining favour over the other proposals made over the years for more liberal
reform of this offence/defence. Section 1(1) of the Infanticide Act now reads:

> Where a woman by any wilful act or omission causes the death of her child being a child
> under the age of twelve months, but at the time of the act or omission the balance of her
> mind was disturbed by reason of her not having fully recovered from the effect of giving
> birth to the child or by reason of the effect of lactation consequent upon the birth of the
> child, then, **notwithstanding that if** the circumstances were such that but for this Act
> the offence would have amounted to murder **or manslaughter**, she shall be guilty of [an
> offence], to wit of infanticide, and may for such offence be dealt with and punished as if
> she had been guilty of the offence of manslaughter of the child. (amendments in bold)

Similar amendments have been made to s. 1(2). It is disappointing to see the confused thinking demonstrated by the Court of Appeal receiving a degree of statutory approval albeit that the most extreme effects of the decision in *Gore* have been
mitigated.

9.3.5.3 Causing or allowing the death of a child or vulnerable adult

Where a child or vulnerable adult dies in circumstances where it is clear that the
death was non-accidental and caused by a parent or someone else who had care of
him, it was often difficult to prove that the death was caused by one or other (or
both) parents or carers. The death may have occurred while one of the parents or
carers was absent. Alternatively, while it may have been possible to prove which
parent was responsible for the act which was the immediate cause of death, it may
have been difficult or impossible to prove whether the other parent was an accomplice in that offence. The Domestic Violence, Crime and Victims Act 2004 seeks to
address this problem by creating in s. 5 an offence punishable with a maximum

of 14 years' imprisonment. The offence is essentially one of negligence. Section 5 provides:

(1) A person ('D') is guilty of an offence if—

    (a) a child or vulnerable adult ('V') dies as a result of the unlawful act of a person who—

        (i) was a member of the same household as V, and

        (ii) had frequent contact with him,

    (b) D was such a person at the time of that act;

    (c) at that time there was a significant risk of serious physical harm being caused to V by the unlawful act of such a person; and

    (d) either D was the person whose act caused V's death or—

        (i) D was, or ought to have been, aware of the risk mentioned in paragraph (c),

        (ii) D failed to take such steps as he could reasonably have been expected to take to protect V from the risk, and

        (iii) the act occurred in circumstances of the kind that D foresaw or ought to have foreseen.

The prosecution does not have to prove which of the alternatives in s. 5(1)(d) applies (s. 5(2)). A person is to be regarded as a 'member of the same household' even if he does not live at the address provided he visits it so often and for such periods of time that it is reasonable to regard him as a member of it. This could cover, for example, a grandparent who looks after a child during the day but does not sleep at the premises. 'Unlawful act' is an act that constitutes an offence (s. 5(5)(a)). For these purposes 'act' includes a course of conduct or an omission (s. 5(6)), for example, failure to feed, or clothe or seek medical attention for a child. Where D is not the person who performs the unlawful act, he will not escape liability by reason of the fact that the person who did perform it was under 10-years-old or insane (see s. 5(5)(b)). Thus, for example, a parent (D) will be liable where a sibling under the age of 10 does the act which causes V's death and D failed to protect V from the risk, being aware of it. Where D is not the mother or father of V, D may not be charged with this offence if he was under 16 at the time of the act that caused V's death (s. 5(3)(a)). In addition, where the death is the result of a course of conduct and D has failed to take reasonable steps to protect V from the risk arising therefrom, his failure will only count against him from the point he attains the age of 16 (s. 5(3)(b)).

The only circumstances where it would appear to be appropriate to charge D under this section where D is responsible for the unlawful act that causes V's death, is where D1 and D2 are the parents/carers of V and both are charged under the section it being unclear which of the two is responsible for the unlawful act. In such circumstances D1 and D2 will either each have perpetrated the act or aided and abetted the other to do so or failed to protect V. Where the prosecution can prove that one or other did the unlawful act and that the other failed to take reasonable steps to protect V in circumstances where he either was aware of the risk or ought to have been aware of it, then both should be convicted.

In *Khan* [2009] EWCA Crim 2, the Court of Appeal was faced with having to determine the meaning of 'vulnerable adult'.

V came to England from a rural part of Kashmir to marry her cousin, H. V spoke no English and had no friends in England. V and H lived with their extended family in one house which included H's mother, his sisters D and E and D's husband, F. V suffered at least three incidents of serious violence at the hands of H, the last of which caused her death. H was convicted of murder. The prosecution case against D, E, and F was that during the three weeks before the final attack on her by H, it must have been apparent to D, E, and F that V had been, and was being, subjected to serious physical violence at the hands of H. The prosecution contended that following the first attack on her three weeks before her death, V thereby became a vulnerable adult. D, E, and F were all convicted of the s. 5(1) offence and appealed. The Court of Appeal dismissed their appeals holding that adults are vulnerable if their ability to protect themselves from violence, abuse, or neglect is significantly impaired which it was here after the major attack on her three weeks before her death. The vulnerability need only be temporary as a result of accident, illness, or injury. The Court left open the possibility that even before this V may have been considered vulnerable on the basis of her situation—lonely and friendless in a strange country and totally dependent upon her husband and his family.

What protective steps might be required of a member of the same household depends upon what is reasonable in the circumstances. In *Khan* the Court of Appeal recognised that if another member of the household is subject to the same violence as V, it might not be reasonable to expect that person to have taken any protective steps.

(The Domestic Violence, Crime and Victims (Amendment) Act 2012 extends the reach of s. 5 to cover non-fatal cases where a child or vulnerable adult has suffered serious physical harm, the maximum penalty for this offence being 10 years' imprisonment.)

FURTHER READING

M. J. Allen, 'Provocation's Reasonable Man: A Plea for Self-control' (2000) 64 JCL 216.

A. Ashworth, 'Reforming the Law of Murder' [1990] Crim LR 75.

A. Bustill and A. McCall Smith, 'Fright, Stress and Homicide' 54 JCL 257.

C. Elliot, 'What Future for Voluntary Manslaughter' (2004) 68 JCL 253; 'Liability for Manslaughter by Omission: Don't Let the Baby Drown!' (2010) 74 JCL 163.

J. Herring and E. Palser, 'The Duty of Care in Gross Negligence Manslaughter' [2007] Crim LR 24.

R. Holton and S. Shute, 'Self Control in Modern Provocation Defence' (2007) 27 OJLS 49.

H. Keating, 'The Law Commission Report on Involuntary Manslaughter: (1) The Restoration of a Serious Crime' [1996] Crim LR 535.

R. D. Mackay and B. J. Mitchell, 'But is this Provocation? Some Thoughts on the Law Commission's Report on Partial Defences to Murder' [2005] Crim LR 44.

R. D. Mackay, B. J. Mitchell and W.J. Brookbanks, 'Pleading for provoked killers: in defence of Morgan Smith' (2008) 124 LQR 675.

D. Maier-Katkin and R. Ogle, 'A Rationale for Infanticide Laws' [1993] Crim LR 903.

J. Miles, 'The Coroners and Justice Act 2009: a "dog's breakfast" of homicide reform' [2009] 10 Arch. News 6.

A. Norrie, 'The Coroners and Justice Act 2009 – Partial Defences to Murder: (1) Loss of Control' [2010] Crim LR 275.

H. Power, 'Provocation and Culture' [2006] Crim LR 871.

O. Quick and C. Wells, 'Getting Tough with Defences' [2006] Crim LR 514.

G. R. Sullivan, 'Complicity for First Degree Murder and Complicity in an Unlawful Killing' [2006] Crim LR 502.

C. Wells, 'The Law Commission Report on Involuntary Manslaughter: (2) The Corporate Manslaughter Proposals: Pragmatism, Paradox and Peninsularity' [1996] Crim LR 545.

G. Williams, '*Mens Rea* for Murder: Leave it Alone' (1989) 105 LQR 387.

G. Williams, 'Gross Negligence Manslaughter and Duty of Care in "Drugs" Cases: R v Evans' [2009] Crim LR 631.

W. Wilson, 'A Plea for Rationality in the Law of Murder' (1990) 10 LS 307; 'The Structure of Criminal Homicide' [2006] Crim LR 471.

D. Yale, 'A Year and a Day in Homicide' [1989] CLJ 202.

10

Non-fatal offences against the person

In this chapter the main offences involving violence against the person will be considered. There are a considerable number of different offences, many of which are contained in the Offences Against the Person Act 1861 (this statute will be referred to by the abbreviation OAPA), but space dictates that only the most common of these can be examined. In the first part of this chapter the main non-sexual offences will be covered and in the second part the main sexual offences will be covered.

10.1 Non-sexual offences

10.1.1 Assault and battery

Common assault and battery were separate common law crimes. Section 39 of the Criminal Justice Act 1988 stipulates that they are summary offences and specifies the maximum penalties which may be imposed. It was believed that they remained common law crimes. However, in *DPP* v *Little* [1992] 1 All ER 299, the Divisional Court held that they are, and have been since 1861, statutory offences. Section 47 of the OAPA prescribed the penalty for these offences. This decision is surprising as the definitions of assault and battery are not found in any statute but in the common law. In *Haystead* v *Chief Constable of Derbyshire* [2000] Crim LR 758, Laws LJ stated that 'in truth, common assault by beating remains a common law offence'. This presents a clear conflict of authority which needs to be resolved.

An indictment charging an indictable offence against the person may include a count of common assault or battery if it is founded on the same facts or evidence as a count charging an indictable offence or is part of a series of offences of the same or similar character as an indictable offence which is also charged (s. 40 of the Criminal Justice Act (CJA) 1988). Thus, if the jury acquit the accused of the more serious indictable offence, they may still convict of the summary offence.

While assault and battery are distinct crimes, judges and statutes often use the term 'assault' or 'common assault' to encompass both these offences (e.g. s. 47 of the OAPA and s. 40(3)(a) of the CJA 1988). In this chapter the term 'assault' will be used in its generic sense to cover both offences. When dealing separately with the offences the terms 'technical assault' and 'battery' will be used. It should be noted that assault and battery are also torts.

10.1.1.1 Technical assault

A technical assault is committed when the accused intentionally or recklessly causes the victim to apprehend immediate and unlawful personal violence (see *Fagan* v *Metropolitan Police Commissioner* [1969] 1 QB 439). This definition was approved by the House of Lords in *Savage and Parmenter* [1991] 1 AC 699 at 740.

10.1.1.1.1 *Actus reus*

V must apprehend immediate and unlawful personal violence. The term 'apprehend' is used as it is not necessary for V to be put in fear; **it is sufficient that she anticipates immediate and unlawful personal violence being applied to here by D**. The term 'unlawful personal violence' may be misleading as it is not necessary for V to apprehend a severe attack; the apprehension of any unwanted touching of her by D is sufficient. **Thus all that V need apprehend is a battery**, which was defined by Lord Lane CJ in *Faulkner* v *Talbot* [1981] 3 All ER 468, 471, as '**any intentional touching of another person without the consent of that person and without lawful excuse**. It need not necessarily be hostile, rude, or aggressive . . .'.

Personal violence is not unlawful where D is justified in using it (e.g. if D is using reasonable force in self-defence, or to prevent a crime or arrest an offender), or D is engaged in lawful correction (see 10.1.1.3.3 *post*).

Technical assault generally requires some act on the part of D causing V to apprehend immediate unlawful personal violence. For example, where D shakes his fist at V or raises a knife as if to stab V or points a gun at V, there would be a technical assault if V apprehended the immediate application of force on her by D. In the example of the gun, however, there would be no assault if V knew or believed that the gun was not loaded (see *Lamb* [1967] 2 QB 981). There are three issues, however, which need to be considered: first, whether an assault may be committed by omission; secondly, whether an assault may be committed by words; and, thirdly, what does 'immediate' mean?

(a) **Omissions** In *Fagan* it was stated that **an omission could not constitute an assault**, but the Divisional Court appeared to leave open the possibility of an assault arising from a continuing act (cf. *DPP* v *Santana-Bermudez* [2003] EWHC Admin 2908, 2.5.2.2.4 *ante*). For example, D, a burglar, is in V's kitchen holding a knife when V enters, coming face to face with D and the knife. V apprehends immediate unlawful personal violence and D, recognising V's fear, continues to hold the knife in the same position. It is suggested that D has not assaulted V by omission, but rather that by failing to terminate his act of holding the knife in what has become a threatening manner he commits an assault (cf. *Kaitamaki* [1985] AC 147, 10.2.1.1.1 *post*).

(b) **Words** **While D's actions may amount to a technical assault, the words he speaks at the time may serve to negative this.** In *Tuberville* v *Savage* (1669) 1 Mod Rep 3, T placed his hand on his sword and said, 'If it were not assize-time, I would not take such language from you'. The Court held that this was not an assault as his declaration indicated that as the judges were in town he would not use force on S. By contrast, if D puts a gun to V's head and says, 'Be quiet or I'll blow your brains out', this should constitute a technical assault as D's forebearance is conditional on V doing as she is told. In *Read v Coker* (1853) 13 CB 850, V sued successfully for assault where D and his servants surrounded him, rolled up their sleeves and threatened to break his neck if he did not leave the premises.

The authorities, until recently, were somewhat confused on the issue whether words alone could constitute an assault. In *Meade and Belt* (1823) 1 Lew CC 184, Holroyd J stated that 'no words or singing are equivalent to an assault'. This created difficulties. For example, if D approached V from behind on a dark night and said, 'I have a gun and I'll shoot if you don't hand over your money', V may well have apprehended immediate unlawful personal violence, but Holroyd J's dictum would suggest this could not constitute a technical assault. In *Wilson* [1955] 1 All ER 744, Lord Goddard stated *obiter* (at p. 745) 'He called out "Get the knives", which itself would be an assault, in addition to kicking the gamekeeper'; this *obiter dictum* was further supported by the civil case of *Ansell v Thomas* [1974] Crim LR 31, where it was held that D's verbal threat to eject V forcibly from a meeting if he did not leave voluntarily constituted an assault.

The matter has now been settled by the House of Lords' decision in *Ireland* [1998] AC 147. D had made a series of silent telephone calls to three women as a result of which the women suffered significant psychological symptoms. D was charged with assault occasioning actual bodily harm contrary to s. 47 of the OAPA. His appeal against conviction to the Court of Appeal was dismissed. Swinton Thomas LJ reasoned backwards from the fact that the three victims suffered psychological harm to conclude that there must have been an assault which caused this. He stated ([1997] 1 All ER 112, 115):

> In our judgment, if the Crown can prove that the victims have sustained actual bodily harm, and that the [appellant]...intended the victims to sustain such harm, or [was] reckless as to whether they did sustain such harm, and that harm resulted from an act or acts of the appellant, namely telephone calls followed by silence, it is open to the jury to find that he has committed an assault. As to immediacy, by using the telephone the appellant put himself in immediate contact with the victims, and when the victims lifted the telephone they were placed in immediate fear and suffered the consequences to which we have referred.

The Court of Appeal certified that the decision involved a point of law of general public importance namely: 'Whether the making of a series of silent telephone calls can amount in law to an assault'. In answering this question in the affirmative the House of Lords resolved several issues. Their Lordships affirmed the definition of assault stated earlier (10.1.1.1 *ante*) and further resolved that **words may constitute an assault**, Lord Steyn stating (at p. 162):

> The proposition that a gesture may amount to an assault, but that words can never suffice, is unrealistic and indefensible. A thing said is also a thing done. There is no reason why something said should be incapable of causing an apprehension of immediate personal violence, e.g. a man accosting a woman in a dark alley saying, 'Come with me or I will stab you.' I would, therefore, reject the proposition that an assault can never be committed by words.

His Lordship went on to conclude that, depending on the facts, a silent call may also constitute an assault stating (at p. 162):

> there is no reason why a telephone caller who says to a woman in a menacing way 'I will be at your door in a minute or two' may not be guilty of an assault if he causes his victim to apprehend immediate personal violence. Take now the case of the silent caller. He intends by his silence to cause fear and he is so understood. The victim is assailed by uncertainty about his intentions. Fear may dominate her emotions, and it may be the fear that the caller's arrival at her door may be imminent. She may fear the possibility of immediate personal violence. As a matter of law the caller may be guilty of an assault: whether he is or not will depend on the circumstances and in particular on the impact of the caller's potentially menacing call or calls on the victim. Such a prosecution case under section 47 may be fit to leave to the jury. And a trial judge may, depending on the circumstances, put a common sense consideration before the jury, namely what, if not the possibility of imminent personal violence, was the victim terrified about? I conclude that an assault may be committed in the particular factual circumstances which I have envisaged.

The crucial question is whether the silent call has caused the victim to apprehend immediate and **unlawful personal violence. 'Unlawful personal violence' must, however, be understood to mean the application of force to the body of the victim.** There undoubtedly was confusion in the Court of Appeal where Swinton Thomas LJ appeared to accept that the apprehension of further psychological symptoms was equivalent to apprehending immediate unlawful violence. Their Lordships did not grapple with this issue and must be taken to have dismissed it by their affirmation of the definition of assault. They were able to side-step this issue in the context of the appeal before them as the appellant had pleaded guilty at his initial trial, thereby implicitly accepting that the victims had been caused to apprehend immediate unlawful personal violence and that he had the requisite *mens rea*.

(c) *Immediate unlawful violence* **There is no assault if V does not apprehend** *immediate* **unlawful violence.** If V apprehends violence at some point in the future, this is not sufficient. For example, if D, standing on one side of a deep, fast-flowing river, shakes his fist at V on the other side, there being no means of crossing, the element of immediacy would be lacking. Likewise, if V, departing from a station in a train, sees D on the platform shaking his fist while shouting, 'You're for a beating when I get my hands on you', there would be no assault as V, while he might fear unlawful personal violence at the hands of D, would fear such occurring at an unspecified future date rather than immediately.

But what does 'immediate' mean? **It is important to emphasise that it is not the apprehension which must be immediate but rather the apprehension must be that violence is going to ensue immediately.** In the Court of Appeal in *Ireland* reliance was placed on *Smith v Chief Superintendent of Woking Police Station* (1983) 76 Cr App R 234, where the Divisional Court found that it was open to the magistrates to find that there was an assault where D looked through V's window at 11pm causing her to fear violence from him. The violence, obviously, could not be applied instantaneously but it could follow 'sufficiently immediately for the purposes of the offence' (*per* Kerr LJ at p. 237). In s. 4(1) of the Public Order Act 1986 the phrase 'immediate unlawful violence' is used. Section 4(1) creates the offence of using 'threatening, abusive or insulting words or behaviour...with intent to cause a person to believe that immediate unlawful violence will be used against him...'. In *R v Horseferry Road Metropolitan Stipendiary Magistrate, ex parte Siadatan* [1991] 1 QB 260, in the Divisional Court, Watkins LJ stated (at p. 269):

> It seems to us that the word 'immediate' does not mean 'instantaneous'; that a relatively short time interval may elapse between the act which is threatening, abusive or insulting and the unlawful violence. 'Immediate' connotes proximity in time and proximity in causation; that it is likely that violence will result within a relatively short period of time and without any other intervening occurrence.

Perhaps the best approximation to 'immediate' is 'imminent'—a word used by Lord Steyn in *Ireland* and which is consistent with the idea that a 'short interval of time' may elapse between the words or acts which constitute the assault and the apprehended violence. This has to be so if it is to be possible to assault via the telephone. In *Ireland* in the Court of Appeal, Swinton Thomas LJ found the New South Wales civil case of *Barton v Armstrong* [1969] 2 NSWR 451, particularly persuasive that an assault could occur over the telephone where Taylor J stated (at p. 455):

> If, when threats...are conveyed over the telephone, the recipient has been led to believe that he is being followed, kept under surveillance by persons hired to do him physical harm to the extent of killing him, then why is this not something to put him in fear or apprehension of immediate violence? In the age in which we live threats may be made and communicated by persons remote from the person threatened. Physical violence and death can be produced by acts done at a distance by people who are out of sight and by agents hired for that purpose. I do not think that these, if they result in apprehension of physical violence in the mind of a reasonable person, are outside the protection afforded by the civil and criminal law as to assault.

Whatever the means used to convey the threat, whether it constitutes an assault depends on the victim apprehending immediate unlawful violence. This will be a matter of evidence and a question for the magistrate or jury to determine. If V contemplates anything more than a short interval of time elapsing between the threatening words, acts or silence on the part of D and the violence ensuing, there will be no assault.

10.1.1.1.2 *Mens rea*

The *mens rea* of technical assault is an intention to cause the victim to apprehend immediate unlawful personal violence or recklessness as to whether such apprehension is caused (*Venna* [1976] QB 421).

With regard to the meaning of recklessness, in *DPP v K (A Minor)* [1990] 1 WLR 1067, the Divisional Court held that the *Caldwell* test of recklessness sufficed. In *Spratt* [1990] 1 WLR 1073, the Court of Appeal held that in every offence against the person recklessness was to be given the *Cunningham* meaning, 'in the sense of taking the risk of harm ensuing with foresight that it might happen' (*per* McCowan LJ at p. 1082). The Court of Appeal went on to state that *DPP v K* had been wrongly decided as the Divisional Court were not referred to *Cunningham* or *Venna*.

In *Parmenter* (1991) 92 Cr App R 68, the Court of Appeal followed *Spratt*. In the joint hearing of the appeals in *Savage and Parmenter* [1991] 4 All ER 698, the

House of Lords was not asked to consider this point but there are dicta in their Lordships' speeches which confirm that advertence to the risk of physical contact is required.

10.1.1.2 Battery

The *actus reus* of battery consists of the infliction of unlawful personal violence by the accused upon the victim. Often a battery follows from a technical assault, as where V sees D swing his fist at him and then suffers the impact of the blow. It is not necessary, however, for there to be a technical assault for D to be liable for battery. For example, if V is blind or D punches him from behind, D will be guilty of battery even though V has no apprehension of unlawful personal violence. **The slightest touching, if unlawful, is sufficient.** The courts, however, have recognised that ordinary everyday life involves many incidents of contact with other persons which should not be treated as criminal. Drawing a line between acceptable and unacceptable forms of contact is not easy. In *Collins v Wilcock* [1984] 3 All ER 374, Robert Goff LJ stated that there was a general exception 'embracing all physical contact which is generally acceptable in the ordinary conduct of daily life'. Whether conduct falls within this exception will depend upon the facts of each particular case, but Robert Goff LJ provided some examples of acceptable conduct (at p. 378):

> So nobody can complain of the jostling which is inevitable from his presence in, for example, a supermarket, an underground station or a busy street; nor can a person who attends a party complain if his hand is seized in friendship, or even if his back is (within reason) slapped....[Also] among such forms of conduct, long held to be acceptable, is touching a person for the purpose of engaging his attention, though of course using no greater degree of physical contact than is reasonably necessary in the circumstances for that purpose.

Thus a police officer may tap a person on the shoulder to gain his attention but he may not restrain the person (*Collins v Wilcock*; cf. *Wilson v Pringle* [1986] 2 All ER 440). In *McMillan v CPS* [2008] EWHC 1457 (Admin) A was in a drunken state and was seen by the police shouting, being abusive, and arguing in the garden of her daughter's house. The Divisional Court held that the police officer committed no assault on A when he took her by the arm to steady her for her own safety and led her (without any resistance) down some steep steps to the street in order to speak to her, as he had been acting within the bounds of what were 'generally acceptable standards of conduct'.

As with technical assault, an omission to act cannot constitute a battery (but cf. *DPP v Santana-Bermudez* [2003] EWHC Admin 2908, 2.5.2.2.4 *ante*) but, if D inadvertently applies force to V and then refuses to withdraw it this may constitute a battery. In *Fagan v Metropolitan Police Commissioner*, D inadvertently parked his car on a police officer's foot. He refused for some time to reverse off when the officer asked him. He was convicted of assaulting a police officer in the execution of his duty. The Divisional Court held that the battery was a continuing act as force continued to be applied to the officer's foot. When D formed the *mens rea* after the inception of the *actus reus*, this was superimposed upon the existing act making it into an assault.

? Question

Can D be liable if his initial act does not apply force to V, but D realises that if he does not terminate it, force will be applied to V?

For example, D places a pole across a darkened corridor. He hears V running along the corridor and deliberately leaves the pole there realising that V will fall over it. If D is not to be convicted of battery it will be on the basis of a very fine distinction which it would be difficult to justify. If D had placed the pole there with the intention of tripping V this has always been assumed to constitute a battery (see *Martin* (1881) 8 QBD 54) (see also *Santana-Bermudez*, 2.5.2.2.4 *ante*).

Martin illustrates another principle namely that **the application of force to V need not be direct.** Although the Court of Appeal overruled the Divisional Court's decision in *DPP* v *K* in respect of *mens rea*, the Court of Appeal did not question its decision with regard to the *actus reus*. In this case D, a schoolboy, had placed acid, which he had removed without permission from the chemistry laboratory, in a hot air drier to conceal it. The next person to use the drier suffered scarring when the machine squirted acid into his face. D was charged with assault occasioning actual bodily harm contrary to s. 47 of the OAPA (see also *Haystead* v *Chief Constable of Derbyshire* [2000] Crim LR 758). Parker LJ stated ([1990] 1 WLR 1067, 1071):

> [I]n my judgment there can be no doubt that if a defendant places acid into a machine with the intent that it shall, when the next user switches the machine on, be ejected onto him and do him harm there is an assault when the harm is done.

In this case, as D was charged with the s. 47 offence, harm had to be proved. There is no need to prove that V suffered harm where the charge is simple battery. Had D simply placed water in the machine, he could have been liable for battery (see *Pursell* v *Horn* (1838) 8 Ad & El 602). Similarly, if D rigs up a 'booby trap' with a bucket of water suspended above a door, he will be liable for battery if the contents spill on to V upon opening the door (see also *Clarence* (1888) 22 QBD 23, at 25; but see discussion of *Wilson* at 10.1.2.1 *post*).

The *mens rea* of battery is intention to apply unlawful force or subjective recklessness as to whether such force might be applied (see *Venna* and 10.1.1.1.2 *ante*).

10.1.1.3 Defences to assault and battery

The main defences which apply in the case of a charge of assault and battery are private defence (e.g. self-defence), acting in the prevention of crime, consent, and lawful correction. For private defence and prevention of crime, see 6.5 *ante*.

10.1.1.3.1 *Consent*

It is the essence of offences against the person that what is done is done unlawfully. Assaults, batteries, woundings, and even killings in certain circumstances may be performed lawfully as where, for example, D injures or kills V in self-defence. The application of force to another may also be lawful in certain circumstances where it is consented to by the recipient. Is the absence of consent a definitional element of the offence which the prosecution have to prove to establish guilt, or is the presence of consent a fact which D may plead as a defence to a charge of an offence of violence? In *Brown* [1993] 2 WLR 556 the majority in the House of Lords treated consent as a limited defence which could apply in some circumstances. It appears that the absence of consent is not a definitional element of the offence implied by the use of the word 'unlawfully' in the definition of offences of violence; their Lordships have implicitly confined the meaning of 'unlawfully' to justifications such as private defence or prevention of crime.

(i) *To what may V consent?*

a. *The common law before 1993* Prior to the cases of *Boyea* [1992] Crim LR 574, *Aitken* [1992] 1 WLR 1006, and *Brown* the common law provided some piecemeal guidance on the limits of consent; public policy considerations could operate to nullify consent. Thus a person could not consent to being killed nor could he consent to run the risk of being killed by duelling (see e.g. *Rice* (1803) 3 East 581; *Young* (1838) 8 C & P 644; *Cuddy* (1843) 1 Car & Kir 210). A person could not consent to being maimed as this would deprive the Sovereign of an able-bodied man for the defence of the realm (see *Wright* (1603) Co Lit f 127 a-b). The consent of the participants in a prize-fight was of no effect on a charge of assault (see *Coney* (1882) 8 QBD 534, CCCR). While consent was generally accepted as an effective answer to a charge of assault, prizefighting was an exception where on grounds of public policy consent was held to be ineffective. In Coney the reasons supporting the decisions of the 11 judges were various: prizefighting was unlawful as a breach of the peace so the parties' consent could not render it lawful; it was against the public interest that the participants should risk serious injury or death; and fists are dangerous weapons and prizefighting should be banned for the same reasons as duelling. Consent is an effective answer to a charge arising from an injury incurred in the course of properly conducted games or sports (see *Attorney-General's Reference (No. 6 of 1980)* [1981] 2 All ER 1057) which includes sports such as wrestling and boxing. Where however, parties agree to settle their differences by means of a fight, consent is not effective if the parties intended to and/or did cause actual bodily harm (*A-G's Reference (No. 6 of 1980)* [1981] 2 All ER 1057). Where, for the purposes of sexual gratification, a person beats another 'with such a degree of violence that the infliction of bodily harm is a probable consequence...consent is immaterial' (Donovan [1934] 2 KB 498, 507 *per* Swift J). The public interest dictates, however, that consent is effective in the context of reasonable surgical interference, dangerous exhibitions (see *Attorney-General's Reference (No. 6 of 1980)* [1981] 2 All ER 1057) or rough and undisciplined horseplay (see *Jones* (1986) 83 Cr App R 375).

The cases discussed in this section do not fit together neatly largely due to the way the common law develops on a case-by-case basis. There is no clear and coherent articulation of fundamental principles which might govern decisions in new situations nor is there any clear identification of the public policy considerations which resulted in each decision. If an individual can consent to run the risk of serious consequences in the context of boxing why can they not consent to much less severe injuries in the context of a sexual encounter? Is there a difference between consenting to the risk of injury (even very serious injury) as compared with consenting to the certainty of injury sufficient to constitute actual bodily harm?

With regard to the way in which consent operates, in *Attorney-General's Reference (No. 6 of 1980)* Lord Lane CJ stated that 'it is an assault if actual bodily harm is intended *and/or* caused' (emphasis added) unless there was a 'good reason' for such harm being risked or caused. In such a case consent would be an effective answer to a charge of assault. The implication from this was that consent could only operate as an effective answer to a charge either where the force applied did not create a risk of, nor lead to, actual bodily harm or, if it did (whether because it was intended or it simply occurred without being intended or foreseen) that there was a good reason for allowing consent so to operate. How has the House of Lords dealt with these problems in *Brown*?

b. *The decision in Brown (1993)* In *Brown* the five appellants were convicted of assaults occasioning actual bodily harm contrary to s. 47 of the OAPA. Three were also convicted of wounding contrary to s. 20 of the OAPA. In addition four of the appellants had pleaded guilty either as principals or aiders and abettors to charges of keeping a disorderly house. One of the appellants, Laskey, also pleaded guilty to two counts of publishing an obscene article, namely video tapes recording some of the activities which formed the subject of some of the other counts. No appeals were lodged against these convictions. The incidents which led to these convictions occurred in the course of consensual homosexual sado-masochistic activities which involved no permanent injuries nor was medical treatment required for any of the participants. The activities were carried out in private but came to light when the police discovered a video recording of the group's practices. Prosecutions for the obvious offence of gross indecency contrary to s. 13 of the Sexual Offences Act 1956 could not be pursued as they were time-barred by s. 7 of the Sexual Offences Act 1967. The appellants' convictions were upheld by the Court of Appeal where Lord Lane CJ, applying the principle stated in *Attorney-General's Reference (No. 6 of 1980)* that 'it is not in the public interest that people should try to cause or should cause each other actual bodily harm for no good reason' concluded that 'the satisfying of sado-masochistic libido does not come within the category of good reason'. The Court of Appeal certified the following point of law of general public importance:

> Where A wounds or assaults B occasioning him actual bodily harm in the course of a sado-masochistic encounter, does the prosecution have to prove lack of consent on the part of B before they can establish A's guilt under s. 20 and s. 47 of the Offences Against the Person Act 1861?

The appellants appealed to the House of Lords which, by a majority of three to two, answered the question in the negative.

The majority started from the premise that the case concerned offences of violence which had a sexual motive, not sexual activity which incidentally involved injury. The language they used throughout their speeches was pejorative. Lord Templeman stated (at p. 564):

> In my opinion sado-masochism is not only concerned with sex. Sado-masochism is also concerned with violence...The violence of sado-masochistic encounters involves the indulgence of cruelty by sadists and the degradation of victims. Such violence is injurious to the participants and unpredictably dangerous.

The words 'violence' and 'cruelty' are suggestive of an unwanted application of force against the person of another resulting in suffering. In a sado-masochistic encounter, however, the force is requested and the pain is desired. The use of pejorative terms, however, served to paint such encounters in a different light which would then lend support to the conclusion at which their Lordships arrived. If the encounters were seen merely as involving violence and cruelty, then they could be dealt with under a statute, the Offences Against the Person Act, which was designed to protect people from violence and cruelty. This position was summarised perfectly by Lord Lowry who stated:

> What the appellants are obliged to propose is that the deliberate and painful infliction of physical injury should be exempted from the operation of statutory provisions the object of which is to prevent or punish that very thing, the reason for the proposed exemption being that both those who will inflict and those who will suffer the injury wish to satisfy a perverted and depraved sexual desire.

It is difficult to believe that the legislators in 1861 had sado-masochism in mind when they framed ss. 18, 20, and 47 of the Act but the majority adopted the position that it was covered unless there was clear authority to the contrary. The majority found none either in precedent or policy.

The majority accepted that consent was a defence to a charge of common assault but not to an assault occasioning actual bodily harm or serious bodily harm or a wounding unless a recognised exception applied. These exceptions, according to Lord Templeman, related to 'lawful activities' which carried the risk of harm such as 'surgery . . . ritual circumcision, tattooing, ear-piercing and violent sports including boxing' and 'parental chastisement'. It is arguable that all of these activities *involve* actual bodily harm (at least) albeit that they also harbour a risk of more serious harm. Perhaps his Lordship was seeking to distinguish between harm which is caused deliberately from motives which he found unacceptable (sexual pleasure) and harm which is incidental to some other purpose which he considered acceptable. The appellants had argued that the line between what was lawful and what was unlawful should be drawn at the level of grievous bodily harm so that the infliction of wounds or actual bodily harm should not be unlawful. The majority, however, accepted that the relevant precedents of *Coney, Donovan, Attorney-General's Reference (No. 6 of 1980)*, and *Boyea* drew the line at the level of actual bodily harm or wounding as, if actual bodily harm is intended or occurs, the act is unlawful in itself (*malum in se*) rendering consent irrelevant. It was, of course, open to their Lordships to consider the issue afresh as none of the authorities they cited were binding on them but they chose not to do so.

The minority, by contrast, started from the premise that the case concerned activity of a sexual nature which involved the infliction of actual bodily harm or wounds on the other party. Lord Mustill made this point at the outset of his speech stating (at p. 584):

> This is a case about the criminal law of violence. In my opinion it should be about the criminal law of private sexual relations, if about anything at all.

That the Offences Against the Person Act was used was 'adventitious'. As the activities engaged in by the appellants were atypical of offences charged under ss. 18, 20, or 47 of the Act, both Lord Mustill and Lord Slynn of Hadley were anxious to determine whether they rightly fell to be included within the prohibition of those provisions. To this end their Lordships engaged in a careful analysis of the previous authorities, concluding that they were not apposite to the facts of the current case and did not bind the House leaving it free to decide (*per* Lord Mustill, at p. 599):

> whether the public interest requires section 47 of the 1861 Act to be interpreted as penalising an infliction of harm which is at the level of actual bodily harm; which is inflicted in private...; which takes place not only with the consent of the recipient but with his willing and glad co-operation; which is inflicted for the gratification of sexual desire, and not in a spirit of animosity or rage; and which is not engaged in for profit.

Both their Lordships accepted that a victim's consent to harm amounting to grievous bodily harm was ineffective and, in addition, the public interest might dictate that the law disregards the consent of the victim where other considerations apply. Thus, in contrast to the majority, the minority were looking for reasons why the activities of the appellants should be brought within the prohibition contained in ss. 20 and 47 rather than looking for reasons why they should be excluded. The issue was not whether their Lordships were disgusted by the conduct (both indicated that they were), nor whether they were endorsing the conduct as morally right (both indicated that they were not approving the activities), but whether the law should be interpreted to render the appellants' conduct criminal.

c. *Developments since Brown* Following the decision of the House of Lords three of the appellants complained to the European Commission of Human Rights that their convictions violated their right to respect for private life guaranteed by Art. 8 of the Convention. In *Laskey, Jaggard and Brown v United Kingdom* (Case No. 109/1995/ 615/703–705) the European Court of Human Rights held that while the prosecution of the applicants interfered in their private lives, this was 'necessary in a democratic society' in pursuance of a legitimate aim, namely that of the 'protection of health'.

Brown **appears to resolve that consent is a defence to common assault**. It is not a defence to assault occasioning actual bodily harm or any more serious offence of violence. The exceptions to this rule are 'lawful activities' which carry the risk of harm such as 'surgery...ritual circumcision, tattooing, ear-piercing and violent sports including boxing' and 'parental chastisement'. **The deliberate infliction of injury in these 'lawful activities' would constitute an offence**, for example, where a rugby player kicks or punches an opponent, or a boxer kicks his opponent or punches him after the bout has ended, or a surgeon removes an organ or limb which the patient did not consent to being removed.

The Court of Appeal has considered the extent of the defence of consent in the context of contact sports in *Barnes* [2004] EWCA Crim 3246. The Court expressed the view that in light of most organised sports having their own disciplinary procedures and the fact that an injured player could use the civil courts to seek to obtain damages, criminal prosecution should be reserved for those situations where the conduct was sufficiently grave properly to be categorised as criminal. If what occurred went beyond what a player could reasonably be regarded as having accepted by taking part in the sport, this would indicate that the conduct was not covered by the defence of consent. Whether conduct reached this level depended on all the circumstances which included the type of sport, the level at which it was played, the nature of the act, the degree of force used, the extent of the risk of injury, and the state of mind of the defendant. In highly competitive sports conduct outside the rules might be expected to occur in the heat of the moment; the fact that such conduct was penalised and even resulted in a warning or a sending off, did not necessarily mean that the threshold level required for it to be regarded as criminal had been reached. In the instant case where V had sustained a serious leg injury as the result of a late tackle by D in a football match, the jury needed to consider whether the contact had been so obviously late and/or violent that it was not to be regarded as an instinctive reaction, error, or misjudgement in the heat of the game.

The list of lawful exceptions was extended by the Court of Appeal in *Wilson* [1996] 3 WLR 125. At his wife's instigation D branded his initials on his wife's buttocks with a hot knife. The Court of Appeal quashed his conviction for assault occasioning actual bodily harm contrary to s. 47 of the Offences Against the Person Act 1861. Russell LJ stated:

> *Brown* is not authority for the proposition that consent is no defence to a charge under section 47 ... in all circumstances where actual bodily harm is deliberately inflicted.

The Court considered that the instant case was distinguishable from *Brown* and *Donovan*. The Court based its decision on several grounds, none of which are particularly convincing: Mrs Wilson instigated the branding (but the appellants in *Brown* willingly engaged in the activities there); there was no aggressive intent on the part of D, his desire being not to injure but to assist his wife in what she regarded 'as the acquisition of a desirable piece of personal adornment' (but there was no aggressive intent in *Brown*; the motivation was sexual and sado-masochistic rather than 'artistic'!); the branding was akin to, and no more dangerous or painful than, tattooing (but branding was involved in *Brown* and none of the injuries required medical attention). Adopting an approach similar to the minority in *Brown* the Court asked whether public policy or the public interest demanded criminal sanctions for D's actions. The Court concluded that they did not, Russell LJ stating:

> Consensual activity between husband and wife, in the privacy of the matrimonial home, is not, in our judgment, normally a proper matter for criminal investigation, let alone criminal prosecution.

Herein, it is suggested, lies the real reason behind the decision—the Wilsons were heterosexual and married; Russell LJ's dictum implicitly suggests that even sado-masochism between husband and wife, in the privacy of the matrimonial home, would not be an offence. Would such liberality be shown towards the unmarried? If so, the decision in *Brown* could be seen to be one based more on prejudice than on principle.

The answer to this question came in the Court of Appeal decision in *Emmett, The Independent*, 19 July 1999. D was convicted of two counts of assault occasioning actual bodily harm arising from consensual sexual activity with his fiancée (involving asphyxiation on the first occasion and the use of lighter fluid on the second) as a result of which she suffered respectively 'subconjunctival haemorrhages in both eyes and some petechial bruising around her neck' and 'a burn, measuring some 6cm by 4cm' on her breast. The trial judge ruled that consent was not available as a defence where the parties foresaw the risk of injury arising from their consensual sexual activities. The Court of Appeal saw no reason in principle 'to draw any distinction between sado-masochistic activity on a heterosexual basis and that which is conducted in a homosexual context'. The Court of Appeal stated that the 'actual or potential damage to which the appellant's partner was exposed in this case, plainly went far beyond that which was established by the evidence in *Wilson*'.

d. *The transmission of disease* In *Clarence* (1888) 22 QBD 23, D, knowing he had a venereal disease, had intercourse with his wife, V, resulting in her contracting the disease. It was argued that his concealment of his condition constituted a fraud which vitiated V's consent thereby rendering the bodily contact an assault. The Court held, however, that there was no deception as to the nature of the act, sexual intercourse, and thus there was no assault and, if there was no assault, there could be no infliction of grievous bodily harm contrary to s. 20 of the OAPA. The court in *Clarence* also took the view that V's consent to sexual intercourse also implied consent to the risk of infection.

The Court of Appeal in the case of *Dica* [2004] EWCA Crim 1103, effectively overruled *Clarence*.

> D, knowing he was HIV, had unprotected sexual intercourse with two long-term sexual partners from whom he concealed his infection, infecting each of them with the disease. D was charged with unlawfully and maliciously inflicting grievous bodily harm contrary to s. 20 of the OAPA. The trial judge considered (1) that *Clarence* had been undermined as an authority, and (2) that the decision in *Brown* deprived the complainants of the legal capacity to consent to such serious harm with the result that even if they had known of D's condition they could not consent to infection. The Court of Appeal, following the House of Lords decision in *Ireland; Burstow* [1998] AC 147, which held that the s. 20 offence could be committed without an assault as where, for example, psychiatric injury is inflicted without direct violence or assault, concluded that *Clarence* had no continuing application as assault is not a necessary prerequisite to establishing the s. 20 offence. In ordering a retrial, however, the Court of Appeal confirmed that the issue for the jury was one of consent; while *Brown* prohibited consent to the deliberate infliction of GBH, V could consent to an activity which merely carried the risk of injury or harm. The Court of Appeal distinguished the present situation from *Boyea* and *Emmett* on the basis that those cases demonstrated that:

>> [V]iolent conduct involving the deliberate and intentional infliction of bodily harm is and remains unlawful notwithstanding that its purpose is the sexual gratification of one or both participants. Notwithstanding their sexual overtones, these cases were concerned with violent crime, and the sexual overtones did not alter the fact that both parties were consenting to the deliberate infliction of serious harm or bodily injury on one participant by the other. To date, as a matter of public policy, it has not been thought appropriate for

such violent conduct to be excused merely because there is a private consensual sexual element to it. The same public policy reasons would prohibit the deliberate spreading of disease, including sexual disease.

It is interesting that the Court characterised both cases as involving consent to the deliberate infliction of serious harm when this is not how either case was presented before the jury or argued before the Court of Appeal. It is clear that the judiciary still struggle with the notion that people may take sexual pleasure from pain. But, by contrast, the Court of Appeal expressed the view that consensual acts of intercourse were not to be rendered unlawful merely because there might be a known risk to the health of one participant. The Court considered a distinction was to be drawn between those who engage in sexual intercourse knowing there might be a risk and those who are intent on spreading or becoming infected with disease. The Court also noted the higher risks in casual sex between complete strangers as compared to those in 'a long-term and loving, and trusting relationship'. The Court did not wish to criminalise, for example, Roman Catholics who were conscientiously unable to use contraception, but who had sexual intercourse in the knowledge that the healthy partner may become infected. Further the Court did not wish to interfere in the sphere of private relationships.

What was not clear from the decision in *Dica* was whether those who engage in casual unprotected sex with the risks attendant upon that, are thereby impliedly consenting to the risk of infection such that the reckless infection of such a person by D would not amount to the s. 20 offence. In *Konzani* [2005] EWCA Crim 706, the Court of Appeal held that consent would only operate as a defence where it was 'informed consent'. Where D concealed his disease from his sexual partners he could not seek to rely on a consent implied from the general risk attendant upon sexual intercourse. The Court placed particular emphasis upon the personal autonomy of the victims. The Court further indicated that it would only be in rare situations that D could seek to raise the defence of honest belief in consent as silence 'is incongruous with honesty, or with a genuine belief that there is informed consent'. One example given was where D honestly believed V had been informed of his condition by someone else.

It is also unclear from *Dica* and *Konzani* whether D has to have actual knowledge of his infected condition or whether it is sufficient that he realises he might be infected. Recklessness is sufficient for the purposes of proving the infliction of grievous bodily harm contrary to s. 20 of the OAPA. Interesting issues will arise where D and V are not in a long-term relationship and where D suspects he is infected with HIV but has not bothered to undergo the necessary testing, and V aware that casual, unprotected sex may result in infection, enquires of D whether he is HIV+, relying on his response 'Not to my knowledge' before having unprotected sex with him.

e. *Further issues relating to consent* A number of matters were left unresolved by the decision in *Brown*. **First, is a person who willingly allows injuries to be inflicted upon him by another an accessory to the other's offence?** Where a statute is designed to protect a certain class of persons, a member of that class who is the victim of the offence cannot be convicted as an accessory (see **7.1.6** *ante*). As ss. 20 and 47 of the OAPA are for the protection of everyone it would be difficult to argue that the recipient of violence in such a case falls within a particular class for whose protection the statute was passed. If this is so a person would be guilty of aiding and abetting the offence committed by the wounder although, had he simply wounded himself, he would have been guilty of no offence.

Secondly, what is the position where actual bodily harm is likely or intended but does not occur? *Dicta* in *Donovan* and *Boyea* suggest that consent is negated, although in *Boyea* these dicta were qualified by the requirement that the assault be accompanied by circumstances of indecency. In *A-G's Reference (No. 6 of 1980)* it was stated that there would be an assault if actual bodily harm was 'intended and/or caused'. The majority in *Brown*, however, considered that consent is a defence to a charge of common assault. Thus if A and B agree to settle their differences by a fight and are arrested after exchanging a few punches which do not result in any harm, and prosecuted for common assault, they may be successful in raising a defence of consent if the majority in *Brown* are followed on this point, although dicta in the Court of Appeal suggest that the defence should not be available where harm is intended. In *Barnes* [2004] EWCA Crim 3246, the Court of Appeal stated, *obiter*, that 'when no bodily harm is caused, the consent of the victim to what happened is always a defence to a charge.'

Thirdly, what is the position if actual bodily harm was not intended but does occur (unforeseen by the accused); does this negate consent? In *Boyea* (which was approved in *Brown*) the appellant's conviction of indecent assault was upheld by the Court of Appeal on the basis of the principle that 'an assault intended or which is likely to cause bodily harm, accompanied by indecency, is an offence irrespective of consent, provided that the injury is not "transient or trifling"' which it derived from *Donovan* and regarded as consistent with the *Attorney-General's Reference (No. 6 of 1980)*. The appeal was argued on the basis that the accused believed the victim was consenting to his touching of her and that he neither intended to cause actual bodily harm nor foresaw the risk of it occurring. Such a belief, it was believed, would negative the *mens rea* for battery as there would be no intention to apply force unlawfully to another nor would there be recklessness thereto. What then is the *mens rea* for assault or battery in these circumstances? The Court held that intention to touch the other is sufficient if actual bodily harm was likely, albeit unforeseen by the accused. This conflicts with the statement of principle by Lord Lane CJ in *Gladstone Williams* (1984) 78 Cr App R 276 (see 3.6.1.1.2 *ante*) who treated consent as pertinent to the question of unlawfulness which was part of the definitional elements of assault, stating (at pp. 279, 280):

> [W]here the victim consents...the application of force to another will, generally speaking, not be unlawful...The mental element necessary to constitute guilt is the intent to apply unlawful force to the victim. We do not believe that the mental element can be substantiated by simply showing an intent to apply force and no more.

This issue was not addressed in *Boyea* or *Brown* but the assumption in *Brown* by the majority is that absence of consent is not a definitional element of the offence and thus this argument about *mens rea* falls by default although, had it been addressed, it would have been difficult to refute. In *Slingsby* [1995] Crim LR 570, however, this approach was rejected where D and V had engaged in vigorous sexual activity to which V fully consented in the course of which a signet ring worn by D caused an internal injury to V from which she subsequently died. Injury was neither intended nor foreseen by D or V. D was tried for manslaughter; Judge J (as he then was), ruled that the injury was the accidental consequence of consensual sexual activity and that it would be contrary to principle to treat as criminal activity which would not otherwise amount to assault merely because an injury occurred. This approach was endorsed by the Court of Appeal in *Meachen* [2006] EWCA Crim 2414 where D's convictions of inflicting grievous bodily harm and indecent assault were quashed where unforeseen injury was caused to V in the course of consensual sexual activity. The Court adopted the approach to *Boyea* which had been adopted in *Dica*, i.e. that that case was decided on the basis that there was no consent and thus the issue that arose in *Slingsby* and the instant case was not before the Court. Thomas LJ stated (at para. 40):

> It is sufficient for the issue that arises in this case to make clear that if the touching was with consent, then the fact that in the course of the consensual activity some bodily injury, even serious bodily injury, resulted accidentally and unintentionally, then as matter of principle no criminality can attach.

It should be noted that now the relevant sexual offence is sexual assault contrary to s. 3 of the Sexual Offences Act 2003 (see **10.2.3** *post*) which differs from indecent assault as the issue of consent is relevant in every case; if V consented to D's touching in sexual circumstances, that consent will negate liability even if harm resulted. It would be strange in such circumstances if a prosecutor chose to prosecute for assault occasioning actual bodily harm.

Fourthly, why is rough and undisciplined horseplay, where serious injuries may be sustained by victims whose consent must be seriously in doubt, included in the list of exceptions? In *Jones* (1986) 83 Cr App R 375 some boys at a youth club tossed two other boys into the air resulting in one suffering a ruptured spleen and the other a broken arm. The Court of Appeal held that they ought to have been able to raise the issue of consent as boys have always indulged in rough and undisciplined play among themselves and probably always will. This case was relied on in *Aitken* where the three appellants and the victim, G, were RAF officers who attended a party where they all became drunk and engaged in horseplay involving setting fire to the fire-resistant suits of two officers who treated it as a joke. Later the appellants sought to set fire to G's suit. They overcame his resistance and poured a large quantity of white spirit over it and ignited it. G was severely burned. At a general court-martial the appellants were charged with inflicting grievous bodily harm contrary to s. 20 of the OAPA. On appeal from their convictions the Courts-Martial Appeal Court quashed the convictions. The Appeal Court confirmed the judge advocate's direction that intoxication was no defence to a s. 20 charge but allowed the appeals on the basis that since the appellants had not intended to injure G, it was arguable both that the pouring of a large quantity of white spirit over him was an accident and that they genuinely believed that G had consented. By excluding these matters from the court's consideration the judge advocate had misdirected the Court on the question of unlawfully causing injury. In effect, the Courts-Martial Appeal Court was holding that G could consent to the risk of serious injury and that an honest belief in such consent negates the element of unlawfulness which had to be proved on a s. 20 charge.

The question which was not answered in *Jones*, *Aitken*, or *Brown* (where their Lordships accepted that rough or undisciplined horseplay was one of the exceptions recognised in the public interest) is, why should the law permit such activities where the injuries risked are life-threatening and where the consents of the victims are highly doubtful? Why should a person be able to consent to the risk of bodily harm (or worse) in the context of horseplay, and another be permitted to risk causing such harm? What public interest is operating here to permit consent (or belief in consent) to operate as an answer to a charge of unlawfully and maliciously inflicting grievous bodily harm? The fact that 'boys will be boys' hardly constitutes a 'good reason' for permitting a person to risk causing severe injury to another. All the courts turned a blind eye both to the degree of injury which may be inflicted and to the element of peer-group pressure which operates in male community life and which impinges upon the voluntariness of the consent of the victim in these situations. 'Horseplay' may be merely a euphemism for 'bullying'. It is worth noting also that if G had asked to be set on fire his consent in this context would have been ineffective.

In *Aitken* the appellants' honest belief that G was consenting to their horseplay, on a conventional understanding of criminal liability (see **5.6.3** and **5.6.4** *ante*), would not have been an effectual defence to the s. 20 charges as the appellants were drunk at the time. The Courts-Martial Appeal Court confirmed that s. 20 created an offence of basic intent so that it was no defence for the appellants to claim that they were deprived of the ability to foresee or appreciate the risk of harm ensuing from their actions; drunkenness substitutes for the *mens rea* requirement of recklessness. But what if they mistakenly believed that the victim was consenting, the mistake being a drunken one? Conventional wisdom, based on the precedents, would have suggested that such a belief in a defence of justification would be of no avail (see *O'Grady* [1987] 3 WLR 321 and *O'Connor* [1991] Crim LR 135 at **5.6.5** *ante*). If a drunken belief in the need to defend oneself is no defence and a drunken belief in consent in relation to rape is no defence, why should a drunken belief in consent be a defence in respect of a s. 20 charge? No answer is supplied in *Aitken* where no reference was made to *O'Grady* or *O'Connor*. The same error was made by the Court of Appeal in *Richardson and Irwin* [1999] 1 Cr App R 392 (see **5.6.5** *ante*).

Fifthly, what is it that determines that there is a public interest in certain activities being regarded as legitimate? Why should a religious motive for wounding (as in the circumcision of boys in a number of religions) be regarded as acceptable whereas a sexual motive is not? Why is boxing, involving the intentional injury of an opponent, acceptable whereas settling a dispute by fists is unacceptable? Why is it a 'manly diversion' to bully others whereas sexual deviation is 'unmanly' and deserving of moral and criminal censure? How is the public interest determined? The cases reek of legal paternalism and legal moralism but little reference is made to ideas of personal autonomy or sovereignty.

Regarding medical treatment a person may consent to surgery where the operation is for a valid purpose recognised by the law. A person's consent is valid where the operation is for a valid therapeutic purpose. This will cover medically prescribed treatment even though such treatment may involve a risk of harm, provided the possible benefits of the operation outweigh the possible harm from the operation or the failure to perform it. Even a sex-change operation performed for therapeutic reasons would be covered (see *Corbett* v *Corbett* [1971] P 83, at 99). However, if a person was to have his hand surgically removed to avoid military service or so that he could claim a disability allowance, his consent would be invalid and the surgeon would be liable at least for assault occasioning actual bodily harm as the operation would have no therapeutic purpose. The area of cosmetic surgery is problematic as it could be argued that such operations have no therapeutic value. It is likely, however, that such operations will be accepted as involving therapeutic value because of the psychological benefits they offer to the patient. If, however, V sought to have cosmetic surgery performed on him to change his appearance in the hope of avoiding detection for the offences he had committed, this would not be a therapeutic purpose nor would it be in the public interest so the consent would be invalid.

(ii) **What constitutes valid consent?** The fact that V apparently consents to D's act does not mean that the law will treat that apparent consent as valid consent. **If V is a child, or mentally retarded, and the prosecution prove that his understanding and knowledge was such that he was not in a position to decide whether or not to consent, his apparent consent will be invalid** (see *Howard* [1965] 3 All ER 684). The issue is whether he was unable to comprehend the nature of the act. In *Burrell* v *Harmer* [1967] Crim LR 169, D was convicted of assault occasioning actual bodily harm arising from tattooing two boys aged 12 and 13 which resulted in their arms becoming inflamed and painful. The Court held that there was no consent as the boys did not understand the nature of the act. Presumably they understood what a tattoo was but, it would appear, they did not understand the pain it would involve. In the case of a young child the absence of consent may be inferred from his/her age as he/she would not have the intelligence or understanding to give consent (see *R* v *D* [1984] AC 778). In the case of an older child it will be for the jury to decide whether the child was of sufficient understanding and intelligence to give consent, and if so, whether it has been proved that the child did not give its consent (*R* v *D*).

Where **V consents only as a result of D's threats or as a result of fear, this will negative consent**. It is not entirely clear what kind of threats will suffice; probably threats to dismiss from employment, or falsely to imprison. The issue will have to be determined on the facts of each case, taking into account the nature of the relationship between the parties and then considering whether the threat would be sufficient to overcome the will of a reasonably firm person. In some situations, the threat may be implied from the relationship, for example where D is in a position of authority over V such as a school teacher.

Fraud may vitiate consent where it relates to the nature of the act involved or the identity of the person performing the act, but not if it relates to the surrounding circumstances in which the act is performed. Thus in *Bolduc and Bird* (1967) 63 DLR (2d) 82, it was held that D, a doctor, was not guilty of assault when he performed a vaginal examination on V, a patient, having told her that E, who was present, was a medical student. E was a voyeuristic musician. This did not vitiate V's consent, however, as D did not deceive her as to the nature of the act. This is undoubtedly a very narrow view as clearly V would not have consented had she known the true circumstances in which the act was to be performed.

In *Richardson* [1999] Crim LR 62, D was charged with six counts of assault occasioning actual bodily harm arising from her continuing to practise as a dentist while suspended by the General Dental Council. The trial judge rejected a defence submission, *inter alia*, that the patients had consented to the treatment albeit that they did not know D was suspended from practice. D then pleaded guilty to all six counts and appealed. On appeal it was argued that the patients had been deceived neither as to the nature and quality of the act nor as to the identity of D. The Crown did not take issue on the first point but concentrated on the identity issue. The Court of Appeal allowed the appeal, there being no fraud as the concealment by D of her suspension from practice did not go to identity.

The Court of Appeal was unwilling to extend the concept of 'identity' to cover qualifications or attributes. This seems an unduly narrow approach as consent can only operate as a defence where the activity involved falls into one of the lawful exceptions—in this case reasonable surgical intervention. A person's qualifications to practice medical or dental surgery would seem to be inextricably linked to their identity for the purposes of relying on this exception. Their identity cannot simply consist of their name, age, sex, and race but must, for the purposes of practising medicine or dentistry, include their qualifications so to do. Would the Court of Appeal have concluded that there was no fraud if Richardson had never been qualified to practise dentistry but had masqueraded as a dentist taking on patients and offering treatment? If the answer is negative it is difficult to find a basis for distinguishing this situation from that in the facts of the case. Further, it is arguable that only a surgeon or dentist can perform a surgical or dental procedure. If performed by someone who is not qualified to practise surgery or dentistry the nature of the act would not be a surgical or dental procedure and thus the actor should be disqualified from relying upon the surgery exception. Clearly the decision in *Richardson* leaves unresolved more problems than it solves.

In *Clarence* (1888) 22 QBD 23, as Mrs Clarence understood the *nature* of this act there was no question of her husband's concealment of his condition amounting to a fraud as to the nature of the act. His concealment, rather, related to an attribute of his conduct, namely its capacity to spread infection. The offence charged, however, was not rape to which that attribute would be irrelevant, but was an offence against the person involving harm to which the attribute is relevant. Much of Stephen J's judgment confuses these issues and his analysis of instances of sexual intercourse which might become rapes if all frauds, without qualification, vitiated consent, do not bear close scrutiny as they lack close attention to the subject to which the fraud relates. It would indeed be anomalous if that to which V could not consent expressly (i.e. infection with disease) could be held to have been implicitly consented to when the risk of such infection was concealed from V by D's fraud.

Clarence is no longer considered a good authority.

> In *Tabassum* [2000] Crim LR 686, D carried out examinations of three women's breasts purporting to be carrying out a study on breast cancer. The women believed he was medically qualified and would not have let him examine them had they known he was not. He was convicted on three counts of indecent assault and appealed arguing that consent could only be negatived where there was deception as to identity or where the nature and quality of the act differed from that to which the victim had consented. The Court of Appeal dismissed the appeal and distinguished *Richardson*

noting that the appeal in that case had proceeded solely by reference to the point on identity. In the present case consent to the touching was given as the victims believed it was for a medical purpose—they were not consenting to indecent behaviour. Thus 'there was consent to the nature of the act but not its quality'.

It should be noted that previous cases stated that fraud as to the *nature* of the act would vitiate consent. The Court of Appeal in this case has used the term 'nature and quality' (a term used in the M'Naghten Rules). What the Court seems to mean here is that the nature of the act the victims consented to was a touching but they believed it to be an examination by a medically qualified person and thus to be performed for a medical purpose rather than performed by an unqualified person for an indecent purpose. By focusing on the act the Court negotiated the problem of identity and the relevance of qualifications thereto. *Tabassum* was followed in *Dica* [2004] EWCA Crim 1103, where the Court of Appeal confirmed that D's concealment of his HIV+ status did not negate consent to sexual intercourse, and thus D could not be liable for rape, as his deceit went not to the nature of the act but a quality of the act. It should be noted that under s. 76 of the Sexual Offences Act 2003, frauds as to the 'nature or purpose' of a relevant act are conclusively presumed to vitiate consent. Frauds as to other matters will only vitiate consent if they negate a person's agreement by choice (see s. 74 of the SOA 2003, **10.2.1.1.2** *post*).

10.1.1.3.2 *Necessity*

The defence of necessity was examined earlier (see **6.3.1** *ante*). *In re F (Mental Patient: Sterilisation)* [1990] 2 AC 1, Lord Goff of Chieveley stated that the common law principle of necessity could justify action which would otherwise be unlawful where, *inter alia*, the 'action [was] taken as a matter of necessity to assist another person without his consent'. Thus there would be no assault where D seizes V and forcibly drags him from the path of an oncoming vehicle thereby saving him from injury or death. A problem which frequently arises is the need to provide care or medical treatment for a person who is incapable of giving consent to it, for example, due to mental incapacity or to being unconscious as a result of illness or accident. Lord Goff concluded that it was the principle of necessity which provided a justification for the care or treatment in these cases. Where there is a situation of emergency, a doctor should do no more than is reasonably required in the best interests of the patient, before he recovers consciousness. Where, however, the inability to consent is permanent or semi-permanent, care or treatment which is in the best interests of the person may be administered if 'it is carried out in order either to save their lives, or to ensure improvement or prevent deterioration in their physical or mental health' (*per* Lord Brandon of Oakbrook). Thus the day-to-day care of those who are unconscious or who lack mental capacity to consent, is justified by this principle. Lord Brandon made the additional point that it is not only the principle of necessity which justifies treatment where a person is incapable of giving consent; where care has been assumed of a person who cannot consent, there is a common law duty to treat them (see further **2.5.2.2.3** *ante*).

One qualification to this point is that 'officious intervention' cannot be justified. Lord Goff stated that intervention would not be justified 'when it is contrary to the known wishes of the assisted person, to the extent that he is capable of rationally forming such a wish'. This raises an interesting problem; suppose P has been diagnosed terminally ill and he takes an overdose of sleeping tablets leaving a note stating that he cannot face the prospect of a slow and painful death and that he does not wish to be resuscitated. Would D, his medically qualified wife, be guilty of assault if she did resuscitate him? Would D's liability depend on whether P was adjudged rational/irrational or on whether D believed him to be irrational?

10.1.1.3.3 *Lawful correction*

It used to be lawful for a parent or other person *in loco parentis* to use reasonable force to discipline their children or charges (see *Cleary* v *Booth* [1893] 1 QB 465; *Mackie* (1973) 57 Cr App R 453) provided the child was old enough to understand its purpose (*Griffin* (1869) 11 Cox CC 402). If corporal punishment was administered out of spite or anger or for gratification, or if the degree of force was unreasonable, it was unlawful (see *Hopley* (1860) 2 F & F 202; *Taylor, The Times*, 28 December 1983). At common law teachers were *in loco parentis* and could administer corporal punishment in respect of the conduct of the child at, or on its way to or from, school. However, the common law only applied to teachers at independent schools which received no public funding and in respect of pupils whose fees were not publicly paid or subsidised. In all other cases no member of staff of a school could administer corporal punishment on a pupil 'by virtue of his position' as a member of staff (Education Act 1996, ss. 548 and 549; originally Education (No. 2) Act 1986). The 1986 provision followed the decision of the European Court of Human Rights which held the United Kingdom in contravention of Art. 3 of the Convention (see *Campbell and Cozans* v *United Kingdom* (1982) 4 EHRR 293). If, however, a parent gave express permission to teachers at his child's school to administer corporal punishment, a teacher who did so would not have done so 'by virtue of his position' but by virtue of being placed *in loco parentis* by the parent. In these cases the burden was on the prosecution to prove that the corporal punishment was not lawful.

In *A* v *UK* (1999) 28 EHRR 603 the European Court of Human Rights held that the United Kingdom was in breach of its obligations under the European Convention on Human Rights in that it failed to provide adequate protection to children and other vulnerable individuals against treatment or punishment which could constitute 'inhuman or degrading treatment' contrary to Art. 3 of the Convention. In the instant case the stepfather of the applicant had been prosecuted for assault occasioning actual bodily harm arising out of his chastisement of A using a cane which was applied with considerable force resulting in a number of severe bruises. He pleaded 'reasonable chastisement' and was acquitted by the jury. The finding of the European Court placed serious doubts over the limits of the defence of reasonable chastisement. The Department of Health issued a consultation document, *Protecting Children, Supporting Parents: A Consultation Document on the Physical Punishment of Children* (2000) and further legislation to clarify this area of the law was promised.

Pending further legislation the Court of Appeal in *R* v *H* [2001] EWCA Crim 1024, [2002] 1 Cr App R 7, gave further guidance on the factors to be taken into account when a jury is considering the reasonableness or otherwise of chastisement:

(i)   the nature and context of D's behaviour;

(ii) the duration of that behaviour;

(iii) the physical and mental consequences in respect of the child;

(iv) the age and personal characteristics of the child;

(v)   the reasons given by D for administering the punishment.

The Court was of the opinion that the common law being evolutionary, standards of reasonableness today would differ from those in the nineteenth century. However, as not every case of corporal punishment would necessarily breach Art. 3 of the Convention, the Court was satisfied that its guidance was consistent with Strasbourg jurisprudence to which English courts had to have regard when applying the common law by virtue of the Human Rights Act 1998. In the instant case, following a preparatory hearing before the trial commenced, the trial judge had sought the guidance of the Court of Appeal on how to direct the jury on the issue of lawful chastisement. The defendant admitted striking his son across the back several times with a leather belt but pleaded lawful chastisement to a charge of assault occasioning actual bodily harm contrary to s. 47 of the Offences Against the Person Act 1861. As there was little to distinguish the facts from those in *A v UK*, should the jury, directed in accordance with the guidance cited earlier, have acquitted and the child had taken his case to the European Court of Human Rights, a finding of a violation of Art. 3 would have been the likely outcome. Leaving it to the jury to evaluate the reasonableness of force used for the purposes of chastisement is hardly likely to be considered an appropriate means of giving effect to a child's Art. 3 rights. It is submitted that the role of the jury should be confined to finding facts in this situation and that the judge should evaluate those findings of fact in light of the jurisprudence of the European Court of Human Rights on what constitutes inhuman and degrading treatment. If the degree of force used falls foul of that evaluation the chastisement would be unlawful and the defence would fail (see further Rogers, 'A Criminal Lawyer's Response to Chastisement in the European Court of Human Rights' [2002] Crim LR 98).

Following the decision in *R v H*, Health Minister Jacqui Smith announced on 8 November 2001:

> Recent developments in the law have answered some of the key concerns that led to the consultation exercise in the first place. And we do not believe that any further change to the law at this time would be appropriate—it would neither command widespread public support nor be capable of consistent enforcement.
>
> However, we will be keeping the use of the 'reasonable chastisement' defence under review to ensure that the Human Rights Act 1998 serves to provide children with adequate safeguards from violence that should not be capable of being justified as reasonable chastisement.

The Government kept its promise to keep this matter under review. The Children Act 2004, s. 58, now provides clarification of the common law defence of lawful correction. Section 58 provides:

(1) In relation to any offence specified in subsection (2), battery of a child cannot be justified on the ground that it constituted reasonable punishment.

(2) The offences referred to in subsection (1) are—

    (a) an offence under section 18 or 20 of the Offences Against the Person Act 1861 (wounding and causing grievous bodily harm);

    (b) an offence under section 47 of that Act (assault occasioning actual bodily harm);

    (c) an offence under section 1 of the Children and Young Persons Act 1933 (cruelty to persons under 16).

This provision renders any physical punishment of a child an offence if it causes any actual bodily harm (see **10.1.1.4.2** *post*) or amounts to cruelty. Cruelty may involve the infliction of unnecessary suffering without any actual injury. It is no defence for D to claim that he did not intend any actual bodily harm as the s. 47 offence does not require *mens rea* in respect of the element of harm. Even if punishment is not cruel and does not cause actual bodily harm, it may still not be lawful if it is not reasonable. Physical punishment of a child for an inability to learn or do something which he could not reasonably be expected to be able to learn or do, is unlikely to be considered reasonable.

10.1.1.4 Aggravated assaults

There are several offences involving assault which are subject to higher penalties because of the presence of aggravating factors. In the case of each of these offences it must be proved that D committed the *actus reus* of technical assault or battery with the requisite *mens rea* and that the aggravating factor was present. In some cases the aggravating factor is the ulterior intent with which the accused committed the assault, for example, assault with intent to rob (s. 8(2) of the Theft Act 1968), and assault with intent to resist or prevent the lawful arrest of the accused or another for any offence (s. 38 of the OAPA; s. 17(1) of and sch. 1 to the Magistrates' Courts Act 1980). In other cases the aggravating factor derives from the circumstances in which the offence is committed, for example, sexual assault (s. 3 of the Sexual Offences Act 2003), and assault on a constable in the execution of his duty (s. 89 of the Police Act 1996).

10.1.1.4.1 *Racially or religiously aggravated assault*

The Crime and Disorder Act 1998 created new offences of racially or religiously aggravated assaults (see s. 29 as amended by s. 39 of the Anti-Terrorism, Crime and Security Act 2001). A racially or religiously aggravated assault is committed where a person commits an offence under s. 20 or s. 47 of the OAPA, or common assault, and either:

(a) at the time of committing the offence, or immediately before or after doing so, the offender demonstrates towards the victim of the offence hostility based on the victim's membership (or presumed membership) of a racial or religious group; or

(b) the offence is motivated (wholly or partly) by hostility towards members of a racial or religious group based on their membership of that group (s. 28(1)).

A 'racial group' means 'a group of persons defined by reference to race, colour, nationality (including citizenship) or ethnic or national origins' (s. 28(4)). A 'religious group' means 'a group of persons defined by reference to religious belief or lack of religious belief' (s. 28(5)).

In the case of assaults based on s. 20 or s. 47 the maximum penalty of five years is increased to seven years and for common assault the maximum penalty is increased from six months to two years. The complexity of this offence is evident from the first reported appeal relating to a prosecution under s. 29, *DPP v Pal* [2000] Crim LR 756. V, a caretaker at a community centre who was of Asian appearance sought to eject D, an Asian youth, from the centre. D assaulted him and called him 'white man's arse licker' and a 'brown Englishman'. The justices acquitted, finding that D used the words because he was aggrieved at being asked to leave and thus he was not demonstrating racial hostility. The Divisional Court dismissed the appeal by the prosecution holding that while the words demonstrated hostility towards V's conduct in ejecting him, they did not demonstrate hostility towards V because of his membership of a racial group (Asian). It seems that D's insults related to what he considered to be V's too close relationship with whites rather than his being an Asian. Thus while the words had a race element within them, this did not fall strictly within the statutory definition of racial aggravation.

The narrow approach adopted by the Divisional Court in *Pal* has not been followed in subsequent cases where the use of racist language has been treated as sufficient to constitute aggravation. In *DPP v Woods* [2002] EWHC Admin 85, D assaulted V, a doorman, who refused to admit one of D's friends to a club. D also called V a 'black bastard'. The magistrates found that D's hostility arose from his frustration and annoyance and that his frame of mind was such that he would have insulted any doorman by reference to an obvious physical characteristic which he happened to possess. Accordingly they found that the assault was not racially aggravated. On appeal by the prosecution, Maurice Kay J (sitting in the Divisional Court), allowed the appeal treating the insult as itself 'a demonstration of hostility based on the victim's membership of a racial group' (see also *DPP v McFarlane* [2002] EWHC 485 (Admin)). The Divisional Court appears now to be treating the use of racist language as sufficient aggravation although this is not what Parliament stipulated in enacting s. 28. In *White* [2001] WLR 1352, the Court of Appeal held that a racially aggravated offence could be committed by one member of a racial group against another member of the same racial group. The Court stated that 'a person may show hostility to his own kind whether racial, ethnic or national'. This suggests that an assault at an international sports event accompanied, for example, by the words 'English bastard' would be a racially aggravated assault regardless of the assailant's race or national origins. The Court also went on to hold that the word 'African' described a racial group despite the numerous racial, ethnic, and national groups within the continent of Africa. The Court took the view that, used in England and Wales, the word 'African' denoted someone who was black. In *A-G's Reference (No. 4 of 2004); R v D* [2005] EWCA Crim 889 the Court of Appeal considered the question whether using the term 'immigrant doctor', which indicated that a person was 'non-British' was specific enough to denote membership of a 'racial group'. The Court of Appeal held that whether the use of this term was only an allegation of 'non-Britishness' or amounted to a demonstration of hostility based on the victim's membership of a racial group was a question of fact which was for a jury to determine. This approach to defining 'racial group' non-inclusively is confirmed by the decision in *Rogers* [2007] UKHL 8 where the same epithet, 'bloody foreigners' was used by D to a group of Spanish women who got in his way as he rode his mobility scooter along the pavement. Their Lordships held that those who were not of British origin constituted a racial group and thus use of the term 'foreigners' fell within s.28(4) provided that the evidence as a whole proved that D's conduct demonstrated, or was motivated by, hostility to such a group. (see also *DPP v M* [2004] EWHC 1453 (Admin) see **14.6** *post*). This seems to imply that everyone who is a different race to D comprises a racial group, albeit that group is multi-racial. This view is supported by their Lordships' reasoning in response to the appellant's argument that a group should be defined by what it is rather than by what it is not. Their Lordships were of the view that the statute intended a broad, non-technical approach to construction. Baroness Hale, delivering the unanimous decision of the House, stated (at paras. 12–13):

> The mischiefs attacked by the aggravated versions of these offences are racism and xenophobia. Their essence is the denial of equal respect and dignity to people who are seen as 'other'. This is more deeply hurtful, damaging and disrespectful to the victims than the simple versions of these offences. It is also more damaging to the community as a whole, by denying acceptance to members of certain groups not for their own sake but for the sake of something they can do nothing about. This is just as true if the group is defined exclusively as it is if it is defined inclusively.
>
> The offences do not require particular words to be used.... Fine distinctions depending upon the particular words used would bring the law into disrepute.

The way in which the group appears to be defined, therefore, is not according to that group's racial characteristics but according to D's; the reference point is D's race as opposed to V's. Thus, rather than being defined as being of X race, they are defined as being non-X, X being D's race. This seems to turn the language of the statute on its head.

If 'African', 'immigrant', and 'foreigner' are treated as referring to a racial group, might 'European bastard' also amount to racial aggravation? Europeans are usually white. Imagine the scene at a Euro referendum debate if one English anti-Euro debater prods in the chest another English pro-Euro debater at the same time saying, 'European bastard'? This is a long way from the kinds of racially aggravated assaults Members of Parliament might have had in mind when the legislation was enacted. Now that religious aggravation is included in the offence the ambit of the offence is even greater (see further **14.6** *post*).

Where s. 28(1)(a) is relied upon to establish the element of racial or religious aggravation, the hostility based on the victim's membership of a racial or religious group must be demonstrated at the time of committing the offence or immediately before or after doing so. 'Immediately before or after' was originally tightly limited. In *Parry* v *DPP* [2004] EWHC 3112 (Admin) the Divisional Court held that a statement made to a police officer 20 minutes after the alleged offence (criminal damage) in which D used racially hostile language in respect of V, was not made immediately after committing the offence. Field LJ stated (at paras. 19 and 21):

> These words must be given their plain and ordinary meaning and so construed their effect is to make the subsection strike at words uttered or acts done in the immediate context of the substantive offence....The statement was not made in the immediate context of the substantive offence, but was made by the appellant after he had quit the scene and was sitting in his own house, at least 20 minutes after the door had been damaged.

By contrast, in *Babbs* [2007] EWCA Crim 2737 a conviction was upheld where D had assaulted V having described V and his companions 15 minutes previously as 'fucking foreigners'. D's annoyance arose as both D and V queued at a takeaway. The insulting words were used at the outset and later, when V was served ahead of D, the assault occurred. The judge directed the jury to consider whether the words had been used immediately before the assault. Later in his summing-up he left them with the question whether they were satisfied that immediately before assaulting V D had demonstrated to him a hostility based on his membership of a particular racial group? The only evidence of such hostility, of course, was the words used. However, in a judgment which massages fact and law, Latham LJ held that s. 28(1)(a) is directed not so much to words but to the hostility which is demonstrated towards a victim with the relevant connotation. Latham LJ was of the view that the words used were capable of colouring D's behaviour towards V throughout the subsequent events and that the jury were entitled to conclude that the hostility based upon race had been evinced over a continuing period from the moment the words were first used to the moment when the assault occurred. The problem with this embroidery of the facts is that there was no evidence of continuing hostility being demonstrated; rather the words were uttered, the queuing continued and 15 minutes later, in response to provocative words ('white trash') and acts (waving his food bag at D) from V, D reacted.

Finally the aggravating factor may be a consequence of the assault such as the occasioning of actual bodily harm (s. 47 of the OAPA). This latter offence will be examined separately later.

10.1.1.4.2 *Assault occasioning actual bodily harm*

An assault occasioning actual bodily harm is an offence triable either summarily or on indictment, the maximum punishment for which is five years' imprisonment.

The *actus reus* is satisfied by proof of a technical assault or battery which, in addition, has caused actual bodily harm. 'Actual bodily harm' means any hurt or injury calculated to interfere with the health or comfort of the victim (*Miller* [1954] 2 QB 282 at 292). **The hurt or injury need not be serious or permanent but must be more than transient and trifling.** In *R (On the application of T)* v *DPP* [2003] EWHC 266 (Admin), the Administrative Court held that momentary loss of consciousness fell within the meaning of the word 'harm' as it involved 'an injurious impairment to the victim's sensory functions' and it was axiomatic, therefore, that the bodily harm was 'actual'. Harm would not be 'actual' where it was so trivial as to be wholly insignificant. The Court emphasised the point that in *Miller* the Court was excluding only harm which was 'transient *and* trifling' not that which was 'transient *or* trifling'. Pain or discomfort are sufficient although there is no discernible injury such as a bruise or swelling (see *Reigate Justices, ex parte Counsell* (1984) 148 JP 193). In *DPP* v *Smith* [2006] EWHC 94 (Admin) the Divisional Court held that hair was a part of the body and that cutting off a substantial part of it was capable of constituting actual bodily harm. Likewise if D put paint or some other unpleasant substance on it which marked or damaged it. While this may undoubtedly be highly distressing for the victim, particularly if not cutting hair has religious significance, it is difficult to see how any hurt or injury or interference with the victim's health or comfort arises. The distress does not amount to actual bodily harm as the next case indicates. An interesting side effect of this decision is that if cutting hair amounts to actual bodily harm, the list of activities for which the public interest requires consent can amount to a defence must be extended to include hairdressing. One hardly thinks the House of Lords would have had this in mind in *Brown* (see **10.1.1.3.1** *ante*).

Psychiatric injury is capable of amounting to actual bodily harm but where a prosecution is brought on this basis expert evidence must be brought unless the matter has been admitted by the defence (*Chan-Fook* [1994] Crim LR 432; affirmed in *Ireland* [1998] AC 147). Hysterical and nervous conditions and mere emotions such as fear, distress, or panic do not constitute psychiatric injury. What is required is something that amounts to a recognised psychiatric illness or condition (see *R v D* [2006] EWCA Crim 1139).

There was some doubt about the *mens rea* of this offence. It was clear that the accused had to intend a technical assault or battery or be reckless (in the *Cunningham* sense) whether the victim apprehended or sustained unlawful personal violence (see *Spratt* [1990] 1 WLR 1073). Whether he had to intend in addition to cause actual bodily harm or be reckless thereto was unclear. In *Roberts* (1971) 56 Cr App R 95, D ordered V, a passenger in his car, to remove her clothes and he tried to pull off her coat. She jumped out of the moving car and suffered concussion and grazing as a result. The Court of Appeal treated the issue of actual bodily harm as purely one of causation to be determined objectively: that is, 'was it the natural result of what the alleged assailant said and did, in the sense that it was something that could reasonably have been foreseen as a consequence of what he was saying or doing?' (*per* Stephenson LJ). There was **no need to prove that the accused intended to cause actual bodily harm or was reckless thereto**. This was confirmed in *Savage* (1990) 91 Cr App R 317. In *Spratt* [1990] 1 WLR 1073, decided by a different panel in the Court of Appeal on the same day as *Savage*, it was held that *mens rea*, amounting to at least subjective recklessness, was required in relation to causing actual bodily harm although this issue was not strictly relevant to the appeal. In neither case was *Roberts* referred to.

In *Parmenter* (1991) 92 Cr App R 68, the Court of Appeal reviewed both cases and expressed a preference for *Spratt*, interpreting it to have decided as *ratio* that foresight of actual bodily harm is necessary for a conviction of the s. 47 offence, when this was strictly *obiter*. In *Savage and Parmenter* [1991] 4 All ER 698, the House of Lords overruled *Spratt* on this point, reversed *Parmenter* and held that the statement of principle in *Roberts* was correct.

The one remaining absurdity in this area is the sentence for the s. 47 offence. The maximum penalty is five years' imprisonment which is the same as that available for the more serious offence of maliciously inflicting grievous bodily harm contrary to s. 20 of the OAPA. So far Parliament has declined to remove this anomaly.

10.1.2 Wounding and inflicting grievous bodily harm

Section 20 of the OAPA provides:

> Whosoever shall unlawfully and maliciously wound or inflict any grievous bodily harm upon any other person, either with or without any weapon or instrument, shall be guilty of a misdemeanour, and being convicted thereof shall be liable...to imprisonment for not more than five years.

10.1.2.1 *Actus reus*

The *actus reus* of this offence consists of unlawful wounding or the unlawful infliction of grievous bodily harm. (For the meaning of 'unlawful' see 10.1.1.1 *ante*.) **To constitute a wound the continuity of the whole skin must be broken** (*Moriarty* v *Brookes* (1834) 6 C & P 684). There need be no profusion of blood; one drop would be sufficient. However, a scratch which does not break the inner skin is not a wound (*McLoughlin* (1838) 8 C & P 635), nor is an internal rupture of blood vessels (*C (A Minor)* v *Eisenhower* [1984] QB 331) but a rupture of the inner skin of the cheek or of the urethra resulting in bleeding is a wound (*Waltham* (1849) 3 Cox CC 442).

Grievous bodily harm means 'really serious harm' (*DPP* v *Smith* [1961] AC 290) and is a question of fact for the jury. **It includes psychiatric injury** (see *Burstow post*). While some wounds may also constitute really serious harm, it is clear that the most minor wound, for example a pin prick, falls within s. 20. It is difficult to see why it was thought necessary to specify wounding as a separate head as minor wounds could have been covered by the s. 47 offence. A number of injuries or wounds which individually would not amount to grievous bodily harm may, in total, do so (see *Grundy* [1989] Crim LR 502; *Birmingham* [2002] EWCA Crim 2608). In the latter case D entered a building as a trespasser and inflicted 11 knife wounds on V, together with bruising to her chest. D was charged with aggravated burglary (see **13.2** and **13.3** *post*) which required proof that he had inflicted grievous bodily harm with a weapon. The wounds were not individually serious but the Court of Appeal relied on *Grundy* to reject D's appeal as the jury were entitled to find that together they amounted to really serious injury. **In determining whether harm is really serious the jury should consider the effect of those injuries on the particular victim, taking into account their age and health** (*Bollom* [2003] EWCA Crim 2846). In this case V, a child aged 17 months, was found to be suffering from non-accidental bruising and abrasions to her body, arms, and legs. D had sought to argue that V's age and health were not relevant considerations. The Court of Appeal stated that injuries had to be viewed in 'their real context' and there was no need for the harm to be life-threatening, dangerous, or permanent, nor was it a requirement that the victim should require treatment or that the harm should have lasting consequences.

Section 20 refers to grievous bodily harm being 'inflicted'. This contrasts with s. 18 of the OAPA (see **10.1.3** *post*) where the relevant word is 'causing' grievous bodily harm. In a series of cases spread over a century, it has been held that the words 'inflict' and 'wound' require proof of an assault (see *Taylor* (1869) LR 1 CCR 194; *Clarence* (1888) 22 QBD 23 (see **10.1.1.3.1** *ante*); *Springfield* (1969) 53 Cr App R 608; *Snewing* [1972] Crim LR 267; *McCready* [1978] 1 WLR 1383; *Beasley* (1981) 73 Cr App R 44). There were, however, cases in which the requirement for an assault appeared to have been ignored (see *Halliday* (1969) 61 LT 701; *Martin* (1881) 8 QBD 54; *Lewis* [1970] Crim LR 647; *Cartledge* v *Allen* [1973] Crim LR 530). Resolution of this matter became important as s. 6(3) of the Criminal Law Act 1967 provides:

> (3) Where, on a person's trial on indictment for any offence except treason or murder, the jury find him not guilty of the offence specifically charged in the indictment, but the allegations in the indictment amount to or include (expressly or by implication) an allegation of another offence falling within the jurisdiction of the court of trial, the jury may find him guilty of that other offence or of an offence of which he could be found guilty on an indictment specifically charging that other offence.

If on a charge under s. 20 of the OAPA the jury concluded that there had not been a wound or that the injury inflicted did not amount to GBH could they convict of the lesser offence of assault occasioning actual bodily harm contrary to s. 47 of the OAPA? In *Wilson* [1984] AC 242 the House of Lords was confronted with this issue. Lord Roskill, with whom all their Lordships agreed, referred to the Australian case of *Salisbury* [1976] VR 452 and stated (at p. 260):

> I am content to accept...that there can be an infliction of grievous bodily harm contrary to section 20 without an assault being committed.

Thus an accused could inflict grievous bodily harm without necessarily committing a technical assault or battery. Thus if the allegation in the indictment for a s. 20 offence does not 'amount to or include' an assault, a conviction of the s. 47 offence as an alternative at that trial would not be possible. If on an indictment for a s. 20 offence the jury is presented with the option of convicting of a s. 47 offence, however, it must be because the prosecution have presented evidence which points to an assault. Lord Roskill stated (at p. 261):

> If it be said that this conclusion exposes the defendant to the risk of conviction on a charge which would not have been fully investigated at the trial on the count in the indictment, the answer is that a trial judge must always ensure, before deciding to leave the possibility of conviction of another offence to the jury under section 6(3), that that course will involve no risk of injustice to the defendant and that he has had the opportunity of fully meeting that alternative in the course of his defence.

Wilson **established that 'inflict' has a wider meaning than 'assault'** but did not resolve the question whether it was as wide as 'cause' in s. 18 of the OAPA. Not having to determine the exact meaning of 'inflict' for the purposes of the case before them, their Lordships were content to cite with approval *Salisbury* where it was stated that (at p. 461):

> grievous bodily harm may be inflicted...either where the accused has directly and violently 'inflicted' it by doing something, intentionally, which, though it is not itself a direct application of force to the body of the victim, does directly result in force being applied violently to the body of the victim, so that he suffers grievous bodily harm.

In *Savage and Parmenter* [1992] 1 AC 699, the House of Lords followed *Wilson* and arrived at the same conclusion regarding wounding, that is, that an alternative verdict of 'Guilty' of the s. 47 offence is permissible on a charge of wounding contrary to s. 20. They accepted that **wounding does not necessarily involve an assault** although they considered that the circumstances in which a wounding might occur without an assault being committed would be 'quite extraordinary'.

> In *Burstow* [1998] AC 147, D was charged with inflicting grievous bodily harm contrary to s. 20 of the OAPA on the basis of a protracted campaign of silent telephone calls to V, 'hate' mail, theft of clothing from her washing line, and scattering condoms in her garden all of which led to V suffering severe depression. The defence conceded that depression amounted to grievous bodily harm and the Crown conceded that there had been no assault or battery as no force had been applied directly to the body of the victim. The trial judge ruled, however, that the House of Lords in *Wilson* had

gone no further than accepting that there can be an 'infliction' without an assault and had not accepted the *Salisbury* judgment in full. Consequently, there was no reason for giving 'inflict' a narrow or restrictive meaning and it should be taken to mean 'impose upon'. In response to this ruling D pleaded guilty and appealed. His appeal was dismissed by the Court of Appeal which certified the following point of law of general public importance for the consideration of the House of Lords:

> Whether an offence of inflicting grievous bodily harm under section 20 of the Offences against the Person Act 1861 can be committed where no physical violence is applied directly or indirectly to the body of the victim.

Their Lordships answered the question in the affirmative, Lord Steyn and Lord Hope of Craighead delivering speeches. Lord Steyn was of the view that any difference in the language in ss. 18 and 20 of the OAPA was not significant. In addition he considered that *Wilson* had not decided what 'inflict' meant before concluding that there is 'no radical divergence between the meaning of the two words ["cause" and "inflict"]'. The only problem remaining was the decision in *Clarence* which Lord Steyn distinguished on the basis that the judges in that case were not concerned with psychiatric injury opining that the case 'no longer assists'. His Lordship concluded that although the words 'cause' and 'inflict' are not exactly synonymous one could 'quite naturally speak of inflicting psychiatric injury'. Lord Hope of Craighead also distinguished *Clarence* without overruling it. He concluded that the words 'cause' and 'inflict' may be taken to be interchangeable and that it was entirely consistent with the ordinary use of the English language to say that the appellant had 'inflicted' psychiatric harm on his victim. It is unfortunate that their Lordships did not explore the problems of *Clarence* in greater detail and that they limited their comments to the infliction of psychiatric harm whereas the question before them concerned the infliction of grievous bodily harm generally. In light of the fact that all their Lordships answered the certified question in the affirmative the only conclusion one can draw is that *Clarence* is no longer a good authority. In *Dica* [2004] EWCA Crim 1103, (see **10.1.1.3.1(i)d** *ante*) where D infected two women with the HIV virus, the Court of Appeal stated that *Clarence* had no continuing relevance in this context and causing someone to suffer GBH through infecting her could amount to an infliction for the purposes of s. 20.

One remaining problem with *Burstow* is a statement by Lord Hope who stated (at p. 164):

> there is this difference [between the meaning of 'inflict' and 'cause'],...the word 'inflict' implies that the consequence of the act is something which the victim is likely to find unpleasant or harmful. The relationship between cause and effect, when the word 'cause' is used, is neutral. It may embrace pleasure as well as pain. The relationship when the word 'inflict' is used is more precise, because it invariably implies detriment to the victim of some kind.

Question

Did Lord Hope mean to throw in doubt the authority of *Brown* [1993] 2 WLR 556?

Clearly masochists do not find injury or pain 'unpleasant or harmful' and do not regard their injuries as detrimental but regard them rather as a means to enhance their sexual fulfilment. It would be strange if a charge of inflicting GBH contrary to s. 20 would fail because of this dictum whereas a charge of causing GBH with intent contrary to s. 18 would succeed. This being so Lord Hope's dictum cannot be taken to contradict the express statements of their Lordships in *Brown*. What the difference in ambit between 'inflict' and 'cause' is must, in the absence of further judicial explanation, remain a mystery.

10.1.2.2 *Mens rea*

D must wound or inflict grievous bodily harm '**maliciously**'. 'Maliciously' does not mean spitefully or with ill-will; rather it **means intentionally or recklessly** and 'recklessly' is given its subjective meaning which requires foresight of the consequence (*Cunningham* [1957] 2 QB 396). What consequence, however, must D be proved to have intended or foreseen? One would have thought that it would be necessary to prove an intention to wound or cause grievous bodily harm or foresight of such a consequence possibly occurring. In *Mowatt* [1968] 1 QB 421, Lord Diplock stated (at p. 426):

> the word 'maliciously' does import on the part of the person who unlawfully inflicts the wound or other grievous bodily harm an awareness that his act may have the consequence of causing some physical harm to some other person....It is quite unnecessary that the accused should have foreseen that his unlawful act might cause physical harm of the gravity described in the section, i.e. a wound or serious physical injury. It is enough that he [foresaw]...that some physical harm to some person, albeit of a minor character, might result.

It is important to read Lord Diplock's speech carefully as the issue is not whether he 'ought' to have foreseen some harm but rather whether he *did* foresee some harm. Thus D will be liable where his foresight is of a lesser degree of harm than that which resulted and which is prohibited by s. 20. This was affirmed by the House of Lords in *Savage and Parmenter* [1991] 1 AC 699, at 721 (see further *Rushworth* (1992) 95 Cr App R 252; *Pearson* [1994] Crim LR 534). This compares with murder where an intention to cause grievous bodily harm is sufficient. Where the harm alleged is psychiatric, it must be proved that the accused foresaw harm of that kind.

Two final points to note are that an intent to frighten V is not sufficient for the s. 20 offence (*Sullivan* [1981] Crim LR 46) unless such an intent is accompanied by foresight of the risk of psychiatric harm, and if D honestly, but mistakenly, believes that he is, for example, acting in self-defence he is not intending to wound *unlawfully* or inflict grievous bodily harm.

10.1.3 **Wounding or causing grievous bodily harm with intent**

Section 18 of the OAPA provides:

> Whosoever shall unlawfully and maliciously by any means whatsoever wound or cause any grievous bodily harm to any person...with intent...to do some...grievous bodily harm to any person, or with intent to resist or prevent the lawful apprehension or detainer of any person, shall be guilty of [an offence and shall be liable to imprisonment for life].

10.1.3.1 *Actus reus*

'Wound' and 'grievous bodily harm' have the same meaning as in s. 20. It is not clear whether a wound, for the purposes of s. 18, must result from an assault. The section states 'whosoever shall unlawfully and maliciously by any means whatsoever wound'; this might imply that a wound may form the basis of a s. 18 charge in a wider range of circumstances than for a s. 20 charge, but the issue is, as yet, unresolved. **The word 'cause' will be satisfied by proof that D's act was a substantial cause of V's injury** (see **2.6** *ante*). Grievous bodily harm may also be caused where D deliberately omits to act where he was under a legal duty to act. One subtle difference between s. 18 and s. 20 is that s. 20 requires the wound or grievous bodily harm to be inflicted on some 'other person' whereas s. 18 only requires that the wound or grievous bodily harm be caused to 'any person'. This raises the interesting possibility that if D caused grievous bodily harm to himself with intent to do so, perhaps seeking to gain discharge from military service or to enable him to claim disability benefit, he could be charged with the s. 18 offence.

10.1.3.2 *Mens rea*

There are two elements to the *mens rea* of s. 18. First D must 'maliciously' wound or cause grievous bodily harm and, secondly, he must do so with an ulterior intent either to cause grievous bodily harm or to resist or prevent the lawful apprehension or detainer of any person.

What does 'maliciously' mean in the context of s. 18? Where D is charged with 'maliciously causing grievous bodily harm with intent to cause grievous bodily harm', the word 'maliciously' is superfluous as D can be convicted only where he intended to cause grievous bodily harm. If D is charged with 'malicious wounding with intent to cause grievous bodily harm' or with 'malicious wounding (or maliciously causing grievous bodily harm) with intent to resist arrest' the word 'maliciously' requires definition. D may intend to cause grievous bodily harm without foreseeing a wound. For example, he may administer a karate chop to V intending to break his arm without foreseeing the ensuing wound caused when V falls over cutting his head on the corner of a table. Likewise he may push a police officer intending to resist arrest and not foresee the officer's resultant fall against a rock resulting in a fractured skull and cut scalp. If further anomalies are not to be created, 'maliciously' should mean the same in s. 18 as it does in s. 20. In *Mowatt* [1968] 1 QB 421, however, the Court of Appeal stated *obiter* that 'in section 18 the word "maliciously" adds nothing'. As the case concerned a charge of inflicting grievous bodily harm under s. 20, little weight should be attached to this dictum.

> In *Morrison* (1989) 89 Cr App R 17, D was seized by a police officer who stated she was arresting him. He dived through a window pane dragging her with him as far as the glass resulting in her sustaining serious facial lacerations. The trial judge directed the jury that if he intended to resist arrest and was reckless in the Caldwell sense as to causing the officer harm, he was guilty of the s. 18 offence. The Court of Appeal quashed the conviction holding that recklessness in the *Cunningham* (subjective) sense was required.

However, the case did not decide what degree of harm D had to foresee to be liable. Under s. 20, foresight of some physical harm is sufficient and this probably suffices for s. 18 but who can predict what the Court of Appeal or House of Lords might decide if directly confronted with this issue?

In respect of the ulterior intent, intention bears the same meaning as for murder, that is either (i) the consequence (causing grievous bodily harm or resisting arrest etc.) was D's aim or purpose or, (ii) if this consequence was not D's aim or purpose, D knew that it was a virtually certain consequence resulting from achieving his aim or purpose, in which case the jury may use this as evidence from which they may find intention proved.

If D mistakenly believes that he is justified in using force in self-defence or prevention of crime etc, and he uses reasonable force in the circumstances (as he believed them to be), he would not be guilty of wounding with intent or causing grievous bodily harm with intent. If D is using force to resist arrest believing the arrest to be unlawful, and it is unlawful, he likewise would not be guilty of the s. 18 offence (*Walker* (1854) Dears CC 358). But if the arrest is lawful, although D honestly believes it is unlawful, he will be guilty of the s. 18 offence (*Bentley* (1850) 4 Cox CC 406; *Lee* [2000] Crim LR 991) as ignorance of the law (in this case the officer's powers of arrest) is no excuse. Thus if D, being innocent of any offence, is arrested by an officer who has reasonable grounds to suspect he had committed an arrestable offence, D would be guilty of the s. 18 offence if he pushed the officer to the ground whereupon he cut his knee (see *Lee ante*). If, however, D believed the person arresting him was not a police officer (rather than believing that an officer had no power of arrest in the circumstances) D's mistake being one of fact rather than of law will, under the principle in *Williams* (1984) 78 Cr App R 276 (see **3.6.1.1.2** *ante*), avail him (see *Blackburn* v *Bowering* [1994] 3 All ER 380).

10.1.4 Administering poison

Section 23 of the OAPA provides:

> Whosoever shall unlawfully and maliciously administer to or cause to be administered to or taken by any other person any poison or other destructive or noxious thing, so as thereby to endanger the life of such person, or so as thereby to inflict upon such person any grievous bodily harm, shall be guilty of [an offence]…and shall be liable…[to a maximum penalty of 10 years' imprisonment].

Section 24 of the OAPA provides:

> Whosoever shall unlawfully and maliciously administer to or cause to be administered to or taken by any other person any poison or other destructive or noxious thing, with intent to injure, aggrieve, or annoy such person, shall be guilty of an [offence]…and shall be liable…[to a maximum penalty of five years' imprisonment].

10.1.4.1 *Actus reus*

Both sections require proof that D administered to, or caused to be administered to or taken by, V some poison or other destructive or noxious thing. Thus, D would commit the offence if he fed V with the poison (administered), if he left the poison in V's food and E subsequently fed him it (caused to be administered), or if he left it in V's food and V subsequently fed himself with it (caused to be taken) (see *Harley* (1830) 4 C & P 369; *Dale* (1852) 6 Cox CC 14). Until V consumes it, however, there is no administration (see *Cadman* (1825) *Carrington's Supplement*) although D's behaviour prior to this could have amounted to an attempt. In *Gillard* (1988) 87 Cr App R 189, the Court of Appeal held that spraying V with a noxious fluid so that it comes into contact with his body amounts to an administration.

In *Kennedy (No. 2)* [2007] UKHL 38 the House of Lords finally sorted out the mess created by the Court of Appeal over a decade in upholding various convictions for manslaughter where heroin-filled syringes had been supplied by one drug-addict to another, the recipient self-injecting and dying as a result. In these cases the Crown Prosecution Service has charged D with manslaughter on the basis of an unlawful and dangerous act, that act being the s. 23 offence of administering or causing to be administered a noxious thing. The House of Lords confirmed that s. 23 creates three distinct offences as set out earlier, namely administering a noxious thing to another, causing a noxious thing to be administered to another, or causing a noxious thing to be taken by another. Where, however, a person supplies a drug to another who with full knowledge freely and voluntarily self-injects, none of these offences is committed (see **2.6.3.5.4** *ante*). In consequence there is no unlawful act and a manslaughter conviction cannot be sustained.

The courts have experienced problems over the definition of 'poison' or 'other noxious thing'. **Ultimately it is for the jury to decide if the substance involved was a poison or noxious thing.** In the context of s. 58 of the OAPA, which relates to the administration of 'poison or other noxious thing' with intent to procure an abortion, the courts have held that the offence may be committed where a 'recognised poison' has been administered although in a quantity too small to be capable of doing any harm (*Cramp* (1880) 5 QBD 307). If the substance is not a 'recognised poison', to constitute a 'noxious thing' it must be administered in such quantity as to be in fact harmful (*Marlow* (1964) 49 Cr App R 49; see also Ormerod and Gunn, 'Criminal Liability for Transmission of HIV' [1996] 1 Web JCLI who argue that body fluids infected with the HIV virus are 'noxious' things). The problem with this distinction is that many things which are poisons are beneficial in small doses. For example, strychnine in small doses is used as a treatment to stimulate the respiratory system where a person has been poisoned by depressants of the central nervous system, but larger doses of strychnine are fatal. Similarly, warfarin is used in the treatment of people with certain heart conditions as an anticoagulant to thin the blood. It is also used as rat poison and in larger quantities can kill humans. Are strychnine or warfarin poisons or noxious things? For the purposes of s. 23 it probably does not matter which category they fall into as it appears that the meaning of noxious thing may differ from s. 23 to s. 24. Section 23 requires not only an administration of the poisonous or noxious substance but that the life of V be thereby endangered or that grievous bodily harm be thereby inflicted on V. If the substance is merely 'noxious' the fact that the life of V has been endangered or he has sustained grievous bodily harm from its administration demonstrates that it has been administered in sufficient quantity to be harmful. These definitional problems may be relevant, however, where an attempt to commit the s. 23 offence is charged. In *Cato* [1976] 1 WLR 110, D was convicted of manslaughter and an offence under s. 23, having injected V, with his consent, with heroin which caused his death. Lord Widgery CJ sought to distinguish between substances in common use which may be harmful when taken in an overdose and those which are liable to injure in common use. The former are not 'noxious' simply because of their aptitude, whereas the latter are. He placed heroin in the latter category and thus it was always a 'noxious' thing although it may not harm experienced addicts who have a high tolerance to it.

It appears that the grievous bodily harm or endangerment of life must result from the administration of the substance and would not cover the situation where, for example, the substance causes drowsiness and V falls down a flight of stairs breaking his neck.

There is no requirement in s. 24 for anything other than proof of administration of the poison or noxious thing. In *Marcus* [1981] 2 All ER 833, D put eight sedative and sleeping pills into her neighbour's bottle of milk. She was convicted of the s. 24 offence and appealed. On appeal it was argued, relying on *Cato*, that as sleeping tablets are harmless in themselves they could not be regarded as 'noxious' simply because D sought to administer an excess quantity of them. The Court of Appeal explained *Cato* taking the view that Lord Widgery was 'not intending to lay down a general proposition that a substance harmless in itself and in small quantities could never be noxious within s. 24...if administered in large quantities'. In the context of s. 24 'noxious thing' had to be interpreted in light of the requisite intent to injure, aggrieve, or annoy. This involved taking into account 'not only the quality or nature of the substance but also the quantity administered or sought to be administered'. Thus a substance harmless in small quantities could be 'noxious' in the quantity administered. In the context of s. 24, 'noxious' was not to be limited to substances which might cause bodily harm but would also include substances which were hurtful or unwholesome or objectionable. The Court gave the example of putting a snail in a bottle of ginger beer intending to aggrieve or annoy V. Similarly it would cover putting a large quantity of laxative in V's milk. In *Marcus*, the sedative quality of the drugs could clearly aggrieve or annoy V but the Court also took the view that they might harm V if, for example, in a sedated condition V were to drive a car or cross a busy street. Thus the 'harmful' quality of the substance may arise indirectly.

10.1.4.2 *Mens rea*

In both sections the word '**maliciously**' is used which **means intentionally or recklessly in its** *Cunningham* sense; it is the administration which must be intentional or reckless. In s. 23 no *mens rea* is required with respect to endangering life or inflicting grievous bodily harm; these are matters of causation (see *Cato*).

D cannot be convicted of the s. 24 offence unless the ulterior intent to 'injure, aggrieve or annoy' V is proved. In deciding if D has such an intent, regard is to be had not only to the effect he intends to produce but also to 'his whole object in acting as he has done' (*per* Robert Goff LJ in *Hill* (1985) 81 Cr App R 206). Thus, if D administered a sleeping pill to a woman with intent to rape her when comatose, the tablet would not be intended to produce injury but his 'ulterior motive' would constitute an intent to injure. In *Hill*, D, a homosexual, gave slimming tablets to two boys which D knew could also produce sleeplessness. Keeping someone awake is not necessarily harmful; but it may be depending on whether D's purpose in doing so is benevolent (for example, to keep the pilot of an aircraft awake) or malevolent (for example, to carry out a prolonged interrogation). In the instant case D's intention in giving the tablets was to disinhibit the boys and thereby render them more susceptible to his sexual advances; this constituted an intent to injure. A problem with this approach is that Robert Goff LJ proceeded, *obiter*, to provide an example which somewhat stretched the meaning of injury. He stated that if D drugged V with a view to stealing his property while asleep, his intention to deprive V of his property amounted to an intent to injure him. It is submitted that this should be regarded as an intent to 'aggrieve or annoy', but Robert Goff LJ considered that depriving V of his property involved more than simply causing him distress or annoyance but was actually injurious to him.

Section 25 of the OAPA provides that a person charged with an offence under s. 23 may be convicted of an offence under s. 24. In such a case, however, the ulterior intent required for s. 24 must be established.

10.1.5 Reform

The Law Commission's Draft Criminal Code (Law Com No. 177) proposed a major overhaul of non-fatal offences against the person. The Law Commission recognised, however, that it was unlikely that the Draft Criminal Code would be implemented *in toto*. As a result it decided to produce a series of Bills, each complete in itself, containing proposals for reform of discrete areas of the criminal law. In *Legislating the Criminal Code: Offences Against the Person and General Principles* (Law Com No. 218) the Law Commission included a Criminal Law Bill which would implement its proposals in respect of non-fatal offences against the person as well as legislating for a number of general principles such as *mens rea* (or 'fault terms' which the Law Commission prefers) and defences which apply throughout the criminal law. The Law Commission's Bill, if enacted, would have repealed, *inter alia*, ss. 18, 20, and 47 on the basis that (at para. 12.6):

> ...the language of the Act is so complicated, obscure and old-fashioned; and the structure of the three sections is so complicated and technical; that mistakes by lawyers and complete unintelligibility to the layman were eventually bound to result.

This obscurity of the law, it argues, results not only in additional expense as it impedes the efficient discharge of business in the criminal courts, but also in injustice.

In February 1998 the Home Office issued a Consultation Document, *Violence: Reforming the Offences Against the Person Act 1861* together with a draft Offences Against the Person Bill. Against a background of 83,000 cases of non-fatal offences against the person before the courts in 1996, the Home Office stated (at para. 1.2):

> It is therefore particularly important that the law governing such behaviour should be robust, clear and well understood. Unclear or uncertain criminal law risks creating injustice and unfairness to individuals as well as making the work of the police and courts far more difficult and time-consuming. The Government's aim is that the proposed new offences should enable violence to be dealt with effectively by the courts and that the law should be set out in clear terms and in plain, modern language.

The Consultation Paper went on to state (at para. 2.1):

> [The] primary purpose [of the reforms] is to replace the outdated offences contained in the Offences Against the Person Act 1861 with a rational and coherent set of new offences. In doing so it is not the Government's intention to alter fundamentally the scope or operation of the law. It does not intend to make the law either tougher or more lenient, but to make it clearer and easier to use.

The Consultation Paper proposed a hierarchy of offences which reflect those proposed by the Law Commission in *Legislating the Criminal Code: Offences Against the Person and General Principles* (Law Com No. 218) and by the CLRC in its Fourteenth Report (Cmnd 7844). The following section details the main offences and maximum sentences proposed.

Intentional serious injury

1. (1) A person is guilty of an offence if he intentionally causes serious injury to another.

(Life imprisonment)

Reckless serious injury

2. (1) A person is guilty of an offence if he recklessly causes serious injury to another.

(On indictment: 7 years; summarily: 6 months and/or a fine not exceeding the statutory maximum)

Intentional reckless injury

3. A person is guilty of an offence if he intentionally or recklessly causes injury to another.

(On indictment: 5 years; summarily: 6 months and/or a fine not exceeding the statutory maximum)

Assault

4. (1) A person is guilty of an offence if—

  (a) he intentionally or recklessly applies force to or causes an impact on the body of another, or

  (b) he intentionally or recklessly causes the other to believe that any such force or impact is imminent.

(2) No such offence is committed if the force or impact, not being intended or likely to cause injury, is in the circumstances such as is generally acceptable in the ordinary conduct of daily life and the defendant does not know or believe that it is in fact unacceptable to the other person.

(Summarily: 6 months and/or a fine not exceeding level 5 on the standard scale)

The Bill spelled out both the meaning of fault terms and of 'injury':

Meaning of fault terms

14. (1) A person acts intentionally with respect to a result if—

(a) it is his purpose to cause it, or

(b) although it is not his purpose to cause it, he knows that it would occur in the ordinary course of events if he were to succeed in his purpose of causing some other result.

(2) A person acts recklessly with respect to a result if he is aware of a risk that it will occur and it is unreasonable to take that risk having regard to the circumstances as he knows or believes them to be.

Meaning of injury

15. (1) In this Act 'injury' means—

   (a) physical injury, or

   (b) mental injury.

(2) Physical injury does not include anything caused by disease but (subject to that) it includes pain, unconsciousness and any other impairment of a person's physical condition.

(3) Mental injury does not include anything caused by disease but (subject to that) it includes any impairment of a person's mental health.

(4) In its application to section 1 this section applies without the exceptions relating to things caused by disease.

The anomaly in the OAPA of wounding being treated as of equal seriousness to inflicting grievous bodily harm, even though the wound is only minor, would have gone as a wound would be dealt with in the same way as any other injury. If there are any remaining distinctions between 'inflicting' and 'causing' following the House of Lords' decision in *Burstow*, these too would disappear. The Draft Bill also provided for a correlation or correspondence between the harm caused and the fault which must be proved on the part of the accused. No longer would foresight of actual bodily harm be sufficient *mens rea* on a charge of inflicting grievous bodily harm. The definition of 'intention' in cl. 14(1) was based on that provided by Professor Sir John Smith in 'Note on Intention' [1990] Crim LR 85. Professor Smith, 'Offences Against the Person: The Home Office Consultation Paper' [1998] Crim LR 317, pointed up a flaw in the cl. 14(1)(b) definition following the House of Lords' decision in *Woollin* [1998] 3 WLR 382 (see **3.2.3.4** *ante*). Woollin in a fit of temper had thrown his baby son on to a hard surface causing his death. His purpose had been simply to vent his anger. Professor Smith suggested that if the child had not died there could be no conviction on a charge under cl. 1(1). He suggested (at p. 318) that cl. 14(1)(b) should be amended to read:

(b) although it is not his purpose to cause it, he knows that it will occur in the ordinary course of events, or that it would do so if he were to succeed in his purpose of causing some other result.

There are some further anomalies which might result from the Draft Bill being enacted. In cll. 1 and 2 a distinction in terms of culpability is drawn between intention and recklessness whereas this is not done in cl. 3 on the basis, according to the Law Commission (which the Government appears to have adopted), that this 'would over-complicate the law' (Law Com No. 218, para. 13.4). This is a lame reason and would leave the potential for injustice in the future. On the question of the transmission of disease the Consultation Paper did not adopt the Law Commission's proposals which would have criminalised the intentional or reckless transmission of disease which resulted in injury. The proposals involved criminalising only the intentional transmission of disease where this causes serious injury. They would only permit prosecution where the transmission was carried out with an intention to cause serious injury. Under the existing law, the reckless transmission of disease resulting in grievous bodily harm falls under s. 20 of the OAPA (see *Dica* and *Konzani ante*). (Ormerod and Gunn, 'Criminal Liability for the Transmission of HIV' [1996] 1 Web JCLI, argue cogently that the transmission of HIV could be prosecuted under ss. 23 or 24 of the OAPA.) The reform proposals would greatly limit the circumstances in which liability could arise for the transmission of disease particularly as the proposed replacement for ss. 23 and 24 of the OAPA, in cl. 11 of the Draft Bill, 'administering a substance capable of causing injury' would not cover illness due to the cl. 15 definition of 'injury'. While it may be difficult to prove causation where an injury is alleged to have arisen from the transmission of a disease, there undoubtedly are circumstances where disease is transmitted intentionally or recklessly (see *Clarence, Dica*, and *Konzani ante*). For example, there were unsubstantiated allegations after the 1995 Rugby World Cup final that the New Zealand rugby players had been served tainted food by South African cooks resulting in food poisoning prior to the final which South Africa won. Imagine a similar situation in England and Wales under the current law and under the proposed Draft Bill. It is difficult to distinguish the culpability of a cook who deliberately serves up salmonella infected food to induce food poisoning from one who serves up food tainted with a strong purgative which is designed to have a similar debilitating effect. Currently, it is arguable that s. 24 of the OAPA, would cover both situations. If the Draft Bill were to be enacted the effects of a strong purgative could amount to an injury and the cook could be liable for causing such injury either under cl. 3 or cl. 11, but he would be guilty of no offence against the person where the food is tainted by salmonella.

The Draft Bill contained a number of other clauses to cover other offences such as assault on a constable (cl. 5), causing serious injury to resist arrest (cl. 6), assault to resist arrest (cl. 7), causing injury or the risk of injury by the use of explosive or dangerous substances (cll. 8 and 9), threats to kill or cause serious injury (cl. 10), torture (cl. 12), and causing danger on the railways (cl. 13). Supervening fault and transferred fault were dealt with in cll. 16 and 17 while all the common law defences currently available were preserved by cl. 18. Clause 19 dealt with the effect of involuntary intoxication on liability. The Bill did not, however, contain any express provision on consent which would continue to be dealt with under the common law.

The Law Commission looked at the problem of consent issuing in 1995 a separate Consultation Paper No. 139: *Consent in the Criminal Law*. The paper sought 'to identify the general principles which ought to underpin the criminal law in this area, and to recommend appropriate reform if the present state of the law conflicts with those principles' (para. 1.11). The paper examined the issue of consent in the context of medical and surgical treatment; circumcision, tattooing, branding, cosmetic piercing, and scarification; religious or spiritual flagellation or chastisement; sado-masochism; chastisement of children; dangerous exhibitions and horseplay; and sports (including boxing) and martial arts. The paper proposed that the intentional or reckless causing of a seriously disabling injury to another person should continue to be criminal, even if the person injured consented to such injury or to the risk of such injury. A 'seriously disabling injury' (SDI) was defined (in para. 4.51) as:

> any injury or injuries which—
>
> (1) cause serious distress, and
>
> (2) involve the loss of a bodily member or organ or permanent bodily injury, or permanent functional impairment, or serious or permanent disfigurement, or severe and prolonged pain, or serious impairment of mental health, or prolonged unconsciousness;
>
> and in determining whether an effect is permanent, no account should be taken of the fact that it may be remediable by surgery.

This proposal was subject to three classes of exceptions. First, a person may consent to a non-fatal injury which amounts to a SDI if it is caused during the course of proper medical treatment or care (para. 8.50). 'Proper medical treatment or care' includes sterilisation operations, sex change operations, lawful abortions, cosmetic surgery, and organ donation (para. 8.50). A similar exception was proposed for injuries caused during the course of properly approved medical research (para. 8.51). Secondly, the paper proposed (at para. 14.20) that:

> (1) the intentional or reckless causing of all types of injury in the course of fighting, otherwise than in the course of a recognised sport, should continue to be criminal, even if the person injured consented to injury or to the risk of injury of the type caused; but
>
> (2) an exception to this rule should continue to be available where any injury, other than seriously disabling injury, is caused in the course of undisciplined consensual horseplay.

While the Law Commission proposed (at para. 12.68) that a person should not be guilty of an offence of causing injury if the relevant injury was caused in the course of playing or practising a recognised sport in accordance with its rules, the proposal (quoted in the preceding section) would clearly criminalise the kind of activity engaged in by the appellants in *Aitken* (see **10.1.1.3.1** *ante*). Thirdly, the paper proposed that any consent given by a person under 18 to injuries intentionally caused for sexual, religious, or spiritual purposes should not be treated as valid consent (see paras. 10.52 to 10.55).

10.2 Sexual offences

There are numerous sexual offences but for the purposes of this chapter discussion will largely be confined to the main offences of rape, assault by penetration, sexual assault and causing a person to engage in sexual activity without consent, and the raft of offences relating to children.

The law on sexual offences was reformed by the passage of the Sexual Offences Act 2003 (SOA 2003). This Act is designed to strengthen and modernise the law with the intention that it be both clearer and more coherent. In 1999 the Home Office announced a review of the law relating to sexual offences with the remit of reviewing the existing law and making recommendations that would:

(i)   Provide coherent and clear sex offences that would protect individuals from sexual violation, especially children and the more vulnerable;

(ii) enable offenders to be appropriately punished;

(iii) be fair and non-discriminatory.

The underlying philosophy was that the intervention of the criminal law into private sexual relations would only be justified where there was harm to an individual and generally the activity was non-consensual. The review resulted in the Report, *Setting the Boundaries: Reforming the Law on Sex Offences* (HO, 2000) which, in turn, led to the publication of the White Paper, *Protecting the Public* (HO, 2002). In the latter the Home Secretary, David Blunkett, described the existing law as 'archaic, incoherent and discriminatory'. The SOA 2003 repealed most of the Sexual Offences Act 1956 and many other provisions and created a new code of sexual offences. It introduced a number of new offences and redefined existing offences to remove the vestiges of stereotyping of masculine and feminine sexuality and discrimination based upon sexual orientation.

10.2.1 Rape

Prior to the enactment of the SOA 2003 rape involved vaginal or anal intercourse by D with a person who did not consent to it, D either knowing that s/he did not consent or being reckless thereto. The inclusion of anal intercourse within the definition of rape (and thus the extension of the protection of the offence to male victims) occurred with the enactment of s. 142 of the Criminal Justice and Public Order Act 1994. Prior to this the courts had extended the reach of the offence to protect married women who were subjected by their husbands to non-consensual sexual intercourse (see *R* v *R* [1991] 1 AC 599). The new offence of rape defined in s. 1(1) of the SOA 2003 further extended the offence of rape to cover other forms of non-consensual penile penetration which are regarded as equally traumatic, abhorrent, and demeaning as vaginal or anal rape. Section 1(1) provides:

A person (A) commits an offence if—

(a) he intentionally penetrates the vagina, anus, or mouth of another person (B) with his penis,

(b) B does not consent to the penetration, and

(c) A does not reasonably believe that B consents.

(Throughout this section the perpetrator will be referred to as A and the complainant as B consistent with the legislation.) While both males or females may be the victims of rape, the offence remains gender-specific in that it may be committed only by males as principals. A female may, of course, aid, abet, counsel, or procure the offence. Where a female causes a male to have non-consensual intercourse with her she may be convicted of the offence of causing a person to engage in sexual activity without consent (SAWC) contrary to s. 4 of the SOA 2003. The maximum penalty for rape is life imprisonment (s. 1(4) of the SOA 2003).

10.2.1.1 *Actus reus*

10.2.1.1.1 *Penetration*

The *actus reus* of rape consists of the penetration of the vagina, anus, or mouth by the penis. Section 79(9) of the SOA 2003 defines 'vagina' to include vulva, thereby confirming that the slightest degree of penetration is sufficient to constitute the complete offence. There is no need for the hymen to be ruptured, nor is it necessary for ejaculation to occur. **Penetration is a continuing act from entry to withdrawal** (s. 79(2) of the SOA 2003). Thus if A penetrates B with consent but B withdraws that consent, A must withdraw his penis; to continue to penetrate B would amount to the *actus reus* of rape (see *Cooper and Schaub* [1994] Crim LR 531). Section 79(3) provides that 'references to a part of the body include references to a part surgically constructed (in particular through gender reassignment surgery)' thereby making it clear that the law covers transsexuals—a male-female transsexual may be the victim of vaginal rape while a female-male transsexual may commit the offence of rape as a principal.

10.2.1.1.2 *Absence of consent*

A's penetration of B's vagina, anus, or mouth may only amount to rape where B does not consent to that penetration. Under the previous law there was no statutory definition of consent. The leading authority on how juries should be directed on this issue was *Olugboja* [1982] QB 320 where Dunn LJ stated:

> They should be directed that consent, or the absence of it, is to be given its ordinary meaning and if need be, by way of example, that there is a difference between consent and submission; every consent involves a submission, but it by no means follows that a mere submission involves consent.... [I]n the less common type of case where intercourse takes place after threats not involving violence or the fear of it... [the jury] should be directed to concentrate on the state of mind of the victim immediately before the act of sexual intercourse, having regard to all the relevant circumstances.... Where [the line between true consent and mere submission] is to be drawn in a given case is for the jury to decide, applying their combined good sense, experience and knowledge of human nature and modern behaviour to all the relevant facts of the case.

One of the complaints about this form of direction was that it left the jury too much leeway and could give rise to inconsistency. The 2003 Act provides a statutory definition of consent which is supported further by presumptions some of which are conclusive that there was no consent and some of which place a burden upon A to raise sufficient evidence as to whether or not B consented.

(a) *The definition of consent* Section 74 provides:

> For the purposes of this Part, a person consents if he agrees by choice, and has the freedom and capacity to make that choice.

Where the facts of the case do not fall within one of the situations covered by the presumptions, the focus will be upon this definition. Often, however, the presumptions will be relevant to the situation. Accordingly, it is important not to consider this section in isolation from the following sections (75 and 76) relating to the presumptions. There are three aspects to this definition of consent which are examined later; these aspects are, however, inter-related and inter-dependent and should not be considered in isolation from each other. It is worth noting at the outset that words such as 'choice' and 'freedom' are philosophically complex. Jurors will have their own notions of 'choice' and 'freedom' deriving from their culture, education, and background. There may be limited common ground between them. The real issue for the jury should not be to struggle to define 'choice' and 'freedom'; rather their focus should be on the issue whether or not B's freedom to choose was in some way constrained. In the Report, *Setting the Boundaries* (2000) it was recommended that there should be a standard direction given to juries on the meaning of consent. In appropriate circumstances juries should be told not to assume that B freely agreed simply because B did not say or do anything, protest, or resist which might indicate the contrary or that B was not physically injured (see para. 2.11.5). The fact that B is frozen by fear of A, and complies with A's demands without resistance, does not mean that B has freely agreed by choice to engage in sexual intercourse with A. A direction along those lines would therefore be appropriate in circumstances such as these to counteract the kind of thinking which considers that if B did not vigorously resist A, B must have been consenting.

(i) *Agreement by choice* **Agreement by choice would seem to imply that B is aware of what the proposed sexual activity is, is aware of who A is, and chooses to agree to that activity with A without any constraint (such as force, coercion, or fraud) impairing that choice.** It must be assumed that the protection offered by the 2003 Act is no less than that which previously pertained. The previous law clearly established that it is not necessary to prove that B positively dissented, it being sufficient to prove that B did not consent; there was no requirement that the absence of consent had to be demonstrated or that it had to be communicated to A for the absence of consent to exist (see *Malone* [1998] 2 Cr App R 447; followed in *H* [2007] EWCA Crim 2056). In *McAllister* [1997] Crim LR 233, Brooke LJ stated:

> The focus of the inquiry in all these cases is based on the sexual autonomy of the complainant. The circumstances of a possibly reluctant consent may be infinitely varied, and on each occasion the jury has to decide whether an alleged agreement to a sexual act may properly be seen as a real consent or whether it should be regarded as a submission founded on improper pressure which this particular complainant could not reasonably withstand from this particular defendant.

Such refined analysis will still be required under the SOA 2003 and the outcome of such analysis is no more predictable under it than under the previous law. The focus on the particular complainant and particular defendant may be important as the existence of a relationship between them, or the fact of a pre-existing relationship between them, may shed additional light on the issue. For example, B may know from past experience with A that a failure to submit to his sexual requests or demands will result in violence even though no violence is threatened. Ultimately, however, the question of how to characterise B's state of mind is one for the jury. Contrasting the nature and propriety of the pressure A may be bringing to bear, and that which B could reasonably be expected to withstand, may be an appropriate exercise for the jury to carry out but it is not immediately clear from the definition of consent that they should. Should promises of benefit which appeal to B's particular tastes or weaknesses be considered sufficient to vitiate consent? For example, the young aspiring film actress who has intercourse with the film director after promises of parts in his films may well be doing something which she finds somewhat distasteful and would not otherwise do, but she is agreeing to intercourse without any external constraint being imposed upon her. The constraint operating is her own internal ambition; no one is forcing her to be a film actress. The choices she is making are between pursuit of her career and preservation of her chastity. Does the protection of sexual autonomy demand that such a transaction be regarded as non-consensual with the potential of founding a charge of rape? By contrast threats of detriment may vitiate consent. A threat of violence or false imprisonment clearly bears upon B's freedom to choose and an agreement to intercourse in such circumstances would not amount to consent. But what is the appropriate outcome where the film director, faced with reluctance from the actress, tells her that he will ensure she never works in films if she does not have sex with him. There is a threat of detriment which may or may not be an idle one. To an extent, the degree of detriment depends upon both the likelihood of the film director carrying out the threat and the depths of the actress's ambition. Balancing the detriment threatened against the detriment of undesired intercourse is thus not a straightforward exercise and how the courts will address the problem of consent is unclear.

If the emphasis under the 2003 Act is upon sexual autonomy, other matters such as the context in which the sexual activity occurs or the consequences of that activity, may have a bearing upon the question whether or not B has truly agreed by choice. **For such a choice to be free and unconstrained, it must be an informed choice.** Concealment of matters relevant to that choice, or deception as to such matters, inevitably impact upon the validity of the agreement which results. For example, in *Linekar* [1995] Crim LR 320, A's conviction of rape was quashed where he had had intercourse with B, a prostitute, on the promise that he would pay her £25 which he did not pay. The Court of Appeal considered that A's false pretence did not destroy the reality of B's consent as the only frauds which could vitiate consent were those as to the nature of the act or the identity of the other party (see now s. 76 of the SOA 2003). This situation, however, was covered by the offence of procuring sexual intercourse by false pretences or false representations contrary to s. 3 of the SOA 1956. This offence has been abolished. The offence which is meant to replace it, causing a person to engage in sexual activity without consent, faces the same problem as the offence of rape as the same definition of consent applies.

The question, therefore, is whether it is possible to argue that as the context was that of prostitution, where the understanding is that the sexual service offered by B is one for which A will pay, there was no real agreement by B as she had been deceived in respect of the very thing, payment, which was fundamental to the conclusion of the agreement.

? Question

If A is infected with a sexually transmitted disease or is HIV+, and does not reveal this when asked by B, is it arguable that B has not agreed to sexual intercourse by choice as she has been deceived as to something fundamental to the conclusion of that agreement?

The old law did not regard this as a matter which vitiated consent. In *B* [2006] EWCA 2945 the Court of Appeal held that the fact that B had not disclosed the fact that he was suffering from a serious sexually transmitted disease is not relevant to the issue of whether a person with whom he engaged in sexual intercourse had consented to it within the meaning of s. 74 and no issues arose under the presumptions in relation to consent under ss. 75 and 76 (discussed later). In particular, s. 76 made reference only to two specific deceptions (as to the nature or purpose of the act or impersonation) which could vitiate consent. (For consideration of liability for inflicting GBH by the transmission of HIV, see *Dica* [2004] EWCA Crim 1103, **10.1.1.3.1(i)d** *ante*). If B expressly asks A about his HIV status before agreeing to sexual intercourse and A lies, can B be said to be 'agreeing by choice' where she has been deceived in respect of a consideration central to her decision? In *B* the Court expressed the *obiter* opinion that express misrepresentations were no different to implied misrepresentations. It is to be hoped that if the Court has to address this issue directly, it will arrive at a different conclusion. In such a situation, if B does not contract HIV, A would not be liable to conviction of the s. 20 offence and there would be no deterrent to him continuing his dangerous activities.

The deficiencies in the reasoning in *B* have, at least, been recognised by the Divisional Court in *Assange* v *Swedish Prosecution Authority* [2011] EWHC 2489 (Admin) in the context of an appeal against extradition under a European Arrest Warrant, where the issue was whether conduct alleged to amount to the Swedish offence of sexual molestation was an offence under the law of England and Wales. The crucial issue was whether A would have been guilty of raping B if B had consented only to protected sex, but A, without B's knowledge, did not use a condom, or removed the condom he had initially worn. The Court concluded that the case raised no issue as to the presumptions in s. 76 (see the following extract) because if there was any deception it was not a deception as to the 'nature or purpose of the relevant act'. Sir John Thomas P stated:

90. …If the conduct of the defendant is not within s.76, that does not preclude reliance on s. 74. *B* goes no further than deciding that failure to disclose HIV infection is not of itself relevant to consent under s. 74. *B* does not permit A to contend that, if he deceived [B] as to whether he was using a condom or one that he had not damaged, that was irrelevant to the issue of [B's] consent to sexual intercourse as a matter of the law of

England and Wales or his belief in her consent. On each of those issues, it is clear that it is the prosecution case she did not consent and he had no or no reasonable belief in that consent. Those are issues to which s. 74 and not s. 76 is relevant; there is nothing in *R v B* which compels any other conclusion....

91. Thus, if the question is whether what is set out in the EAW is an offence under the law of England and Wales, then it is in our view clear that it was; the requirement of dual criminality is satisfied.

The Divisional Court was satisfied, quite rightly, that the fact that conduct does not fall within s. 76 (a provision which relates to very limited circumstances in which conclusive presumptions arise) does not preclude reliance upon s. 74. Sir John Thomas P stated (at para. 88):

It would, in our view have been extraordinary if Parliament had legislated in terms that, if conduct that was not deceptive could be taken into account for the purposes of s. 74, conduct that was deceptive could not be.

(ii) *Freedom to make the choice* The absence of free choice whether or not to agree to penetration of the vagina, anus, or mouth by A's penis, vitiates consent. Clearly where that agreement is brought about by violence or the threat of force, such freedom to choose is negated. The relationship that exists between A and B may be of particular relevance when considering whether undue pressure or influence has been brought to bear by A upon B to secure apparent agreement to the relevant sexual act. The law on undue influence may provide some assistance in dealing with those situations where B is not a person of impaired capacity, albeit that s/he is naive and gullible. In *Royal Bank of Scotland plc v Etridge (No. 2)* [2001] UKHL 44, Lord Nicholls stated the general position regarding undue influence in the civil law as follows (at paras. 8 and 9):

Equity identified broadly two forms of unacceptable conduct. The first comprises overt acts of improper pressure or coercion such as unlawful threats. Today there is much overlap with the principle of duress as this principle has subsequently developed. The second form arises out of a relationship between two persons where one has acquired over another a measure of influence or ascendancy, of which the ascendant person then takes unfair advantage.... In cases of this latter nature the influence one person has over another provides scope for misuse without any specific overt acts of persuasion. The relationship between the two individuals may be such that, without more, one of them is disposed to agree a course of action proposed by the other. Typically this occurs when one person places trust in another to look after his affairs and interests, and the latter betrays this trust preferring his own interests. He abuses the influence he has acquired.

For regular readers of the tabloid papers, it will be easy to recall the many stories of doctors, psychotherapists, and priests who take advantage of vulnerable patients or parishioners who have looked to them for help and support in times of bereavement, illness, or crisis, and end up having sexual relationships with them. While the SOA 2003 expressly deals with abuse of positions of trust in relation to those under the age of 18 and creates a range of offences to deal with such situations (see ss. 16–19), it is unclear to what extent the abuse of a position of trust in relation to an adult of full capacity may be taken into account in considering whether or not there has been consent.

> **? Question**
>
> B suffers a traumatic marital breakdown and looks to her priest, A, for support. Over a period of months, having recognised B's vulnerability and desperation for acceptance and intimacy, A encourages B to pour out her most intimate secrets. He further persuades her that a sexual relationship with him, with no ties or commitment, would assist her in getting over her divorce. B, having been brought up to trust her priest, eventually agrees, after a period of increasing physical intimacy, to engage in full sexual intercourse with A. Several years later, when B has recovered from the trauma of the divorce, she complains that A raped her having exercised undue influence over her and having taken advantage of her vulnerability for his own purposes. Has A engaged in undue influence such as to negate B's freedom to make a choice?

While A's actions may attract moral censure, it is submitted that this is not the kind of situation which should fall within the law of rape. Emotional blackmail should not be regarded as a negation of B's freedom, as ultimately B still made the choice unconstrained by threat, force, fear, or coercion. By contrast, if her psycho-therapist had hypnotised her, and when under hypnosis had instructed her that she would willingly respond to his sexual demands, her apparent willing response subsequently when not under hypnosis may constitute a choice that was not truly free as the decision to agree was involuntary.

> The boundary between consent and submission set in the context of taking unfair advantage of a person in desperate straits, received some attention in *Kirk and Kirk* [2008] EWCA Crim 434. JM (aged 14) had for many years been sexually abused by P Kirk, her aunt's husband. T Kirk had also abused her on occasions. She regularly ran away from home because of pressure from her brother who was bullying and blackmailing her over what P Kirk had done to her. JM had been living on the streets for some time. Tired, dirty, and hungry, with nowhere to go, in desperation she went to the minicab office where T Kirk worked, as the only place left where she might get help and something to eat. In return for £3.25 which she used for food, she had sexual intercourse with T Kirk. The case was left to the jury on the basis that T took advantage of a hungry and vulnerable child whom he knew had been abused by his brother and himself, the prosecution contending that her will was overcome through hunger and desperation such that she submitted but did not consent. It was left to the jury to draw the line between submission and consent. T was convicted and the Court of Appeal upheld the conviction satisfied that it was appropriate to leave the issue of submission and consent to the jury against the background circumstances of this case.

While the circumstances in which intercourse took place have some similarity to prostitution, there were several factors which transformed the transaction: there was a history of abuse by T and his brother P (of which T was aware) which created the circumstances giving rise to JM's vulnerability; and JM was a child in desperate circumstances of which T was fully aware. If anything, this case demonstrates the importance which context may play in determining whether in any particular case the agreement to intercourse arises from free choice or constrained choice. T's responsibility for JM's circumstances suggest that any advantage he took of those circumstances for his own gratification would be unfair.

(iii) *Capacity to make a choice* If B does not have capacity to make a choice, there can be no consent. Capacity, however, is not defined. In the offence of sexual activity with a person with a mental disorder impeding choice contrary to s. 30(1) of the SOA 2003, a requirement of the *actus reus* is that 'B is unable to refuse because of or for a reason related to a mental disorder'. Section 30(2) provides that:

> B is unable to refuse if—
>
> (a) he lacks the capacity to choose whether to agree to the touching (whether because he lacks sufficient understanding of the nature or reasonably foreseeable consequences of what is being done, or for any other reason), or
>
> (b) he is unable to communicate such a choice.

The inability to refuse in either case must be the result of a mental disorder. The phrase by 'any other reason' has the potential to be very wide. In C [2009] UKHL 42, the House of Lords considered that it covered B who suffered from schizo-affective disorder, an emotionally unstable personality disorder, an IQ of less than 75, and had a history of alcohol abuse. Her mental disorder did not mean that she did not understand what was involved when A asked her to perform oral sex on him; however, because of her very unstable condition at the time, which gave rise to an irrational fear, she lacked the capacity to choose. The test is person- and situation-specific in that on a different day, or in a different situation, B may have had the capacity to choose as her mental disorder had a fluctuating impact upon her.

The remainder of s. 30(2)(a) relates to whether B has sufficient understanding of the nature of the sexual act involved and what its foreseeable consequences might be; if sexual intercourse, obviously pregnancy; all forms of penetration, the possibility of contracting a STD; if anal intercourse, the possibility of pain and injury. It is submitted that incapacity for the purposes of ss. 1–4 of the SOA 2003 is both a broader and a narrower concept. It is a broader concept as matters which may impair a person's capacity to choose are not confined to mental disorders. Clearly a lack of understanding is relevant as a person may not be deceived as to what the sexual act is, but have no comprehension of what it involves, as where, for example, a person has a severe learning disability. By contrast, a person generally may have such understanding but, in a particular circumstance, may lack the capacity to make a choice, as where, for example, s/he is voluntarily intoxicated by drink or drugs or is acting as an automaton in a state of impaired consciousness. It is a narrower concept as an inability to communicate a choice does not prevent a person who understands the nature of the sexual act, and its foreseeable consequences, from positively agreeing to it albeit s/he may be unable to communicate that agreement other than by submitting to the act. If it had been intended that such a person should not be deemed capable of giving consent, this should have been dealt with by means of including in s. 76 a conclusive presumption to this effect. (For a different view see Stevenson, Davies and Gunn, *Blackstone's Guide to the Sexual Offences Act 2003* (OUP, 2004).)

In *Bree* [2007] EWCA Crim 804 the Court of Appeal provided some guidance on how the regularly occurring issue of a complainant's intoxication should be treated. The question is not whether alcohol might have removed inhibitions such that B may have done something which she would not have done if sober; nor is it relevant that B later regrets what she did, or that she has little recollection of what precisely happened, or that A or B or both of them were behaving irresponsibly. The essential question was whether or not B consented. On a proper construction of s. 74 the issue was whether or not B had temporarily lost her capacity to choose whether to have intercourse on the relevant occasion; if she had, she was not consenting. However, where B, despite the consumption of substantial amounts of alcohol, remained capable of choosing whether or not to have intercourse, and in drink had agreed to do so, that consent would mean there was no rape. But, as a matter of practical reality, the capacity to consent might have evaporated well before B became unconscious. Each case would depend on its own facts and it would be for the jury to decide. The Court recognised that no legislative structure could further define the issue as the problems arose not from the legislation but the infinite circumstances of human behaviour, usually taking place in private without independent evidence and the consequential difficulties of proof to which this gave rise.

(b) *Consent and presumptions* In order to provide assistance in determining whether or not B consented to the relevant sexual act, the SOA 2003 created two sets of presumptions, namely conclusive presumptions and evidential or rebuttable presumptions. The presumptions have an impact in terms of both the *actus reus* and *mens rea* elements of the offences in ss. 1–4 of the SOA 2003. The 'relevant act', which must be proved by the prosecution before a presumption may arise, is defined in s. 77 of the SOA 2003. In the case of rape the relevant act is the defendant penetrating the complainant's vagina, anus, or mouth with his penis.

(i) *Conclusive presumptions* Section 76(1) of the SOA 2003 provides that where the prosecution prove that the defendant did the relevant act and that one of the two circumstances specified in s. 76(2) existed, it is to be conclusively presumed—

(a) that the complainant did not consent to the relevant act, and
(b) that the defendant did not believe that the complainant consented to the relevant act.

Paragraph (b) does not create a strict liability offence as the circumstances in s. 76(2) require proof of intention in respect of them on the part of the defendant. The relevant circumstances are that:

(a) the defendant intentionally deceived the complainant as to the nature or purpose of the relevant act;
(b) the defendant intentionally induced the complainant to consent to the relevant act by impersonating a person known personally to the complainant.

As there must be an intentional deception or inducement, A will have the relevant knowledge about the circumstances. Under the previous law deception as to the nature or purpose of the relevant act negated consent (see *Williams* [1923] 1 KB 340; *Flattery* (1887) 2 QB 410). In *Jheeta* [2007] EWCA Crim 1699 the Court of Appeal expressed the view that s. 76 required stringent scrutiny as the presumptions are conclusive on the issue of consent. The Court took the view that s. 76(2)(a) was limited to the nature or purpose of the sexual act involved. The Court cited as examples of cases where the presumption would now arise *Flattery*, *Williams*, *Tabassum* (*ante*), and *Green* [2002] EWCA Crim 1501. In *Green* a qualified doctor carried out bogus examinations of young men in the course of which they were wired to monitors and asked to masturbate so that he could assess their potential for impotence. The deception related to the 'purpose' of the physical act. By contrast the Court considered that *Linekar* (*ante*) fell outside the ambit of s. 76(2)(a) as the deception was as to A's intentions rather than the nature or purpose of the act. In *Jheeta* A created a 'bizarre and fictitious fantasy' relating to B's safety and his own suicidal intentions designed to encourage her to have sex with him more often. There was no deception as to the nature (vaginal intercourse) or purpose (sexual gratification) of the act but as to the situation in which she found herself with the result that s. 76(2)(a) had no application. A's deceptions, however, would be relevant evidence for a jury in considering if there was consent under s. 74. (For a bizarre case which appears to have been wrongly decided under s. 76(2)(a) when it more appropriately fell under s. 76(2)(b) see *Devonald* [2008] EWCA Crim 527).

Impersonation of a woman's husband negated consent for the purposes of rape, but there was doubt whether the impersonation of anyone else did so (see *Elbekkay* [1995] Crim LR 163). Section 76(2)(b) dispels such doubt and applies to the full range of sexual offences where the absence of consent is an element of the offence.

One question worth raising, however, is why these particular deceptions necessitate a conclusive presumption that consent is negated when arguably more heinous acts, such as the use of violence, or the administration of a stupefying substance, to overcome a complainant's resistance, do not give rise to a conclusive presumption.

(ii) *Evidential presumptions* An evidential presumption is a rebuttable presumption. Section 75(1) provides:

> If in any proceedings for an offence to which this section applies it is proved—
> (a) that the defendant did the relevant act,
> (b) that any of the circumstances specified in subsection (2) existed, and
> (c) that the defendant knew that those circumstances existed, the complainant is to be taken not to have consented to the relevant act unless sufficient evidence is adduced to raise an issue as to whether he consented, and the defendant is to be taken not to have reasonably believed that the complainant consented unless sufficient evidence is adduced to raise an issue as to whether he reasonably believed it.

On proof by the prosecution of (a), (b), and (c) the presumption arises and a burden is cast upon the defendant to adduce sufficient evidence (1) to raise an issue as to whether the complainant, despite the existence of the specified circumstances, nonetheless consented, and/or (2) that the defendant reasonably believed the complainant consented. If the judge considers there is sufficient evidence to raise such an issue, he will direct the jury accordingly. If there is not sufficient evidence, upon proof of the necessary facts or circumstances in (a), (b), and (c), the presumption will arise and will be conclusive of a lack of consent on the part of the complainant and a lack of reasonable belief in consent on the part of the defendant.

The relevant circumstances in s. 75(2) are set out in the following paragraphs interspersed with comments.

> (a) any person was, at the time of the relevant act or immediately before it began, using violence against the complainant or causing the complainant to fear that immediate violence would be used against him.

'Violence' is not defined in the SOA 2003. In s. 161(3) of the Powers of Criminal Courts (Sentencing) Act 2000, 'violent offence' is defined as an offence 'which leads, or is intended or likely to lead, to a person's death or to physical injury to a person, and includes an offence which is required to be charged as arson'. The stereotypical case of rape is that where violence, or threat thereof, is employed by A to overcome B's resistance. While violence, or the fear thereof, will normally impact upon B's freedom to agree by choice, the fact that the presumption is rebuttable allows for the situation where A and B voluntarily engage in sado-masochistic sex. By contrast, the nature of the relationship between A and B may be such that A's apparently innocuous actions are recognised by B as signals of impending violence unless B agrees to A's sexual demands. If A knows that his actions have this effect upon B, the relevant circumstance of 'causing the complainant to fear' would be made out.

> (b) any person was, at the time of the relevant act or immediately before it began, causing the complainant to fear that violence was being used, or that immediate violence would be used, against another person.

Clearly this would cover the situation where violence is used on C to persuade B to consent to A's sexual demands. It would also cover the situation where the relationship between A and B is such that B recognises the signals of A's impending violence against C (perhaps B's child) unless B agrees to A's sexual demands. While there will probably be a relationship between B and C in most circumstances where this presumption is relied upon, there is no requirement for there to be a pre-existing relationship.

> (c) the complainant was, and the defendant was not, unlawfully detained at the time of the relevant act.

A need not be the person unlawfully detaining B, but he has to know of B's unlawful detention. The fact of unlawful detention undoubtedly will impact upon B's ability to make free and unconstrained choices. It is not, however, beyond the bounds of possibilities for B to still exercise a free choice to engage in sexual activity with A for which the rebuttable nature of the presumption provides.

> (d) the complainant was asleep or otherwise unconscious at the time of the relevant act.

Under the previous law a person who was asleep was regarded as being unable to provide consent (see *Larter and Castleton* [1995] Crim LR 75). The rebuttable nature of this presumption relating to sleep or unconsciousness leaves the defendant with the opportunity of seeking to rely on reasonable belief in consent despite knowing of the complainant's somnolent or unconscious state. While such might be highly unlikely, it is not beyond the bounds of possibility. In *Ciccarelli* [2011] EWCA Crim 2665, A touched B sexually while she was drunk and asleep. He did not know her well having only met her a couple of times before and there had never previously been any sexual activity between them. He nevertheless tried to argue that he had believed she would consent. On appeal from his conviction, Lord Judge CJ explained the operation of s. 75:

> It was suggested that section 75 of the 2003 Act reverses the ordinary principles relating to the burden of proof in criminal cases. We do not agree. Section 75 is an evidential provision. It relates to matters of evidence, and in particular evidential presumptions about consent in circumstances where, as we have already indicated, as a matter of reality and common sense, the strong likelihood is that the complainant will not, in fact, be consenting. If, however, in those circumstances there is sufficient evidence for the jury to consider, then the burden of disproving them remains on the prosecution. Therefore, before the question of the appellant's reasonable belief in the complainant's consent could be left to the jury, *some evidence beyond the fanciful or speculative had to be adduced to support the reasonableness of his belief in her consent.* (emphasis added)

While A had given evidence to the effect that he did believe she would consent, the trial judge's view was that there was nothing that might even begin to suggest a reasonable basis for such a belief. The Court of Appeal agreed; there was accordingly no evidence capable of rebutting the evidential presumption. Simply asserting a belief (if, indeed, A ever had such a belief) is a long way from providing evidence to support the reasonableness of that belief.

> (e) because of the complainant's physical disability, the complainant would not have been able at the time of the relevant act to communicate to the defendant whether the complainant consented.

Such a presumption may offer protection to those who due to physical disability are unable to communicate. The rebuttable nature of the presumption, however, provides for the situation where despite an inability to communicate, B does consent.

> (f) any person had administered to or caused to be taken by the complainant, without the complainant's consent, a substance which, having regard to when it was administered or taken, was capable of causing or enabling the complainant to be stupefied or overpowered at the time of the relevant act.

There have, in recent years, been widespread fears about the use of drugs, such as Rohypnol and GHB, to stupefy victims for the purpose of having sexual intercourse with them. This provision covers such drugs but would also cover the situation where B's drink is laced with alcohol in sufficient quantity to effect the same purpose. A need not be the person who administers the substance but he has to know of its administration and that it was without the complainant's consent. The use of a substance (perhaps alcohol or some other drug) to reduce B's inhibitions to make it more likely that B will agree to sexual activity with A, will not be sufficient to raise the presumption as the drug must be capable of stupefying or overpowering B at the time. This requires that a sufficient quantity is used for that purpose. This provision, however, cannot be intended to require B to be rendered unconscious, this being covered by (d) quoted earlier. The effect of some drugs, however, is to impair consciousness rendering B compliant, suggestible, disorientated, and less able to resist demands without being reduced to unconsciousness. It will be necessary for the courts to interpret 'stupefy' and 'overpower' in a way which reflects this or this provision could be rendered nugatory.

10.2.1.2 *Mens rea*

There are several mental elements which the prosecution must prove. Additional mental elements arise where the prosecution seek to rely on any of the conclusive or evidential presumptions detailed earlier.

10.2.1.2.1 *Intentional penetration*

The prosecution must prove that the defendant intended to penetrate the vagina, anus, or mouth of another. Is it sufficient that A intentionally penetrates B or must A intend to penetrate a particular organ. For example, A and B agree to have vaginal intercourse with A entering B from behind. A is inexperienced and in the dark by mistake slightly penetrates B's anus. On realising his mistake A immediately withdraws. Must the prosecution prove intentional penetration of B's anus or simply intentional penetration of B? Under the previous law, rape was charged as having sexual intercourse with B without consent, there being no need to specify whether intercourse was vaginal or anal. As the definition in s. 1(1) of the SOA 2003 refers to intentional penetration of vagina, anus or mouth, rather than using a term such as 'sexual intercourse' to embrace all forms of prohibited penetration, it is submitted that the intent must relate to the particular form of penetration.

10.2.1.2.2 *Intention and knowledge in relation to the presumptions*

Where the prosecution wish to rely on either of the conclusive presumptions of consent in s. 76 of the SOA 2003, they must prove that either—

(a) the defendant intentionally deceived the complainant as to the nature or purpose of the relevant act; or

(b) the defendant intentionally induced the complainant to consent to the relevant act by impersonating a person known personally to the complainant.

Recklessness as to either of these matters will not suffice. If A is reckless, however, as to either of these matters, this would be a circumstance highly relevant to the consideration of the question whether A does not reasonably believe that B consents.

Where the prosecution wish to rely on any of the evidential presumptions of consent in s. 75 of the SOA 2003, they must prove that the defendant knew of the existence of the particular circumstance in s. 75(2) upon which they are relying to raise the presumption. Recklessness as to those circumstances will not suffice, but again, this would be a circumstance highly relevant to the consideration of the question whether A does not reasonably believe that B consents.

10.2.1.2.3 *Reasonable belief in consent*

(a) *The previous law* In *Morgan* [1976] AC 182 (see **3.6.1.1.1** *ante*) the House of Lords held that a defendant could not be guilty of rape where he honestly believed that the woman consented to sexual intercourse, even if he was mistaken in that belief. The belief held by the man need not be reasonable, although as a matter of common sense the more unreasonable a belief is the less likely it is to have been honestly held. Following the decision in *Morgan* the *mens rea* for rape was put into statutory form by s. 1 of the Sexual Offences (Amendment) Act 1976 requiring proof either of knowledge that the other person did not consent or recklessness as to their consent. Recklessness was interpreted as covering knowledge that there was a risk that the other person did not consent or indifference whether s/he consents or not, that is a 'couldn't care less' attitude (see *Kimber* [1983] 1 WLR 1118; *Satnam and Kewal* (1983) 78 Cr App R 149).

There was considerable controversy at the time of the decision in *Morgan* and the subsequent statutory amendment, with the law being described by some as 'a rapist's charter'. It was also argued that the law both reduced the likelihood of convictions and also reduced the likelihood of victims of rape reporting the offence. The controversy has continued resulting in a change in the law being effected by the SOA 2003. The change requiring reasonable belief in consent is designed to respect and protect sexual autonomy, recognising the serious ramifications for victims where their sexual autonomy is breached. The change also recognises the context in which sexual activity occurs, namely that the parties are in close proximity thereby facilitating enquiry. Whether the change will break down outmoded and offensive attitudes about the nature of sexual relationships, which are sometimes deeply culturally rooted, only time will tell.

(b) *Reasonable belief in consent* In ss. 1–4 of the SOA 2003 the prosecution must prove first that B did not consent to the relevant sexual activity involved and that 'A does not reasonably believe that B consents'. Subsection (2) of each of those sections provides:

> (2) Whether a belief is reasonable is to be determined having regard to all the circumstances, including any steps A has taken to ascertain whether B consents.

The fact that the steps A has taken to ascertain whether B consents is relevant to the consideration whether A's belief is reasonable is an important reform. It will be more difficult to argue the reasonableness of his belief where A has not taken any steps to ascertain whether B consents. Where A does enquire, and B says 'No', it will also be difficult for A to argue that his belief that 'women always say no when they mean yes' was reasonable. However, the question arises whether 'all the circumstances' embraces A's culturally conditioned beliefs based on the inferior position accorded to women within his culture and the view that it is their duty to submit to men's sexual desires. Of course, the interplay with the evidential presumptions should not be ignored. Where the cultural conditioning of women involves the use of violence to enforce those cultural norms regarding their position vis-à-vis men, it may be that A's sexual advances were causing B to fear that immediate violence would be used against her if she did not comply with A's demands (see s. 75(2)(a) of the SOA 2003).

An issue which the courts will have to resolve is whether 'all the circumstances' include the characteristics of the defendant—such as his mental capacity or his view of sex which may be culturally conditioned. It is clear that we live in a society where there are diverse cultural traditions which include the way in which sexual relationships are conducted based on cultural norms relating to the respective roles and duties of men and women. If the dominant culture seeks to promote the equality of the sexes and the need for respect for individual autonomy and freedom of choice (values which seem to underpin the SOA 2003), should A be able to place reliance on the fact that he belongs to a different cultural tradition where the position of women is totally subservient to that of men and where a married woman's duty is to comply with the sexual demands of her husband? In *The Government Reply to the Fifth Report from the Home Affairs Committee Session 2002–2003* HC 639: *Sexual Offences Bill* (Cm. 5986, 2003) the Government stated (at para. 3):

> it is for the jury to decide whether any of the attributes of the defendant are relevant to their deliberations, subject to directions from the judge where necessary.

In determining this matter a relevant consideration will be the Human Rights Act 2000 and the rights protected by the European Convention. A defendant may argue that his Art. 8 right to respect for his private and family life is engaged. Of course this right is not absolute but is subject to limitations which are necessary in a democratic society in the interests of '...the prevention of...crime,...or for the protection of the rights and freedoms of others.' Article 14 seeks to secure that the rights and freedoms guaranteed are enjoyed without discrimination. A relevant consideration would be the State's obligation to protect its citizens from 'inhuman or degrading treatment' (see *A v UK* (1999) 28 EHRR 603, see **10.1.1.3.3** *ante*). If victims are to be provided equal protection under the law, it is difficult to see, in this light, that a defendant's cultural conditioning could be regarded as a relevant circumstance.

A further undetermined issue is whether 'all the circumstances' includes B's behaviour, whether at the time or previously. Will A be permitted to tender evidence, or cross-examine B, about his and B's prior relationship to provide support for his reasonable belief in consent? As the words 'at the time of the relevant act' are not included in sub-s. (2), this would seem to be permissible.

10.2.2 Assault by penetration

The Review concluded in *Setting the Boundaries* that the offence of indecent assault, for which the maximum sentence was 10 years' imprisonment, did not adequately reflect the gravity of a range of serious assaults involving penetration of the complainant by objects or parts of the defendant's body other than his penis. The new offence of assault by penetration contrary to s. 2 of the SOA 2003 carries a maximum sentence of life imprisonment.

The offence is defined as follows:

(1) A person (A) commits an offence if—
    (a) he intentionally penetrates the vagina or anus of another person (B) with a part of his body or anything else,
    (b) the penetration is sexual,
    (c) B does not consent to the penetration, and
    (d) A does not reasonably believe that B consents.

10.2.2.1 *Actus reus*

10.2.2.1.1 *Penetration*
Penetration of the vagina or anus of another must be proved. Vagina includes a surgically constructed vagina (s. 79(3) of the SOA 2003). Penetration is a continuing act from entry to withdrawal (s. 79(2)). The slightest degree of penetration is sufficient. The penetration may be by a part of the body, e.g. a finger, or by an object.

10.2.2.1.2 *Penetration which is sexual*
The penetration must be sexual. Section 78 defines sexual as follows:

penetration, touching or any other activity is sexual if a reasonable person would consider that—
(a) whatever its circumstances or any person's purpose in relation to it, it is because of its nature sexual, or
(b) because of its nature it may be sexual and because of its circumstances or the purpose of any person in relation to it (or both) it is sexual.

This is a somewhat awkwardly worded provision. It excludes from liability, for example, bona fide medical examinations and surgical procedures; but as such procedures or examinations would be covered by consent or necessity (see *In re F* [1990] 2 AC 1, **6.3.1** and **10.1.1.3.2** *ante*) it might be considered superfluous. The complexity arises from the inclusion in the definition of the offence the requirement that the penetrative assault be sexual. Where A's purpose is not sexual gratification but to demean and humiliate B, this could present a problem. (From B's point of view the trauma of the assault would not seem to differ whether A's purpose is sexual gratification of himself or humiliation of B.) The solution in the legislation is to create an objective definition of 'sexual' based upon a reasonable person's view which in (a) focuses on the nature of the act and takes no account of A's purpose. Undoubtedly the vast majority of reasonable people would regard the non-consensual penetration of another's vagina or anus as a sexual act. In (b) the circumstances in which the act is committed and the purpose of A may convert an act which might not appear sexual into one which is. In this situation A's purpose may be sexual gratification, for example, where a doctor performs an intimate examination not because this is necessary but because he derives sexual gratification from it. However, in such a case his deception as to the purpose of the act negates consent under the conclusive presumption in s. 76 and thus, again, the complexity of s. 78 serves no purpose. It is submitted that the requirement in s. 2

for penetrative assaults to be sexual is unnecessary. It may be that for the offences in ss. 3 and 4 of the SOA 2003 the requirement that the assault or activity be sexual does serve a purpose and that the definition of 'sexual' in s. 78 is necessary to deal with acts which may be ambiguous. Penetration of another's anus or vagina without their consent, it is submitted, permits of no such ambiguity and the combination of s. 2(1)(b) and s. 78 makes for the very complexity and confusion which the new law was meant to counteract.

10.2.2.1.3 *Absence of consent*
See **10.2.1.1.2** *ante.*

The presumptions in ss. 75 and 76 apply to this offence. The 'relevant act' which must be proved under s. 77 is:

> The defendant intentionally penetrating, with a part of his body or anything else, the vagina or anus of another person ('the complainant'), where the penetration is sexual.

10.2.2.2 *Mens rea*
See **10.2.1.2** *ante.*

The presumptions in ss. 75 and 76 apply to this offence.

10.2.3 **Sexual assault**

The maximum sentence for this offence is 10 years' imprisonment. Sexual assault is the second offence which covers activities previously covered by indecent assault. It will cover non-penetrative touchings of another which are sexual. Penetrative touchings of B's mouth with anything other than a penis, may fall within this offence. Indecent assault did not require touching (battery), as a technical assault (causing B to apprehend being touched) in circumstances of indecency would suffice. While s. 3 has the heading 'sexual assault' the definition of the offence does not refer to assault but to 'touching' and thus the offence is narrower than the offence of indecent assault. The offence of causing a person to engage in sexual activity without consent contrary to s. 4 will catch many situations previously falling within indecent assault where there was no touching involved (see, for example, *Sargeant* [1997] Crim LR 50). Requiring B at knife point to undress for A's sexual gratification would have been an indecent assault; it will not be a sexual assault as there is no touching and it will only amount to the s. 4 offence if B does undress and the court concludes that this activity does amount to a sexual activity. If B does not undress there is only an assault.

Section 3 of the SOA 2003 provides:

> (1) A person (A) commits an offence if—
>   (a) he intentionally touches another person (B),
>   (b) the touching is sexual,
>   (c) B does not consent to the touching, and
>   (d) A does not reasonably believe that B consents.

10.2.3.1 *Actus reus*

10.2.3.1.1 ***Touching***

Section 79(8) of the SOA 2003 provides:

> Touching includes touching—
>
> (a) with any part of the body,
>
> (b) with anything else,
>
> (c) through anything,
>
> and in particular includes touching amounting to penetration.

Touching a person with an object or through their clothing is included.

10.2.3.1.2 ***Touching which is sexual***

In the offence of indecent assault the House of Lords identified three situations which could pertain which determined whether or not the assault was indecent (*Court* [1989] AC 28). First, the act and its surrounding circumstances when viewed objectively could not be considered indecent by right-minded persons; in such a situation it did not matter that A had a secret indecent motive. Thus in *George* [1956] Crim LR 52, there was no indecent assault where A attempted to remove B's shoe even though this was something A found sexually gratifying, as there were no circumstances of indecency. Secondly, when viewed objectively, an incident could be inherently indecent regardless of D's purpose or motives. An example given was of a man stripping a woman of her clothing against her will. Thirdly, an incident might be capable of being indecent in which case the crucial factor would be A's motive. The instant case fell within this category where A had spanked B, a 12-year-old girl, across the seat of her pants. When asked by the police why he had done so, he replied 'I don't know, buttock fetish'. A's motive converted an incident which was capable of being indecent into an indecent assault.

A touching can only support a conviction for sexual assault where the touching is 'sexual'—the term preferred by the legislature in place of 'indecent'. While the overlap between these terms is substantial, it may be the case that the word 'sexual' will embrace situations not caught by the word 'indecent'. 'Sexual' is defined in s. 78 of the SOA 2003 (see **10.2.2.1.2** *ante* and the discussion thereafter). The test is objective and depends upon the reasonable person's assessment of the situation. A touching may be sexual under (a) where a reasonable person would consider that because of its nature it is sexual regardless of its circumstances or the purpose with which it is done. This seems to suggest that some touchings, by their very nature, are inherently sexual even though A may not have as his purpose sexual gratification. This would seem to cover any touching of another's genitals. It is not immediately clear, however, that stripping someone of their clothing is necessarily sexual, although it may be indecent. If A is doing so to humiliate B rather than for personal sexual gratification, his actions if not caught by (a) would not fall within (b). Secondly, a touching may be sexual under (b) because a reasonable person would consider it has the potential to be sexual and because of its circumstances and/or the purpose with which it is done, it is sexual. In this situation context and purpose become crucial. A coach patting a player on the buttocks when he comes off the pitch to say, in effect, 'well done', may not be regarded as sexual. Where the patting, however, is done by an adult stranger, in a park to a teenager, the context may convert this potentially sexual touching, in the eyes of a reasonable person, into a sexual touching. If A says something at the time of patting B to indicate his sexual motives, his purpose will combine with the circumstances to inform the decision on its sexual nature. In *H* [2005] EWCA Crim 732, the Court of Appeal emphasised that s. 78(b) creates a two stage process. In considering the first question, whether because of its nature the touching may be sexual, the jury has to do so without taking any account of the circumstances before and after the touching and any evidence as to A's purpose. In the instant case A had approached B, a stranger, and asked her, 'Do you fancy a shag?' This question by A would have to be discounted by a jury when considering whether the touching he subsequently performed was capable of being sexual. When B had sought to walk away, A had grabbed her by her trouser pocket and sought to pull her towards him covering her mouth with his hand. As all kinds of acts are capable of having sexual significance for those performing them, it is arguable that the ambit of the first category in *Court* (acts which could not be considered indecent) has been greatly narrowed. An alternative way of putting this is that the ambit of the new offence of sexual assault, is potentially broader than the offence of indecent assault. Might a reasonable person consider that touching another's foot is capable of being sexual? If A obtains particular sexual gratification from such an act, his purpose would seem to have the potential to render his act 'sexual' when it might not be indecent (cf. *George ante*). The Court of Appeal avoided providing an answer to this conundrum in *H* stating that this would be a matter for a jury to determine. Whether a jury could exclude from their minds A's expressed motive when considering the first question is open to doubt.

10.2.3.1.3 *Absence of consent*
See **10.2.1.1.2** *ante*.

The presumptions in ss. 75 and 76 apply to this offence. The 'relevant act' which must be proved under s. 77 is:

> The defendant intentionally touching another person (the complainant), where the touching is sexual.

10.2.3.2 *Mens rea*

The *mens rea* is an intention to touch and an absence of a reasonable belief that B consents. See **10.2.1.2** *ante*. The offence, however, is one of basic intent and A is unable to rely on intoxication in his defence (see *Heard* [2007] EWCA Crim 125, 5.6.3 *ante*).

The presumptions in ss. 75 and 76 apply to this offence.

While it has to be proved only that A intended to touch B, and not that he intended to touch B sexually, A's purpose in touching B may be crucial to the determination whether or not the touching was sexual (see **10.2.3.1.2** *ante*).

10.2.4 Causing a person to engage in sexual activity without consent

The previous law did not catch all the various forms of compelled sexual activity that might arise. In *Setting the Boundaries* it was recommended (at para. 2.20.4) that a new offence be created of compelling another to perform sexual acts. This was intended to cover, *inter alia*, cases of women forcing men to have sex with them, forcing others to perform sexual acts together, and forcing a person to perform a sexual act on himself or with an animal. Section 4 of the SOA 2003 provides:

> (1) A person (A) commits an offence if—
>
>   (a) he intentionally causes another person (B) to engage in an activity,
>
>   (b) the activity is sexual,
>
>   (c) B does not consent to engaging in the activity, and
>
>   (d) A does not reasonably believe that B consents.

The maximum sentence for this offence is 10 years' imprisonment, unless the activity caused falls within s. 4(4) in which case it is life imprisonment. The activities in s. 4(4) are:

> (a) penetration of B's anus or vagina,
>
> (b) penetration of B's mouth with a person's penis,
>
> (c) penetration of a person's anus or vagina with a part of B's body or by B with anything else, or
>
> (d) penetration of a person's mouth with B's penis.

There are several anomalies arising from this provision. If B is compelled to submit to penetration of his anus by an animal's penis, the maximum sentence is life imprisonment. But if he is compelled to submit to penetration of his mouth with an animal's penis, the maximum sentence is 10 years. Likewise, if B is compelled to penetrate another person's anus or vagina with his penis or other part of his body, or is compelled to penetrate another's anus or vagina with an object, the maximum sentence is life imprisonment. But if B is compelled to penetrate an animal with his penis the maximum sentence is 10 years. It is difficult to understand how such distinctions have arisen. It is submitted that those activities which attract only a 10-year maximum penalty are every bit as abhorrent, and doubtless cause to B every bit as much trauma, as those for which the maximum penalty is life imprisonment.

10.2.4.1 *Actus reus*

For discussion of the meaning of 'sexual' see **10.2.2.1.2** and **10.2.3.1.2** *ante*. If A compels B to take off his clothes, this is not necessarily a sexual activity. A's purpose, if it is one of sexual gratification, may make it so, but if it is simply to humiliate B will not.

For a discussion of causation see **2.6** *ante*. A may cause B to engage in the sexual activity with himself (A), or with another (C), or to perform the act on himself (B) (e.g. masturbation), or with an animal. There must be a direct causal link between A's actions and the activity which B performs or submits to. If B is compelled by threats, sufficient to amount to duress, to commit a sexual act with C who is not consenting, B, as well as being a victim of the offence, will have a defence in so far as he has perpetrated an offence upon C. But if the threats are not of death or serious injury, albeit that they are sufficient to vitiate B's consent, B would not have a defence if charged in respect of the offence he commits on C.

10.2.4.1.1 *Absence of consent*
See **10.2.1.1.2** *ante*.

The presumptions in ss. 75 and 76 apply to this offence. The 'relevant act' which must be proved under s. 77 is:

> The defendant intentionally causing another person ('the complainant') to engage in an activity, where the activity is sexual.

10.2.4.2 *Mens rea*

The *mens rea* is an intention to cause B to engage in a sexual activity and an absence of a reasonable belief that B consents. See **10.2.1.2** *ante*.

The presumptions in ss. 75 and 76 apply to this offence.

A's purpose may be crucial to the determination whether or not the activity he has caused B to engage in is sexual (see **10.2.3.1.2** *ante*).

Where A visits a brothel suspecting that the prostitutes are girls held there against their will and forced by threats and violence to offer sexual services to those who frequent the brothel, A's visit to the brothel and payment for the relevant sexual services, will have a causal connection to the performance of that activity by B, and A could be liable for the s. 4 offence as his knowledge or suspicion would be relevant to the consideration whether he reasonably believed that B consented to the sexual activity. If A has actual knowledge of the circumstances in which the prostitutes operate, this could give rise to one of the evidential presumptions in s. 75(2)(a) or (c) being raised.

10.2.5 **Offences against children**

Five new categories of offences, in addition to the offences in ss. 1–4 of the SOA 2003, have been created to protect children. The statutory scheme is complex, the offences overlap, and it is not clear whether some are or are not offences of strict liability. The age of consent to sexual activity remains at 16 such that any sexual activity with a child under that age remains unlawful. There is an assumption underlying the SOA 2003 that children under the age of 13 are incapable of giving consent but this is not actually expressed in the Act. Those between the ages of 13 and 15 may give consent but where the other person is aged 18 or over such consent will not prevent the other being liable for a range of offences. In addition, the offences relating to those under the age of 16 and 13 or over do not require proof of the absence of consent. Consensual acts by teenagers or pre-teens are caught by the legislation. It would have been possible to draft the legislation to exclude from liability consensual acts between those of a similar age but the Government were adamant that all consensual acts involving children should in principle be criminal with it being left to the Crown Prosecution Service to ensure by written guidelines that there were no oppressive prosecutions. The legislation therefore criminalises acts which the Government does not wish to have punished. This smacks of exceedingly muddled thinking. If it is possible to draw up guidelines relating to the circumstances in which prosecutions should or should not be pursued, it is equally feasible to draft the legislation in the first place to exclude the need for such guidelines. The breadth of these offences also offends against the principle in *Tyrrell* [1894] 1 QB 710 under which a child victim could not be convicted as a participant in the offence of unlawful sexual intercourse (see **7.1.6** *ante*). Now if two 12-year-olds engage in sexual intercourse they both may be prosecuted.

The prosecution of children for offences against other children where the activity was consensual raises the question whether this could amount to a breach of their Art. 8 right to respect for their private life. This question was answered negatively by the House of Lords in *G* [2008] UKHL 37 (see **4.2.6** *ante*).

10.2.5.1 Offences against children under 13

10.2.5.1.1 *Rape of a child under 13 (s. 5 of the SOA 2003)*

A's intentional penetration with his penis of B's vagina, anus, or mouth, where B is under 13, is an offence with a maximum sentence of imprisonment for life. The offence is one of strict liability as to age (see *G* [2008] UKHL 37; cf. *K* [2001] UKHL 41, **4.2.3.1** *ante*). It had been contended that as the acts covered by s. 5 are also covered by s. 9, which is a strict liability offence in respect of children under 13 but requires proof of an absence of a reasonable belief that B is 16 or over where B is under 16 but 13 or over, and carries a lesser sentence (14 years maximum), the more serious offence created by s. 5 is one requiring *mens rea* as this is normally read in where the statute is silent (see further Spencer, 'The Sexual Offences Act 2003: (2) Child and Family Offences' [2004] Crim LR 347; see also **4.1.2** and **4.2.3** *ante* and **10.2.5.2.1** *post*). This argument failed to persuade the House of Lords. The absence of consent is not an element of this offence and thus belief in consent is irrelevant.

> In *R v G* [2006] EWCA Crim 821, G, aged 15, had sexual intercourse with B, aged 12. He was charged with the s. 5 offence and pleaded guilty on the basis that he believed B was 15 as she had told him she was, and that B had willingly agreed to sexual intercourse. G appealed his conviction on the basis that if s. 5 could not be read down by inclusion of a defence of reasonable belief that B was over 13, it was incompatible with Art. 6(2) of the European Convention. Further, that the conviction and sentence (a 12-month detention and training order), constituted a disproportionate interference with respect for his private life under Art. 8 of the European Convention. He drew attention to the contrast between conviction for the s. 5 offence as compared to conviction of the s. 13/s. 9 offence. Under s. 5 he could be liable to a sentence of detention for life and would be subject to notification requirements as a sex offender being labelled a child rapist. Under s. 13 the maximum sentence would be detention for five years, there would be no notification requirement unless the sentence imposed was for more than 12 months, and the label applied to him would be that of a child who had had sexual activity with another child. G contended that it was inappropriate to prosecute a child for the s. 5 offence where intercourse had been consensual relying on a statement during the passage of the Bill that one would not expect the full weight of the criminal law to be used against children where sexual activity took place with mutual consent. To rely

on the discretion of prosecutors not to prosecute was not consonant with the rule of law. The Court of Appeal refused to read down s. 5, finding that the presumption of *mens rea* was negatived by necessary implication arising from the express references in other sections to reasonable belief. Strict liability offences did not breach Art. 6(2) as that article was concerned with procedural fairness and not with the substantive law. As for Art. 8, while prosecution could produce consequences that interfered with a child's rights under Art. 8(1), where the facts turned out to be less serious than anticipated when the charge was preferred, a judge could reflect this in sentencing to ensure that there was no interference with the defendant's rights that could not be justified under Art. 8(2); he was not, however, under a duty to substitute a lesser charge if the prosecution, themselves, did not seek leave to withdraw the s. 5 charge in favour of a s. 13/s. 9 charge. On further appeal the House of Lords endorsed the decision of the Court of Appeal.

The fears of many about the oppressive potential of the Sexual Offences Act when it is brought to bear upon child defendants are all too sadly justified by this decision. If the prosecution decide to over-charge by pursuing a s. 5 prosecution rather than a s. 13/s. 9 prosecution, or no prosecution at all, or, on discovering the true facts refuse to withdraw the s. 5 charge, the courts will stand back and do nothing to protect the child defendant other than to reduce their sentence. In the instant case, G having served five months in detention had his sentence reduced to a conditional discharge. While he avoided the notification requirements as a sex offender, he remains labelled a child rapist. This outcome strikes this author as a disproportionate response to what the prosecution accepted was a case of consensual sexual activity where G believed B was over 13. An attempt to apply to the European Court of Human Rights alleging breaches of Arts 6 and 8 was ruled inadmissible (see *G v UK* [2011] ECHR 1308).

10.2.5.1.2 *Assault of a child under 13 by penetration (s. 6 of the SOA 2003)*
A's intentional penetration with a part of his body or anything else of B's vagina or anus, is an offence where the penetration is sexual and B is under 13. The maximum sentence is life imprisonment.

For the meaning of 'sexual' see **10.2.2.1.2** *ante.*

The absence of consent is not an element of this offence and thus belief in consent is irrelevant. As this offence overlaps with the offence in s. 9 (see **10.2.5.2.1** *post*) it will probably be held to be one of strict liability (see *R v G ante*).

10.2.5.1.3 *Sexual assault of a child under 13*
A's intentional touching of B where B is under 13 and the touching is sexual is an offence carrying a maximum sentence of 14 years' imprisonment (see s. 7 of the SOA 2003).

See **10.2.3.1.2** *ante* for the meaning of 'sexual touching'.

While it has to be proved only that A intended to touch B, and not that he intended to touch B sexually, A's purpose in touching B may be crucial to the determination whether or not the touching was sexual (see **10.2.3.1.2** *ante*). The absence of consent is not an element of this offence and thus belief in consent is irrelevant. As this offence overlaps with the offence in s. 9 (see **10.2.5.2.1** *post*) it will probably be held to be one of strict liability (see *R v G ante*).

10.2.5.1.4 *Causing or inciting a child to engage in sexual activity*

A's intentional causing B to engage in sexual activity or inciting B to do so where B is under 13 is an offence (see s. 8(1) of the SOA 2003). The maximum sentence for inciting or causing non-penetrative sexual activity is 14 years' imprisonment, but where the activity caused or incited falls within s. 8(2) the maximum is life imprisonment. The activities in s. 8(2) are:

(a) penetration of B's anus or vagina,

(b) penetration of B's mouth with a person's penis,

(c) penetration of a person's anus or vagina with a part of B's body or by B with anything else, or

(d) penetration of a person's mouth with B's penis.

For a discussion of the meaning of 'Causing another person to engage in a sexual activity' see **10.2.4.1.1** *ante*. The absence of consent is not an element of this offence and thus belief in consent is irrelevant. As this offence overlaps with the offence in s. 10 (see **10.2.5.2.2** *post*) it will probably be held to be one of strict liability as regards the element of the age of the child (see *R v G* **10.2.5.1.1** *ante*).

The differential sentencing structure means that the section creates four separate offences: (1) intentionally causing, or (2) intentionally inciting, non-penetrative sexual activity and (3) intentionally causing, or (4) intentionally inciting, penetrative sexual activity (see *Grout* [2011] EWCA Crim 299. Where the offence is charged as 'inciting' a child to engage in sexual activity, there is no need to prove that any sexual activity occurred. It is sufficient that A incited B so to do. The Court of Appeal has adopted a wide interpretation to incitement holding in *Walker* [2006] EWCA Crim 1907 that the essence of the offence of incitement is encouragement. It is this which has to be intentional or deliberate and there is no need to prove that A intended that any sexual activity should actually happen. This is contrary to the common law on incitement but has been confirmed by *Jones* [2007] EWCA Crim 1118.

> A wrote graffiti on toilet walls seeking girls aged 8–13 for sex in return for payment and left his mobile number. B, a police officer, pretending to be aged 12, contacted A and he incited her to penetrative sexual activity. A was arrested when he turned up to a meeting arranged with her. In upholding A's conviction for attempt to incite based on the text messages, the Court observed that the offence could be committed by general statements, such as the graffiti, which were not made to any specific or identifiable person.

10.2.5.2 Offences against children under 16

The common elements in the offences which follow (ss. 9–12 of the SOA 2003) are firstly, that B is under 16 and A does not reasonably believe that B is 16 or over. Thus, with regard to the age of B, the offence is not one of strict liability. However, where B is under 13 the necessary implication of the drafting is that the offence is one of strict liability as to age. Secondly, A must be aged 18 or over to be liable to conviction for one of these offences. By a strange piece of legislative drafting, however, s. 13 of the SOA 2003 provides that the activities comprised in ss. 9–12 amount to offences when committed by A who is under 18, the only difference being that the maximum sentence is five years whereas the maximum sentence for the offences under ss. 9 and 10 is 14 years and for those under ss. 11 and 12 is 10 years.

10.2.5.2.1 *Sexual activity with a child*
Section 9 of the SOA 2003 provides:

> (1) A person aged eighteen or over (A) commits an offence if—
> (a) he intentionally touches another person (B),
> (b) the touching is sexual, and
> (c) either—
>   (i) B is under 16 and A does not reasonably believe that B is 16 or over, or
>   (ii) B is under 13.

While this offence refers to 'sexual activity', it is, in fact, limited to sexual touching.

For discussion relevant to the *actus reus* of this provision see **10.2.3, 10.2.3.1.1** and **10.2.3.1.2** *ante*. Touching includes penetration.

The *mens rea* is an intention to touch.

While it has to be proved only that A intended to touch B, and not that he intended to touch B sexually, A's purpose in touching B may be crucial to the determination whether or not the touching was sexual (see **10.2.3.1.2** *ante*).

If B is under 13, strict liability as to age applies. Where B is 13 or over but under 16 the prosecution have to prove either that A did not believe that B was over 16, or if he did, that that belief was not reasonable.

It is worth noting that two 14-year-old teenagers engaging in mutual consensual petting would commit this offence subject to the maximum penalty of five years under s. 13 of the SOA 2003.

10.2.5.2.2 *Causing or inciting a child to engage in sexual activity*
Section 10 of the SOA 2003 provides:

> (1) A person aged eighteen or over (A) commits an offence if—
> (a) he intentionally causes or incites another person (B) to engage in an activity,
> (b) the activity is sexual, and
> (c) either—
>   (i) B is under 16 and A does not reasonably believe that B is 16 or over, or
>   (ii) B is under 13.

For a discussion of the meaning of 'Causing another person to engage in a sexual activity' see **10.2.4.1.1**. For the meaning of 'inciting' see **8.2.1** *ante*.

Where the offence is charged as 'inciting' a child to engage in sexual activity, there is no need to prove that any sexual activity occurred. It is sufficient that A incited B so to do.

If B is under 13, strict liability as to age applies. Where B is 13 or over but under 16 the prosecution have to prove either that A did not believe that B was over 16, or if he did, that that belief was not reasonable.

It is worth noting that A, a 14-year-old who suggests to B, another 14-year-old, that they remove their clothes to see each other's genitals, would commit this offence subject to the maximum penalty of five years under s. 13 of the SOA 2003, even before an item of clothing is removed. Similarly, if A describes to B the mechanics of masturbation and suggests he do it when he gets home, A and B both being under 16, A would commit this offence even if B did nothing pursuant to A's encouragement. One cannot help but feel that the breadth of the law is much greater than is necessary to deal with the evils of child sex abuse.

10.2.5.2.3 *Engaging in a sexual activity in the presence of a child*
Section 11 of the SOA 2003 provides:

> (1) A person aged eighteen or over (A) commits an offence if—
>> (a) he intentionally engages in an activity,
>> (b) the activity is sexual,
>> (c) for the purpose of obtaining sexual gratification, he engages in it—
>>> (i) when another person (B) is present or is in a place from which A can be observed, and
>>> (ii) knowing or believing that B is aware, or intending that B should be aware, that he is engaging in it, and
>> (d) either—
>>> (i) B is under 16 and A does not reasonably believe that B is 16 or over, or
>>> (ii) B is under 13.

This is another example of a complex piece of drafting. The purpose in (c) of obtaining sexual gratification links to the fact that it is done in circumstances where B may observe it. In fact it is sufficient that A believes B is aware of the sexual activity or intends that B should be aware of it, even though B may not become aware of it. For example, if A engages in a sexual activity in B's presence, intending B to be aware of this but B, unknown to A is blind, A will nonetheless commit this offence. (On sexual gratification, see *Abdullai* [2006] EWCA Crim 2060 *post*.)

While this offence is aimed at those who may seek to corrupt children by exposing them to inappropriate sexual behaviour by adults, or even sexual behaviour by children directed by adults, the offence is wide enough to catch other situations. For example, A and B masturbate in each other's presence, both being under the age of 16. They would commit this offence subject to the maximum penalty of five years under s. 13 of the SOA 2003.

If B is under 13, strict liability as to age applies. Where B is 13 or over but under 16 the prosecution have to prove either that A did not believe that B was over 16, or if he did, that that belief was not reasonable.

10.2.5.2.4 *Causing a child to watch a sexual act*
Section 12 of the SOA 2003 provides:

> (1) A person aged eighteen or over (A) commits an offence if—
>
> (a) for the purpose of obtaining sexual gratification, he intentionally causes another person (B) to watch a third person engaging in an activity, or to look at an image of any person engaging in an activity,
>
> (b) the activity is sexual, and
>
> (c) either—
>
>   (i) B is under 16 and A does not reasonably believe that B is 16 or over, or
>
>   (ii) B is under 13.

For the definition of 'sexual' see **10.2.2.1.2** *ante.*

Section 79(4) defines 'image' to mean 'a moving or still image and includes an image produced by any means and, where the context permits, a three-dimensional image'. Section 79(5) states that references 'to an image of a person include references to an image of an imaginary person'. Thus the offence may be committed where the child is shown a live sexual activity involving a third party, or a video, picture or photograph of a sexual activity, or computer-generated images or pseudo photographs, or even a hologram.

The causing of the child to watch such a sexual activity must be intentional.

If B is under 13, strict liability as to age applies. Where B is 13 or over but under 16 the prosecution have to prove either that A did not believe that B was over 16, or if he did, that that belief was not reasonable.

A problematical requirement of the offence, however, is that A must cause the watching of the sexual activity 'for the purpose of sexual gratification'. This suggests that it must be proved that A sought to obtain sexual gratification from causing B to watch the activity. The main menace to children, which the offence might be thought to be designed to deal with, is that of predatory paedophiles who seek to groom children over a period of time to render them more susceptible to their sexual advances. Often this process involves giving children alcohol and cigarettes and permitting them to watch pornographic videos. A may not be present during the watching of the videos; paedophiles often allow their houses to become gathering places for children and teenagers where the rules which parents might impose are not observed. A may obtain no sexual gratification from B actually watching the pornographic video, but his aim ultimately is to bring B to the point where B's view of sex has become distorted, his inhibitions have been worn away, and his trust for A developed such that he will consent to engaging in sexual activity with A. This is virtually the situation which pertained in *Abdullai* [2006] EWCA Crim 2060. The Court of Appeal held there is nothing to suggest that the offence would only be committed if the sexual gratification and the causing of the child to watch the sexual act are simultaneous, contemporaneous, or synchronised. The Court further stated that sexual gratification may take any of the myriad forms which sexual pleasure or indulgence may take, and it may simply involve the defendant enjoying the sight of the child watching the sexual act. Whatever form it takes, however, there is no temporal restriction which operates so as to stop the section applying to a longer-term plan to obtain further or greater sexual gratification in the form of the eventual working out of a particular sexual fantasy or activity involving the child.

10.2.5.2.5 *Arranging or facilitating commission of a child sex offence*
The maximum sentence for this offence is 14 years' imprisonment. Section 14 of the SOA 2003 provides:

> (1) A person commits an offence if—
>
>> (a) he intentionally arranges or facilitates something that he intends to do, intends another person to do, or believes that another person will do, in any part of the world, and
>>
>> (b) doing it will involve the commission of an offence under any of sections 9 to 13.

Once again an offence is created in language which is opaque. The offence is, essentially a preparatory offence aimed at criminalising behaviour which is carried out for the purpose of enabling a child sex offence to be committed by A or by another anywhere in the world. It is aimed at those who procure children for use in the child sex industry or those who avail of their services. The offence could be committed by something as simple as A permitting C to use his mobile phone to contact B who A believes is a child with whom C is planning to commit a child sex offence.

There is a defence to this offence set out in sub-ss. (2) and (3) as follows:

> (2) A person does not commit an offence under this section if—
>
>> (a) he arranges or facilitates something that he believes another person will do, but that he does not intend to do or intend another person to do, and
>>
>> (b) any offence within subsection (1)(b) would be an offence against a child for whose protection he acts.
>
> (3) For the purposes of subsection (2), a person acts for the protection of a child if he acts for the purpose of—
>
>> (a) protecting the child from sexually transmitted infection,
>>
>> (b) protecting the physical safety of the child,
>>
>> (c) preventing the child from becoming pregnant, or
>>
>> (d) promoting the child's emotional well-being by the giving of advice,
>
> and not for the purpose of obtaining sexual gratification or for the purpose of causing or encouraging the activity constituting the offence within subsection (1)(b) or the child's participation in it.

This defence (which overlaps with that in s. 73 see **10.2.5.2.8** *post*) will cover, for example, police officers using a child as a decoy to seek to catch child sex offenders. It will also cover healthcare workers providing advice on contraception and sexually transmitted diseases and, in addition, providing contraceptives to children under the age of 16 (cf. discussion of *Gillick* at **3.2.3.2, 3.2.3.5, 6.3.1,** and **6.3.3** *ante*). But for this defence, the healthcare worker, for example, who provides contraceptives to two 15-year-olds who are having a sexual relationship, would be facilitating the commission of a child sex offence. Of course, the two 15-year-olds will have to rely on the good sense of the Crown Prosecution Service not to prosecute them.

10.2.5.2.6 *Meeting with a child following sexual grooming*
Section 15 of the SOA 2003 (as amended by the Criminal Justice and Immigration Act 2008, sch. 15, para. 1), for which the maximum sentence is 10 years' imprisonment, provides:

> (1) A person aged eighteen or over (A) commits an offence if—
>
> (a) having met or communicated with another person (B) on at least two earlier occasions, he—
>
>   (i) intentionally meets B, or
>
>   (ii) travels with the intention of meeting B in any part of the world, or
>
>   (iii) B travels with the intention of meeting A in any part of the world,
>
> (b) A intends to do anything to or in respect of B, during or after the meeting mentioned in paragraph (a)(i) to (iii) and in any part of the world, which if done will involve the commission by A of a relevant offence,
>
> (c) B is under 16, and
>
> (d) A does not reasonably believe that B is 16 or over.

A 'relevant offence' is any offence under Part 1 of the SOA 2003, one of a specified range of traditional sexual offences in Northern Ireland, or any conduct done outside England, Wales, or Northern Ireland which would be an offence if done in England and Wales (s. 15(2) of the SOA 2003). The original meetings, subsequent meeting, communications with B, and intended location for the 'relevant offence' may be in any part of the world. Thus, for example, A, a British citizen resident in England, would commit this offence where he twice contacts over the internet B, a child aged 13 resident in Thailand, and arranges to meet B when he travels to Thailand intending to have sex with B. The offence is complete as soon as A sets off on his journey to Thailand.

10.2.5.2.7 *Offences outside the United Kingdom*
Section 72 of the SOA 2003 (as substituted by s. 72 of the Criminal Justice and Immigration Act 2008), which replaces s. 7 of the Sex Offenders Act 1997, extends the jurisdiction of courts in England and Wales, and Northern Ireland to cover sex offences against children committed abroad. It covers not just British nationals or residents but also persons who subsequently become nationals or residents. Under s. 72(1) a United Kingdom national will be guilty of an offence if he does an act abroad which is an offence covered by s. 72. Previously it had to be proved that the act was also an offence in the country where it was committed but this requirement has been dispensed with in the new s. 72. Where a person who is a United Kingdom resident does any act abroad which is an offence in that country and would be an offence if done in England and Wales, or in Northern Ireland, he is also guilty of an offence in that part of the United Kingdom (s. 72(2)). If a person who is not a United Kingdom national or resident does an act abroad which is an offence in that country and would be an offence if done in England and Wales, or in Northern Ireland, and he subsequently becomes a United Kingdom national or resident, he may be prosecuted for that offence (s. 72(3) and (4)). The acts covered

are any of the offences under ss. 5–19, 25 and 26 and 47 to 50 of the SOA 2003; any offence under ss. 1–4, 30 to 41 and 61 where the victim of the offence was under 18 at the time of the offence; and a range of other offences including abuse of a position of trust, offences against persons with a mental disorder, prostitution offences, certain offences relating to pornography, and administering a substance with intent where, again, the victim is under the age of 18.

10.2.5.2.8 *Exceptions for aiding, abetting, and counselling*
Section 73 provides a defence which gives statutory effect to, and extends the law deriving from, the decision in *Gillick v West Norfolk and Wisbech AHA* [1986] AC 112 (see **3.2.3.2**, **3.2.3.5**, **6.3.1**, and **6.3.3** *ante*).

  The defence applies, *inter alia*, to offences under ss. 5–7, 9, and 13 where the act would be an offence under s. 9 if the offender were aged 18. A person will not be guilty of aiding, abetting, or counselling the commission of such an offence against a child where he acts for the purpose of—

(a) protecting the child from sexually transmitted infection,

(b) protecting the physical safety of the child,

(c) preventing the child from becoming pregnant, or

(d) promoting the child's emotional well-being by the giving of advice,

and not for the purpose of obtaining sexual gratification or for the purpose of causing or encouraging the activity constituting the offence within subsection (1)(b) or the child's participation in it.

10.2.5.3 Abuse of a position of trust
Sections 16–24 of the SOA 2003 create four offences of sexual offences with children by persons who are in a position of trust. These offences are essentially those that are provided for under ss. 9–12, the only essential differences being that A is in a position of trust in relation to B and B may be up to 18 years of age instead of under 16 as required by ss. 9–12. The sections are unnecessarily convoluted, complex, and complicated. All that would have been necessary to achieve the same result would have been one section defining 'position of trust' and one section stating that where a position of trust existed the age limit in the offences under ss. 9–12 should be 18 rather than 16. Once again the aim of making the law clearer and more coherent has not been achieved.

  As the maximum penalty for any of these abuse of trust offences is five years' imprisonment it is clear that where B is under 16 the offences under ss. 9–12 would be charged as the maximum sentence is much greater. The purpose of the offences, therefore, is to protect those between the ages of 16 and 18 from abusive or predatory sexual behaviour by those in a position of trust in relation to them. Of course, the 17-year-old pupil at a college may be the one seducing the young teacher; such a fact will not stop his sexual activity with her from constituting an offence. Again the law is drafted so broadly that it catches situations which involve no abuse.

  The range of situations where a position of trust will be deemed to exist is set out in s. 21 of the SOA 2003. The following is a non-exhaustive list of the main situations. A is in a position of trust in relation to B if A looks after persons under 18 who are:

- detained by virtue of a court order and B is so detained (e.g. a young offender institution);
- resident in a home or other place where accommodation is provided under the Children Act 1989 and B is resident in that place;
- accommodated and cared for in a hospital, independent clinic, care home, residential care home, children's home, private hospital, community home, voluntary home, residential family centre, or a home provided under s. 82(5) of the Children Act 1989, and B is accommodated and cared for in that institution;
- receiving full-time education at an educational institution, and B is receiving education at that institution.

Many people who might generally be regarded as being in a position of trust such as doctors and healthcare employees outside of residential units, priests and clergymen, youth leaders, and child-minders are not covered by s. 21 leaving one to question what the real purpose of the section is.

If B is under 13, strict liability as to age applies. Where B is 13 or over but under 18, A will be taken not to have reasonably believed that B was 18 or over unless sufficient evidence is adduced to raise an issue whether A reasonably believed B was 18 or over.

In the main situations detailed earlier it must be proved that A knew, or could reasonably be expected to have known, that he was in a position of trust in relation to B where A adduces sufficient evidence to raise an issue as to whether he knew or could reasonably have been expected to known this fact.

There are two defences which A may rely upon and the burden of proving them rests on him. The first under s. 23 is that B is over 16 and A and B are lawfully married. The second under s. 24 is that prior to the position of trust arising a lawful sexual relationship existed between A and B. For example, in the teacher/pupil example given earlier there would not be an offence if A and B had a sexual relationship while A was training to become a teacher which relationship they continued when A, upon qualifying, obtained employment at the school which B attended.

10.2.6 Familial sex offences

Under the SOA 1956 there were two offences relating to incest. Section 10 made it an offence for a man to have sexual intercourse with a woman he knew to be his granddaughter, daughter, sister, or mother. Section 11 made it an offence for a woman aged 16 or over to permit a man whom she knew to be her grandfather, father, brother, or son to have sexual intercourse with her. The offences did not depend upon the absence of consent and made no distinction based on age other than the limitation in s. 11 on the age of the woman. The offence was also limited to vaginal sexual intercourse. The SOA 2003 has replaced these offences with four offences; first, under s. 25 sexual activity with a child family member; and secondly, under s. 26 inciting a child family member to engage in sexual activity. The sexual activity covers both penetrative sexual acts and sexual touching and may be homosexual. The person touched or incited (B) must be under 18. The range of relationships covered (see s. 27 of the SOA 2003) is greater including adopted children, half-brother and half-sister, aunt and uncle, and foster-parent. It also covers in certain situations, step-relationships and cousins as well as situations where A lives in the same household as B and is regularly involved in the care of B.

Penetrative sexual acts between persons in prohibited degrees of relationship are covered by two offences created by ss. 64 and 65. Section 64 covers the situation where A, aged 16 or over, sexually penetrates B, aged 18 or over, while s. 65 covers the situation where A, aged 16 or over, consents to being sexually penetrated by B, aged 18 or over. In each case there is an offence if A and B are related as parent (including adoptive parent), grandparent, child (including adopted child), grandchild, brother, sister, half-brother, half-sister, uncle, aunt, nephew, or niece.

10.2.7 Offences against persons with a mental disorder

The SOA 2003 creates three sets of offences where the victim is a person with a mental disorder. Sections 30–33 create four offences mirroring the child sex offences in ss. 9–12, dealing with aspects of improper sexual activity with people with a mental disorder impeding choice. Sections 34–37 create four offences, again mirroring ss. 9–12, but relating to persons with a mental disorder which does not impede choice such that they are capable of deciding whether to engage in sexual activity, but their agreement in the particular case is obtained by inducement, deception, or threat. Sections 38–41 create four offences relating to the same activities but where the defendant is a care worker and the offence may be committed regardless of consent.

10.2.8 Preparatory offences

Three offences seek to address behaviour which is engaged in with the intent of committing a sexual offence.

10.2.8.1 Administering a substance with intent

Section 61 of the SOA 2003 creates an offence aimed at dealing with the phenomenon of drug-assisted rape. The offence is drafted in broad terms and covers any form of sexual activity providing much greater protection than s. 4 of the SOA 1956 which it replaces which only covered administering a drug to a woman to enable a man to have unlawful sexual intercourse with her. Section 61(1) provides:

> A person commits an offence if he intentionally administers a substance to, or causes a substance to be taken by, another person (B)—
>
> (a) knowing that B does not consent, and
>
> (b) with the intention of stupefying or overpowering B, so as to enable any person to engage in a sexual activity that involves B.

This is an offence of ulterior intent which is complete upon the substance being administered with the necessary intent, it being unnecessary to prove that any sexual activity actually took place. In most cases, however, proof of sexual activity at least being attempted will be the most straightforward way of establishing the prohibited intent. A must know that B does not consent. B's lack of consent relates to taking the substance by which A is seeking to stupefy or overpower him, rather than to the sexual activity which A intends to enable to take place. The offence would cover putting a drug, such as Rohypnol, into B's drink or putting, for example, vodka into B's orange juice with the necessary intent. For the definition of 'sexual activity' see s. 78 of the SOA 2003 (**10.2.2.1.2** *ante*). The maximum sentence for the offence is six months on summary conviction and 10 years' imprisonment following conviction on indictment.

10.2.8.2 Committing an offence with intent to commit a sexual offence

Section 62 of the SOA 2003 provides:

> (1) A person commits an offence under this section if he commits any offence with the intention of committing a relevant sexual offence.

'Relevant sexual offence' means any offence under Part 1 of the SOA 2003 including aiding, abetting, counselling, or procuring such an offence. The primary offence that might be thought to be covered by this offence would be kidnapping and false imprisonment. If such an offence is committed with the requisite intent the maximum sentence is life imprisonment. In respect of other offences committed the maximum sentence is six months' imprisonment on summary conviction and 10 years following conviction on indictment. The main purpose behind the offence would appear to be to enable the offender to be categorised as a sex offender with the consequence of being placed on the Sex Offenders' Register.

10.2.8.3 Trespass with intent to commit a sexual offence

Formerly the offence of burglary included entering a building, or part of a building, as a trespasser with intent to rape any person therein (Theft Act 1968, s. 9(1)(a)). Section 63 of the SOA 2003 replaces this form of burglary with a more broadly drafted offence. Section 63(1) provides:

> A person commits an offence if—
> (a) he is a trespasser on any premises,
> (b) he intends to commit a relevant sexual offence on the premises, and
> (c) he knows that, or is reckless as to whether, he is a trespasser.

'Relevant sexual offence' means any offence under Part 1 of the SOA 2003 including aiding, abetting, counselling, or procuring such an offence. For the meaning of 'trespasser' see **13.2.1.2** *post*. Unlike burglary, it is not necessary for A to enter the premises as a trespasser: it is enough that he has become a trespasser, for example, by the removal of permission to be there or the breach of any implied condition attaching to that permission. Thus, where B invites A back for coffee following their meeting at a disco, and A starts to act in a way which makes B feel uncomfortable such that she tells A she is not attracted to him and she asks him to leave, an attempt by A to touch B sexually could amount to this offence provided A has the necessary intent and is at least reckless as to his status as a trespasser. 'Premises' includes a structure or part of a structure; 'structure' includes a tent, vehicle, or vessel or other temporary or movable structure. In the previously used example, if A was in B's car when he was asked by her to leave, his remaining with the necessary intent could amount to this offence. The maximum sentence is six months' imprisonment for summary conviction and 10 years' for conviction on indictment.

10.2.9 Other sexual offences

The SOA 2003 creates a range of other offences which are listed without further exposition as follows:

- indecent photographs of persons aged 16 or 17 (ss. 45–46);
- abuse of children through prostitution and pornography (ss. 47–51);
- exploitation of prostitution (ss. 52–54);
- trafficking for sexual exploitation (ss. 59A–60);
- exposure (s. 66);
- voyeurism (ss. 67–68);
- intercourse with an animal (s. 69);
- sexual penetration of a corpse (s. 70);
- sexual activity in a public lavatory (s. 71).

FURTHER READING

M. J. Allen, 'Consent and Assault' (1994) 58 JCL 183; 'Look Who's Stalking: Seeking a Solution to the Problem of Stalking' [1996] 4 Web JCLI 182.

B. Bell and K. Harrison, '*R v Savage, DPP v Parmenter* and the Law of Assault' (1993) 56 MLR 83.

C. M. V. Clarkson, 'Law Commission Report on Offences against the Person and General Principles: (1) Violence and the Law Commission' [1994] Crim LR 324.

S. Cooper and M. James, 'Entertainment – The Painful Process of Rethinking Consent' [2012] Crim LR 188.

S. Cooper and A. Reed, 'Informed Consent and the Transmission of Sexual Disease: *Dadson* Revivified' (2007) 71 JCL 461.

C. Elliott and C. de Than, 'The Case for a Rational Reconstruction of Consent in Criminal Law' (2007) 70 MLR 225.

E. Finch and V. E. Munro, 'Intoxicated Consent and Drug Assisted Rape Revisited' [2004] Crim LR 789.

I. Hare, '*R v Savage, DPP v Parmenter* —A Compelling Case for the Code' (1993) 56 MLR 74.

P. Murphy, 'Flogging Live Complainants and Dead Horses: We May No Longer Need to Be in Bondage to Brown' [2011] Crim LR 758.

D. C. Ormerod and M. J. Gunn, 'The Second Law Commission Consultation Paper on Consent: Consent—A Second Bash' [1996] Crim LR 694; 'Criminal Liability for the Transmission of HIV' [1996] 1 Web JCLI; 'The Legality of Boxing' (1995) 15 LS 181; 'In Defence of *Ireland*' [1997] 3 Web JCLI.

J. Rogers, 'A Criminal Lawyer's Response to Chastisement in the European Court of Human Rights' [2002] Crim LR 98.

S. Ryan, 'Reckless Transmission of HIV; Knowledge and Culpability' [2006] Crim LR 981.

S. Shute, 'The Second Law Commission Consultation Paper on Consent: Something Old, Something New, Something Borrowed: Three Aspects of the Project' [1996] Crim LR 684.

J. R. Spencer, 'Child and Family Offences' [2004] Crim LR 347.

J. Stannard, 'Sticks, Stones and Words: Emotional Harm and the English Criminal Law' (2010) JCL 533.

J. Temkin and A. Ashworth, 'Rape, Sexual Assaults and the Problems of Consent' [2004] Crim LR 328.

J. Tolmie, 'Consent to Harmful Assaults: The Case for Moving Away from Category Based Decision Making' [2012] Crim LR 656.

S. Wallerstein, '"A drunken consent is still consent" – or Is It? A Critical Analysis of the Law on a Drunken Consent to Sex Following Bree' (2009) 73 JCL 318.

M. Weait, 'Knowledge, Autonomy and Consent: *R v Konzani*' [2005] Crim LR 763.

G. Williams, 'Force, Injury and Serious Injury' (1990) 140 New LJ 1227.

11

Offences under the Theft Acts 1968 and
1978: theft and related offences

11.1 Introduction

In 1968 the Theft Act (hereafter referred to as the TA 1968) was passed. For seven years the Criminal Law Revision Committee had considered the area of property offences, previously covered by the Larceny Act 1916. Appended to its *Eighth Report: Theft and Related Offences* (Cmnd 2977, 1966) was a draft Bill which, with some amendment, was passed by Parliament as the TA 1968. This Act was a new code which swept away the previous law creating a new range of offences which were framed, so far as possible, in simple language to avoid the technicality and complexity of the old law. The Theft Act 1978 (hereafter referred to as TA 1978) was passed to replace s. 16(2)(a) of the TA 1968 which had proved highly unsatisfactory. The TA 1978 also contains other provisions to fill some gaps left by the TA 1968. In 1996 the Theft (Amendment) Act (hereafter referred to as the TAA 1996) was passed inserting new ss. 15A and 15B into the TA 1968 to fill further gaps in that Act.

While TA 1968 and TA 1978 aimed to avoid technicality, problems have materialised. The Acts used words, like 'dishonestly', which the courts have sought to leave to juries to define. This creates a problem of inconsistency. A second problem, which also involves inconsistency, is that the courts in applying the law contained in the Acts have often done so in disregard of the civil law. Theft and related offences are concerned with interferences with the rights and interests others have in property. It would seem first to be necessary to determine to whom the property belonged; this cannot be done without reference to the civil law. Unfortunately the criminal courts have often disregarded the civil law in a misplaced desire to keep the criminal law simple. If a criminal statute uses civil law terms such as 'trust', 'trespasser', 'proprietary right or interest', or 'equitable interest', one would have thought that Parliament intended the recognised civil law meaning to apply. The result is that the law relating to offences against property remains confused, inconsistent, and, at times, obscure. A third problem is the continuing tendency of appellate courts to consider particular aspects of the definition of theft in isolation from the other elements of the offence and statutory provisions relating thereto. The outcome, inevitably, is inconsistency, incoherence, and contradiction as the meaning of particular words or concepts cannot accurately be determined in isolation from their context. In *Hallam and Blackburn* [1995] Crim LR 323, the Court of Appeal called for urgent reform as an Act passed to simplify the law had become over-complicated by technicalities grafted onto it since its passage.

In the next chapter fraud will be examined. The Fraud Act 2006 (hereafter referred to as the FA 2006) has repealed various sections of the TA 1968 and TA 1978 replacing a number of individual offences based on deception with a new offence of fraud which may be committed in three ways. It also creates a new offence of dishonestly obtaining services to replace the offence of obtaining services by deception under s. 1 of the TA 1978. These new offences are designed to overcome problems in the old law and to simplify the law. On occasions in both this chapter and the next chapter it will be necessary to refer to the old law. The FA 2006 came into force on 15 January 2007 but the repeal does not affect 'any liability, investigation, legal proceeding or penalty for or in respect of any offence' partly committed before the repeal comes into force (FA 2006, sch. 2).

One final preliminary point is that many offences of dishonesty involve schemes or activities which cross international borders. Reference should be made to **8.5** *ante* where this topic is dealt with. Briefly, theft, blackmail, handling, and fraud may be prosecuted in England and Wales where at least one element of the offence (an act, omission, or the result) occurs in England and Wales.

11.2 Theft

Section 1(1) of the TA 1968 provides that:

> A person is guilty of theft if he dishonestly appropriates property belonging to another with the intention of permanently depriving the other of it; and 'thief' and 'steal' shall be construed accordingly.

The maximum penalty on conviction on indictment is seven years' imprisonment (s. 7 of the TA 1968, as amended by s. 26(1) of the CJA 1991).

Five facts must be proved to lead to a conviction of theft; three relate to the *actus reus* and two to the *mens rea*. The *actus reus* consists in (i) the appropriation (ii) of property (iii) belonging to another. The *mens rea* consists in (i) the dishonest (ii) intention permanently to deprive the other of the property. These five elements of theft will be examined separately for convenience, but it should be noted that they are interconnected and sometimes difficult to separate.

11.2.1 *Actus reus*

11.2.1.1 Property

Conduct which may constitute 'appropriation' must occur in relation to 'property belonging to another'. It is important to determine first what constitutes property for the purposes of theft. Before examining s. 4 of the TA 1968 an important exclusion should be noted. **At common law neither a corpse, nor parts of a corpse, could be stolen as there was no property in a corpse** (see *Sharpe* (1857) Dears & B 160). The Court of Appeal confirmed this principle in *Kelly* [1998] 3 All

ER 741, making it clear that if this principle was to be changed only Parliament could do so. However, Rose LJ went on to state (at p. 749) that:

> parts of a corpse are capable of being property within s. 4 of the Theft Act, if they have acquired different attributes by virtue of the application of skill, such as dissection or preservation techniques, for exhibition or teaching purposes.

The Court confirmed the convictions for theft of K, an artist, and L, a junior technician employed by the Royal College of Surgeons. L had removed, at K's request, 35 to 40 body parts which were used by doctors training to be surgeons. K made casts of the parts. He retained some of the parts but disposed of others. The Court of Appeal followed an earlier Australian case, *Doodeward* v *Spence* (1908) 6 CLR 406, the authority of which had previously been accepted in a civil case, *Dobson* v *North Tyneside Health Authority* [1996] 4 All ER 474. Rose LJ went on to say (at p. 750):

> Furthermore, the common law does not stand still. It may be that if, on some future occasion, the question arises, the courts will hold that human body parts are capable of being property for the purposes of s. 4, even without the acquisition of different attributes, if they have a use or significance beyond their mere existence. This may be so if, for example, they are intended for use in an organ transplant operation, for the extraction of DNA or, for that matter, as an exhibit in a trial.

The property which may be the subject of theft is defined by s. 4 of the TA 1968. Section 4(1) defines property to include ' **money and all other property, real or personal, including things in action and other intangible property'**. This is a sweeping definition subject to some limitation in the ensuing subsections relating to land, things growing wild on land, and wild creatures. Subject to these exceptions, however, the only limitation is whether the property is capable of being appropriated; and it does not matter that the person from whom the property is appropriated is unlawfully in possession of the property (see *Smith* [2011] EWCA Crim 66 where drugs were stolen from a drug dealer and it was unsuccessfully argued on appeal that items unlawfully possessed could not constitute property).

11.2.1.1.1 *Money and cheques*

Money refers only to current coins and banknotes, including foreign coins and notes. While I may assert that I have £100 in my bank account, if D steals a cheque of £100 I have made payable to X, D has not stolen any money. He has stolen the cheque, which is a piece of paper; he only steals £100 if he manages to cash the cheque and receives coins or notes to that value (see *Davis* (1988) 88 Cr App R 347). The property in the bank in which I have a proprietary right or interest is not £100 in money but rather a debt of £100 owed to me by the bank; a debt is a 'thing in action'. Once a cheque has been drawn by the authorised drawer, it becomes a valuable security. A 'valuable security' is defined in s. 20(3) of the TA 1968 as:

> ...any document creating, transferring, surrendering or releasing any right to, in or over property, or authorising the payment of money or delivery of any property or evidencing the creation, transfer, surrender or release of any such right, or the payment of money or delivery of any property, or the satisfaction of any obligation.

A cheque authorises the drawer's bank to pay the sum specified on it to the payee. If the cheque is given for valuable consideration it will create a thing in action, namely a debt between the bank and the payee which the payee could enforce by legal proceedings (see **11.2.1.1.2** *post*). The debt in such a case is property but it belongs to the payee not the drawer (see *Preddy* [1996] AC 815). But a cheque can constitute property in another sense: Professor Smith in 'Obtaining Cheques by Deception or Theft' [1997] Crim LR 396, 400, describes a cheque as not just a piece of paper but as a piece of paper which has 'special properties'—'it is an effective key to the drawer's bank account'. When a cheque is paid it reverts to being just a piece of paper as it then loses its 'special properties' and can no longer be used to instruct the bank to pay money to a payee. Section 20(2) of the Theft Act 1968 created the offence of procuring the execution of a valuable security by deception (this offence has been replaced by fraud: s. 1 of the Fraud Act 2006). The obtaining of the cheque itself could be an obtaining of property by deception contrary to s. 15 of the Theft Act 1968 (which has also been replaced by fraud) or it could be theft where D appropriates the cheque. For example, V draws a cheque for £50 in favour of D to pay D for tidying his garden and leaves it on the kitchen table intending to pay D when the work is completed. D sees the cheque and enters the kitchen and takes it and leaves without finishing tidying the garden. D has appropriated a valuable security, the cheque, which at this point still belonged to V although the thing which the cheque represents, a debt between the bank and the payee, D (a thing in action, see **11.2.1.1.2** *post*), would belong to D. In such a situation it should be possible to charge D with theft of the cheque as a valuable security. Unfortunately, because of an *obiter dictum* of Lord Goff in *Preddy* (to the effect that there could be no intent to permanently deprive V of the cheque form itself as it would be returned to V via his bank following presentation and payment), the Court of Appeal has held in *Clark (Brian)* [2001] EWCA Crim 884, [2002] 1 Cr App R 14, that a cheque is not capable of being stolen. The Court felt itself bound by Lord Goff's *obiter dictum* because in *Graham* [1997] 1 Cr App R 302, the Court of Appeal had assumed Lord Goff's *dictum* was *ratio* and quashed convictions on the assumption that it is not an offence to obtain a cheque by deception. The Court's mistake in *Graham* was not to distinguish between a cheque as a piece of paper and a cheque as a valuable security. In *Clark* the Court of Appeal was not prepared to treat Lord Goff's *dictum* as *obiter* because it had previously regarded it as *ratio* in *Graham*. The Court seems to consider that there is some virtue in compounding error. This decision also stands in conflict with *Marshall* [1998] 2 Cr App R 282 (see **11.2.2.1.1** *post*) where the defendants were convicted of stealing London underground tickets, things in action, the Court of Appeal dismissing an argument that if a cheque cannot be stolen from the drawer, a ticket cannot be stolen from the issuer. Prior to 1968 a cheque was recognised as a valuable security which could be the subject of simple larceny. It is difficult to believe that in enacting the Theft Act 1968 with its broad definition of property in s. 4(1), Parliament would have intended to exclude cheques from this definition. Somehow the Court of Appeal contrives to maintain this belief!

11.2.1.1.2 *Things in action and other intangible property*
A thing in action is intangible property but not all items of intangible property are things in action. **A 'thing in action' is a personal right of property which**

can only be claimed or enforced by legal action and not by taking physical possession (see *Torkington* v *Magee* [1902] 2 KB 427). Examples of things in action are debts, a right under a trust, a copyright or a trade mark, a credit balance in a bank account, and a contractual right to overdraw the account. If D purports to sell my copyright in this book to X, this is appropriation of a thing in action belonging to me (see *Mensah Lartey and Relevey* [1996] Cr App R 143). If D, an accountant authorised to draw cheques on X Co's behalf, takes a cheque from X Co's chequebook and makes it payable to himself for the sum of £100, when he pays this cheque into his own bank account he will be appropriating a thing in action, namely the debt which the bank owes to X Co (see *Kohn* (1979) 69 Cr App R 395). On the other hand, if D knows that his own account is not in credit and he has no overdraft facility (or if he has exceeded the limit of his overdraft facility), and he writes a cheque for £50 on his own account made payable to X and backs it with a banker's card so that the bank is obliged to meet the cheque, D does not commit theft. Although the bank's funds will be diminished by this transaction, D has not appropriated a thing in action; he has not taken for himself or another someone else's right to sue as, prior to the cheque being written, there was no specific debt of £50 (or any greater amount of which it formed a part) owed by the bank to anyone (see *Navvabi* [1986] 3 All ER 102; but D may be liable for fraud (previously for obtaining a pecuniary advantage by deception, see **Chapter 12** *post*).

Question

Where a cheque is drawn by P in favour of D, the thing in action which the cheque represents, namely a right in the payee to sue the drawer for £x, belongs to D and thus cannot be stolen by D. However, if D presents the cheque for payment, the effect of this is to diminish by £x (or destroy) P's credit balance in his bank account. Could D be guilty of stealing this?

In *Williams (Roy)* [2001] 1 Cr App R 362, D ran a building business and targeted vulnerable, elderly householders. D's practice was to charge a modest sum for an initial piece of work to gain the customers' trust and then to charge exorbitant sums for subsequent work. D was charged with several counts of theft of the customers' credit balances by causing cheques to be drawn in his favour and then presenting them for payment. The trial judge directed the jury that the prosecution had to prove that D had appropriated the credit balances of the customers stating, 'If you get a householder to draw a cheque on a bank or building society and cause the cheque to be presented, you cause the householders' credit balance to be diminished, and accordingly take that credit balance for your own use.' In upholding D's convictions the Court of Appeal referred to *Kohn* and *Graham* [1997] 1 Cr App R 302, where the Court had sought to make clear that nothing it said should cast doubt on *Kohn* and 'the principle that theft of a chose in action may be committed when a chose in action belonging to another is destroyed by the defendant's act of appropriation' (see also *Burke* [2000] Crim LR 413).

By s. 30 of the Patents Act 1977, a patent, or an application for a patent, is declared not to be a thing in action but it is personal property; it is 'other intangible property' and thus is capable of being stolen. An export quota issued by the Government confers an expectation that a licence will be granted to export goods to the amount of the quota, but there is no legally enforceable right to such a licence and thus an export quota is not a thing in action. As a person with an export quota may sell it, it has been held that an export quota is 'other intangible property' and therefore capable of being stolen (see *A-G for Hong Kong* v *Nai-keung* (1987) 86 Cr App R 174). Confidential information, such as the questions on an examination paper, is not 'property' (see *Oxford* v *Moss* (1978) 68 Cr App R 183), and by analogy, trade secrets are not property. If D, however, takes the document on which the information is written, he may be guilty of theft of the document. By contrast, s. 7(2)(b) of the Patents Act 1977 treats an invention for which no patent has been granted or applied for as intangible property. As an invention is essentially information it is difficult to see why confidential information cannot constitute property; the information has value and that value will be lost or diminished if its confidentiality is lost. It is arguable that if D takes that information (for example, by making a copy of the document), while he does not deprive P of the information he does deprive him of its secrecy which is an intangible quality giving the information value. It is argued by Griew, *The Theft Acts 1968 & 1978* (7th edn), that confidential information is not capable of being appropriated (paras. 2–144). While Griew's view is worthy of consideration, it is submitted that it is not necessarily correct. To read confidential information is to assume a right of an owner as it is the right of the owner to determine who should have access to it; it is arguable, therefore, that confidential information should be regarded as property which may be appropriated (see further **11.2.2.1.1** *post*).

It appears that electricity is not 'other intangible property' as s. 13 of the TA 1968 creates a specific offence of dishonestly using, wasting, or diverting electricity (see *Low* v *Blease* [1975] Crim LR 513). Thus, if D dishonestly reconnects his electricity supply after it has been cut off for non-payment of his electricity bill, he will commit this offence. Using a private telephone without authority also falls within the scope of this offence, as would switching on the appliances in P's home, when he is away, with the intention that he should incur higher electricity bills.

11.2.1.1.3 *Limitations on the theft of land*

Section 4(2) of the TA 1968 provides a general limitation that **land cannot be stolen subject to three exceptions.** Section 4(2) provides that, subject to certain exceptions, **a 'person cannot steal land, or things forming part of land and severed from it by him or by his directions'.** Thus, as a general rule, land is not stealable. If I dishonestly move my boundary fence to incorporate part of my neighbour's garden within my own garden, this will not constitute theft. Land for the purposes of s. 4(2), however, does not include incorporeal hereditaments. Thus **easements, profits, and rents are all capable of being stolen by anyone.**

There are three exceptions to the general rule where land may be stolen. First, under s. 4(2)(a), **a person may steal land:**

> ...when he is a trustee or personal representative, or is authorised by power of attorney, or as liquidator of a company, or otherwise, to sell or dispose of land belonging to another, and he appropriates the land or anything forming part of it by dealing with it in breach of the confidence reposed in him.

For example, if D is authorised as a trustee to sell 100 acres of land and he sells 99 acres and appropriates the remainder for himself, he would be guilty of theft of that acre of land.

Secondly, under s. 4(2)(b), **a person may steal land**:

> …when he is not in possession of the land and appropriates anything forming part of the land by severing it or causing it to be severed, or after it has been severed.

This provision is subject to s. 4(3) quoted in the succeeding paragraph. The difficulty with it is in determining when something forms part of the land. If it is growing on the land or is a permanent structure or integral part of such a structure or a fixture it is part of the land. Thus, if I dig up my neighbour's rose bushes to plant them in my garden, I will be appropriating them by severing them from the land; similarly if I chop down one of his trees for firewood. If my neighbour digs up his rose bushes to move them to another part of the garden and I remove them, I will be appropriating something that has been severed. Likewise I will be appropriating property by severing it from the land where I remove the tiles from his roof or the topsoil from his garden. If, however, I am in possession of the land as a tenant or a licensee and I remove the topsoil or the rose bushes I will not be guilty of theft (but see s. 4(2)(c) *post*).

A further gloss has been added to this second exception by s. 4(3) which provides:

> A person who picks mushrooms growing wild on any land, or who picks flowers, fruit or foliage from a plant growing wild on any land, does not (although not in possession of the land) steal what he picks, unless he does it for reward or for sale or for other commercial purpose.
>
> For purposes of this subsection 'mushroom' includes any fungus, and 'plant' includes any shrub or tree.

If I uproot a sapling growing wild on my neighbour's land I will not be within this subsection as I am not picking from a plant but rather taking the whole plant; if done dishonestly this is theft. Similarly, if I chop down a tree growing wild for firewood I will not be within this subsection as chopping is not 'picking'; if done dishonestly this is theft. Apart from such examples, if I confine myself to picking from plants growing wild, for example, taking blackberries or mistletoe or flowers, or picking mushrooms, this will not be theft subject to a further exception. If I pick these items for a commercial purpose this will be theft provided dishonesty is also proven. D picks blackberries growing wild along a hedgerow to make blackberry jelly to sell at a 'Blue Peter Bring and Buy Sale'. The picking would thus be 'for sale' and D will be guilty of theft provided dishonesty is proved. A jury would be unlikely to find D dishonest in this case, but if D is a market trader picking wild mushrooms, mistletoe, or blackberries for sale on his stall, his enterprise being of a more commercial nature may persuade a jury to find that this is dishonest.

Thirdly, under s. 4(2)(c), **a person may steal land**:

> …when, being in possession of the land under a tenancy, he appropriates the whole or part of any fixture or structure let to be used with the land.

If I am the tenant of the property and appropriate a fixture, such as a washbasin or a fireplace or the fitted kitchen cupboards, I will be guilty of theft. Similarly if I appropriate a structure such as a garden shed or a greenhouse. There is no need to prove a severance of the property in this case; it would be sufficient if I contracted with X to sell the fireplace or greenhouse to him. However, I will not be guilty of theft if I remove the topsoil or rose bushes. If a person in possession of the land as a licensee appropriates fixtures he will not be guilty of theft as he is not within the provision, but, if a licensee appropriates a greenhouse, as this is not part of the land, he will be guilty of theft. The distinctions highlighted here are fine and technical and reflect no distinction in culpability. It appears that the differences in liability between licensees and tenants are the result of legislative oversight rather than legislative intent.

Section 4(4) deals with the position of wild creatures. It provides:

> Wild creatures, tamed or untamed, shall be regarded as property; but a person cannot steal a wild creature not tamed nor ordinarily kept in captivity, or the carcase of any such creature, unless either it has been reduced into possession by or on behalf of another person and possession of it has not since been lost or abandoned, or another person is in course of reducing it into possession.

The effect of this provision is to limit the circumstances in which theft of wild creatures may occur to the following cases:

 Key Point

(1) If a creature is tamed or ordinarily kept in captivity it may be stolen. Thus animals kept in a zoo or wildlife safari park may be stolen, even if they escape, as they are ordinarily kept in captivity. If P tames a wild animal it may be stolen.

(2) Other wild creatures, including game, while at large are not owned by anyone, not even the landowner or someone with shooting rights on his land. But once an animal, or its carcass, has been reduced into possession by or on behalf of another, or while it is being reduced into possession, it may be stolen. If D takes a rabbit caught in a trap set by P, this will be theft as P was in the course of reducing it into possession. If D takes a pheasant shot by P, for example, before P's dog retrieves it or from the back of P's vehicle, this will be theft. If D, P's gamekeeper, shoots pheasant on P's instructions and keeps one for himself, this will be theft as he has reduced the pheasant into possession on behalf of another. If, after a day's shoot, a grouse is not retrieved and D finds it, this will not be theft as possession has been lost or abandoned.

11.2.1.2 Belonging to another

In order to be the subject of theft, the property D appropriates must, at the time of the appropriation, belong to another. The Theft Act is not concerned to protect only rights of ownership in property but also other interests in property. Accordingly s. 5(1) defines 'belonging' for the purposes of theft:

> Property shall be regarded as belonging to any person having possession or control of it, or having in it any proprietary right or interest (not being an equitable interest arising only from an agreement to transfer or grant an interest).

The different elements of this definition will be examined separately.

11.2.1.2.1 *Possession or control*

(a) *Possession* In the normal case a person who owns property also has possession of it.

> ### Example
>
> P owns a tool hire business storing the tools at his shop. If D enters the shop and dishonestly appropriates a power drill he will be stealing from P the owner who has possession of the power drill at that moment. If P hires a lawnmower to Q, P retains the ownership of the lawnmower but Q has possession of it. If D dishonestly appropriates the lawnmower from Q's garage he will be stealing from both Q who has possession of it and P who has owner-ship of it. If Q's son R is mowing the lawn when D seizes the lawnmower from him, he will be stealing from R who has control of the lawnmower, if not possession of it, as well as from P and Q.

The inclusion of 'possession and control' in the definition of 'belonging' serves two purposes. First, if someone has possession or control of the article it absolves the prosecution from having to prove who the legal owner of the article was at the moment of appropriation. Secondly, a person with a greater interest in property may steal from a person with a lesser interest. If during the period of hire, P had removed the lawnmower from Q's garage he could be convicted of theft provided he had done so dishonestly. For example, he may have taken the lawnmower as a preliminary to demanding payment from Q for the cost of replacing it or so that he could obtain the hire fee from another customer.

In *Turner (No. 2)* (1971) 55 Cr App R 336, the Court of Appeal, in an ill-considered judgment, appears to have extended liability further. D left his car at P's garage for repair. When he completed the repair P parked the car on the road outside the garage. D, using his spare set of keys, removed the car without paying for the repair. P had a lien on the car entitling him to retain possession of it until the repair bill had been paid. The judge directed the jury to ignore the question of liens and D was convicted of theft. If lien was ignored P was a bailee at will. Bailment at will may be terminated at any time by the bailor. The Court of Appeal held, however, that the words 'possession or control' were not to be qualified in any way. The decision creates obvious problems for a bailor who now may be liable for theft of his own goods if he terminates a bailment at will by surreptitiously removing the goods from the bailee's possession, even though the bailee could not have prevented the bailor from doing so had he done it openly (cf. *Meredith* [1973] Crim LR 253).

While *Turner (No. 2)* may be criticised because of the problem created by the statement on lien, one aspect of the decision is to be supported. Part of the argu-ment by the defence was that the words 'possession or control' should be qualified by the word 'lawful'. In *Kelly* [1998] 3 All ER 741, the Court of Appeal confirmed that **the word 'lawful' is not to be read into s. 5(1).** Thus, property may be stolen from a person who is not in lawful possession of it; for example, a thief may steal property which has been stolen and remains in the possession of another thief. Or a drug user may steal drugs from his dealer, the dealer being in sufficient posses-sion thereof to satisfy the requirements of the Theft Act even though his posses-sion of proscribed drugs is unlawful (see *Smith* [2011] EWCA Crim 66). In *Smith* the

Court of Appeal were sensitive to the havoc that might be caused were they to construe the Theft Act in such a way as to permit drug-users to steal from dealers with impunity, Lord Judge CJ stating (at para. 10) that 'the criminal law is concerned with keeping the Queen's peace, not vindicating individual property rights'.

(b) *Control* The problem sometimes arises of determining whether property belongs to anyone. **A person may be in control of property without knowing that he possesses it.** Generally the owner of land is in 'control' of any property on his land even if he does not know it is there. Thus, for example, golf balls lost on a golf course will ordinarily be considered as belonging to the club that owns the course (see *Hibbert* v *McKiernan* [1948] 2 KB 162; *Rostron* [2003] EWCA Crim 2206). In *Woodman* [1974] QB 754, English China Clays (ECC) sold all the scrap metal on its site to another company which removed the bulk of it but left some behind which was too inaccessible to remove economically. ECC, believing that all the metal had been removed, erected a barbed wire fence and notices warning trespassers to keep out. D entered the site and removed the remaining scrap metal. D was convicted of theft. The Court of Appeal upheld that conviction as there was ample evidence that ECC were in control of the site, had sought to exclude trespassers and thus were prima facie in control of property on the site. The Court did go on to say that if a third party had, for example, hidden explosives or drugs on the site and the occupier had no means of knowledge, this would rebut the general presumption that the occupier had control.

(c) *Abandonment* If property is lost, for example P's wallet falls out of his jacket pocket, P continues to possess it until someone else assumes control of it. The wallet still belongs to P and may, in certain circumstances, be stolen by a finder (see **11.2.2.2.1** *post*). The position is different, however, if P abandons his property, for example, where P buys a new wallet and throws his old wallet into a hedge the old wallet ceases to belong to anyone and thus cannot be the subject of theft. **Property will be regarded as abandoned only when the owner is indifferent as to what becomes of it.** Abandonment is not readily inferred by the courts. The fact that P has no further use for it is not conclusive. Thus if P had put the wallet in his dustbin rather than throwing it away, he would not be abandoning it as he would be putting it there to be collected by the council refuse collectors rather than presenting an invitation to others to take it (see *Williams* v *Phillips* (1957) 41 Cr App R 5). Where A left items in a black bag outside a charity shop, while the obvious inference was that A had intended the goods to be a gift to the charity, the charity at that point did not have possession or control of them. However, the property was not abandoned; although A had divested himself of possession, he would not be treated as having given up ownership of the property until the point the charity took possession of it (see *R (Ricketts)* v *Basildon Magistrates' Court* [2010] EWHC 2358 (Admin).

11.2.1.2.2 *Proprietary right or interest*
A full examination of the civil law relating to property would be necessary to explain proprietary rights or interests; this is outside the scope of this book. It is proposed to examine briefly some of the situations which may arise.

(a) *The owner* **A person with a proprietary right or interest in property includes the legal owner of the property but this concept is wider than that**

of ownership. If a co-owner sells property without the other co-owner's consent, or if a partner sells partnership property without his partner's consent, this will be theft as each co-owner or partner has a proprietary right in the property which is defeated by such a sale (see *Bonner* [1970] 2 All ER 97).

(b) *Equitable interests* **While a trustee is the legal owner of property, the beneficiaries under the trust have equitable interests in the property.** Thus, if a trustee dishonestly appropriates trust property this will be theft from the beneficiaries as persons with proprietary interests (see *Clowes (No. 2)* [1994] 2 All ER 316). Similarly, if an executor dishonestly appropriates property under a will, this will be theft from the legatee(s) (see *Sanders* [2003] EWCA Crim 3079).

Section 5(1) excludes from the meaning of property belonging to another 'an equitable interest arising only from an agreement to transfer or grant an interest'. For example, D contracts to transfer shares to P who pays for them. Before the transfer is effected D transfers the shares to Q. As P, until the transfer is executed, has only an equitable interest in the shares, D is not guilty of theft of the shares. Depending on what D has done, or intends to do, with the money P has paid him, he may be guilty of theft of the money or obtaining property by deception.

A particular problem which has arisen relates to constructive trusts. A constructive trust is one imposed by the principles of equity in order to satisfy the demands of justice and good conscience without reference to any presumed intention of the parties, for example, where a person in a fiduciary position makes a profit a constructive trust is imposed. In *Westdeutsche Landesbank Girozentrale* v *Islington London BC* [1996] 2 All ER 961 at 998, Browne-Wilkinson LJ stated:

> Although it is difficult to find clear authority for the proposition, when property is obtained by fraud equity imposes a constructive trust on the fraudulent recipient: the property is recoverable and traceable in equity.

In *A-G's Reference (No. 1 of 1985)* [1986] QB 491, D, the manager of a tied public house, was obliged by his contract of employment with P Brewery to obtain all liquor from them and pay all takings into their bank account. D secretly bought beer elsewhere and sold this keeping the profits. If he was the constructive trustee of these profits holding them on behalf of P, he could be guilty of theft. The Court of Appeal held there was no constructive trust, but even if there was, a constructive trust would not create a proprietary interest covered by s. 5(1). To exclude constructive trusts from the purview of s. 5(1) would seem to involve adding words to the statutory language which, it is submitted, is not an appropriate task for a court. The authority of this decision, however, is now in doubt. In *Shadrokh-Cigari* [1988] Crim LR 465, the Court of Appeal applied the principle derived from the civil case of *Chase Manhattan Bank N.A.* v *Israel-British Bank (London) Ltd* [1981] Ch 105 that where P transfers property to D under a mistake of fact, P retains an equitable proprietary interest in the property transferred. If D subsequently dishonestly appropriates the property he will be guilty of theft. If P retains an equitable interest in the property it must be because the demands of justice and good conscience impose a constructive trust (see *Re Holmes* [2004] EWHC 202 (Admin); see further **11.2.1.3.3** *post*). In *Hendricks* [2003] EWCA Crim 1040, the Court of Appeal upheld a conviction of attempted theft where D had sought to withdraw £41,000 from his account at Lloyds Bank. The credit balance in his account was the result of a stolen cheque made out for £41,000 having been altered and paid into D's business account. The prosecution avoided the problems of constructive trusts by the simple device of charging D with attempting to steal the cash belonging to Lloyds Bank. Clearly money in the bank belongs to the bank whether or not anyone else might have an equitable interest in it.

Further doubt as to the authority of *A-G's Reference (No. 1 of 1985)* results from the Privy Council case of *A-G for Hong Kong v Reid* [1994] 1 AC 324 (see **11.2.1.3.2** *post*). It is also worth noting that if, for example, D had agreed with his barman to sell the beer bought elsewhere, there would be a conspiracy to defraud (see *Adams v The Queen*, **8.3.4.1.1** *ante*). In *Re Holmes* [2004] EWHC 202 (Admin), where a transfer from one bank account to another was brought about by fraud by D, the Divisional Court stated, *obiter*, that D held the proceeds under a constructive trust. The Court distinguished *A-G's Reference (No. 1 of 1985)* on the basis that that case involved secret profits whereas the instant case dealt with a fraudulent taking of property (see further **11.2.1.3.1** *post*).

11.2.1.3 Special cases

Although s. 5(1) of the TA 1968 is quite widely drafted there are certain cases which it has been considered appropriate to label as theft, even though the property in question does not belong to another. In these cases, others either suffer loss or D makes an unconscionable gain, although technically the property with which D is dealing legally belongs to him.

11.2.1.3.1 *Trust property*
Section 5(2) provides:

> Where property is subject to a trust, the persons to whom it belongs shall be regarded as including any person having a right to enforce the trust, and an intention to defeat the trust shall be regarded accordingly as an intention to deprive of the property any person having that right.

Under s. 5(1) property in a trust is regarded as belonging to both the trustees and the beneficiaries. However, there are some trusts which do not have specific beneficiaries. Charitable trusts do not have specific beneficiaries who could enforce the trust so, if trustees dishonestly appropriated the property of the trust, it would not be property belonging to another. Charitable trusts are enforceable, however, by the Attorney-General and thus this provision deems him to have a beneficial interest in the trust property so that theft by a trustee is theft from him (see *Dyke and Munro* [2001] EWCA Crim 2184, [2002] 1 Cr App R 30).

11.2.1.3.2 *Property received under an obligation*
Section 5(3) provides:

> Where a person receives property from or on account of another, and is under an obligation to the other to retain and deal with that property or its proceeds in a particular way, the property or proceeds shall be regarded (as against him) as belonging to the other.

This provision is designed to deal with the situation where D receives property from or on account of P and, in so doing, he obtains not only possession but also legal ownership of the property. It may be that P retains an equitable interest (see **11.2.1.2.2** *ante*) but the subsection is designed to avoid the necessity for complex technical analysis. Thus cases which fall within s. 5(3) are probably also covered already by s. 5(1). Section 5(3) would apply where D receives property from P who attaches to it a requirement that he use it in a particular way.

 Example

P employs D to paint his house and gives him a cheque for £50 to buy paint. D obtains possession and ownership of the cheque but he is under a legal obligation to use the 'proceeds' of that cheque to buy paint. If D cashes the cheque and uses the proceeds to bet on a horse he will be guilty of theft. Alternatively, if he cashes the cheque, buys the paint and uses it to paint his own house, while he has applied the money for the correct purpose of buying paint, he has appropriated the proceeds of the original cheque by using the paint on his own house. By contrast, if P had paid D a deposit of £50 without imposing any obligation on D on how this money was to be used, D would be free to do with it whatever he liked. Even if he never painted P's house he would not be guilty of theft as there was no legal obligation to use that money or its proceeds in a particular way, although if it was his intention at the outset not to paint the house this might be theft or the offence of obtaining property by deception.

In *Hall* [1973] QB 126, D, a travel agent received deposits and payments from clients who had booked air trips to America. D paid the money into the firm's general account but never arranged the trips and was unable to repay the money. His conviction of theft was quashed, however, as it was not proved that he was under an obligation to the clients to retain and deal with the money in a particular way. It would have been different if D had been under an obligation to preserve the money in a separate fund (see *Brewster* (1979) 69 Cr App R 375). A case which contrasts with *Hall* is that of *Hassall* (1861) Le & Ca 56. D was the treasurer of a club into which members paid money each week on the understanding that D would return the money to each member at Christmas. D became the legal owner of the money as it was never expected that he would return the identical coins to each member. However, it is a situation where D is expected to retain the property or its proceeds and deal with it in a particular way. If he dishonestly appropriates it he will be guilty of theft. While the facts in cases will vary, it is clear that **the crucial question is what the clear understanding of the parties to the transaction was.** It is necessary for the prosecution to prove that both the accused and the client clearly understood that the client's money was to be kept separate from the accused's business money (see *McHugh* (1993) 97 Cr App R 335).

In *Klineberg and Marsden* [1999] 1 Cr App R 427, a company, Powerhouse Canaries Ltd, operated by the appellants sold timeshare apartments in Lanzarote to customers in England. The purchasers paid over the purchase price on the understanding (supported by both documents and oral representations from the defendants) that the money would be held by an independent trust company, Timeshare Trustees

International (TTI), which would act as stakeholders to protect the purchaser until the apartment in question was ready for occupation. Between October 1990 and November 1991, 237 people paid over £500,000 to Powerhouse in connection with intended purchases of timeshares but only £233 found its way to TTI. The appellants' convictions for theft were upheld as there was a legal obligation imposed on them to deal with the intending purchasers' property in a particular way which they had breached. The documents and oral representations the purchasers had received had played a crucial part in inducing them to hand over their money and thus evidenced both the appellants' and purchasers' understanding of the transaction (see also *Kumar, Re* [2000] Crim LR 504; cf. *Floyd* v *DPP* [2000] Crim LR 41 and commentary thereon).

In some situations it may be unclear in which sense 'property belonged to another', whether under s. 5(1), (2), or (3), or whether it was the original property which D appropriated dishonestly or the proceeds thereof. It will still be possible to secure a conviction of theft, however, where it is clear that whatever category the property fell into it belonged to V and D had, with the requisite *mens rea*, appropriated it. In *Hallam and Blackburn* [1995] Crim LR 323, the appellants were financial advisers working as Abbeyfield Ltd. In some cases they paid investors' cheques into their own account or into the Abbeyfield account and did not invest them on their clients' behalf. In other cases policy surrender cheques received from insurance companies were never passed on to the investors. Their convictions for theft were upheld by the Court of Appeal on the basis that the clients retained an equitable interest in any cheques they drew in favour of the appellants or any cheques drawn by the insurance companies, and in the proceeds of those cheques or the balance of any account operated by the appellants or Abbeyfield Ltd. It was immaterial at what point in time the appellants appropriated the property and thus it was irrelevant whether it was a chose in action at that time (i.e. a credit balance in a bank account) or the proceeds thereof. The evidence established that they had failed to account to their clients for the sums with which they had been entrusted and had done so with the intention of permanently depriving them of their interest in the property or its proceeds.

Section 5(3) also covers the situation where D receives money on account of P.

 Example

If D is employed as P's agent to collect the rent from tenants of property owned by P, the tenants will pay the money to D on account of P. If D dishonestly appropriates this money he may be guilty of theft depending upon the nature of the arrangements operating between himself and P. If D is under an obligation to maintain a distinct fund containing the money obtained from the tenants and pay this over to P, D will be guilty of theft. By contrast, if D is merely under a duty to account to P in due course for an equivalent sum (less any commission) there will be no obligation to retain and deal with the property in a particular way; the relationship is merely that of debtor and creditor. Thus, if D was the rent agent for several property owners and paid all rent collected into one account from which he withdrew his commission and then subsequently paid each property owner the amounts they were due, he would not be guilty of theft if he absconded with the money he collected (see *Robertson* [1977] Crim LR 629).

In *Lewis v Lethbridge* [1987] Crim LR 59, D obtained sponsorship for a particular charity to be paid if X ran the London Marathon. D collected the sponsorship money but did not pay the charity. It was held that there was no obligation upon D to maintain a fund consisting of the money collected or its proceeds; his relationship with the charity was merely that of debtor and creditor. This case has been overruled by the Court of Appeal in *Wain*, 12 October 1993, unreported. W organised various events to raise money for 'The Telethon Trust', a charitable body created by the Yorkshire Television Company. With the permission of a representative of the company he transferred the money he had raised from a special bank account into his own personal account. He then dissipated the credit in his own account and was charged with theft of £2,833.25, the amount he had originally raised. The Court of Appeal considered that the Divisional Court had overlooked the trust aspect of the facts in *Lewis v Lethbridge* and found itself agreeing with Professor Smith's criticisms of the case in *The Law of Theft* (6th edn) where he stated (at p. 39):

> Sponsors surely do not give the collector…the money to do as he likes with. Is there not an overwhelming inference (or, at least, evidence on which a jury might find) that the sponsors intend to give the money to the charity, imposing an obligation in the nature of a trust on the collector?

The Court of Appeal stated:

> …by virtue of s. 5(3), [W] was plainly under an obligation to retain, if not the actual notes and coins, at least their proceeds, that is to say the money credited in the bank account which he opened for the trust with the actual property. When he took the money credited to that account and moved it over to his own bank account, it was still the proceeds of the notes and coins donated which he proceeded to use for his own purposes, thereby appropriating them.

One final point the Court of Appeal made was that the test whether a person is a trustee is an objective one depending on the law and not that person's own understanding (see also *Dyke and Munro* [2001] EWCA Crim 2184, [2002] 1 Cr App R 30).

While civil law may place D under an obligation to account for property in particular circumstances, this will not necessarily bring D within the reach of s. 5(3). At civil law, an employee who takes a bribe or makes a secret profit by misusing his employer's property or his own position is bound to account to his employer for the profit. This duty to account, however, only creates the relationship of debtor and creditor; D does not receive the bribe 'on account of' the employer (*Powell v McRae* [1977] Crim LR 571), nor the profit 'on account of' the employer (*A-G's Reference (No. 1 of 1985)* [1986] QB 491). The latter two cases under the 1968 Act followed a decision of long-standing authority, *Lister v Stubbs* (1890) 45 Ch D 1 which Lord Lane CJ in *A-G's Reference (No. 1 of 1985)* considered the draftsman of the 1968 Act must have had in mind. In *A-G for Hong Kong v Reid* [1994] 1 AC 324 the Privy Council, in a civil case, ruled that *Lister v Stubbs* had been wrongly decided and that a person in a fiduciary position who received a bribe became not only a debtor for the amount of the bribe but also held the bribe (and its proceeds) on constructive trust. If the English courts follow this highly persuasive authority a person in a fiduciary position who makes a secret profit, whether by accepting a bribe or by use of his employer's property for his own purposes, will be a trustee of that property and the property may, accordingly, be the subject of theft. Should an English court follow this course it would be, to quote Professor Smith, '*Lister* v *Stubbs* and the criminal law' (1994) 110 LQR 180, at p. 184:

> ...an odd situation when an extension of the criminal law which Parliament has declined to make is made...by the decision of a civil court; but that court cannot be criticised for stating what it believes the civil law to be.

It is difficult to formulate any general rules in relation to s. 5(3) as each case will hinge upon its own particular facts. **The obligation upon D, however, must be a legal obligation** (see *Gilks* (1972) 56 Cr App R 734; *Mainwaring* (1981) 74 Cr App R 99). The judge must initially decide whether the possible facts are capable of being construed to give rise to a legal obligation. It is then for the jury to determine what the actual facts of the case are; if they fall within those that would give rise to a legal obligation, they then have to consider whether the other criteria for theft are established. If they do not, they should acquit D. **The legal obligation should exist at the time D dishonestly appropriates the property or its proceeds.** This last proposition, however, appears to conflict with the case of *Meech* [1974] QB 549. P gave D a cheque which D agreed to cash and pay the proceeds to P. D then discovered that P had obtained the cheque by fraud. Together with E and F, D planned to stage a fake robbery so that he could tell P that the money had been stolen. D, E, and F were convicted of theft of the money being the proceeds of property that D had received from P under an obligation within s. 5(3). It was argued on appeal that P could not have enforced any such obligation having acquired the cheque illegally. The Court of Appeal, turning the law on its head, concluded that the question was to be looked at from D's point of view; he initially assumed an obligation which he believed was legally binding. But the fact that D believes an element of the *actus reus* of an offence exists does not render him guilty of that offence (as opposed to an attempt to commit it) if that element does not exist in fact. It was further argued by D that, as at the time of appropriation (which the Court had held to be when D, E, and F divided the proceeds from the cashing of the cheque), D knew the truth, he was not then under any 'obligation'. Again, amazingly, the Court held that the crucial time was 'the time of the creation or acceptance of the obligation'. But, if there was no obligation at the time of the appropriation, there was no property deemed to belong to another. It is essential for the commission of theft that the property belong to another at the time of the dishonest appropriation. Doubtless D, E, and F had criminal intentions, and may indeed have been guilty of attempted theft or conspiracy to steal, but this does not justify the Court of Appeal throwing principle out of the window in order to uphold the convictions of those it considers to be undeserving appellants.

11.2.1.3.3 *Property 'got' by another's mistake*
Section 5(4) provides:

> Where a person gets property by another's mistake, and is under an obligation to make restoration (in whole or in part) of the property or its proceeds or of the value thereof,

> then to the extent of that obligation the property or its proceeds shall be regarded (as against him) as belonging to the person entitled to restoration, and an intention not to make restoration shall be regarded accordingly as an intention to deprive that person of the property or proceeds.

This provision is designed to cover the situation where P transfers property to D under a mistake which does not operate to prevent ownership of the property passing to D. In many cases this provision is not necessary.

In some situations, however, P's mistake will not prevent legal ownership in the property passing to D. In such a situation D may commit theft of the property, its proceeds or value thereof, if he dishonestly appropriates it being under a legal obligation to restore it to P.

An example of a situation covered by s. 5(4) would be that disclosed by the facts in *Moynes v Cooper* [1956] 1 QB 439. D, having received a partial advance on his week's wages, was paid his full wages by the wages clerk. When D opened his wage packet he discovered the mistake but decided to keep the money he had been overpaid. D was acquitted of larceny. The wages clerk had transferred ownership of the money to D so D could not steal what was his own property. Under s. 5(4), D would be guilty of theft as he would be under a legal obligation to make restitution of the part, or value thereof, overpaid. In *A-G's Reference (No. 1 of 1983)* [1985] QB 182, this provision was held to cover the case where an employee received an overpayment of wages by means of a direct debit transaction between the employer's account and the employee's account. In this case, the thing in action, the debt owed by the bank to D, to the value of the overpayment, had been 'got' by the employer's mistake, and D was under an obligation to make restitution of that amount to her employer. If D had spent all the money in her account on drinking and gambling before realising that she had been overpaid, a subsequent refusal to restore the sum overpaid to the employer could not amount to theft as there would no longer be property (in this case a thing in action in the form of the debt owed by the bank to D) which D could appropriate. If, however, D had bought jewellery this would represent the proceeds of the overpayment in which the employer would have a proprietary interest and which D could steal.

In *Davis* (1988) 88 Cr App R 347, D was in receipt of housing benefit. By computer error he received additional cheques, some before and some after his entitlement to benefit had ceased. While a machine cannot make a mistake a computer error is the manifestation of a human error, namely that of the operator. D could have been charged with theft of the cheques (which would have fallen within s. 5(1)) but the prosecution charged him with theft of the money he received when he cashed the cheques. His conviction of theft was upheld as the cash represented the proceeds of the cheques and he was under an obligation to make restoration of the proceeds of all cheques paid after entitlement to benefit ceased and of the amount by which he was overpaid while entitled to benefit.

D will be guilty of theft only where there is a legal obligation to make restitution; a moral obligation will not suffice. In *Gilks* (1972) 56 Cr App R 734, D had won £10.62 betting on horses. When he claimed his winnings the betting shop manager paid him £117.25 mistakenly believing he had backed one more winner than he had. D realised the mistake but decided to keep the overpayment. He was convicted of theft. The Court of Appeal held that the conviction could not be sustained under s. 5(4) as 'obligation' meant 'legal obligation' and gaming transactions were not legally enforceable. The Court upheld the conviction, however, relying on an old case, *Middleton* (1873) LR 2 CCR 38, stating that, as the property had been transferred under a mistake, ownership did not pass, so the property belonged to the betting shop when D decided to keep it. In *Middleton*, however, the mistake was as to the identity of the recipient of the overpayment; there was no such mistake in this case. Nor was there a mistake as to the amount paid; the manager paid D the sum he intended to pay him. There would only have been a mistake as to the property if he had miscounted or mistaken, for example, a £20 note for a £10 note. The *ratio* of the case is thus wrong. If such a situation were to recur it is submitted that a conviction might be secured under *Shadrokh-Cigari* [1988] Crim LR 465, on the basis that where property is obtained as a result of a mistake on P's part, P retains an equitable interest in the property or its proceeds. Thus, although D may become the legal owner he may steal from P who retains a proprietary interest in the property (see **11.2.1.2.2** *ante*). This rule, it is submitted, should be confined to mistakes as to the identity of the recipient or the property transferred (which are already adequately covered) or mistake on P's part that he is under an obligation to transfer the property to D (as was the case in *Shadrokh-Cigari*). It should not be extended to cover other mistakes, for example, where P gives D a painting believing it has little value, although D knows that it is valuable. If D sells the painting he is currently guilty of no offence and should not become so by any further extension of the rule in the absence of legislative intervention.

11.2.1.4 The property must belong to another at the time of appropriation

The fact that property at one time belonged to P does not mean that it necessarily continued to belong to him at the time D did the act alleged to constitute an appropriation of it. In some situations it will be important to determine when ownership in property passes. This will involve the law of contract and sale. The general rule stated in s. 17 of the Sale of Goods Act 1979 is that the property (i.e. ownership) in goods passes to the buyer at the time the parties intend it to pass. In the case of shops, the courts attribute to the parties the intention that ownership shall pass only on payment by the customer. If D dishonestly removes goods from a shop without paying for them he will be appropriating property belonging to another. By contrast, where D fills his tank with petrol at a self-service station and then decides to make off without paying for the petrol, this is not theft as under s. 18, Rule 5 of the 1979 Act, property in the petrol (i.e. ownership of it) passed to him at the time of filling his tank; when he drives off the petrol is his (see *Edwards v Ddin* (1976) 63 Cr App R 218; but D would now be guilty of making off without payment under s. 3 of the TA 1978). In the case of other sales, s. 18, Rule 1 of the 1979 Act provides that ownership may pass under a contract of sale as soon as the contract is made and before the price has been paid. Thus, if this was the intention of the parties and P hands over the property to D and D then absconds with it, this would not be theft as the property D appropriated was his own as it belonged to him from the time the contract was concluded.

In seeking to determine when ownership was intended to pass 'regard shall be had to the terms of the contract, the conduct of the parties and the circumstances of the case' (s. 17(2) of the 1979 Act). In *Dobson* v *General Accident Fire and Life Assurance Corporation* [1990] QB 274, P offered for sale some jewellery which X agreed to buy and pay for by a building society cheque. The cheque had been stolen and thus was invalid. When P sought to claim under his insurance policy with D, D refused to pay arguing that the property had not been stolen but obtained by deception. The Court of Appeal held that there had been a theft. Looking at the facts they found that property was not intended to pass except in exchange for a valid cheque. Thus when X took delivery of the jewellery it was property belonging to another and he appropriated it at that point. The contract had been induced by X's fraud and thus was voidable. Property does pass under a voidable contract. In this case the very act which passed the property to X, delivery, was also X's appropriation of it, and at that time it still belonged to P. The act by which P divested himself of ownership of the property, delivery, also involved X assuming ownership of the property. In support of his view that it is no defence to say that property has passed under the terms of a voidable contract, Parker LJ quoted from the speech of Lord Roskill in *Morris* [1984] AC 320, at p. 334:

> I respectfully suggest that it is on any view wrong to introduce into this branch of the criminal law questions whether particular contracts are void or voidable on the grounds of mistake or fraud or whether any mistake is sufficiently fundamental to vitiate a contract. These difficult questions should so far as possible be confined to those fields of law to which they are immediately relevant and I do not regard them as relevant questions under the Theft Act 1968.

In *Gomez* [1992] 3 WLR 1061, Lord Keith of Kinkel approved of Parker LJ's reasoning, finding further support for this position in the speech of Viscount Dilhorne in *Lawrence* [1972] AC 626, at p. 633, who stated that '"belonging to another" in section 1(1)…in my view signifies no more than that, at the time of the appropriation…the property belonged to another'. It seems that what is important is the history of the property up to the moment when the rogue appropriates it. If it belonged to someone other than the rogue then that is sufficient to satisfy the requirements of the Act. Whether or not the rogue had acquired a voidable title to the property is treated as irrelevant. It follows from this (and the decision of their Lordships in relation to the issue of consent, see **11.2.1.5.2** *post*) that the person who fills his car with petrol at a self-service filling station intending not to pay for it, appropriates property belonging to another as up to the point when the petrol enters his tank it belongs to another. As a result, it appears that in all contractual situations involving deception (or false representation) by D where property is intended to pass under the contract, D may be convicted of either theft or fraud (previously, obtaining property by deception contrary to s. 15 of the TA 1968). Incredibly, following the decision of the House of Lords in *Hinks* [2000] 3 WLR 1590 (**11.2.1.5.3** *post*), it appears that D may even steal property which indefeasibly belongs to him, it being sufficient that before it became D's property it belonged to another and D is considered to be dishonest in accepting the property (in this case, a gift).

11.2.1.5 Appropriation

The definition of theft requires that D appropriate property belonging to another. The simplest example of appropriation is where D surreptitiously removes P's wallet from his pocket. It is not every appropriation, however, which amounts to theft; **the appropriation must be accompanied by dishonesty and an intention to deprive the owner permanently of the property.** Thus the pickpocket who intends to spend the money he finds in P's wallet would have the necessary *mens rea*. By contrast, if D is P's son, and is removing the wallet as an April Fools' Day prank, with no intention to deprive his father of it permanently, there would be no theft, not because of a lack of appropriation, but because of the absence of *mens rea*.

When the Criminal Law Revision Committee, in its *Eighth Report, Theft and Related Offences* (Cmnd 2977, 1966), framed the concept of 'dishonest appropriation' it did so in the hope and belief that this concept would be easily understood without the aid of further definition (see para. 34). Unfortunately, even after 40 years of judicial consideration involving four decisions of the House of Lords, one cannot be certain that the meaning of appropriation has finally been resolved. The last pronouncement of the House of Lords in *Hinks* (**11.2.1.5.3** *post*) appears almost surreal and it is difficult to believe it bears any resemblance to the legislature's understanding of this concept.

11.2.1.5.1 *Assuming the rights of an owner*
Section 3(1) of the TA 1968 provides:

> Any assumption by a person of the rights of an owner amounts to an appropriation, and this includes, where he has come by the property (innocently or not) without stealing it, any later assumption of a right to it by keeping or dealing with it as owner.

For the moment we are concerned only with the first part of this definition; cases of later assumption of rights to property will be dealt with later (see **11.2.1.5.5** *post*). **The phrase 'any assumption of the rights of an owner' cannot mean that D actually acquires rights of ownership; rather it suggests that he is taking to himself rights which he does not have and that he is dealing with the property as if he was the owner.** As the word 'assume' may be defined to mean 'to usurp, to arrogate, to seize', **the idea sought to be conveyed is the ousting or supplanting of the owner's rights vis-à-vis the property** as D seeks to occupy the owner's place in relation to it. Seen in this light the word 'assumption' (or 'assume') has a pejorative connotation and is not a value-neutral word. (Had Parliament wanted to use a value-neutral word, it could have used a word such as 'exercise'.) **The suggestion is that D is asserting a right, which he neither has, nor has authority to assert, over the property of another.** The principal rights of the owner are, for example, to possess, use, consume, sell, hire, lend, or destroy his property. The paradigm case of theft is that of D, a pickpocket, removing a wallet from P's pocket. In taking the property D is clearly assuming and exercising rights which he does not have to the property. But theft may occur in many and varied situations and the act of stealing itself may not be physical but mental in the sense of a decision made in respect of property (as envisaged by the second part of s. 3(1)).

Example

P lends D a book for a week but at the time of taking possession of it D intends to sell it. In this situation P is permitting D to take possession of the book for a limited period; D, however, in taking the book is taking it to dispose of outright and thereby is, in his mind, assuming rights of ownership over the book which P had not transferred to him. It would not be inaccurate to say in this situation that D is arrogating to himself rights which P had not granted, or that he is usurping P's rights.

It should be noted that the offence of theft protects not just ownership but also lesser interests such as possession or control. Thus **even the acts of an owner, if designed to usurp or defeat the interests of another in the owner's property, may amount to theft.**

Example

If D hires a lawnmower to P he has divested himself of his right to possession of the lawn-mower for the period of hire. If D surreptitiously removes the lawnmower from P's posses-sion prior to the expiry of the hire period, he will be usurping P's right to possession (see *Turner (No. 2)* **11.2.1.2.1** *ante*). Similarly, if E removes it from P intending to return it to him after the period of hire has expired, he will be assuming a right of an owner, namely pos-session.

Of course, in the context of the statutory definition, appropriation is inextricably linked to the concept of dishonesty. **Theft, consequently, is concerned with dis-honest appropriations.** (This is a point which we will return to when considering *Hinks*.) But an issue which arises is whether all the mischief with which the offence of theft is concerned is locked within the concept of dishonesty or whether some of it is to be found in the concept of appropriation. There is a danger that if insuf-ficient attention is paid to the meaning of appropriation, actions which do not fit paradigms of theft may be sucked within the boundaries of theft by juries (or magistrates) determining, as a moral reaction, whether what D did was dishonest. Such an undiscriminating approach could lead to uncertainty, inconsistency and injustice, all of which might be avoided by adopting a definition of 'appropria-tion' which is more discriminating. Such discrimination between actions which Parliament intended to fall within theft and those which it did not, demands that **'appropriation' should have a pejorative connotation**. A value-neutral view of appropriation leaves everything to hinge on the ill-defined concept of dishonesty.

A problem which s. 3(1) presents is that it states that any assumption by a per-son of 'the rights of an owner' amounts to an appropriation. In some cases, how-ever, only one such right is assumed, namely, possession. In *Morris* [1984] AC 320, two appeals were heard by the House of Lords relating to dishonest shoppers in supermarkets:

> D and E switched the price labels on goods intending to buy the goods at a lower price at the till. D was arrested after paying the lower price while E was arrested

before he paid the lower price. D would, if charged, have been liable to conviction of obtaining property by deception contrary to s. 15 of the TA 1968. E may have reached the point of attempting the s. 15 offence. Both D and E, however, were charged with theft. It was clearly one of the owner's rights to fix the price at which his property would be sold. Switching the price labels was an assumption of this right and it did not matter that the dishonest shoppers had not yet assumed all the owner's rights.

Lord Roskill stated (at pp. 331, 332) that **it is sufficient to prove that an accused assumed *any* of the rights of an owner.** This is a necessary construction of the provision as there are cases where D has clearly not assumed some of the owner's rights. For example, D may appropriate property without ever being in possession of it, as where D offers to sell, without authority, P's goods to Q; at that point D is assuming a right of the owner, namely to sell his property (see *Pitham and Hehl* (1976) 65 Cr App R 45). A problem with this decision, however, is that P knew D was not the owner of the goods, and D knew that P knew this; on its actual facts, therefore, it would appear that D did not truly assume the rights of an owner, but this should not be taken to undermine the general principle. In such a case the theft is committed at the time of the offer to sell; it does not matter that P was never deprived of his property (although it must, of course be proved that D intended to deprive P of his property permanently).

The decision in *Morris* has important implications relating to when and where theft is committed. If D draws an unauthorised cheque on P's bank account, making it payable in favour of himself or in favour of Q and presents it to Q, D is assuming the rights of an owner as he is doing that which only an owner is entitled to do (see *Kohn* (1979) 69 Cr App R 395; *Governor of Pentonville Prison, ex parte Osman* (1989) 90 Cr App R 281; *Hilton, The Times*, 18 April 1997 where the chairman of a charity faxed instructions to the bank to transfer sums from the charity's account to another account). The property D is appropriating is the debt owed by the bank to P. The offence of theft of this thing in action occurs when D delivers the cheque to Q, even if it is never presented (see *Osman*; this case actually involved sending telex instructions to debit P's account) or, if the cheque is made out in his own favour, when D presents it (see *Chan Man-sin* [1988] 1 All ER 1). The offence is committed where D delivers or presents the cheque even though the account may be held in a bank outside the jurisdiction (see *Osman*). If the bank honours such a cheque and debits P's account, such a transaction is a complete nullity; P's rights against the bank remain exactly as before, that is, the debt owed him by the bank is in the same sum as stood in his account prior to the honouring of the unauthorised cheque (see *Chan Man-sin* v *A-G for Hong Kong*). Although P ends up not being deprived of anything by such a transaction, D remains guilty of theft as it is the appropriation which constitutes the *actus reus* of theft; there is no need to prove 'deprivation' (see *Hilton*; see also *Wheatley* v *Commissioner of Police of the British Virgin Isles* [2006] UKPC 24). These principles also cover other transactions. In the present example, if D purports to sell P's property to E, the appropriation occurs where the offer to sell is made even though the property may be situate outside the jurisdiction.

11.2.1.5.2 *Consent and appropriation*

The major problem in relation to appropriation has been whether there could be an appropriation where the owner of the property had consented to the 'taking' of it by the alleged thief. In *Gomez* [1992] 3 WLR 1061, as with *Lawrence* [1972] AC 626 and *Dobson* v *General Accident Fire and Life Assurance Corp plc* [1990] QB 274 (see **11.2.1.4** *ante*) the owner consented to the taking of the property but only because of a deception practised upon him by the rogue. While these facts could have supported, at the time, a conviction for the offence of obtaining property by deception contrary to s. 15(1) of the Theft Act 1968 (and now, fraud), would they also enable a conviction to be obtained for the simple offence of theft contained in s. 1(1)? *Lawrence* suggested an affirmative answer while *Morris* had been construed in several Court of Appeal decisions as suggesting the contrary.

> In *Gomez* the accused was the assistant manager of an electrical goods shop. X approached him seeking to acquire goods from the shop in exchange for two building society cheques which were stolen. The cheques were undated and bore no payee's name. Gomez approached the manager seeking his authorisation for a sale totalling the amount of £7,950, the amount of one of the cheques. The manager instructed him to confirm with the bank that the cheque was acceptable. Gomez later falsely told the manager that the bank had said the cheque was 'as good as cash'. The sale was authorised and the goods were duly supplied to X. A few days later Gomez presented the manager with the second cheque which was in the amount of £9,250 in support of a further sale and again this transaction was authorised by the manager and the goods supplied to X. Several days later the cheques were returned marked 'Orders not to pay. Stolen cheque'. Gomez was convicted of theft. The Court of Appeal quashed his conviction on the basis that there was no appropriation at the moment when X took possession of the goods because he was entitled to do so under a contract of sale (which although voidable had not been avoided at the time). The Court of Appeal took the view that the manager's consent and authority negated the element of appropriation. In reaching its decision the Court purported to follow *Morris* although the question of property being obtained by trickery had not been considered in that case. Lord Lane CJ, in dealing with the conflict between *Lawrence* and *Morris*, stated 'suffice it to say that if there is a difference between the two decisions, that was not the view taken by their Lordships in *R v Morris*, and that is the decision we must follow'.
>
> The House of Lords gave the Crown leave to appeal and the Court of Appeal subsequently certified that a point of law of general public importance was involved in the decision, namely:
>
> When theft is alleged and that which is alleged to be stolen passes to the defendant with the consent of the owner, but that has been obtained by a false representation, has (a) an appropriation within the meaning of s. 1(1) of the Theft Act 1968 taken place, or (b) must such a passing of property necessarily involve an element of adverse interference with or usurpation of some right of the owner?
>
> By a majority of four to one (Lord Lowry dissenting) their Lordships allowed the appeal and approved *Lawrence*, answering the certified question (a) in the affirmative and (b) in the negative. The leading speech was delivered by Lord Keith of Kinkel with whom Lords Jauncey of Tullichettle, Slynn of Hadley, and Browne-Wilkinson agreed. His Lordship reviewed the earlier decisions of the House in *Lawrence* and *Morris* highlighting the conflict to which the two decisions gave rise.
>
> In *Lawrence* D, a taxi-driver, was convicted of theft where he represented to P, his Italian passenger, that the £1 tendered was insufficient to cover the fare and removed a further £6 from the passenger's wallet, the true fare for the journey being

52p. D argued on appeal that the conviction of theft of this £6 could not stand as P had consented to him taking it. D was seeking to have the words 'without consent of the owner' implied into s. 1(1) of the TA 1968. The House of Lords rejected this argument stating that there may be an appropriation 'even though the owner has permitted or consented to the property being taken'. At the time D removed the money from the wallet, it was property belonging to P. In removing it D was doing something which only an owner could do. His removal of the money constituted an appropriation. Whether this was theft would hinge on whether D was dishonest. He would not have been dishonest if he believed that P, knowing the circumstances (i.e. that he was being charged a fare far in excess of the legal fare) consented to his appropriation of the money. Viscount Dilhorne stated (at p. 632):

> Belief or the absence of belief that the owner had with such knowledge consented to the appropriation is relevant to the issue of dishonesty, not to the question whether or not there has been an appropriation.

When D took the £6 from the wallet he appropriated it whether or not P consented to him taking it. D was dishonest because he did not believe that P knew the circumstances and, with that knowledge, consented to the £6 being taken. The transaction was one coloured by D's fraud.

Viscount Dilhorne's view finds support in another provision of the Act. Section 2(1)(b) provides that an appropriation of property belonging to another is not to be regarded as dishonest:

> (b) if D appropriates the property in the belief that he would have the other's consent if the other knew of the appropriation and the circumstances of it.

The section contemplates that an appropriation may be consented to. Viscount Dilhorne expressly stated in *Lawrence* (at p. 632):

> [A] person is not to be regarded as acting dishonestly if he appropriates another's property believing that with full knowledge of the circumstances that other person has in fact agreed to the appropriation.

In *Morris* the House of Lords did not question the decision in *Lawrence*, Lord Roskill taking the view that the facts of the case clearly disclosed a dishonest appropriation. Section 3(1) of the Theft Act 1968 provides that 'Any assumption by a person of the rights of an owner amounts to an appropriation...'. A question which arose in *Morris* was whether or not D had to assume all the rights of an owner in order to appropriate property. Lord Roskill answered this by stating:

> [I]t is enough for the prosecution if they have proved...the assumption...of any of the rights of the owner of the goods in question...

In *Gomez*, after approving this dictum, Lord Keith proceeded to label as unnecessary and incorrect certain of the observations which Lord Roskill had made in his speech in *Morris*.

First, Lord Roskill **gave the example of the practical joker** who switches price labels on items in a supermarket concluding that this act, without more, would not amount to an appropriation. Lord Keith was of opinion that label switching in itself constitutes an appropriation as it involves an assumption of one of the rights of the owner irrespective of whether or not it is accompanied by some other act. **It is, accordingly, the absence of dishonesty and an intention to deprive the owner permanently of the property which renders the practical joker not guilty of theft.**

Secondly, and flowing directly from the previous point, **Lord Roskill defined 'appropriation' pejoratively**, stating that it 'involves not an act expressly or impliedly authorised by the owner but an act by way of adverse interference with or usurpation of those rights'. There would have been no real problem with Lord Roskill's dictum if he had excised from it the words 'not an act expressly or impliedly authorised by the owner' as the essential point was that an appropriation is something adverse to the owner, something which usurps the owner's rights. The shoplifter clearly seeks to do so whereas the honest shopper intends nothing adverse to the owner's interests. **The context in *Lawrence* was one of consent or authorisation being induced by fraud.** In such a situation P is giving consent on one basis but D is taking the goods on a different basis. In *Lawrence* **P was consenting to D taking the correct fare whereas D was taking more than the correct fare**; his act was not truly consented to by P. **Likewise, in *Morris*, there was fraud** as D was seeking to deceive the shop assistant as to the correct price for the goods. While the shop owner consented to shoppers taking goods from the shelves for the purpose of purchasing them, he did not consent to them changing price labels to purchase them at a lower price. In response to Lord Roskill's dictum, Lord Keith stated (at p. 1076):

> While it is correct to say that appropriation for purposes of section 3(1) includes the latter sort of act, it does not necessarily follow that no other act can amount to an appropriation and in particular that no act expressly or impliedly authorised by the owner can in any circumstances do so. Indeed, *Lawrence v Commissioner of Metropolitan Police* is a clear decision to the contrary since it laid down unequivocally that an act may be an appropriation notwithstanding that it is done with the consent of the owner. It does not appear to me that any sensible distinction can be made in this context between consent and authorisation.

The distinction between consent and authorisation had been the basis of an attempt by Parker LJ in *Dobson* v *General Accident Fire and Life Assurance Corporation plc* to reconcile the two conflicting schools of thought following *Lawrence* and *Morris*. *Skipp* [1975] Crim LR 114 and *Fritschy* [1985] Crim LR 745 supported the *Morris* line of reasoning whereas *McPherson* [1973] Crim LR 191, approved in *Anderton* v *Wish* (1980) 72 Cr App R 23 at p. 25 supported the *Lawrence* line of reasoning. Parker LJ sought to distinguish the cases of *Skipp* and *Fritschy* on the basis that the owners of the goods in these cases had expressly authorised the physical acts of the defendants in that they had instructed them to take possession of the goods alleged to have been stolen and deal with them in a particular manner, rather than simply consenting to the defendants taking the goods. It is no longer necessary to attempt to make such fine distinctions; Lord Keith concluded that the decisions in *Skipp* and *Fritschy* were wrong as they were inconsistent with *Lawrence*. Lord Keith saw no purpose in referring to the Eighth Report of the CLRC concluding that (at p. 1080):

> The decision in *Lawrence* was a clear decision of this House upon the construction of the word 'appropriate' in section 1(1) of the Act, which had stood for twelve years when doubt was thrown upon it by obiter dicta in *Morris*. *Lawrence* must be regarded as authoritative and correct, and there is no question of it now being right to depart from it.

Following *Gomez*, accordingly, appropriation was seen as something which could be done even though the owner apparently consented to the act. In *Gomez* the shop manager was only consenting to D taking the goods in return for full payment. There was no actual consent (based on full knowledge of the facts) to what the thief was actually doing. **The problem with *Gomez*, however, is that in correcting errors which crept in as a result of Lord Roskill's speech in *Morris* , their Lordships also answered the second part of the certified question in the negative, holding that appropriation is not necessarily something adverse to the owner's rights or something which usurps the owner's rights.** The way in which the question for their Lordships' consideration was framed assumed that consent and adverse interference or usurpation could not co-exist. In all the cases where the issue of consent or authorisation arose there was an element of usurpation arising from the deception involved. If sight is lost of this idea, appropriation may be perceived of as a value-neutral word and be stripped of its pejorative connotation. It is not clear that Lord Keith intended to do so as his dictum cited earlier simply seeks to state that consent does not, in all circumstances, prevent an appropriation occurring. The circumstances he must have had in mind because of the context in *Lawrence*, *Morris* and *Gomez* together with the civil case of *Dobson*, were those of a deception being involved which runs counter to the apparent consent. There is a suggestion, however, in Lord Keith's dictum that not every act which amounts to an appropriation is necessarily an adverse interference with or usurpation of the owner's rights. This leaves then the question whether consent, which is not induced by fraud (or some other circumstance which might render the transaction voidable), is relevant to the question of appropriation.

 Question

Can D appropriate property where that which he does in relation to it is done with the full knowledge and consent of the owner, that is, does not amount to any adverse interference with or usurpation of the owner's rights?

This question will be considered in **11.2.1.5.3**.

It is clear following the decision in *Gomez* that the degree of overlap between theft contrary to s. 1 and obtaining property by deception contrary to s. 15 of the Theft Act 1968 was considerable (see further *Atakpu and Abrahams* [1994] Crim LR 693). It had been suggested in argument before their Lordships that by following *Lawrence* rather than *Morris*, s. 15 would be rendered otiose since a person who, by

deception, persuades an owner to consent to parting with his property will necessarily be guilty of theft within s. 1. An example of a situation which would constitute the s. 15 offence but which would not amount to theft, would be where D
deceives P into sending him property. At the point when P despatches the property
he passes ownership of it to D. At the time when D receives the property it belongs
to him so he cannot appropriate it. He has, however, obtained it by deception. In
his speech Lord Browne-Wilkinson provided a further example, namely where the
property obtained is land which cannot be stolen (subject to the exceptions in
s. 4(2) of the Theft Act 1968). For practical purposes, however, most s. 15 offences
also amounted to thefts. This gave the prosecution considerable discretion in
deciding which charge to level. Given that consent is irrelevant, it was easier to
prove theft than to prove the s. 15 offence which required the prosecution to prove
that P was deceived by D into parting with his property. The offence of fraud,
which replaces the s. 15 offence, is a conduct crime rather than a result crime and
does not require any proof that P is deceived (see **12.3.2** *post*). While the overlap
between fraud and theft remains as great as that between theft and s. 15, there is
no particular benefit to the prosecution charging theft in the situation which arose
in *Gomez* rather than the new fraud by false representation offence.

    Problems persist in this area where a victim is deceived to give their consent
to some transaction involving their property. In *Briggs* [2004] 1 Cr App R 34, the
Court of Appeal managed to give a judgment without referring to the House of
Lords' decisions in *Lawrence, Gomez*, or *Hinks*. The outcome is further confusion. In
Briggs, D had been convicted of the theft of a credit balance. She had deceived her
elderly relatives who were selling their house, to give her a signed authority, which
she presented to the conveyancers dealing with the house sale, whereby the proceeds of the sale were transferred to an account used to purchase another property
in D's name. The trial judge directed the jury that it was open to them to conclude
that there had been an appropriation of the credit balance, notwithstanding that
it had been transferred with the victims' consent, if that consent was induced by
fraud. Such a direction was consistent with *Gomez* and *Hilton* (**11.2.1.5.1** *ante*). In
quashing the conviction the Court of Appeal placed reliance on *Naviede* [1997]
Crim LR 662, which they took to have established that where a victim causes a
payment to be made in reliance on deceptive conduct by the defendant, there is no
appropriation by the defendant.

    Three factors fortified the Court of Appeal in this conclusion. First, no case
had been cited to them where it had been held that an 'appropriation' occurs
where the relevant act is committed by the victim albeit as a result of deception. One might have expected the Court to be aware of *Gomez* and *Hinks* even
if counsel did not cite them! The Court of Appeal, relying on Sir John Smith's
commentary to *Naviede*, placed significance on the distinction between (a) D's
direct acts to V's property done with V's fraudulently obtained consent (this
would cover *Gomez*-type situations) and (b) D's acts which cause V to transfer his
property (or, in the case of a chose in action, to extinguish it), V's acts resulting
from D's fraud. Sir John Smith took the view that in (b) V's acts broke the chain
of causation. However, it is arguable that V's acts would not be 'free, deliberate
and informed' and thus would not amount to intervening acts breaking the
chain of causation. Further, whatever the criticisms which may be levelled at
the decision in *Hinks*, if consent which is not induced by fraud does not prevent

an appropriation occurring, how much more should consent induced by fraud not do so?

Secondly, the Court of Appeal considered that if they found an appropriation in the instant case, there would be little need for many deception offences because of the overlap there would be with theft. Since the decision of the House of Lords in *Lawrence*, such an overlap has been a reality; and despite ample opportunity since, the House of Lords has steadfastly increased, rather than endeavoured to diminish, this overlap.

Thirdly, the Court took the view that the word 'appropriation' 'connotes a physical act rather than a more remote action triggering the payment which gives rise to the charge'. Their preferred definition was that in the *Oxford English Dictionary* 'to take possession for one's own, to take to oneself'. They could not see why an act of deceiving an owner to do something should fall within the meaning of appropriation. Had this been a decision which pre-dated *Lawrence*, such reasoning may have had some merit; that the Court can engage in it 32 years after that decision defies belief. The case law on appropriation over that period clearly indicates that 'appropriation' is not confined to purely physical acts. There clearly cannot be a taking where the theft involves a chose in action being extinguished (see *Graham* [1997] 1 Cr App R 302); nor is there a taking where the property involved is intangible; nor was there a taking in *Pitham and Hehl* (*ante*); nor is there a taking where D has previously come by property and appropriates it subsequently by assuming a right to it by keeping it.

Whether the decision in *Briggs* is an aberration, remains to be seen. It is clearly undesirable and detrimental to the rule of law for the Court of Appeal to make pronouncements on appropriation which ignore and, in turn, contradict, decisions by the House of Lords however flawed those decisions might be.

11.2.1.5.3 *Appropriating gifts*

A problem arose in several cases involving purported gifts *inter vivos* which highlighted a weakness in the reasoning in *Gomez* and *Lawrence*. In both of those cases the consent of the owner had been obtained by deception. One reading of the cases would be to confine the circumstances in which there can be an appropriation where the owner has consented to D taking property to those where that consent has been obtained by some false representation or, to put it more broadly, by some other wrongful means (for example, coercion or undue influence). In *Gomez* the title D obtained to the property he took from the shop was voidable due to the deception. The same applied in *Lawrence*. The question certified for their Lordships' consideration in *Gomez* was also framed in terms of the property having been obtained by means of a false representation. **Could a theft occur where there is no false representation and the property D receives indefeasibly belongs to him?** This issue arose in the context of several cases involving *inter vivos* gifts.

In the context of the law of gift, if a donor who has capacity makes a gift to a donee, the donor thereby transfers ownership of the property to the donee. If the donor lacks capacity, the transaction is void and the donee would not become the owner of the property. However, if there is coercion, undue influence, or fraud, the transaction is merely voidable, that is, it may be avoided by the donor. Could a donee be considered to have committed theft by accepting a gift from a donor who had capacity, even though there was no coercion, undue influence, or fraud on the donee's part, where, for example, the donee is manipulative and takes advantage of a gullible or vulnerable donor? Clearly it would be undesirable for the criminal law to find a donee guilty of theft where the civil law would find that a valid gift had been made and that the allegedly stolen property belonged to the alleged thief.

> In *Mazo* [1997] 2 Cr App R 518, D, a maid to Lady S, was convicted of theft having cashed cheques totalling £37,000 made payable to her by Lady S. There was evidence to the effect that Lady S was elderly and suffered from confusion at times and short-term memory lapses. D's convictions were quashed as the trial judge had not given an adequate direction to the jury to consider whether Lady S had capacity to make valid gifts. This being so, the jury may have wrongly convicted D of theft without considering the question of whether the property she received had been a gift. The Court of Appeal accepted that it was common ground that if the gifts were valid there could not be a theft, Pill LJ stated (at p. 521):

>> It is clear that a transaction may be a theft...notwithstanding that it was done with the owner's consent if it was induced by fraud, deception or a false representation: see *Gomez*...It is also common ground that the receiver of a valid gift, *inter vivos*, could not be the subject of a conviction for theft...In *Gomez*, reference was made to the speech of Viscount Dilhorne in Lawrence [who stated]: 'A fortiori, a person is not to be regarded as acting dishonestly if he appropriates another's property believing that, with full knowledge of the circumstances, that other person has in fact agreed to the appropriation'. It is implicit in that statement that if in all the circumstances, there is held to be a valid gift there can be no theft.

Thus the Court of Appeal was reading *Gomez* in its context and taking account of the voidable nature of the transaction induced by the deception.

> In *Kendrick and Hopkins* [1997] 2 Cr App R 524, the appellants' convictions for conspiracy to steal were upheld where they had drawn a large number of cheques on the victim's account. The victim, aged 99 and virtually blind, was a resident in a small residential home for the elderly run by the appellants. The Court of Appeal stated that they found it unnecessary to consider whether the narrow reading of *Gomez* adopted in *Mazo* was well founded, being satisfied in the instant case that the jury had received an adequate direction on the question of the capacity of the victim to make valid gifts. The Court of Appeal did, however, criticise *Mazo* as they took the view that appropriation was a concept distinct from dishonesty and thus could be looked at in isolation; questions such as incapacity or fraud were only relevant to dishonesty. This ignores several crucial matters; first, that none of the elements of theft is completely self-contained and to be considered in isolation from the remainder (support for this proposition deriving from Viscount Dilhorne's speech in *Lawrence* as approved in *Gomez*); and secondly, that if the donor lacks capacity, the gift is void, whereas, if the gift is valid (there being no fraud, undue influence, or coercion), unlike the situations in *Lawrence* and *Gomez*, full title to the property passes to the donee and the transaction is not voidable.

The actual decisions in *Mazo* and *Kendrick and Hopkins* were not in conflict; a legitimate reading of them would be that liability for theft would not arise where there was a valid *inter vivos* gift. This position, however, has been thrown into disarray by the case of *Hinks* [2000] 3 WLR 1590.

> D befriended P, a man of low IQ, and over a period of eight months accompanied him to his building society on most days where he made withdrawals totalling £60,000 which were deposited in her account. In addition he gave D a television. There was evidence that D had encouraged, coerced or influenced P to make these gifts and that he was naive and trusting and had no idea of the value of his assets. The trial judge in directing the jury, however, did not clearly put to them the question whether P either lacked capacity to make the gifts or had been unduly influenced or coerced by D, leaving everything to be considered under the question of dishonesty, namely whether P was 'so mentally incapable that the defendant herself realised that ordinary and decent people would regard it as dishonesty to accept that gift from him?' This left the possibility that D could have been convicted of theft of valid gifts on the basis solely of the jury's view on dishonesty. The Court of Appeal dismissed her appeal taking the view that the validity or otherwise of the gifts was irrelevant to the question whether there had been an appropriation; indeed, they even stated that a gift itself might be clear evidence of appropriation!

This involves treating 'appropriation' as a completely value-neutral word. The problem this gives rise to is that if the gift is valid, D has acquired indefeasible title to the property; the transaction is neither void nor voidable. That being so, how could D appropriate (assume the rights of the owner to) property which was her own? If the decisions in *Lawrence* and *Gomez* are applied without any recognition of their context (transactions voidable because of fraud), the outcome could be absurd. Commenting on the Court of Appeal decision, Professor Smith states in *The Law of Theft* (8th edn) para. 2–22:

> If [the property] were seized from [D] by the police, D, not the donor or anyone else would be entitled to recover it. [D] would have an action in conversion against the police—or the donor, if the police returned the property to [the donor].

The Court of Appeal certified a question for consideration of the House of Lords:

> Whether the acquisition of an indefeasible title to property is capable of amounting to an appropriation of property belonging to another for the purposes of section 1(1) of the Theft Act 1968.

Amazingly, **by a majority of four to one, their Lordships answered the question in the affirmative.** Thus D's receiving of a gift can amount to an appropriation; guilt of theft will hinge on whether the jury consider she was dishonest to accept the gift. (Lord Hutton, although answering the question in the affirmative, considered that there could not be dishonesty where a valid gift was made and thus would have quashed the conviction on that ground.) The majority took this issue to have been settled by *Gomez* ignoring the fact that that case involved a deception which rendered the transaction voidable. Lord Steyn, with whom Lords Slynn of Hadley and Jauncey of Tullichettle agreed, was of opinion that the judgments in *Gomez* did not 'differentiate between consent induced by fraud and consent given in any other circumstances'. Their Lordships came to this conclusion despite the fact that the question certified for consideration in *Gomez* expressly referred to the context of property being 'obtained by a false representation'. **'Appropriation'**, in their Lordships' view, **was a totally value-neutral word.** Lord Steyn approved of a dictum of Lord Browne-Wilkinson in *Gomez* that the word **'appropriation' is 'an objective description of the act done irrespective of the mental state of either the owner or the accused'.** Lord Steyn stated (at p. 1599) that *Gomez* **treated the word 'appropriation' as 'a neutral word comprehending "any assumption by a person of the rights of an owner".'** This strips the act which might constitute an appropriation entirely from its context. It also ignores the fact that in paradigm cases of theft, thieves are assuming rights of ownership to which they have no entitlement. A donor making a valid gift divests himself of all title to the property gifted in favour of the donee; the donee, in accepting the gift, receives her own property to which she has indefeasible title. It is ridiculous to state that she is assuming the rights of an owner—she is the owner so there is no assumption. She is not supplanting the owner or arrogating to herself any rights which the owner has not, with full knowledge and consent, transferred to her.

Such arguments, however, had no effect on the views of the majority who were even unconcerned that their decision would create inevitable conflict between the criminal law and the civil law, Lord Steyn blithely stating (at p. 1601) that 'it would be wrong to assume on a priori grounds that the criminal law rather than the civil law is defective'. Indeed, his Lordship considered it a great virtue to seek to eliminate civil law concepts from the deliberations of juries. This leads to the absurd position that what the civil law permits may yet constitute a crime under the Theft Act if 12 people in a jury, or a magistrate on summary trial, consider that D's behaviour is morally reprehensible and therefore dishonest.

The bizarre reasoning of the majority stands in stark contrast to the carefully crafted speech of Lord Hobhouse of Woodborough who was conscious of the danger of construing each word or phrase in s. 1(1) of the Theft Act in isolation from its context. In his speech he sought to negotiate the inter-relationship of the different elements of the offence. He also sought to respect the civil law in relation to property as, in using terms such as 'belonging to another', the Act presumes the existence and relevance of the civil law. His Lordship highlighted the anomaly to which the decision of the majority gave rise, namely that s. 5, which builds upon the civil law and is concerned with deeming property to belong to another in circumstances where D has acquired legal title (albeit that his title is defeasible), makes no provision for the situation where D 'has been validly given the property' and in such a situation D 'can no longer appropriate property belonging to another...There is no law against appropriating your own property as defined in s. 5.' It was not only s. 5 which led Lord Hobhouse to his conclusion. He also considered ss. 2, 3, and 6. On the relationship of appropriation to dishonesty, picking up on the point made by Viscount Dilhorne in *Lawrence*, his Lordship looked at the wording of s. 2 relating to belief in a right to deprive another of property or belief in consent to the appropriation of property, which both serve to negate dishonesty, and asked (at p. 1614):

[H]ow can it be said that [D's] knowledge that he has such a right or the actual consent of the person to whom the property belongs is irrelevant? How can it be said that the right

> of the defendant to accept a gift is irrelevant—or the fact that the transferor has actually and validly consented to the defendant having the relevant property?

In the context of a gift, the property once gifted by the donor belongs to the donee. Even if acceptance of a gift could be an appropriation (which Lord Hobhouse strenuously contested), difficulties arise in relation to s. 2(1)(a). His Lordship stated (at p. 1615):

> The defendant did have the right to deprive the donor of the property. The donor did consent to the appropriation; indeed, he intended it. There are also difficulties with s. 6 as she was not acting regardless of the donor's rights; the donor has already surrendered his rights. The only way that these conclusions can be displaced is by showing that the gift was not valid. There are even difficulties with s. 3 itself. The donee is not 'assuming the rights of an owner': she already has them.

His Lordship concluded that the Court of Appeal's decision was based on a misreading of the authorities as the context of decisions such as *Lawrence* and *Gomez* in the House of Lords, and *Dobson* in the Court of Appeal was one of consent induced by fraud. Speaking of Parker LJ's judgment in *Dobson* and Lord Keith of Kinkel's in *Gomez*, Lord Hobhouse stated (at p. 1620):

> Neither is saying that consent and authorisation are irrelevant to appropriation but, rather, that they do not necessarily exclude the possibility of appropriation. The consent or authority may be limited in its scope and not cover the acts done by the defendant because the defendant has an unauthorised purpose (Parker LJ; and *Morris*) or the consent or authorisation may have been obtained by fraud (*Lawrence*; and *Gomez*).

Rose LJ's reading of the cases in the Court of Appeal led to a conclusion that consent can never negative appropriation when all that Lord Keith and Parker LJ were confirming was that appropriation may occur although there is consent—but it is consent in the context of fraud or some unauthorised purpose.

Sadly, Lord Hobhouse was in the minority and a speech which resonates with sound reasoning, common sense, and astute legal analysis failed to persuade the majority. Receiving that which the donor wishes her to receive may nonetheless be theft if 12 people conclude she should not have accepted it. Appropriation, therefore, is a value-neutral term. **When s. 3(1) uses the word 'assumption' it simply means 'exercise'.** Thus any dealing with property or any exercise of a right of an owner (even the exercise of that right with the owner's express authorisation in a situation where the owner has full knowledge and there being no circumstances which might render the transaction voidable) amounts to an appropriation. As Oliver Hardy would say to Stan Laurel, 'That's another fine mess you've got us into'.

11.2.1.5.4 *Appropriating company assets*

In law a company is a person. As a company may own property it may also be the victim of theft. A company, however, has no mind of its own; the board of directors is the directing mind and will of the company. A director who has authority to deal with the property of the company for the company's purposes can steal from the company where he applies company property for his own purposes 'dishonestly and in fraud of the company' (see *A-G for Hong Kong* v *Nai-keung* (1987) 86 Cr App R 174). A problem arises, however, where a company is wholly owned by one director or several directors. If the sole director, or all the directors together, apply company property for their own purposes, can he or they appropriate property with which he or they, as the mind and will of the company, have authorised him or them to deal? The dictum in *Morris* that 'appropriation involves not an act expressly or impliedly authorised by the owner...' spawned a number of conflicting decisions. In *Attorney-General's Reference (No. 2 of 1982)* [1984] QB 624, the two defendants who were shareholders and directors of various companies were charged with theft from those companies. It was conceded by counsel that an appropriation had taken place and the case was argued on the sole issue of dishonesty. The Court of Appeal approved the concession that counsel had made and stated *obiter* that where all the directors and shareholders of a company acted illegally or dishonestly in relation to the company, their consent to the illegal or dishonest acts was not to be attributed to the company. In *McHugh and Tringham* (1988) 88 Cr App R 385, the Court of Appeal upheld a conviction of theft by a company director on the basis that the company had not authorised his actions. The Court stated as a proposition that '(4) An act done with the authority of a company cannot in general amount to an appropriation'. On the facts of the case the Court was not required to determine the correctness of this proposition. Mustill LJ, however, stated (at p. 394):

> If we had thought that this was a case of express authority, it would have been necessary to look closely at proposition (4) to work out the extent of the qualification which we have indicated by the words in general: for qualification there must be, since even an express authority which is either obtained by the actor with a view to abuse, or is actually abused, can scarcely render innocuous what would otherwise be a misappropriation.

By 'misappropriation' Mustill LJ presumably meant a 'dishonest appropriation'.

By contrast in the Supreme Court of Victoria in *Roffel* [1985] VR 511, it was held that a sole director and shareholder could not be convicted of theft of the company's assets because the company had consented to Roffel's acts thereby preventing an appropriation from taking place. In *Philippou* (1989) 89 Cr App R 290, the Court of Appeal upheld the convictions of two sole directors of three companies in the United Kingdom who had used assets of one of those companies to purchase property in Spain in the name of another company of which they were also the sole directors and shareholders. The Court of Appeal took the view that the purchase of the property in Spain for their own benefit displayed the directors' dishonest intention permanently to deprive the first company of its property which, in turn, indicated that the original transfer of funds was adverse to the company and thereby was an act without its consent amounting to a dishonest appropriation.

In *Gomez*, Lord Browne-Wilkinson stated that the decision in *Roffel* and the statement of principle in *McHugh and Tringham* (namely proposition (4)) 'are not correct in law and should not be followed'. This was so whether or not the dictum in *Morris* was correct, his Lordship stating (at pp. 1110, 1111):

> Where a company is accused of a crime the acts and intentions of those who are the directing minds and will of the company are to be attributed to the company. That is

> not the law where the charge is that those who are the directing minds and will have themselves committed a crime against the company.... In any event, your Lordships' decision in this case, re-establishing as it does the decision in *Lawrence*, renders the whole question of consent by the company irrelevant. Whether or not those controlling the company consented or purported to consent to the abstraction of the company's property by the accused, he will have appropriated the property of the company.

His Lordship went on to conclude that in each case the question to be asked is whether or not the taking of the property from the company has been done dishonestly.

The speeches in *Gomez* make it clear that those who are the directing minds and wills of companies who use their position to pillage company assets have always been liable to convictions for theft on the basis of the ruling in *Attorney-General's Reference (No. 2 of 1982)* irrespective of the decisions in either *Lawrence* or *Morris*. In deciding whether or not a company director could be convicted of theft it should not have been necessary to refer to either *Lawrence* or *Morris*, but the decision of the majority in *Gomez* puts the issue beyond doubt by making the question of consent irrelevant.

11.2.1.5.5 *Appropriation by keeping or dealing*

The second part of s. 3(1) of the TA 1968 deals with the situation where D originally comes by property without stealing it. A later assumption of a right to the property by keeping or dealing with it as owner amounts to an appropriation.

 Example

If P lends D his book for a week, D obtains possession of it but he is not a thief if he has no intention of depriving P of it. If, however, D subsequently decides to keep the book permanently or if he subsequently sells it (dealing with it), this conduct represents an appropriation as D is assuming the rights of an owner. The same would apply where D receives property as a result of a mistake by P of which D was unaware at the time. For example, P agrees to lend D his books on criminal law. He gives D a pile of books which D later discovers contains a book on contract. If D decides to keep this or otherwise deal with it he would be appropriating it at that time. Similarly if D finds a book and has no means of discovering its owner at the time this would not be theft. If, however, P later tells D that he has lost a book and the facts revealed indicate that the book lost was the one D found, a decision by D at that time to keep it would be an appropriation.

If D appropriates property abroad and brings it into the jurisdiction, his acts within the jurisdiction cannot amount to appropriation as his acts outside the jurisdiction constitute stealing even though D cannot be prosecuted here for them (see *Atakpu and Abrahams* [1994] Crim LR 693). In *Atakpu* the Court of Appeal quashed convictions for conspiracy to steal. The appellants were arrested at Dover driving cars which they had hired in Germany and Belgium using false driving licences and passports. The prosecution alleged they intended to 'ring' the cars and sell them in England. The Court of Appeal held, however, that as their fraudulent obtaining of the cars was an appropriation following *Gomez*, they had come by the property by stealing it and thus their later dealing with the cars within the jurisdiction could not amount to appropriations within s. 3(1). (At the time the court's jurisdiction for conspiracy required that the plan would involve the commission of theft in England: see now **8.5** *ante*.) If goods have once been stolen they cannot be stolen again by the same thief who has continued in possession of them. The appropriation was complete abroad; it was not a continuing act which continued to occur within the jurisdiction (cf. *Ascroft* [2003] EWCA Crim 2365, where, in upholding a confiscation order imposed following a conviction for conspiracy to steal, the Court of Appeal arrived at a different conclusion).

11.2.1.5.6 *Excluding the bona fide purchaser from liability*
Section 3(2) provides:

> Where property or a right or interest in property is or purports to be transferred for value to a person acting in good faith, no later assumption by him of rights which he believed himself to be acquiring shall, by reason of any defect in the transferor's title amount to theft of the property.

This provision excludes from liability bona fide purchasers who otherwise might be guilty of theft under s. 3(1) (see **11.2.1.5.5** *ante*).

 Example

If D buys a car from E in good faith believing that E has good title to the car, D's subsequent discovery that E had stolen the car from P will not render D liable to conviction for theft if he then keeps the car. The relevant moment when considering D's belief is when he purchased the property (see *Adams* [1993] Crim LR 72).

Should D in the this example decide to sell the car and then advertise it for sale, impliedly representing thereby that he has good title to it, he would be liable for fraud by false representation contrary to s. 1 of the Fraud Act 2006 (previously he would have been liable for obtaining property by deception contrary to s. 15(1) of the TA 1968 if Q bought the car from him). This exception under s. 3(2) does not apply to anyone who does not acquire the property in good faith and for value. Thus, where E merely gave the car to D as a gift, he would be liable under s. 3(1) if, on discovering that the car was stolen, he decided to keep it. Similarly, if E, a thief, hires stolen property to D, D would be guilty of theft if he discovered that the property was stolen and then sold it or destroyed it, as he would be assuming rights which as a bailee he had not acquired when the initial bailment took place.

11.2.2 *Mens rea*

The *mens rea* of theft is made up of two elements: an intention of permanently depriving the owner of his property and dishonesty. It is important at the outset to make plain that both these states of mind must be proved. It should also be understood that while most thieves steal property for personal gain, this is not an element of the offence. Section 1(2) of the TA 1968 provides that 'it is immaterial whether the appropriation is made with a view to gain, or is made for the thief's own benefit'.

Thus D may be guilty of theft where he destroys P's property. In such a situation he will usually be charged with criminal damage contrary to s. 1 of the Criminal Damage Act 1971. If, however, P is simply deprived of the property without it being damaged, for example, D throws P's jewellery into the Thames, there is no criminal damage but there may be theft.

11.2.2.1 With the intention of permanently depriving the other of it

There is no requirement that P be actually deprived of his property permanently; the crucial question is what was D's intent at the time he appropriated the property? As a general rule, an intention to borrow the property cannot amount to an intention to deprive permanently. If, however, D takes P's money, intending to return to P an equivalent amount, D does have the requisite intention as he does not intend to return to P the exact coins or notes he removed. Where P has only a limited interest in the property, for example, where P has hired a lawnmower from Q for the weekend and D takes it knowing of P's limited interest and intending to return it on Monday, this would amount to an intention to deprive P permanently of his interest in the property. In this example, D steals from P because he intends to deprive P of his limited interest in the property; he does not steal from Q because there is no intention permanently to deprive Q of it. If D did not know the facts and, thinking that P owned the lawnmower, he took it intending to keep it for a week, this would not be theft even though P was permanently deprived of his interest in it.

In most cases, D's intention may be inferred from the circumstances. For example, if D takes P's wallet and spends the contents, or if he takes P's video recorder and sells it, or if he takes P's sandwiches and eats them, the evidence of an intention permanently to deprive P of his property is virtually irrefutable. In other cases, however, the correct inference to draw from the facts will not be so obvious. For example, if D removes P's book from his bag and is found reading it in the library, or if D removes P's bicycle from the cycle stands and is found riding it home, it is far from clear whether D was merely borrowing P's property or whether he intended to deprive P of it permanently. Further evidence would be necessary to found a charge of theft.

The issue of intention may usually be left to the jury without too much elaboration. Section 6 of the TA 1968, however, provides a partial definition of 'intention of permanently depriving'. **Section 6 operates to deem a person's intention to amount to an intention to deprive permanently even though he may have intended to return the property or even had returned the property. The section should not be referred to if the issue of D's intention may be resolved without reference to it; it should be referred to in exceptional cases only** (see *Lloyd* [1985] QB 829). There are two reasons for this: first, the section is only a partial definition designed to deal with a particular form of mischief; secondly, the section is particularly obscurely drafted. Regarding this latter point it should be noted that the section refers to 'property' and 'the thing itself', but appears to mean the same by both terms. In s. 6(1) the word 'meaning' is used as well as 'intention'; it appears that 'meaning' was used in the sense of 'intending'.

11.2.2.1.1 *Section 6(1)*

Section 6(1) provides:

> A person appropriating property belonging to another without meaning the other permanently to lose the thing itself is nevertheless to be regarded as having the intention of permanently depriving the other of it if his intention is to treat the thing as his own to dispose of regardless of the other's rights; and a borrowing or lending of it may amount to so treating it if, but only if, the borrowing or lending is for a period and in circumstances making it equivalent to an outright taking or disposal.

This provision may be divided into two parts which will be examined separately.

(a) *Disposing of the property regardless of the other's rights* 'A person...is...to be regarded as having the intention of permanently depriving the other of it if his intention is to treat the thing as his own to dispose of regardless of the other's rights'. In such cases, D may intend the property to be returned to P so that P is not actually deprived of it. **D will be deemed to have the requisite intention, however, on the basis of his treating the property as his own to dispose of regardless of P's rights.**

Several situations may fall within this provision. If D takes P's property intending to sell it back to P (the 'buy back principle'), D will not intend to deprive P of it permanently, but he will be treating the property as his own to dispose of regardless of P's rights; it is one of the rights of the owner to sell his property (see *Hall* (1849) 1 Den 381, and most recently *Raphael* [2008] EWCA Crim 1014). The same principle may be applied to the situation where D removes a ticket from a booking office for a pop concert. The organisers of the concert own the ticket which will be returned to them by D when he hands it to the attendant on the door to gain admission to the concert. The organisers, however, are effectively paying for the return of the ticket by providing D with admission to the concert. Professor Smith states, in *The Law of Theft* (8th edn) para. 2–144, that the same principle would cover someone who takes, for example, milk tokens from a dairy intending to return them in exchange for milk. Similarly, if D takes P's property intending to return it only when P pays for it or fulfils some other condition (the 'ransom principle'), he will again be treating the property as his own to dispose of regardless of the other's rights: only an owner may attach conditions to the use or possession of his property (but cf. *Coffey* [1987] Crim LR 498). In *Lloyd* (11.2.2.1 *ante*), the Court of Appeal affirmed that these situations fell within s. 6(1). The Court, however, considered that s. 6(1) should be given a restricted meaning stating that they would endeavour to interpret the section so that '**nothing is construed as an intention permanently to deprive which would not prior to the 1968 Act have been so construed**'. It was a requirement of larceny at common law and under the Larceny Act 1916 that D have an intention of permanently depriving P of his property. Other decisions of the Court of Appeal and of the Privy Council, however, have not taken so restrictive a view of s. 6. In *Downes* (1983) 77 Cr App R 260, D was in lawful possession of vouchers from the Inland Revenue which could be used to obtain certain exemptions from deduction of tax. D sold the vouchers to others who would then use them for this purpose. D was guilty of theft as although the vouchers which belonged to the Inland Revenue would return to them, D was treating them as his own to dispose of regardless of the other's rights by selling them. In *Chan Man-sin* v *A-G for Hong Kong* [1988] 1 All ER 1, D, a company account-ant, drew a forged cheque on the company's account. If the fraud was discovered the company's credit balance would have to be restored by the bank as a debit made on a forged cheque is a nullity; but it was, of course, D's hope that the fraud would not be discovered. The Privy Council held that there was 'ample evidence' that D intended to treat the credit balance in the account (a thing in action) as his own to dispose of regardless of the company's rights. In *Fernandes* [1996] 1 Cr App R 175 Auld LJ, reading the judgment of the Court of Appeal, provided, it is submit-ted, the correct interpretation of s. 6, stating (at p. 188):

> In our view, section 6(1), which is expressed in general terms, is not limited in its appli-cation to the illustrations given by Lord Lane CJ in *Lloyd*. Nor, in saying that in most cases it would be unnecessary to refer to the provision, did Lord Lane suggest that it should be so limited. The critical notion…is whether a defendant intended 'to treat the thing as his own to dispose of regardless of the other's rights'. The second limb of sub-section (1), and also subsection (2), are merely specific illustrations of the application of that notion. We consider that section 6 may apply to a person in possession or control of another's property who, dishonestly and for his own purpose, deals with that property in such a manner that he knows he is risking its loss.

In *Marshall* [1998] 2 Cr App R 282, the Court of Appeal applied *Fernandes*. The appellants obtained used, but unexpired, tickets from passengers leaving London Underground stations and sold them on to other travellers thereby depriving London Underground of revenue. They appealed against convictions for theft of the tickets. The Court of Appeal dismissed their appeals holding that the tickets belonged at all times to London Underground which had the exclusive right to sell tickets. By acquiring and reselling the tickets the appellants had the intention to treat the tickets as their own to dispose of regardless of London Underground's rights. This decision has been subjected to fairly rigorous criticism by Professor Smith in 'Stealing Tickets' [1998] Crim LR 723 who counsels that the answer will not necessarily be the same for all tickets as the question whether the original vendor of the ticket retains property in the ticket will depend on the terms of the contract. Professor Smith states (at p. 724):

> But a person is not bound by a condition printed on a ticket unless reasonable steps have been taken to bring it to his attention. If such steps have not been taken, the condition does not form part of the contract and it cannot be relied on to show that the ownership in the ticket did not pass. Where a ticket is obtained from a machine, the supplier must give reasonable notice to the purchaser before he inserts his money. A term printed on the ticket issued by the machine is too late; the contract is already made.

In certain circumstances D's borrowing of P's property may fall within the second limb of s. 6(1). If D borrows P's book to read on a train or plane journey and, hav-ing read it, abandons it in the station or airport on his arrival at his destination, his abandonment would tend to show an indifference as to whether P recovers the book, particularly if there is little likelihood of P recovering it. He is dealing with it in a way in which only an owner may do and is treating it as his own to dispose of regardless of the owner's rights. In a case such as this there would not appear to be any need to resort to the second part of s. 6(1). In *DPP* v *J and others* [2002] All

ER (D) 260 the Administrative Court held that snatching V's stereo headphones and breaking them before returning them to him provided evidence from which the justices could have inferred an intention permanently to deprive. The Court considered that this action amounted to a disposal of the property and was no different from an action which risked the loss of the article. In *Mitchell* [2008] EWCA Crim 850 a violent carjacking was held not to amount to robbery as D intended only to use the car to make his getaway before abandoning it.

It is important, however, in dealing with cases under the first part of s. 6(1) that meaning is attributed to all the words. It is not enough that D 'treat the thing as his own'; **some meaning must be given to the further requirement 'to dispose of regardless of the other's rights'.** In *Cahill* [1993] Crim LR 142, the Court of Appeal approved the following passage in Professor Smith, *The Law of Theft* (6th edn) p. 73:

> It is submitted, however, that an intention to use the thing as one's own is not enough and that 'dispose of' is not used in the sense in which a general might 'dispose of' his forces but rather in the meaning given by the *Shorter Oxford Dictionary*: 'To deal with definitely: to get rid of; to get done with, finish. To make over by way of sale or bargain, sell.'

Unfortunately in *DPP* v *Lavender* [1994] Crim LR 297 the Divisional Court, without referring to *Cahill*, ruled that the dictionary definition of 'dispose of' was too narrow and a disposal could include 'dealing with' property. L had been charged with theft of two doors from the council. He had taken the doors from a council property undergoing repair and used them to replace damaged doors in his girlfriend's council flat. The justices had dismissed the information. The Divisional Court allowed the prosecution's appeal and remitted the case to the justices with a direction to convict. The Divisional Court's substitution of 'deal with' for 'dispose of' greatly widens the ambit of s. 6(1). If 'dispose of' means 'deal with', it is submitted that the words are superfluous as they simply repeat the previous phrase 'to treat the thing as his own'. If the words are not superfluous they can only mean what the Court of Appeal in *Cahill* accepted they meant and, in line with precedent, the decision in *Cahill* should be followed.

One final situation worth mentioning is where D purports to sell P's property to Q. By selling it D is appropriating it. He may have no intention that P be deprived of his property; his intention rather being that he deprive Q of his money by means of the deception. His case does, however, fall within s. 6(1) as he is treating the property as his own to dispose of regardless of P's rights and thus 'is ... to be regarded as having the intention of permanently depriving the other of it'. If there was no risk of P ever being deprived of his property this may be stretching the bounds of theft too far. A more appropriate charge now would be fraud by false representation contrary to s. 1 of the Fraud Act 2006 (previously the appropriate charge would have been obtaining, or attempting to obtain, property by deception contrary to s. 15 of the TA 1968).

(b) *Borrowing or lending* The second part of s. 6(1) simply expands on the first part; a borrowing or lending of P's property by D may amount to an intention to treat the thing as his own to dispose of regardless of P's rights if 'the borrowing or lending [of it] is for a period and in circumstances making it equivalent to an outright taking or disposal'. In *Lloyd* (**11.2.2.1** *ante*), Lord Lane CJ stated (at p. 836) that this provision:

> [I]s intended to make clear that a mere borrowing is never enough to constitute the necessary guilty mind unless the intention is to return the thing in such a changed state that it can truly be said that all its goodness or virtue has gone.

This was a statement of the **'essential quality principle'**. If D takes P's railway season ticket, intending to return it to him after it has expired, P will receive back a worthless piece of paper. Similarly if D borrows P's battery and uses it only returning it to P when it is exhausted, the thing returned will be deprived of all virtue.

This principle applies equally to the situation where D is the bailee of P's property and he lends it to E, telling E to keep it for as long as he likes. Thus, if P had gone on holiday leaving some of his valuables with D and D lent P's battery operated torch to E, D's lending of the batteries would seem to be for a period and in circumstances making it equivalent to an outright disposal. In the examples used earlier, if D returns the season ticket one day before the expiry date, or returns the battery with a little power remaining in it, the question will be whether this is equivalent to an outright taking. It could be argued that not all 'its goodness or virtue' has gone.

In **11.2.1.1.2** *ante* the question arose whether confidential information or trade secrets could constitute property. In *Oxford* v *Moss* (1978) 68 Cr App R 183, it was held that confidential information in a university examination paper was not 'property'. It was submitted that this was questionable and that the secret quality of the information was a form of intangible property; by reading such a document D was assuming the right of an owner and permanently depriving the owner of the secrecy of the information. It is further submitted that a person borrowing a document containing confidential information so that he may copy it, or even simply to read it, could be held to intend to deprive the lender of it permanently; the document, when it is returned, has lost its virtue, namely its confidentiality, the very thing which gave it, or enhanced, its value. Thus it is submitted, even if confidential information is not to be regarded as a form of intangible property, D may be guilty of the theft of documents containing confidential information where he only borrows such documents.

11.2.2.1.2 *Section 6(2)*
Section 6(2) provides:

> Without prejudice to the generality of subsection (1) above, where a person, having possession or control (lawfully or not) of property belonging to another, parts with the property under a condition as to its return which he may not be able to perform, this (if done for purposes of his own and without the other's authority) amounts to treating the property as his own to dispose of regardless of the other's rights.

This section covers both the situation where D is the bailee of P's property, or D surreptitiously borrows P's property. In either case if D pledges the property as security for a loan (pawning being the usual situation envisaged), even though he intends to redeem it and return it to P, he will be deemed to intend to deprive P of the property permanently. It is obvious that at the time of pledging the property D cannot be certain that he will be able to redeem it. If D foresees the slightest possibility that he may not be able to perform the condition, he will fall within the section. It is only where D honestly believes that there is no possibility of him being unable to fulfil the condition that he will not be deemed to have had the necessary intent.

11.2.2.1.3 *Conditional intent*

Will a conditional intent suffice for theft? For example, D takes P's handbag intending to search through it and steal any money he may find; upon finding no money he replaces the handbag where he found it. In such a case D has no intention to deprive P of the handbag, and the property of which he seeks to deprive P does not exist so there is no appropriation of money. He is, however, guilty of attempted theft as a conditional intention suffices for attempt (see **8.4.2** *ante*).

11.2.2.2 Dishonesty

The final element of theft which must be proved is that at the time D appropriated property belonging to another intending permanently to deprive the other of it, he did so dishonestly. As the concept of appropriation has been stripped of all pejorative connotations and is a neutral word (see the discussion of *Hinks* **11.2.1.5.3** *ante*), this means that dishonesty has become the crucial concept in theft used to discriminate between those appropriations which may amount to theft and those which may not. This being the case, it might be considered important that there be a clear definition of dishonesty. Sadly, there is **no such definition in the Theft Act** and the cases which have considered this concept have failed to achieve precision in defining the concept. Rather than provide a definition, **s. 2 of the TA 1968 specifies three situations in which D's appropriation is not to be regarded as dishonest** (s. 2(1)) **and one situation in which it may be regarded as dishonest** (s. 2(2)). If D raises a defence which falls within s. 2(1) he will be entitled to an acquittal unless the prosecution disproves his alleged belief beyond reasonable doubt.

11.2.2.2.1 *Section 2*

Section 2 provides:

(1) A person's appropriation of property belonging to another is not to be regarded as dishonest—

(a) if he appropriates the property in the belief that he has in law the right to deprive the other of it, on behalf of himself or of a third person; or

(b) if he appropriates the property in the belief that he would have the other's consent if the other knew of the appropriation and the circumstances of it; or

(c) (except where the property came to him as trustee or personal representative) if he appropriates the property in the belief that the person to whom the property belongs cannot be discovered by taking reasonable steps.

(2) A person's appropriation of property belonging to another may be dishonest notwithstanding that he is willing to pay for the property.

(a) *Belief in a right to deprive* **If D believes he has a legal right to appropriate P's property he is not dishonest no matter how unreasonable his belief may**

be. If D believes the property is his own, there is no intention to deprive another of the property permanently. Section 2(1)(a), however, relates to mistakes as to the law. For example, if D sells and delivers goods to P and P fails to pay for them, D may wrongly believe he has the right in law to take possession of the goods. In such a case D may rely on s. 2(1) (a). If E, D's employee, is instructed to seize the goods from P for non-payment and believes that D has a legal right to them, he similarly may rely on s. 2(1)(a) if charged with theft.

(b) *Belief in the other's consent* D is hungry and has no money. He goes to P's house and admits himself using a key P has given him for the purposes of checking on the property while P is on holiday. D takes food from P's cupboards believing P would have consented to him doing so had he known the circumstances. If such a belief is honestly held, D is not dishonest.

(c) *Belief that the owner cannot be found* Although s. 2(1)(c) does not refer to 'finding' property this is the situation which most clearly falls within this provision. Where D finds property and honestly believes that the owner cannot be discovered by taking reasonable steps, D's appropriation of the property will not be dishonest. In considering what steps would be reasonable regard would be paid to the nature of the property, whether there were any identification marks or distinguishing features, the nature and value of the property and the place where it was found; but, it must be stressed, ultimately the question is what was D's belief. If D honestly believed there were no reasonable means of discovering the owner he will not be dishonest even if the reasonable person would have recognised an obvious and simple means of tracing the owner. It should be noted that if, after finding the property and concluding that the owner cannot be traced, D discovers who the owner is, or how he may be traced, any subsequent keeping or dealing with the property as owner by D would amount to theft (see s. 3(1), **11.2.1.5.5** *ante*).

If the beneficiaries under a trust or will cannot be found, in the absence of a specific clause that the property reverts to the trustee or personal representative, the Crown will be entitled to the property as *bona vacantia*. If a trustee honestly believes the beneficiaries cannot be found and that he is entitled to the property he would appear to fall within s. 2(1)(a), but if he knows he is not entitled to it he is not covered by the exception in s. 2(1)(c).

(d) *Willingness to pay* Section 2(2) states that D's appropriation of property may be dishonest even though D is willing to pay for it. A wide variety of situations may arise, hence the provision is framed in permissive rather than mandatory terms. For example, D unexpectedly has visitors but has no coffee. He goes to his flatmate's cupboard and removes a jar of coffee leaving a note and the price of the coffee. A jury would have to decide if this was dishonest in all the circumstances. It may be that D could also rely on s. 2(1)(b). By contrast, P has a valuable painting which D covets but P refuses to sell to him. D removes the painting leaving a sum in excess of the value of the painting. In this case D's willingness to pay would have to be set in the context of P's clear unwillingness to sell and it is submitted that this should be regarded as dishonest.

In *Wheatley* v *Commissioner of Police of the British Virgin Isles* [2006] UKPC 24 the Privy Council held that although in most cases of theft there would be an original owner of money or goods who would be poorer because of the defendant's conduct, the prospect of loss was not determinative of the dishonesty necessary to establish the offence.

> D1, while employed by the Government as financial secretary of the British Virgin Islands, acting contrary to orders and regulations which forbade him from engaging in any private activity which might place him in a position to use his official position for his private benefit, awarded construction contracts to D2, in whose companies D1 had a personal interest. D1 and D2 conceded that they had appropriated property belonging to the Government, namely the payments due under the contracts. They argued, however, that there could be no dishonesty where the contract had been made and services rendered for an appropriate price. The Privy Council held that the fact that services pursuant to the contract had been rendered for an appropriate price was no bar to conviction for theft. In providing that an appropriation might be dishonest even where there was a willingness to pay, the law showed that the prospect of loss was not determinative of dishonesty.

11.2.2.2.2 *Situations not covered by section 2*

The fact that D cannot rely on any of the provisions in s. 2(1) does not mean that D is necessarily dishonest. Where D does not raise any of these defences his case will fall to be considered under the general test of dishonesty. Who is to decide, however, what dishonesty means? As the Act only gives a partial definition one might have expected the courts to provide a general definition of this concept and then leave it to the jury in each case to determine whether the facts fall within this definition. The courts, however, have adopted the contrary approach, determining that **what is 'dishonest' is not a question of law but a matter for the tribunal of fact.** In *Ghosh* [1982] QB 1053, the Court of Appeal laid down a two-part test to be applied by juries. **Was what was done dishonest according to the ordinary standards of reasonable honest people? If so, did D realise that what he was doing was by those standards dishonest?**

In most cases there will be no dispute regarding dishonesty; if D is shop-lifting, or robbing a bank, or breaking into and stealing from houses, it would be impossible to argue that this was not dishonest according to ordinary standards of reasonable honest people, or that D did not realise it was dishonest. There are, however, some situations which may give rise to difficulty. In *Feely* [1973] QB 530, the manager of a betting shop took £30 from his employer's safe, a practice which the employer had prohibited. When charged with theft he claimed he had only borrowed it and was going to replace an equivalent sum. His conviction was quashed as the trial judge had ruled that this did not amount to a defence. **The Court of Appeal held that the question of what was dishonest was for the jury to determine.**

Where an employee borrows his employer's money an infinite variety of circumstances may arise: the employer may have expressly prohibited such a practice in all circumstances; the amount taken may be large or small; the period for which it is taken may vary; D's likelihood of paying it back may vary; D may or may not leave an 'IOU'; D may take the money because some unforeseen emergency has arisen or he may take it for some less creditable reason such as betting on a horse race. As the situations vary so may the conclusions of different juries. Even judges have been known to differ greatly. In *Sinclair* v *Neighbour* [1966] 2 QB 279, D removed money from his employer's till to bet on a horse race. The trial judge thought that this was reprehensible conduct but that it was not dishonest. In the Court of Appeal, Sachs LJ considered that the conduct was dishonest while Sellers LJ considered that views as to the honesty of the conduct might differ. If judges, who share the same or similar class, cultural, educational, and professional backgrounds cannot agree on what is dishonest, how can we hope for consistency from juries in an increasingly heterogeneous society? At least if judges make errors on questions of law these may be rectified on appeal and a body of precedent is thereby built up to guide future decisions. Jury decisions on questions of fact are not amenable to rectification nor do they provide any guide for the future. In the situation given earlier it is arguable that if D, when removing the money, did not believe that he would have had his employer's consent (s. 2(1)(b)) he should not be allowed by other means to raise a defence.

It is arguable, therefore, that the decision in *Feely* was unnecessary. Unfortunately it has been built upon by *Ghosh* so that it is now the law, whether sensible or not, that the question of what is dishonest is one of fact for the jury to determine. The Law Commission in its consultation paper, *Legislating the Criminal Code, Fraud and Deception* (Law Com. CP No. 155) provisionally concluded (at para. 5.20) that:

> juries and magistrates should not be asked to set a moral standard on which criminal liability essentially depends. As a general rule, the law should say what is forbidden, and that should be informed by insights. A jury or magistrates should then be asked to apply the law by coming to *factual* conclusions, not moral ones.

The dangers are exemplified in the case of *Hinks* (**11.2.1.5.3** *ante*) which prompted the Law Commission further to conclude (at para. 5.32) that:

> it is undesirable in principle that conduct which is otherwise unobjectionable should be rendered criminal merely because fact-finders are willing to characterise it as 'dishonest'.

The second question in *Ghosh* need only be posed where there is some evidence to suggest that D believed that what he did was honest by ordinary people's standards (see *Roberts* (1987) 84 Cr App R 117; *Price* (1989) 90 Cr App R 409; *Squire* [1990] Crim LR 341). It raises a question: why should being out of touch with normal standards of honesty generally held in the community avail D? The Court of Appeal did not address this issue. Indeed the creation of the second question appears to have been based on a misconception. The Court of Appeal asserted that 'dishonestly' was not intended to characterise D's conduct but his state of mind which cannot be established independently of his knowledge and belief. Examining s. 2(1), the Court found that the matters covered related to the accused's belief which could only be established subjectively. It is important therefore to determine what his state of mind was, and for the jury then to determine if this is dishonest. Under s. 2(1), if D claims he believed he had a right to take the property, or that he believed the owner would have consented to his taking it, or that the owner could not reasonably have been found, the jury would find him not dishonest if he may have had that belief. If he claims he was willing to pay, having determined if he might have been willing to pay, the jury would then decide if ordinary people would regard that, in the circumstances, as dishonest. But strangely, if D claims he did not believe that ordinary people would regard what he did as dishonest, a jury, if they find he may have had this belief, must acquit. This is a strange conclusion; if D, charged with murder, claims he did not believe that a jury would regard his state of mind as 'intention' (another ordinary word for the jury to define), this will not avail him if the jury conclude that he did intend to kill regardless of how he might define intention or characterise his own state of mind. In such a case, the jury determine what his state of mind was, and then characterise it either as intention or not. Where dishonesty is involved, why should D's characterisation of his state of mind be relevant? The answer to this conundrum is that the Court of Appeal did not understand their own test. The Court provided the following example (at p. 1063):

> ...a man...comes from a country where public transport is free. On his first day here he travels on a bus. He gets off without paying. He never had any intention of paying. His mind is clearly honest; but his conduct, judged objectively by what he has done, is dishonest. It seems to us that in using the word 'dishonestly' in the Theft Act 1968, Parliament cannot have intended to catch dishonest conduct in that sense, that is to say conduct to which no moral obloquy could possibly attach.

If one ignores the fact that there is no offence under the Theft Acts of which such a visitor could be convicted (which indicates the ludicrous nature of the example Lord Lane CJ chose to illustrate the principle), this example is riven with misconceptions. How can D's conduct, judged objectively by what he has done, be dishonest if one of the objective facts is that he did not believe a fare had to be paid? If there was any offence with which D could be charged and the jury had to consider whether he was dishonest, the first question would be whether what he had done was dishonest by the standards of ordinary honest people. The ordinary honest person would have to be placed in the situation as D believed it to be, that is, is it dishonest not to pay a fare if you believe no fare is due? To frame the question thus exposes the ludicrous nature of the example. This was a case of simple mistake of fact, not one of conflicting beliefs as to what is or is not honest. Because the Court of Appeal wrongly adjudged their alien objectively dishonest they then had to create the second question to render him honest. The second question, thus, appears to have been an unnecessary construct. No moral obloquy ever attached to his conduct because he acted in furtherance of a mistake as to facts; his mistake did not relate to his assessment of what ordinary people would regard as dishonest.

  Ghosh, however flawed its reasoning, is a decison of the Court of Appeal which has been applied without question in subsequent cases. The outcome, however, is that **if D is totally out of touch with ordinary community standards, the *Ghosh* direction would dictate that he be acquitted.** For example, if D, a latter-day Robin Hood who is incensed by the plight of the homeless, decides to steal from the rich who can easily afford it and give the money to charities for the homeless, and he honestly believes that no ordinary reasonable person would regard his charitable activities as dishonest, he is entitled to be acquitted. (Strangely Lord Lane CJ thought that the *Ghosh* test would not avail such a person!) In such a case there is no claim by D of a belief that he had a legal right to take the property or that he believed the owners would have consented to him taking their property; on the contrary he is well aware of the fact that he is depriving them of what is rightfully theirs. As Professor Smith, *The Law of Theft* (8th edn), states (at para. 2–122). 'The law fails in one of its purposes if it does not afford protection to a person against what he quite reasonably regards as a straightforward case of theft'.

This mess would have been avoided if the courts had accepted their responsibility to define what the law is rather than leaving it to juries. Professor Smith (*ante*) suggests (at para. 2–124) that it would be open to the House of Lords to reinterpret 'dishonestly' to mean 'knowing that the appropriation will or may be detrimental to the interests of the owner in a significant practical way'. This would remove the risk of inconsistency between juries as to how they define dishonesty and would also negate the defence which the latter-day Robin Hood might raise. Regardless of his or the jury's assessment of what may or may not be regarded as dishonest by ordinary people, he would know that taking another's property may be detrimental to the owner's interests; if he does not have his property he cannot possess it, use it, sell it, spend it, or do anything else he might wish to do with it. Professor Smith states that the inclusion of the words 'in a significant practical way' is simply to rule out cases where only minimal detriment may be caused to the owner—it is 'no more than an application of the well-known *de minimis* principle to the law of theft'.

A further pit into which a judge may fall is that of giving the *Ghosh* direction to the jury where it is not necessary. This may have the effect of confusing the jury and leading to the quashing of the accused's conviction on appeal. In *Wood (Peter)* [2002] EWCA Crim 832, D was convicted of burglary having entered a building as a trespasser and removed various items of property from it. In his defence D contended that he believed that the property had been abandoned. The prosecution contended that such a belief was unreasonable. The Recorder, however, gave the full *Ghosh* direction to the jury. In quashing his conviction Rix LJ stated (at para. 26):

> It was common ground that if the goods were abandoned then there could be no dishonesty and no offence. The sole question was as to the genuineness of the defendant's belief as to the factual situation *not* as to the ordinary person's idea of honesty. In these circumstances we think the jury were not adequately assisted but rather liable to have been confused by the Recorder's directions on the sole critical issue in the case.

The Court of Appeal emphasised the point that the unreasonableness of D's belief was a matter which went to the honesty of that belief and might satisfy the jury that the belief was not honestly held. It was necessary, however, in such circumstances to remind the jury that an unreasonable belief may nevertheless be an honest one. The focus, however, is on D's subjective belief not the ordinary person's view of dishonesty.

The reverse of the unnecessary *Ghosh* direction arose in *Rostron and Another* [2003] EWCA Crim 2206, a case which attracted considerable public attention. The defendants were caught at night in diving gear diving for golf balls in a lake on a golf course. They were charged with theft. The trial judge directed the jury that if the defendant knew he was not entitled to go on the golf course and remove golf balls, this amounted to dishonesty and it would not matter what other people might think as he could not, in such circumstances, have had an honest belief that he was entitled to do what he had done. Even if the defendants believed they had no legal right to the golf balls, they may have believed that reasonable honest people would not regard their enterprise as dishonest. As to what is dishonest is for the jury to determine; it is arguable that the judge's direction removed this matter from the jury's consideration. If this position were to be followed, a defendant could be convicted of theft on the basis of a belief on his part that he was acting dishonestly, such belief being so out of touch with reality that no reasonable honest person would hold it. This would turn *Ghosh* on its head. If the Court of Appeal in *Ghosh* decided that dishonesty is a matter for juries to determine (a position which has never been gainsaid since), the Court must live with the consequences of this decision; one such consequence is that juries may deliver verdicts with which judges might disagree. The solution to this problem is to overrule *Ghosh* and provide a definition of dishonesty.

11.3 Abstracting electricity

Electricity does not fall within the definition of 'property' for the purposes of theft. A separate offence covers the dishonest use of electricity. Section 13 provides:

> A person who dishonestly uses without due authority, or dishonestly causes to be wasted or diverted, any electricity shall on conviction on indictment be liable to imprisonment for a term not exceeding five years.

The partial definition of 'dishonestly' in s. 2 does not apply to this offence. A person who uses electricity, believing, for example, that the supplier or consumer would have consented if he had known of the circumstances of its use, will not be treated as a matter of law as not being dishonest; the issue will be left to be considered by the jury according to the standards of ordinary honest people.

The normal situation in which this offence may be committed will be where D uses some device to by-pass his electricity meter. The offence is wide enough, however, to cover using P's battery-operated torch. The offence need not be committed for D's benefit; it is sufficient that he dishonestly wastes or diverts electricity.

11.4 Robbery

Section 8(1) of the TA 1968 provides:

> A person is guilty of robbery if he steals, and immediately before or at the time of doing so, and in order to do so, he uses force on any person or puts or seeks to put any person in fear of being then and there subjected to force.

Both robbery and assault with intent to rob are punishable with life imprisonment (s. 8(2)).

11.4.1 **The need to prove theft**

As robbery is an aggravated form of theft it is necessary to prove theft. For the offence of assault with intent to rob it is necessary to prove an intent to steal. If D has not committed a theft, for example, because he believes he has a right to the property, he cannot be convicted of robbery even though he used force to deprive P of the property and even though he knew he was not entitled to use force (see *Robinson* [1977] Crim LR 173). Similarly, if D uses force to deprive P of his property temporarily, thus lacking the intention to deprive P of his property permanently, there is no theft. In either case, of course, D could be charged with the appropriate offence against the person arising from his threat or use of force.

Robbery is complete when the theft is complete, that is when D has appropriated the property (see **11.2.1.5** *ante*). It can apply where the enterprise may be unsuccessful. In *Corcoran* v *Anderton* (1980) 71 Cr App R 104, there was found to be a robbery where D tugged a handbag from a woman's grasp, although he then dropped it and made off without it. The Court said that taking hold of the bag could be an appropriation. But if D does not have the intent permanently to deprive at the time force is used in order to take V's property, even though he may form that intent subsequently and his actions then may amount to appropriation and the completed offence of theft, he has not committed robbery (see *Vinall* [2011] EWCA Crim 6252).

11.4.2 **The need to prove force or threat of force**

11.4.2.1 Force on a person

In *Dawson and James* (1976) 64 Cr App R 170, D and E jostled P so that he lost his balance at which point F was enabled to take his wallet. The Court of Appeal held that 'force' was an ordinary word and that the trial judge was correct in leaving it to the jury to determine whether jostling P constituted force. This approach was confirmed in *Clouden* [1987] Crim LR 56.

Prior to the Theft Act 1968 robbery required that the force be used to overpower P or to make him give up his property; it was not sufficient if the force was applied to the property to wrench it from P's possession. In *Clouden*, however, the Court of Appeal held that the Act had removed all such distinctions. In this case D approached P from behind and wrenched her shopping basket out of her grasp. In using force on the property, force is also applied to the person and the judge was not at fault in leaving the question to the jury whether D had applied force to a person in order to steal.

11.4.2.2 Threat of force

It is sufficient that D 'puts or seeks to put any person in fear of being then and there subjected to force'. A threat of future force will not suffice (but this may constitute blackmail; see **13.4** *post*). While most cases will involve awareness on P's part of D's threat to use force, the provision also covers the situation where D seeks to put P in fear of being subjected to force but P remains oblivious to the threat. Thus D would be guilty of robbery where he waved a knife at P and issued verbal threats in order to steal P's property but P, unknown to D, was deaf and blind. If V is aware of D's threat of force (whether express or implicit) but is not in fact put in fear thereby, D will nonetheless be liable to conviction as it is D's intention that matters (see *B and R* v *DPP* [2007] EWHC 739 (Admin)).

11.4.2.3 On any person

In most cases, the force, or threat of force, will be used against P, the person in possession or control of the property. D will be liable for robbery, however, where the force, or threat, is used or issued against another in order to steal. For example, D breaks into P's house and is disturbed by the butler, Q. D knocks Q unconscious and proceeds to steal P's silver. Similarly, if D holds a knife to Q's throat threatening to cut it if P does not hand over the contents of his safe, this would fall within s. 8(1).

11.4.2.4 Immediately before or at the time of the stealing

In the previous example of the attack on the butler, D used force immediately before he appropriated the silver. The phrase, however, may be interpreted expansively to cover a wider range of situations. It is submitted that it would cover the case where D uses force on Q at the house to acquire the keys to P's shop or factory from which D then steals property.

If Q, the butler, had disturbed D as he was leaving P's dining room with a bag of silver and D had knocked him unconscious, the question would arise whether the force was used at the time of the stealing. Appropriation was complete when D laid hands on the silver. For these purposes, however, appropriation is treated as a continuing act (cf. rape **10.2.1.1.1** *ante*). This problem arose in *Hale* (1978) 68 Cr App R 415. D and E entered P's house and, having taken her jewellery box, tied her up. It was submitted that the theft was complete when they laid hands on the jewellery box and thus they did not use force at the time of stealing. Eveleigh LJ stated (at p. 418):

> To say that the conduct is over and done with as soon as he lays hands upon the property, or when he first manifests an intention to deal with it as his, is contrary to common-sense and to the natural meaning of words...the act of appropriation does not suddenly cease. It is a continuous act and it is a matter for the jury to decide whether or not the act of appropriation has finished. Moreover, it is quite clear that the intention to deprive the owner permanently...was a continuing one at all times....As a matter of common-sense the appellant was in the course of committing theft; he was stealing.

This case rectifies a flaw in the statute so that the whole course of conduct is regarded as stealing rather than the act which satisfies the minimum requirement for appropriation. A line must be drawn somewhere, however, and it would appear that it would be drawn at the point where D ceases to be engaged in removing the property from P (see also *Atakpu and Abrahams* [1994] Crim LR 693). For example, if D had reached the street with the jewellery box before being confronted by P, it is submitted that the stealing would have been completed prior to this point.

11.4.2.5 In order to steal

The force or threat of force must be used or issued in order to steal. For example, if D uses force to rape P and then, having committed the rape, makes off with P's handbag which she had dropped, this would not be robbery as the force was used in order to rape rather than to steal. The force, or threat of it, need not be used only to remove the property from P; it is sufficient if it is used to enable D to commit the theft more safely, for example, where he knocks unconscious a night-watchman before stealing from a factory, in case the watchman might discover him and raise the alarm.

11.5 Offences involving temporary deprivation

Theft requires an intention of permanently depriving the other of the property. The Theft Act 1968 contains two offences to cover particular situations where this intention does not exist. Apart from these offences and those situations which fall within s. 6(1) (see **11.2.2.1.1** *ante*), unauthorised borrowing is not an offence under the Act.

11.5.1 Removal of articles from places open to the public

This offence was created to deal with the particular mischief of the removal of property from places, such as art galleries, museums, cathedrals, and other buildings open to the public in which valuable property may be housed or displayed, where there may have been no intention of permanently depriving the owner of the property. A work of art, for example, might be taken as a means of making a political statement, or to obtain publicity for a particular cause, or simply as a prank. It is difficult, however, to envisage a more complicated statutory provision. As more things seem to be excluded than are included, and often the only basis for distinction appears to be whim, one is left wondering whether there really was a need for this offence. The maximum punishment for this offence is five years' imprisonment (s. 11(4)).

Section 11(1) provides:

> Subject to subsections (2) and (3) below, where the public have access to a building in order to view the building or part of it, or a collection or part of a collection housed in it, any person who without lawful authority removes from the building or its grounds the whole or part of any article displayed or kept for display to the public in the building or that part of it or in its grounds shall be guilty of an offence.

For this purpose 'collection' includes a collection got together for a temporary purpose, but references in this section to a collection do not apply to a collection made or exhibited for the purpose of effecting sales or other commercial dealings.

11.5.1.1 *Actus reus*

This offence is confined to buildings, or parts of buildings, where the public have access to view the building (or part of it) or a collection (or part of a collection) housed in it. If access is given to the public for some other purpose, for example, a theatre may display paintings in the foyer, removal of such exhibits will not be covered as access to the theatre is for the purpose of viewing performances of plays. If a separate part of the theatre is set aside purely for the display of exhibits, access to this part would be to view the collection. Where, for example, paintings are exhibited in a gallery for the purpose of sale, such exhibits are not protected by this provision. By contrast, where the purpose is to display the paintings to the public and they are incidentally for sale by the individual artists, the exhibitor's purpose is not that of sale and thus they would be protected by the provision.

Strangely, the offence covers only situations where the public have access to a building to view exhibits. If there are also exhibits in the grounds around such a building, these are also protected. By contrast, if the grounds alone are open to the public and, for example, sculptures are displayed there, removal of a sculpture from the grounds would not be covered. The sculptures would also not be covered even though the public had access to the building if that access was not for the purpose of viewing exhibits as where, for example, they are given access to the house to buy teas or souvenirs or to use lavatories. This would seem to be the result of an oversight by the draftsman.

The articles which are protected by this provision are those which are displayed or kept for display. If D removes a painting from the store in the National Gallery, this would be covered as it is kept for display. If D, by contrast, removed a chair from the gallery, this would not fall within the provision as it is not kept for display. A cross placed in a church for purely devotional purposes is not 'displayed' (*Barr* [1978] Crim LR 244).

If an item is displayed in a building or its grounds, D must remove it from the building or the grounds respectively before he will be liable to conviction. It is not enough that he has moved the item to some other place in the building and hidden it there, or likewise in respect of the grounds. It is sufficient, however, that he removes the item from the building and hides it in the grounds (and presumably vice versa).

Where the article taken is part of a collection intended for permanent exhibition (or an article on loan and exhibited with such a collection) the offence may be committed at any time (s. 11(2)). An item in store remains part of a collection intended for permanent exhibition where the items on display from the collection are rotated as it is the collection which is intended for permanent display (see *Durkin* [1973] QB 786). Where the item is not part of a permanent exhibition, the offence will be committed only where it is removed during the times when the building is open to the public. The articles in a privately owned stately home, which is open to the public only at particular times, would not form a collection intended for permanent exhibition (but where the home was owned, for example, by the National Trust, they probably would). This leads to the ludicrous position that if D enters on a day when the home is open to the public and removes a painting he will be guilty of this offence, whereas if he enters on such a day and hides in a cupboard until after midnight and then removes the painting on a day when the home is not open to the public, he will not be guilty of this offence. The distinction between the two situations is one without substance in so far as it relates either to D's moral culpability or the harm, loss, or inconvenience caused to the owner of the home.

11.5.1.2 *Mens rea*

D must intend to remove the article. He will not be guilty of the offence, however, 'if he believes that he has lawful authority for the removal of the thing in question or that he would have it if the person entitled to give it knew of the removal and the circumstances of it' (s. 11(3)).

11.5.2 **Taking a conveyance without authority**

Where D takes a vehicle it is often difficult to prove an intention of permanently depriving the owner of it; D may take a car, for example, to joyride or to use on a criminal enterprise or to use for his own convenience. Whatever the reason, such behaviour may create a social nuisance, a public danger, and personal inconvenience for the person temporarily deprived of his vehicle. Section 12 covers such taking of motor vehicles and also covers the taking of other conveyances such as boats or bicycles.

11.5.2.1 Taking a conveyance other than a pedal cycle

Section 12(1) provides:

> ...a person shall be guilty of an offence if, without having the consent of the owner or other lawful authority, he takes any conveyance for his own or another's use or, knowing that any conveyance has been taken without such authority, drives it or allows himself to be carried in or on it.

This section creates two summary offences punishable with a fine not exceeding level five on the standard scale or up to six months' imprisonment or both (s. 12(2) as amended by s. 37(1) of the Criminal Justice Act 1988). On a trial on indictment for theft, a jury may return a verdict of guilty of the s. 12(1) offence if they are not satisfied that the accused is guilty of theft but it is proved that he committed this offence. As the s. 12(1) offence is a summary offence, an attempt to commit it is not an offence, but s. 9 of the Criminal Attempts Act 1981 creates a separate offence of interference with a motor vehicle with the intention that an offence under s. 12(1) shall be committed (interference with something like a yacht, however, would not be covered).

11.5.2.1.1 *Conveyance*

A 'conveyance' is something 'constructed or adapted for the carriage of a person or persons whether by land, water, or air' excluding a vehicle where the person controlling it is not carried in or on it (see s. 12(7)(a)). Implicit in the definition of the offence in s. 12(1) is the requirement that it be a conveyance which can be driven. Thus the vehicle, vessel, or aircraft must be one which carries its 'driver' on it. This is a broad definition and covers cars, lorries, motor-cycles, boats, and aircraft. The definition is wide enough to cover a 'soap-box', a wheelchair, a rowing-boat, or a hang-glider but it would not cover roller skates or skis. In *McDonagh* [1974] QB 448, a case concerned with the meaning of 'driving' in the Road Traffic Acts, it was stated that the essence of driving was the use of 'the driver's controls for the purpose of directing the movement of the vehicle'. According to this definition, roller skates or skis would be excluded as there are no 'controls' of even the most rudimentary nature. An animal is not a 'conveyance' (*Neal* v *Gribble* (1978) 68 Cr App R 9).

11.5.2.1.2 *Takes for his own or another's use*

A person 'takes' a conveyance when he (1) assumes possession or control of it and (2) intentionally causes it to move or be moved (see *Bogacki* [1973] QB 832). There is no need for D to ride on or 'drive' the conveyance; thus the offence was committed where D took a boat, loaded it on a trailer, and drove away (*Pearce* [1973] Crim LR 321).

A person in lawful control or possession of a vehicle, such as an employee or a bailee, may, in certain circumstances, 'take' it. In *McKnight* v *Davies* [1974] RTR 4, D, a lorry driver, was under a duty to return the lorry to his employer's depot after completing his deliveries. D drove the lorry to a public house for a drink, drove several friends to their homes, called at another public house for a drink and then drove home and parked the lorry overnight near his home, returning it to the depot in the morning. He was convicted of the s. 12(1) offence, Lord Widgery CJ stating when dismissing his appeal (at p. 8):

> Not every brief, unauthorised diversion from his proper route by an employed driver in the course of his working day will necessarily involve a 'taking' of the vehicle for his own use. If, however, . . . he returns to the vehicle after he has parked it for the night and drives it off on an unauthorised errand, he is clearly guilty of an offence. Similarly, if in the course of his working day, or otherwise while his authority to use the vehicle is unexpired, he appropriates it to his own use in a manner which repudiates the rights of the true owner, and shows that he has assumed control of the vehicle for his own purposes, he can be properly regarded as having taken the vehicle within s. 12.

Lord Widgery CJ was satisfied that D took the lorry when he left the first public house as 'at that point he assumed control for his own purposes in a manner which was inconsistent with his duty to his employer to finish his round and drive the vehicle to the depot'. Presumably, D's driving to the first public house was regarded as a 'brief, unauthorised diversion'.

An employee only has control of the conveyance; a bailee, who has possession, may also commit the offence if he uses the vehicle for some purpose other than that for which he received permission, or if he uses it after the period of the bailment has ended. In *Phipps and McGill* [1970] RTR 209, D borrowed P's car to take his wife to Victoria Station on the express condition that he would return it by 9.30pm. D kept the car overnight and drove the following day to Hastings. It was held that at the time D decided not to return the car and drove it for his own purposes, he took it.

The taking of a conveyance must be purposive; that is, D must take it for his own or another's use as a conveyance. Thus the conveyance must either be used as such while it is being taken, as where D, or another, rides in or on it as it moves or is being moved (see *Bow* (1976) 64 Cr App R 54), or D must take it intending it to be used in future as a conveyance (see *Pearce, ante; Marchant and McCallister* (1984) 80 Cr App R 361). Pushing a car down a hill as a prank, or to remove an obstruction it is causing, would not amount to using it as a conveyance.

11.5.2.1.3 *Without the consent of the owner or other lawful authority*

The taking of the vehicle must be without the consent of the owner or other lawful authority. The latter phrase will cover, for example, cases where the police or local authority have a statutory power to remove vehicles. It is no answer to a charge under s. 12(1) that the owner would have given consent had he been asked (*Ambler* [1979] RTR 217; but cf. **11.5.2.1.4** *post*). Consent obtained by intimidation or force is not true consent (see *Hogdon* [1962] Crim LR 563).

Where consent has been obtained by fraud it appears that the consent is valid consent for the purposes of this section. In *Whittaker* v *Campbell* [1984] QB 318, D, who had no driving licence, pretended to be X and presented X's driving licence in order to obtain the hire of a van. The Divisional Court held that even if a mistake induced by fraud rendered a contract void, this would not affect the validity of the consent to the taking of the vehicle. As the parties were dealing face to face, this was not truly a case of mistaken identity as P hired the van to the person before him who asked to hire it. The principle in the case, however, is stated widely enough to cover cases of mistaken identity; thus if P had intended to hire the van to X (but not to Y) and Y, X's twin brother, had taken possession of it, this would have been a fundamental mistake rendering the contract void. It is submitted that Y's taking of the van should be an offence under s. 12 and that the *ratio* in *Whittaker* v *Campbell* should be limited to the facts of the case which involved a mistake as to D's attributes rather than his identity; such a mistake only serves to render a contract voidable.

A further problem, however, arises in the fraud cases which highlights a conflict between these cases and those discussed earlier (**11.5.2.1.2** *ante*). In *Peart* [1970] 2 QB 672, P obtained the loan of a car by representing to P that he needed to drive from Newcastle upon Tyne to Alnwick, a journey of some 30 miles. D drove in the opposite direction to Burnley, some 100 miles away. D's conviction of the s. 12 offence was quashed as he had not 'taken' the vehicle as P had consented to him using it. This case seems to conflict with *Phipps and McGill*. In that case it was a 'taking' to use the vehicle for an additional purpose after the permitted purpose had been completed. It is difficult to see why the immediate use of the vehicle for some unauthorised purpose should not constitute 'taking' because possession or control of the vehicle has been obtained by a misrepresentation. In *Peart*, had D driven to Alnwick and then gone to Burnley he would have committed an offence; it is difficult to see how driving straight to Burnley alters the substance of what he did. It is submitted that the decision in *Peart* is wrong and that *Phipps and McGill* should be regarded as the correct authority.

11.5.2.1.4 *Belief in lawful authority or consent*
Section 12(6) provides:

> A person does not commit an offence under this section by anything done in the belief that he has lawful authority to do it or that he would have the owner's consent if the owner knew of his doing it and the circumstances of it.

This provision is similar to s. 2(1)(a) and (b) relating to dishonesty for the purposes of theft. D must adduce evidence of his belief but, having done so, the burden is on the prosecution to disprove that belief beyond reasonable doubt.

In *McMinn* v *McMinn and another* [2006] 3 All ER 87, QBD, the Divisional Court held that where D, an employee, who was permitted to drive a vehicle owned by his employer, allowed a third party to drive it, D would be guilty of the s. 12 offence if it could be said that 'he had appropriated the vehicle for use in a manner which repudiated the rights of the true owner, and showed that he had assumed control of the vehicle for his own purposes'. The crucial question would be whether D knew or believed that his employer would not have permitted the third party to drive the vehicle. As it would be unlikely in most cases that the employer would have insurance cover for non-employees to drive his vehicles, the prospects of a defendant being able to raise a reasonable doubt that he did not know or believe his employer would not permit the driving would appear to be very slim.

11.5.2.1.5 *Driving or allowing oneself to be carried in or on a conveyance*
Where a conveyance has been taken by another without lawful authority (this covers theft or the s. 12 offence; see *Tolley* v *Giddings* [1964] 2 QB 354), and D knows this (wilful blindness will probably suffice), he will be guilty of the second offence created by s. 12(1) if he drives the conveyance or allows himself to be carried in or on it. If D aids, abets, counsels, or procures the taking of the vehicle by E he will be liable as an accessory to E's offence of taking. This second offence created by s. 12(1) extends the ambit of secondary liability. If E takes a car and then meets D and offers him a ride, D would commit the s. 12(1) offence if, knowing that E had taken the car without lawful authority, he accepted the offer and was carried as a passenger in the vehicle. He would not, however, be guilty of aiding and abetting the original taking by E, as this offence was complete prior to D being offered a ride.

To be liable for this second offence, D must either drive the vehicle himself, or he must 'allow himself to be carried' which requires that the vehicle must move while he is in or on it (see *Miller* [1976] Crim LR 147; *Diggin* (1980) 72 Cr App R 204).

11.5.2.2 Aggravated vehicle-taking
Because of the perceived problem of 'joyriding' Parliament decided that further legislation was necessary in this area. In many cases of joyriding the vehicle involved ends up being damaged or even destroyed. If several individuals were involved it might prove difficult to establish which of them caused the damage. To counter this and other problems the Aggravated Vehicle-Taking Act was passed in 1992. This inserts a new s. 12A into the Theft Act 1968 which provides:

(1) Subject to subsection (3) below, a person is guilty of aggravated taking of a vehicle if—
  (a) he commits an offence under section 12(1) above (in this section referred to as the 'basic offence') in relation to a mechanically propelled vehicle; and
  (b) it is proved that, at any time after the vehicle was unlawfully taken (whether by him or another) and before it was recovered, the vehicle was driven, or injury or damage was caused, in one or more of the circumstances set out in paragraphs (a) to (d) of subsection (2) below.
(2) The circumstances referred to in subsection 1(b) above are—
  (a) that the vehicle was driven dangerously on a road or other public place;
  (b) that, owing to the driving of the vehicle, an accident occurred by which injury was caused to any person;
  (c) that, owing to the driving of the vehicle, an accident occurred by which damage was caused to any property, other than the vehicle;
  (d) that damage was caused to the vehicle.
(3) A person is not guilty of an offence under this section if he proves that, as regards any such proven driving, injury or damage as is referred to in subsection (1)(b) above, either—

(a) the driving, accident or damage referred to in subsection (2) above occurred before he committed the basic offence; or

(b) he was neither in nor on nor in the immediate vicinity of the vehicle when that driving, accident or damage occurred....

The maximum penalty on conviction on indictment is two years' imprisonment but if it is proved that, in circumstances falling within sub-s. (2)(b) cited earlier, the accident caused the death of the person concerned, the maximum is 14 years (increased from five years by s. 285 of the Criminal Justice Act 2003).

Upon proof of the basic offence in relation to a mechanically propelled vehicle under s. 12(1) of the Theft Act 1968, guilt of the aggravated offence will be established on proof of one of the three circumstances specified in s. 12A(2). Proof of a certain degree of fault is required in respect of driving dangerously in that it must be proved that 'it would be obvious to a competent and careful driver that driving in that way would be dangerous' (s. 2A(1)(b) of the Road Traffic Act 1988). No degree of fault, however, need be proved in relation to the other two circumstances. D could be liable for the aggravated offence where the vehicle is hit by another vehicle through no fault of D's. Similarly, D would be liable where, even though he was driving carefully, he had to swerve to avoid another vehicle being driven dangerously and he damaged a parked car. His liability arises from the fact that the vehicle was being driven as s. 12A(2)(b) does not refer to the 'manner' in which it was being driven (see *Marsh* [1997] 1 Cr App R 67). In *Marsh*, through no fault of D's, the vehicle he was driving hit P who had run into the road in front of it. Had P died, would D have been convicted of unlawful act manslaughter? It is arguable that had D not taken the vehicle it would not have been on the road at the time P ran out. There is a connection in this case between D's culpable act and the consequence of P's death (cf. *Dalloway* **2.6.3.1** *ante*). It is also arguable that driving a vehicle on a public road harbours the risk of some harm resulting therefrom (cf. *Church* **9.3.3.1.2** *ante*).

It is also worth noting that anyone who allows himself to be carried in a vehicle which he knows has been taken without the owner's consent commits the basic offence and will be guilty of the aggravated offence simply if the eventualities in sub-s. (2) occur. For example, E a hitch-hiker, obtains a lift from D who is committing the s. 12(1) offence. On learning this E continues to ride in the vehicle. However, when D starts to drive the vehicle in a dangerous manner, thereby committing the aggravated offence under s. 12A(1), E pleads to be let out. It would appear from the wording of the section that E is also guilty of the aggravated offence and there is no possibility of withdrawal. By contrast, E would not be guilty as an accessory to the offence of dangerous driving contrary to s. 2 of the Road Traffic Act 1988 as he would not be aiding or abetting that offence. Similarly, if D did stop to let E out and then either drove off immediately hitting another vehicle or a pedestrian, or set fire to the vehicle, E would again be liable for the aggravated offence as he was in the vicinity when one of the eventualities in s. 12A(2) of the Theft Act 1968 occurred. It is submitted that the net has been cast too widely by the legislators and that some degree of complicity on the part of E should have been required.

'Accident' in the context of s. 12A was held by the Court of Appeal in *Branchflower* [2004] EWCA Crim 2042 to describe the consequences of what occurred and is not concerned with how they occurred. D had driven off in V's car while V was closing his garage door. In driving off D drove over V killing him. D was convicted of both murder and the s. 12A offence and appealed the latter on the basis that if he had driven over V intentionally, this could not amount to an accident. The Court held that the fact that a moving vehicle caused V's death was enough to constitute an accident in the context of s. 12A. 'Accident', accordingly, describes the incident which is a result of the driving rather than being descriptive of D's state of mind. If this were not so, a defendant who intended to cause injury or damage would be in a more advantageous position than one who caused injury or damage negligently; such an outcome could hardly be the intent of Parliament.

11.5.2.3 Taking a pedal cycle

Where the conveyance involved is a pedal cycle, s. 12(5) provides that it is an offence where a person either takes it for his own or another's use, without having the consent of the owner or other lawful authority, or rides it knowing it to have been taken without such authority. This is a summary offence punishable with a fine not exceeding level two on the standard scale. The defence of honest belief in s. 12(6) also applies to this offence.

FURTHER READING

A. Ashworth, 'Robbery Re-assessed' [2002] Crim LR 851.

A. L. Bogg and J. Stanton-Ife, 'Theft as Exploitation' (2003) Legal Studies 402.

R. Brazier, 'Criminal Trustees' (1975) 39 Conv (NS) 29.

C. Clarkson, 'Theft and Fair Labelling' (1993) 56 MLR 554.

A. Coleman, 'Trade Secrets and the Criminal Law: The Need for Reform' (1985) 5 Comp L&P 111.

S. Cooper and M. Allen, 'Appropriation after *Gomez*' (1993) 57 JCL 186.

D. W. Elliott, 'Dishonesty in Theft: A Dispensable Concept' [1982] Crim LR 395.

S. Gardner, 'Is Theft a Rip-off?' (1990) 10 OJLS 441; 'Property and Theft' [1998] Crim LR 35.

E. Griew, 'Dishonesty—the Objections to *Feely* and *Ghosh*' [1985] Crim LR 341; 'Theft and Obtaining by Deception' [1979] Crim LR 292.

A. Halpin, 'The Test for Dishonesty' [1996] Crim LR 283.

R. G. Hammond, 'Theft of Information' (1984) 100 LQR 252.

E. Melissaris, 'The Concept of Appropriation and the Offence of Theft' (2007) 70 MLR 581.

S. Parsons, 'Dishonest Appropriation After *Gomez* and *Hinks*' (2004) 68 JCL 520.

S. Shute, 'Appropriation and the Law of Theft' [2002] Crim LR 450.

S. Shute and J. Horder, 'Thieving and Deceiving: What is the Difference?' (1993) 56 MLR 548.

A. T. H. Smith, 'Shoplifting and the Theft Acts' [1981] Crim LR 586.

J. C. Smith, 'Obtaining Cheques by Deception or Theft' [1997] Crim LR 396.

J. N. Spencer, 'The Aggravated Vehicle-Taking Act 1992' [1992] Crim LR 699.

12

Fraud

12.1 Introduction

The Theft Acts created a range of offences which contain the common element that the proscribed consequence is brought about as a result of the accused's dishonest deception. These offences covered obtaining property, services or a pecuniary advantage by deception and evading liability by deception. The Fraud Act 2006 (hereafter referred to as the FA 2006) has repealed various sections of the TA 1968 and TA 1978 replacing a number of individual offences based on deception with a new offence of fraud which may be committed in three ways. It also creates a new offence of dishonestly obtaining services to replace the offence of obtaining services by deception under s. 1 of the TA 1978. These new offences are designed to overcome problems in the old law and to simplify the law. The FA 2006 came into force on 15 January 2007 but the repeal does not affect 'any liability, investigation, legal proceeding or penalty for or in respect of any offence' partly committed before the repeal comes into force (FA 2006, sch. 2). This means that for some time the old law will continue to form the basis of prosecutions where 'any act, omission or event' in respect of the offence occurred before the commencement date (FA 2006, sch. 2). Before examining the offence of fraud, however, the previous law will be examined as it remains relevant where the *actus reus* was committed, or partly committed, before 15 January 2007, and some elements of the old offences are carried over to the new. The major difference to grasp at the outset, however, is that the old deception offences were result crimes as the deception had to lead to either the obtaining of property, services or a pecuniary advantage, or the evasion of a liability, whereas the new offence of fraud is a conduct crime there being no need to prove that any result ensued. The FA 2006 also creates a new offence of obtaining services dishonestly; this is a result crime like the offence of obtaining services by deception which it replaces but it is not limited by the concept of a deception.

12.2 Offences under the Theft Acts

12.2.1 Common elements

12.2.1.1 Deception

Section 15(4) of the TA 1968 provided:

> For the purposes of this section 'deception' means any deception (whether deliberate or reckless) by words or conduct as to fact or as to law, including a deception as to the present intentions of the person using the deception or any other person.

This definition applied to all the offences (see s. 16(3) of the TA 1968 and s. 5(1) of the TA 1978).

12.2.1.1.1 *Deceiver and deceived*

The deception had to arise from D's words or conduct and, in addition, operate to deceive another person. If D made a representation believing it to be false but it was, in fact, true, there was no offence as P had not been deceived (see *Deller* (1952) 36 Cr App R 184, **2.3** *ante*), but D could be guilty of an attempt. **Using a false coin to obtain items from a vending machine did not constitute obtaining property by deception as no person was deceived.** If D succeeded in obtaining an item from the machine in these circumstances he could always be prosecuted for theft (see *Wise and Candy*, *The Independent*, 21 August 1990), and if he failed, for attempted theft. Where he obtained a service, for example the use of a washing machine in a launderette, he could be guilty of abstracting electricity contrary to s. 13 of the TA 1968 or making off without payment contrary to s. 3 of the TA 1978. This paragraph amply demonstrates deficiencies in the old law which the FA 2006 has swept away. The new law requires a false representation but there is no requirement to prove that anyone was deceived.

12.2.1.1.2 *Deliberate or reckless*

D was liable to conviction where he made a representation knowing it to be false or where he was aware that it may be false (see *Staines* (1974) 60 Cr App R 160). As deception offences required the proof of dishonesty which is a subjective concept recklessness was similarly subjective.

12.2.1.1.3 *Words or conduct*

A deception could arise from D's words or conduct. The representation contained in the words or conduct could be express or implied. If D, wrongfully in possession of a charity collecting box, stood on a street corner shaking the box, his conduct would involve an implied representation that he was entitled to collect for the charity concerned and that money so collected would be handed over to the charity. Similarly a person who ordered a meal in a restaurant, registered as a guest in a hotel, or took a taxi represented that he intended to pay for the service rendered (see *DPP v Ray* [1974] AC 370; *Harris* (1975) 62 Cr App R 28; cf. *Waterfall* [1970] 1 QB 148).

12.2.1.2 The 'obtaining' must be by deception

'Obtaining' is the term used in ss. 15 and 16 of the TA 1968 and s. 1 of the TA 1978 to cover the consequence which D had to produce by means of his deception; different terms are used in s. 2 of the TA 1978, but 'obtaining' will be used in this context as a generic term.

D had to make a false statement but there would be no offence unless it deceived P and caused him to act in the way appropriate to the relevant offence, for example, to hand over property for the s. 15 offence. If D had already obtained the property before seeking to deceive P, the obtaining could not be as a result of the deception (see *Collis-Smith* [1971] Crim LR 716; *Coady* [1996] Crim LR 518). Likewise, **if P was not deceived**, for example, because he did not believe D, or did not hear or see the words or conduct which constituted the deception, **the obtaining was not the result of the deception.** In addition, even though D may have been deceived, the actual deception may not have been operative in causing the obtaining, that is D may not have acted in reliance on the false representation but for some other reason. This was a question of fact for the jury to decide applying their common sense (see *King* [1987] 1 All ER 547).

It was important that the prosecution identified the representation which they alleged caused the obtaining.

> In *Laverty* [1970] 3 All ER 432, D changed the number plates of a stolen car and sold it to P. He was charged with obtaining the price from P by the deception that it bore its original plates. P stated in evidence that what induced him to buy the car was, rather, the representation that D had title to sell the car. D's conviction was quashed as there was no evidence that P acted in reliance upon the alleged representation, nor could it safely be inferred that he would not have bought the car if he had known the number had been changed.

Had the representation alleged been that D had been the owner of the car, then the conviction would have been upheld. The new offence of fraud by false representation avoids this difficulty as there is no requirement that anyone be deceived.

In other cases, however, the courts were more prepared to permit inferences that P had been deceived and induced to act in reliance upon the false representation even though the representation involved did not appear to have been at the forefront of P's mind. The problem arose in particular where the false representation was implied from D's conduct.

> In *Metropolitan Police Commissioner* v *Charles* [1977] AC 177, P accepted D's cheques because they were backed by a cheque card which guaranteed that they would be honoured; he was totally unconcerned as to the state of D's account or whether his authority to use the card had been withdrawn. P did state, however, that had he known D had no funds in his account or no authority to overdraw he would not have accepted the cheques. As the false representation construed from the facts was that D had authority to use the card, it would appear that this was a matter of indifference to P who may not have had any belief that the representation was true. The House of Lords, however, upheld D's conviction.

This decision is only explicable if deception did not require a positive belief in the truth of the representation which was, in fact, false, it being sufficient that P was ignorant of the truth and acted in reliance upon the representation of authority. *Charles* was followed in *Lambie* [1982] AC 449 where the House of Lords held that the only inference to be drawn from the evidence of D's use of a credit card to purchase goods was that P relied upon D's implicit representation that she had authority to use the card and that had P known the truth she would not have concluded the transaction and supplied D with goods. P's evidence, however, was to the effect that the only thing she was concerned about was that the store be paid which would be assured if the conditions on the card were observed. Again, the House seemed to have been satisfied that **the property was *obtained by* deception if P would not have concluded the transaction had she known the truth**; this was somewhat different from saying that P supplied the goods or service etc. because she *believed* that D had authority.

One final point to note is that it was sufficient if the property, services, pecuniary advantage etc. which D obtained were obtained from someone other than the person who was deceived and the obtaining resulted from that deception. In *Charles* and *Lambie* it was the casino employee and shop assistant, respectively, who were deceived but in both cases D obtained a pecuniary advantage from his bank or credit card supplier respectively.

12.2.1.3 'Dishonestly'

The obtaining also had to be dishonest. No definition of 'dishonestly' for the purposes of deception offences was given in either Theft Act. Dishonesty, however, remained a subjective concept so that the *Ghosh* direction (see **11.2.2.2.2 ante**) was also applicable to deception offences (see *Woolven* (1983) 77 Cr App R 231). Doubtless, the fact that D had used a deception would tend to indicate that he was dishonest, but it did not necessarily follow that he was guilty of an offence as, in the case of property, he may have believed that he had a right to the property.

12.2.2 Obtaining property by deception

Section 15(1) of the TA 1968 provided:

> (1) A person who by any deception dishonestly obtains property belonging to another, with the intention of permanently depriving the other of it, shall on conviction on indictment be liable to imprisonment for a term not exceeding ten years.

It is worth noting that because of the expansive definition of 'appropriation' in theft, many situations which involved deception were also thefts. In *Gomez* [1992] 3 WLR 1061 (see **11.2.1.4** and **11.2.1.5.2 ante**) the theft occurred when D took delivery of the electrical goods which was the same point at which D 'obtained' the property by deception.

12.2.2.1 *Actus reus*

The definitions of 'property' in s. 4(1) and 'belonging to another' in s. 5(1) (see **11.2.1.1** and **11.2.1.2 ante**) apply generally to other offences (s. 34(1)). The limitations contained in s. 4(2) relating to the theft of land do not apply so that a person could obtain land by deception in circumstances where he could not steal land. As a person 'obtains' property if he 'obtains ownership, possession or control of it...' (s. 15(2)), D could be guilty of the s. 15 offence even though he never gained possession of the property. For example, in a sale of goods situation where ownership passes on contract, D could be guilty of the s. 15 offence upon inducing P, by deception, to conclude the contract and thereby transfer ownership of the goods to him, even though he never subsequently received delivery of the property.

The offence under s. 15 may be committed where D obtained the property for himself or for another or where the deception enabled another to obtain or retain the property (s. 15(2)). D would 'enable' another to 'obtain' property where, for example, E offered to sell a painting to P for £10,000 but P rejected E's offer whereupon D dishonestly represented to P that the painting was an 'Old Master' and was worth considerably more resulting in P agreeing to buy the painting and paying E £10,000. D's deception enabled E to obtain the purchase price. D would 'enable' another to 'retain' property where, for example, P lent a book to E for a week, and at the end of the week, D dishonestly represented to P that E required the book for a longer period and P agreed not to seek its return.

12.2.2.2 *Mens rea*

The deception had to be deliberate or reckless and D's obtaining of the property had to be dishonest. In addition he had to intend to deprive the other of the property permanently. Section 6 (see **11.2.2.1** *ante*) applied also to s. 15 with the necessary amendment that for 'appropriating' the word 'obtaining' had to be substituted (s. 15(3)).

12.2.3 **Obtaining a money transfer by deception**

As with theft, the obtaining of cheques (and of credit transfers of money by CHAPS (clearing house automated payment system) or telegraphic transfers) has presented problems. Where A draws a negotiable cheque in favour of P this creates a thing in action, namely a debt. If the cheque is not honoured, P may sue A on the cheque. If by deception D caused P to sign over the cheque to him, D obtained property belonging to another, namely the thing in action (the debt) which P owned. A problem arose, however, where D by deception caused P to draw a cheque in his favour (or to cause a CHAPS or telegraphic transfer to be made from P's bank account to D's).

> In *Preddy* [1996] AC 815, the appellants obtained a substantial number of mortgage advances from building societies to purchase houses, intending to repay the mortgages when, as they hoped, they sold the houses at a profit. All the mortgage applications contained false representations. The mortgage advances were paid by cheque or telegraphic transfer or by CHAPS. The appellants' convictions of obtaining property by deception were quashed by the House of Lords on the basis that no property belonging to another had been obtained. When payments were made by cheque, the thing in action represented by the cheque belonged to the payee not the drawer. Similarly when payments were made by electronic means no identifiable property passed from the payer to the payee; rather the thing in action, the credit balance in the payer's bank account, was extinguished or reduced and a new thing in action was created in the payee's bank account which necessarily belonged to him.

There were a number of possible offences which could have been charged in the situation which pertained in *Preddy*. One possibility was procuring the execution of a valuable security contrary to s. 20(2) of the TA 1968 in respect of advances made by cheques (a cheque is a valuable security) and possibly for advances made by CHAPS order (see *King* [1992] 1 QB 20) but a telegraphic transfer was not a valuable security (see *Manjdadria* [1993] Crim LR 73). A second possibility was a charge of theft based on D's dealings with the new credit balance in his account on the basis that the building society retained an equitable interest in this property (see *Shadrokh-Cigari*, **11.2.1.2.2** *ante*). In *Nathan* [1997] Crim LR 835, the Court of Appeal described this proposition 'as in principle sound'. An alternative was to bring a charge of obtaining services by deception contrary to s. 1 of the TA 1978 as the provision of a loan constituted a service (see s. 1(3) of the TA 1978 inserted by s. 4(1) of the Theft (Amendment) Act 1996). (The Theft (Amendment) Act 1996 was quickly passed by Parliament enacting the draft Bill appended to the Law Commission's Report, *Offences of Dishonesty: Money Transfers* (Law Com No. 243) which was published following the decision in *Preddy*.) Obtaining services by deception was not charged in *Preddy* because an earlier decision of the Court of Appeal in *Halai* [1983] Crim LR 624 had held that a mortgage advance could not be regarded as a service. The Theft (Amendment) Act 1996 overruled *Halai* prospectively. Following its passage the Court of Appeal overruled *Halai* retrospectively (see *Graham* [1997] 1 Cr App R 302 and *Cooke* [1997] Crim LR 436). The third possible charge was a new offence created by the 1996 Act of dishonestly obtaining a money transfer by deception contrary to s. 15A of the TA 1968 (inserted by s. 1 of the 1996 Act, since repealed by the FA 2006). This provided:

(1) A person is guilty of an offence if by any deception he dishonestly obtains a money transfer for himself or another.

(2) A money transfer occurs when—

    (a) a debit is made to one account,

    (b) a credit is made to another, and

    (c) the credit results from the debit or the debit results from the credit.

This offence covered all transfers made by CHAPS order, electronic or telegraphic transfer, or by cheque. The offence did not, however, cover the case of D who obtained a cheque by deception but who did not pay it into his bank account. In this case either the s. 20(2) offence had to be charged or D could be charged with theft of, or obtaining by deception, the cheque as a valuable security (see **11.2.1.1.1** and **11.2.2.1.1(a)** *ante*). Section 2 of the 1996 Act also inserted a new s. 24A into the Theft Act 1968, supplementing the law on handling by creating a separate offence of dishonestly retaining a wrongful credit where the credit has derived from an offence under s. 15A, theft, blackmail, or any stolen goods (see **13.5** *post*). This offence has not been repealed by the FA 2006.

12.2.4 Obtaining services by deception

Section 1 of the TA 1978 provided:

(1) A person who by any deception dishonestly obtains services from another shall be guilty of an offence.

(2) It is an obtaining of services where the other is induced to confer a benefit by doing some act, or causing or permitting some act to be done, on the understanding that the benefit has been or will be paid for.

The deception had to be deliberate or reckless and the obtaining had to be dishonest. The services had to be obtained by means of the deception. There would be no offence where, for example, D slipped secretly into a theatre to watch a production, or slipped secretly into an hotel and spent the night in an unoccupied room as in neither case has anyone been deceived.

The services obtained had to be rendered 'on the understanding that the benefit has been or will be paid for'. If D dishonestly told P, his neighbour, that he was afraid of heights and asked him to clear leaves from his gutter and P agreed as an act of neighbourliness, there was no offence. By contrast, if D had, in addition, offered him £5 to do the job there was potentially an offence even though D intended to pay, and did pay, for the service.

'Services' for the purposes of this offence involved the conferring of a benefit by doing some act or causing or permitting some act to be done. The benefit could be conferred on D or another. Whether something constituted a benefit would generally be settled by the fact that there is an understanding that it has been or will be paid for; people do not generally pay for something if it is not beneficial.

Following the decision of the House of Lords in *Preddy* [1996] AC 815, Parliament enacted the Theft (Amendment) Act 1996 providing a new sub-s. (3) to s. 1 of the 1978 Act which provided:

> (3) Without prejudice to the generality of subsection (2) above, it is an obtaining of services where the other is induced to make a loan, or to cause or permit a loan to be made, on the understanding that any payment (whether by way of interest or otherwise) will be or has been made in respect of the loan.

12.2.5 Evasion of liability by deception

Evasion of liability was originally dealt with by s. 16(2)(a) of the TA 1968. This provision proved problematic. Following the Criminal Law Revision Committee's *Thirteenth Report: Section 16 of the Theft Act 1968* (Cmnd 6733), s. 16(2)(a) was repealed and replaced by s. 2 of the TA 1978 which provided:

> (1) Subject to subsection (2) below, where a person by any deception—
>   (a) dishonestly secures the remission of the whole or part of any existing liability to make a payment, whether his own liability or another's; or
>   (b) with intent to make permanent default in whole or in part on any existing liability to make a payment, or with intent to let another do so, dishonestly induces the creditor or any person claiming payment on behalf of the creditor to wait for payment (whether or not the due date for payment is deferred) or to forgo payment; or
>   (c) dishonestly obtains any exemption from or abatement of liability to make a payment;
>
> he shall be guilty of an offence.

The deception had to be deliberate or reckless. The securing, inducing, or obtaining had to be dishonest.

The liability in s. 2(1)(a) and (b) had to be an existing one at the time of the deception albeit that the date when payment was due had not arrived. Section 2(1)(c) referred simply to a 'liability' and thus covered prospective liabilities. In all cases the liability had to be a legally enforceable one (s. 2(2)). Thus, for example, if D owed money to his bookmaker, he would not be guilty of this offence if he evaded liability to pay that debt by deception as gaming debts are not legally enforceable. Similarly, if the debt concerned was no longer enforceable because it was statute-barred, D would not commit this offence.

'Remission' of a liability involved the reduction of, or cancellation of, the debtor's debt. This offence could be committed only where the creditor knew that there was a debt and that he was cancelling or reducing the debtor's liability to make payment.

Stalling a creditor is not generally an offence but it could be where D dishonestly induced the creditor to wait for or forgo payment by means of a deception with intent to make permanent default in whole or in part of the liability. Section 2(3) expressly provided that if D paid P by cheque this did not constitute payment as P was being induced to wait for payment. A creditor was induced to 'forgo' payment where, for example, he was deceived into believing that the debt had been paid already, or he was deceived into believing that the debt was irrecoverable and he wrote it off.

The s. 2(1)(b) offence would be committed where D obtained the exemption or abatement for himself or for another or he enabled another to obtain it (s. 2(4)). The liability could be a prospective one. The Criminal Law Revision Committee *Thirteenth Report*, envisaged that this provision would cover the ratepayer who obtained a rebate by making a false statement. It also covered the case where a person obtained services free or at a reduced rate, for example, gaining admission to a theatre or cinema at a reduced rate by falsely representing that he was a student or a pensioner, or gaining free travel on public transport by representing that he was a pensioner. These cases were also be covered by s. 1.

Section 2(1)(c) suffered from the same potential problem as s. 2(1)(a) in that a person who obtained, for example, a reduction in his council tax by means of false statements on the assessment form that he was a student did not actually obtain an abatement of his liability; his actual liability remained the same. The complexities of these offences are avoided by the new fraud offence.

12.2.6 Obtaining a pecuniary advantage by deception

Section 16 of the TA 1968 provided:

(1) A person who by any deception dishonestly obtains for himself or another any pecuniary advantage shall on conviction on indictment be liable to imprisonment for a term not exceeding five years.

(2) The cases in which a pecuniary advantage within the meaning of this section is to be regarded as obtained for a person are cases where—

(a) [repealed]

(b) he is allowed to borrow by way of overdraft, or to take out any policy of insurance or annuity contract, or obtains an improvement of the terms on which he is allowed to do so; or

(c) he is given the opportunity to earn remuneration or greater remuneration in an office or employment, or to win money by betting.

Deception had the same meaning as for s. 15 (s. 16(3)) and had to have been made deliberately or recklessly. The obtaining had resulted from the deception. The pecuniary advantage could be for D or another. D had to have acted dishonestly.

D committed the s. 16(2)(b) offence where he was allowed to borrow by way of overdraft. This might occur where D deceived the bank into granting him an overdraft facility in which case the offence was complete even though D never used the facility (see *Watkins* [1976] 1 All ER 578). Alternatively, D committed this offence where he wrote cheques using a cheque card which the bank was then bound to honour, and either went into overdraft when he had no authorisation to do so or exceeded his overdraft limit (see *Charles* **12.2.1.2** *ante*).

This offence could also be committed where D was allowed to take out an insurance policy or annuity contract, or where he obtained improved terms in relation to either of these. For example, if D took out an endowment policy falsely representing that he was a non-smoker when he was a smoker, or that he had not had a test for HIV when he had, and obtained improved terms either in the level of cover or a reduction in the payments, or obtained cover when he would not otherwise have done so, he would be guilty of this offence.

If D by deception obtained employment (or a promotion) he could be guilty of the s. 16(2)(c) offence even if he never drew any remuneration. The offence was confined, however, to the earning of remuneration in an 'office or employment' but 'employment' was construed widely to include contracts for services and was not confined to contracts of service (see *Callender* [1992] 4 All ER 51).

Where D by deception obtained an opportunity to bet, for example, on a horse race, and won, the winnings were not obtained by deception but rather because D chose the winning horse (*Clucas* [1949] 2 KB 226). He could not, therefore, be guilty of the s. 15 offence but he would fall within the bounds of s. 16(2)(c) whether or not he placed a winning bet; it was the 'opportunity' to win money by betting which he obtained by his deception.

12.3 Offences under the Fraud Act 2006

12.3.1 Introduction

In 2002 the Law Commission published its Report, *Fraud* (Law Com No. 276) in which it recommended the creation of a unitary offence of fraud which could be committed in three different ways. The aim was to simplify and rationalise the law on fraud. In particular, the proposed offence of fraud was a conduct crime designed to avoid the problems with the deception offences under the Theft Acts which arose from having to prove both that a person had been deceived and that the deception had caused the relevant obtaining or evasion (see *Charles, Lambie,* and *Preddy ante*). The particularity of the existing offences meant that on occasions new and unforeseen methods of committing fraud, often due to the exploitation of new technology, were not covered by existing offences, as where, for example, computers had been introduced to dispense services automatically without the need for any human intervention. In addition, the complexity of the existing law often meant that prosecutors charged the wrong offence or, in seeking to avoid this possibility, charged too many offences thereby unnecessarily complicating trials. The requirement of proof of a deception also meant that certain dishonest activities which caused loss to another might not be covered, for example, where D abused a position of trust he held in relation to V, or where he failed to disclose information thereby taking advantage of V's ignorance. The offence of fraud was to be supplemented by a new offence of obtaining services dishonestly to replace the offence of obtaining services by deception and cover both the prevalent behaviour of deceiving a machine, which the existing offence did not cover, and other forms of dishonest conduct where a service was obtained without anyone being deceived.

In 2004 the Government, while broadly accepting the Law Commission's proposals, issued a Consultation Paper, *Fraud Law Reform: Consultation on Proposals for Legislation* (Home Office, 2004), followed by its response to the consultation in *Fraud Law Reform: Government Response to Consultations* (Home Office Criminal Policy Unit, 2005). In 2005 the Government introduced the Fraud Bill which largely adopted the Law Commission's recommendations with the exception that it did not provide for the abolition of the common law offence of conspiracy to defraud because of concerns expressed in the consultation as to limitations on the scope of statutory conspiracy which meant that certain types of secondary participation in fraud might only be caught by the common law offence. In November 2006 the Fraud Act 2006 was enacted, coming into force on 15 January 2007. The FA 2006 repealed the deception offences in ss. 15, 15A, 16, and 20(2) of the TA 1968 and ss. 1 and 2 of the TA 1978. The FA 2006 also creates the offences of possession of articles for use in frauds (s. 6), making or supplying articles for use in frauds (s. 7), participating in fraudulent business carried on by sole trader (s. 9), and participating in fraudulent business carried on by company (s. 10).

12.3.2 Fraud

Section 1(1) of the FA 2006 creates the general offence of fraud which is committed where a person breaches ss. 2, 3, or 4 which provide for different ways of committing the offence. On summary conviction the maximum sentence is 12 months' imprisonment or a fine up to the maximum or both. Following conviction on indictment the maximum sentence is 10 years' imprisonment or a fine or both.

In the text which follows reference will be made to cases under the Theft Acts as these are still relevant when construing some of the terminology and considering some of the concepts in the FA 2006.

12.3.2.1 Fraud by false representation

Section 2(1) provides that a person is in breach of s. 2 if he:

  (a) dishonestly makes a false representation, and
  (b) intends, by making the representation—
      (i) to make a gain for himself or another, or
      (ii) to cause loss to another or to expose another to a risk of loss.

12.3.2.1.1 Actus reus

Fraud is a conduct crime which means that there is no need to prove that any particular result ensued. The *actus reus* consists of the making of a false representation. There is no requirement that anyone should actually believe or act upon the representation. The offence is complete upon a false representation being made with the requisite *mens rea*. Thus, for example, D would be guilty of fraud where he writes a letter to V, his elderly aunt, falsely stating that he is penniless and asking her for a loan, even though the letter is lost in the post and never delivered to V. Unlike the old offences of obtaining by deception under the Theft Acts, there is no requirement to prove that D obtained anything as a result of the false representation, although this may be D's purpose when making the false representation. The new offence, accordingly, is much broader than the old offences and, indeed, has the potential to cover conduct which would not even have been caught by the offence of attempt. This offence, consequently, has the potential to criminalise many commercial practices which exploit the gullibility of consumers. In effect misleading or exaggerated advertising claims, which clearly have a financial motive in boosting sales, have the potential to found convictions for fraud where everything would hinge on a jury's assessment of dishonesty. Much, ultimately, will depend on the discretion of prosecutors in determining which cases to prosecute. Undoubtedly they will place considerable store on the question whether or not a gain or loss has arisen even though this need not be proved as an element of the *actus reus*.

(a) *What is a representation?* Section 2(3) of the FA 2006 defines 'representation' as meaning:

> any representation as to fact or law, including a representation as to the state of mind of—
>
> (a) the person making the representation, or
>
> (b) any other person.

Before analysing this provision in any detail, it should be noted that, as with deception, **a representation may arise from words or conduct and**, as s. 2(4) makes clear, **may be express or implied** (see **12.2.1.1.3** *ante*). For example, if D offers to sell a painting (even though he does not own it), he is impliedly representing that he has a right to do so.

What s. 2(3) does not define, of course, is what amounts to a 'representation' albeit that this word is in everyday usage and 'misrepresentation' is a familiar civil law concept. **The provision, rather, seeks to define what the representation must be about, namely, any fact, law, or state of mind.**

A representation as to law would cover, for example, the situation where D misrepresents to P the legal effect of a document P is executing. Representations, however, generally relate to facts whether past or present. A straightforward representation of fact would be, for example, 'this bracelet is solid 24 carat gold' when D knows it is only gold plated. Such representations of fact are unlikely to be problematic. A problem arises, however, in relation to statements of opinion. It is the practice of those selling goods or supplying services to make extravagant claims about those goods or services. How many times do secondhand car salesmen seek to induce sales by declaring, 'this car is a good little runner' or 'a genuine bargain'?

While this is a statement of opinion, it is also an implied representation of fact, namely that it is D's opinion honestly held. If D knows that the car in question has several mechanical defects which cause it to stop regularly or break down and which would necessitate a considerable expenditure of money to rectify, it would not be his honest opinion that the car is either a 'good little runner' or 'a genuine bargain'. Thus, if D's opinion is not honestly held, his statement, although appearing to be one of opinion, is, in reality, a false representation of fact because he does not hold the opinion expressed.

A statement of present intention is a representation as to state of mind and is also a statement of fact. For example, if D asks P for money to fund his university course, his intention being to use the money to bet on a horse, he would be falsely representing his state of mind (i.e. his intention). A statement of intention may be implied from D's conduct as in *DPP* v *Ray* [1974] AC 370.

> D ordered a meal in a restaurant intending to pay for it. After eating the meal he decided not to pay and sat at his table until the waiter left the room at which point he departed without paying. The House of Lords held that there was a deception. Lord MacDermott took the view that the initial representation that he would pay, implied from ordering a meal, was a continuing one which remained live and operative and became false upon his change of mind. Lords Morris and Pearson took the view that by remaining at the table after he had changed his mind he continued to make from moment to moment, but now falsely, the representation that he intended to pay.

The principle in *Ray* has wide application. For example, P telephones D, in response to D's advertisement that he has a cooker for sale, and D represents that it is in good working order. Subsequently D discovers that the oven is not working. The representation he made was true when he made it. When P inspects the cooker, which is disconnected, and agrees to buy it, D may be guilty of fraud by false representation either on the basis that the original representation was a continuing one which remained live and operative until the contract was concluded, or that, while negotiations were being conducted, D continued to make from moment to moment, but now falsely, the representation that the cooker was in good working order. In effect, in situations such as this D is under a duty to correct P's misapprehension as soon as the situation has changed such that the earlier representation is falsified.

Ray was applied in *Rai* [2000] 1 Cr App R 242 where D had applied to the council for a grant to provide a bathroom downstairs in his house for the use of his mother who was infirm. The grant was approved but two days after D received notification of this, his mother died. D did not inform the council of this fact and the building work went ahead. D was charged with obtaining services by deception contrary to s. 1(1) of the Theft Act 1978. On appeal against conviction, the Court of Appeal held that D's acquiescence in letting the work be done amounted to deception by conduct as the local authority continued to believe the property would be occupied by his mother. D's offence now would be fraud by false representation. Similarly, if D asks P for a loan he impliedly represents that he will repay it by using the term 'loan' rather than 'gift'. If it is not his present intention to repay he will be guilty of fraud by false representation. If D's intention at the time of his request was to repay the loan, but having received the loan, D decides not to repay it, he will not be guilty of fraud by false representation as his representation was not false at the time of making it and the representation is not of a continuing nature.

Of course, if D makes some further false representation to P to seek to discourage P from enforcing the debt, he would at that point be liable for fraud.

Generally, where contracts for services or for the sale of property are involved, the provider of the service or vendor of the property may charge whatever he likes. An excessive quotation, however, may constitute a false representation where a situation of mutual trust exists between D and his customer or, perhaps, where D knows that his customer is naive or inexperienced and is relying on D's expertise and honesty. In *Silverman* [1987] Crim LR 574, D was known to two elderly sisters having done work for them for many years. He charged them grossly excessive prices for work he did on their property. In this situation of mutual trust, the implied representation was that his charge was fair and proper, which D knew to be untrue. The Court of Appeal found that 'his silence on any matter other than the sums to be charged was as eloquent as if he had said that he was going to make no more than a modest profit'. (See further *Jones, The Times*, 15 February 1993.)

The use of cheques, cheque cards, and credit cards has presented the courts with particular problems. Where D draws a cheque in favour of P, for example, in payment for property supplied by P, the act of drawing the cheque involves certain implied representations. First, D is representing that he has an account with the bank upon which the cheque is drawn; if D has stolen the cheque his conduct in drawing it in favour of P will involve a false representation. In many cases, however, the problem is not that D does not have an account, but rather relates to the state of the account he does have. Where D draws a cheque in favour of P he is representing that the present facts are such that, in the ordinary course of events, the cheque will be honoured by the bank when presented (see *Metropolitan Police Commissioner v Charles* [1977] AC 177). This representation will be true provided either (i) D believes that there are currently sufficient funds in the account to meet the cheque; (ii) he intends to pay in sufficient funds; (iii) he believes a third party will pay in sufficient funds (for example, his employer may pay his salary directly into his account); or (iv) in the case of a post-dated cheque, he believes that by the time the date for presenting the cheque arrives his account will contain sufficient funds to meet the cheque (see *Gilmartin* [1983] QB 953). If D does not have such a present intention or belief, his drawing of the cheque amounts to a representation of a present fact (his intention or belief) which is untrue.

Where a cheque is supported by a cheque card, the situation is not quite so straightforward. Provided the conditions on a cheque card are observed, the bank is legally bound to honour the cheque even though D's authority to use the card may have been withdrawn or D has neither sufficient funds in his account nor sufficient overdraft facility to cover the cheque. When a person presents a cheque card he makes a contract on behalf of the bank with the payee to the effect that the bank will honour the cheque.

> In *Charles (ante)*, D obtained gambling chips at a casino in return for 25 cheques for £30 each, all supported by a cheque card. D knew his account was overdrawn and that he had no authority to overdraw and thus no authority to draw further cheques. The conditions on the card, however, had been observed so D could not be guilty of a deception in representing that each cheque would be honoured by his bank. In upholding D's conviction of obtaining a pecuniary advantage by deception contrary to s. 16(1), the House of Lords held, however, that D's presentation of the cheque

card involved the implied representation that he had the authority of the bank to use the card so as to create a contractual relationship between the bank and the payee.

In a prosecution for fraud by false representation, the same implied representation could be relied upon.

The principle in *Charles* was extended to credit cards in *Lambie* [1982] AC 449. Suppliers of goods and services accept credit cards in pursuance of agreements they have entered into with the credit card companies under which the companies agree to honour credit card transactions provided the supplier complies with certain conditions relating to the validity of the card.

> In *Lambie* D had a credit card which gave her credit facilities up to a limit of £200. Knowing she had exceeded this limit and that authority to use the card had been withdrawn by the credit card company, D purchased goods from a shop using her credit card. The shop complied with the relevant conditions so that a valid transaction was concluded which the credit card company was bound to honour. The House of Lords held that in presenting the credit card D was representing (falsely) that she had the authority of the credit card company to use the card.

The Explanatory Notes to the FA 2006 provide a contemporary example of false representation, 'phishing' (para. 16):

> where a person disseminates an email to large groups of people falsely representing that the email has been sent by a legitimate financial institution. The email prompts the reader to provide information such as credit card and bank account numbers so that the 'phisher' can gain access to others' assets.

(b) **When is a representation false?** Section 2(2) provides that **a representation is false if (a) it is untrue or misleading, and (b) D knows that it is, or might be so.** This provision contains an element of the *actus reus* in (a) and an element of the *mens rea* in (b). The representation must be either untrue as a matter of fact or misleading. In their 2005 response to the consultations, the Home Office provided the following explanation of 'misleading' as meaning '**less than wholly true and capable of an interpretation to the detriment of the victim**' (para. 19).

Example

D drafts an email with the heading 'Sponsored Swim to Support Cancer Research' and sends it to family, friends, and neighbours. D carries out the swim, collects the sponsor money from those who responded to his email, and donates 5% to Cancer Research and keeps the rest. While D has carried out the swim and money he has collected has been donated to support Cancer Research, it is likely that a jury would consider his email to be misleading.

(c) **When is a representation made?** Ordinarily a representation will be made when D communicates it to the person he is seeking to deceive. The Act, however, does not impose any requirement that the representation be heard or received by another. Thus if D speaks to V and makes a false representation with the necessary *mens rea*, the offence is complete even though V is deaf and did not hear D's representation. Likewise, if the representation is made in a letter, the offence will be complete on D posting the letter even if it never reaches the addressee.

Section 2(5) makes express provision for the situation where the representation D makes is made to a machine and no human agent is involved in receiving or perceiving it.

Section 2(5) provides:

> For the purposes of this section a representation may be regarded as made if it (or any-thing implying it) is submitted in any form to any system or device designed to receive, convey or respond to communications (with or without human intervention).

The Explanatory Notes to the FA 2006 (at para. 17) express the main purpose of this provision to be to cover the situation where D makes a representation to a machine and a response can be produced without any need for human involve-ment. An obvious example would be where D acquires V's cashcard and PIN and uses them at a cash machine (ATM) to obtain money. The cash machine responds to the insertion of the card, accompanied by the correct PIN, and responds to the request for cash without any human agent playing a part in the process before the cash is dispensed. Section 2(5) is not confined to situations involving modern tech-nology. As the Explanatory Notes make clear it covers the situation where 'a false statement is submitted to a system for dealing with communications but is not in fact communicated to a human being (e.g. postal or messenger systems)'. Similarly, a message left on an answerphone or voicemail system would be covered.

12.3.2.1.2 Mens rea

There are three elements to the *mens rea* of this offence namely, knowledge, inten-tion, and dishonesty. They will be considered in turn.

(a) *Knowing the representation is or might be false* As stated earlier, liability can only arise where the representation made is actually false in the sense of being untrue or misleading. For D to be found guilty it must be proved that he either knew that the representation he made was untrue or misleading or he knew that it might be so (s. 2(2)(b) of the FA 2006). **What is required is either actual knowledge or a recognition that the representation might be untrue or misleading and a decision to make it nonetheless.** While the latter state of mind is akin to recklessness, it is not entirely the same as recklessness as recklessness involves taking a recognised risk where it is unreasonable in all the circumstances to do so. There is no element of unreasonableness for the jury to consider under s. 2(2)(b) but, of course, the element of dishonesty will be crucial in the ultimate assessment of guilt. In the Consultation concern was raised over art sales, for example, where D offers a painting for sale as a Renoir. In art sales there is always a risk that a painting either may be incorrectly attributed to an artist or be a fake. The Government's *Response to Consultations* states (at para. 18):

> An example was given of a seller of a Renoir painting which turns out to be incorrectly attributed. It was argued that, given the inevitable uncertainties in such areas, the seller would only be able to protect himself from a fraud charge if he had said 'I honestly believe this to be a Renoir' rather than 'This is a painting by Renoir'. We do not agree as the 'dishonesty' requirement will assist in drawing the line in marginal cases. But if the consequence were that sellers became more cautious in their statements this does not seem an undesirable result.

(b) *Intending to make a gain or cause a loss* The offence is one of ulterior intent. Section 2(1) provides that a person is in breach of the section if he:

> (b) intends, by making the representation—
>> (i) to make a gain for himself or another, or
>> (ii) to cause loss to another or to expose another to a risk of loss.

As the *actus reus* is complete upon a false representation being made, there is no need that anyone suffer any loss, or be exposed to the risk of loss, or that D, or another, actually make any gain. What is crucial is that **D's intent in making the false representation must be that of making a gain or causing a loss or exposing another to the risk of loss.** This provision is similar to blackmail under s. 21 of the TA 1968 where an unwarranted demand with menaces is made 'with a view to gain for himself or another or with intent to cause loss to another'. In blackmail the term used is 'with a view to' which it is difficult to distinguish from intent. Blackmail lacks, however, the alternative element of exposing another to a risk of loss.

This provision was introduced at the recommendation of the Law Commission to cover situations where V's economic interests are imperilled such as occurred in *Adams* v *The Queen* [1995] 1 WLR 52, *Allsop* (1976) 64 Cr App R 29, and *Wai Yu-tsang* v *R* [1991] 4 All ER 664 (see **8.3.4.1.1** and **8.3.4.1.2** *ante*). These cases involved conspiracy to defraud but the same activities carried out by an individual would now fall under the offence of fraud. The provision is included largely out of an abundance of caution as the purpose of most schemes promoted by false representations is to make a gain for someone. It will be rare, indeed, for a scheme to involve only the risk of loss without there also being an intent for someone to make a gain.

Section 5 defines 'gain and loss'.

 Example

> D falsely represents to V that he has inside information and that a particular horse is a certain winner and encourages V to bet £100 on it. If the horse wins, V will suffer no loss—indeed, he will make a considerable gain. D's intent, however, is to expose V to the risk of loss. Whether or not he is acting dishonestly will be a matter for the jury.

Even in this example, there is a gain to someone if the bet fails, namely the bookmaker, and the concept of oblique intent could readily be applied to satisfy the requirement of an intention to make a gain for another as, while that may not be D's direct intent, it is an inevitable consequence if the horse loses. Indeed, as a gain need only be temporary, there is a gain to the bookmaker upon receipt of the bet.

> (2) 'Gain' and 'loss'—
>> (a) extend only to gain or loss in money or other property;
>> (b) include any such gain or loss whether temporary or permanent;
>
> and 'property' means any property whether real or personal (including things in action and other intangible property).

This definition is consistent with that of 'property' in s. 4(1) of the TA 1968 (see **11.2.1.1** *ante*).

> (3) 'Gain' includes a gain by keeping what one has, as well as a gain by getting what one does not have.
>
> (4) 'Loss' includes a loss by not getting what one might get, as well as a loss by parting with what one has.

'Gain' and 'loss' are defined consistently with s. 34(2)(a) of the TA 1968 (see **13.4.4** *post*). If D uses false representations with the intention of obtaining from V what V already owes him (and thus D is only seeking to acquire that to which he has a lawful claim), this may nevertheless fall within s. 5 of the FA 2006. In *Lawrence and Pomroy* (1971) 57 Cr App R 64, the Court of Appeal assumed that such would be the case in a blackmail case (see **13.4.2** *post*).

In *Parkes* [1973] Crim LR 358 (Sheffield Crown Court), D was charged with blackmail on the basis that he demanded with menaces money owed to him by V. It was submitted that to demand what is lawfully owing to you was not a demand 'with a view to gain'. Judge Dean QC ruled that by demanding money lawfully owing to him D did have a view to gain as 'gain' included 'getting what one has not'. By intending to obtain hard cash as opposed to a mere right of action in respect of the debt, D was getting more than he already had.

(c) **Dishonesty** This is a crucial element in the offence. Section 2(1) provides that a person only commits the offence of fraud by false representation where he 'dishonestly makes a false representation'. Both the Law Commission and the Home Office consider that the *Ghosh* test applies, that is first whether D's conduct would be regarded as dishonest by the ordinary standards of reasonable and honest people, and secondly, whether D was aware that his conduct would be so regarded (see **11.2.2.2** *ante* noting that s. 2 of the TA 1968 does not apply to fraud offences).

12.3.2.2 Fraud by failing to disclose information

Section 3 of the FA 2006 provides:

A person is in breach of this section if he—

> (a) dishonestly fails to disclose to another person information which he is under a legal duty to disclose, and
>
> (b) intends, by failing to disclose the information—
>
> > (i) to make a gain for himself or another, or
> >
> > (ii) to cause loss to another or to expose another to a risk of loss.

The Law Commission recommended in its Report, *Fraud* (Law Com No. 276, paras. 7.22–7.34) a wider offence which would have incorporated situations falling short of a legal duty of disclosure where there was a moral duty to do so because V trusted D to make disclosure of information and it was reasonable to expect him to do so. The Law Commission provided the following example (at para. 7.33):

> For example, a dealer buying an antique is guilty of fraudulent nondisclosure if she knows that the seller is trusting her to disclose any marked discrepancy between the

price offered and the true value of the item, *and* it is reasonable to expect her to do so. This is a question of degree. If the dealer knows that she can resell the item for £10,000, but does not disclose this and offers only £2,000, it would be open to a jury to conclude that her failure to disclose the true value was unreasonable. It would be otherwise if she did not expect to be able to resell the item for more than, say, £4,000, because it is not reasonable to expect a dealer to disclose the full extent of the reasonable profit she hopes to make, and such a mark-up would be within the bands of what is reasonable. In such a case we would expect the court to direct an acquittal, on the basis that no reasonable jury could be sure that it was reasonable to expect the defendant to disclose the information in question.

There would be a large number of imponderables in this situation which a jury would be left to determine before convicting the antique dealer. The Law Commission identified these (para. 7.34):

> Whether the defendant is trusted to make disclosure, and if so whether a failure to disclose the information in question is unreasonable, will depend on a variety of factors— for example, whether the defendant is believed by the other to have special expertise, and if so whether the defendant has induced the other to believe this; whether the other has such expertise; the value of the transaction, from the other's point of view; whether the other is in receipt of legal, financial or other advice; and so on. A trial judge would of course remind a jury of any such factor that may have particular relevance to the facts of the case.

The Government in its response to the consultation concluded that this proposal would create an undesirably wide offence with the potential for conflict between the civil law and criminal law as it would become criminal to fail to provide information which D was not under any civil law duty to provide. Such a conflict would mirror that which already exists in theft following the decision in *Hinks* (see **11.2.1.5.3** *ante*). In extreme cases, in any event, it may be possible to charge fraud by false representation where D's conduct involves an implied representation (see *Silverman* **12.3.2.1.1** *ante*). In this case, however, a crucial factor was the course of previous dealing which had built up an expectation on the part of V that D would quote a fair price for any work done.

12.3.2.2.1 Actus reus

The *actus reus* comprises a failure to disclose to another information which D is under a legal duty to disclose. The mischief which is targeted is that of V acting, or omitting to act, to his economic detriment in reliance upon his trusting D to disclose to him information relevant to his decision and D failing to make such disclosure. The Law Commission provided the following explanation which is reproduced in the Explanatory Notes to the FA 2006 (para. 18):

> 7.28...Such a duty may derive from statute (such as the provisions governing company prospectuses), from the fact that the transaction in question is one of the utmost good faith (such as a contract of insurance), from the express or implied terms of a contract, from the custom of a particular trade or market, or from the existence of a fiduciary relationship between the parties (such as that of agent and principal).

7.29 For this purpose there is a legal duty to disclose information not only if the defendant's failure to disclose it gives the victim a cause of action for damages, but also if the law gives the victim a right to set aside any change in his or her legal position to which he or she may consent as a result of the non-disclosure. For example, a person in a fiduciary position has a duty to disclose material information when entering into a contract with his or her beneficiary, in the sense that a failure to make such disclosure will entitle the beneficiary to rescind the contract and to reclaim any property transferred under it.

The Explanatory Notes give the following examples (at para. 19):

For example, the failure of a solicitor to share vital information with a client within the context of their work relationship, in order to perpetrate a fraud upon that client, would be covered by this section. Similarly, an offence could be committed under this section if a person intentionally failed to disclose information relating to his heart condition when making an application for life insurance.

In *Firth* (1990) 91 Cr App R 217, D, a consultant obstetrician, referred private patients to an NHS hospital for treatment, omitting to declare that they were private patients. D was convicted of obtaining an exemption from liability to make payment contrary to s. 2(1)(c) of the TA 1978. The Court of Appeal affirmed the conviction as D was under a duty to give the relevant information to the hospital. By deliberately and dishonestly refraining from so doing, with the result that no charge was levied on himself or his patients, he had obtained the exemption by deception. The relevant offence now would be fraud under s. 3 by failing to disclose information. It is arguable that D's act of sending the patients to an NHS hospital would also amount to an implied false representation that they were NHS patients bringing D also within the offence of fraud by false representation.

In an era where inflated claims within, and omissions from, CVs has become almost *de rigueur, Razoq* [2012] EWCA Crim 674 is a timely reminder that such actions may amount to crimes. D, who was a doctor suspended from practice by the hospital where he worked, applied for, and obtained, several locum positions failing to disclose his suspension, and falsely claiming qualifications and experience he did not have. He was convicted of seven offences involving breaches of ss. 2 and 3. As regards the s. 3 offences, as the contractual documents relating to each position required disclosure, his failure to disclose his suspension breached an express legal duty arising under contract. Even if the contracts had not contained such express terms, it would have been open to the jury to convict if satisfied that the legal duty arose (1) as an implied term of the contract and the conditions under which the doctor was registered with the GMC, or (2) because the contracts into which he entered were contracts of utmost good faith.

12.3.2.2.2 Mens rea

The *mens rea* for this offence is (1) an intention to make a gain or cause a loss (or expose to the risk of loss) as for fraud by false representation, and (2) dishonesty. There is no requirement that D should know that he is under, or might be under, a legal duty to disclose information. D's ignorance of such a legal duty, however, will be highly relevant to the question whether or not he was dishonest.

12.3.2.3 Fraud by abuse of position

Section 4 of the FA 2006 provides:

> (1) A person is in breach of this section if he—
>
>   (a) occupies a position in which he is expected to safeguard, or not to act against, the financial interests of another person,
>
>   (b) dishonestly abuses that position, and
>
>   (c) intends, by means of the abuse of that position—
>
>   (i) to make a gain for himself or another, or
>
>   (ii) to cause loss to another or to expose another to a risk of loss.
>
> (2) A person may be regarded as having abused his position even though his conduct consisted of an omission rather than an act.

This provision aims to deal with the mischief where V has voluntarily placed D in a privileged position in relation to V's financial interests such that D is able to act in relation to those interests without reference to V. The Law Commission provided (at para. 7.36) the example of an 'employee who, without the knowledge of his employer, misuses his or her position to make a personal profit at the employer's expense'. For example, the cinema employees who lent films temporarily to S so that he could make copies of them to sell would now be guilty of the s. 4 offence (see *Scott v Metropolitan Police Commissioner* [1975] AC 819, **8.3.4.1.1** *ante*). In such a situation of trust D will be expected to safeguard V's financial interests or not act against them. The Law Commission explained their thinking (at paras. 7.37–7.38):

> Such an expectation to safeguard or power to damage may arise, for example, because the defendant is given authority to exercise a discretion on the victim's behalf, or is given access to the victim's assets, premises, equipment or customers. In these cases the defendant does not need to enlist the victim's *further* co-operation in order to secure the desired result, because the necessary co-operation has been given in advance.
>
> The necessary relationship will be present between trustee and beneficiary, director and company, professional person and client, agent and principal, employee and employer, or between partners. It may arise otherwise, for example within a family, or in the context of voluntary work, or in any context where the parties are not at arm's length. In nearly all cases where it arises, it will be recognised by the civil law as importing fiduciary duties, and any relationship that is so recognised will suffice. We see no reason, however, why the existence of such duties should be essential. This does not of course mean that it would be entirely a matter for the fact-finders whether the necessary relationship exists. The question whether the particular facts alleged can properly be described as giving rise to that relationship will be an issue capable of being ruled upon by the judge and, if the case goes to the jury, of being the subject of directions.

12.3.2.3.1 Actus reus

The offence may be committed both by act or omission. The question whether or not D is in the necessary position in relation to V and his financial interests is initially one for the judge who will determine whether the relationship is capable of falling within the section, and then it is for the jury to determine whether or not it does. The Explanatory Notes to the FA 2006 provide the following examples (at paras. 22 and 23):

> An employee of a software company who uses his position to clone software products with the intention of selling the products on would commit an offence under this section.
>
>   Another example covered by this section is where a person who is employed to care for an elderly or disabled person has access to that person's bank account and abuses his position by transferring funds to invest in a high-risk business venture of his own.

In the first example, if D went ahead with his scheme he would hold the profits on constructive trust for his employer, but there is some doubt whether or not he could be convicted of theft of those profits (see *A-G's Reference (No. 1 of 1985)* [1986] QB 491 at **11.2.1.2.2** *ante*). The care assistant, however, could be convicted of theft of V's credit balance (cf. *Williams (Roy)* [2001] 1 Cr App R 362 at **11.2.1.1.2** *ante*). The advantage of the fraud offence, of course, is that it may be charged when D first acts to abuse his position before any loss might be suffered by V. In *Doukas* [1978] 1 WLR 372, D, a waiter at a hotel, was found in possession of bottles of wine which he intended to substitute for his employer's bottles when a customer ordered wine.

He would then make out a separate bill and pocket the money paid by the customer. D would now be guilty of fraud by abuse of position.

The Explanatory Notes provide the following example of a commission of this offence arising from an omission (at para. 21):

> an employee who fails to take up the chance of a crucial contract in order that an associate or rival company can take it up instead at the expense of the employer, commits an offence under this section.

12.3.2.3.2 Mens rea
The *mens rea* for this offence is (1) an intention to make a gain or cause a loss (or expose to the risk of loss) as for fraud by false representation, and (2) dishonesty. There is no requirement that D should know that he is in a position of trust in relation to V, although it is difficult to believe a judge would leave to a jury such a relationship if there was no evidence of knowledge on D's part. In any event, D's ignorance of the position of trust, however, will be highly relevant to the question whether or not he was dishonest.

12.3.2.4 Ancillary offences
Section 6 of the FA 2006 creates the offence of possession of articles for use in fraud. This replaces the offence of going equipped to cheat under s. 25 of the TA 1968. The latter offence has been amended to become the offence of going equipped for burglary or theft.

Section 6(1) provides:

> A person is guilty of an offence if he has in his possession or under his control any article for use in the course of or in connection with any fraud.

This is potentially a very wide offence and could cover possession of pen and paper to write a letter containing a false representation, or possession of something as sophisticated as a cloning machine to clone credit cards. Mr Doukas, on his way to work in possession of the bottles of wine he intends to use to sell to customers in the restaurant, would now commit this offence. There is no need to prove that D possessed the relevant article to be used in the course of or in connection with a specific fraud, it being sufficient to prove that he had a general intention (see *Ellames* 60 Cr App R 7). This will be easier to do, however, where the relevant article has no legitimate purpose, for example, the credit card cloning machine.

Section 8 defines 'article' to include 'any program or data held in electronic form'. D's draft email in the Example at **12.3.2.1.1** *ante* would clearly fall within this provision as would his possession of the email program (e.g. Outlook Express) on his computer and the computer itself.

Section 7 of the FA 2006 creates the offence of making or supplying articles for fraud. Section 7(1) provides:

> A person is guilty of an offence if he makes, adapts, supplies or offers to supply any article—
>
> (a) knowing that it is designed or adapted for use in the course of or in connection with fraud, or
>
> (b) intending it to be used to commit, or assist in the commission of, fraud.

For example D would commit this offence if, knowing E intends to seek to defraud customers in his pub, he makes E a fake charity collection box to place on his counter, E intending to keep the proceeds himself. Likewise D would commit this offence where he supplies a credit card cloning machine to E. The Explanatory Notes to the FA 2006 give as an example, a person who makes devices to attach to electricity meters to cause them to malfunction and not record the electricity used.

12.3.2.5 Obtaining services dishonestly

Section 11 of the FA 2006 creates the offence of obtaining services dishonestly to replace the offence of obtaining services by deception contrary to s. 1 of the TA 1978. The maximum penalty on summary conviction is the same as for fraud but on conviction on indictment the maximum penalty is five years' imprisonment (s. 11(3) of the FA 2006). Unlike the offence of fraud, this is a result crime as it must be proved that the services have actually been obtained. Unlike the offence of obtaining services by deception, this offence does not require there to be any deception and thus there is no need to prove that the provider of the service has been deceived. The Explanatory Notes to the FA 2006 give the example of D climbing over a wall to watch a football match without paying the entrance fee. D does not deceive anyone in order to gain admission to the ground, but he does obtain a service which is provided on the basis that people pay for it. The absence of requirement that anyone be deceived also catches the situation where D engages in a transaction resulting in the obtaining of a service without any human agent determining that the service should be provided to D. The Explanatory Notes give the example of D using false credit card details to obtain data or software via an automated process over the internet where that data or software is made available only to those who have paid for access rights to that service. A further example given is that of D attaching a decoder to her television to enable viewing access to cable/satellite television channels for which she has no intention of paying.

Section 11 of the FA 2006 provides:

> (1) A person is guilty of an offence under this section if he obtains services for himself or another—
>
>   (a) by a dishonest act, and
>
>   (b) in breach of subsection (2).
>
> (2) A person obtains services in breach of this subsection if—
>
>   (a) they are made available on the basis that payment has been, is being or will be made for or in respect of them,
>
>   (b) he obtains them without any payment having been made for or in respect of them or without payment having been made in full, and
>
>   (c) when he obtains them, he knows—
>
>   (i) that they are being made available on the basis described in paragraph (a), or
>
>   (ii) that they might be,
>
> but intends that payment will not be made, or will not be made in full.

12.3.2.5.1 Actus reus

(a) *Dishonest act* **The offence requires that there be a dishonest act**—thus it cannot be committed by omission—resulting in D or another obtaining services. In the earlier example of the football match, the act would be climbing into the ground. If the relevant act is a false representation, for example, D says to the turnstile operator at the football ground that the person behind is paying for him, D could also be liable to conviction for fraud by false representation. If D is stopped immediately after he goes through the turnstile and before he has an opportunity to view the football match, he would not have obtained any service at that point but would have committed the fraud offence.

Dishonesty is a *mens rea* element.

(b) *Obtains* It must be proved **that as a result of D's dishonest act he obtained a service** to which the section applies. If, for example, owing to someone else's mistake, D is given access to satellite television channels which are only available to customers who have paid in advance for them, D's use of the channels would not amount to an offence as he has not performed any act which led to the obtaining of them. His omission to inform the provider of their mistake cannot amount to a dishonest act. Of course, a convoluted argument could be constructed that each time D switches to the relevant channel there is a separate obtaining. Everything would then hinge on whether or not a jury would be satisfied that tuning into that channel was a dishonest act and that it was done with the requisite knowledge and intent.

(c) *Services* The offence only applies to **services which are made available on the basis that 'payment has been, is being or will be made for or in respect of** them'. If the services are obtained on the understanding that no payment will be made for them, D cannot be guilty of this offence. For example, if D approaches a taxi and falsely represents to the taxi driver that she has been robbed and is unable to pay for the fare and he agrees to drive her to her destination for no charge, she has not obtained 'services' under s. 11 as the service was not made available on the basis that it would be paid for. D could be liable to conviction of fraud by false representation. By contrast, if D orders a taxi intending not to pay the fare and, when it arrives at her address, she gets into it and is driven to her destination where she then runs off without paying the taxi driver, D will have obtained services dishonestly. She would also be liable to conviction for fraud by false representation as by getting into the taxi she impliedly represents she is an honest customer who will pay for the fare. In addition, she could be convicted of making off without payment (see **13.1** *post*).

'Services' are not defined in the Act which leaves room for argument over what constitutes a service. Where a credit card is obtained or bank account opened as a result of a false representation, the card or account does not, itself, amount to a service but rather provides access to a range of facilities which underlie the card or account (see *Sofroniou* [2004] 1 Cr App R 35). This participation in the banking system is a service (*Sofroniou*) and could support a conviction for the s. 11 offence provided there is some charge for the service whether through an annual fee or other bank charges. It is arguable that the low interest rate on a current account or the higher interest rate on a credit card (and the commission fee levied on shops and businesses) means that these services are made available on the basis that payment has been or will be made for them. Thus inducing a bank to open an account with the intention of running up an overdraft on it and not repaying it, or to issue a credit card with the intent of spending up to the credit limit and not paying off the debt thereby incurred or interest charges on that debt, could constitute obtaining services dishonestly provided D had the necessary knowledge and intent.

(d) *Payment* The services which may be the subject of the s. 11 offence must be services made available on the basis that payment has been, is being or will be made for or in respect of them. **D must obtain the relevant service either without paying for it or without paying in full for it.** If D obtains a service by means of a false representation but pays for it in full, he would not appear to commit this offence. For example, D, aged 14, gains access to a cinema to watch an 18 plus film by convincing the sales assistant that he is 18. D pays for his ticket and watches the film. D does not commit the offence of fraud by false representation as he does not make a gain in terms of property or cause any loss to the cinema operator. D would have committed an offence under s. 1 of the TA 1978. The Law Commission in their Report of 2002 provide a further example where an offence would not be committed which would have been an offence under s. 1 of the TA 1978, namely 'where parents, who have every intention of paying all relevant fees, lie about a child's religious upbringing in order to obtain a place at a fee paying school.' Both the Law Commission and the Home Office in its *Response to the Consultations* considered that this type of behaviour should not be covered by the new offence which should be confined to situations where there is an intention not to pay.

12.3.2.5.2 **Mens rea**

There are three elements to the *mens rea* for this offence.

(a) *Dishonesty* In determining whether D's act was dishonest, the *Ghosh* test applies. This involves two questions: first, whether D's act would be regarded as dishonest by the ordinary standards of reasonable and honest people, and secondly, whether D was aware that his act would be so regarded (see **11.2.2.2** *ante* noting that s. 2 of the TA 1968 does not apply to this offence).

(b) *Knowledge* D must know either that the services are being made available on the basis that payment has been, is being or will be made for or in respect of them or that they might be being made available on that basis.

(c) *Intention* D must intend either not to pay for the service or not to pay in full for it. This intention must exist at the point that D obtains the service. It would appear, however, that the intent should also exist when D does the relevant act which leads to the obtaining if that act is to be considered dishonest. If D has the intent on doing the dishonest act but changes his mind before the obtaining occurs, he will not be liable for the s. 11 offence although, of course, he may be liable for attempt.

It is not clear whether the intent not to pay means an intent never to pay as opposed to an intent not to pay at the time when payment is due. By analogy with making off without payment, it is assumed that an intent never to pay is what is required (see *Allen* [1985] AC 1029, **13.1.2** *post*).

FURTHER READING

J. Collins, 'Fraud by Abuse of Position: Theorising Section 4 of the Fraud Act 2006' [2011] Crim LR 513.

R. Sullivan, 'Fraud–The Latest Law Commission Proposals' (2003) 67 JCL 139.

13

Further offences under the Theft Acts

13.1 Making off without payment

There are certain situations where D obtains property or services, or seeks to evade his liability to pay, which do not fall within the offence of theft or the fraud offences examined in **Chapter 12**. For example, if D obtains ownership and possession of property from P and then decides not to pay, he is not guilty of theft as the property belongs to him (see *Edwards* v *Ddin* (1976) 63 Cr App R 218). If D makes no false representation to obtain the property he is not guilty of fraud by false representation. If D makes off from the place where he obtained the property and where payment was due, for example, by simply driving away from a self-service filling station without any false representation, he does not commit fraud. Section 3 of the TA 1978 was enacted to cover situations such as these where a debtor, seeking to avoid paying his debt, removes himself from the scene where his liability was incurred. Such conduct is commonly referred to as 'bilking'. Section 3 does not require proof that the property involved belonged to another, or that there was any false representation practised.

Section 3(1) of the TA 1978 provides:

> Subject to subsection (3) below, a person who, knowing that payment on the spot for any goods supplied or service done is required or expected from him, dishonestly makes off without having paid as required or expected and with intent to avoid payment of the amount due shall be guilty of an offence.

The offence is punishable on conviction on indictment with up to two years' imprisonment (s. 4(2)(b)), and on summary conviction with up to six months' imprisonment and/or a fine not exceeding £2,000 (s. 4(3)).

13.1.1 *Actus reus*

13.1.1.1 Goods supplied or service done

The goods must be supplied. This is satisfied either by P delivering the goods to D or D being permitted to take them, for example, by filling his petrol tank at a self-service filling station or by taking goods from a supermarket shelf. If D takes goods from a shop which is not self-service he does not commit this offence although he may commit theft. If he takes goods in a self-service supermarket he may be guilty of both offences.

Where services are involved the service must be 'done'. Mending D's shoes, letting a room in an hotel, supplying a meal in a restaurant, or hiring D a car are all examples of a 'service done'. The latter two examples also, incidentally, involve the supply of goods. The use of a facility which P provides, for example, using a car park, would also be regarded as a 'service done' so that D would commit this offence if he drove out without paying the charge due. By contrast, if D surreptitiously enters P's theatre, watches a performance, and leaves without paying, it would be difficult to construe the performance as a 'service done' as P has not permitted D's entry in the way entry is permitted to a car park.

Section 3(3) provides that:

> Subsection (1) above shall not apply where the supply of the goods or the doing of the service is contrary to law, or where the service done is such that payment is not legally enforceable.

The supply of goods would be contrary to law, for example, when P sells prohibited drugs to D, or serves alcohol to D who is under 18. Likewise the supply of the service may be contrary to law, for example, in a brothel or an unlicensed casino. Finally, payment for the service may not be legally enforceable, for example, gaming debts are not legally enforceable, a prostitute cannot sue her client for payment for her services, and payment for the provision of lawful services to a minor is only legally enforceable where the service provided is a 'necessary'. If a minor has a course of beauty treatment at an expensive salon and makes off without paying she would commit no offence as the treatment is not a 'necessary' and, accordingly, payment is not legally enforceable. By contrast if she goes to the nearest branch of 'Boots' and is supplied with expensive beauty products and leaves without paying, although these are not 'necessaries' and payment would not be legally enforceable, she would be guilty of the s. 3 offence and probably of theft.

13.1.1.2 Making off

D must make off from the spot where payment is required (*McDavitt* [1981] Crim LR 843). There may be more than one 'spot' or the 'spot' may cover a very wide area; where a passenger on the underground fails to buy a ticket, the spot where he commits the offence includes the exit barrier to the underground and is not confined to the place where a ticket should be bought before the journey commences (see *Moberly* v *Alsop*, *The Times*, 13 December 1991, DC; see further *Aziz* [1993] Crim LR 708). If D is caught climbing through a window to leave a hotel he will not have made off but he may be guilty of attempt. 'Makes off' is a broad term which will cover the situation where D leaves by stealth or where he openly runs off, for example, by jumping out of a taxi and running away when it stops at his destination. It was suggested at one time that there could not be a 'making off' where P consented to D's departure as a result of a deception by D, for example, D tells the hotel manager that he has settled the bill with the receptionist and is then assisted into his taxi by the manager. The Court of Appeal in *Brooks and Brooks* (1983) 76 Cr App R 66, did not accept that the term was limited in this way taking the view that 'makes off' means 'departs' regardless of how that departure is effected. The Court emphasised that the crucial consideration was whether the 'making off' was dishonest.

13.1.1.3 Without having paid as required or expected

Payment on the spot for the goods or services must be required or expected. Section 3(2) provides that '"payment on the spot" includes payment at the time of collecting goods on which work has been done or in respect of which service has been provided'. D's departure must be made without paying in the way required or expected. Where D, by false representation, obtains the agreement of the person to whom payment is owed to his paying at some later date, the s. 3 offence is not committed as the requirement or expectation of payment on the spot no longer exists and the court should not explore whether that agreement was induced by deception (see *Vincent* [2001] EWCA Crim 295). The appropriate offence to charge in such a case is fraud by false representation. If D gives forged banknotes he does not pay. Where D pays by means of a worthless cheque the appropriate charge again would be fraud by false representation. The offence under s. 3 should not be charged. Where the cheque is supported by a cheque card, even though there are no funds in D's account, he will have paid P as the bank will be obliged to honour the cheque. Similarly, where D pays by credit card P will be paid as required or expected even if D uses it without authority (whether because his authority has been revoked or it is stolen) (see *Re Charge Card Services Ltd* [1988] 3 All ER 702). In these situations the appropriate charge is fraud by false representation.

13.1.2 *Mens rea*

The making off must be dishonest. In addition it must be proved that D knew that payment on the spot was required or expected of him. If D honestly believed that the goods were supplied or the service done on credit and that he would be invoiced later he would not be guilty. Similarly, if D believed that someone else had paid or was going to pay, he would not be guilty.

It was originally believed that the offence was committed where D's intention in making off was merely to avoid payment on the spot at that time, even though he may have intended to pay later. In *Allen* [1985] AC 1029, the House of Lords held that an intention to permanently avoid payment was required.

13.2 Burglary

Section 9 of the TA 1968 provides:

(1) A person is guilty of burglary if—
  (a) he enters any building or part of a building as a trespasser and with intent to commit any such offence as is mentioned in subsection (2) below; or
  (b) having entered any building or part of a building as a trespasser he steals or attempts to steal anything in the building or that part of it or inflicts or attempts to inflict on any person therein any grievous bodily harm.

(2) The offences referred to in subsection (1)(a) above are offences of stealing anything in the building or part of a building in question, of inflicting on any person therein any grievous bodily harm, and of doing unlawful damage to the building or anything therein.

(3) References in subsections (1) and (2) above to a building shall apply also to an inhabited vehicle or vessel, and shall apply to any such vehicle or vessel at the times when a person having a habitation in it is not there as well as at times when he is.

(4) A person guilty of burglary shall on conviction on indictment be liable to imprisonment for a term not exceeding fourteen years.

Section 9 creates two separate offences of burglary. The first offence under s. 9(1)(a) requires proof of entry as a trespasser and of the ulterior intent at that time to commit one of the three offences specified in sub-s. (2). (Subsection (2) used to include a fourth offence of rape; rape was removed from the list by s. 63(1) of the Sexual Offences Act 2003 which creates a much broader offence of trespassing on any premises with intent to commit a relevant sexual offence.) **The second offence requires proof of entry as a trespasser and of commission of theft or inflicting grievous bodily harm or an attempt to commit either of these offences.** In most cases where the second offence is committed D will also have committed the first offence at an earlier stage. The two offences in sub-s. (1), however, are separate and on an indictment for one there can be no conviction of the other (*Hollis* [1971] Crim LR 525). The second offence, however, also covers cases where D entered as a trespasser without having the requisite ulterior intent at that time but subsequently did commit theft or inflict grievous bodily harm or attempt to do so.

13.2.1 Entry as a trespasser

13.2.1.1 Entry

In *Collins* [1973] QB 100, D climbed a ladder and observed P lying naked on her bed asleep. He descended, stripped naked (apart from his socks) and ascended again stopping on the window sill. P, thinking this naked person was her boyfriend, beckoned him in and they had sexual intercourse before she discovered her mistake. D was convicted of burglary on the basis that he entered as a trespasser intending to commit rape. One of the issues in the case was whether D had entered before P beckoned to him. Edmund-Davies LJ stated that it had to be proved that D had made 'an effective and substantial entry' before consent had been apparently given.

This appeared to abandon the old common law rule that insertion of any part of the body, however minimal, was sufficient to constitute an entry whether the purpose of the insertion was to commit the ulterior felony or merely to effect entry (see *Bailey* (1818) R & R 341). In *Brown* [1985] Crim LR 611, **the Court of Appeal took the view that all that was required was that the entry be 'effective' and that the question was one of fact for the jury.** In the instant case the jury were entitled to find that there had been an effective entry where D was found with the top half of his body inside a shop window rummaging for goods. This left a problem unresolved, namely, what was the purpose for which the entry must be effective? Was the requirement simply that sufficient of D's body be inside the building to effect the purpose he had in mind? A hand inside a building would be sufficient entry to steal if some item was close to the point of entry. By contrast, if D's purpose was rape, on the facts of *Brown* there would not be an effective entry as his lower body remained outside the building. **As a burglary is complete when D has entered with the ulterior intent whether or not he commits the ulterior offence, it would seem to be going too far to require that his entry be sufficient to effect that purpose.**

> In *Ryan* [1996] Crim LR 320, D was found by an elderly householder trapped with his head and arm inside a window. He was convicted of burglary but appealed, contending that his actions could not constitute an 'entry' as he could not have stolen anything as he was firmly stuck. The Court of Appeal held, following *Brown*, that entry of part of his body could constitute an entry and it was irrelevant whether or not he was capable of stealing anything. The Court did not go so far as to declare that the insertion of any part of D's body is sufficient to constitute an entry preferring to leave the matter to juries to decide.

It is likely that the question of 'effectiveness' is now no longer relevant but a firmer declaration of the law by the Court of Appeal would have resolved the matter once and for all. Furthermore, by leaving the issue to the jury to decide, rather than expressly affirming the common law rule, similar cases may end up being decided differently by different juries.

A further problem relates to the insertion of instruments into a building either to effect the ulterior offence or to facilitate entry. At common law, if the instrument was inserted to effect the ulterior offence, this constituted an entry whereas, if it was inserted to facilitate access, this did not constitute entry. This probably remains the case. Where the instrument is used to facilitate access there will certainly be an attempt. If it is used to effect the ulterior offence, for example, to grab goods, it can be regarded as an extension of D's body.

If D uses an innocent agent to enter the building it is submitted that D commits trespass by that means. There is no reason in principle why burglary should be excluded from the principles relating to the commission of offences by means of innocent agents.

13.2.1.2 As a trespasser

In establishing whether a person enters as a trespasser, three questions arise: (1) what is trespass for the purposes of burglary? (2) did the person entering have permission to enter? (3) had he exceeded the limits of that permission?

13.2.1.2.1 *What is trespass for the purposes of burglary?*

Trespass is a civil concept. **Trespass, for the purposes of civil liability, is committed where a person intentionally, recklessly, or negligently enters a building in the possession of another without either permission to do so or a legal right to enter. D's entry must be voluntary.** There would be no trespass where D tripped and stumbled into a building or where he was dragged unwillingly into a building.

Mere proof of a trespass for the purposes of civil liability is not sufficient, however, for the purposes of criminal liability for burglary. In tort trespass may be committed negligently. **For the purposes of burglary *mens rea* must be proved.** In *Collins*, **13.2.1.1** *ante*, Edmund-Davies LJ stated (at p. 105):

> [T]here cannot be a conviction for entering premises 'as a trespasser'... unless the person entering does so knowing that he is a trespasser and nevertheless deliberately enters, or, at the very least, is reckless as to whether or not he is entering the premises of another without the other party's consent.

'Reckless' for these purposes has its '*Cunningham*' meaning (see **3.4.2.1** *ante*). It was not clear whether Collins was on the inside window sill when P beckoned to him; if he was he had already entered as a trespasser. On the assumption that he was outside, his conviction had to be quashed as the trial judge had directed the jury that a civil trespass was sufficient for the purposes of burglary and thus the question of D's *mens rea* had not been left to the jury. **If D does not enter as a trespasser, he cannot, generally, commit burglary. The exception is where P requests D to leave; if he does not do so within a reasonable time he becomes a trespasser and thus would commit burglary if he then entered another part of the building and, for example, stole P's purse.**

13.2.1.2.2 *Permission to enter*
The person who is in possession of a building or a part of it is the person who may give permission to others to enter. Thus it is the tenant of a flat who may give that permission and not the landlord who owns the property. A lodger or a guest in a hotel, however, is not in possession of his room but is a mere licensee so that permission may only be given by the licensor, in this case the landlord or hotelier. The person in possession, however, may authorise others to give permission to enter. For example, parents who own the family home expressly or impliedly authorise their children to invite others into the home. Similarly, they may forbid the entry of certain persons, for example, their daughter's boyfriend, D. If the daughter invites D into the house and he enters knowing his entry is forbidden, or being reckless thereto, and then steals, he will be guilty of burglary as he entered as a trespasser. It was suggested in *Collins* that if a person enters having been given permission by one who has no authority to do so, he is not in fact a trespasser for the purposes of burglary. It is submitted that this is wrong. If D enters without the permission of the occupier, this is trespass for civil purposes but only becomes trespass for the purposes of burglary where D knows he does not have the occupier's permission in the circumstances or is reckless thereto. Where the parents had changed their minds and, unknown to D, had given their daughter permission to invite him into the house, if D entered believing he was forbidden from entering and then stole, he would be guilty of theft and attempted burglary (cf. **8.4.4** *ante*).

13.2.1.2.3 *Exceeding permission*
A problem which may arise, however, is that of a person exceeding the permission granted. For example, if D had permission to enter but entered intending from the outset to steal, would this nevertheless be burglary on the basis that his permission was impliedly limited to lawful purposes?

> In *Jones and Smith* (1976) 63 Cr App R 47, S had general permission to enter his father's house. On the occasion in question he entered with J to steal a television

set. The Court of Appeal upheld his conviction of burglary on the basis that the jury were entitled to find that in entering his father's house with the intent to steal, S had knowingly exceeded the permission given to him.

Thus a person who is given permission to enter a building for one purpose and enters for another will be a trespasser. For example, if P gives a key to D to enter her house and water her plants while she is on holiday, and D enters to steal her video recorder, he will be trespassing and guilty of burglary (see *Barker* v *R* (1983) 153 CLR 338, High Court of Australia). Similarly, if D has permission to enter one part of a building and enters another he will be trespassing. For example, if D is invited into P's house to mend her television in the living room and enters P's bedroom to search for her purse to steal it, he would commit burglary as he has entered this part of the building as a trespasser.

How far does this principle extend? Will D necessarily become a trespasser when he enters with one of the requisite ulterior intents on the basis that this exceeds the permission granted? *Jones and Smith* would suggest that this is the case, even though the permission granted to Smith by his father had not been expressly limited to a specific purpose. The decision in *Collins* appears to contradict this. It would defy credulity if D had pleaded that he believed P had authority to permit persons to enter to commit rape. But the Court of Appeal quashed Collins's conviction, which might tend to suggest that entry in excess of permission does not negative that permission. It is submitted that, as the effect on permission of an ulterior intent was not directly adverted to in *Collins*, the case cannot be considered an authority on this point; it should be seen as a case relating to the requirement of *mens rea*. Further, as Professor Smith argues, in *The Law of Theft* (8th edn) at para. 11–06, 'as the girl saw him to be a "naked male with an erect penis" it seems clear that she invited him in for the purpose of sexual intercourse, that he knew he was so invited and that any intention to rape must have lapsed' although his intention to have intercourse obviously persisted. **Thus, if a person enters with an ulterior intent, the entry will generally be trespassory unless the occupier has granted permission to enter for that purpose.** For example, if P invites D into his house to beat up his lodger, D would not enter as a trespasser. It would be burglary, however, where D enters a shop intending to steal at the outset. The permission the shop-keeper gives to the public is impliedly limited to entry for the purpose of inspecting or purchasing goods. The Court in *Barker* were not prepared to go this far but it would seem to be implicit in the decision in *Jones and Smith*, and it is submitted, rightly so. Thus a person should be regarded as a trespasser where he enters with an intention contrary to the purposes for which permission to enter was granted. If the shopper enters without an intent to steal, but then forms that intent inside the shop, this is not burglary, even if he then proceeds to steal, as the initial entry was not a trespass.

Where D has a legal right to enter a building, for example, a police officer with a warrant to search for stolen goods, or a British Gas official entering to trace a gas leak, his entry for that purpose will not be trespass. If, however, the officer or the official enter intending, for example, to steal this will be a trespass. It will also be trespass where D gains entry into a building by fraud, for example, by deceiving P that he is a British Gas official seeking to read the meter.

13.2.2 **Any building or part of a building**

13.2.2.1 'Building'

For the purposes of burglary the trespassory entry must be made into a building or a part of a building. The maximum sentence varies depending on the type of building entered. Section 26 of the Criminal Justice Act 1991 introduced a two-tier system, substituting new sub-ss. (3) and (4) into s. 9 of the TA 1968. If the building burgled is a 'dwelling', the maximum penalty is 14 years' imprisonment, whereas it is 10 years for any other building. **There is no definition of 'building' but it appears that it must be a fairly permanent structure.** Thus a temporary prefabricated structure (such as is used by many schools for temporary classrooms) would be a building but whether transportable containers connected to an electricity supply on a fairly permanent site are buildings is not yet settled (cf. *B* and *S* v *Leathley* [1979] Crim LR 314 and *Norfolk Constabulary* v *Seekings and Gould* [1986] Crim LR 167). **A tent is not a building.** It is not clear when a structure in the process of erection becomes a building. If D enters a structure which is complete apart from the roof, doors, and windows, with intent to cause criminal damage, has he entered a building? As yet there is no answer to this problem (cf. *Manning* (1871) LR 1 CCR 338).

   An inhabited vehicle or vessel is a building (s. 9(3)). Thus both caravans and house-boats are buildings provided they are occupied, although the occupier does not have to be in at the time D enters it as a trespasser. Problems, however, may arise in defining the limits of 'inhabited'. Is a caravan inhabited when left on a site over the winter months when P does not use it? Is a 'dormobile' inhabited when P is using it simply as a vehicle and not as a holiday home? It is likely that neither of these cases would be covered as P is not actively inhabiting the vehicle. The extension to the meaning of 'building' which s. 9(3) provides is a limited one. It would not cover, for example, a mobile library or shop, or a mobile blood transfusion unit or a mobile army recruitment office, all of which are essentially vehicles converted for a particular purpose but which are not 'inhabited'. Thus, if D enters a mobile library intending to set fire to the books, he would not be guilty of burglary although if he entered a library building with the same intent he would. The mischief involved would not seem to be any different but Parliament has ordained that the offence of burglary should be restricted. If D is to be liable for burglary where he enters a vehicle or vessel it will have to be proved that he knew that it was inhabited or was reckless thereto.

13.2.2.2 'Part of a building'

For the purposes of burglary it is sufficient that D enters *part* of a building as a trespasser. Thus while D may have permission to be in certain parts of the building there may be other parts to which his permission does not extend. For example, a guest in a hotel has permission to enter his own room and communal rooms, but has no permission to enter another guest's room or parts of the building exclusively for the use of hotel staff. **If D, in the hotel bar, goes behind the counter to steal from the till he would be guilty of burglary; the same applies to a customer who goes behind the counter in a shop to steal** (see *Walkington* [1979] 2 All ER 716). The intent, however, must be to commit the ulterior offence in that part of the building which he has entered as a trespasser. If D hides between several racks of clothes in a shop waiting for it to close before removing items of clothing, he would not be guilty of burglary as he has simply remained in a part of the shop which he entered with permission. Of course, if at the time of his original entry into the shop he intended to steal, he would have committed burglary at that point.

Certain problems may arise, however, regarding the extent of a building or its constituent parts. If D enters as a trespasser a flat above a shop intending to gain access to the shop and steal therein, has he committed burglary at the point when he entered the flat? Provided the flat and shop are regarded as one building, he has. But what if D is lawfully in flat A and he uses an interconnecting fire door to enter flat B as a trespasser for the purpose of gaining access to the shop below to steal therein—has he entered a building or part of a building as a trespasser with the requisite ulterior intent? If he enters the shop there is no problem, but if he is apprehended in flat B he would not appear to have entered a part of a building with intent to steal therein. A conviction of burglary would only be possible if the remainder of the building, beyond the part which D lawfully entered, was treated as 'part' of the building. This would involve treating the shop and flat B as one part rather than two separate parts (see Professor Smith, *The Law of Theft* (8th edn) paras. 11–18 to 11–21; cf. Griew, *The Theft Acts* (7th edn) para. 4–23). This would seem to be straining the statutory language which should not be justified by a desire to convict D. A charge of attempted burglary would be more appropriate.

13.2.3 The ulterior offence

As we have already seen burglary is committed either (1) where D enters the building or part of it as a trespasser with intent to commit one of the offences in s. 9(2) (s. 9(1)(a)), or (2) having entered the building or part of it as a trespasser he steals or attempts to steal or he inflicts grievous bodily harm on any person therein or attempts to do so (s. 9(1)(b)).

13.2.3.1 Section 9(1)(a)

Under s. 9(1)(a) it is necessary to prove an ulterior intent to commit one of the three offences specified in s. 9(2). A conditional intent is sufficient (*A-G's References (Nos. 1 and 2 of 1979)* [1979] 3 All ER 143). Thus, if D enters as a trespasser intending to steal anything of value he might find, and there is nothing there, he will have a sufficient intent for burglary. In the case of these ulterior offences it must be proved that D *intended* to commit the relevant offence.

The Act speaks of entering a building and stealing anything in it or inflicting grievous bodily harm upon a person 'therein' or doing unlawful damage to the building or anything 'therein'. The word 'therein' is ambiguous as it could mean simply performing the act on a person inside the building (this would cover the case of D dragging P into a building with intent to inflict grievous bodily harm on her), or it may mean with intent to inflict grievous bodily harm upon a person already in the building before D enters it as a trespasser. As the purpose of burglary is the protection of persons or property in a building it might be suggested that the latter interpretation is the correct one.

13.2.3.2 Section 9(1)(b)

Under s. 9(1)(b), the theft, infliction of grievous bodily harm, or attempt to commit either of these offences must be proved. This requires that both the *actus reus* and *mens rea* of these ulterior offences must be proved. 'Inflicting grievous bodily harm' would appear to cover the offences under ss. 20, 18, or 23 of the Offences Against the Person Act 1861. Recklessly inflicting grievous bodily harm would be sufficient for this form of burglary. Presumably if D murders P he will also be guilty as the commission of grievous bodily harm is a step on the way to causing death and it would be ludicrous to suggest that D intended to kill but did not intend to inflict grievous bodily harm. If D took property intending only to borrow it, there would be no theft and thus no burglary. It is submitted that D in *Dobson* v *General Accident Fire and Life Assurance Corp plc* [1990] QB 274 (**11.2.1.4** *ante*) committed burglary as his permission to enter was on the basis that he had come to purchase P's jewellery; his intention was to steal it from the outset. When he appropriated it he committed theft, therefore, having entered the building as a trespasser.

If D has a defence to any of these offences he will not be guilty of burglary. For example, if D enters a building as a trespasser intending to shelter from the rain and P, the occupier, attacks him with an axe seeking to eject him, D would not be guilty of burglary if he inflicted grievous bodily harm on P in reasonable self-defence. Likewise, if D takes property believing he has in law a right to it, he would not commit theft and therefore would not be guilty of burglary.

13.2.3.3 Intoxication

Where D is intoxicated this will be of no relevance in relation to the question whether he knew he was trespassing or was reckless thereto. Intoxication may be relevant, however, in respect of the ulterior offence. Where D is charged with burglary with intent to steal, this is an offence of specific intent (see *Durante* [1972] 3 All ER 962; see also **5.6.3** *ante*). It is submitted that all forms of burglary under s. 9(1)(a) are offences of specific intent. Where D is charged with burglary contrary to s. 9(1)(b) on the basis of theft, this is an offence of specific intent as theft is such an offence (see *Ruse* v *Read* [1949] 1 KB 377). Where D is charged with burglary on the basis of inflicting grievous bodily harm, however, it would appear that the offence is one of basic intent as the *mens rea* for inflicting grievous bodily harm is intention or recklessness. If the burglary charge is based upon an attempt to steal or to inflict grievous bodily harm, it is an offence of specific intent as attempt is an offence of specific intent.

13.3 Aggravated burglary

Section 10 of the TA 1968 provides:

> (1) A person is guilty of aggravated burglary if he commits any burglary and at the time has with him any firearm or imitation firearm, any weapon of offence, or any explosive; and for this purpose—

(a) 'firearm' includes an airgun or air pistol, and 'imitation firearm' means anything which has the appearance of being a firearm, whether capable of being discharged or not; and

(b) 'weapon of offence' means any article made or adapted for use for causing injury to or incapacitating a person, or intended by the person having it with him for such use; and

(c) 'explosive' means any article manufactured for the purpose of producing a practical effect by explosion, or intended by the person having it with him for that purpose.

(2) A person guilty of aggravated burglary shall on conviction on indictment be liable to imprisonment for life.

The element of aggravation in this offence is the fact that D *at the time has with him* a firearm or imitation firearm, a weapon of offence, or an explosive. Whether something is an imitation firearm will be a question of fact for the jury (cf. *Morris and King* (1984) 79 Cr App R 104). 'Weapon of offence' is a wider term than 'offensive weapon' under s. 1(4) of the Prevention of Crime Act 1953 as it includes items not only made or adapted for use for causing injury or intended for such use but also items made or adapted for use for incapacitating a person or intended for such use. For example, a broken bottle would be an item adapted for use for causing injury, while a hammer could be an item intended for such use. Handcuffs are items made for incapacitation while a rope or a cloth soaked in chloroform could amount to an item intended for use to incapacitate a person, where, for example, D intends to incapacitate the night-watchman at a factory. If a question arises whether an article is made or adapted for use for causing injury or incapacitating a person, it will be for the jury to decide (*Williamson* (1977) 67 Cr App R 35). But, with certain items which have no other purpose, for example, a flick-knife or knuckleduster, the jury must take judicial notice that it is so made (*Simpson* [1983] 3 All ER 789). If an article is made or adapted for use for causing injury or incapacitating a person, it is offensive *per se* and it will be sufficient for the prosecution to prove that D had it with him even if he did not intend to use it. If an article is not offensive *per se*, but may be used to cause injury or incapacitate a person, the prosecution must prove that D intended it to be used for such purpose.

D must have the firearm, weapon of offence, or explosive with him at the time he commits the burglary. It is not enough that an accomplice who remains outside the building has a weapon with him (see *Klass* [1998] 1 Cr App R 453; *Wiggins* [2012] EWCA Crim 885). 'Has with him' requires that D knows that he has an article of aggravation with him (cf. *Cugullere* (1961) 45 Cr App R 108), so that if D is unaware of the fact that there is a flick-knife in his tool bag, or if he does not know his accomplice is carrying a weapon, he will not be guilty of aggravated burglary. If D has forgotten that he has, for example, a flick-knife in his bag, he does not know that he has it with him (*Russell* (1984) 81 Cr App R 315). D will have an article with him where he has custody of it or where he knows that an accomplice has custody of it and is carrying it into the building.

The meaning of 'at the time of committing the burglary' depends on whether burglary is committed contrary to s. 9(1)(a) or s. 9(1)(b). Under s. 9(1)(a) the relevant time is the time when D entered the building as a trespasser. Under s. 9(1)(b) burglary is committed where D, having entered as a trespasser, commits an ulterior offence; **he must have the weapon etc. with him at the time of committing this offence** (*Francis* [1982] Crim LR 363). Thus, if D enters as a trespasser, picks up a knife from the kitchen and then commits the ulterior offence, he would be guilty of aggravated burglary (see *O'Leary* (1986) 82 Cr App R 341). If D enters carrying with him, for example, a rope to tie together items he intends to steal and, upon being disturbed by the householder, uses it to tie him up, does he commit aggravated burglary, i.e. does he have with him at the time of committing the burglary an article intended for use to incapacitate a person? The authorities under the Prevention of Crimes Act 1953, on the question whether a person has with him in a public place an offensive weapon, suggested that the person must have formed the intention to use the article for the purpose of causing injury at some time before the occasion for that use occurred (see *Ohlson v Hylton* [1975] 2 All ER 490; *Humphreys* [1977] Crim LR 225). These cases can be distinguished, however, as in both cases D was in a public place lawfully going about his business carrying the relevant article without any criminal intent. In the burglary example, D is already engaged in an unlawful purpose and is carrying that article to effect that purpose which he then uses for an additional unlawful purpose. It is difficult to make out a case for extending the reasoning of those two cases to burglary and thus it is suggested that s. 10 should be construed strictly: at the time of committing the ulterior offence did D have the article in his custody intending it for use to cause injury or to incapacitate at that time regardless of any intention in respect of it he may previously have had? The Court of Appeal adopted this position in *Kelly* (1992) 97 Cr App R 245, holding that the screwdriver D used to break into a house became an offensive weapon when he used it to threaten the occupier who disturbed him, as he intended to use it at that time for causing injury to or incapacitating her.

13.4 Blackmail

Section 21 of the TA 1968 provides:

(1) A person is guilty of blackmail if, with a view to gain for himself or another or with intent to cause loss to another, he makes any unwarranted demand with menaces; and for this purpose a demand with menaces is unwarranted unless the person making it does so in the belief—

(a) that he has reasonable grounds for making the demand; and

(b) that the use of menaces is a proper means of reinforcing the demand.

(2) The nature of the act or omission is immaterial, and it is also immaterial whether the menaces relate to action to be taken by the person making the demand.

(3) A person guilty of blackmail shall on conviction on indictment be liable to imprisonment for a term not exceeding fourteen years.

13.4.1 Demand

D must, expressly or impliedly, make a demand of P to do or refrain from doing something. The nature of the act or omission demanded is immaterial

(s. 21(2)). In *Collister and Warhurst* (1955) 39 Cr App R 100, two police officers intimated to P that he would be prosecuted for an offence and arranged to meet him the following day intimating that the report of the offence would be held up and was to be filed only if P failed to keep the appointment. At that meeting W asked P if he had brought anything with him, and P handed him £5. C and W were convicted of demanding money with menaces contrary to s. 30 of the Larceny Act 1916, the judge having directed the jury that they did not need to be satisfied that there had been express threats or demands it being sufficient that:

> [T]he demeanour of the accused and the circumstances of the case were such that an ordinary reasonable man would understand that a demand for money was being made upon him and that that demand was accompanied by menaces...so that his ordinary balance of mind was upset...

In *Lambert* [2009] EWCA Crim 2860, V owed D money. D pretended to be V and rang V's grandmother claiming he was tied up and the people holding him wanted £5,000. The Court of Appeal held that this was capable of being an unwarranted demand and it did not matter whether D was pretending to be the victim or the person holding the victim. A demand did not have to be made in terms of a requirement or obligation. Indeed, the more suave and gentle the request, the more sinister it might be in the circumstances.

It is enough that the demand is made regardless of whether P complies with it. A problem may arise, however, in deciding when or where a demand has been made. Is, for example, the posting of a letter, the sending of a fax, the speaking of words, a demand at that point or only when received or heard by P? In *Treacy v DPP* [1971] AC 537, D posted a letter in England containing a demand to P in Germany. D argued that the demand was made in Germany when P read the letter and thus she was not triable in England. The House of Lords held, by a majority, that the demand was made when the letter was posted. The same would apply to a telex or fax. Where D makes a verbal demand, it is made when he utters the words even though P is deaf. If D posts a letter abroad addressed to P in England the offence will be committed when it is delivered to P (see *Treacy* and cf. *Baxter* [1972] 1 QB 1).

13.4.2 Menaces

As with the demand, the menaces may be express or implied from the circumstances (see *Lawrence and Pomroy* (1971) 57 Cr App R 64). Menaces is not defined in the Act but it had developed a wide meaning under the former law. In *Thorne v Motor Trade Association* [1937] AC 797, Lord Wright stated (at p. 817):

> I think the word 'menace' is to be liberally construed and not as limited to threats of violence but as including threats of any action detrimental to or unpleasant to the person addressed. It may also include a warning that in certain events such action is intended.

It is immaterial whether the menaces do or do not relate to action to be taken by the person making the demand (s. 21(2)); thus it is sufficient that the act may be carried out by someone else. Further, it does not matter that D is in no position to carry out the menace (*Lambert*). The threats, however, must cross some threshold of seriousness to constitute 'menaces'. In *Clear* [1968] 1 QB 670 (a pre-1968 Act case; see also *Lawrence and Pomroy*) Sellers LJ stated (at p. 679) that **the threat must be 'of such a nature and extent that the mind of an ordinary person of normal stability and courage might be influenced or made apprehensive so as to accede unwillingly to the demand'.** Thus in *Harry* [1974] Crim LR 32, Judge Petre directed the jury to acquit as 'menaces' was a strong word and could not be established on the evidence in the case. The accused was the organiser of a Student Rag Appeal who had written to shopkeepers offering immunity from any 'inconvenience' arising from Rag activities.

As blackmail is committed when the demand with menaces is made, it does not matter that P is not actually intimidated if the threats would have affected the mind of an ordinary person of normal stability (see *Garwood* [1987] 1 All ER 1032, 1034). If, however, P is unusually timorous and would be intimidated by threats where a person of normal stability and courage would be unmoved, this will only constitute 'menaces' if 'the accused...was aware of the likely effect of his actions on the victim' (*Garwood*).

13.4.3 Unwarranted demand

If D demands from P that to which he is legally entitled, for example, payment of a debt or the return of bailed property, and threatens to institute legal proceedings to enforce the demand, this would not constitute an 'unwarranted' demand as D is simply seeking to do that which he is legally entitled to do. By contrast, if D demands something to which he is not entitled accompanied by menaces, or demands something to which he is entitled but threatens action which he is not legally entitled to use to enforce the demand, his demand may be found to be 'unwarranted'. **Whether or not a demand is unwarranted depends on D's belief. The prosecution must prove beyond doubt either (1) that he did not believe he had reasonable grounds for making the demand, or (2) that he did not believe that the use of menaces was a proper means of reinforcing the demand.** The question is 'what was D's subjective belief?' If D does not introduce any evidence that he had both these beliefs, the judge need not direct the jury on this issue (see *Lawrence and Pomroy*). The relevant beliefs will be examined separately.

13.4.3.1 Belief in reasonable grounds for making the demand

The question is not whether there *were* reasonable grounds for making the demand but rather whether D *believed there were* reasonable grounds for making the demand. Many situations may arise where D could have such a belief. For example, P may owe him money, or P may have committed a tort and D may believe he is entitled to compensation. D may believe that a demand for payment in these circumstances is reasonable. He may have that belief even though it is founded upon a mistake as where, for example, he believes that Q broke his window and he mistakes P, Q's twin brother, for him. The mistake D makes may be an unreasonable one but this will not matter provided D's honest belief is that he has reasonable grounds for making the demand (see *Harvey* (1981) 72 Cr App R 139).

D's belief need not relate to the law. In the examples given earlier he may have believed that he was legally justified in demanding payment but D's belief may be that he is morally justified in demanding something. For example, Q dies without leaving a will and D, a neighbour who is not entitled to inherit anything on the intestacy, demands from P, Q's daughter, some property from the estate believing that she is morally justified in doing so in recognition of all the help she rendered Q. If D honestly believes that the help she rendered provides reasonable grounds for her demand, the requirements of s. 21(1)(a) are satisfied. In all cases, however, D must also have the belief specified in s. 21(1)(b). This is a provision which it is more difficult to satisfy.

13.4.3.2 Belief that menaces are a proper means of reinforcing the demand

While D may plausibly say that he believed P owed him money, or that he believed he was entitled to certain property, credulity is much more likely to be strained when he states he believed he was entitled to threaten P with violence or defamatory disclosures to enforce the demand. If the jury consider that D may possibly have believed that the menaces he used were a proper means of reinforcing the demand, they must acquit. To this extent, the standard against which the appropriateness of the menaces is measured is D's understanding of what is morally and socially acceptable in English society.

> In *Harvey*, **13.4.3.1** *ante*, D, E, and F paid £20,000 to S for what was thought to be a consignment of cannabis but which turned out to be a load of rubbish. They kidnapped S's wife and child and told S they would rape, maim, and kill them unless he gave them their money back. The judge directed the jury that threats which were to commit what everybody knew were serious criminal offences could not be proper. D, E, and F were convicted of blackmail and appealed. The Court of Appeal applied the proviso and upheld their convictions as, although the trial judge had not left the question of their belief to the jury, they were satisfied that any jury properly directed would inevitably have convicted as there was no suggestion on the part of the accused that they did not know that rape, murder, and maiming were crimes. Bingham J stated (at p. 142):
>
>> 'Proper'...is, however, plainly a word of wide meaning, certainly wider than (for example) 'lawful'. But the greater includes the less and no act which was not believed to be lawful could be believed to be proper within the meaning of the subsection. Thus no assistance is given to any defendant, even a fanatic or a deranged idealist, who knows or suspects that his threat, or the act threatened, is criminal, but believes it to be justified by his end or his peculiar circumstances.

In the circumstances of this case there was no room for doubt in light of the crimes actually threatened. If what D threatens is not known to him to be a crime, he may still be convicted if he did not believe it to be socially and morally acceptable as a means of enforcing his demand. For example, D demands payment from P of a debt threatening to show to P's neighbours and the editor of a Sunday newspaper explicit photographs of P performing an unnatural sexual act if P does not pay. D may believe that he has reasonable grounds for making the demand. D may not know that showing an obscene photograph to another person may constitute the offence of publishing obscene matter contrary to s. 2 of the Obscene Publications Act 1959. If he believed that showing the photographs was not unlawful, he could only be convicted of blackmail if it was proved that he did not believe that this would generally be regarded as morally and socially acceptable. It is difficult to imagine that D would have a strong chance of success on this point. However, if D, for example, is a person of low intelligence, poor education, and from a social background where it is generally accepted that debts may be enforced by threats, he may genuinely believe his threat to be proper, in which case he would have to be acquitted.

13.4.4 With a view to gain or intent to cause loss

In s. 34(2)(a) of the TA 1968 **'gain' and 'loss' are defined as being limited to gain or loss of money or other property, whether temporary or permanent.** Many demands may be regarded as improper but they will found a charge of blackmail only if made by D 'with a view to gain for himself or another or with intent to cause loss to another'. Thus, for example, if D threatens to expose P's adultery to her husband unless she has sexual intercourse with him, this is not blackmail as it does not involve any gain in money or property to D or similar loss to P. By contrast if D's demand had been for money or property in return for not revealing P's adultery, this would found a charge of blackmail.

Section 34(2)(a) further provides:

(i) 'gain' includes a gain by keeping what one has, as well as a gain by getting what one has not; and
(ii) 'loss' includes a loss by not getting what one might get, as well as a loss by parting with what one has.

The following examples may serve to illustrate what is covered by s. 34(2)(a), the threat in each case being to expose P's adultery, P being his secretary:

Example

(a) D demands that P allow him to keep the camera she has lent him (see (i));
(b) D demands that P forgo her salary for a month (see (ii));
(c) D demands that P repay a loan he made to her (see (i): this is a gain even though D is legally entitled to repayment of the loan; see *Lawrence and Pomroy*);
(d) D demands that P lend him her car for the weekend (both a gain to D and a loss to P);
(e) D demands that P withdraw her writ for damages for injuries sustained due to D's negligence (D has a view to keeping what he has and P will sustain loss by not getting what she might get);
(f) D demands that P destroy photographs of D in a compromising situation which she has (see (ii));
(g) D demands that P feature in a pornographic video he is making and proposing to sell (D has a view to gain, i.e. the proceeds of sale of the video);
(h) D (who has a grudge against Q) demands that P set fire to Q's car (this constitutes a 'loss to another'; there is no requirement that the loss be caused to the person against whom the threats are made).

13.5 Handling

Section 22 of the TA 1968 provides:

> (1) A person handles stolen goods if (otherwise than in the course of the stealing) knowing or believing them to be stolen goods he dishonestly receives the goods, or dishonestly undertakes or assists in their retention, removal, disposal or realisation by or for the benefit of another person, or if he arranges to do so.
>
> (2) A person guilty of handling stolen goods shall on conviction on indictment be liable to imprisonment for a term not exceeding fourteen years.

A person who handles stolen goods may also, incidentally, commit theft if his act involves an appropriation. The offence of handling, however, is regarded as more serious than theft, as the maximum sentence available indicates, as the existence of professional handlers (commonly referred to as 'fences') helps to generate thefts; many thieves might not be so keen to steal if they did not have a person readily available who was prepared to dispose of their goods.

The offence of handling is quite complex as it may be committed in many different ways. In addition terms like 'stolen' and 'goods' have their own definitions.

13.5.1 *Actus reus*

13.5.1.1 'Stolen'

The goods handled must be 'stolen' goods at the time of the handling. If the handler believes the goods to be stolen but they are not, he will not be guilty of handling (see *Haughton* v *Smith* [1975] AC 476) but he may be guilty of attempted handling (see *Shivpuri* [1987] AC 1). For example, goods would not be 'stolen' if the alleged thief believed he had a claim of right to the property. If, however, the alleged thief successfully pleaded the defence of duress on his trial for theft, this would not avail the handler as the defence of duress only operates as an excuse; D admits to committing the offence but is excused from the consequences of conviction and punishment due to the duress operating upon him. If the alleged thief has been tried and acquitted, this is not necessarily inconsistent with a conviction of the handler as, for example, the evidence against the handler may be much stronger than that against the alleged thief. If the thief has been convicted, the alleged handler may, nevertheless, dispute that the goods were stolen, in which case he will have to prove on a balance of probabilities that the thief's conviction was wrong (see s. 74(2) of the Police and Criminal Evidence Act 1984). If the alleged thief has not been tried or, if tried, has not been convicted, the question whether the goods were stolen must be decided on the basis of the evidence produced pointing to that fact in the trial of the alleged handler. The handler's belief that the goods were stolen does not constitute proof that they were (see *A-G's Reference (No. 4 of 1979)* [1981] 1 All ER 1193) but D's admissions in respect of facts within his knowledge (such as the circumstances in which he acquired the goods) may provide a legitimate basis for inferences to be drawn by the jury that the goods were stolen (see *McDonald* (1980) 70 Cr App R 288; *Barnes* [1991] Crim LR 132).

For the purposes of the offence of handling, 'stolen' has an extended meaning to include goods obtained by blackmail or by fraud contrary to s. 1 of the Fraud Act 2006 (previously it covered goods obtained by deception contrary to s. 15(1) of the TA 1968) (see s. 24(4)). The words 'steal', 'theft', and 'thief' are also to be construed accordingly. Furthermore, the theft etc. need not take place in England or Wales provided that the activity amounts to theft etc. and is an offence in the country where it was committed (s. 24(1)). It is necessary to prove that the conduct complained of amounted to an offence in the relevant foreign country; it is not enough to rely on the fact that it would have been an offence if it had been performed in England (see *Ofori and Tackie* (1994) 99 Cr App R 223).

The goods must remain stolen at the time of the handling. Section 24(3) provides:

> But no goods shall be regarded as having continued to be stolen goods after they have been restored to the person from whom they were stolen or to other lawful possession or custody, or after that person and any other person claiming through him have otherwise ceased as regards those goods to have any right to restitution in respect of the theft.

This provision relates to the two situations dealt with in the following paragraphs.

13.5.1.1.1 *Restoration of goods*

When do goods cease to be stolen? This problem arises most often when the owner (or his agent) or the police repossess the goods and then return them to the thief to entrap the handler. **If the police take possession of the goods this constitutes 'other lawful possession or custody'. In these situations the handler generally will not be guilty of handling as the goods will have ceased to be stolen** (see *Haughton v Smith, ante*; *Dolan* (1855) 6 Cox CC 449; *Schmidt* (1866) LR 1 CCR 15; *Villensky* [1892] 2 QB 597). There is one situation where the handler may be convicted, however, namely where it is alleged that he 'arranged' to handle the goods provided that the arrangement was made after the goods were stolen and before they were restored to lawful possession. For the goods to cease to be stolen there must be an act by the owner etc. amounting to the deliberate exercise of control over the goods. Simply to mark goods which have been stolen for the purpose of identifying them later when transferred by the thief to the handler does not constitute the exercise of control over the goods (see *Greater London Metropolitan Police Commissioner v Streeter* (1980) 71 Cr App R 113).

In deciding whether goods have been restored to lawful possession, the question whether a person has taken possession of goods for this purpose depends primarily on his intentions when he acted (see *A-G's Reference (No. 1 of 1974)* [1974] QB 744). In this case a police officer correctly suspected that goods in a car were stolen. He immobilised the car by removing the rotor arm and kept watch. When D returned to the car he questioned him and then arrested him. The Court of Appeal (at p. 753) held that:

> if the jury came to the conclusion that the proper explanation of what had happened was that the police officer had not intended at that stage to reduce the goods into his possession or to assume the control of them, and at that stage was merely concerned to ensure that the driver, if he appeared, could not get away without answering questions, then in that case the proper conclusion of the jury would have been to the effect that the goods had not been reduced into the possession of the police...

13.5.1.1.2 *The right to restitution has ceased*

Goods cease to be stolen when the person from whom they were stolen, or any person claiming through him, no longer has any right to restitution of the goods. For example, if E deceives P into agreeing to sell him property, this is a voidable contract of sale. If P discovers the deception but decides to ratify the contract by delivering the property to E, the goods cease to be stolen. Thus, if E sells the property to D who believes that it is stolen, there is no offence of handling as P's right to restitution of the property ceased upon ratification of the voidable contract.

13.5.1.2 Goods and their proceeds

Section 34(2)(b) defines 'goods' to include 'money and every other description of property except land, and includes things severed from land by stealing'. The definition of 'goods' is largely co-extensive with that of 'property' for the purposes of theft with the exception that land, if it is to be the subject of handling, must be severed. The requirement of severance acts as a limitation in respect of property obtained as a result of deception or blackmail.

Section 24(2) provides:

> ... references to stolen goods shall include, in addition to the goods originally stolen and parts of them (whether in their original state or not)—
>
> (a) any other goods which directly or indirectly represent or have at any time represented the stolen goods in the hands of the thief as being the proceeds of any disposal or realisation of the whole or part of the goods stolen or of goods so representing the stolen goods; and
>
> (b) any other goods which directly or indirectly represent or have at any time represented the stolen goods in the hands of a handler of the stolen goods or any part of them as being the proceeds of any disposal or realisation of the whole or part of the stolen goods handled by him or of goods so representing them.

The effect of this provision is to extend the range of property which may be regarded as 'stolen' for the purposes of supporting a charge of handling. Thus, if the thief or the initial handler converts the stolen goods into money or other property (i.e. 'proceeds' of the disposal or realisation of the stolen goods), these proceeds are also regarded as 'stolen' so that anyone who knowingly handles them will be guilty of handling. This can lead to considerable multiplication of the 'goods' which may be regarded as 'stolen' for the purposes of handling.

 Example

These examples serve to illustrate the operation of this provision.

(i) A steals P's car and sells it for £500 to B, who knows it is stolen. Both the car and the money are stolen. The money directly represents the original stolen goods in the hands of the thief being the proceeds of its realisation or disposal (s. 24(2)(a)).

(ii) A gives the £500 to C in payment of a debt, C knowing of its provenance; C would be guilty of receiving stolen goods.

➡

(iii) B breaks the car into parts and sells most of the parts to D and E for £300 each. The £600 is now proceeds of stolen goods which were 'in the hands of a handler' resulting from the disposal of part of the stolen goods and the remaining parts represent part of the stolen goods (s. 24(2)(b)). If D and E knew of the provenance of the parts they would be guilty of handling.

(iv) B buys another car for £300. This car is also 'stolen goods' as it is 'goods so represent-ing' the 'proceeds of any disposal or realisation of the whole or part of the stolen goods handled by him' (s. 24(2)(b)).

(v) C buys a painting for £500 from Q. The painting is 'stolen goods' being the pro-ceeds of the realisation or disposal of stolen goods (money) in the hands of a handler (s. 24(2)(b)).

A problem created by s. 24(2) relates to funds in a bank account. D steals jewellery which he sells to E for £1,000. The £1,000 represents the proceeds of D's disposal of the stolen goods. D then deposits the £1,000 in his bank account and asks the bank to transfer £500 to W's account (W being his wife who knows of the provenance of this transfer) which W then withdraws. Is W a handler? A. T. H. Smith, *Property Offences*, states (para. 30.15):

[W]here the thief pays stolen money into the handler's bank account[,] the chose in action represented by the bank debt and the cash that the handler takes from [her] account have never been proceeds 'in the hands of' the thief or a handler, even though they have been under the thief's control. The same point appears to have been overlooked in *Attorney-General's Reference (No. 4 of 1979)*, where it was stated that the transfer of a bank credit from the account of the thief to the account of an accomplice would amount to handling. Such a result is incompatible with the plain words of the section.

The Law Commission, *Offences of Dishonesty: Money Transfers* (Law Com No. 243) agreed with this analysis which it considered was confirmed by the decision in *Preddy* (see paras. 6.5 to 6.7). The decision in *Preddy* had created the additional problem that the obtaining of a transfer of money by means of a CHAPS order, telegraphic or electronic transfer, or by cheque, where the obtaining resulted from deception, did not constitute the offence of obtaining property by deception con-trary to s. 15 of the TA 1968 (see **12.2.2** *ante*). Consequently, the credit balance in the recipient's account could not constitute 'stolen goods' for the purposes of the offence of handling in respect of subsequent dealings with the account. The Law Commission recommended two solutions to these problems, both of which have been implemented by the enactment of the Theft (Amendment) Act 1996: first, the creation of a new offence of dishonestly retaining a wrongful credit (see s. 24A of the TA 1968; **13.6** *post*); and secondly, the expansion of the definition of 'stolen goods' to catch, by the general law of handling, dishonest withdrawals from accounts to which 'wrongful credits' have been made. Section 24A(8) provides:

References to stolen goods include money which is dishonestly withdrawn from an account to which a wrongful credit has been made, but only to the extent that the money derives from the credit.

Section 24A(2) of the TA 1968 provides that 'references to credit are to a credit of an amount of money' and s. 24A(2A) and (5) provide:

> (2A) A credit to an account is also wrongful to the extent that it derives from—
>
>   (a) theft;
>
>   (b) blackmail;
>
>   (c) fraud (contrary to section 1 of the Fraud Act 2006); or
>
>   (d) stolen goods.
>
> (5) In determining whether a credit to an account is wrongful, it is immaterial (in particular) whether the account is overdrawn before or after the credit is made.

The Law Commission provides the following examples of how these provisions would operate (Law Com No. 243, para 6.20):

> (7) A obtains a money transfer by deception, theft or blackmail, withdraws the proceeds from his account and hands the cash to B. The cash is stolen goods. If B knows this or believes this, she is guilty of handling.
>
> (8) A obtains a money transfer by deception, theft or blackmail and transfers the proceeds to B's account. B dishonestly withdraws the proceeds and hands the cash to C. The cash is stolen goods, and C is guilty of handling if he knows or believes this....

13.5.1.3 Handling

'Handling' may be committed in one of four basic ways provided that the conduct involved takes place 'otherwise than in the course of stealing'. There is, however, only one offence (see *Griffiths* v *Freeman* [1970] 1 All ER 1117; *Nicklin* [1977] 2 All ER 444), and 'handling' is simply a generic term to cover the various ways in which the offence may be committed. Accordingly, an indictment which simply alleges 'handling' is not bad for duplicity but the better practice is to particularise the form of handling alleged (see *Griffiths* v *Freeman, ante*, and *Alt* (1972) 56 Cr App R 457). If one particular mode of handling is alleged, such as 'receiving', D cannot be convicted on the basis of a different mode (see *Nicklin, ante*). In any case where there is uncertainty as to the appropriate mode to allege, the indictment should contain separate counts alleging different modes (see *Sloggett* [1972] 1 QB 430).

 Key Point

The four basic modes of committing the offence are:

(1) *receiving* stolen goods; or

(2) *undertaking* the retention, removal, disposal, or realisation of the goods for the benefit of another person; or

(3) *assisting* in the retention, removal, disposal, or realisation of the goods by another person; or

(4) *arranging* to do (1), (2), or (3).

Two points in particular should be noted. **First, in all cases the goods must be stolen at the time the receiving, undertaking, assisting, or arranging takes place.** If, for example, D arranges with A to receive goods which A is going to steal, D is not guilty of handling as there are no goods then stolen, but he may be guilty of conspiracy to handle stolen goods. **Secondly, apart from receiving or arranging to receive, the other forms of handling are subject to a qualification: in (2) the acts must be done 'for the benefit of another person' and in (3) the handler must assist another person to do the relevant acts. If D is charged with arranging to undertake or assist the same qualification applies.**

13.5.1.3.1 *Receiving and arranging to receive*

Receiving involves D in taking possession or control of the stolen goods either alone or with others, which may include joint possession with the thief. It is a finite act so that, where D receives on different occasions goods from different thefts, these occasions must be specified as separate counts on the indictment (see *Smythe* (1980) 72 Cr App R 8). If D's servant or agent takes possession of stolen goods with his authority this will constitute receiving by D (see *Miller* (1854) 6 Cox CC 353). **There is no requirement that D should receive the goods to keep or otherwise dispose of them nor that he should gain any profit or other benefit from their receipt.** It is sufficient that he has possession or control even if he is only receiving them temporarily to hide them (see *Richardson* (1834) 6 C & P 335). There must be evidence, however, that D has possession or control. If D is merely inspecting the goods in the thief's presence during negotiations, he has neither possession nor control of them. Helping a thief to remove stolen goods from a lorry does not amount to receiving (see *Hobson v Impett* (1957) 41 Cr App R 138) although it may amount to one of the other forms of handling. If D finds stolen goods and takes possession of them this does not amount to receiving (see *Haider*, unreported, 22 March 1985) although this may amount to theft (see **11.2.2.2.1** *ante*).

Negotiating with the thief to purchase stolen goods is not itself a complete act of arranging to receive. When agreement is reached that D will receive the goods, this will constitute the offence of arranging to receive. The arrangement need not be made with the thief; an arrangement made with a person innocently in possession of stolen goods would suffice provided D knew the goods were stolen. Although an agreement may not be concluded, an offer by D to receive stolen goods may constitute an attempt to handle.

13.5.1.3.2 *Undertaking or assisting*

There are four activities which may constitute handling where either D undertakes those activities for the benefit of another, or D assists another to perform those activities or arranges to undertake or assist in those activities. In *Bloxham* [1982] 1 All ER 582, the House of Lords held that 'the other person' must have the same meaning whether it is alleged that D assisted or undertook the relevant activity. Thus something may only be undertaken for the benefit of another if that other person could have done the act himself.

> In *Bloxham*, D, believing that a car he had bought was stolen, sold it to E. He was charged with handling stolen goods on the basis that he had undertaken the realisation of the car for the benefit of another person, namely E. The House of Lords was

of the view that the person for whose benefit this transaction was undertaken was D and not E. E's purchase of the car may have been of benefit to him, but this was irrelevant as it was D's act of sale (realisation) which was required to have benefited him. D could only be convicted where the sale was for the benefit of another person as where, for example, he was selling the car as an agent for C (the thief or another handler of it).

Furthermore, the act of sale of the car (realisation) was not one which could have been performed *by* E as he did not possess the car. Where A and B are jointly charged in one count on an indictment with handling 'by or for the benefit of another person', the other person must be someone other than the co-accused (see *Gingell* [2000] 1 Cr App R 88).

The four activities involved each have a separate meaning and appear to cover all the various things a person may seek to do with stolen goods.

(a) *Retention* In *Pitchley* (1972) 57 Cr App R 30, **the Court of Appeal defined 'retain' to mean 'keep possession of, not lose, continue to have'.** A person undertakes the retention of stolen goods where, for example, he stores the goods for the thief or another handler. As retention is a continuing activity, D may commit the offence where, after taking possession of property to retain for another, he discovers that it is stolen. By continuing to keep possession of it he would be undertaking to retain it (but cf. *Pitchley* where the Court of Appeal appears to have treated this as assisting in the retention of stolen goods). D will be guilty of assisting another to retain stolen goods where he does something 'intentionally and dishonestly, for the purpose of enabling the goods to be retained' (*per* Cantley J in *Kanwar* [1982] 2 All ER 528). Examples of such conduct would be where D helps to hide the goods or he puts the thief in touch with someone else who agrees to store them, or where he tells lies to make it more difficult for the police to find or identify the goods (see *Kanwar*).

 Example

If E is a thief and the police visit E's flat seeking particular goods and D tells the police that items fitting the description of the stolen goods in fact belong to him and he lent them to E, D would be assisting E to retain those goods. By contrast, however, if D is, for example, a lodger in E's flat and knows where the stolen goods are hidden, but simply refuses to answer any police questions (as opposed to giving untruthful answers), this does not constitute assisting (see *Brown* [1970] QB 105).

In *Brown*, the Court of Appeal took the view that to hold that a failure to answer questions amounted to 'assisting' would encroach on the principle that a person is not bound to answer police questions. If, however, the stolen goods were hidden in D's room, this would be circumstantial evidence which may point to him having permitted them to be hidden there initially and thus may support a charge of handling on the basis of undertaking to retain the stolen goods.

It appears that D will be convicted only where a purposive intent is proved. In *Kanwar*, D's husband brought home stolen goods which D used to furnish the home being aware of their provenance. Cantley J stated that D would not be guilty of handling where 'she was merely willing for the goods to be kept and used in the house and was thinking it was nice to have them there, although they were stolen goods'. Similarly a person does not assist in the retention of stolen goods merely by using them (see *Sanders* (1982) 75 Cr App R 84).

(b) *Removal* **This involves transporting or carrying stolen goods.** If D transports stolen goods for E's benefit he will have undertaken their removal; if he assists E to transport goods, for example, by lending him a van, he will have assisted in their removal.

(c) *Disposal* **This covers destroying, dumping, giving away, or transforming stolen goods.** An example of transformation would be where D melts down stolen silver items. The fact that D benefits from a disposal of stolen property does not, in itself, amount to assisting in its disposal; assisting requires an act of helping or encouraging (see *Coleman* [1986] Crim LR 56). In *Coleman*, D and his wife purchased a flat in their joint names; the wife, to D's knowledge, used stolen money to pay some of the fees involved. While the purchase of the flat benefited D, this did not establish that he had assisted her; there had to be proof that D encouraged her to do so or agreed to her doing so. On a proper direction, however, a jury may have inferred this from the facts.

(d) *Realisation* **Realisation involves the selling of stolen goods or their exchange for anything else of value.** If D sells stolen goods as agent for E (the thief or another handler) he undertakes their realisation for the benefit of another. If D introduces a purchaser to E who is seeking to sell stolen goods, he assists in their realisation. If D arranges a meeting between D and E he would be arranging to assist in the realisation of stolen goods.

13.5.1.3.3 *Otherwise than in the course of the stealing*

This limitation in s. 22(1) protects the original thief from liability for handling in respect of the course of conduct which constituted the original theft. This is necessary where two or more persons participate in the original theft. As theft is committed as soon as D appropriates property, subsequent acts to remove the property might otherwise amount to handling but for this limitation (see *Gregory* (1981) 77 Cr App R 41). For example, D and E agree to burgle a house. D enters and passes property through the window to E outside. D and E then carry the goods to a van to transport them to a fence who will pay them for the property. If s. 22(1) did not contain this limitation, E would be guilty of receiving when D hands him the goods and both D and E would be guilty of assisting each other to remove the goods and to realise them. The phrase 'course of the stealing' extends beyond the time of the appropriation of the property. **The difficulty, however, is determining when the course of the stealing ends.** For example, if D removes a statue from P's house and hides it in P's shed to return later with E to remove it from the premises, it is submitted that 'the course of the stealing' was over when D first removed the statue so that when E later assisted D to remove it from the shed he was assisting another to remove stolen goods. By contrast, if E had accompanied D and waited in the shed to help D, the whole transaction would have been a continuing one and E would have been an aider and abettor to the burglary or theft rather than a handler. It is, essentially, a question of fact when a course of stealing ends.

A case which has been regarded by some as problematic is *Pitham and Hehl* (1976) 65 Cr App R 45. M offered to sell P's furniture to D and E. D and E inspected the furniture, agreed to buy it, paid M, and then removed it from P's house. They were convicted of handling and appealed, contending that their acts did not take place 'otherwise than in the course of the stealing'. The Court of Appeal upheld their convictions on the basis that M's offer to sell the furniture amounted to a completed theft as he was assuming the rights of the owner at that point. Everything D and E did thereafter was after the course of the stealing had transpired. The case has been subjected to criticism but the decision may be supported. Clearly nothing else was necessary to commit theft other than the making of the offer to sell. If the purpose of the limitation in s. 22(1) was to protect accessories from liability for handling arising from their acts which aided and abetted the principal, the decision does not conflict with this purpose as there was no evidence to suggest that D and E had aided, abetted, counselled, or procured M's theft. Rather, it appeared that he committed the theft independently of D and E. It may be, however, that in removing the goods D and E themselves committed a theft but this was a separate theft from M's initial theft (cf. *Gregory ante*).

Where D is found in possession of stolen goods several days after the theft it may not be clear whether he is the thief or a handler. If D is charged with handling, must the prosecution prove that he came by the goods 'otherwise than in the course of the stealing'? The Court of Appeal held in *Cash* [1985] QB 801, that unless there was some evidence pointing to D being the thief, the jury were entitled to infer from the evidence of recent possession that he was the handler and, in such a case, the words 'otherwise than in the course of the stealing' should not be mentioned to the jury.

Once the 'course of the stealing' is over a thief may be guilty of handling the goods he has stolen, for example, by helping a receiver of the goods to move them or dispose of them. Similarly, if D is an accessory to the theft and several days later another party to the theft delivers to him his share of the items stolen, D will be guilty of receiving stolen goods.

It is worth noting that a handler generally commits a separate offence of theft by means of his subsequent dealing with the goods as virtually any act of handling (apart from the 'arranging' cases) will amount to an appropriation of property with the intention of permanently depriving the owner of it.

13.5.2 *Mens rea*

D will be guilty of handling only where he knows or believes that the goods are stolen goods at the time when he does the act which constitutes handling. In the case of receiving or arranging to receive or to do any of the other prohibited acts, this knowledge or belief must exist at the time D receives the goods or makes the arrangement (see *Brook* [1993] Crim LR 455). Where D's acts constitute *undertaking* or *assisting* in the prohibited acts, D will be liable if he learns the truth and continues to undertake or assist in, for example, the disposal of the stolen goods even though his initial participation in this activity was innocent. If D comes by the stolen goods innocently as a bona fide purchaser, his subsequent dealing with the goods, after he learns of their provenance, cannot amount to theft (see s. 3(2) of the TA 1968, **11.2.1.5.6** *ante*) but there is no similar provision excluding liability for handling. If, for example, D subsequently assisted E to sell the goods he would appear to have assisted another to realise the goods. By contrast, if D initially received the goods as a gift his keeping of or dealing with them after discovering their provenance would amount to theft (see s. 3(1), TA 1968, **11.2.1.5.5** *ante*); any dealing with the goods thereafter may also constitute handling.

13.5.2.1 What constitutes knowledge or belief?

Actual knowledge or belief on the part of D must be proved; it is not sufficient that any reasonable person would have realised that the goods were stolen (see *Atwal* v *Massey* (1971) 56 Cr App R 6). It is enough that D knows or believes in the existence of facts which render the goods 'stolen' in law. D need not know the law and, indeed, it would not avail him if he believed the goods had been stolen when, in fact, they had been obtained as a result of blackmail. **In addition, D need not know the nature of the goods;** if he takes possession of a suitcase having been told that it contains stolen goods, he will be guilty of handling if it does contain stolen goods even though they differ from the goods which D believed the case contained (see *McCullum* (1973) 57 Cr App R 645).

If D has direct evidence as to the provenance of the goods, for example, he witnesses the theft or the thief tells him the goods are stolen, he 'knows' the goods are stolen (*Hall* (1985) 81 Cr App R 260). **'Belief' that goods are stolen**, according to Boreham J in *Hall* (at p. 264):

> ...may be said to be the state of mind of a person who says to himself: 'I cannot say I know for certain that these goods are stolen, but there can be no other reasonable conclusion in the light of all the circumstances, in the light of all that I have heard and seen'.

Suspicion, on the other hand, that goods are stolen is not sufficient (see *Hall*; *Grainge* (1974) 59 Cr App R 3; *Pethick* [1980] Crim LR 242), nor does foresight that goods are probably stolen constitute belief (*Reader* (1977) 66 Cr App R 33). Similarly, wilful blindness does not amount to knowledge or belief, although the fact that D suspects that goods are stolen and deliberately shuts his eyes to this is evidence which may point to him having the requisite knowledge or belief, that is it is evidence from which knowledge or belief may be inferred (see *Griffiths* (1974) 60 Cr App R 14; *Moys* (1984) 79 Cr App R 72). This latter proposition, which was approved in *Forsyth* [1997] 2 Cr App R 299 (where it was stated that the *Hall* dictum was confusing), is difficult to follow; if the jury conclude that D suspected the goods were stolen, and suspicion does not constitute knowledge or belief, how can they infer from this knowledge or belief? The only way to avoid problems is for the judge to refuse to elaborate on the meaning of 'belief' and leave it to the jury to define as an ordinary word with the warning that suspicion, however great, is not belief.

13.5.2.2 Proof of knowledge or belief

The prosecution may be assisted in their task of proving knowledge or belief by the common law doctrine of '**recent possession**' and by s. 27(3) of the TA 1968. **Where D is found in possession of recently stolen goods and offers no explanation for his possession, or the jury are satisfied beyond reasonable doubt that any explanation offered is untrue, the jury *may* infer guilty knowledge from this**

fact (see *Abramovitch* (1914) 11 Cr App R 45). The jury are not obliged to draw such an inference and should convict only where satisfied beyond reasonable doubt that D had such knowledge or belief (*Abramovitch*). There is no particular magic in this doctrine; it is, in fact, simply an example of circumstantial evidence.

Section 27(3) is very different. This provision permits the admission of evidence which may have little or no probative value but will have a highly prejudicial effect upon the accused's case. Where D is charged with handling *and* evidence has been given of his having performed an act which could amount to handling, then for the purpose of proving that D knew or believed the goods to be stolen, **two classes of evidence may be admitted:**

(a) evidence that he has had in his possession, or has undertaken or assisted in the retention, removal, disposal or realisation of, stolen goods from any theft taking place not earlier than twelve months before the offence charged; and

(b) (provided that seven days' notice in writing has been given to him of the intention to prove the conviction) evidence that he has within the five years preceding the date of the offence charged been convicted of theft or of handling stolen goods.

This subsection is strictly construed. Under (a) it is only permissible to tender evidence of the actual handling; no evidence as to D's state of mind nor as to the circumstances in which D came into possession of them, is admissible (*Bradley* (1979) 70 Cr App R 200). This has the potential of wreaking injustice as the other incident of handling may not have constituted an offence as D may not have known or believed the goods to be stolen. Thus, if D had innocently bought stolen goods and been acquitted on a charge of handling and then is subsequently found in possession of stolen goods, the other incident may be proved. The only purpose of proving it is to try to persuade a jury to conclude that it is stretching credulity to believe that both incidents are innocent. D may simply have been unfortunate, however, rather than dishonest. The trial judge, of course, has a discretion to refuse to admit evidence under (a) which the prosecution might tender (see *Rasini, The Times*, 20 March 1986).

Under para. (b) the prosecution may merely prove the fact of D's previous conviction (*Fowler* (1988) 86 Cr App R 219), but again the risk of prejudice is obvious.

13.5.2.3 Dishonesty

The test of dishonesty is the same as for theft (see **11.2.2.2.2** *ante*). Obviously, if D receives stolen goods to hand them back to the owner or the police, he would not be dishonest.

13.6 Dishonestly retaining a wrongful credit

Prior to the decision of the House of Lords in *Preddy* [1996] AC 815 (see **12.2.3** *ante*), a credit balance obtained by deception from another account would have constituted 'stolen goods' for the purposes of the offence of handling. The Law

Commission, *Offences of Dishonesty: Money Transfers* (Law Com No. 243, para. 6.2) states:

> On this assumption, the offence of handling would be committed if, knowing or believing the funds to be stolen goods, a person dishonestly receives them or deals with them in any of the other ways set out in section 22(1). According to *Preddy*, however, the funds are not obtained in the circumstances described in section 15(1); therefore they are probably not stolen goods, and subsequent dealings with them fall outside section 22(1).

The Theft (Amendment) Act 1996 created the offence of obtaining a money transfer by deception to cover the lacuna in s. 15 resulting from *Preddy* (since abolished by the Fraud Act 2006 and now covered by the offence of fraud contrary to s. 1 of that Act). A second offence was created by s. 2 inserting a new s. 24A into the Theft Act 1968 making it an offence dishonestly to retain a wrongful credit. This offence is analogous to handling, but it goes further than simply restoring the status quo as it was prior to *Preddy*, as certain conduct is made criminal which was not previously criminal. Section 24A of the TA provides:

> (1) A person is guilty of an offence if—
>> (a) a wrongful credit has been made to an account kept by him or in respect of which he has any right or interest;
>> (b) he knows or believes that the credit is wrongful; and
>> (c) he dishonestly fails to take such steps as are reasonable in the circumstances to secure that the credit is cancelled.
> (2) References to a credit are to a credit of an amount of money.

This offence will cover a person whose account is credited with any wrongful credit as defined in s. 24A(2A) (see **13.5.1.2** *ante*). Thus D who obtains a wrongful credit by fraud commits this further offence if he dishonestly retains that credit. This stretches liability beyond that which exists for the offence of handling. Liability is further extended by the definition of 'wrongful credit' in s. 24A(2A). For example, if D steals £100 and places it in his own money box he cannot be convicted of handling stolen goods by retaining it (see **13.5.1.3** *ante*). By contrast, if D deposits the £100 in his bank account, this amounts to a wrongful credit and he will be guilty of the s. 24A(1) offence if he does not take reasonable steps to cancel that credit by returning £100 to his victim. (The same would apply if D had obtained the £100 by fraud or by blackmail.) If D had deposited the £100 in E's account, E would commit the s. 24A(1) offence if he knew or suspected that this was a wrongful credit and did not take reasonable steps to divest himself of it. The Law Commission provided the following examples of how it envisaged the new offence would operate (see Law Com No. 243, para. 6.20):

> (4) A, by deception, theft or blackmail, obtains a transfer of funds from V's account into B's. A is guilty of obtaining a money transfer by deception or of theft or blackmail (as the case may be). The credit to B's account is therefore wrongful. B is guilty of

retaining a credit from a dishonest source if, knowing or believing the credit to be wrongful, she dishonestly fails to take reasonable steps to cancel it.

(5)   A, by deception, theft or blackmail, obtains a transfer of funds from V's account into his own, and transfers the proceeds to B's. B's position is the same as in example (4). If B transfers the proceeds to C's account, the same rules apply in respect of C's liability; and so on ad infinitum.

A person guilty of an offence under s. 24A is liable on conviction on indictment to imprisonment for a term not exceeding 10 years (s. 24A(6) of the TA 1968).

FURTHER READING

P. Alldridge, 'Attempted Murder of the Soul: Blackmail, Piracy and Secrets' (1993) 13 OJLS 368.

J. R. Spencer, 'The Mishandling of Handling' [1981] Crim LR 682; 'Handling, Theft and the Mala Fide Purchaser' [1985] Crim LR 92 and 440.

14

....

Criminal damage

14.1 Introduction

The Criminal Damage Act 1971 contains the main offences involving damage to property. The Act is mainly the result of work by the Law Commission (see in particular Law Com No. 29). The Act largely complements the law of theft.

14.2 Destroying or damaging property belonging to another

Section 1(1) of the Criminal Damage Act 1971 provides:

> A person who without lawful excuse destroys or damages any property belonging to another intending to destroy or damage any such property or being reckless as to whether any such property would be destroyed or damaged shall be guilty of an offence.

The maximum punishment for this offence following trial on indictment is 10 years' imprisonment (s. 4(2)). Where, however, the offence is committed by fire it is charged as arson and the maximum punishment is life imprisonment (ss. 1(3) and 4(1)). This reflects the extra danger arising from fire-raising.

14.2.1 *Actus reus*

14.2.1.1 Destroy or damage

Whether property is damaged is a question of fact and degree (see *Cox v Riley* (1986) 83 Cr App R 54). **It includes physical harm, whether permanent or temporary, and the permanent or temporary impairment of the value or usefulness of property.** Physical harm may result to property in many ways. Trampling down grass, or other vegetation, may constitute damage (see *Gayford v Choulder* [1898] 1 QB 316). Dumping rubbish on land may amount to damage where the owner of the land is put to expense in removing it, even though the land underneath is not damaged (*Henderson and Battley*, 29 November 1984, unreported). Drawing or painting on a pavement using water soluble chalks or paints constitutes damage where the local authority is involved in expense in cleaning the pavement (*Hardman v Chief Constable of Avon and Somerset Constabulary* [1986] Crim LR 330).

Spitting on a policeman's coat, however, does not constitute damage where the spittle can be removed with a damp cloth (*'A' (a juvenile)* v R [1978] Crim LR 689).

The requirement appears to be that if expense on the part of the owner of the property is incurred to restore it to its previous condition a jury or magistrates may conclude that damage has been caused (see *Roe* v *Kingerlee* [1986] Crim LR 735). Had the policeman's coat required dry cleaning, for example, the result might have been different. The nature of the property involved may also be relevant in addition to the degree of harm caused. In *Morphitis* v *Salmon* [1990] Crim LR 48, the Divisional Court held that a scratch to a scaffold bar could not constitute damage as it involved no impairment of its value or usefulness since scratching was a normal incident of scaffolding components. By contrast, a scratch to the bonnet of a car could constitute damage as this would involve expense on the part of the owner in remedial work albeit that the secondhand value of the car might not be affected. Of course, if the damage to the paintwork is substantial this might also affect the value of the vehicle. **There is no need for the property to be rendered useless if the damage involves diminution in its value.** For example, if water is added to beer its value is diminished but it is not useless; this amounts to damage (see *Roper* v *Knott* [1898] 1 QB 868).

Damage arising from the impairment of the usefulness of property occurs where, for example, a part is removed from a machine (*Tacey* (1821) Russ & Ry 452) **or a machine is dismantled or tampered with so that it will not work** (*Fisher* (1865) LR 1 CCR 7; *Getty* v *Antrim County Council* [1950] NI 114). Where a part is removed or a machine dismantled, D should be charged with damaging the machine and not the parts unless these have also been damaged (see *Woolcock* [1977] Crim LR 104 and 161; *Morphitis* v *Salmon*). Simply to deny P the use of his property, for example, by placing a wheel clamp on his car, does not amount to damage (*Lloyd* [1992] 1 All ER 982). In *Cox* v *Riley* (1986) 83 Cr App R 54, erasure of the programmes on a printed circuit card used to control a computerised saw was held to be damage to the card. This was affirmed in *Whiteley*, *The Times*, 6 February 1991, where D had hacked into a computer network and altered data stored on disks. This was held to be damage even though the physical nature of the disks had not been altered or impaired; their usefulness, however, was impaired. The effect of these decisions in so far as they relate to computers has been reversed by s. 3(6) of the Computer Misuse Act 1990 (the offence in *Whiteley* was committed before the Act came into force) which provides:

> For the purposes of the Criminal Damage Act 1971 a modification of the contents of a computer shall not be regarded as damaging any computer or computer storage medium unless its effect on that computer or computer storage medium impairs its physical condition.

When the Police and Justice Act 2006 comes into force it will repeal s. 3(6) of the 1990 Act but, at the same time, it will insert a new sub-s. (5) into s. 10 of the 1971 Act which will provide:

> (5) For the purposes of this Act a modification of the contents of a computer shall not be regarded as damaging any computer or computer storage medium unless its effect on that computer or computer storage medium impairs its physical condition.

The accused in *Cox* v *Riley* and *Whiteley* would now be guilty of the offence of unauthorised modification of computer material contrary to s. 3 of the 1990 Act (or when the Police and Justice Act 2006 comes into force the new offence under a substituted s. 3 of 'Unauthorised acts with intent to impair, or with recklessness as to impairing, operation of computer, etc.'). The Law Commission, *Computer Misuse* (Law Com No. 186), whose recommendations resulted in the passage of the 1990 Act, did point out, however, (at para. 3.78) that:

> This recommendation would not of course prejudice the operation of the 1971 Act in cases where the unauthorised modification [of a computer's memory or computer storage medium] leads to actual physical damage. For example, if a computer-operated saw were reprogrammed so that it ruined a load of timber, then (subject in both cases to the presence of the appropriate *mens rea*) the re-programming would amount to an unauthorised modification and the consequent damage to the timber would come within section 1 of the Criminal Damage Act 1971.

The 1990 Act does not affect the authority of *Cox* v *Riley* and *Whiteley* in so far as they are appropriate to other situations where information is stored in electro-magnetic form. For example, if D alters or erases P's audio tapes or video tapes, this would constitute damage even though the physical nature of the tapes had not been altered. In *Whiteley* it was argued that tampering with the disks altered only intangible information contained on them but caused no tangible or perceptible damage to the disk itself. Lord Lane CJ responded:

> That contention contained a basic fallacy. What the Act required to be proved was that tangible property had been damaged, not necessarily that the damage itself should be tangible. There could be no doubt that the magnetic particles on the metal disks were a part of the disks and if the appellant was proved to have intentionally and without lawful excuse altered the particles in such a way as to cause an impairment of the value or usefulness of the disk to the owner, there would be damage within the meaning of s. 1. The fact that the alteration could only be perceived by operating the computer did not make the alterations any the less real, or the damage . . . any the less within the ambit of the Act.

This statement of principle will continue to apply if the words 'audio or video tape' and 'tape recorder or video recorder' are substituted for 'metal disk' and 'computer' respectively.

Criminal damage is also committed where D destroys property, for example, by demolishing a building, breaking up a machine, killing an animal, laying waste crops (e.g. by mowing a field of wheat, or spraying it with herbicide), incinerating books etc. It is difficult to envisage a case where damage will not be done to the property in the process of destroying it.

14.2.1.2 Property

Section 10(1) provides:

> In this Act 'property' means property of a tangible nature, whether real or personal, including money and—
>
> (a) including wild creatures which have been tamed or are ordinarily kept in captivity, and any other wild creatures or their carcasses if, but only if, they have been reduced

> into possession which has not been lost or abandoned or are in the course of being reduced into possession; but
>
> (b) not including mushrooms growing wild on any land or flowers, fruit or foliage of a plant growing wild on any land.
>
> For the purposes of this subsection 'mushroom' includes any fungus and 'plant' includes any shrub or tree.

There are some differences between this definition of 'property' and that in s. 4 of the Theft Act 1968, necessitated by the differing mischief to which each Act is directed. First, land may not be stolen but it may be damaged or destroyed; indeed arson is generally committed against land in the form of buildings. Secondly, 'property' is confined to tangible property in the Criminal Damage Act. Thirdly, wild mushrooms, flowers, fruit, or foliage cannot be the subject of criminal damage although they may, in certain circumstances, be the subject of theft.

14.2.1.3 Belonging to another

Section 10 provides:

> (2) Property shall be treated for the purposes of this Act as belonging to any person—
>
> (a) having the custody or control of it;
>
> (b) having in it any proprietary right or interest (not being an equitable interest arising only from an agreement to transfer or grant an interest); or
>
> (c) having a charge on it.
>
> (3) Where the property is subject to a trust, the persons to whom it belongs shall be so treated as including any person having a right to enforce the trust.
>
> (4) Property of a corporation sole shall be so treated as belonging to the corporation notwithstanding a vacancy in the corporation.

Again these provisions are broadly similar to s. 5 of the Theft Act 1968. In s. 5 of the TA 1968 theft may be committed where a person has 'possession or control' of property; the equivalent words in s. 10(2) are 'custody or control' suggesting that P must have physical custody of it and were used to provide a clearer concept than the word 'possession' which is a technical term sometimes giving rise to difficulty (see *Warner* v *Metropolitan Police Commissioner* [1969] 2 AC 256). Another difference from the Theft Act is the inclusion of para. (c) in sub-s. (2) relating to charges on property. This provision is superfluous, however, as a charge on property amounts to a proprietary right or interest in property.

Property may be the subject of criminal damage, therefore, where some person has custody or control of it or a proprietary right or interest in it. As with theft, where D may steal property he owns if another also has a proprietary right or interest in it or possession or control of it, a person may cause criminal damage to property he owns if another has such an interest in it. For example, if D hires a car to P and then removes the rotor arm from it rendering it inoperable, he may be guilty of criminal damage. In cases where D is alleged to have damaged property in which he has a proprietary interest proof of *mens rea* or disproof of lawful excuse may be difficult. If D destroys his own property for a dishonest purpose, for example to make a fraudulent insurance claim, this is not an offence under s. 1(1) despite

D's dishonesty as an insurance company has no proprietary interest in property it insures. But if D mistakenly believes property is his when it is not, he may be liable for criminal damage if he also believes someone else has a proprietary interest in it (see *Seray-Wurie v DPP* [2012] EWCH 208 (Admin)).

14.2.2 *Mens rea*

The destruction or damage to property belonging to another amounts to an offence only if it is done intentionally or recklessly and without lawful excuse.

14.2.2.1 Intention and recklessness

As to the meaning of intention see 3.2.3 *ante*. If D is charged with intentionally damaging property belonging to another, it must be proved that he intended to cause damage by his act (or omission) and that he intended to damage property belonging to another. If D mistakenly believes that the property he is damaging or destroying is his own, he will lack the requisite intention (but if he believes another also has a proprietary interest in the property his mistake will not save him—see *Seray-Wurie* mentioned earlier). In *Smith (David)* [1974] QB 354, D, not knowing property law, damaged fixtures he had installed in the flat of which he was a tenant when removing wiring for his stereo equipment. He believed that the fixtures belonged to him when, in law, they belonged to the landlord. His conviction of criminal damage was quashed, James LJ stating (at p. 360):

> Applying the ordinary principles of *mens rea*, the intention and recklessness and the absence of lawful excuse required to constitute the offence have reference to property belonging to another. It follows that in our judgment no offence is committed under this section if a person destroys or causes damage to property belonging to another if he does so in the honest though mistaken belief that the property is his own, and provided that belief is honestly held it is irrelevant to consider whether or not it is a justifiable belief.

In this case D's mistake was one of law; it would make no difference if the mistake was one of fact. For example, after his exams D burns a textbook believing it is his when, in fact, it is his flatmate P's textbook which he has picked up by mistake. It is also not necessary to prove that D knows or realises that what he is doing to the property of another constitutes 'damage' in law; in *Seray-Wurie* (mentioned earlier) D wrote on a parking notice with a black marker pen, something which amounted in law to damage even though he may not have believed it did. D agreed he wrote on the notice, intending to do so; his motives for doing so could not alter the fact that his action amounted to damage and his action was intentional.

Recklessness in the context of criminal damage was originally defined by the House of Lords in *Caldwell* to include inadvertence to an obvious risk of damage to property. In *G* [2003] UKHL 50, the House of Lords reversed *Caldwell* and provided the following fully subjective definition for recklessness (see **3.4.2.2.6** *ante*):

> A person acts recklessly within the meaning of section 1 of the Criminal Damage Act 1971 with respect to—
>
> (i) a circumstance when he is aware of a risk that it exists or will exist;
>
> (ii) a result when he is aware of a risk that it will occur; and it is, in the circumstances known to him, unreasonable to take the risk.

Where the accused is charged with recklessly damaging property belonging to another, the offence is one of basic intent. If the prosecution charge the accused in the alternative, that is intentionally *or* recklessly damaging property belonging to another, he will also be denied the possibility of raising intoxication as a factor relevant to his state of mind as criminal damage where recklessness is charged is an offence of basic intent but where the aggravated offence is charged under s. 1(2) (see **14.3** *post*) it is an offence of specific intent (see **5.6.3** *ante*).

14.2.2.2 Lawful excuse

Section 5(2) provides a partial definition of 'lawful excuse' (see s. 5(5)). Thus D may also avail himself of any other defence, e.g. duress, prevention of crime, arrest of offenders, and self-defence. For example, where D is being attacked by P he may damage property to defend himself where (i) he jumps through a window, breaking it, in seeking to escape from P; or (ii) he pushes P through the window; or (iii) he hits P over the head with a vase belonging to X and breaks it. In (i) D's defence would be duress of circumstances and in (ii) and (iii) it would be self-defence. In each case D will succeed provided the measures he took were objectively reasonable in the circumstances.

Section 5 provides:

> (2) A person charged with an offence to which this section applies shall, whether or not he would be treated for the purposes of this Act as having a lawful excuse apart from this subsection, be treated for those purposes as having a lawful excuse—
>
> > (a) if at the time of the act or acts alleged to constitute the offence he believed that the person or person whom he believed to be entitled to consent to the destruction of or damage to the property in question had so consented, or would have so consented to it if he or they had known of the destruction or damage and its circumstances; or
> >
> > (b) if he destroyed or damaged or threatened to destroy or damage the property in question or, in the case of a charge of an offence under s. 3 above, intended to use or cause or permit the use of something to destroy or damage it, in order to protect property belonging to himself or another or a right or interest in property which was or which he believed to be vested in himself or another, and at the time of the act or acts alleged to constitute the offence he believed—
> >
> > > (i) that the property, right or interest was in immediate need of protection; and
> > >
> > > (ii) that the means of protection adopted or proposed to be adopted were or would be reasonable having regard to all the circumstances.
>
> (3) For the purposes of this section it is immaterial whether a belief is justified or not if it is not honestly held.
>
> (4) For the purposes of subsection (2) above a right or interest in property includes any right or privilege in or over land, whether created by grant, licence or otherwise.

Section 5(2)(a) is equivalent to s. 2(1)(b) of the TA 1968 (see **11.2.2.2.1** *ante*). The only issue is whether D's belief was honestly held regardless of whether or not it was reasonable. It does not even matter that D's mistake was a drunken one (see *Jaggard v Dickinson* [1980] 3 All ER 716, **5.6.5** *ante*). The burden is on the prosecution to prove beyond reasonable doubt the absence of lawful excuse once the accused has adduced some evidence to raise the issue. D's mistake may relate to one of several matters (or to a combination of these matters): (i) D may mistakenly believe that he has been told to damage or destroy the property; (ii) D may mistakenly believe that the person telling him to damage or destroy the property (or whom he believes is telling him to do so) is the person entitled to consent to its damage or destruction; (iii) D may mistakenly believe that the person entitled to consent to the damage or destruction of the property would do so if he knew of the circumstances in which D has damaged or destroyed it; (iv) D may believe that the person whom he mistakenly believes is entitled to consent to the damage or destruction of the property would do so if he knew of the circumstances in which D has damaged or destroyed it.

If D honestly believes that the owner of property (or some other person entitled to give consent) has consented to his damaging the property, the reason for the damage is irrelevant even if it is for the purpose of perpetrating a fraud. This results from the fact that criminal damage is not an offence of which dishonesty is an element. In *Denton* [1982] 1 All ER 65, D, who was employed at a cotton mill, set fire to the mill and machinery in it because he thought his 'employer' T had asked him to do so in order to make a fraudulent claim against the insurers. Indeed, it appeared that T had asked D to do so. The Court of Appeal quashed his conviction, Lord Lane CJ stating (at p. 68):

> [O]ne has to decide whether or not an offence is committed at the moment that the acts are alleged to be committed. The fact that somebody may have had a dishonest intent which in the end he was going to carry out, namely a claim from the insurance company, cannot turn what was not originally a crime into a crime. There is no unlawfulness under the 1971 Act in burning a house. It does not become unlawful because there may be an inchoate attempt to commit fraud contained in it; that is to say it does not become a crime under the 1971 Act, whatever may be the situation outside the Act.

If T had asked D to set fire to the mill for the purpose of making a fraudulent insurance claim, both D and T could have been convicted of conspiracy to defraud. But where D claims 'God' commanded him to damage the property, 'God' is not a 'person' capable of giving such consent (see *Blake* v *DPP* [1993] Crim LR 587).

Section 5(2)(b) provides that D has a lawful excuse where he believes his property or that of another (or property which he believes is his property or another's) is in need of immediate protection and he damages or destroys property in order to protect property belonging to himself or another believing that this is reasonable in all the circumstances. D will satisfy the requirement of immediacy in s. 5(2)(b) if the threat to his property has already materialised. In *Chamberlain* v *Lindon, The Times*, 6 April 1998, the Queen's Bench Division upheld the decision of Nuneaton Justices to acquit D of criminal damage where he had demolished a wall built by C on C's land as D honestly believed such action was necessary to protect his right of vehicular access across C's land and that delay would prejudice his rights. The Court also held that s. 5(2) did not contain any requirement that the defendant had to exhaust any alternative remedies, for example in the civil courts, before self-redress was permitted.

Whether or not D believed the means he adopted to protect the property were reasonable is a subjective question and not a matter of objective fact (see *Jones (Iorwerth)* [2003] EWCA Crim 894). The objective element of this defence, however, is whether what D did could be said to have been done 'in order to protect property'. This assessment is made on the basis of the facts as D believed them to be (see *Jones and others* [2004] EWCA Crim 1981); and there is no requirement that the damage to property which D seeks to prevent would be the result of an illegal act—it could arise from some natural disaster. If D's purpose is something other than the protection of property this defence will not be available (see *Hunt* (1978) 66 Cr App R 105; *Hill and Hall* [1989] Crim LR 136). Having determined what D's purpose was, it is for the court to rule as a matter of law whether this amounts to a purpose of protecting property; the cases hold, however, that the fact that D believes he is protecting his property is irrelevant. The approach adopted in the cases is open to criticism as what D's purpose was would appear to be something which may only be determined by examining his subjective state of mind. Whether the means he chose to effect his purpose were capable of doing so is, strictly speaking, irrelevant. While the efficacy of the means chosen may be circumstantial evidence which may help the jury determine what his purpose was (namely the less likely the means chosen were to be effective, the less likely it is that the protection of property was D's purpose), the fact of their inefficacy should not be determinative of that issue. If D honestly believed that what he was doing would protect the property, no matter how unreasonable that belief might be, he was acting 'in order to protect property'.

The courts' approach, however, is to impose an objective test on this defence. In *Hill and Hall*, the fact that D and E, members of CND, believed that, by cutting the fence surrounding a United States naval base at Brawdy, they would protect their homes was of no avail as the judge ruled that their acts were not for the purpose of protection. D's and E's convoluted reasoning was that if the Russians attacked this nuclear base, their homes would be damaged by the blast or fall-out from a nuclear attack. If enough people breached the perimeter fence the Americans might decide to remove the base and thereby remove the threat of nuclear attack. The trial judge's conclusion was that D's and E's purpose was to encourage the Americans to leave and this was not a purpose of protecting their property. The Court of Appeal affirmed that he had adopted the correct approach which was to decide (i) what was in D's mind (the subjective test) and (ii) whether it could be said, as a matter of law, on the facts as believed by D, that cutting the strand of wire could amount to something done to protect her home or those of others (the objective test). Thus, the question whether property is damaged or destroyed by D 'in order to protect property belonging to himself' is one of law and not a matter of D's belief. The trial judge had also concluded that D and E had not adduced any evidence that they believed that their property was 'in immediate need of protection'. The Court of Appeal held that he was correct in withdrawing this part of the case from the jury. This decision was followed in *Blake* v *DPP, ante* where the Divisional Court ruled that it was for the court objectively to decide whether, on the facts believed by the accused, the action taken did protect, or was capable of protecting, property. D, a vicar, protesting outside Parliament against the use of force by the allies in Iraq and Kuwait, wrote a biblical quotation on a concrete pillar. The Court ruled that he could not rely on s. 5(2)(b) as the damage done was not capable of protecting property in the Gulf states as it was too remote. (See also *Johnson* v *DPP* [1994] Crim LR 673.)

In *Jones (Iorwerth)* D, in a roof-top protest over planning permission for a lorry park which he believed would lead to further diminution in the value of his bungalow adjacent to the lorry park, caused £65,000 worth of damage to council offices.

Upholding his conviction, the Court affirmed the objective nature of the test stating (at para. 19):

> The court has to decide whether what the appellant claims to be doing can be characterised in law as the protection of property. That, as it seems to us, is no different from, for instance, the court having to decide whether, when a person says that their intent was to break the victim's nose, that in law amounts to an intent to cause grievous bodily harm.

The Court explained its reasoning on the basis of the purpose behind the legislation (at para. 22):

> Although we have, of course, approached section 5 on the basis of its plain wording and not sought to reflect upon its reasons or motivation, we have no doubt at all, being to some extent familiar with the origins of that section, that it was not intended in any way to encompass a case like this. It was not intended to encompass a deliberate and lawless attack on a person's property, with a view to attempt to make him change his mind. It was intended to excuse interference with one part of property that was directly and proximately threatening the property of the appellant.

14.3 Destroying or damaging property with intent to endanger life

Section 1(2) of the Criminal Damage Act 1971 provides:

> A person who without lawful excuse destroys or damages any property, whether belonging to himself or another—
>
> (a) intending to destroy or damage any property or being reckless as to whether any property would be destroyed or damaged; and
>
> (b) intending by the destruction or damage to endanger the life of another or being reckless as to whether the life of another would be thereby endangered; shall be guilty of an offence.

The maximum punishment for this offence is life imprisonment (s. 4(1)). In many cases where D damages property and endangers life he will do so with the specific intent to kill and would be liable to conviction of attempted murder. This offence, however, is wider in some respects than attempted murder, as it is sufficient that D is reckless whether life will be endangered (but attempted murder does not require proof of damage to property). This offence, if appropriate on the facts, also avoids the difficulties of proving that D has done a 'more than merely preparatory act'.

14.3.1 *Actus reus*

The meaning of 'damage', 'destroy', and 'property' is the same as for s. 1(1). **There is a major difference, however, in that the property destroyed or damaged need not belong to another; D may commit this offence where he destroys or damages his own property if he does so with intent to endanger life or being**

reckless thereto. For example, if D, a landlord wishing to evict a squatter who is refusing to leave, throws a petrol bomb into the house thereby damaging the property, he is liable to conviction of the s. 1(2) offence if he had the requisite *mens rea* specified in s. 1(2)(b). There is no need to prove that a life was in fact endangered (*Parker* [1993] Crim LR 856).

14.3.2 *Mens rea*

D must intend to damage or destroy property or be reckless thereto. In addition, **D must intend *by* that damage to endanger life or be reckless thereto.**

> In *Steer* [1987] 2 All ER 833, D fired a shot through a window pane behind which P and Q were standing. It was accepted that he did not intend to endanger their lives. The question remained, however, whether he damaged property being reckless as to whether the life of another would be endangered. D was convicted and appealed submitting that it had to be proved that the endangering arose from the damage to the window and not the act which caused the damage to the window (i.e. the firing of the bullet which smashed it). The House of Lords affirmed the decision of the Court of Appeal allowing his appeal as it was the shooting which endangered the lives and not the breaking of the window.

This requirement has been reiterated in the two cases which follow where the Court of Appeal, by a process of intellectual gymnastics, managed to uphold the convictions. In *Asquith, Webster, and Seamans* [1995] 1 Cr App R 492, the appellants had pushed a coping stone from a bridge on to a train passing below. It hit a carriage showering the passengers with debris from the roof but it did not fall into the carriage. In the conjoined appeal of *Warwick* [1995] 1 Cr App R 492 the appellant was the passenger in a stolen car who hurled bricks at a police car, smashing a window and showering the officers with glass. The stolen car also rammed the police car and another brick was thrown which hit an officer. Lord Taylor CJ conceded that s. 1(2)(b) can produce some anomalous distinctions. He emphasised that the issue was not whether and how life was endangered but rather 'whether and how it was intended to be endangered or there was a...risk of it being endangered' of which D was aware (see *G, ante*). In addition the reference in s. 1(2)(b) to 'destruction or damage' referred to 'such destruction or damage as the defendant intended'. Lord Taylor CJ stated (at p. 497):

> [I]f a defendant throws a brick at the windscreen of a moving vehicle, given that he causes *some* damage to the vehicle, whether he is guilty under s. 1(2) does not depend on whether the brick hits or misses the windscreen, but whether he intended to hit it and intended that the damage therefrom should endanger life or whether he was reckless as to that outcome. As to the dropping of stones from bridges, the effect of the statute may be thought strange. If the defendant's intention is that the stone itself should crash through the roof of a train...and thereby directly injure a passenger or if he was reckless only as to that outcome, the section would not bite....If, however, the defendant intended or was reckless that the stone would smash the roof of the train or vehicle so that metal or wood struts from the roof would or...might descend upon a passenger, endangering life, he would surely be guilty. This may seem a dismal distinction.

The Court of Appeal proceeded to uphold the conviction in *Warwick* as the broken glass, or ramming of the vehicle, could have caused the driver to lose control thereby endangering the lives of the driver and passengers and there was adequate evidence from which the jury could infer an intention to endanger life in this way or recklessness thereto. In *Asquith* the Court of Appeal quashed the conviction as it was based on an erroneous direction that an intent to endanger life by the stone falling on a passenger would suffice. The Court, however, substituted a conviction based on recklessness, Lord Taylor CJ stating (at p. 498):

> However, the jury's finding of an intent by each appellant to endanger life…must, in common sense, carry the implication that they were each reckless as to endangering life (by whatever damage the stone might do) when it fell. If the intention was for the stone to penetrate the roof, there was clearly an obvious risk that it might endanger life by bringing parts of the roof down into the compartment, quite apart from other obvious risks such as derailment if it fell in front of the train or struck the driver's cab incapacitating him or the controls.

Following the House of Lords' decision in *G* (*ante*) the test now is not whether the risk was obvious but rather whether D was aware of the risk and unreasonably took it. The unreasonableness of taking a risk is assessed in light of the circumstances known to D (see *Castle* [2004] All ER (D) 289 (Oct.). Following *Heard* [2007] EWCA Crim 125, the s. 1(2) offence is one of specific intent as the element of intent or recklessness as to endangering life is an ulterior *mens rea*. Thus D may rely on his intoxication if it is such that he did not form the requisite intent or did not appreciate the risk to life (see **5.6.3** *ante*).

In the latest Court of Appeal decision, *Wenton* [2010] EWCA Crim 2361, D's conviction for damaging property being reckless whether life was endangered, was quashed. D had first broken a window using a brick; he then threw a container of petrol into the house with a lighted piece of paper but the petrol did not ignite. The Court of Appeal considered *Asquith* and *Warwick*, and pointed out, somewhat exasperatedly, that the act which caused the damage was throwing the brick whereas the act which caused the endangerment was throwing the petrol container and lighted paper into the house, the two acts being unrelated. Had the petrol ignited and damage had been caused by the fire, D could have been convicted of arson being reckless whether life was endangered (see *Dudley, post*).

The fact that lives are not endangered is irrelevant if it was D's intention by the damage to endanger life (see *Dudley* [1989] Crim LR 57) or he was reckless thereto (*Sangha* [1988] 2 All ER 385).

> In *Dudley*, D had set fire to P's house in pursuit of a grievance. D threw a fire bomb at the house but P and his family quickly extinguished the fire and only trivial damage was caused. D's conviction of arson being reckless whether life would be endangered was affirmed by the Court of Appeal. The relevant time was when D did the act which caused the damage; if at that time he was aware of a risk of danger to life or if he intended to endanger life, he had the requisite *mens rea*.

14.3.3 Without lawful excuse

'Without lawful excuse' in s. 1(2) does not have the same meaning as for s. 1(1). **The definition in s. 5 does not apply to offences under s. 1(2).** Thus, even though D may have P's consent to damage his property, if he does so intending to endanger the life of another or being reckless thereto, he will be guilty of the s. 1(2) offence. In *Merrick* [1996] 1 Cr App R 130 (**3.4.2.2.4** *ante*) counts of simple criminal damage were dismissed on the basis of lawful excuse but the trial proceeded for the counts under s. 1(2) where, according to the Court of Appeal, 'the defence of lawful excuse did not apply'. There was no investigation of who actually owned the cabling and the trial proceeded on the basis that the householder did and could consent to its removal. If this was so, D was not placing reliance on s. 5(2)(a) but rather on the fact of consent which is an 'excuse apart from this subsection' (see *Denton*, **14.2.2.2** *ante*; Professor J. C. Smith, Commentary, *Merrick* [1995] Crim LR 804). The suggestion is that more should have been made of the excuse point on appeal in *Merrick* and that the dictum of the Court of Appeal is *obiter* and wrong.

The limited circumstances in which D would have a lawful excuse appear to be confined to situations where he damages property to prevent crime or defend himself or apprehend an offender and the reasonable force he uses endangers life. For example, if E is attacking D with a hatchet and D smashes P's vase over E's head to defend himself intending to kill E, D will have damaged property belonging to another intending to endanger the life of another. If the force used, however, was reasonable in the circumstances, D will have been acting with lawful excuse in damaging the property and thereby endangering life.

14.4 Threats to destroy or damage property

Section 2 of the Criminal Damage Act 1971 provides:

> A person who without lawful excuse makes to another a threat, intending that that other would fear it would be carried out—
>
> (a) to destroy or damage any property belonging to that other or a third person; or
>
> (b) to destroy or damage his own property in a way which he knows is likely to endanger the life of that other or a third person; shall be guilty of an offence.

On conviction on indictment the maximum punishment for this offence is 10 years' imprisonment (s. 4(2)).

The threat may be made by any means. The Law Commission stated that 'the only limitation that needs to be imposed is that the threats should be intended to create fear that what is threatened will be carried out' (Law Com No. 29, para. 55). There is no requirement that D intend to carry out the threats; the essence of the offence is the intention to create fear. If P is not, in fact, put in fear as he does not believe D would carry out the threat, this will not avail D provided it is proved D intended to cause fear in P.

The conduct threatened must be an offence under s. 1 of the Act. If D threatens an offence under s. 1(1), the definition of 'without lawful excuse' in s. 5 applies, but if he threatens an offence under s. 1(2) this definition is inapplicable.

14.5 Possessing anything with intent to destroy or damage property

Section 3 of the Criminal Damage Act 1971 provides:

> A person who has anything in his custody or under his control intending without lawful excuse to use it or cause or permit another to use it—
>
> (a) to destroy or damage any property belonging to some other person; or
>
> (b) to destroy or damage his own property in a way which he knows is likely to endanger the life of some other person; shall be guilty of an offence.

On conviction on indictment the maximum punishment for this offence is 10 years' imprisonment (s. 4(2)).

It is necessary to prove a purposive intention, that is that D possessed the item for the purpose of committing an offence under s. 1 himself or for another to use it to commit such an offence. A conditional intention, to use the item to cause damage should it prove necessary, will suffice (*Buckingham* (1976) 63 Cr App R 159). 'Without lawful excuse' applies in the same way as for the s. 2 offence (see **14.3** *ante*). D must have actual custody or control of the item at the time he formulates the intention. If, for example, D gives E a brick and subsequently suggests to him that he should use it to damage P's property, D has the necessary intention but he does not have custody or control of the brick (he would, however, be liable to conviction for incitement). By contrast, if D picks up a brick intending to give it to E so that he can damage P's property, D will have custody and control of the brick with the intention to permit E to use it to cause criminal damage.

There is no definition of 'anything'; the essence of the offence is D's intent. If D has the requisite intent it does not matter what the thing is which he has in his custody or control.

14.6 Racially or religiously aggravated criminal damage

The Crime and Disorder Act 1998 has created a new offence of racially aggravated criminal damage (see s. 3). Criminal damage is racially aggravated where a person commits criminal damage, and:

> (a) at the time of committing the offence, or immediately before or after doing so, the offender demonstrates towards the victim of the offence (i.e. the person to whom the property belongs or is treated as belonging) hostility based on the victim's membership (or presumed membership) of a racial or religious group; or
>
> (b) the offence is motivated (wholly or partly) by hostility towards members of a racial or religious group based on their membership of that group (see ss. 28(1) and 30(3)).

The maximum penalty for criminal damage is increased to 14 years where the offence is racially aggravated. For further analysis of this offence see Leng, Taylor and Wasik, *Blackstone's Guide to the Crime and Disorder Act 1998* (for the meaning of 'racial group' or 'religious group' see **10.1.1.4.1** *ante*).

The tendency for the CPS to charge racially or religiously aggravated offences where the actual reason for the offence has nothing to do with race or religion, and for courts to uphold convictions in such circumstances, risks bringing these laws into disrepute. In *DPP* v *Green* [2004] EWHC 1225 (Admin), the Divisional Court considered *DPP* v *Woods* (**10.1.1.4.1** *ante*) and confirmed that an offence may be considered racially or religiously aggravated if accompanied by any racial or religious abuse even where the defendant does not in fact act from any racial or religious motive. The effects of this approach are amply illustrated by the fact of *DPP* v *M* [2004] EWHC 1453 (Admin). D, who was involved in a dispute over whether an order had been paid for in a Turkish kebab shop, broke a window in the shop in the course of the argument. What may, in other circumstances have been regarded as a minor incident, escalated into a serious offence in the eyes of the Crown Prosecution Service as D was intemperate enough to mutter in the course of the argument the words 'bloody foreigners'. The offence was charged as racially aggravated criminal damage and, although the justices found as a fact that the cause of the dispute was an argument over money, the Divisional Court held that the words 'bloody foreigners' were capable of describing a racial group by reference to nationality and the word 'bloody' could demonstrate hostility. Dare one suggest that the term 'foreigner' lacks a certain specificity; to what nationality is reference being made? Such an argument, however, has recently fallen on deaf ears in *Rogers* [2007] UKHL 8 where the same epithet, 'bloody foreigners', was used by D to a group of Spanish women who got in his way as he rode his mobility scooter along the pavement. The best advice to persons such as Mr M and Mr Rogers, is to utter the words 'bloody chefs' or 'bloody pedestrians'! (See further **10.1.1.4.1** *ante*.)

FURTHER READING

D. W. Elliott, 'Endangering Life by Destroying or Damaging Property' [1997] Crim LR 382.

INDEX